Categorical perception

Categorical perception

The groundwork of cognition

Edited by
STEVAN HARNAD

Behavioral and Brain Sciences
Princeton, New Jersey

CAMBRIDGE UNIVERSITY PRESS
Cambridge
New York   New Rochelle   Melbourne   Sydney

Published by the Press Syndicate of the University of Cambridge
The Pitt Building, Trumpington Street, Cambridge CB2 1RP
32 East 57th Street, New York, NY 10022, USA
10 Stamford Road, Oakleigh, Melbourne 3166, Australia

© Cambridge University Press 1987

First published 1987

Printed in the United States of America

Library of Congress Cataloging-in-Publication Data
Categorical perception.
Includes index.
1. Categorization (Psychology) 2. Perception.
I. Harnad, Stevan R.
BF445.C38   1987   153   86-34286

British Library Cataloguing in Publication Data
Categorical perception.
1. Social perception
I. Harnad, Stevan
302.1'2   HM291

ISBN 0-521-26758-7

Contents

List of contributors	*page* vii
Preface	ix
Introduction: Psychophysical and cognitive aspects of categorical perception: A critical overview Stevan Harnad	1

Part I Psychophysical foundations of categorical perception

1	Categorical perception: Some psychophysical models Richard E. Pastore	29
2	Beyond the categorical/continuous distinction: A psychophysical approach to processing modes Neil A. Macmillan	53

Part II Categorical perception of speech

3	Phonetic category boundaries are flexible Bruno H. Repp and Alvin M. Liberman	89
4	Auditory, articulatory, and learning explanations of categorical perception in speech Stuart Rosen and Peter Howell	113
5	On infant speech perception and the acquisition of language Peter D. Eimas, Joanne L. Miller, and Peter W. Jusczyk	161

Part III Models for speech categorical perception

6	Neural models of speech perception: A case history Robert E. Remez	199
7	On the categorization of speech sounds Randy L. Diehl and Keith R. Kluender	226

v

8 Categorical partition: A fuzzy-logical model of categorization behavior 254
   Dominic W. Massaro

Part IV Categorical perception in other modalities and other species

9 Perceptual categories in vision and audition 287
   Marc H. Bornstein
10 Categorical perception of sound signals: Facts and hypotheses from animal studies 301
   Günter Ehret
11 A naturalistic view of categorical perception 332
   Charles T. Snowdon
12 The special-mechanisms debate in speech research: Categorization tests on animals and infants 355
   Patricia K. Kuhl
13 Brain mechanisms in categorical perception 387
   Martha Wilson

Part V Psychophysiological indices of categorical perception

14 Electrophysiological indices of categorical perception for speech 421
   Dennis L. Molfese
15 Evoked potentials and color-defined categories 444
   D. Regan

Part VI Higher-order categories

16 Categorization processes and categorical perception 455
   Douglas L. Medin and Lawrence W. Barsalou
17 Developmental changes in category structure 491
   Frank C. Keil and Michael H. Kelly
18 Spatial categories: The perception and conceptualization of spatial relations 511
   Ellen Bialystok and David R. Olson

Part VII Cognitive foundations

19 Category induction and representation 535
   Stevan Harnad

Author index 566
Subject index 577

Contributors

Lawrence W. Barsalou, Department of Psychology, Emory University, Atlanta GA 30322

Ellen Bialystok, Department of Psychology, York University, North York, Ontario, Canada M3J 1P3

Marc H. Bornstein, Department of Psychology, New York University, New York NY 10003

Randy L. Diehl, Department of Psychology, University of Texas, Austin TX 78712

Günter Ehret, Fakultät für Biologie, Universität Konstanz, D-7750 Konstanz, Federal Republic of Germany

Peter D. Eimas, Department of Psychology, Brown University, Providence RI 02912

Stevan Harnad, Behavioral and Brain Sciences, 20 Nassau Street, Princeton NJ 08542

Peter Howell, Department of Psychology, University College London, London WC1 6BT England

Frank C. Keil, Department of Psychology, Cornell University, Ithaca NY 14853

Michael H. Kelly, Department of Psychology, Cornell University, Ithaca NY 14853

Keith R. Kluender, Department of Psychology, University of Texas, Austin TX 78712

Patricia K. Kuhl, Department of Speech and Hearing Sciences, University of Washington, Seattle WA 98195

Peter W. Jusczyk, Department of Psychology, University of Oregon, Eugene OR 97403

Alvin M. Liberman, Haskins Laboratories, New Haven CT 06511

Neil A. Macmillan, Department of Psychology, Brooklyn College, Brooklyn NY 11210

Dominic W. Massaro, Department of Psychology, University of California, Santa Cruz CA 95064

Douglas L. Medin, Department of Psychology, University of Illinois, Champaign IL 61820

Joanne L. Miller, Department of Psychology, Northeastern University, Boston MA 02115

Dennis L. Molfese, Department of Psychology, Southern Illinois University, Carbondale IL 62901

David R. Olson, Ontario Institute for Studies in Education, Toronto, Ontario, Canada M5S 1V6

Richard E. Pastore, Department of Psychology, SUNY, Binghamton NY 13901

D. Regan, Department of Psychology, York University, North York, Ontario, Canada M3J 1P3

Robert E. Remez, Department of Psychology, Barnard College, Columbia University, New York NY 10027

Bruno H. Repp, Haskins Laboratories, New Haven CT 06511

Stuart Rosen, Department of Phonetics and Linguistics, University College London, London WC1E 6BT, England

Charles T. Snowdon, Department of Psychology, University of Wisconsin, Madison WI 53706

Martha Wilson, Department of Psychology, University of Connecticut, Storrs CT 06268

Preface

How do we sort the objects, people, events, and ideas in the world into their proper categories? What transforms the "booming, buzzing confusion" that enters our eyes and ears at birth into that orderly world we ultimately experience and interact with? These most basic of questions about human (and animal) perception and cognition are the subject of this exhaustive survey and synthesis of the findings from a diversified area of research on what has come to be called "categorical perception."

Categorical perception occurs when the continuous, variable, and confusable stimulation that reaches the sense organs is sorted out by the mind into discrete, distinct categories whose members somehow come to resemble one another more than they resemble members of other categories. The best-known example is color categories: Physically speaking, colors differ only in their wavelengths, which gradually get shorter across the spectrum of visible colors. What we see, however, are qualitative changes, from red to orange to yellow to green, and so forth. The same is true of musical pitches: Gradually increasing frequencies can come to be heard as categorical changes from C to C-sharp to D to E-flat. A lesser-known example is "stop-consonants": (synthesized) "ba," "da," and "ga" also vary along a physical continuum, yet we hear them as three qualitatively distinct and discrete categories. In all three cases, perceptual *boundaries* have somehow arisen along the physical continuum, dividing it into discrete regions, with qualitative resemblances *within* each category and qualitative differences *between* them. These bounded categories may provide the groundwork for higher-order cognition and language.

This book brings together all the known examples of categorical perception, in humans and animals, infants and adults, in all the sense modalities that have been studied: hearing, seeing, and touch. The perceptual findings are then interpreted in terms of the available cognitive and neuroscientific theories about how categorical perception is accomplished by the brain: Is it inborn? Is it learned? What is it that the mind does to the incoming continuous information to sort it into the discrete categories we can see, manipulate, name, and describe? This research on our elementary perceptual and psychophysical categories (colors, sounds) is then integrated with the work on higher-order categories: objects, patterns, abstract concepts. From a focus on the most thoroughly investigated case of categorical perception – speech perception – the chapters proceed to an integrative overall view of category cognition.

The objective of the book is to survey and unify the diverse and interdisciplinary experimental and theoretical work on categorical perception and to guide future research on categorization in general. The volume will be of general interest to cognitive scientists, neuroscientists, developmental and comparative psychologists, behavioral biologists, linguists, anthropologists, and philosophers. It will be especially useful to experimentalists, theoreticians, and students who are concerned with any aspect of category representation: from threshold psychophysics, speech perception, and animal signaling systems to perceptual learning, language acquisition, and concept formation.

Stevan Harnad

Introduction
Psychophysical and cognitive aspects of categorical perception: A critical overview

Stevan Harnad

The categorization problem

One of the most basic questions of cognitive science is, How do organisms sort the objects of the world into categories? The problem is very general, for an "object" can be any recurring class of experience, from a concrete entity, such as a cat or a table, to an abstract idea, such as goodness or truth. And "sorting" can be any differential response to the object category, from detecting and instrumentally manipulating it to identifying and verbally describing it. Categorization hence plays a critical role in perception, thinking, and language and is probably a significant factor in motor performance too.

There are many entry points into the problem of categorization. Two particularly important ones are the so-called "top-down" and "bottom-up" approaches. *Top-down* approaches, such as artificial intelligence, start with the symbolic names and descriptions for some categories already given; computer programs are written to manipulate the symbols. Cognitive modeling involves the further assumption that such symbol interactions resemble the way our brains do categorization. An explicit expectation of the top-down approach is that it will eventually join with the *bottom-up* approach, which tries to model how the hardware of the brain works: sensory systems, motor systems, and neural function in general. The assumption is that the symbolic cognitive functions will be implemented in brain function and linked to the sense organs and the organs of movement in roughly the way a program is implemented in a computer, with its links to peripheral devices, such as transducers and effectors.

Another entry point is human-performance modeling. What people categorize, and how, is studied experimentally; then models are devised to account for people's performance, especially their efficiency and their errors. These models try to capture why it is that we can categorize some things more easily or quickly or reliably than others. A related approach is the study of cognitive development: how the child acquires categories. These lines of inquiry have their counterparts in comparative psychology, where the behavior of animals is studied to determine how they categorize their worlds. The comparative approach is also concerned with the evolutionary origins and the adaptive value of categories.

One last approach is less easy to classify: the "psychophysical" one. Psychophysics is concerned with the relationship between physical stimulation and sensation, for example, that between the physical intensity of a stimulus and the psychological intensity of the sensation it causes. Categorization is studied by examining the limits of discrimination (how small a physical difference we can tell apart) and of identification (what classes of stimuli we can reliably label). The approach is "bottom-up," although not in the usual hardware-to-software sense, but rather in the sense the name implies: physical-to-psychological. Psychophysics is close to the level of neural mechanisms and is often pursued in close collaboration with parallel work on sensory psychophysiology, although it is methodologically independent of such work.

Learning and representing categories. A theme running through the various approaches to categorization is that of *learning.* Clearly, no organism is born a blank slate. Some categories are innate. The comparative and psychophysical approaches tend to be concerned primarily with the mechanisms of innate categorization, although learning factors are not necessarily excluded. The developmental and neural approaches deal with both innate and acquired categories, whereas the top-down and human-performance research concentrates mainly on learned categories. The general problem of the origins of categories – both phylogenetic and ontogenetic – is something that looms large for all the approaches to categorization. This is the problem of induction: How does any mechanism learn to form, on the basis of a finite sample of particular cases, a reliable generalization about future cases?

A second theme that runs through all the approaches to categorization is that of *representation:* How are categories represented? What structures and processes make it possible to categorize appropriately? Top-down research tends to favor symbolic representations, whereas bottom-up work focuses on sensory representations. All approaches are concerned with the question of which representations are innate and which are learned. The problem of the origins of representations – in evolution, development, and learning – coalesces with the problem of the origins of categories.

The psychophysics of categorical perception. All of these approaches to categorization are represented to some degree in this volume, but the emphasis is on a psychophysical phenomenon that may help to unify the diverse lines of inquiry. The phenomenon is "categorical perception" (henceforth CP). CP was first observed with color perception and the perception of speech sounds, but it has since been found in a variety of domains. The effect is best described as a qualitative difference in how similar things look or sound depending on whether or not they are in the same category. The experimental paradigm for demonstrating CP is psychophysical: Discrimination and identification performance (telling things apart and labeling them) are compared for a set of stimuli. Usually the stimuli vary along a physical continuum and regions of that continuum have been or can be assigned labels.[1]

An example of CP is the color spectrum as it is subdivided into color categories, or an acoustic continuum called the "second-formant transition" as it is subdivided into the (synthesized) stop-consonant categories /ba/, /da/, and /ga/. In both cases, equal-sized physical differences between stimuli are perceived as larger or smaller depending on whether the stimuli are in the same category or different ones. Indeed, the effect is not only quantitative but qualitative: A pair of greens of different shades look more like one another than like a shade of yellow (which may be no more different in wave length from one of the greens than the other green is), and this difference is one of quality. The same is true of /ba/'s and /da/'s.

Qualitative differences in perception cannot be demonstrated objectively; we have only the subject's word (and our own introspective experience) as evidence for them. Quantitative differences, however, can be tested experimentally. The method is to compare discrimination and identification performance. *Discrimination* requires a subject to tell apart stimuli presented in pairs (by indicating whether they are the same or different). *Identification* requires the subject to categorize individual stimuli using labels (to say, for example, whether they are /da/ or /ga/). A CP effect occurs when (1) a set of stimuli ranging along a physical continuum is given one label on one side of a category "boundary" and another label on the other side and (2) the subject can discriminate smaller physical differences between pairs of stimuli that straddle that boundary than between pairs that are within one category or the other. In other words, in CP there is a quantitative discontinuity in discrimination at the category boundaries of a physical continuum, as measured by a peak in discriminative acuity at the transition region for the identification of members of adjacent categories.[2]

Categorical perception as the groundwork for category cognition. The unifying hypothesis of this volume is that this highly specific psychophysical phenomenon may be related in an important way to the general problem of categorization: that CP may not only furnish the building blocks – the elementary units – for higher-order categories, but it may also provide a representative model for the categorization process in general. The provisional "may" is used because, as already mentioned, there are still many questions to be answered about CP: How are CP categories formed? What is the role of innate mechanisms? What is the role of learning? What is the nature of the underlying representations? There are even questions about how general CP is as a psychophysical phenomenon. However, the reason for bringing together the diverse and seemingly disparate contributions in this book is that the answers to these questions, as they are currently emerging from the many different areas where the pertinent research is being conducted, appear to be promising. The time has come to promote a mutually informed, unified research strategy.

The objective is therefore to raise the basic questions about categorization in general in the context of CP in particular, to survey the currently available answers, and to focus future investigation of categorization on CP as a unifying model. We accordingly begin with a survey of the contributions to this volume.

Psychophysical foundations of categorical perception

Analog/digital conversion. The CP phenomenon can be seen as an analog-to-digital transformation that recodes a continuous region of physical variation as a discrete, labeled equivalence class. The a.m./p.m. indicator on a digital watch illustrates the main features of this transformation: Time varies continuously, but in one region (from midnight to noon) the watch labels it all "a.m." and in the other (noon to midnight), "p.m." In this case, noon would be the category "boundary" (if we ignore the 24-hour cyclicity). The analogy also holds at a finer-grained level, for exactly the same digitization is going on at the watch's minutest scale of resolution, say, seconds. Here too the continuum 11:59–12:01 is being treated as two discrete "chunks," with the boundary at 12:00. And the analogy goes still further, for although the nearest second is as fine a category as the watch can identify, its internal-analog pacemaker is presumably making still finer discriminations, which could in principle be expressed by a signal indicating whether one event had occurred before or after another. Even this comparator, however, would have limits on its resolving capacity, so that sufficiently tiny time differences would simply not be discriminable by the watch.

There is a CP counterpart for most of these features. The category boundary can be viewed as a threshold for identifying the nearest second. If the device were being used as an automatic stopwatch, one second would be the threshold amount of time that had to elapse to determine whether an event was to be labeled as occurring within the foregoing second or the following one. If two events were being timed, however, the smallest difference that the device could discriminate (as before/after or same/different) would be smaller than the smallest difference that it could label with a specific time. Moreover, the device would make fewer errors with tiny differences that straddled the boundary between a pair of adjacent intervals (i.e., if one event came just before the boundary and one just after) than with tiny differences that occurred in the middle of an interval, because near the boundary the accuracy of the analog difference comparator could be augmented by the accuracy of the digital threshold comparator.

1. Pastore. Chapter 1 by Pastore proposes that the boundary effect (rather than 0% within-category discriminability or 100% identification accuracy) is the hallmark of CP, which he interprets as a threshold phenomenon. In perception, thresholds tend to delineate all-or-none, qualitative differences as opposed to graded, quantitative ones. The threshold for flicker-fusion (the flicker-rate above which a light is per-

Critical overview

ceived as being on continuously) is an example of such a qualitative change, and Pastore shows that it displays all the requisite features of CP. Even an external reference point – such as the one involved in visually discriminating and identifying v's and Y's with variable stem-lengths – will mimic all the features of the CP phenomenon.

Pastore shows that multiple boundary effects can arise from higher-order interactions (both acoustic and neural) that can occur with complex stimuli such as two tones, one fixed and one varying in intensity or frequency. He also argues that some complex acoustic CP effects thought to be unique to speech may arise from higher-order effects of the threshold for perceiving which of two sounds occurs first. Similarly, "trading relations" (see Chapter 3 by Repp & Liberman) – in which the location of CP boundaries seems to be influenced by variations along other acoustic dimensions (perhaps constrained by how a combination of sounds would have had to be pronounced) – may be an effect of intensity/duration tradeoffs with complex stimuli.

Pastore uses this interpretative framework to review the many lines of investigation of CP, from their origins in phenomena assumed to be peculiar to speech perception and production, to the much more general view of CP that seems to be emerging currently. He suggests that regions of "natural sensitivity" underlie the CP boundary effect and that exposure, practice, and selective attention may influence its location, as well as the acuity of discrimination and the accuracy of identification. Other questions his account calls to mind will echo throughout this book: What are the functions of categorical and continuous perception? Can category boundaries arise as a result of learning alone, and if so, how? What are the representations and processes underlying categorization, both psychophysical and cognitive? And what is the relation between CP and higher-order categorization and language?

2. *Macmillan.* The standard CP experiment tests how well subjects can identify individual stimuli that vary along a continuum and how well they can discriminate pairs of these stimuli as being the same or different. Macmillan has proposed in Chapter 2 some refinements on both the experimental method and the analysis of the results that may lead to a more perspicuous and general interpretation of the processes involved. He distinguishes between "fixed" discrimination, in which subjects are tested repeatedly with the same pair of stimuli in a block of trials, and "roving" discrimination, in which the stimulus pairs may come from anywhere in the range of the continuum being tested. He also recommends using signal detection analysis (which yields a standardized measure of detectability that is independent of various response biases) instead of the percent-correct scores that are ordinarily used.

With this refined methodology, CP data can be interpreted in terms of Durlach and Braida's (1969) psychophysical model, which has two interesting parameters: The "trace" parameter is interpreted as reflecting a processing "mode" that compares a stimulus with the sensory trace of another stimulus; it is influenced by how long the delay between the two stimuli is (presumably because of the decay of the iconic trace in immediate memory) and it contributes to both fixed and roving discrimination. The "context" parameter is interpreted as reflecting a processing mode that compares the stimulus with its overall context (including possible "anchor" features); it is influenced by how large the stimulus range is and it contributes to roving discrimination and to identification (presumably involving short- and long-term memory effects, respectively).

The conclusion from this more general analysis is that the continuous/categorical distinction in CP is an oversimplification, and that continua actually differ in how much they draw on the trace and context modes and in where and what their "anchors" are. Anchors may be the extremes of continua (as in the loud and soft end of a range of loudnesses) or they may occur in the middle of the range, in which case they may be boundary regions of heightened sensitivity (for discrimination) or central "prototypes" (for identification).

Macmillan's analysis makes it clear that many questions about CP can be instructively reformulated as questions about the nature, origin, and functional role of "anchors." What are anchors (apart from the special case of edges of continua)? Are some innate and some learned? Of those that are learned, are some anchors short-term context effects (as in roving discrimination and adaptation effects) and some long-term, overlearned effects (as in object naming)? What about multidimensional stimuli? In general, what are the underlying representations of stimuli and of stimulus categories (and the processing "modes" operating on them) that give rise to different trace, context, and anchor effects in different continua?

Categorical perception of speech

The motor theory of speech perception. Of the two phenomena that originally stimulated the special interest in CP, color boundaries (see Chapter 9 by Bornstein and Chapter 15 by Regan), and phoneme boundaries, it was the latter that came to be far more intensively studied. The reason for this was that, until the discovery of the physiological bases for color vision, the only theory of color CP was the Whorf Hypothesis (Whorf, 1964), according to which the location of color boundaries is determined by where languages happen to put them. This was apparently too nonspecific a hypothesis to generate focused research (and once it did, it turned out that color boundaries were largely determined by species-specific color receptors rather than by language). Phoneme boundaries, on the other hand, were explained by the "motor theory of speech perception," a more specific and testable theory (Liberman, Harris, Hoffman, & Griffith, 1957).

According to the motor theory, speech perception is special, and different from other perceptual domains, auditory and nonauditory, in that how speech is heard is influenced by how it is produced. The discontinuities among /pa/, /ta/, /ka/, /ba/, /da/, and /ga/, for example, arise from the discontinuities required to pronounce them. Although there is a continuum in a single acoustic dimension varying from, say, /pa/ to /ta/, there is a discontinuity between the movement of the two lips required to produce /pa/ and the tongue-to-palate movement for /ta/. Hence, just as Helmholtz hypothesized that the basis for many perceptual constancies (see Chapter 5 by Eimas, Miller, & Jusczyk) is "unconscious inference" (e.g., we perceive that an object remains the same size even though the size of its image on our retina is shrinking, because we unconsciously infer that as the image gets smaller the object is moving farther away), Liberman et al. (1957) hypothesized that we perceive what sound we are hearing by unconsciously inferring how it would have had to be pronounced.

The motor theory generated a large body of valuable research on how speech was special, and how our hearing system may have a specialized module for processing speech sounds. Among the possible sounds that humans can produce, a certain finite subset of them has been used by the existing languages. This is our "phonetic" repertoire. Any given language, however, uses a still smaller subset of these, consisting only of those sounds – called "phonemes" – that signal differences in meaning, plus whatever variation they undergo because of the other sounds they are pronounced together with: For example, the sounds of the *o* in *ton* and the *u* in *turn* do not function as distinct phonemes in American English, but as positional variants of the *same* phoneme, the pronunciation of which is determined by whether or not it precedes an *r*; the two variants never contrast to signal two different meanings. The *o* sound in *ton* and the *a* sound in *tan*, on the other hand, are distinct American English phonemes. (The positional variant does not occur, for example, in Irish English.)[3]

According to the motor theory, these minimal meaning-signaling units, called "phonemes," are processed by special phonetic mechanisms of hearing. Specialized for speech perception, these mechanisms "analyze" the distinctive features of phonemes by what it would take to "synthesize" (i.e., pronounce) them. Using an internal model of the vocal apparatus of production (the mouth, tongue, larynx, and so on) and what it can and cannot do, this "analysis-by-synthesis" mechanism is even able to make allowances for the positional variants of phonemes as a function of what sounds they are copronounced with, how quickly, even by how high a voice. Some of the constraints on this mechanism are "phonetic," or universal to all human languages, and some are "phonemic," depending on what the meaning-signaling units in a particular language happen to be. CP boundaries would be special cases of the role of this mechanism in perceptual discontinuities between sounds that require motor discontinuities in order to be produced.

The original motor theory assumed that the internal language-production model had to be learned. But later evidence that preverbal infants (see Chapter 5 by Eimas et al.) and nonverbal animals (see Chapter 12 by Kuhl) have many of the same CP boundaries that mature language speakers do suggested that some of the functions of the specialized speech perception mechanism must have been biologically "prepared" by evolution rather than being learned from experience. Evidence for auditory CP with nonspeech stimuli (see Chapter 4 by Rosen & Howell) has cast some further doubt on whether CP boundaries are mediated by a speech-production model. However, there remain some effects suggesting that speech CP may still be special among other varieties of CP in virtue of its specific links to production.

3. Repp and Liberman. Chapter 3 by Repp and Liberman reviews the evidence for the speech CP effects that still seem to be best explained by a mechanism that infers how the sounds would have had to be pronounced. These effects include changes in a phoneme's CP boundary depending on the following:

1. The sounds that came immediately before or after it (or even its more global context)
2. Differences in the effects of adaptation to a frequently presented sound depending on the listener's native language
3. "Trading relations," or the equivalence of different combinations of cues in producing the same CP effect (where the combinations are explicable by how they would have had to be copronounced)
4. Overall speaking rate
5. Other overall speaker characteristics (whether the voice is high or low, or even more specific individual speaking traits)
6. Effects of expectations arising from grammar and meaning (e.g., shifts in the boundary between *s* and *sh* depending on whether one is expecting to hear a plural ending)
7. Differences between speakers of different languages (as in the absence of a CP boundary between *r* and *l* for Japanese speakers)

All these findings continue to suggest that speech CP is special. The question for the purposes of this volume, however, concerns what aspects of speech CP can be generalized: Are there shared properties of CP in all domains where there is an analog relation between perception and production? (Other cases would include sign language, facial expression, lip reading, music, certain motor skills and certain animal signaling systems.) What about the role of learning? Is it mere "parameter setting" and fine tuning (modulating "prepared" boundaries that already exist innately) or can CP boundaries be built up entirely from learning? Can the "analysis-by-synthesis" model be generalized to a domain where there is no perception/production analog? Finally, are there any inferences to be made from the functional role of bounded phonemes in speech perception to the role of bounded categories in general, in perception and cognition? Numerous chapters in this volume are accordingly devoted to the available evidence from this best-studied of CP phenomena, speech CP.

4. Rosen and Howell. There are three contending kinds of theories to account for speech CP:

1. The *motor theory* (see Chapter 3 by Repp & Liberman) attributes the discontinuities in speech perception to mediation by discontinuities in speech production. (A Gibsonian variant of this theory turns it on its head, claiming that invariant cues in the sounds themselves signal the discontinuities, and hence how the mouth produced them.)
2. The hypothesis of *innate sensitivity* attributes the discontinuities to inborn enhancement and reduction of the sensory system's sensitivity in selected portions of

certain physical continua (i.e., violations of Weber's law that perceived differences should be proportional to relative physical differences). Sometimes such boundary effects are even generated by higher-order interactions of components of the physical signal itself (i.e., some complex physical continua may not be strictly continuous, as Pastore's chapter also suggests).
3. The *label-learning* hypothesis has several variants: The weakest is that labels are learned by mere exposure and association, and that label differences then come to mediate identification and to influence discrimination in much the way the motor theory claims motor discontinuities do. A stronger version is that label learning, through selective attentional effects and learned expectations, actually alters the encoded similarity structure of stimuli, making those with the same label look more alike. This "acquired similarity" view can be contrasted with a still stronger "acquired distinctiveness" view, whereby stimuli with different labels come to look more different. According to the strongest (Whorf-like) version, label learning produces not just quantitative, but qualitative effects.

Hypotheses 1 to 3 have tended to vie for exclusive sovereignty as explanations of speech CP. Rosen and Howell, however, in a masterly review of the evidence for all sides, show in Chapter 4 that none of the theories is able to account for all the findings alone and that it is more realistic to see the three, not as competitors, but as each making an independent contribution to the CP phenomenon in the special case of speech.

There is strong evidence – for example, with the /ba/, /da/, /ga/ (place-of-articulation) discontinuities – that motor mediation plays a role in phoneme boundary effects. But the absence of CP along the *sh/ch* (frication) continuum makes the motor explanation of the *p/b* (voicing) boundary sound ad hoc. Animal and infant CP-boundary findings support the innate-sensitivity hypothesis, but heightened discrimination by language speakers and boundary-location differences between speakers of different languages implicate learning. Learning seems to be the primary explanation for why musicians show stronger CP for semitone boundaries than nonmusicians; but innate sensitivities may be playing some role in this effect too, as well as in unlearned CP for certain buzz, noise, and relative-timing continua.

Rosen and Howell favor a two-process CP model of the kind discussed by Macmillan. One process involves a rapidly decaying echoic or analog representation of the stimulus and is involved in immediate comparisons; the factors of recency and innate sensitivity would have their effects here. The other process involves a longer-term, context-dependent categorical representation influenced by factors such as the range and relative frequency of the stimuli (i.e., interconfusability); this would be the locus of the speech-specific effects of motor analysis/synthesis as well as of label-learning factors.

In projecting conclusions from the special case of speech CP to CP in general, it is clear that the motor factor will be the least useful (except in production-analog media such as pitch perception). Innate sensitivities clearly do play a role in other modalities such as vision (see Bornstein's chapter). But the most general and potentially interesting factor is that of label learning, for not only is the process underlying label learning critical to all domains of categorization, but the subsequent use of labels (and their underlying representations) also extends into the most general problems of language and cognition. This theme is elaborated later in the volume.

5. Eimas, Miller, and Jusczyk. Some natural questions to ask about CP in adults are, When does it arise? Is it learned or inborn? If learned, how early is it learned? And if inborn, how early is it manifested? Eimas, Jusczyk, and Miller in Chapter 5 provide some of the answers for the special case of speech CP and then go on to review the evidence in other modalities.

Eimas and his coworkers trained preverbal infants to perform an operant response (sucking a nonnutritive device) in order to hear sounds. When a sound is new, infants respond vigorously. When they get used to it after repeated presentations, their response becomes weak. The measure of discrimination is how much a new sound strengthens the response (on the assumption that the strength of the response reflects how discriminable the new sound is from the familiar one).

With this measure Eimas et al. found that four-month-old infants, never having spoken a word, not only have CP boundaries for speech sounds, but even show sensitivity to some of the modulations caused when certain sounds are pronounced together (see Chapter 3 by Repp & Liberman). Eimas et al. concluded that infants are born with "categorical representations" for speech sounds, perhaps encoded in syllabic "chunks." These take the form of "prototypes" that facilitate language learning and can be updated and fine-tuned on the basis of experience with specific languages. This modification of prototypes by experience may either take the form of an irreversible "imprinting" effect or a reversible selective-attentional effect.

Eimas et al. review parallel evidence for innate categorical representations in other modalities. Two CP-like phenomena are perceptual constancy (the tendency to see objects as looking the same despite variations in distance, size, and orientation, or to hear speech as sounding the same despite variations in speaker, rate, and articulatory context) and equivalence classes (the tendency to generalize over certain stimulus variations, responding to them as being equivalent). Using operant discriminative responses, investigators have found CP-like effects in the way infants perceive pattern orientation, faces, and other objects and properties.

Eimas et al. propose a general schema for the formation and revision of categorical representations: innate prototypes, with their parameters fine-tuned by learning. What is unclear is just what a "prototype" really is – other than whatever must be encoded in the brain in order to generate CP. The most prevalent notion of a prototype is that it is some sort of characteristic or ideal category member, one that other members resemble to varying degrees. This is intended to contrast with a rival kind of representation: a set of distinctive features necessary and sufficient to determine category membership (see Chapter 16 by Medin & Barsalou). At the level of the one-dimensional parameters involved in most sensory CP, however, the prototype/feature distinction would appear to collapse. The substantive questions seem to concern the nature of the information represented: how much of it is innate in the case of speech and form perception, how it is modified by experience, and

Critical overview 11

how speech and form CP are related to higher-level categorization (e.g., classification and abstraction).

Models for speech CP

The theories of CP in the special case of speech sounds are at some level all feature-detection models (as the theories of higher-level categorization will also prove to be) even though they may, like prototype models and higher-level knowledge models, be formulated as the rivals of some *specific* type of feature-detection theory. This is true because categorization is concerned with picking out classes of objects in the world; hence if this can be accomplished by a categorizer at all (and not by trivial rote enumeration or by magic), then its success must be the result of having picked out some reliable *basis* for the categorization – something that makes it possible to sort the members from the nonmembers. Although it may not be simple or direct, it may require much computation to find and act on, and it may involve a complex of conditional or either/or properties, in the end this process must nevertheless amount to detecting the *features* of the objects that provide a reliable basis for the categorization. To deny this is either to deny that a reliable basis for the categorization exists in the objects or to deny that the categorizer finds or uses it, which amounts in both cases to denying that the categorization is possible.[4]

6. *Remez*. One special class of feature-detection models in speech-perception research is the neural detectors, which are based on an analogy with feature detectors in vision. Visual feature detectors seem to be organized in an orderly network of dot, line, and edge detectors arranged promisingly in a rising hierarchy of abstraction. This picture was carried over into speech-perception research where it was hoped that the substrates for either the phonetic features peculiar to speech or else some general auditory features, or both, would turn out to have specialized neural detectors. The experimental method used was selective adaptation, on the assumption that if the detector for one of a pair of opponent processes analogous to those in, say, color perception, were selectively fatigued by repeated stimulation, the CP boundaries it governed would accordingly shift in favor of its opponent detector.

In Chapter 6, Remez likens this view to Selfridge's "pandemonium" model of pattern analysis, in which low-level "image demons" detect physical attributes of the stimulation, middle-level "computational demons" detect features peculiar to certain objects, and high-level "cognitive demons" detect objects. The model is called pandemonium because the signaling function of these demons is analogous to yelling, with the demons who yell the loudest calling the shots, so to speak.

At first the empirical results were promising, but then they became more complicated and inconsistent with the phonetic and auditory theories that had indicated what features to look for. Eventually, Remez indicates in his review, something as complex as a homunculus would have had to be performing the functions of the detectors, which now even called for sensitivity to the meaning of the stimulus. Hence feature detectors were abandoned in speech-perception research.

The selective-adaptation method may indeed be an unprofitable way of testing feature-detection theories, because the complex, higher-order correlations and interactions involved in speech perception may not correspond one to one with the activity of any fixed set of neurons. Moreover, there may not be a special neural "module" devoted specifically to speech perception. Indeed, even the sense modalities themselves (hearing, vision, etc.) may not be functionally independent of one another or of higher-order cognition, either in speech perception or in other complex categorical activities. There is little doubt that a pandemonium-like "yelling" model (which is to say, a summation model) is too simple for sophisticated categorization. – But whatever the right model is, it will still have to do feature detection (and the feature detection will have to have a neural substrate).

7. Diehl and Kluender. In Chapter 7, Diehl and Kluender argue that "tacit knowledge" plays a large role in speech recognition. The cues that guide phonetic categorization are not of the local, isolable kind that would have to exist if there were to be specific feature detectors for them. Speech perception is sensitive to holistic and global context effects. To account for this, Diehl and Kluender suggest that there is relatively little analysis of the raw signal in the sensory representation (the "neural spectrogram"). Instead, the hard work is done at a "decision-making stage," on the basis of tacit knowledge about the physical and physiological constraints on speech production.

The authors stress that theirs is not a "motor theory," which depends on the mediation of speech recognition by a production template, but an argument for a knowledge-driven, top-down computational theory. Two actual speech recognition models are discussed: LAFS, a bottom-up feature-detecting model, is rejected as having too many primitive features and not capturing their higher-order regularities. The earlier model, HEARSAY, is preferred because it is more computational.

Assigning a dominant role to knowledge and decision processes amounts to preferring computations on symbolic descriptions of sensory data rather than direct sensory analysis of the sensory data themselves. The questions it leaves unanswered are:

1. What are the symbolic descriptions on which knowledge operates?
2. How does the speech recognizer get from the sensory data to the symbolic descriptions?
3. What is the knowledge that is applied to these descriptions?
4. Where does that knowledge come from?

The detection of the regularities that allow speech to be categorized appropriately amounts formally to "feature detection" whether or not it is done formally. If there are, in fact, no innate or learned sensory feature detectors, then the model must "know" (tacitly?) what they would have had to do, had they existed.

Critical overview 13

8. *Massaro*. As several contributors to this volume point out, in the initial uncertainty about what was and was not special about CP, too much was made of the congruence between discrimination and identification; some investigators had even assumed that what made perception categorical was the impossibility of making any within-category discriminations. A little reflection shows that this cannot be true, for we certainly can tell apart members of the same CP category (although we may not be able to identify them reliably in isolation).

Massaro suggests in Chapter 8 that the failure to find complete within-category indiscriminability argues for abandoning the categorical/continuous distinction altogether: All sensory processes are continuous, and CP boundary effects arise only because of discrete "decision" processes. Such all-or-none decision processes may be engaged by tasks that make memory demands exceeding the capacity of the rapidly decaying sensory trace, forcing the subject to recode the stimulus by giving it a verbal label. Another source of discontinuity would be to provide an external reference stimulus (as described in Chapter 1 by Pastore) or to extend the range of a stimulus continuum across a singularity, such as a zero-crossing.

Massaro calls this decision-governed discontinuity "categorical partitioning" instead of "categorical perception" and offers two kinds of evidence for the fact that the underlying sensory representation is continuous: "goodness" judgments (e.g., "how good a /ba/ is this?") and identification reaction times. Both of these do indeed vary continuously, rather than in the all-or-none fashion characteristic of the identification boundary. Massaro proposes a "fuzzy-logical" model for the underlying continuous aspects of perception, based on graded degrees of category membership.

Massaro's findings and conclusions are consistent with the fact that discrimination performance is not all or none. They do not seem, however, to account for the "anisotropy" of the discrimination continuum, with compression of equal-sized physical differences within categories and amplification between. Moreover, as with the work in the prototype tradition described in Chapter 16 by Medin and Barsalou, the all-or-none character of identification and labeling does not seem to be explained by attributing it to a partitioning by a decision process. Determining the nature of the decision process, how it originates and how it operates on the sensory data, is itself the problem of CP.

CP in other modalities and species

The phenomenon of CP is by no means restricted to speech or to human beings. Although its investigation in other modalities and other species is only beginning, this work is already helping to place CP into clearer functional and ecological perspective.

9. *Bornstein*. Chapter 9 by Bornstein is concerned with whether CP effects are universal or language-relative. According to the "relativist" (Whorf) hypothesis,

language determines how we view reality. The location of CP boundary effects is determined by how we elect to carve the world into nameable parts. The alternative, "universalist" view is that category boundaries tend to occur where nature has put them, either because there are discontinuities in the world or because our nervous system innately imposes discontinuities.

Bornstein examines how the evidence about color categories bears on the two hypotheses. On the basis of color-discrimination performance by animals and infants, as well as by adults in different cultures (with different languages and different named subdivisions of the color spectrum), together with the data on physiological mechanisms of color vision, Bornstein concludes that there is overwhelming support for the universalist hypothesis: Color categories depend on innate detectors, and language and experience probably only influence the fine-tuning or short-term modifications of color boundaries. To ascertain whether color CP is somehow unique or special, Bornstein goes on to make systematic comparisons between color CP and phoneme CP, finding the pattern of data to be very similar in both cases (and recommending where further parallels might be looked at).

Bornstein's findings are important in that they increase our understanding of the special innate mechanisms of color CP and help place phoneme CP into context as less of a special case than it was thought to be. However, color perception and speech perception may still turn out to be "special," in that they are both biologically "prepared" phenomena. The real test of the scope and generality of CP is the case of learning categories for which there is no specially prepared discontinuity, either in the nervous system or in the environment. Can a CP boundary arise in our perception of initially confusable objects purely on the basis of experience with sorting them into different labeled categories?[5]

10. Ehret. Ethologists are interested in what Lorenz called "releasers" or "key stimuli," which trigger specific behaviors, often biologically prepared ones, sometimes learned ones. A prominent class of key stimuli is the communicative signals of animals. Specific calls signal differences between species, between individuals, and between "meanings" (e.g., courtship versus threat).

Ehret reviews in Chapter 10 the evidence that many of these calls are perceived categorically. The strict way to demonstrate this is of course with discrimination and identification tests for the existence of a CP boundary that mediates identification and modulates discrimination within and between categories. Although much of the ethological evidence is incomplete – consisting only of identification data or between- but not within-category discrimination data – CP has been unequivocally confirmed in some cases, and the probability of similar findings is high in many of the analogous incomplete cases in species of many different classes, including insects.

Ehret emphasizes that key stimuli are typically multidimensional and occur in a particular ecological context. Whereas human CP research tends to focus on the variation of a single unidimensional stimulus parameter at a time, ethological CP research is concerned with variation of the whole signal and with its ecological signaling function. Ehret hypothesizes that the adaptive function of CP is to differentiate discrete species-specific, individual-specific, and call-type-specific parameters reliably within noisy and variable multidimensional signals that also vary in continuous motivational parameters. He proposes a specific selective-attentional model for CP, involving the detection of critical durations and frequency bandwidths by means of innate (or learned) templates.

The ethological aspect of CP is important and promising, but some questions arise concerning the commensurability of human and animal CP. For example, it is not clear why categorical *perception* should be needed in animal communication at all, as long as calls can be kept sufficiently discrete by categorical *production*. If natural call types are suitably discrete, then the interpolation of continuous parameters that is involved in testing discrimination would be, in a sense, unecological (in much the same way that "generalization gradients" are unecological). This may also be why CP has so far been confirmed for species and call-type discrimination, but not for discriminating or identifying individual animals: Differences among the calls of individuals may be continuous rather than discrete. Another question concerns the role of biological "preparation" in CP: Do CP boundaries occur only where there is a natural discontinuity, internal or external, or can they occur anywhere? This of course leads to the recurrent and central question about the role of learning in CP. Finally, how representative and critical is the factor of communication and the existence of production/perception homologies? Is there CP in other psychophysical continua as well? In any case, both the continuities and the discontinuities between human and nonhuman CP should help clarify the origins and functions of the phenomenon.

11. Snowdon. The ecological themes raised by Ehret are extended in Chapter 11 by Snowdon, who suggests that the functional role of categorization is to contribute to "cognitive economy" by parsing environmental variation into units that can be processed and manipulated more efficiently than continuous variation, both in sensorimotor performance and in communication. He too provides evidence that, as already noted, one of the provisional criteria for CP – total indiscriminability among members of the same category – was probably unrealistic (and perhaps an artifact of using unnatural stimuli and unnatural testing conditions).

Snowdon reports that pygmy marmosets can discriminate and categorize calls of familiar individuals even though these all belong to the same superordinate category (say, contact calls). Whether or not the subordinate differences are responded to depends on context (e.g., whether the call issues from inside or outside the perceiver's cage). Since such subordinate differences must be learned rather than innate, Snowdon concludes that experience may play a larger role in CP than some theorists have assumed, and he even conjectures that all CP could be the result of learning.

The observation of subordinate-category discriminability is perhaps less surprising in view of the fact that many categorizations are hierarchical, with multiple levels of abstraction (each, presumably, having its own distinctive context of relevant alternative categories); however, the observation provides a valid corrective to the assumption that CP must involve within-category indiscriminability. Snowdon does not test subordinate discriminability directly, but merely infers it from the stronger finding of subordinate identifiability; hence, it remains to determine the shape of the within-category discrimination functions (which will presumably vary with the stimulus domain). Logic suggests that there will have to be some absolute limits on subcategorizability "grain," but evidence suggests that discriminability "grain" will always be somewhat finer.

12. Kuhl. The original CP findings with speech stimuli were interpreted as evidence that speech was somehow "special" – that there existed a level of processing specialized for speech sounds rather than other kinds of sounds. As discussed earlier, the "motor theory of speech perception" was actually a conjecture that incoming speech sounds were recognized by checking them against how they would have to be produced in speaking, and that CP boundaries arose from the discreteness of certain vocal gestures (such as the bilabial /ba/ and the alveolar /da/). Eimas et al.'s (Chapter 5) demonstration of CP in infants reduced considerably the likelihood that a learned vocal template was involved (as the infants had not yet begun to speak). The second possibility for the motor theory was that it was an evolutionarily "prepared" speech analyzer, inherited from the adaptive advantages of speech for our vocal ancestors. In Chapter 12, Kuhl has provided evidence that this cannot be the way in which speech is special either.

Using operant procedures, Kuhl has found that chinchillas and monkeys not only display CP, but that their discrimination and identification boundaries also occur on the same continua (voicing and place-of-articulation) and at roughly the same points (/ba/, /da/, /ga/; /pa/, /ta/, /ka/) that human CP boundaries do. As these animals never speak, this must be a natural auditory discontinuity, which still leaves open the possibility for speech to be special in two senses: These natural sensitivities could have been capitalized on and specialized for speech by natural selection, and the human auditory system may still treat speech and speechlike sounds specially as a consequence. Kuhl still considers these questions open.

Kuhl has also found evidence of "perceptual constancy" and "equivalence classification" for speech sounds in infants. It is hard to imagine such speech-specific equivalence-detection occurring in animals. Still more unlikely in animals is a counterpart of the infant's apparent ability to correlate a speech sound with a face that looks as if it is pronouncing that sound. These phenomena have yet to be checked in animals, however.

It is hard to know yet what to make of these instances of innate auditory CP in animals, on the one hand, and these elements of speech-specific motor-theoretic effects in infants on the other. Perhaps the most prominent question they raise is, How specific to speech is speech CP, and how representative is it of CP in general?

13. Wilson. Wilson offers an interpretation of CP in terms of adaptation-level theory in Chapter 13. According to adaptation-level theory, when stimuli varying in one sensory attribute (or more) are presented to a subject repeatedly, sensory adaptation always takes place, yielding a neutral level for that attribute that is roughly in the midpoint of the range of variation. It is relative to this average value that the other stimuli are perceived as varying. Wilson shows that a calculation of this adaptation level from paired comparison judgments as to which stimulus is relatively greater in the attribute in question will also predict discrimination and identification functions, with the adaptation level corresponding to the category boundary. Wilson conjectures that the nervous system computes adaptation levels and that this underlies our ability to categorize. She goes on to describe some data in animals and normal and brain-damaged humans to suggest that an analysis in terms of adaptation level can be informative about brain locus and underlying function.

There seem to be three problems with adaptation-level theory as a general account of categorical perception:

1. Since every set of stimuli always has an adaptation level, the theory suggests that there should be many more instances of CP than there actually are. In fact, it seems to imply that all sensory continua should be perceived categorically, with qualitative perceptual differences across the adaptation level. This does not appear to be the case.
2. There seems to be no natural way of accounting for long-term effects with adaptation-level theory. One can claim that long-term averaging is always going on, but this does not seem to be a satisfactory predictive account of some of the very dramatic and robust long-term CP effects. (Why are there long-term effects in some continua and not others? Why do short-term adaptation effects not alter long-term boundaries appreciably or permanently?) Yet long-term effects – including innate, "natural" boundaries in some cases – seem to be what is distinctive about CP.
3. In a sense, adaptation-level theory does not really seem to explain function (or predict data) since, by definition, it is calculable a posteriori in all cases. It is not even clear whether its results are really equivalent to standard discrimination and identification functions, even though it simulates their shape, because discrimination and identification derive from independent relative and absolute measures of performance, respectively (paired comparison vs. individual labeling), whereas adaptation level is derived only from relative judgments.

Hence it may be that adaptation-level theory's relevance to CP is more limited, namely, it may describe the short-term plasticity (adaptability) of the category boundary, but not its origins or long-term plasticity.[6]

Psychophysiological indices of CP

Some of the questions that arise about the processes and representations underlying CP are difficult to answer using only discrimination and identification data. Furthermore, there are subjects (such as infants and animals) with whom the ordinary psychophysical procedures cannot be used. Event-related potentials may provide an extension to behavioral methodologies.

When an event occurs and one looks at the scalp electrical activity accompanying it, it looks like noise. However, if the event is repeated many times and the electrical activity is averaged, the noise cancels out and a characteristic waveform called the event-related potential (EP) becomes measurable. Early components of this waveform seem to reflect sensory processes that are relatively constant across individuals and tasks. Later components are influenced by cognitive variables such as attention and expectation.

14. Molfese. As reported in Chapter 14, Molfese has examined EPs accompanying speech and nonspeech auditory stimuli that give rise to CP boundaries. He has found components that are sensitive to between-category differences in 2-month-old infants – younger than could be tested by any other means. He has also found left–right differences in the distribution of these components across the scalp and has been able to study the developmental course of changes in some of them. Although it is too early to be confident in any specific interpretation of these effects, the psychophysiological methodology seems promising and is certainly a welcome supplement to psychophysical methods.

15. Regan. Regan gives a brief sketch in Chapter 15 of how visual EPs might be used to study color categories. There are distinct components of the waveform that are sensitive to hue, although it is sometimes difficult to disentangle them from components sensitive to luminance. EP features have been found to vary in their shape and distribution over the head as a function of the color of the stimulus. EP patterns are also differentially correlated with red, green, and blue stimuli, consistent with the known existence of the three parallel color channels.

Apart from their possible utility in the study of color categories, EPs may also contribute to the study of visual form categories. And, as mentioned, later components may be informative about cognitive processes such as expectation, selective attention, match/mismatch detection, and perhaps also the subliminal time course of the unconscious processes underlying perceptual judgments.

Higher-order categories

Research on people's everyday categorization of concrete and abstract objects has focused on (a) how quickly and easily an instance is judged to be a member of a category, (b) how typical a member it is judged to be, and (c) how subjects *report* that they are accomplishing the categorization (i.e., what features or rules they feel they use).[7] For example, the reaction time for identifying a robin as a bird is shorter than for identifying a penguin as a bird (whether the stimulus is the name or the image of the bird), a robin is rated as being a better or more typical example of a bird than a penguin is, and subjects report that a robin has more of the features characteristic of a bird than a penguin does. From these data it has been inferred that the representation of a bird does not consist (as some had believed) of a set of

Critical overview 19

"defining" features that all birds share, features that provide necessary and sufficient conditions for identifying birds. Rather, the representation is a "prototype" that specific members such as robins and penguins resemble to a greater or lesser degree (hence the variation in reaction time and typicality judgments). It is still an open question what a prototype really is, but it seems to consist of the features of either a typical or an "ideal" category member, rather than invariant features common to every member.

16. Medin and Barsalou. The research on CP and on higher-order categories has been proceeding more or less independently (although prototypes and related concepts have lately found their way into CP theory – see Chapters 5 and 8 by Eimas et al. and Massaro). Chapter 16 by Medin and Barsalou describes parallels between the two lines of categorization research – one concerned with what they call "sensory perception" (SP) categories and the other with "generic knowledge" (GK) categories – in the hope of integrating and unifying them (which is also the objective of this volume as a whole). The authors point out similarities, differences, and empirical questions whose investigation would contribute to both lines of research.

Medin and Barsalou distinguish between two different kinds of categories: (1) all-or-none categories and (2) graded ones. There are two subtypes of all-or-none categories: (1a) In "well-defined" categories all members share a common set of features and a corresponding rule defines these as necessary and sufficient conditions for membership (an example would be "bachelor"). (1b) In "defined" (but not well-defined) categories the features need not be shared by all members, and the rule can be an either/or one (e.g., for a "strike" in baseball). Graded categories (2) are not defined by an all-or-none rule at all, and membership is a matter of degree.

Clearly, the nature of the representations of both SP and GK categories (e.g., whether they consist of defining features or prototypes) and how categorization is accomplished (e.g., whether by detecting defining features or degree of similarity to a prototype) will depend on whether the categories in question are all or none or graded. GK research examines the *ease* or *speed* of identification, whereas CP research focuses on discrimination and identification performance itself. The all-or-none question hinges on whether the identification boundary itself is graded, which remains to be examined in GK research. In SP research it is in fact the all-or-none nature of the boundary (apart from some psychophysical variance near threshold) that sets apart CP and non-CP continua. A convergence of methods and questions is certainly desirable and promising.

Medin and Barsalou's integration of SP and GK categorization research by analyzing their *parallels* is very suggestive. A complementary integrative approach is to consider them *hierarchically* (as I do in Chapter 19), with higher-order concrete and abstract categories (GK) built out of elementary psychophysical ones (SP). The parallels would still exist, for categorization is involved at all levels. But some differences and asymmetries may be accounted for by the fact that the GK categories are being *grounded* in the SP categories in a bottom-up fashion.

17. Keil and Kelly. The representations underlying children's categories, especially as reflected in their word meanings, seem to undergo critical developmental changes. Keil and Kelly suggest in Chapter 17 that categories are initially represented by "characteristic" or "instance-bound" features. These are the features of typical members of the category, but not necessarily the features that reliably "define" membership in the category in general. The shift to such defining features is gradual rather than all or none and it is domain specific, occurring at different times with different categorization problems, even in adulthood. Such shifts seem to occur in all cultures and do not depend on specific changes in parental instructional practices.

Parallel to the characteristic-to-defining shift, there is a shift from "integral" to "separable" dimensions in perception. Initially, children see objects holistically, unable to pay selective attention to some features and ignore others. Gradually, certain perceptual dimensions such as size and color become separable and can be used to categorize things. Other dimensions, however, such as hue and saturation, remain integral (although this may be a matter of relative ease of separation, rather than absolute unseparability).

Keil and Kelly suggest that in the holistic stage the child is categorizing on the basis of prototypes: characteristic features with integral dimensions. The only way he can sort things is by their overall similarities. In the later, analytic stage, representations consist of separable, defining features. The child is then sorting things the way we do, and can usually even verbalize the basis for his categorization in the form of a rule or definition.

The questions this raises concern the nature of the initial and final representations and the nature of the experience and the processing that produce the "shift" from one kind of representation to the other. If I may use the editor's prerogative to make some unifying conjectures: Perhaps the first, "holistic" representation is chiefly analog, and the second, "analytic" one consists of distinctive features that have been picked out by the category-induction process. (As Keil and Kelly indicate, learning the correct names of objects is the crucial task here.) Then, once learned, perhaps the labels that identify categories function as symbols in a third representational system, the one underlying language. The function of the three representational systems would then be, respectively, discrimination, identification, and description, with CP being responsible for the shift from the first to the second representational system by the formation of discrete category boundaries that "separate" the pertinent features.

18. Bialystok and Olson. Propositions are the abstract meanings that are expressed by sentences. One simplified way to think of a proposition is as predicating something to be true of its subject: "Straight (line)" proposes that the line is straight. "On (cat, mat)" proposes that the cat is on the mat. Some cognitive theorists (e.g., Pylyshyn 1980) have hypothesized that all cognitive processes are propositional – not conscious English sentences, but strings of abstract symbols in the brain formulated in the "language of thought" (Fodor, 1975). These theorists have argued that until and unless the objects we see, and any imagelike copies our brains make of them, are turned into these abstract descriptions, we are not yet doing cognition, but relying on a homunculus to look at our images and do our cognition for us.

One of the prominent features of any propositional code is that it must operate on discrete symbols. Hence, in (say) vision, a physical object is viewed, it makes an analog projection on the retina, and then, at some stage in processing, that analog information must somehow be filtered, digitized, and turned into symbols for the propositional system to be able to operate on. CP would be an obvious candidate for mediating this sort of analog/digital (A/D) conversion – if and when it really takes place. Some investigators, however, have tried to show that, at least in some areas of perception, the A/D conversion never happens. These counterexamples have tended to involve spatial perception, a domain in which continuity is particularly important.

Shepard showed that the length of time it takes subjects to make same/different judgments about pairs of shapes, one in standard position and the other rotated, is proportional to the degree of rotation (see Shepard & Cooper, 1982). He concluded that subjects mentally rotate images to perform the comparison. To answer him, propositionalists would have to claim that the rotation angle was somehow categorical, with the propositional process taking longer in proportion to the number of rotation increments that had to be encoded symbolically. This has strained some theorists' sense of parsimony, but others have accepted that even spatial perception may be better explained propositionally.

Bialystok and Olson advocate such a propositional theory of spatial representation in Chapter 18. They hypothesize that spatial relations are encoded as structural descriptions, each consisting of a spatial predicate with two arguments (as in the example, "On [cup, table]"), and that this accounts for a large body of spatial performance data. They make a distinction between spatial properties that are "implicit" in a representation (e.g., "round," for a child who has the category "ball" but not yet the category "roundness") and properties that are "explicitly" represented as categories (as demonstrated by the subject's capacity to name and use the property in describing and solving spatial problems such as judging how an object looks from another orientation). All implicit properties are potentially explicit, presumably. The authors also emphasize the relational character of spatial properties (usually described by two-place predicates) and the fact that they tend to be binary (e.g., above/below), which Bialystok and Olson call "categorical." The authors write that whereas object boundaries are often fuzzy, spatial property boundaries are "strict." To confirm this hypothesized CP effect, however, discrimination/identification tests still remain to be performed.

Bialystok and Olson emphasize that they are not proposing a theory of the source of propositional spatial representations – only that the assumption that subjects have and use them accounts for their spatial performance. The authors do express doubts, however, that these spatial descriptions are the output of feature detectors, either innate or learned (chiefly because they do not consider relations to be features and because there are too many relations), suggesting instead that the predicates themselves may be innate.

The propositional approach to spatial representation raises many unanswered questions. For, if correct descriptions are indeed mediating spatial performance, then the substantive problem in modeling spatial categorization seems to be that of accounting for how we get from viewing objects to correct (or correctable) descriptions of their spatial properties. Behind every reliable problem-solving performance there is always a description of the successful solution, but proposing that the subject is actually *using* that description, rather than that he is merely describable as performing in accordance with it, presupposes the solution to the antecedent problem of how he *arrived at* the right description (or any description at all). CP itself is one possible hypothesis about the origins of spatial categories and their names ("on," "behind," "beside," etc.).

Cognitive foundations

19. Harnad. What features of CP can be generalized to categorization as a whole? The hypothesis underlying my own chapter is that the "identification" in the psychophysical labeling task, the "identification" in object recognition, and the "identification" in linguistic naming are one and the same. This implies that learning to label regions of a one-dimensional stimulus continuum should be representative of the sorting and naming of all the multidimensional objects in the world. The representations and processes underlying elementary psychophysical label learning should accordingly be like the representations and processes underlying categorization in general. In addition, it is noteworthy that higher-order categories are constituted of elementary psychophysical ones. The bounded CP category may also be the "chunk" out of which the rest is built.

If psychophysical labeling performance is representative of categorization in general, then what sort of model would be needed to generate it? CP is defined by the discrimination and identification function. Discrimination requires analog stimulus traces for relative comparisons and for other analog operations. These representations need not – indeed cannot – be categorical. Identification requires a feature detector that reliably picks out the features distinguishing the members of a category from confusable nonmembers. Features that are not innate must be learned from experience, so categorical representations for learned categories consist of learned feature detectors. Finally, the labels of the bounded CP categories provide the elementary terms for a third representational system, the symbolic descriptions of natural language (and perhaps also of the "language of thought").

My concluding chapter describes such a three-level representational system – iconic, categorical, and symbolic – with a special emphasis on the role of learning processes and context. Every category is based on a specific *context* of alternatives. Without this representative sample of the relevant, confusable *complement* of a category, the highly underdetermined search for features may never converge (i.e., it may never yield reliable, successful categorization performance). Moreover, convergence is always provisional: Categories always remain context relative and approximate. Yet, when they are well learned, most categories are nevertheless all-or-none, not graded or fuzzy, even though a new, anomalous case could foil the provisional feature detector at any time.

The model does not answer all the questions I have raised in connection with the other chapters. Its most prominent weakness is that it does not give an algorithm for learning; it merely assumes that learning is possible, and takes place somehow. The model is not particularly useful if either the role of learning in CP turns out to be minimal or (what amounts to the same thing) feature detection turns out not to be a hard (i.e., underdetermined) problem. The model's contribution to the problem of language and meaning is also inconsequential if perceptual representations of objects don't turn out to have much to do with what we can do with words, and how.

The model does suggest a strategy for further investigating categorization and CP, however. If the induction/representation hypotheses have any validity then we ought to be studying and modeling the time course of changes in discrimination and identification performance (and perhaps their psychophysiological correlates) during actual label learning as a function of the context of alternatives sampled and the degree of informational underdetermination of the features (invariants) that are sufficient to subserve reliable categorization. The experimental paradigm would be a time-series elaboration of the discrimination and identification paradigm of CP research, beginning, systematically and parametrically, with concrete one-dimensional sensory continua and working up to multidimensional and eventually even abstract categories to be identified and discriminated.

Microcomputers make it very easy to generate new and unfamiliar visual and auditory patterns, in one and many dimensions. Interactive programs can provide subjects with instances and feedback as to the correctness of their provisional labeling while at the same time gathering data on how their identification performance develops in real time, from trial to trial, as the sample grows and the context of confusable alternatives widens. Parallel discrimination tests can determine the cumulating effects of the label-learning process on perceived similarity structure – acquired distinctiveness and similarity – and especially CP *boundary formation*. The roles of direct experience and verbal description can also be compared.

We have George Miller's (1956) famous limits on informational capacity. They could be supplemented by an assessment of the limits on just *how* underdetermined (confusable) the features of a category can be before they make the category unlearnable altogether. Data on how categorization performance improves with time under feedback conditions may provide clues about those early childhood learning processes and "tabula rasa" mechanisms that the study of old, overlearned categories and their recombination does not seem able to provide. And how label learners use cumulative information and contend with anomalous instances could also be informative about the "real time" nature of category learning and revision.

Pari passu with this bottom-up approach to category learning, it would be necessary to model category formation computationally. However, instead of modeling the higher-order, overlearned categories that we know people have (but for which we have no idea of a realistic entry point), we could try to model psychophysical labeling performance bottom-up too, implementing the three-way division of labor in the representational architecture that has been proposed here.

Conclusions

This volume brings together a diversity of research united only by the organizing principle offered by the CP phenomenon. Whether it will have been a stimulus to unified and productive inquiry into how organisms sort the objects of the world into categories, or merely a symposium on some of the false starts and side alleys peculiar to speech-perception research, will depend on how special CP really is: whether it can indeed furnish the groundwork for cognition in general.

Notes

1. The question of the origins of the labels touches on the problem of innateness and learning and is ordinarily not addressed directly by the psychophysical approach.

2. For the more classical definition of CP in speech perception, see Studdert-Kennedy, Liberman, Harris & Cooper (1970) and Repp's (1984) review.

3. Bruno Repp (personal communication) has suggested that this classical example of the phonemic/phonetic distinction may no longer be accurate on the basis of current phonetic analysis because the *ur* sound is really a single "rhotecized" vowel. As a better example he suggests the subtler case of the *a* in *fat* versus the nasalized *a* in *fan*.

4. The related Gibsonian concepts of "invariants" and "affordances" are discussed in a companion volume by Neisser (1987) on higher-order categories.

5. This question was already raised by Lane (1965) in his famous critique of the motor theory.

6. Martha Wilson (personal communication) has provided replies to the questions raised in the critical overview. The following is a summary of her replies: (i) Long-term effects of experience on categorization are part and parcel of adaptation-level (AL) theory and are discussed specifically in the chapter. (ii) Conventional identification functions were presented. The AL is not ordinarily derived solely from relative judgment; the relative method was specially devised for studying CP in animals, infants, and aphasic subjects. (iii) The AL is not necessarily in the middle of the range. (iv) The quantitative theory makes it plain that well-established boundaries cannot be moved within an experimental session. (v) It is not at all clear in what respect the theory fails to predict data. (vi) The theory does predict boundaries for all sensory continua; it is an empirical question whether this hypothesis is confirmed. Data are reported in the chapter showing that if the adaptation level is taken into account, the prediction holds for the five continua studied. It is also shown why other approaches may fail to find boundaries. (vii) It is not at all clear how AL theory fails to explain the "origins and long-term plasticity" of CP. In contrast to the other approaches, it does so explicitly.

7. See Neisser's (1987) companion volume for a more extensive exposition of this line of research.

References

Durlach, N. I., & Braida, L. D. (1969). Intensity perception. I. Preliminary theory of intensity resolution. *Journal of the Acoustical Society of America, 46,* 372–383.
Fodor, J. (1975). *The language of thought.* New York: Crowell.
Lane, M. (1965). The motor theory of speech perception: A critical review. *Psychological Review, 72,* 275–309.
Liberman, A. M., Harris, K. S., Hoffman, H. S., & Griffith, B.C. (1957). The discrimination of speech sounds within and across phoneme boundaries. *Journal of Experimental Psychology, 54,* 358–368.
Miller, G. A. (1956). The magical number seven, plus or minus two: Some limits on our capacity for processing information. *Psychological Review, 63,* 81–97.
Neisser, U. (1987). *Concepts and conceptual development: Ecological and intellectual factors in categorization.* Cambridge University Press.
Pylyshyn, Z. W. (1980). Computation and cognition: Issues in the foundation of cognitive science. *Behavioral and Brain Sciences, 3,* 111–169.
Repp, B. H. (1984). Categorical perception: Issues, methods and findings. In N. J. Lass (Ed.), *Speech and language: Advances in basic research and practice* (Vol. 10). New York: Academic Press.
Shepard, R. N., & Cooper, L. A. (1982). *Mental images and their transformations.* Cambridge, MA: MIT Press/Bradford.
Studdert-Kennedy, M., Liberman, A. M., Harris, K. S., & Cooper, F. S. (1970). Motor theory of speech perception: A reply to Lane's critical review. *Psychological Review, 77,* 234–249.
Whorf, B. L. (1964). *Language, thought and reality.* Cambridge, MA: MIT Press.

Part I

Psychophysical foundations of categorical perception

1 Categorical perception: Some psychophysical models

Richard E. Pastore

Categorical perception (CP) was originally believed to involve a unique, discrete recoding of speech stimuli by species-specific perceptual processes. During the last decade, the empirical basis for the CP phenomenon has changed in a number of significant ways. While undergoing these changes, the phenomenon itself has taken on an identity of its own with an importance that transcends and is in many ways orthogonal to the original demonstrations of speech CP. This chapter first discusses the original conceptualization of CP in terms of expected psychophysical measures, comparing that conceptualization with less discrete modes of perception. The nature of the metamorphosis of this phenomenon and the contribution of its various changes to its current status in the auditory perception literature is then examined. It is argued that CP and category boundary effects differ qualitatively rather than quantitatively, and that both are indicative of restricted regions of perceptual sensitivity, but not necessarily of a discrete perceptual recoding of the physical stimulus information. A number of psychophysical models of nondiscrete stimulus processing which should yield data meeting the criterion for categorical perception are discussed. Finally, a number of CP results are reanalyzed in terms of the psychophysical models, and the implications of these results for specialized processing of complex stimuli are reexamined.

Categorical perception (CP) originally referred only to a phenomenon in which a range of stimuli from a physical continuum gave rise to a limited set of discrete perceptual responses. This notion of a discrete perceptual recoding of a physical continuum can be contrasted with more traditional psychophysical functions that crudely approximate the continuous monotonic recoding implied by Fechner's Law and Stevens's Power Law.[1] One early conceptual version of CP is summarized in Figure 1.1, where a continuum of physical stimuli is processed or transduced into a monotonically related sensory continuum, which is then recoded into a discrete set of perceptual responses. In the speech-perception literature, an additional assumption was added to this notion, giving rise both to the conception that CP was truly discrete and to an operational definition for CP. The assumption was that the recoding resulted in loss of subsequent access to the earlier sensory distinctions among stimuli;[2] the only stimulus distinctions that can be accessed by the listener are those that exist subsequent to the discrete recoding. The mystique of CP was further enhanced by assertions that most acoustic continua (as well as most sensory continua) are perceived continuously, assertions that are, at best, oversimplified.

In Figure 1.1, perceptual responses a'', b'', c'', d'' are equivalent and would be

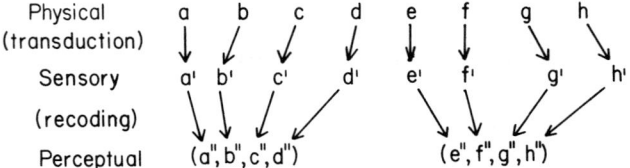

Figure 1.1. Classical model of absolute CP. Stimuli from a physical continuum (unprimed letters) are transduced by the receptor system into sensory analogs (single primes). The sensory continuum is presented here as single dimensional with the stimulus order montonically related to the ordering of the physical stimuli that give rise to those sensations. The sensory representations of the stimuli are then recoded into two discrete perceptual states. One can add further assumptions to this model, such as that the sensory representations do not reach a level of conscious awareness, or that they affect behavior only through their recoded perceptual form.

assigned a single label; they are distinct from the other set of equivalent perceptual responses, e'', f'', g'', h'', which would be assigned a different single label. Both the assignment of differential labels to the perceptual responses resulting from the stimulus continuum and the discriminability among pairs of those stimuli can be based only on the distinction between these two sets of perceptual responses because distinctions within a set of perceptual responses do not exist. Where one finds discrete labeling categories that indicate this absolute recoding of the stimulus information one would expect to find both chance performance in discriminating among the perceptually equivalent stimuli drawn from a single perceptual category (whose membership is estimated from the labeling data) and a higher degree of discriminability between stimuli drawn from separate perceptual categories (again estimated from the labeling data). Thus, except for measurement error, the discrimination and labeling functions should be perfectly correlated. In fact, one definition for CP is "the equivalence of discrimination and identification measures," assuming that the measures are equated for task differences (Macmillan, Kaplan, & Creelman, 1977). Any case of absolute or perfect CP would produce a difference limen[3] (DL) for the lower category equal to the physical difference between the given stimulus magnitude, S, and the category boundary, B. For the upper category, the DL should be determined by the next higher category boundary, B' (should one exist). These conditions are shown in Figure 1.2 for an arbitrary continuum.

I will develop the various concepts of CP in terms of the DL. The upper panel of Figure 1.3 plots some arbitrary discrimination results in terms of d' for a constant stimulus difference, while the lower panel plots these same results in terms of the DL.[4] Here we have used $d' = 1.0$ as our measure of the DL and have assumed additivity of d'; when actually tested, additivity of d' usually is found to be only roughly approximated (see Chapter 2 by Macmillan). Note that the DL function is not simply the inverse of the d' function. I find the DL function easier to use than the d' function in examining CP because the discrimination-function step size can always be compared directly with the DL, whereas the direct use of a theoretical (or empirical) d' function depends on the use of a stimulus difference equal to the step

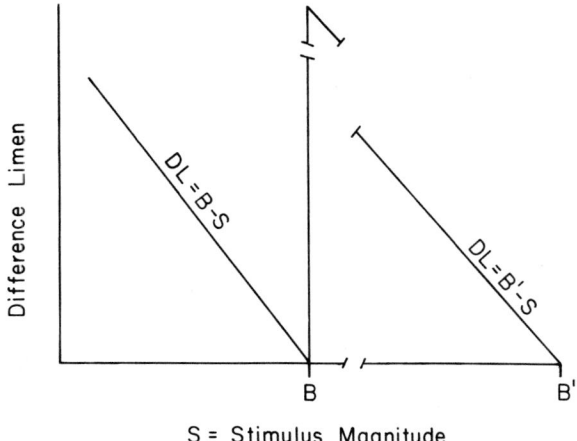

Figure 1.2. The difference limen (DL) as a function of physical-stimulus magnitude based on the model presented in Figure 1.1. Stimulus-magnitude, B, would fall between stimuli d and e in Figure 1.1 and represents the category boundary. The assumption here is that we are measuring the smallest identifiable stimulus difference. The DL is then determined by the stimulus distance from the category boundary, B. If we assume measurement errors of magnitude c, the DL should have an additive constant of c. If we always have the standard stimulus lower in value than the comparison, the DL would be a large, constant value for all stimulus magnitudes above B; if another category boundary, B', exists for the stimulus values above B, the DL should abruptly increase at B, then be a function of the stimulus distance between the ordinate value, S, and the new category boundary.

size. Although a DL function provides an important way to examine the underlying psychophysical relationship (one that is not available in more classical presentations of percent or d' as a function of stimulus magnitude), it cannot directly reveal the natural versus learned boundary anchor effects analyzed by Macmillan (Chapter 2) using d' analyses.

In using the DL function, it is important to keep in mind that the DL represents a measure of central tendency for a discriminability distribution at the given stimulus value. When the stimulus step size is larger than the DL, average discrimination performance is better than the criterion used to measure the DL (e.g., $d' = 1.0$) by an amount proportional to the difference between the step size and the DL. Conversely, when the stimulus step size is smaller than the DL, average discrimination performance will be less than that criterion level of performance, again by a degree proportional to the difference between the DL and the step size.

Historical review

In the human speech perception literature, CP was found to occur with consonants (in vowel context) varying over single physical continua, but not when these were presented in isolation (Liberman, Harris, Hoffman, & Griffith, 1957; Liberman, Harris, Kinney, & Lane, 1961; Mattingly, Liberman, Syrdal, & Halwes, 1971). CP

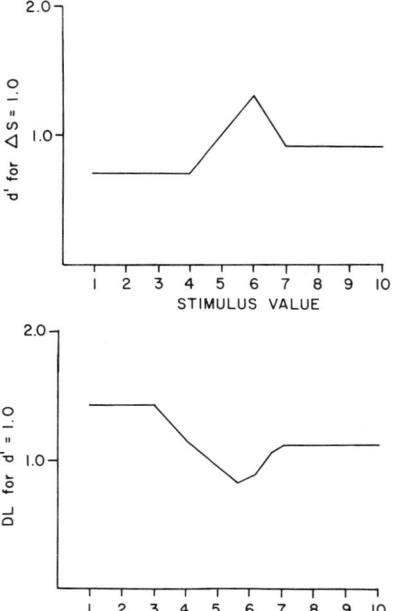

Figure 1.3. The upper panel plots a hypothetical psychometric function relating d' to stimulus magnitude for a constant stimulus difference. The lower panel plots the difference limen (DL) for $d' = 1.0$ derived from the d' function.

was claimed to be unique to speech stimuli, and not to occur with other types of stimuli, thus supporting the developing speech-is-special claims (Liberman et al., 1961; Mattingly, 1972). Lane's (1965) challenge to this claim led to a strong rebuttal by Studdert-Kennedy and associates in which a set of four operational criteria for CP were proposed (Studdert-Kennedy, Liberman, Harris, & Cooper, 1970). In their conception, CP requires (a) distinct labeling categories with sharp boundaries, (b) regions or "troughs" of chance performance in discriminating stimuli drawn from the same labeling category, (c) a discrimination performance peak at the category boundary, and (d) a close correspondence between the actual discrimination performance and discrimination performance predicted from the labeling results based on the assumption of absolute categorization. Although it was conjectured that categorically perceived speech "stimuli are responded to, and *can only be responded to, in absolute terms* [their italics]" (Studdert-Kennedy et al., 1970, p. 234), the second criterion clearly allows for less than absolutely discrete perception, requiring only regions of chance performance rather than uniform chance performance. This operational definition of CP is the standard one used in the auditory-perception literature, although there are several auditory-perception studies that have ignored significant aspects of this definition in claiming to find CP (for discussion, see Pastore, 1976; Pastore, Szczesiul, Wielgus, Nowikas, & Logan, 1984). We note that the definitions of CP used in other perceptual research areas (many are described in this volume) differ from this operational definition and are often more like the definition for category boundary effects described below.

There have been a number of problems with the various "demonstrations" of CP for auditory stimuli. Whereas labeling results usually exhibited relatively sharp boundaries among categories, stimuli two or three "steps" into categories were still identified as members of the alternative category at rates of at least 5% to 10%. One might attribute this discrepancy to measurement errors, although the same measurement errors are not seen with stimuli further into categories. A more likely hypothesis, borrowed from quantum-threshold theory, was that the category boundary has some instability due to stimulus variability, recoding variability, or both factors. Thus, the absence of a discrete labeling boundary is only a minor problem with the concept of CP.

A second, more critical problem with demonstrations of CP was the finding that the discrimination function (and especially its peak at the category boundary) was usually better than predicted on the basis of the labeling data alone. Better-than-predicted discrimination performance has been reported for speech stimuli defining place continua (Liberman et al., 1957), voice-onset-time (VOT) continua (Liberman et al., 1961; Pisoni & Lazarus, 1974), fricative-affricate continua (Cutting & Rosner, 1974), and musical rise-time continua (Cutting & Rosner, 1974). Other factors were therefore assumed to play a role in the measurement of CP. For example, it was conjectured that there was some short-lived residual or echoic memory for the original sensory information that was useful in the performance of any discrimination tasks that involved the comparison of stimuli presented within a single trial (Pisoni & Lazarus, 1974; Cutting & Rosner, 1974). Another conjecture was based on the notion of a dual processing of the signals in terms of discrete or categorical speech perceptions and continuous acoustic perceptions with some access to the continuous process possible in a discrimination task (Wood, 1976; Pisoni, 1975; Fujisaki & Kawashima, 1970; for further discussion, see Macmillan, Repp and Liberman, and Harnad, this volume). The original formula for predicting discrimination performance from the labeling results assumed only absolute categorization; this formula was subsequently modified to include the assumption that other factors, such as memory, allowed for better-than-predicted discrimination data (Fujisaki & Kawashima, 1970). In their evaluation of CP tasks, Macmillan et al. (1977; see also Chapter 2 by Macmillan in this volume) estimate that the "other" factors typically produce an average discrimination performance level of 67%, or better, in those tasks. Thus, although the finding of CP was, and often still is, interpreted in terms of an *absolute* recoding, neither the actual data demonstrating CP nor the criteria used to evaluate those data support the view that the perceptual categories are absolutely discrete. We have a phenomenon that is assumed to be more discrete than its demonstrations indicate.

Selective adaptation

In the mid-1970s, research on CP led to several significant developments. Eimas and Corbit (1973) conjectured that CP for speech stimuli might be the result of the activation of specialized speech feature detectors. The notion of specialized neural units that respond to a specific, limited range of stimulus characteristics had been proposed for the visual system based on electrophysiological research (Hubel & Wiesel, 1962). If the perception of speech stimuli were mediated by a limited set of specialized feature detectors, then we would expect to find the type of discrete perceptual behavior characteristic of CP. In the human-vision literature, feature detectors had been conjectured to be involved with adaptation aftereffects apparently involving a fatiguing of the detector (Riggs, 1973; Weisstein, 1970). If specialized feature detectors were responsible for the categorical nature of speech perception, then one should be able to modify the location of the category boundary by selectively adapting one of the feature detectors.

The basic idea was that the range of adequate stimuli for a feature detector overlaps to a limited degree with the stimulus range for the detectors whose range is adjacent along the stimulus continuum. This overlap in stimulus range would account for the less than perfectly discrete labeling boundary for the identification categories mediated by the feature detectors. Fatiguing one feature detector by repeated stimulation should reduce its responsiveness (or raise its activation threshold), thus increasing the likelihood that stimuli in the overlapping stimulus region will activate the other, nonfatigued detector. This fatigue would result in a shift in the location labeling boundary toward the adapting stimulus. If the feature detectors are responsible for CP, then one also would expect a corresponding shift in the discrimination boundary. These results have been reported by Eimas and Corbit (1973) and by a number of subsequent researchers (see Chapter 5 by Eimas, Miller, & Jusczyk and Chapter 7 by Diehl and Kluender).

Although the phenomenon of selective adaptation for the auditory system was originally investigated to provide evidence for the feature-detector explanation of CP, in subsequent research the two phenomena tended to be treated as separate and largely independent. With only a few exceptions, later research on selective adaptation tended to use only a labeling task, ignoring the discrimination task necessary to relate the results to CP. Also, later models for selective adaptation conjectured that stimulus range effects (Parducci, 1974) or response contrast (Diehl, 1975) were responsible for selective adaptation. Implicit in these models is the notion that stimuli drawn from within a labeling category are not completely identical in their resulting perceptual responses, thus allowing for the modification of the role of specific stimulus characteristics in defining the range of response activation for subjects undergoing selective adaptation. Because selective adaptation has apparently developed into a phenomenon with its own identity and independent existence, we shall not dwell on it further in our examination of CP (chapters by Bornstein, Remcz, & Wilson in this volume focus on selective adaptation).

Nonspeech demonstrations and models

Auditory stimuli

The second major development in the CP literature was the demonstration of CP for nonspeech continua. CP was demonstrated for musical triads (Locke & Kellar,

Psychophysical models

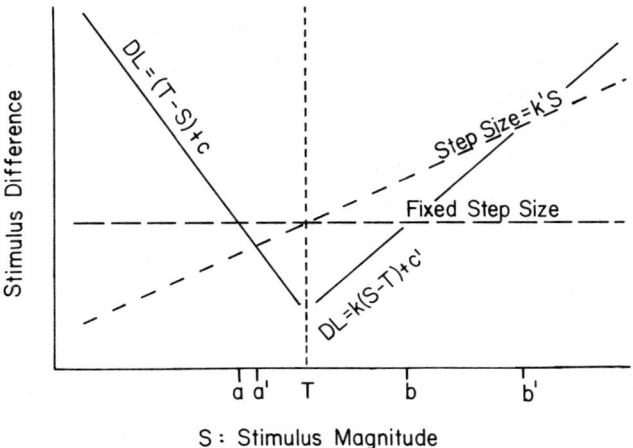

Figure 1.4. Hypothetical stimulus difference as a function of stimulus magnitude for an absolute threshold model of CP. The DL stimuli below threshold (to the left of T) are equal to the stimulus distance from threshold (plus a constant representing measurement error, threshold variability, and so on). Above threshold the DL follows a Weber's law relationship. In addition to indicating the DL (solid lines), a constant or fixed step size and a proportional ($k'S$) step size for a discrimination task are indicated. When the DL is larger than the step size ($S < a$ or a'; $S > b$ or b' for fixed [unprimed] and variable [primed] step size), discrimination performance should be at chance. When the DL is smaller than the step size ($a < S < b$ or $a' < S < b'$), discrimination performance will be proportional to the degree to which the DL has been exceeded.

1973; Pastore, Schmuckler, Rosenblum, & Szczesiul, 1983), musical intervals (Burns & Ward, 1978), and a rise-time continuum (Cutting & Rosner, 1974; although see the later section on artifacts). Categorical perception was also demonstrated for noise-buzz sequences modeled after speech VOT continua, whereas continuous perception was found for the isolated noise component of these stimuli (Miller, Wier, Pastore, Kelly, & Dooling, 1976). Miller et al. proposed that CP could be due to the existence of an absolute threshold (limen) along a continuum; subliminal stimuli would be perceived as being equivalent and discriminated at chance. Supraliminal stimuli would differ from subliminal stimuli and would probably exhibit a Weber's law discrimination function; if the discrimination step size were smaller than the difference limen (DL) for supraliminal stimuli several steps above the threshold, one would find chance-discrimination performance. This condition is illustrated in Figure 1.4.

With stimuli below absolute threshold, T, the DL for a stimulus is equal to the difference between the magnitude of that stimulus and the magnitude of a stimulus at threshold (plus some constant, c, which allows for stimulus, threshold, and measurement variability); the assumption here is that whereas subliminal stimuli may not be discriminably different from each other, all subliminal stimuli should be different from any supraliminal stimuli. This assumption was used to predict the DL in Figure 1.2 based on the notion of absolute categorization (although here we have added an arbitrary constant, c). The DLs for supraliminal stimuli are assumed to follow Weber's law, and are thus equal to a constant fraction, k, of the suprathreshold magnitude (S-T) plus a constant, c'. Note that if the Weber constant, k, is equal to unity and c' is negligible, this condition for the DL is psychophysically equivalent to the absolute CP condition shown in Figure 1.2; empirically measured Weber constants, however, are significantly less than unity. In practice, however, few continua are orderly or follow a Weber's law relationship, and few thresholds are indicative of an absolute limit to stimulus processing (a high threshold). Most absolute limits on performance are conceptualized in terms of low-threshold theory, where the lower limit on measured performance is some form of noise or a factor other than the threshold. We can assume that the threshold described in Figure 1.4 represents some average effect of noise in the perceptual system, which, for "subliminal" stimuli, masks or otherwise limits the detection of the relevant stimulus parameter(s) for the continuum, whereas other noise limits the discriminability of "supraliminal" stimuli. The latter formulation of the model in Figure 1.4 is consistent with statistical decision theory.

Discriminability is usually measured by comparing stimuli that differ by a constant stimulus difference (or fixed step size). This measurement condition is indicated in Figure 1.4. When the step size is less than the DL, we should find chance performance; in Figure 1.4, this condition is found for $S<a$ and $S>b$. When the step size is greater than the DL, discrimination performance is proportional to the difference between the DL and the step size in Figure 1.4; better-than-chance performance is found for $a < S < b$, with the discrimination peak at $S = T$. We have also plotted the condition where the step size for discrimination performance is a constant proportion of the stimulus magnitude ($k'S$). The rationale for a proportional step size is based on the assumption that, at least as a very rough approximation, a Weber's law relationship (or logarithmic transformation of stimulus information) is appropriate for the given continuum. This condition yields essentially the same results, only with the better-than-chance discrimination region shifted to between a' and b'. This model describes conditions that should meet all four criteria for CP, predicting CP for both the constant step size and the proportional step-size conditions. In this model, increasing the step size (or mean step size) will increase the height and the width of the discrimination peak but will continue to yield CP. Although the model does not represent absolute CP, it does indicate that the category boundary represents a discontinuity in the transduction of the physical continuum into its perceptual representation. Thus, the results indicate that there is something unique or critical happening at the category boundary and, according to this model, that that critical condition is the existence of a perceptual threshold.

Visual stimuli

An example of the application of this model is our demonstration of CP for flickering visual stimuli (Pastore, Ahroon, Baffuto, Friedman, Puleo, & Fink, 1977). The

Psychophysical models

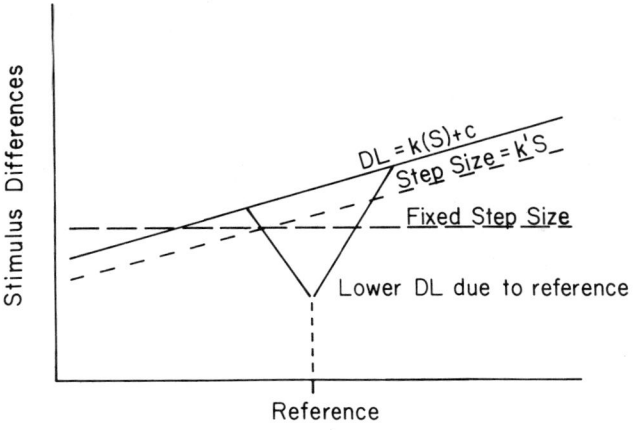

Figure 1.5. Hypothetical stimulus difference as a function of stimulus magnitude for a continuum that follows Weber's law. The addition of a reference stimulus lowers the DL in the region of the reference. The fixed and proportional step sizes are explained in Figure 1.3.

absolute threshold is that for flicker fusion or CFF. We find a sharp labeling boundary between the "flicker" and "fused" responses. Short-period (therefore, high-frequency) stimuli are all subliminal to the flicker threshold and are consistently discriminated at chance. There is a discrimination peak for cross-threshold comparisons that contrast flickering and fused stimuli. Although discrimination performance for stimuli with longer periods (lower frequency) has a "trough" of chance performance, these stimuli, which are supraliminal to the fusion threshold, tend to be discriminated at better than a chance level.

In our 1977 paper we proposed a second condition under which CP should be found (Pastore et al., 1977). This condition is summarized in Figure 1.5. Here we take a continuum where the DL obeys Weber's law at least as an approximation. We assume that the magnitude of the DL is limited by some form of noise, stimulus uncertainty, or variability in the physical stimulus or the encoding of the stimulus information. One type of stimulus uncertainty might be a task requirement that the subject must use long-term memory for certain aspects of the stimulus parameters. The various sources of variability represent a limit on the ability to label differentially or respond to stimuli. In signal-detection-theoretic terms, the discriminability of two stimuli is inversely proportional to the magnitude of the variability (or noise) for the given stimuli, whereas the DL is directly proportional to that variability. If we add a constant stimulus reference, we can reduce uncertainty for stimulus parameters near the reference, thus reducing the effective noise in the perceptual system and creating a local DL minimum along the continuum near the reference. The subjects can also readily label the stimuli in terms of their relationship to the reference. This condition has been plotted in Figure 1.5. Note that both the fixed step size and the proportional step-size condition would meet the four criteria for CP. I demonstrated such CP for a visual line-length continuum by adding a reference that mediates the perception of the letter contrasts v-Y and D-P (Pastore, 1978). Returning to our hypothetical condition, we note that a small increase in the fixed step size (relative to that shown in Figure 1.5) will result in the discrimination performance for the subreference stimulus category always exceeding chance, while discrimination performance for suprareference stimuli may remain at chance. With the proportional step-size condition, a sufficient increase in the mean step size will push discrimination performance to above chance levels for most or all of the stimulus continuum.

Psychophysical discontinuities

The CP models summarized in Figures 1.4 and 1.5 both conjecture a local increase in the size of the perceptual distance between stimuli along an otherwise relatively orderly continuum. Although auditory continua often have been asserted to be perceived continuously, Stevens (1975, 1981) has reminded us on several occasions that the perceptual transfer function for the auditory system is not simple and is not uniform across a physical continuum. Thus, small uniform changes in the physical parameter of a stimulus may, for some region of the continuum of variation, produce small uniform changes in perception, while in other regions of the continuum, the same uniform physical change may result in a large or significant change in perception. This can be demonstrated by reference to the classic stimulus-interaction results mapped 60 years ago by Wegel and Lane (1924). A portion of their results has been redrawn in Figure 1.6.

Wegel and Lane presented subjects with two simultaneous tones: The primary tone was fixed at 1200 Hz at 80 dB, while the secondary tone varied in frequency and intensity. The subjects were asked to report the nature of their perception. If the secondary tone was 1600 Hz and one systematically varied its intensity, the subjects heard only the primary tone for secondary-tone intensities below a masked threshold of approximately 46 dB; then they heard an additional difference tone varying in intensity as the intensity was increased above 46 dB. At approximately 58 dB the perception of the secondary tone was added. If, instead, intensity was held constant at 60 dB and frequency was varied, increasing from 500 Hz, the subject first heard both tones, then both tones plus a difference tone, then only the primary tone, then the primary tone plus beats, then only the primary tone again, and so forth. These two variations in physical continua should give rise both to relatively uniform changes in perception within the perceptual classes and to relatively abrupt changes in perception at the perceptual class boundaries. If the boundaries are relatively stable and distinct, we would expect to find the conditions described in Figure 1.5, and thus CP.

Note that with the 1600-Hz intensity-variation condition and a limited binary-response set, the location of the category boundary would depend on whether the

Psychophysical models

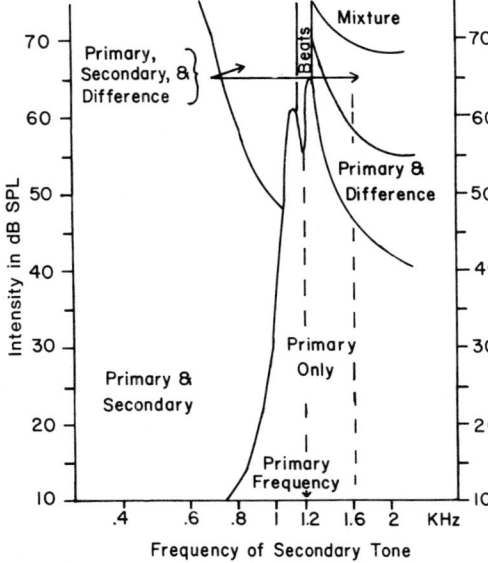

Figure 1.6. The perceptual consequences of presenting two simultaneous tones. The primary tone is 1200 Hz at 80 dB while the secondary tone varies in frequency (abscissa) and intensity (ordinate). This figure is based upon Wegel and Lane (1924) and is used to illustrate various effects related to CP.

subject decides (or is instructed) to respond on the basis of the difference tone or the secondary tone. Labels mapped to a contrast between "primary alone" versus "primary plus" would yield a lower boundary than labels mapped to "no secondary tone" versus "secondary tone." These are conjectures concerning CP that we have not tested, but that are somewhat analogous to our demonstration of CP for flickering visual stimuli described in the section on visual stimuli.

Noncategorical aspects of categorical perception

Practice effects

In 1977, two studies demonstrated that although certain speech continua were perceived categorically by naive subjects, experience with the given continuum reduced the categorical nature of the perception of the continuum. With practice, the labeling function became less distinct while discrimination performance improved (Samuel, 1977; Carney, Widen, & Viemeister, 1977). These studies are important in further demonstrating that these "categorically perceived" continua are not necessarily perceived in an absolute or discrete manner.

I offer two hypotheses to explain these results. Both hypotheses are based on the notion of uncertainty described in the section on visual stimuli presented earlier in the chapter. The noise hypothesis assumes that naive subjects have a less than optimal knowledge of the relevant stimulus continuum. This limited knowledge (thus, uncertainty) can be represented as greater variability (or noise) in the processing system and would result in a large DL. Practice provides the subject with increased knowledge of the specific nature of the stimulus continuum, thus reducing noise in the processing system. Reduced noise yields a reduced magnitude of the DL. This condition can be modeled, using Figures 1.4 and 1.5, by reducing the magnitude of the DL.

My second hypothesis is similar to the levels-of-processing notion proposed in the cognitive literature (Craik & Lockhart, 1972). I assume that under normal listening conditions speech stimuli vary along a large number of dimensions. Under such conditions, an effective listener would ignore much of the stimulus information available in the stimuli, with the perceptual response based on the most salient characteristics of the stimuli (or the most relevant characteristics, as defined by past experience). The noise hypothesis might begin with this same basic idea, but there one would conjecture a narrowing of processing capacity. The second hypothesis proposes a broadening of processing, with the experienced subjects responding on the basis of previously less distinct characteristics of the stimuli. In a sense, the subject will have shifted to a finer grain, or level, of processing. The finest level of processing might be useful only for stimulus distinctions in the fixed continuum used in a given study; such distinctions would not normally be sufficiently reliable to provide a basis for perceptual responding and would thus usually be ignored.

This condition can be modeled, using Figures 1.1 and 1.2, by assuming learned access to some of the information at the transducer stage. Using the model in Figures 1.4 and 1.5, we assume the addition of stimulus dimensions to the processing that would alter the DL in a manner appropriate to the stimulus distinctions characteristic of those dimensions. For the conditions described in Figure 1.6, the subject who had been responding only on the basis of the perception of the primary and secondary tones would, with practice, be able to differentiate among the various difference tones produced by the interaction of the primary and secondary tones. This level-of-processing hypothesis is typical of that found in the CP literature (Pastore, Ahroon, Puleo, Crimmins, Golowner, & Berger, 1976), whereas the noise hypothesis is typical of the signal detection theory literature (Swets, 1964; Pastore & Scheirer, 1974). To date, these two hypotheses have not been tested for CP conditions.

Artifacts

One of the original demonstrations of CP for nonspeech acoustic stimuli was with a rise-time continuum using sawtooth stimuli; sinusoidal stimuli were perceived less categorically (Cutting & Rosner, 1974). Recently, using fixed step sizes, Rosen and Howell (1981) failed to replicate this finding with new sawtooth stimuli meeting Cutting and Rosner's stimulus description, but they did replicate the CP finding with the original Cutting and Rosner stimuli. An analysis of the original Cutting and Rosner stimuli indicated a larger physical difference at the obtained categorical boundary. Cutting (1982) replicated Rosen and Howell's noncategorical findings with fixed step sizes, but found CP for the rise-time continuum when using a proportional step size. An explanation for these findings can be provided using the models summarized in Figures 1.4 and 1.5 by assuming that k (the Weber constant) and k' (the proportional constant for step size) are much smaller than arbitrarily depicted in these figures. Clearly, the rise-time continuum is not discrete, but, under appropriate listening conditions (i.e., proportional step size), does meet the requirements for CP (see Chapter 4 by Rosen & Howell).

Another recent study attempting to follow up on the Rosen and Howell (1981) finding was published by Hary and Massaro (1982), who created two rise-time continua for stimulus onset. For positive rise-times, the stimulus envelope increased from zero amplitude to a constant amplitude, A, over a given time interval, t, where t was varied to create the continuum. For negative rise-times, the stimulus envelope increased quickly to twice the base amplitude, then decreased to the base amplitude over the given time interval, t. Although Hary and Massaro claim that this last condition represents a negative rise-time continuum that is a logical extension of the positive rise-time continuum, the negative rise-time continuum is really a fall-time continuum placed at stimulus onset. Not surprisingly, these investigators find a perceptual discontinuity when they treat the initial rise- and fall-time continua as part of a single bipolar rise-time continuum, and they find a category boundary effect under that condition (within-category discrimination is consistently above chance). With the "unipolar" positive rise-time continuum alone, they replicate the Rosen and Howell findings. Their finding of a category boundary effect for their "bipolar continuum" is clearly the result of semantics – their unusual labeling of the two physically very different continua as a single continuum. The most important aspect of CP (and category boundary effects) is that a single, continuous physical dimension is perceived in a discontinuous manner; the mere finding of a type of direct mapping of physical characteristics to perception is, by modern standards, relatively trivial and theoretically uninteresting (Pastore et al., 1984). Other aspects of the results of the Hary and Massaro study are discussed by Macmillan (Chapter 2) and Massaro (Chapter 8).

Auditory onset time continua

Temporal-order identification has been conjectured to be a possible basis for voicing contrasts found with time-varying VOT speech continua (see Miller et al., 1976). Hirsh (1959) had found that the threshold for the identification of the temporal order of onset for acoustic signals was approximately 17 msec. This threshold was independent of both the spectral composition of the component stimuli and the relative intensity (for a 20-phon range) of those stimuli. This 17-msec threshold does not hold for very brief stimuli (less than 10 msec duration) where spectral composition and phase may serve as the basis for temporal judgment (Patterson & Green, 1970). The category boundary for both a bilabial stop consonant (VOT) speech continuum (Abramson & Lisker, 1970) and the noise-buzz (Noise-onset-time [NOT]) continuum (Miller et al., 1976) was approximately 20 msec. CP with a similar boundary was also found for a continuum created by two tones varying in their temporal-onset asynchrony (Pisoni, 1977). As with the VOT continua, the tone-onset time (TOT) continuum exhibited selective adaptation effects (although no cross-adaptation was found between a VOT and a TOT continuum) (Pisoni, 1980). Thus, there is the qualified possibility that CP for NOT, TOT, and VOT are all due to the temporal-order identification or judgment (TOJ) threshold reported by Hirsh (1959) and that all follow the threshold model described in Figure 1.4.

The category boundary for VOT is not fixed at a 20-msec onset asynchrony as originally assumed, but is a function of a number of factors, including place of articulation (Lisker & Abramson, 1970), and the vowel in the CV syllable. For example, the category boundary was found to range from approximately +22 msec for bilabial (/ba-pa/) contrasts to +35 and +42 msec for alveolar (/da-ta/) and velar (/qa-ka/) contrasts (Lisker & Abramson, 1970). Also, Miller and Eimas (1981) have found that the VOT boundary for a /da-tha/ continuum is a direct function of the duration of the formant transitions (which covaries with the stimulus rise-time). We investigated several acoustic factors that might explain the dependency on the nature of the vowel in the hope of learning more about the perception of these continua. Because vowels differ in both their formant frequencies and their duration, I investigated the effect of stimulus duration and component frequency on the temporal-order judgment (TOJ) threshold (Pastore, Harris, & Kaplan, 1982). With practiced subjects, TOJ for tone onset is a direct function of both stimulus duration and stimulus rise-time. Replicating Hirsh (1959), we found an independence of TOJ from spectral composition. With 300 msec stimuli, TOJ threshold had a mean value of approximately 15 msec. In light of the difference among vowels in duration and formant frequency, it is possible that the dependence of the VOT boundary on vowel context might be a function of the vowel duration, whereas the dependence of VOT on the manner of articulation cue defined by transition duration may be a function of rise-time. To date, we have no solid evidence for the category-boundary dependency on place of articulation, but there is at least one hypothesis.

My research on TOJ demonstrated an interesting practice effect: Naive subjects consistently exhibited initial thresholds on the order of 120 to 150 msec. After practice with the tonal stimuli, subjects exhibited different thresholds, which had seemed to change in stages to 80 to 100, 35 to 50, and 15 to 20 msec. With significant additional practice, two of our subjects exhibited an additional stage of improvement to a range of 2 to 10 msec. A subject would sometimes move briefly to a lower TOJ threshold stage, slipping back to the previous stage, then moving again to that lower threshold. Each subject seemed to exhibit stable performance for several sessions at a given threshold before demonstrating a discrete improvement to the next stage. Pisoni, Aslin, Perey, and Hennessy (1982) have reported similar results with voicing contrasts. My conjecture is that subjects were initially responding to gross differences in temporal order. Those gross differences define the threshold for the subject under the given measurement conditions. With increased stimulus-continuum familiarity, the subjects were able to respond on the basis of other, less obvious parameters of the continuum. Finally, the well-practiced subjects were able to respond to the stimuli on the basis of subtle stimulus cues, which might very well be valid only for a stimulus continuum with very limited parameter variance, such as a continuum used in a controlled research experiment. It would seem that TOJ threshold is not a single threshold, but rather a series of relative perceptual discontinuities. If a TOJ threshold defines a CP condition, one would expect that the boundary location will depend on stimulus duration, stimulus rise-time, continuum stability, the familiarity of the subjects with the stimulus continuum, and possibly several other factors. It may be that stimulus transition is one of those factors that determines TOJ threshold.

Another somewhat analogous result occurs with speech VOT continua. It is well established that adults of different linguistic backgrounds exhibit CP for voicing contrasts with category boundaries that are characteristic of their language (Lisker & Abramson, 1964; Abramson & Lisker, 1970; Simon & Fourcin, 1978). Because the category boundaries for voicing contrasts are not uniform across languages, there would appear to be a strong case for the argument that because adults fail to perceive nonnative distinctions in voicing (chance performance within categories), linguistic experience must influence the development or degeneration of the neural mechanisms that mediate VOT perception (Eimas, 1978) and that voicing contrasts must be based on something other than the auditory threshold for temporal-order identification. I will examine this argument from several different perspectives. Rosen and Howell (Chapter 4) provide a further discussion of temporal-order effects, providing a different perspective on the nature of such effects and their relationship to speech categories.

Category boundary differences

Animal studies

Using a conditioned-avoidance paradigm based on a generalization of responses to "good exemplars" of each voicing category (e.g., 0-msec VOT and +80-msec VOT for /da/ and /ta/), Kuhl and Miller (1975) examined the identification boundaries of VOT continua (10-msec steps) for chinchillas. They found that the identification boundaries for chinchillas were a function of the place of articulation and that the boundaries did not differ significantly from those exhibited by adult humans. Using a generalization of a habituated heart-rate response to exemplars from a synthetic-place continuum, Morse and Snowdon (1975) similarly demonstrated category boundaries for rhesus monkeys corresponding to those found with adult humans for the given-place continuum. Thus, there is some evidence of a response boundary in animals for human speech that roughly corresponds to that found for human listeners. (See also Chapter 11 by Snowdon and Chapter 12 by Kuhl).

Kuhl has extended this line of research with chinchillas to examine within- and cross-category discriminability for VOT continua. In one study using an alveolar continuum, Kuhl (1981) found that the difference limen (DL) for VOT was minimal near the phonetic boundary and was maximum at within-category VOTs. These results are consistent with the discussion of the relationship of the DL to categorical perception in my introduction. In a second study, Kuhl and Padden (1982) used a same-different procedure to examine the discriminability of a 20-msec VOT difference for Japanese macacques of a contrast within each voicing category and across the human voicing boundary for initial bilabial, alveolar, and velar consonants. The monkeys exhibited significantly better discrimination for cross-boundary contrasts than for the within-category contrasts, with the within-category contrasts approaching chance (or threshold) levels of performance. With the very important qualification that I am generalizing across studies, I have evidence that animals exhibit behavior consistent with CP for human-speech stimuli and that the boundaries for the continua seem to roughly reflect the dependency on place of articulation found for human listeners. It would appear that the category boundaries are indicative of perceptual discontinuities.

Infant studies

Research with human infants, some as young as one month, has tended to find poor discriminability for speech stimuli drawn from within phonetic categories and relatively enhanced discriminability for stimuli in the region of the adult category boundary (Eimas, 1974; Eimas, Siqueland, Jusczyk, & Vigorito, 1971; Jusczyk, 1981). These studies used infants from English-speaking families and the results were compared with the category boundary for English-speaking adults. The results are suggestive of CP in infants and have been interpreted as evidence for a biologically based linguistic mode of perception (Eimas et al., 1971; Eimas & Miller, 1980). (See also Chapter 5 by Eimas et al. and Chapter 14 by Molfese.)

An important but largely unresolved issue concerns whether infants discriminate speech contrasts that do not exist in the language of their parents. A common example is the absence of a category boundary for negative VOT stimuli for English-speaking adults; the negative VOT boundary is used in Thai (Lisker & Abramson, 1964). Eimas (1975) found some weak evidence for a negative VOT boundary in infants from an English-speaking environment. Other researchers have also reported very mixed results with infants. For example, Streeter (1976) found evidence for a labial voicing contrast with Kikuyu infants; Kikuyu adults do not use a voicing contrast for labial stimuli, but do use a voicing contrast for velar components.

Recently, Aslin, Pisoni, Hennessy, and Perey (1981) attempted to evaluate directly the discriminability of bilabial VOT stimuli in young (5.5 to 11.5 months) infants from English-speaking environments using a conditioned headturn response with a staircase psychophysical procedure. Adults were tested with an analogous procedure. Aslin claimed that their results demonstrate that their infants "reliably and consistently respond to a phonologically-irrelevant VOT contrast located in the minus region of the VOT continuum . . ." (Aslin et al., 1981). In Figure 1.7, I have replotted the results from their Table 2 in terms of the DL as a function of the VOT value of the stimulus with the less positive magnitude; in the psychophysical

Psychophysical models 45

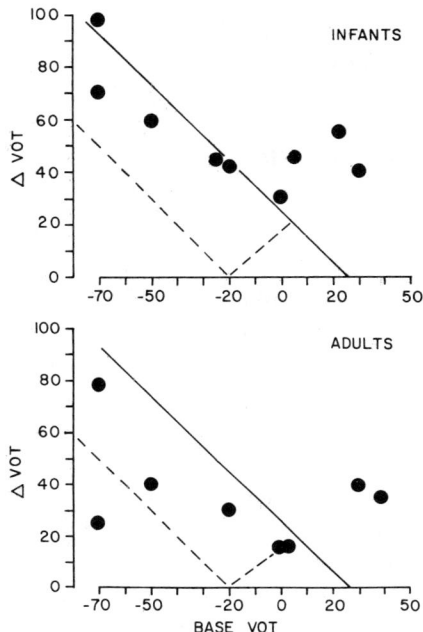

Figure 1.7. The DL for VOT in adults and infants redrawn from Aslin et al. (1981) with the lower value of VOT always on the abscissa. The linear functions are the DL predicted for perfect CP with boundaries at the 25.5 msec (solid line) and the −20 msec (broken lines locations reported by Aslin et al., 1981).

literature this is the typical way of plotting DL. I have indicated the expected function for perfect CP (as summarized in Figure 1.2) for a category boundary at +25.5 msec VOT (solid line) and for a category boundary at −20 msec (dashed line). These boundary values were selected on the basis of the published research cited by Aslin et al. (1981). Both the infants and adults exhibit DLs that are typically smaller (or better) than that predicted on the basis of absolute categorization with only positive VOT boundary (solid line). Thus, contrary to the original claim, neither the infants nor the adults exhibit evidence of absolute categorization for the minus VOTs, with the DLs being larger than predicted. Finally, the DLs for adults are smaller than those for infants – a finding that probably reflects a better ability to understand the task. However, I interpret these results as exhibiting performance that is better than absolute categorization based on the positive VOT boundary; I find no convincing evidence of an effective category boundary (or, therefore, of a DL minimum) in the negative VOT region. Obviously, there must be some form of stimulus information that cues the minus VOT contrast; due to a lack of attention or learning, these subjects do not respond to this information.

Direct comparison of continua

Recently, Summerfield (1982) compared the perception of three types of continua by naive listeners: tone-onset-time (TOT or TOJ), noise-buzz stimuli similar to those used by Miller et al. (1976) creating a noise-onset-time (NOT) continuum, and VOT continua. The TOT and NOT stimuli each had two stationary components, whereas the VOT continuum had three formants with a flat first formant ($F1$). This study compared the simultaneity-successiveness threshold for TOT and NOT with the voicing-contrast category boundary for VOT as a function of the frequency of the lowest stimulus component. Although Summerfield did find changes in the mean threshold and threshold variability for both TOT and NOT, with shifts in the lower-frequency components, these differences were not robust. The VOT category boundaries were typically far more stable than these thresholds and required a significantly larger onset difference (e.g., 40 msec for VOT with $F1$ = 200 Hz, versus 21 msec for TOT and NOT). Summerfield interpreted his results as suggesting that, in the perception of voicing, the role of $F1$ does not have purely an auditory basis.

Summerfield's results should be viewed in the context of the existing auditory-perception literature. Summerfield's naive subjects exhibited average simultaneity-successive thresholds between 9 and 27 msec for TOT and NOT. Hirsh (1959), using reasonably practiced subjects, reported that the threshold for detecting an onset asynchrony (the simultaneity-successivity threshold) was approximately 2 msec, whereas the threshold for reporting order of onset asynchrony was 17 msec. Hirsh's 2-msec figure is an order of magnitude smaller than Summerfield's thresholds, and, in any case, the threshold for identifying the order of onset asynchrony (not *detecting* that asynchrony) is what has been conjectured to be the basis for the category boundary for VOT stimuli. Reexamining my own temporal-order identification research (Pastore et al., 1982; see the section on auditory onset time continua), I found that those thresholds decreased in relatively discrete steps with practice. The example in Figure 1.6 of an 80-dB/1200-Hz primary tone and a 1600-Hz secondary tone that varies in intensity provides an hypothesis to account for the findings. Suppose we determine the threshold for our subjects to detect the presence of the secondary tone which is held constant at 1600 Hz. Naive subjects who listen carefully for the 1600-Hz tone will yield thresholds of approximately 58 dB. More practiced subjects, who have learned that the presence of difference tones is correlated with the presence of the secondary tone, will produce thresholds of approximately 46 dB. If we determine the threshold for hearing a complex mixture of sounds, we will obtain a value of approximately 70 dB. Turning to the other example cited for Figure 1.6, if we hold intensity constant and systematically vary the frequency of the secondary tone from 1400 Hz upward, we will find a different set of distinct perceptual boundaries. In effect, we can ask (or allow) subjects to tell us about different perceptual aspects of a given physical continuum. To return to the Summerfield (1982) study, it is unclear whether his subjects were providing equivalent perceptual responses to physically and perceptually distinct continua, or different perceptual responses to physically different, but perceptually equivalent, continua.

Trading relationships

A number of recent CP studies using special stimuli have tended to focus on trading relationships among cues. It is well known that there are a number of stimulus parameters that are important for any distinction between speech categories. For example, Lisker (1978) has categorized 16 parameters that contribute to the distinction between /b/ and /p/ in intervocalic positions. In trading studies, a second parameter for a stimulus contrast is manipulated, causing a shift in the location of the category boundary along the primary-stimulus dimension. For example, the boundary for the labial /p-b/ stop contrast along a VOT continuum in "rapid"–"rabid" was shown to be a function of the duration of the silent interval prior to the stop (Port, 1978; Lisker, 1978). Silence is claimed to be traded with VOT to maintain constant perception. In addition, cues from the two stimulus dimensions can be combined so that they both indicate the same category, resulting in a sharpening of the category boundary; or they can be combined in such a way that each dimension cues a different perceptual category, resulting in a less precise category boundary for the stimulus set. Trading relationships have been reported between silence and $F1$ onset frequency for a "say"–"stay" contrast (Best, Morrongiello, & Robson, 1981), between silence and vocalic formant transition onsets in a "slit"–"split" contrast (Fitch, Halwes, Erickson, & Liberman, 1980), between VOT and aspiration noise amplitude (Repp, 1979) for $F1$ onset frequency and VOT, and for many other conditions. These trading relationships have been interpreted as being too complex to be explained in terms of either selective attention to individual cues or acoustic integration of information prior to the processing of that information as speech.

Relationships such as these are quite common in the auditory-perception literature. For example, auditory threshold is a function of total energy in a stimulus: At least within a range of intensities and durations, threshold follows an auditory analog to Block's law in vision ($IT = k$). Thus, if one doubles the duration, the threshold intensity per unit time is halved. In a sense, one is trading time for duration (this type of trading relation has also been noted by Repp, 1982). Looking at the damage-risk criteria for noise exposure, a 5-dB increase in intensity can be tolerated for half as long (Henderson, Hamernik, Dosanjh, & Mills, 1976). These trading relationships for intensity would seem to be relatively simple, and they are in fact claimed to be too simple to account for the trading relationships found with speech stimuli (Repp, 1982; Chapter 3 by Repp & Liberman).

Turning to Figure 1.6, we can see how more complex trading relationships might occur. To continue with our example of a 1600-Hz secondary tone varying in intensity, assume that CP is based on the detection of the presence of the secondary tone (consistently due to either its actual perception or the perception of the difference tones). Increasing the frequency of the secondary tone from 1600 to 2000 Hz would shift the category boundary to a lower intensity. One could claim that we have been able to trade frequency for intensity. A more productive way to view this situation is that the masked threshold for the secondary tone is a complex function of a number of factors including the frequency difference between the masking stimulus (the primary stimulus) and the masked or target stimulus (the secondary stimulus). Increasing the frequency differences between the masker and the target stimulus reduces the amount of masking (other things being equal). As with masking, we can learn a great deal about complex stimulus relationships by a careful and systematic mapping of the relations among the various stimulus parameters in defining the various perceptually equivalent categories. Once we have accomplished such a mapping we will have a basis for beginning to understand the nature of CP in the given circumstance. Relatively limited studies of CP, or trading relationships in CP, provide only a very limited perspective on what are probably very complex stimulus-perception relationships. In the absence of such a systematic investigation, conjectures about the nature of perceptual processing and either the uniqueness of the CP phenomena in the given condition, or their similarity to other phenomena, would seem to be premature.

Summary and conclusions

I have reviewed some of the existing models and data relevant to the concept of CP. I began with the notion of a discrete perceptual processing into absolute categories; the label "categorical perception" still implies that notion even though the empirical results are usually indicative of less than absolute categorization. I examined the way that absolute categorization should manifest itself in a difference limen (DL) as a function of the physical continuum. I then examined several other possible models, expressed in terms of the DL, that are not based on an absolute categorization but should yield results meeting the criteria for CP. These models are all based on the notion that there is something different about the continuum at the category boundary that causes a local minimum in the DL. I would argue that examining the perceptual properties of a continuum in terms of the DL can provide far more information about the relationship between the physical continuum and the perception of that continuum than attempts to find "categorical perception" for that continuum. Taking my argument to an extreme, CP, unless demonstrated to be absolute, really only tells us that there is something special about the boundary stimulus (a finding Wood [1976] describes as the "category boundary effect") and that observers' sensitivity should be equivalent across the identification and discrimination tasks (a point already made by a number of others [Durlach & Braida, 1969; Braida & Durlach, 1972; Macmillan, Kaplan, & Creelman, 1977]). Furthermore, meeting the operational criteria for CP implicitly attributes to the continuum a property of being perceptually discrete – a property that probably is not valid. An analysis in terms of the DL, or in terms of other psychophysical variables that do not assume absolute perceptual discreteness, would allow us to begin to understand more fully the nature of the underlying relationships between perception and the physical stimuli. Such analyses would avoid the implicit attribution of an assumed discreteness and uniqueness to continua that meet the criteria for CP. This would also leave the term CP to those continua, should they exist, that actually are perceived in an absolutely discrete manner, as was originally implied by the term "categorical perception."

Notes

1. Fechner's Law and Stevens's Law attempt to specify the relationship between sensory or perceptual magnitude and physical-stimulus magnitude. Fechner's Law claims that logarithmic changes in physical magnitude cause linear changes in sensation. Stevens's Power Law claims that sensation is a power function of physical magnitude; logarithmic changes in physical magnitude cause logarithmic changes in sensation. These laws are reasonably accurate for specific types of continua, at least for a limited range of stimulus magnitudes.
2. Another version of this condition is where the sensory continuum never exists; rather, there is a direct processing of the physical continuum into the discrete perceptual continuum (e.g., Wood, 1976), in a top-down process with limited downward processing.
3. The Difference Limen (DL) or difference threshold is the minimal change in stimulus physical magnitude which is detectable as a difference at a specified rate or criterion. A 50% DL will be perceived as a difference half of the time.
4. Signal Detection Theory (SDT) attempts to provide independent measures of sensory (or perceptual) ability and bias (or motivational) factors. In the Equal Variance Gaussian Model of SDT, d' is the unbiased measure of sensory ability. Although SDT assumes that noise, rather than a threshold, limits performance, it is sometimes convenient to estimate a measure equivalent to a threshold. One convention is to estimate as the DL that stimulus difference resulting in $d' = 1.0$, which approximates 67% correct detection in a same/different task.

References

Abramson, A. S., & Lisker, L. (1970). Discriminability along the voicing continuum: Cross-language tests. *Proceedings of the Sixth International Congress of Phonetic Sciences, 1967*, Prague: Academia.
Aslin, R. N., Pisoni, D. B., Hennessy, B. L., & Perey, A. J. (1981). Discrimination of voice-onset-time by human infants: New findings concerning phonetic development. *Research on Speech Perception*, Report 6, 1981.
Best, C. T., Morrongiello, B., & Robson, R. (1981). Perceptual equivalence of acoustic cues in speech and nonspeech perception. *Perception & Psychophysics, 29*, 191–211.
Braida, L. D., & Durlach, N. I. (1972). Intensity perception II: Resolution in one-interval paradigms. *Journal of the Acoustical Society of America, 51*, 483–502.
Burns, E. M., & Ward, W. D. (1978). Categorical perception—phenomenon or epiphenomenon: Evidence from experiments in the perception of melodic musical intervals. *Journal of the Acoustical Society of America, 63*, 456–468.
Carney, A. E., Widen, B., & Viemeister, N. (1977). Non-categorical perception of stop consonants differing in VOT, *Journal of the Acoustical Society of America, 62*, 961–970.
Craik, F. I. M., & Lockhart, R. S. (1972). Levels of processing: A framework for memory research. *Journal of Verbal Learning & Verbal Behavior, 11*, 671–684.
Cutting, J. E. (1982). Plucks and bows are categorically perceived, sometimes. *Perception & Psychophysics, 31*, 462–476.
Cutting, J. E., & Rosner, B. S. (1974). Categories and boundaries in speech and music. *Perception & Psychophysics, 16*, 564–570.

Diehl, R. L. (1975). The effect of selective adaptation on the identification of speech sounds. *Perception & Psychophysics, 17,* 448–452.
Durlach, N. I., & Braida, L. D. (1969). Intensity perception I: Preliminary theory of intensity resolution. *Journal of the Society of America, 46,* 372–383.
Eimas, P. D. (1978). Developmental aspects of speech perception. In R. Held, H. Lebowitz, & H. L. Teuber (Eds.), *Handbook of Sensory Physiology* (Vol. 8), New York: Springer.
Eimas, P. D. (1975). Auditory and phonetic coding of the cues for speech: Discrimination of the /r-l/ distinction by young infants. *Perception & Psychophysics, 18,* 341–347.
Eimas, P. D. (1974). Auditory and linguistic processing of cues for place of articulation by infants. *Perception & Psychophysics, 16,* 513–521.
Eimas, P. D., Siqueland, E. R., Jusczyk, P., & Vigorito, J. (1971). Speech perception in infants. *Science, 171,* 303–306.
Eimas, P. D., & Miller, J. L. (1980). Contextual effects in infant speech perception. *Science, 209,* 1140–1141.
Eimas, P. D., & Corbit, J. D. (1973). Selective adaptation of linguistic feature detectors. *Cognitive Psychology, 4,* 99–109.
Fitch, H. L., Halwes, T., Erickson, D. M., & Liberman, A. M. (1980). Perceptual equivalence of two acoustic cues for stop-consonant manner. *Perception & Psychophysics, 27,* 343–350.
Fujisaki, H., & Kawashima, T. (1970). Some experiments on speech perception and a model for the perceptual mechanism. *Annual Report of the Engineering Research Institute, 29,* 207–214. Tokyo: University of Tokyo, Faculty of Engineering.
Hary, J. M., & Massaro, D. W. (1982). Categorical results do not imply categorical perception. *Perception & Psychophysics, 32,* 409–418.
Henderson, D., Hamernik, R. P., Dosanjh, D. S., & Mills, J. H. (Eds.). (1976). *Effects of Noise on Hearing.* New York: Raven Press.
Hirsh, I. J. (1959). Auditory perception of temporal order. *Journal of the Acoustical Society of America, 31,* 759–767.
Hubel, D. H., & Wiesel, T. N. (1962). Receptive fields, binocular interaction, and functional architecture in the cat's visual cortex. *Journal of Physiology, 160,* 106–154.
Jusczyk, P. W. (1981). Infant speech perception: A critical appraisal. In P. D. Eimas and J. L. Miller (Eds.), *Perspectives on the study of speech.* Hillsdale, NJ: Erlbaum.
Kuhl, P. K. (1981). Discrimination of speech by nonhuman animals: Basic auditory sensitivities conducive to the perception of speech-sound categories. *Journal of the Acoustical Society of America, 70,* 340–349.
Kuhl, P. K., & Miller, J. D. (1975). Speech perception by the chinchilla: Voiced-voiceless distinction in alveolar plosive consonants. *Science, 190,* 69–72.
Kuhl, P. K., & Padden, D. M. (1982). Enchanced discriminability at the phonetic boundaries for the voicing feature in macaques. *Perception & Psychophysics, 32,* 542–550.
Lane, H. (1965). The motor theory of speech perception: A critical review. *Psychological Review, 72,* 275–309.
Liberman, A. M., Harris, K. S., Hoffman, H. S., & Griffith, B. C. (1957). The discrimination of speech sounds within and across phoneme boundaries. *Journal of Experimental Psychology, 54,* 358–368.
Liberman, A. M., Harris, K. S., Kinney, J. A., & Lane, H. (1961). The discrimination of relative onset-time of the components of certain speech and nonspeech patterns. *Journal of Experimental Psychology, 61,* 379–388.
Lisker, L. (1978). Rapid *vs.* rabid: A catalogue of acoustic features that may cue the distinction. *Haskins Laboratories Status Report on Speech Research* (SR-54, pp. 127–132).
Lisker, L., & Abramson, A. S. (1964). Cross-language study of voicing in initial stops: acoustical measurements. *Word, 20,* 384–422.
Lisker, L., & Abramson, A. S. (1970). The voicing dimension: Some experiments in comparative phonetics. *Proceedings of the Sixth International Congress of Phonetic Sciences, 1967.* Prague: Academia.
Locke, S., & Kellar, L. (1973). Categorical perception in a non-linguistic mode. *Cortex, 9,* 355–369.

Macmillan, N. A., Kaplan, H. L., & Creelman, C. D. (1977). The psychophysics of categorical perception. *Psychological Review, 84,* 452–471.
Mattingly, I. G. (1972). Speech cues and sign stimuli. *American Scientist, 60,* 327–337.
Mattingly, I. G., Liberman, A. M., Syrdal, A. K., & Halwes, T. (1971). Discrimination in speech and nonspeech modes. *Cognitive Psychology, 2,* 131–157.
Miller, J. D., Wier, C. C., Pastore, R. E., Kelly, W. J., & Dooling, R. J. (1976). Discrimination and labeling of noise-buzz sequences of categorical perception. *Journal of the Acoustical Society of America, 60,* 410–417.
Miller, J. D., & Eimas, P. D. (1981). Contextual perception of voicing by infants, Paper presented to the Biennial Meeting of the Society of Research in Child Development, 25 April, Boston, MA (cited in Summerfield, 1981).
Morse, P. A., & Snowdon, L. T. (1975). An investigation of categorical speech discrimination by rhesus monkeys. *Perception & Psychophysics, 17,* 9–16.
Parducci, A. (1974). Contextual effects: A range-frequency analysis. In E. C. Carterette & M. P. Friedman (Eds.), *Handbook of Perception 2.* New York: Academic Press.
Pastore, R. E. (1976). Categorical perception: A critical re-evaluation. In S. K. Hirsh, D. H. Eldredge, I. J. Hirsh, & S. R. Silverman (Eds.), *Hearing and Davis: Essays Honoring Hallowell Davis.* St. Louis, MO: Washington University Press.
Pastore, R. E. (1978). Phonemes and alphanumeric characters: Possible components of parallel human communication systems. *Visible Language, 12,* 27–42.
Pastore, R. E., Szczesiul, R., Wielgus, V., Nowikas, K., & Logan, R. (1984). Categorical perception, category boundary effects, and continuous perception: A reply to Hary and Massaro. *Perception & Psychophysics, 35,* 583–585.
Pastore, R. E., Schmuckler, M. A., Rosenblum, L., & Szczesiul, R. (1983). Duplex perception with musical stimuli. *Perception & Psychophysics, 33,* 469–474.
Pastore, R. E., Harris, L. B., & Kaplan, J. K. (1982). Temporal order identification: Some parameter dependencies. *Journal of the Acoustical Society of America, 71,* 430–436.
Pastore, R. E., Ahroon, W. A., Baffuto, K. J., Friedman, C., Puleo, J. S., & Fink, E. A. (1977). Common-factor model of categorical perception. *Journal of Experimental Psychology: Human Perception & Performance, 3,* 686–696.
Pastore, R. E., Ahroon, W. A., Puleo, J. S., Crimmins, D. B., Golowner, L., & Berger, R. S. (1976). Processing interaction between two dimensions of nonphonetic auditory signals. *Journal of Experimental Psychology: Human Perception & Performance, 2,* 267–276.
Pastore, R. E., & Scheirer, C. J. (1974). Signal detection theory: Considerations for general application. *Psychological Bulletin, 81,* 945–958.
Patterson, J. H., & Green, D. M. (1970). Discrimination of transient signals having identical energy spectra. *Journal of the Acoustical Society of America, 48,* 894–905.
Pisoni, D. B. (1975). Auditory short-term memory and vowel perception. *Memory & Cognition, 3,* 7–18.
Pisoni, D. B. (1977). Identification and discrimination of the relative onset time of two-component tones: Implications for voicing perception in stops. *Journal of the Acoustical Society of America, 61,* 1352–1361.
Pisoni, D. B. (1980). Adaptation of the relative onset time of two-component tones. *Perception & Psychophysics, 28,* 337–346.
Pisoni, D. B., Aslin, R. N., Perey, A. J., & Hennessy, B. L. (1982). Some effects of laboratory training on identification and discrimination of voicing contrasts in stop consonants. *Journal of Experimental Psychology: Human Perception and Performance, 8,* 297–314.
Pisoni, D. B., & Lazarus, J. H. (1974). Categorical and non-categorical modes of speech perception along the voicing continuum. *Journal of the Acoustical Society of America, 55,* 328–333.
Port, R. F. (1978). Effects of word-internal versus word-external tempo on the voicing boundary for medial stop closure. *Journal of the Acoustical Society of America, 63,* Suppl. 20 [A].
Repp, B. H. (1982). Phonetic trading relations and context effects: New experimental evidence for a speech mode of perception. *Psychological Bulletin, 92,* 81–110.

Repp, B. H. (1979). Relative amplitude of aspiration noise as a voicing cue for syllable-initial stop consonants. *Language and Speech, 22,* 173–189.
Riggs, L. A. (1973). Curvature as a feature of pattern vision. *Science, 181,* 1020–1072.
Rosen, S. M., & Howell, P. (1981). Plucks and bows are not categorically perceived. *Perception & Psychophysics, 30,* 156–168.
Samuel, A. G. (1977). The effect of discrimination training on speech perception: Noncategorical perception. *Perception & Psychophysics, 22,* 321–330.
Simon, C., & Fourcin, A. J. (1978). Cross-language study of speech-pattern learning. *Journal of the Acoustical Society of America, 63,* 925–935.
Stevens, K. N. (1981). Constraints imposed by the auditory system on the properties used to classify speech sounds: Evidence from phonology, acoustics, and psychoacoustics. In T. Myers, J. Laver, & J. Anderson (Eds.), *Advances in Psychology: The Cognitive Representation of Speech* (pp. 61–74). Amsterdam: North-Holland.
Stevens, K. N. (1975). The potential role of property detectors in the perception of consonants. In G. Fant & M. A. A. Tatham (Eds.), *Auditory analysis and perception of speech* (pp. 303–330). New York: Academic Press.
Streeter, L. (1976). Language perception of two-month-old infants shows effects of both innate mechanisms and experience. *Nature, 256,* 39–41.
Studdert-Kennedy, M., Liberman, A. M., Harris, K. S., & Cooper, F. S. (1970). Motor theory of speech perception: A reply to Lane's critical review. *Psychology Review, 77,* 234–249.
Summerfield, Q. (1981). On articulatory rate and perceptual constancy in phonetic perception, *Journal of Experimental Psychology: Human Perception & Performance, 7.*
Summerfield, Q. (1982). Differences between spectral dependencies in auditory and phonetic temporal processing: Relevance to perception of voicing in initial stops. *Journal of the Acoustical Society of America, 72,* 51–61.
Swets, J. A. (Ed.) (1964). *Signal Detection and Recognition by Human Observers.* New York: Wiley.
Wegel, R. L., & Lane, C. E. (1924). The auditory masking of one sound by another and its probable relation to the dynamics of the inner ear. *Physics Review, 23,* 266–285.
Weisstein, N. (1970). Neural symbolic activity: A psychophysical measure. *Science, 168,* 1489–1491.
Wood, C. C. (1976). Discriminability, response bias, and phoneme categories in discrimination of voice onset time. *Journal of the Acoustical Society of America, 60,* 1381–1389.

2 Beyond the categorical/continuous distinction: A psychophysical approach to processing modes

Neil A. Macmillan

Perception is traditionally deemed categorical if discrimination performance peaks in the midrange of a continuum and can be predicted from identification; otherwise, perception is said to be continuous. In this chapter, a detection-theory based model of perceptual processing, developed by Durlach and Braida for intensity perception, is offered as a framework for categorical perception research. According to the theory, two memory modes are used in processing perceptual continua. In the *trace mode,* observers compare stimuli with the memory traces of other stimuli, and performance is limited by the interstimulus interval. In the *context mode,* observers compare stimuli to *perceptual anchors,* and performance is limited by stimulus range.

For a variety of continua, the Durlach-Braida model fits well. Stimulus dimensions differ, according to the model, in the amounts of trace and context variance limiting performance, and in the location of perceptual anchors. Contrary to the categorical perception hypothesis, identification and discrimination are never exactly equivalent. For some continua, peaks occur in discrimination tasks with insignificant memory demands; these peaks are interpreted as regions of high basic sensitivity. For other continua, peaks occur in tasks that make substantial demands on memory; these peaks reveal the existence of perceptual anchors. The theory offers a more sophisticated taxonomy of processing modes than the categorical/continuous distinction, and has methodological implications for the psychoacoustics of speech perception.

Categorical perception (CP), through its association with nonspeech stimuli and nonlinguistic organisms, has fallen from its original status as a touchstone for the existence of processing unique to speech. But it is still widely considered to be a special type of processing, distinct from more mundane, "continuous" perception. This distinction rests primarily on two aspects of data collected using categorically perceived continua.

First, when discrimination of stimuli differing by a fixed amount is measured

This chapter was written in part while I was on leave at the Research Laboratory of Electronics at MIT. I wish to thank Lou Braida and Nat Durlach for many helpful comments and discussions about this material. In particular, Dr. Braida suggested the analysis presented in the section entitled "Efficiency of the trace and context modes." I am also grateful to Doug Creelman, Norma Graham, Howard Kaplan, Dom Massaro, Clark McCauley, Dick Pastore, Dave Pisoni, Bruno Repp, Burt Rosner, and Rosalie Uchanski for their comments on earlier drafts of the manuscript, and to Dave Pisoni, Bruno Repp, and Burt Rosner for providing their data. The work was supported by a National Research Service Award from NIH, and research grants from NSF and the PSC-CUNY Research Foundation.

across the range of a continuum, performance on categorical continua reaches a peak near the middle. This phenomenon, the *category boundary effect* (Wood, 1976), is contrary to Weber's law, which characterizes many perceptual dimensions to a first approximation. According to Weber's law, discrimination is constant for stimuli separated by a fixed *ratio* of physical magnitudes, and decreases monotonically for stimuli separated by a fixed *difference* (see Chapter 1 by Pastore).

The second psychophysically unusual aspect of CP concerns the relation between discrimination and identification. For most continua, discrimination is the easier of these tasks: Two stimuli that can be distinguished perfectly when they are the only stimuli ever presented cannot be labeled perfectly in the context of other stimuli (Miller, 1956). Categorically perceived continua are said to provide an exception to Miller's generalization, in that stimuli can be discriminated only to the extent they can be identified (Studdert-Kennedy, Liberman, Harris, & Cooper, 1970).

According to this analysis, CP is interesting because it contradicts psychophysical laws. The thesis of this chapter is that, on the contrary, categorically perceived continua and continuously perceived ones can be described by a single psychophysical model.[1] Most perceptual continua violate Weber's law in ways that generalize naturally to categorically perceived dimensions. Miller's principle *is* generally true, for categorical continua and for other stimulus domains.

It will be useful to distinguish between *psychophysics* and *psychoacoustics*. By psychoacoustics I mean theories that relate abstract constructs such as thresholds or sensitivity to stimulus characteristics. Because the stimulus continua used in speech research and in other areas in which CP is found are typically complex, speech perception has yielded rather grudgingly to psychoacoustic attack. Examples of this approach include attempts to specify invariant features for phonemes (Stevens, 1981) and the study of simpler stimuli, analogous to those that comprise speech, which are easier to characterize and control (e.g., Miller, Wier, Pastore, Kelly, & Dooling, 1976).

Psychophysical models, on the other hand, relate sensitivity and other constructs to experimental design, and may apply equally to simple and complex stimulus sets. In the first section of this chapter, I review the two most popular psychophysical models of CP: the *Haskins model* and the *dual-process model*. We shall see that wide application of these models has generally yielded only a qualitative description of data. Furthermore, because these are discrete-state models, they are difficult to relate to the larger body of psychophysical work based on signal detection theory (SDT) and Thurstonian models. CP data can be analyzed with SDT tools, however. I review a straightforward strategy for doing so, and discuss practical aspects of using SDT in this context.

The remainder of the chapter generalizes the SDT-based psychophysical theory for auditory-intensity perception of Durlach, Braida, and their colleagues to other perceptual continua. The theory has two parts. In the second section, the *preliminary theory* is used to estimate variability due to sensation and to two different types of memory. A taxonomy of processing modes is proposed that is more general than the categorical/continuous distinction. In the third section, the *revised theory* is used to distinguish between two possible explanations of discrimination peaks in CP: that they reflect regions of natural sensitivity and that they reflect the operation of perceptual anchors.

Whatever the perceptual distinction between categorical dimensions and continuous ones, the differences in how these stimuli have been investigated are substantial. By bringing the same psychophysical tools to bear on both, we can hope to provide a taxonomy of processing modes that is not also a taxonomy of methodology.

Threshold and signal-detection models of categorical perception

Traditional (threshold) models of categorical perception

The first attempt to predict discrimination from identification of a speech continuum was by Liberman, Harris, Hoffman, and Griffith (1957), who used a set of consonant-vowel syllables in which the consonant ranged from /b/ to /d/ to /g/. Their discrimination experiment used an ABX design: Two different sounds (A, B) were presented, followed by a sound (X) that matched one of them. The model generating their predictions assumed that each syllable was covertly classified phonemically by the observer, whose decision was then based on these classifications; stimuli that were classified the same way were therefore indiscriminable. The labeling probabilities were estimated from an identification experiment that allowed three responses, one corresponding to each phonemic category. This model has come to be called the *Haskins model;* it is an example of what psychophysicists later dubbed a *low-threshold* theory of discrimination (Luce, 1963a,b).[2]

Liberman et al. (1957) found that discrimination reached a peak between phonemic categories, as expected under the Haskins model, but that it was systematically better than predicted. Of the many experiments against which the Haskins model has been tested, virtually every one has found this same result. This failure of the Haskins model led Fujisaki and Kawashima (1969, 1970) to conclude that "the so-called categorical and continuous modes of perception . . . [are] not absolutely dichotomous" (1970, p. 207). They proposed that the observer in ABX discrimination proceeds as in the Haskins model, covertly classifying each signal; but if no decision is possible based on phonemic information (i.e., if the first two signals in an ABX trial are classified as the same), the "timbre" of the stimuli serves as the basis for judgment. Discrimination is better than identification because, of the two processes used in discrimination, only one is used in identification. Pisoni (1975) dubbed this the *dual process* model.

For each pair of stimuli in a discrimination experiment, the dual-process model has two parameters: the *phonemic sensitivity* $P(C/L)$, the probability of being correct via the labeling process; and the *auditory sensitivity* $P(C/A)$, the probability of

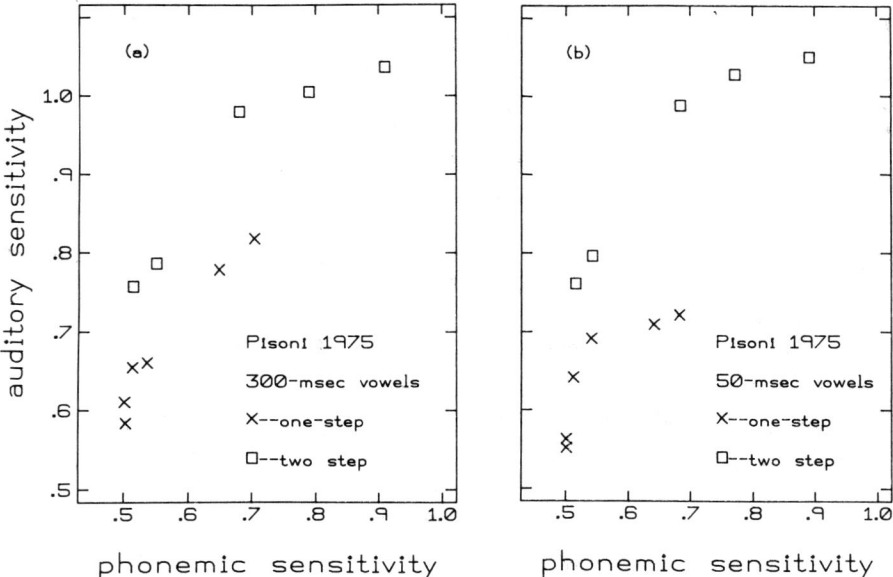

Figure 2.1. Evaluation of the dual-process model, as applied to the data of Pisoni (1975). Auditory sensitivity (the probability of a correct response due to the auditory process) is plotted against phonemic sensitivity (the probability of a correct response due to the labeling process). The vowel continuum is from /i/ to /I/.

being correct via the auditory ("timbre") process. The dual-process model asserts that $P(c)$, the probability of correctly discriminating these two stimuli in an ABX paradigm, is

$$P(c) = P(C/L)P(L) + P(C/A)[1-P(L)], \qquad (1)$$

where $P(L)$ is the probability that the labeling process leads to a decision.

Both Fujisaki and Kawashima (1969, 1970) and Pisoni (1975) performed identification and discrimination experiments to test the dual-process model. Fujisaki and Kawashima used data from a variety of continua to estimate sensitivity to timbre, which was assumed constant over the stimulus range. The model fit their data well, and the authors used the value of timbre sensitivity to characterize the degree of categoricality of each dimension.

Later tests of the dual-process model have not generally been as successful. I have estimated $P(C/L)$ and $P(C/A)$ (see Appendix A) from two experiments by Pisoni (1975; Perey & Pisoni, 1977); the relation between these parameters is shown in Figures 2.1 and 2.2. Three aspects of these plots are interesting. First, auditory sensitivity $P(C/A)$ is not a constant, but varies with phonemic sensitivity: The correlations between the two sensitivities exceed 0.8 for all four of the experiments analyzed in Figures 2.1 and 2.2. In Pisoni's experiments, unlike those of Fujisaki and Kawashima, the two processes are tapping the same information, or,

A psychophysical approach to processing modes

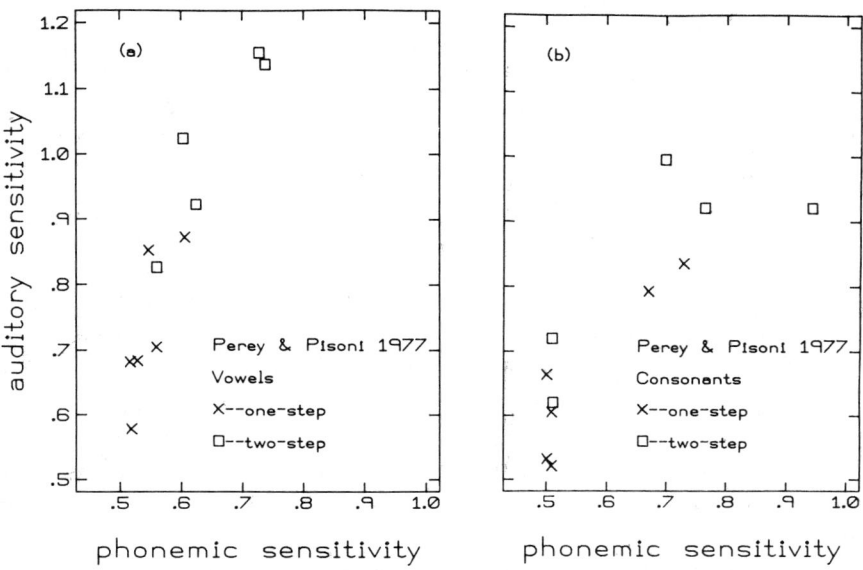

Figure 2.2. Evaluation of the dual-process model, as applied to the data of Perey and Pisoni (1977). The vowel continuum is /i/-/I/, and the consonant continuum /ba/-/pa/.

more simply, only one process is operating. The same conclusion could be reached by examining Pisoni's original data (see, for example, Pisoni, 1975, Fig. 3): When $P(C/A)$ is calculated so as to accurately predict discrimination at the extremes of the vowel continuum, predicted performance near the middle of the range is too low. Logically, $P(C/A)$ could either be constant or variable, but if it is variable the model becomes impossible to test because there is a free parameter for every data point.

Second, for 43 of the 44 points plotted in Figures 2.1 and 2.2, auditory sensitivity is higher than phonemic, although the model postulates that the auditory process is not consulted unless the phonemic process fails to yield a result. A similar result was obtained by Fujisaki and Kawashima (1970, Fig. 4). Thus the model leads to the conclusion that observers use a nonoptimal strategy; it has been argued that this occurs because the labeling process is overlearned and requires less attention than the auditory process.

Finally, the figures contain seven data points for which the model fails, in that an auditory sensitivity greater than 100% would be needed to fit the data.

The dual-process model has other shortcomings that are not directly related to the preceding analysis. For example, it cannot be applied to same-different discrimination, as has been attempted by both Pisoni (1973) and Repp, Healy, and Crowder (1979). In a same-different paradigm, the phonemic process cannot lead to an ambiguous decision – the two intervals are classified "same" or "different," either of which leads directly to a response – so the auditory process is never consulted. Although two processes could certainly be at work in these experiments, they must combine in some manner other than that proposed by Fujisaki and Kawashima for ABX.

We shall see that some of the qualitative conclusions of dual-process theorists are robust, that is, they can be supported by a different quantitative analysis of these and other data. But the evidence supporting the quantitative statement, particularly the discrete-state assumptions, of the model, is weak. If one is accustomed to thinking in threshold terms it is hard to imagine how these models could be wrong. A great deal of inventive theorizing has been done in response to this dilemma.

The history of low-threshold investigations of intensity perception offers an instructive analogy. Building on neural quantum theory (Békésy, 1960), researchers asked whether the perception of intensity was continuous or discrete. Tests of this issue required narrowly circumscribed experimental designs; failures to support threshold predictions were generally attributed, by proponents, to failure to implement the prescribed design appropriately. Ultimately, the substantive question of discreteness was lost amid controversy over methods; investigators using continuous models, notably SDT, concerned themselves with other questions, which came to be seen as more central. Perhaps the discreteness of speech dimensions (or the lack of it) will also reveal itself to be a less than crucial issue for the understanding of speech perception.

A final weakness of the threshold approach to CP is the short list of conclusions to which data can lead. A continuum can be found to be "categorical," "continuous," or sometimes "less categorical." But not all categorical continua yield the same data; in fact, not all continuous ones do either, and a rich array of psychophysical concepts has been developed to characterize the ways in which the latter differ. One of my purposes here is to extend the usefulness of these concepts.

SDT models of categorical perception

Predicting discrimination from identification using SDT. Signal detection theory has a number of advantages over threshold theory that recommend its use in analyzing CP experiments. For example, it permits separation of sensitivity and response bias in discrimination, given a 2 × 2 confusion matrix; and it extends naturally to the analysis of multiresponse identification. In a sense, the usefulness of SDT is argued by the rest of this chapter. This preliminary section summarizes the simplest SDT model for CP (for a more detailed discussion, see Macmillan, Kaplan, & Creelman, 1977); the following section discusses some practical experimental implications of using this model.

The measure of sensitivity used in SDT is not percent correct, but d', the psychological distance between two stimuli expressed in units of their internal variability. This parameter can be estimated from both discrimination and identification experiments; Macmillan et al. (1977) proposed that perception be said to be categorical if the d' values from the two tasks correspond.

Testing the CP hypothesis with the SDT model is more trouble than with the

Haskins model. Estimating d' from discrimination data is fairly straightforward in yes-no and two-interval-forced-choice discrimination tasks (Green & Swets, 1974), but these tasks are rarely used in studying categorical perception. Models for estimating d' from same-different and ABX tasks, which are commonly used, are contained in Macmillan et al. (1977); tables for using the models have been presented by Kaplan, Macmillan, and Creelman (1978). For identification data, estimates of d' are obtained by converting proportions to z-scores and subtracting; if the identification task allows more than two responses, more complex data processing is needed (Braida & Durlach, 1972). The usual conclusion to which this analysis leads, when applied to identification and discrimination experiments using the same stimulus set, is that discrimination d' exceeds, but is correlated with, d' predicted from identification. Because the same conclusion can be reached by the simpler threshold analysis, it is reasonable to ask, Why bother?

There are two quite different answers to this question. One is that the SDT approach will turn out to be parsimonious: In extending this simple model to fit the data, we will be able to use concepts from other areas of auditory research, drawing connections that threshold theory has failed to make.

The second justification for using detection theory is the same as the response SDT proponents gave to their threshold-theory critics in the 1950s and 1960s: d' is an unbiased measure of sensitivity, according to SDT; its value does not depend on the tendency of the observer to favor one response over the other. Percent correct is not unbiased, according to threshold (or any other) theory. In detailed threshold models (Luce, 1963a,b), an estimate of "true" sensitivity can be obtained by collecting an entire ROC curve, but this is rarely done. The Haskins and dual-process models simply assume their subjects are unbiased; in fact, an examination of studies in which hit and false alarm rates are presented reveals that the same-different and ABX paradigms typically yield significant amounts of bias.

Experimental design considerations. The use of SDT and Thurstonian methods has implications for experimental design. Because d' is, in the simplest cases, an inverse Gaussian (or z) transform of a proportion, it is important to avoid hit or false alarm rates of 0 or 1. Once confusable stimuli have been selected (probably by pretesting), enough data should be collected for an individual subject so that 0s and 1s do not arise through sampling variability if the true proportions are, say, 0.95 or 0.05. Since d' is, at best, a nonlinear transformation of proportion correct, one should not average proportions before computing d', but average the d' values across subjects. Thus many trials should be run for all subjects, who will therefore be well-trained, experienced observers, at least by the end of the experiment.

These considerations can be used to argue against applying SDT in CP research. It is known that experience in listening to speech sounds helps in discriminating and identifying them (Carney, Widin, & Viemeister, 1977; Samuel, 1977); the improvement is probably greater in regions where performance was initially poor. Whether training alters the phenomenon of CP has elicited much controversy. Certainly peaks in discrimination can be measured in trained subjects (see Miller et al., 1976). This question of perceptual learning is very important, and needs to be approached experimentally. If SDT could be applied to group data, the apparent restriction to well-trained observers could be lifted.

Fortunately, the penalty for averaging proportions from different subjects before computing d' is slight. Macmillan and Kaplan (1985) have compared the *group d'* statistic, in which d' is estimated from averaged hit- and false-alarm rates, with *average d'*, the mean d' for individual observers. They reach two comforting conclusions: (1) Group d' is, on the average, less than average d', but the discrepancy is not great unless observers differ greatly in sensitivity or, especially, response bias. (2) The variability of group d' is *less* than that of average d'. The most serious potential distortion concerns averaging subjects with very different biases. As far as one can tell from published reports, this problem does not arise in practice. In same-different tasks, subjects (especially the customary untrained ones) display a bias toward "same"; in ABX, they display a bias toward responding that X matches B rather than A. Remember that it is not the bias itself that is potentially troublesome, but the possibility of a wide range of biases. Apparently, such a range of biases does not occur; if it does, however, it distorts threshold as well as SDT analysis.

The problem of 0s and 1s can also be easily solved. The problem arises not only because small numbers of trials are used; according to some "definitions" of CP (including the classic one by Studdert-Kennedy et al., 1970), the *ideal* case of the phenomenon occurs when identification proportions are perfect at almost all points along a continuum. Success in satisfying this definition accordingly guarantees ceiling and floor effects. That is, if stimuli 1 and 2 are each identified as /ba/ 100% of the time, the threshold model will predict that, because subjects identify them as the same, they will be indiscriminable. The possibility that subjects could identify them as different if they were permitted more than two responses is neglected. In fact, the problem of perfect proportions, which arises mostly in identification, can generally be avoided by using more than two responses; a few studies of this type have been reported (see Perey & Pisoni, 1977, and Rosner, 1984), but two-response paradigms are far more popular.

In the next section the Durlach and Braida model is described and then data from several experiments are reanalyzed in SDT terms. In most of these studies, data from groups of observers have been averaged together, so that group d', not average d', is estimated. When proportions of 0 and 1 are reported, no attempt is made to interpret them in SDT terms.

Applications of Durlach and Braida's preliminary theory of intensity resolution: The relation between discrimination and identification

A summary of Durlach and Braida's theory

The theory of intensity perception developed by Durlach, Braida, and their colleagues has been presented in a series of 13 papers over the last 15 years. In this section, I summarize the "preliminary theory" (see especially Durlach & Braida, 1969; Braida & Durlach, 1972; and Berliner & Durlach, 1973), and use it to evaluate the relation between identification and discrimination on categorical continua. A "revised theory" has recently been proposed (Braida, Durlach, Lim, Berliner, Rabinowitz, & Purks, 1984); it is used in the section on revised theory to interpret the category boundary effect.

The theory is primarily psychophysical, not psychoacoustic; that is, its theoretical constructs are related to aspects of the experimental design, rather than to stimulus characteristics. In fact, the experimental work that has been undertaken to test the theory has used only pure tones differing in intensity, and detailed models for the perceptual effects of these stimuli have not been incorporated into the model. Of course, this is an advantage from the point of view of the present enterprise. Ades (1977) first recognized the potential of the Durlach-Braida model for an understanding of CP. Although his analysis was limited by the fact that SDT analyses of the most popular discrimination designs were not yet available, his general approach (and some of his specific conclusions) foreshadows my own.

The basic model of internal processing derives from SDT and Thurstonian scaling. Each stimulus is imagined to lead to a normal distribution of internal effect; the distributions vary along one dimension. The variances of the distributions have three components: sensory, trace, and context. The *sensory variance* originates from irreducible neural fluctuations, and is assumed to be equal for all stimuli on a given continuum. Observers operate in the *trace mode* and/or the *context mode*. In the trace mode, the memory of one signal is compared with the percept of the previous one; the variance of this process is proportional to the interstimulus interval. In the context mode, each signal is compared with the overall stimulus context; the variance of this process is assumed to be proportional to the square of the stimulus range (in intensity perception, R is measured in bels). The preliminary model does not propose a specific process for context coding; this lack is remedied in the revised theory. (See also Harnad's model, in Chapter 19 of this volume, which hypothesizes distinct representations underlying trace mode – *unbounded* and *iconic* – and [long-term, overlearned] context mode – *bounded* and *categorical*.)

The parameter d' can be estimated from both discrimination and identification experiments. The key postulates of the theory relate d' and the three sources of variance to performance in three tasks: identification, fixed discrimination, and roving discrimination. In *identification*, the observer uses M responses to classify N stimuli. Whereas in CP research M is usually 2, in psychophysical experiments it is most commonly greater than 2; it can be any integer larger than 1, however. Because only one signal is presented per trial, the context mode is used exclusively, and performance is limited by sensory variance β^2 and context variance $(GR)^2$:

$$d'_{ident} = \frac{\Delta\mu}{(\beta^2+(GR)^2)^{1/2}}, \qquad (2)$$

where $\Delta\mu$ is the mean perceptual separation between two signals, R is the stimulus range, and G is a constant.

Discrimination can be either "fixed" or "roving." In *roving discrimination*, the two signals being discriminated are varied from trial to trial. That is, the first trial might require that the observer discriminate between stimuli 1 and 2, the next trial between stimuli 8 and 9, and so on. Because at least two signals must be presented on each trial, the trace mode as well as the context mode affect performance. Trace variance (AT) is proportional to the interstimulus interval T. The two modes combine in an optimal fashion, so that the addition of a second mode improves, rather than harms performance. To pose an electrical analogy, trace and context variances add in the manner of resistances in parallel, yielding:

$$d'_{roving} = \frac{\Delta\mu}{\left[\beta^2 + \frac{1}{\frac{1}{AT} + \frac{1}{(GR)^2}}\right]^{1/2}} \quad (3)$$

When one type of memory variance is much less than the other, the process with the larger variance affects performance very little. For example, equation (2) is a special case of equation (3) for $(GR)^2 \ll AT$.

In *fixed discrimination* experiments, the two signals being discriminated are fixed for a block of trials. (The correct answer on each trial remains, of course, unpredictable.) The context variance, being proportional to R^2, is effectively zero, because the range is of the order of one jnd (just-noticeable-difference); total memory variance, which is less than the smaller of trace and context variance, also approaches 0, and only the sensory variance matters, which is to say:

$$d'_{fixed} = \frac{\Delta\mu}{\beta} \quad (4)$$

A concise summary of the sources of variance presumed to limit performance in each of these tasks is provided in Table 2.1.

The values of d' given in equations (3) and (4) are for yes-no (one-interval) discrimination, which cannot be performed in a roving design, and is rarely performed even when levels are fixed. Values estimated from two-interval forced-choice experiments are larger by a factor of $\sqrt{2}$. Models for extracting d' for same-different and ABX discrimination designs are given in Macmillan et al. (1977).

Equations (2) to (4) have four unknowns (three variance terms and the mean difference $\Delta\mu$), but if all three values of d' are available, both context and trace variance can be estimated, in units of the sensory variance. In addition, the dependence of trace variance on T can be evaluated in experiments where T is varied. (The dependence of context variance on R is less helpful, as the physical specification of R is only defined, so far, for the intensity continuum.) When just two experimental conditions are run, as is typical, one variance ratio can be estimated only as a function of the other, but even this much information can be enlightening.

A psychophysical approach to processing modes 63

Table 2.1. *Tasks and sources of variance according to Durlach and Braida's preliminary theory*

Task	Description	Sources of variance
Discrimination: Two possible designs are same-different (SD) and two-interval-forced-choice (2IFC)	Two stimuli from the set {AB} are presented. In SD, observer must say SAME (if AA or BB) or DIFFERENT (if AB or BA); in 2IFC, observer must give order (AB or BA).	—
Fixed	Only two different stimuli occur in an entire block of trials.	Sensory (β^2)
Roving	Stimuli may be drawn from entire range.	Sensory (β^2) Context $((GR)^2)$ Trace (AT)
Identification	One stimulus is presented per trial, and the observer must assign an appropriate label.	Sensory (β^2) Context $((GR)^2)$

We are now in a position to apply the preliminary theory to experiments from the CP literature. The most useful data come from experiments in which identification and both fixed and roving discrimination have been measured, but few such experiments have been conducted. Experiments not satisfying this requirement have been selected when data collected by the same investigator can plausibly be combined across studies, or when the variety of stimuli used makes even a partial analysis worthwhile.

Time-dependent memory variance in discrimination: Trace mode

Speech perception researchers have claimed that some speech continua, particularly those along which consonants vary, are relatively unaffected by trace decay. Pisoni (1973) conducted a straightforward test of this hypothesis, which he formulated in terms of the dual-process model: "Consonants and vowels differ in the degree to which distinct auditory and phonetic memory codes are employed in discrimination" (p. 254). This led him to expect different results for stimulus pairs that varied between phonetic categories (and thus could be discriminated phonetically) and for pairs that varied only within a category (and thus could be discriminated only using the "auditory" process).

Some understanding of these data in terms of the Durlach and Braida model can be gained by looking at discrimination alone if we are willing to assume that the trace variance is substantially less than the context variance, so that the trace mode

Table 2.2. *Estimating relative trace variance* (AT/β^2) *using the equation:*
$d'^{-2} = \Delta\mu^{-2}(\beta^2 + AT)$

Reference and stimulus condition	Between or within categories	Goodness of fit (r)[a]	AT/β^2
Pisoni (1973)			
Vowels (300 msec)	Between	.9987	.592
	Within	.991	.916
Vowels (50 msec)	Between	.980	.239
	Within	.9996	1.216
Voiced stops	Between	.921	.521
	Within	.489	—[b]
Bilabial stops	Between	.123	—[b]
	Within	−.670	—[b]
Berliner & Durlach (1973)			
Tones (54-dB range)	—	.997	5.4

[a]The values of r are based on four points; $p < .05$ two-tailed tests require $r > .87$ for significance.
[b]Model does not apply $(r < .87)$.

dominates discrimination. (Evidence that this is in fact true for the data to be analyzed will be presented in the section on the efficiency of the trace and context modes.) In that case, sensory and trace variance combine to limit performance. Rewriting equation (3) for the case $(GR)^2 \gg AT$ we have:

$$d'_{roving}{}^{-2} = \Delta\mu^{-2}(\beta^2 + AT) \qquad (5)$$

Linear regression can be used to test the model, and if it provides a good fit, to obtain estimates for the ratio between the slope and the intercept, A/β^2, which is the ratio between trace and sensory variance when $T = 1$.

Pisoni (1973) used a same-different design to study the discrimination of vowels and consonant-vowel syllables. He reported both $P(D/D)$, the probability of correctly reporting that a pair was different, and d'_s, or apparent d', which is obtained by computing z(hit rate) $- z$(false-alarm rate). I have used his numbers to estimate true d' values: A table of the normal distribution was used to find $P(D/S)$, and the tables in Kaplan et al. (1978) were then consulted to find d' values. The data are shown in Figures 2.3a for vowels and 2.3b for consonants; values of A/β^2 are presented in Table 2.2.

Equation (5), which was used to generate the lines in Figure 2.3 (ignoring $T = 0$, where temporal masking appears to reduce sensitivity), provides an excellent fit to the vowel data, accounting for more than 96% of the variance in all cases. The relative proportion of trace variance is greater for long (300-msec) than for short (50-msec) vowels, and greater for within-category than for between-category pairs. For consonants, the model fits adequately only for the between-category com-

A psychophysical approach to processing modes

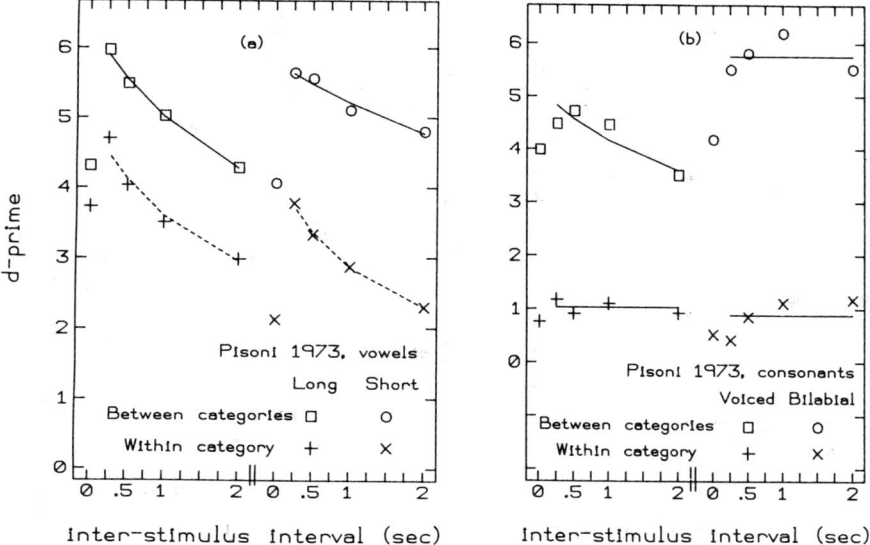

Figure 2.3. Trace-mode analysis of data from Pisoni (1973). For panel (a) and the upper-left segment of panel (b), lines are best fits to equation (5), which describes the decay in discrimination performance with increasing ISI. For the rest of panel (b), equation (5) provides a poor fit, and lines are horizontal at the mean. Vowel continuum is /i/-/I/, voiced consonants are /bae/-/dae/, bilabial consonants are /ba/-/pa/.

parison /bae/ vs /dae/; trace variance turns out to be as important for these stimuli as for long vowels. In the within-category condition and for the bilabial syllables /ba/ and /pa/, ISI has little effect; this would happen, according to the model, if the listener operated largely in the context mode. In general, the conclusions reached by applying the Durlach-Braida model to these data parallel those reached by Pisoni using the dual-process model.

Using identification and fixed and roving discrimination to estimate memory variance: Context mode

In the typical CP experiment, identification and roving discrimination are performed. The preliminary theory predicts that identification d' will be proportional to discrimination d', as dividing equation (3) by equation (2) yields:

$$\frac{d'_{roving}}{d'_{ident}} = \left[\frac{\beta^2 + (GR)^2}{\beta^2 + \dfrac{1}{(GR)^{-2} + (AT)^{-1}}} \right]^{1/2} \quad (6)$$

If an estimate of trace variance is available, equation (6) can be used to assess the contribution of the context mode.

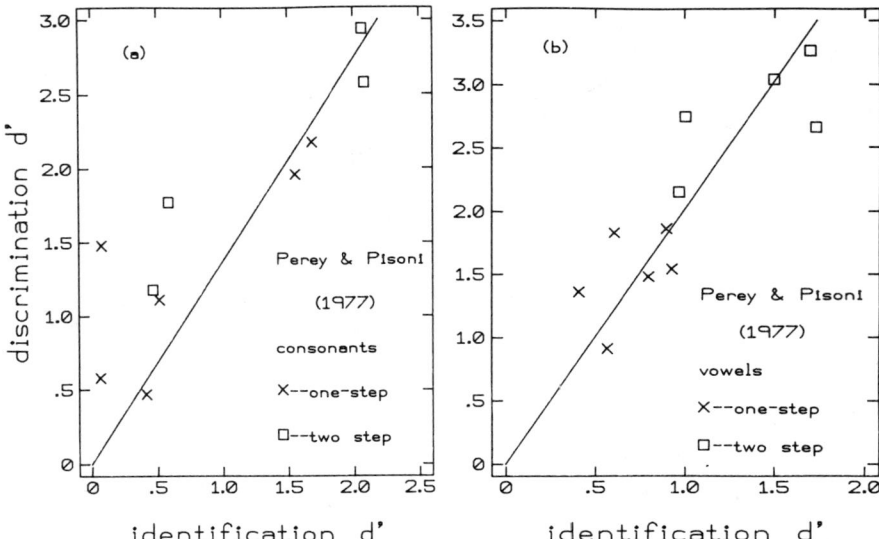

Figure 2.4. Signal-detection analysis of data from Perey and Pisoni (1977). The Durlach-Braida model predicts discrimination d' will be proportional to identification d'. Lines of best fit constrained to pass through the origin are shown.

Because a major aim of this analysis is to compare the processing of different stimulus types, experiments using a variety of stimuli will be analyzed. The experiments to be discussed are those of Perey and Pisoni (1977), on vowels (/i/-/I/) and consonants (bilabials differing in VOT); Rosner (1984), also on VOT; Macmillan (1979), on plucks and bows; and Healy and Repp (1982), on consonants, vowels (/i/-/I/), timbres, and fricatives.

Vowels and consonants (Perey & Pisoni, 1977). In analyzing the Perey and Pisoni data, we can take advantage of the fact that the stimuli were identical to the "long vowels" and "bilabial consonants" in the experiment of Pisoni (1973) discussed above (Pisoni, personal communication, 1983). We shall assume, therefore, that A/β^2 is essentially zero for consonants, and about 0.74 (the geometric mean of the between- and within-category values) for vowels.

For their ABX discrimination experiment, Perey and Pisoni report values of d'_s or apparent d', which is obtained by computing z(hit rate) $- z$(false-alarm rate). I have converted each d'_s value to true d', using the tables of Kaplan et al. (1978). Identification d' values are computed by Perey and Pisoni in the manner already described, by applying the z-transformation to proportion identified. Discrimination d' is plotted against identification d' in Figure 2.4a for a consonant continuum and in Figure 2.4b for a vowel continuum. In each figure, the least-squares line passing through the origin is drawn.

For consonants, the best-fit line explains 58% of the variance. The line has a slope of 1.14, which means that variances limiting performance in the two tasks are of similar magnitude. It is still impossible to tell, however, whether the listeners were operating in the trace or the context mode.

For vowels, discrimination is better than identification – the slope of the line in Figure 2.4b is 1.72. The prediction that d' in the two tasks is proportional is again upheld, as the line accounts for 59% of the variance. To obtain an estimate of $(GR)^2/\beta^2$, the ratio of context to sensory variance, we combine Pisoni's (1973) same-different data with Perey and Pisoni's (1977) identification data. The ratio between discrimination d' and identification d', as given in equation (6), can be expressed in terms of two parameters: the *relative trace variance* AT/β^2, which we have estimated to be 0.74; and the *relative context variance* $(GR)^2/\beta^2$. The best (minimum least-squares fit) value of $(GR)^2/\beta^2$ for Pisoni's (1973) data can be found by iteration to be about 14.6. Relative context variance is clearly substantial for vowels; at a 1-sec ISI, it is almost 20 times as great as the relative trace variance. Listeners apparently operate in the trace mode in discriminating vowels; that is, they compare the two stimuli in each trial with each other, not with the overall context.

Consonants (Rosner, 1984). Rosner (1984) also studied the VOT (voice-onset time) continuum; his experiment can be straightforwardly analyzed in terms of the preliminary theory, as he conducted both fixed and roving discrimination as well as identification.[3]

The (two-step) discrimination d's calculated by Rosner can be compared with identification d's, as was done for Perey and Pisoni's data (Figure 2.4). The two d' values are again proportional, but there is somewhat more scatter: For both fixed and roving conditions, the line of proportionality explains about half of the variance. The slopes of the lines are 3.01 for fixed discrimination versus identification, 1.98 for the roving paradigm. Solving equations (2) through (4), we find that the relative context variance is 8.1, whereas the relative trace variance is 0.61. Rosner's listeners perceive his VOT continuum much as Pisoni's listeners do vowels, in the trace mode. This means that very little context-coding, or labeling, is used for either continuum, contrary to the spirit of the CP hypothesis. Both Rosner and Pisoni used naive listeners; I will argue later that training improves the efficiency of context coding, so the dominance of the trace mode may reflect the lack of training.

Vowels, timbres, and fricatives (Healy & Repp, 1982). In many experimental investigations of CP, fixed discrimination is not tested. If only roving discrimination and identification are examined, the ratio of d's in the two tasks can be inserted into equation (6), and relative trace variance can be computed as a function of the relative context variance. The resulting relation defines the locus of possible variances yielding the observed performance ratio. To illustrate this approach, I will examine some data collected by Healy and Repp (1982).

Healy and Repp investigated four stimulus continua: consonants, vowels, tim-

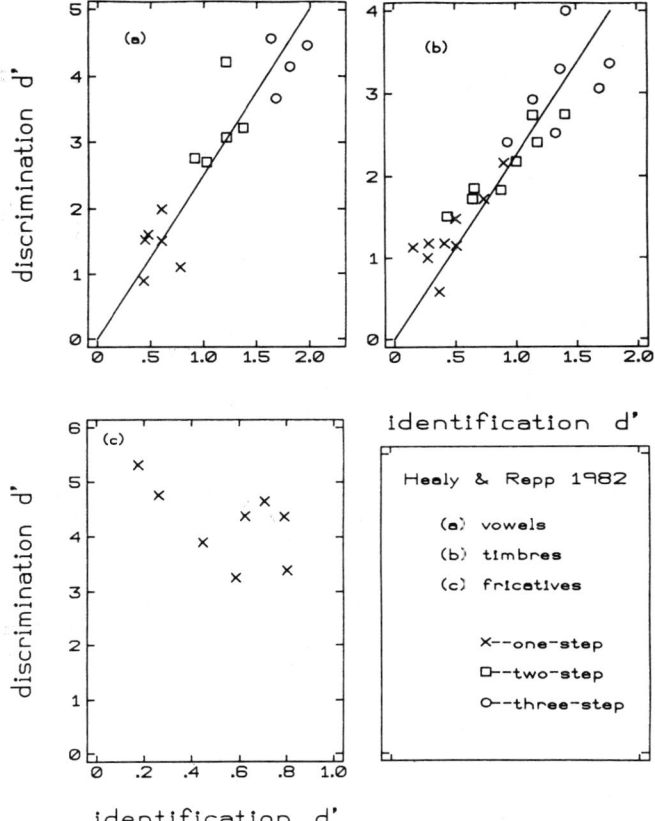

Figure 2.5. Signal-detection analysis of data from Healy and Repp (1982). Vowel continuum is /i/-/I/; timbres are second-formant resonances from 2156 to 2837 hertz, driven by a 124-hertz fundamental; fricative continuum is /sh/-/s/. The lines in panels (a) and (b) are as in Figure 2.4.

bres, and fricatives. For all four, they found that discrimination exceeded that predicted by the Haskins model. Because their discrimination task was same-different, they could not apply the dual-process model; they nonetheless concluded that the discrepancy between identification and discrimination could be explained by reference to a second, auditory process.[4]

No SDT analysis of the consonant data is possible because of ceiling effects: Most identification proportions are either 0 or 1. The results for the other continua are shown in Figure 2.5. For vowels and timbres, discrimination d' and identification d' are proportional, the line of proportionality accounting for, respectively, 82% and 76% of the variance.

For fricatives (Figure 2.5c) the preliminary theory clearly fails, implying that one of its assumptions is false; a natural suspect is the assumption of one-dimensionality. That the model can be shown to fail in one situation is reassuring because it means that our tests have some point; that fricatives particularly may be multidimensional is interesting, as Repp (1981) has argued from identification and discrimination experiments that fricatives may be processed in more than one manner. I discuss the dimensionality question at greater length in a later section.

Applying our psychophysical model to Healy and Repp's data has led us to conclusions quite different from those reached by the authors, who ordered their continua by a categoricality criterion, as follows: consonants, timbres (fricatives and vowels). My analysis suggests that timbres and vowels are perceived quite similarly; fricatives appear to differ fundamentally from the other sets in being perceptually multidimensional.

Plucks and bows (Macmillan, 1979). The experiments to be described in this section do not concern speech continua, but the allegedly musical continuum that contains plucks and bows; this stimulus set has repaid psychoacoustic investigation to a certain extent. Plucks and bows are far simpler than speech, but considerably more complex than intensity; they are more likely to yield to psychoacoustic analysis than are other stimuli that are categorically perceived.

A brief history of pluck-bow research follows; a fuller one is contained in Rosen and Howell's contribution to this volume (Chapter 4). In 1974, Cutting and Rosner reported identification and discrimination experiments performed with sawtooth stimuli varying in rise time. Stimuli with short rise times were called "plucks," those with long rise times, "bows." A category-boundary effect was observed: Discrimination of stimuli differing in rise time by 20 msec peaked in midrange. Although both the Haskins and dual-process models fit poorly, Cutting and Rosner (1974, 1976) described their results as implying the categorical perception of plucks and bows.

Rosen and Howell (1981) discovered that the nominal rise times of Cutting and Rosner's stimuli were incorrect. Using stimuli whose rise times really were 0, 10, 20 msec, and so on (instead of 4, 6, 15, and so on, as in Cutting and Rosner's study), they found that discrimination decreased monotonically with increasing rise time, as predicted by Weber's law. This confirmed the work of van Heuven and van den Broecke (1979), who had reached a similar conclusion using a different procedure, the method of adjustment. Cutting (1982) replicated Rosen and Howell's nonreplication, but also reported that a discrimination peak could be found when stimuli were spaced logarithmically, rather than arithmetically. An explanation of this finding has been offered by Pastore in Chapter 1.

The data to be described in this section are from an unpublished experiment of my own (Macmillan, 1979). Nominal rise times were between 0 and 50 msec, but the method of stimulus generation produced distributions of actual rise time corresponding to each nominal rise time. Postexperimental analysis of the stimuli revealed that the actual rise times of the stimuli were different from the nominal values,[5] but the spacing of the stimuli does not matter for present purposes.

Table 2.3. *Comparison of d' values for 2IFC and ABX fixed designs*

Stimulus rise times (msec)	Observer MM		Observer DG		Observer BW		Average	
	2IFC	ABX	2IFC	ABX	2IFC	ABX	2IFC	ABX
0,10[a]	1.44	1.26	.65	.77	.42	.70	.84	.91
10,20	2.49	2.34	2.75	1.99	3.07	1.91	2.77	2.08
20,30	1.76	1.22	1.76	2.36	2.60	2.36	2.04	1.98
30,40	1.43	1.31	1.83	1.89	2.21	1.41	1.83	1.54
40,50	1.03	.94	.31	1.54	.84	1.26	.73	1.25
Total d'	8.15	7.07	7.30	8.55	9.14	7.64	8.21	7.76

[a]Nominal 0-msec stimulus actually had a mean rise time between 5 and 10 msec.
Source: Data are from a pluck-bow experiment (Macmillan, 1979).

Three well-trained subjects performed in identification and discrimination conditions; both roving and fixed discrimination trials were run, in both ABX and 2IFC paradigms (see Table 2.1). One purpose of collecting discrimination data of different types was to test some assumptions of the SDT model. As can be seen in Table 2.3, d' estimated from 2IFC and ABX agreed quite well, in support of the Macmillan et al. (1977) models. The small (6%) advantage of 2IFC over other discrimination paradigms has been found with other stimuli (Creelman & Macmillan, 1979; Jesteadt & Sims, 1975); observers seem to be especially efficient in this paradigm.

Here I use the fixed and roving 2IFC discrimination,[6] and the identification data, to estimate the variances of the model. The trace model in the preliminary theory was developed for the 2IFC paradigm, so the data are entirely appropriate for the analysis. The plots of discrimination d' versus identification d' are well fitted by a line through the origin, 98% of the variance being accounted for in each case. Roving discrimination is a factor of 1.41 better than identification; fixed discrimination is better by a factor of 1.82. Solving equations (2) through (4) reveals that context variance is 2.3 times as large as sensory variance, trace variance 0.91 times as large. The ISI (interstimulus interval) in this experiment was only 200 msec, so the relative trace variance for a 1 sec-ISI is 4.55. Pluck-bow listening, according to these data, uses both memory modes, the context mode being more efficient.

Efficiency of the trace and context modes: Characterizing the processing space

The perception of stimuli that vary along a single dimension depends, according to the preliminary theory, on the efficiency of two memory modes. The variances of the trace and context modes, relative to basic sensory variability, define a two-dimensional *processing space* in which stimulus continua can be represented; such a

A psychophysical approach to processing modes

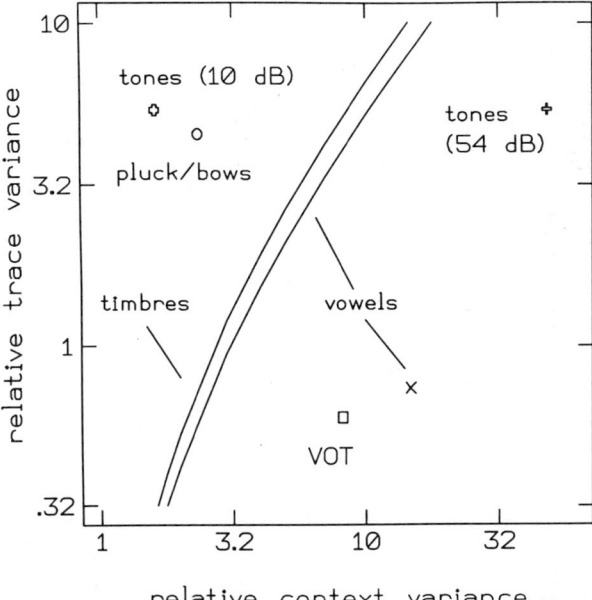

Figure 2.6. Perceptual processing space for consonants and vowels. The axes are the relative memory variances for the two processing modes of Durlach and Braida (1969); trace variance is for an ISI of 1 second. Performance in identification and in roving discrimination determines a curve through the space; if fixed discrimination performance is also known, the processing locus can be identified uniquely. Sources of data and numerical values of relative trace and context variance are given in Table 2.2.

space is portrayed in Figure 2.6. To obtain values of A/β^2, the relative trace variance for an ISI of one second, estimates of AT/β^2 were divided by the ISI.

The figure locates the stimulus sets discussed so far in the processing space; values of the relative trace and context variances are given in Table 2.4. The figure also contains two points for discrimination and identification of tone intensity, based on the parameter estimates provided by Berliner and Durlach (1973). The points represent tones varying over a 10-dB intensity range and over a 54-dB range; both points are based on the same parameters, which were estimated using data from several values of the range.

Because Healy and Repp (1982) collected only roving discrimination and identification data, the continua they studied cannot be localized at single points. However, the locus of possible values of the relative trace and relative context variance can be found. The slopes of the best-fitting lines in Figure 2.5 provide an estimate of d'_{roving}/d'_{ident}; equation (6) then generates the curves drawn in Figure 2.6 for these continua.

The figure illustrates a wide range of coding strategies, from context-coding

Table 2.4. *Sources of variance in roving-level discrimination*

Stimuli	Reference	Relative context variance $(GR)^2/\beta^2$	Relative trace variance AT/β^2	Relative trace variance, ISI = 1 sec A/β^2
Vowels (/i/-/I/)	Pisoni (1973)	14.7	.74	.74
	Perey & Pisoni (1977)			
Consonants (/ba/-/pa/)	Rosner (1984)	8.13	.61	.61
Pluck-bows	Macmillan (1979)	2.33	.91	4.55
Tones, 54-dB range	Berliner & Durlach (1973)	47.6	5.44	5.44
Tones, 10-dB range	Berliner & Durlach (1973)	1.62	5.44	5.44

dominance (for a 10-dB range of tone intensities) to trace-coding dominance (for Pisoni's [1973] vowels and Rosner's [1984] consonants). If the relative context variance is interpreted as a measure of the psychological range, then the speech sounds in these experiments have a large range, compared to plucks and bows, and vowels span a larger range than consonants, as conjectured by Ades (1977). Healy and Repp's (1981) vowel (and timbre) data reveal relatively more trace variance, and thus more context coding, than Pisoni's, although the same stimuli were used in both experiments. This discrepancy could have an analytic cause (recall that parameter estimation was unusual for Pisoni's data) or a procedural one.

It is interesting to compare the taxonomy offered by Figure 2.6 with the traditional categorical/continuous dichotomy. Theoretical CP, in the Macmillan et al. (1977) sense of identification-discrimination equivalence, implies a relative context variance of zero, and clearly does not occur. More pragmatically, we may ask whether dimensions commonly thought to be categorical are grouped together in Figure 2.6. Vowels and consonants, generally said to be categorical but to different degrees, are indeed in a different part of the space from the other continua, but their processing cannot be said to be categorical. Rather, context variance is so great that little labeling takes place, and perception of vowels and consonants is mostly in the trace mode.

Comments on perceptual dimensionality

We discovered earlier that the fricative stimulus set used by Healy and Repp (1982) violated the prediction of the preliminary theory that d's in different tasks should be proportional. I speculated that this might have resulted from the stimuli being perceptually multidimensional. The unidimensionality of stimulus sets used in CP experiments can be conveniently tested. Since d' is a distance measure, and both one- and two-step discrimination is measured in most studies, we can ask whether

$$d'(i, i+2) = d'(i, i+1) + d'(i+1, i+2). \tag{7}$$

Equation (7) is a basic axiom of the preliminary theory. In Table 2.5, total two-step d' is compared with total one-step d' for those studies in which d' can be estimated. On the average, one-step d' is greater by about 8%, suggesting that if there are other perceptual dimensions, they are unimportant here. Unfortunately, no one seems to have collected both one- and two-step data for fricatives, except Healy and Repp (1982); one-step percent correct was near 100, so two-step d's could not be estimated.

Applications of Durlach and Braida's revised theory: The shape of the discrimination function

In experimental tests, the preliminary theory has generally been found to fit tone-intensity data well, but some consistent discrepancies have been observed. The

Table 2.5. *Additivity tests. Two-step* d' *versus the sum of one-step* d's

Reference	Stimuli	Total d' (two-step)	Total d' (one-step)	Percent difference
Healy & Repp (1982)	Timbres	8.75	9.08	3.8
	Vowels	12.03	10.81	−10.1
Pisoni (1975)	Vowels (300 msec)	6.77	7.96	17.6
	Vowels (50 msec)	6.66	7.08	6.3
Perey & Pisoni (1977)	Consonants	6.00	6.85	14.1
	Vowels	6.83	8.19	19.9

Note: Mean percent difference (geometric mean of the ratio of column four to column three, converted to percent) is 8.1.

major failure of the theory, first acknowledged in Braida and Durlach (1972), is that sensitivity in identification (and roving discrimination) is not strictly proportional to sensitivity in fixed discrimination, as implied by equations (2) and (4). Instead, identification is relatively good at the edges of the stimulus range. Figure 2.7 shows that this effect can be substantial, especially when the stimulus range is large.[7]

Braida et al. (1984) have formulated a model of context coding, which proposes that these edge effects result from *perceptual anchors* located at the edges of the range. According to this model, observers make their judgments in the context mode by comparing stimuli with well-remembered stimulus values, located at edges. Stimuli that are close to an anchor can be identified accurately; to identify those far away, the observer measures off the distance from an anchor, using a "noisy" perceptual ruler, and performs less well. Because no stimulus is many steps from an anchor the presence of anchors is less noticeable for small stimulus ranges.

Perceptual anchors occur only at the edges of the range in auditory-intensity experiments, but it is natural to ask whether interior anchors might exist for other dimensions. In this section, I use the perceptual anchor model to determine whether the category boundary effect for categorical continua results from the existence of a perceptual anchor interior to the range.

The anchor concept is quite different from a second, more popular, explanation for the category boundary effect: the possibility of a natural boundary, or region of heightened basic sensitivity, in the region of the peak (see Miller et al., 1976; Wood, 1976; Stevens, 1981). The theoretical distinction between these two possible explanations was drawn by Ades (1977), but the preliminary theory with which he was working did not suggest an empirical method for separating them.

According to the revised theory, anchors reveal themselves by improving identification and roving discrimination performance in their vicinity. Anchors cannot, however, differentially affect fixed performance, which is constrained only by sensory variance. Thus regions in which fixed discrimination performance is high

A psychophysical approach to processing modes

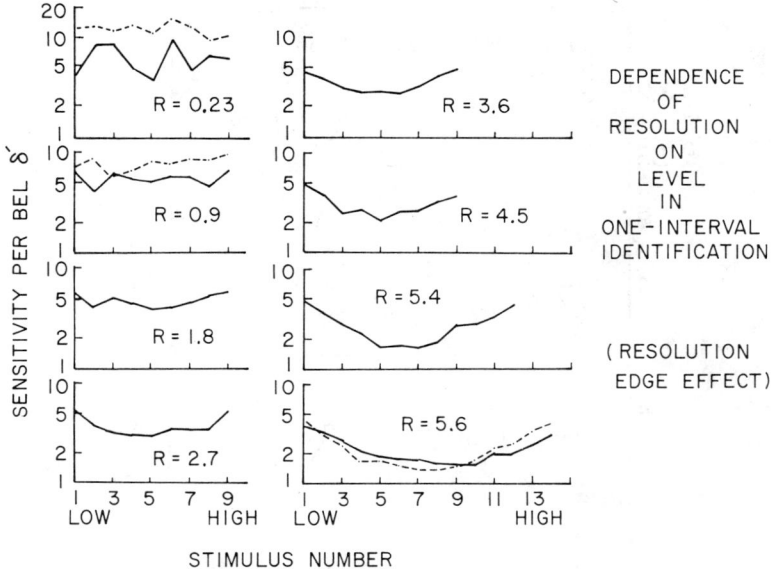

Figure 2.7. d' as a function of intensity for eight different ranges; the range R is measured in bels. The data have been adjusted to take account of differences in fixed discriminability, so the preliminary theory predicts the curves will be horizontal lines. Instead, sensitivity is better at the edges of the range, when R is large. (Based on Berliner, et al., 1977, Fig. 4.)

correspond to areas of natural sensitivity; regions in which identification or roving discrimination performance is high *relative to fixed performance* contain perceptual anchors. In the next two sections, data from VOT and pluck-bow continua are analyzed in this way.

VOT: A continuum with a region of high sensitivity and an interior anchor

Rosner's (1984) VOT experiment is well designed for testing the anchor model: He conducted fixed discrimination and eight-response identification trials.[5] Such an identification task is less likely to yield proportions of 0 or 1 than the conventional two-response paradigm. Identification and same-different discrimination data (ISI = 1 second) for 20-msec differences from 0 to 70 msec are presented in Figure 2.8.

Both tasks show a peak in midrange; the discrimination peak, at least, must reflect a region of natural sensitivity because fixed discrimination does not afford a context in which anchor-related peaks could arise. The identification data, however, show a sharper peak than discrimination, as can be seen from the plot of the ratio of identification d' to discrimination d'. The peak in *relative* performance is evidence for an interior anchor on the VOT dimension. Analysis of Rosner's other fixed

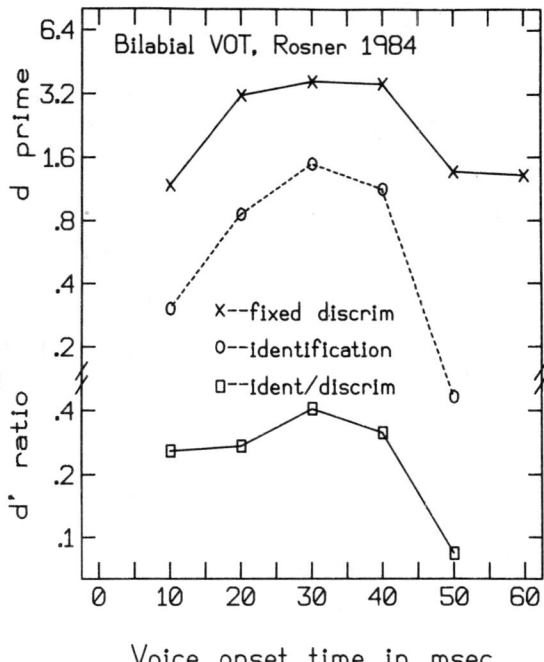

Figure 2.8. d' values for identification and fixed discrimination, and the ratio between them, for a VOT experiment (Rosner, 1984). If the preliminary theory were correct, the two discrimination curves would be parallel on these log coordinates. Instead, the ratio of identification d'/discrimination d' has a peak in midrange, reflecting the operation of an interior anchor. (No identification point is given for the 50–70 msec pair; estimated d' was -0.14.)

discrimination tasks leads to the same conclusion. (More recent studies of the VOT continua are discussed in Macmillan, Braida, & Goldberg, 1987.)

Pluck/bows: A continuum with edge anchors

Macmillan (1979) used fixed 2IFC discrimination and six-response identification tasks (among others) to investigate a pluck-bow continuum. Figure 2.9 presents the data. From 10 to 50 msec resolution decreases monotonically with rise time, as in other recent reports (see Rosen & Howell, 1981); because the nominal 0-msec rise time is actually longer (see footnote 5), the leftmost points are consistent with the trend.

The plot of the identification-discrimination d' ratio reveals that the anchors in this experiment were at the endpoints of the range, as in intensity, a conclusion that is not affected by the exact rise time of the nominal 0-msec stimulus. This continuum provides us with examples of anchors that do not correspond to regions of

A psychophysical approach to processing modes

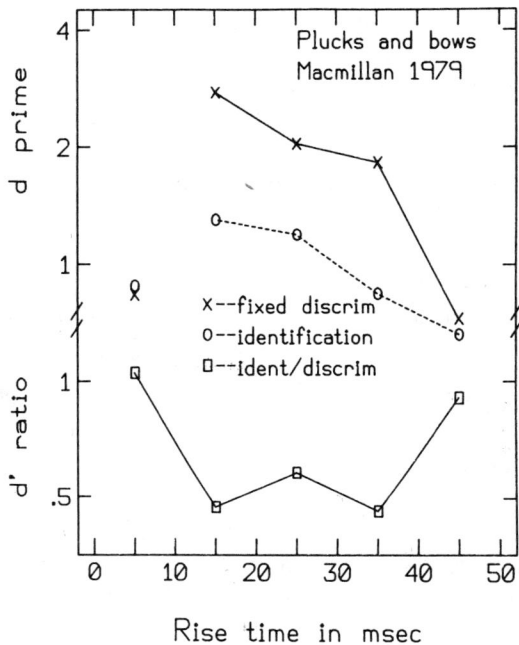

Figure 2.9. d' values for identification and fixed discrimination, and the ratio between them, for a pluck-bow experiment (Macmillan, 1979). The ratio (identification d')/(fixed d') has peaks that reflect the operation of anchors at the edges. Nominal 0-msec rise time is actually longer.[5]

high sensitivity. The anchors may have arisen, as in intensity, because they define the limits of the stimulus range for the (well-trained) observers. However, the 0-msec stimulus may be a special case. I have elsewhere (Macmillan, 1983) analyzed some pluck-bow data reported by Hary and Massaro (1982), and concluded that the 0-msec stimulus can serve as an anchor even when it is interior to the range. Although this is an ad hoc conclusion, it could easily be tested by performing fixed discrimination for such a stimulus set.

The analysis of these two continua, VOT and pluck/bows, suggests the power of Durlach and Braida's perceptual anchor model. Voice-onset time has a region of natural sensitivity, and an anchor, in midrange. Plucks and bows, like tones differing in intensity, show no peaks in basic sensitivity, and display edge anchors. Before generalizing from these two data points, we should be aware of one important procedural difference between the experiments. Macmillan's listeners were highly trained, and received feedback throughout; Rosner's were naive, and received none. Although even Rosner's listeners served longer than those in many other speech experiments, they had much less experience than Macmillan's subjects, or the observers in the Braida-Durlach tone experiments. Figure 2.6 shows that context variance was small in the latter studies. Anchors are presumably acquired through experience, and their locations may well shift during training, as context coding improves; in any case, comparisons across experiments in which different amounts of learning experience were provided must be made with caution.

Conclusions, implications, and connections to other research

This attempt to provide a psychophysical framework for CP raises a number of rather broad questions about the processing of stimuli that differ psychologically in one dimension. In some cases, the conclusions to which this approach leads have been reached by other investigators following different paths. This final section addresses five issues:

1. the relation between identification and discrimination
2. the category boundary effect
3. effects of perceptual learning
4. context effects
5. limitations of the models.

Relation between identification and discrimination

Early writers on CP (see Studdert-Kennedy et al., 1970) believed identification and discrimination to be equivalent for categorical continua. Our earlier characterization of CP (Macmillan et al., 1977) agreed with this, using an SDT rather than a discrete-state model for the equivalence. It is now clear that few if any dimensions have this property.

One way to see this is to examine Figure 2.6. For a continuum to be categorical by the identification-discrimination equivalence criterion, the context variance would have to be a small fraction of the sensory variance; yet no points are shown in the figure for which the relative context variance is less than one. Pynn, Braida, and Durlach (1972) did find near equivalence of identification and discrimination for a very small range of tone intensities (2.25 dB); apparently none of the other continua discussed here has a comparably small psychological range. As a rule, identification and roving discrimination of unidimensional stimulus sets is dominated by memory variance, not sensory variance.

Massaro (Chapter 8, this volume; see also Hary & Massaro, 1982) has argued that the relation between identification and discrimination cannot be evidence for the categoricality of a dimension. I am in essential agreement, but find the situation both better and worse than this statement suggests. Relations between tasks *can* provide useful information about the manner in which stimuli are processed, however such processing is named; the implication that CP is a well-defined mode that can be studied (by other means) seems to me doubtful.

Another aspect of the traditional view of the identification-discrimination relation can now be seen to be, at best, an exaggeration. Continuous perception was characterized by Studdert-Kennedy et al. (1970) as a mode in which discrimination and identification were essentially unrelated. My analysis (see Figures 2.4 and 2.5) shows that in most cases there is a simple relation between these tasks: Sensitivity in identification is proportional to sensitivity in discrimination. The two tasks measure the same thing, but identification has a coarser grain. Historically, most psychophysicists (S. S. Stevens was a notable exception) have believed that resolution provided a basic sensory metric that was tapped by many tasks, and it is not surprising that this is as true for speech continua as it is for auditory intensity.

The category boundary effect

If the category boundary effect is not to be understood in terms of identification-discrimination equivalence, how can it be interpreted? One possibility, discussed above and by several other contributors to this volume (Repp & Liberman in Chapter 3 and Rosen & Howell in Chapter 4) is that some continua contain psychoacoustic discontinuities, or regions of natural sensitivity. An attractive feature of this hypothesis is that it motivates psychoacoustic experimentation on the complex stimuli that are typical in CP research. My analysis makes a strong assertion about the methodology used in pursuing this goal.

In psychoacoustics, an attempt is made to relate d' to stimulus characteristics. If d' is determined primarily by sensation noise, this enterprise is at least possible, whereas if sensation noise is overwhelmed by memory noise, or if sensitivity results largely from the existence of an anchor, the likelihood that d' will be systematically related to the stimulus is slight. This suggests that psychoacoustic investigations of dimensions having a category boundary effect should use fixed discrimination because that task minimizes the contribution of memory. Rosner's (1984) VOT data (see Figure 2.8) provide an example of a peak that occurs even in fixed experiments.

But if roving discrimination is used, a category boundary effect can arise, not because of natural sensitivity, but because of anchors. The possibility that peaks may arise from memory effects of some kind has been recognized by many writers, including Ades (1977) and Rosen and Howell (see Chapter 4, this volume). Dimensions with anchors are those, according to the present analysis, in which sharper peaks occur in identification or roving discrimination than in fixed discrimination.

Rosen and Howell dub this explanation of the category boundary effect "learned labels." Indeed, a likely distinction between regions of natural sensitivity and anchors is the time course over which they are established; I discuss perceptual learning explicitly in the next section. But Rosen and Howell's terminology suggests that what observers learn are good examples of stimulus categories, rather than the boundaries between them; in this, Repp and Liberman (Chapter 3) agree, attributing the boundary effect to the use of "prototypes." Although this may be the case for some continua, it apparently is not true for all: Anchors can occur in regions of natural sensitivity (as in Rosner's VOT data), at the edges of the stimulus range (as in Macmillan's pluck-bow data [Figure 2.9], or in loudness [Figure 2.7]), or, in principle, at any other location. The particular perceptual landmarks observers use in processing stimuli must be determined empirically.

Perceptual learning

As observers perform in psychophysical tasks, their sensitivity improves. The improvement is nonuniform in at least two respects. First, learning is more rapid, and reaches an earlier asymptote, in fixed discrimination than in roving discrimination or identification (Watson, 1980). Thus the location of dimensions in the processing space (Figure 2.6) is determined in part by the experience of the observers. This dictates caution in interpreting old data in terms of the processing space; for example, as already indicated, the pluck/bow dimension may have a small relative context variance because the subjects were well-trained. On the other hand, the model provides a powerful tool for analyzing experiments in which learning is studied explicitly, provided both identification and fixed and roving discrimination are performed.

The second nonuniform aspect of perceptual learning is that performance may improve in some regions of a continuum more than in others. Berliner, Durlach, and Braida (1978) showed that presentation of a standard could induce a peak in intensity identification; something similar may occur over a much longer term in the development of speech perception. An analysis of the development of anchors, using the methods described in the section on Durlach and Braida's revised theory, could provide useful insight into perceptual learning of speech and other continua (e.g., in music) in which sensitivity improves substantially over time (see Harnad, Chapter 19, this volume).

Context effects

An observer's response to a stimulus presented in a discrimination or identification task depends on other recently presented stimuli. Examples of this phenomenon include sequential effects (Repp et al., 1979), changes due to the presentation of standards (Sawusch, Nusbaum, & Schwab, 1980), and possibly changes owing to the use of "adapting stimuli" (see Chapter 6 by Remez). Some writers (Repp & Liberman, Chapter 3) have argued that context effects pose a problem for a psychophysical approach to CP.

In general terms, changes in responding can result from changes in bias or sensitivity, either of which may be interesting. In roving intensity discrimination experiments, Berliner, Durlach, and Braida (1977) found a *bias-edge effect* as well as the *resolution-edge effect* (anchor effect) seen in Figure 2.7. (Cf. Chapter 13, by Wilson, this volume.)

As both Repp and Liberman and Rosen and Howell point out in Chapters 3 and 4 (this volume), such effects cannot be attributed to regions of natural sensitivity. Some more short-term learning process is presumably involved, and the present analysis suggests two possibilities: Sensitivity may change when anchors are established, or response criteria may be shifted. Many experiments have focused on the location of the "boundary," the stimulus value in two-response identification at

A psychophysical approach to processing modes 81

which the two responses are used equally often. The Thurstonian tools used here are hard to apply to the two-response task, because of ceiling and floor effects (see the section on experimental-design considerations in the discussion of traditional models), so it is often unclear how such changes are to be interpreted. The use of more than two responses in identification, which can be accomplished by adding a confidence judgment to a binary response, is very useful in disentangling sensitivity and bias changes in identification.

Limitations

Many of the most interesting classes of sounds in the real world, such as the set of all vowels in a language, are perceptually multidimensional; Ehret (Chapter 10, this volume) also stresses the multidimensionality of signals available to nonhuman animals. CP research in general, and Durlach and Braida's models in particular, are explicitly one-dimensional. This discrepancy limits the potential of CP experiments as a tool for understanding speech and other complex sounds.

The problem is not that several physical variables may change as sounds vary in, say, VOT (see Soli, 1983); as long as the resulting stimulus set is *perceptually* unidimensional, in the sense of equation (7), the models described here can still be applied. Rather, the difficulties are that (1) apparently simple stimulus sets, perhaps generated by changing only one physical variable, may turn out to be multidimensional; and (2) exposing observers to a perceptually unidimensional stimulus set drawn from a larger multidimensional set may eliminate the most important aspects of real-life perception of the stimuli.

I have speculated in my earlier comments on perceptual dimensionality that the failure of the preliminary theory to describe fricative perception (Figure 2.5c) may result from the multidimensionality of fricatives. Another content area in which stimuli may be multidimensional is color (see Chapter 9 by Bornstein). Certainly the two-dimensional chromaticity diagram used to describe color mixture has served as a model for perceptual confusability; in spite of the occurrence of category boundary effects in the discrimination of wavelength, this dimension may be fundamentally different from those typically studied in speech.

However, the psychophysical issues with which this chapter is concerned, namely, the existence of regions of above-average sensitivity and the relation between identification and discrimination, are not exclusively one-dimensional ideas. Although it is useful to be able to identify stimuli for which CP is not a well-defined notion, it would be more useful to relate the concept to a wider set of stimulus domains. A variety of scaling tools for studying multidimensional stimuli have been developed, but they are not easy to generalize to discrimination, and little is known about the relation between identification and discrimination of stimuli differing in more than one dimension beyond Miller's (1956) observation that added dimensions increase the information transmitted in identification. The dimensionality limitation may be one of the reasons so little contact has been made between the CP literature and work on cognitive categories (see Chapters 16 by Medin & Barsalou, 17 by Keil & Kelly, and 18 by Bialystok & Olson, this volume). As the complexity of the stimuli that can be practically studied in the laboratory grows, so does the need for a thorough psychophysical understanding of multidimensional stimuli. One-dimensional psychophysics, as exemplified by the Durlach-Braida models, does a good job of describing tone-intensity perception and, I have argued here, many other continua. The study of more complex stimuli provides a challenge to speech perception and psychophysics alike.

Appendix A. Estimating phonemic and auditory sensitivity from identification and ABX discrimination data

In the dual-process model, let:

$p_i = P$ (identifying stimulus i with response R_1);
$p_j = P$ (identifying stimulus j with response R_1);
$p_L = P$ (reaching a decision in ABX by labeling);
$p(C|L)$ = phonemic sensitivity = P (reaching a correct decision in ABX, given that labeling leads to a decision); and
$p(C|A)$ = auditory sensitivity = P (reaching a correct decision in ABX, given that labeling does not lead to a decision).

It suffices to consider trials on which the stimuli $\langle ABA \rangle$ or $\langle ABB \rangle$ are presented. (Capital letters indicate signals, the corresponding small letters, responses.) The probability of reaching a *correct* labeling decision is:

$$p(C \cap L | \langle ABA \rangle) = P(aba) + P(bab) = p_i^2(1 - p_j) + (1 - p_i)^2 p_j.$$
$$p(C \cap L | \langle ABB \rangle) = P(abb) + P(baa) = p_i(1 - p_j)^2 + (1 - p_i)p_j^2.$$

The probability of an *incorrect* labeling decision is:

$$p(\bar{C} \cap L | \langle ABA \rangle) = P(abb) + P(baa)$$
$$= p_i(1 - p_j)(1 - p_i) + (1 - p_i)p_j p_i.$$
$$p(\bar{C} \cap L | \langle ABB \rangle) = P(aba) + P(bab)$$
$$= p_i(1 - p_j)p_j + (1 - p_i)p_j(1 - p_j).$$

Since

$$p_L = p(C \cap L) + p(\bar{C} \cap L),$$
$$p(C|L) = \frac{p(C \cap L)}{P(C \cap L) + P(\bar{C} \cap L)}.$$

Thus the phonemic sensitivity $P(C|L)$ depends only on p_i and p_j, which can be estimated from identification data. The auditory sensitivity $P(C|A)$ can then be computed from the following relation (equation [1] in the text):

$$p(C|A) = \frac{P(C) - P(C \cap L)}{1 - p_L}.$$

Notes

1. The phrase "categorically perceived continuum" sits uncomfortably in a chapter that is critical of the categorical/continuous distinction. It is a hard term to do without, however, and I will use it, as others do, to refer to dimensions with discrimination peaks in midrange.
2. Threshold models of detection postulate two discrete internal states, "detect" and "nondetect." A signal may lead to either event. In high-threshold models, a catch-trial, on which no signal is presented, can never lead to the detect state, whereas in low-threshold models it can. In speech-discrimination experiments there is no stimulus that has the special status of a null signal, so symmetric, low-threshold assumptions are more natural.
3. Rosner's experiments 1, 3, and 4 (in experiment 2, the stimulus conditions were different) actually include five conditions: identification, fixed ABX, roving ABX, fixed AX with ISI = 1 second, and fixed AX with ISI = 4 seconds. The fixed AX d's were systematically higher than the fixed ABX d's. The ABX data are used here so that fixed and roving conditions can be compared even though the Durlach and Braida (1969) model for the trace mode assumes a two-interval task.
4. In fact, Healy and Repp attributed the difference in part to "context effects," and performed a same-different labeling task to assess the contribution of context to discrimination. Except for the consonants, however, discrimination exceeded even "in-context" identification, due to "auditory information."
5. Plucks and bows were generated by modulating an analog 150-hertz sawtooth; the onset was random with respect to the phase of the sawtooth. A sample of waveforms reveals that the 0-millisecond stimuli had rise times very similar to the 10-millisecond stimuli, although it is difficult to assign a precise value because of the low frequency of the sawtooth. Thus the data, which were originally thought to display a category boundary effect, are in fact consistent with Rosen and Howell's (1981) study.
6. I use two-interval discrimination (here, 2IFC) where available, rather than ABX. In this experiment, the two procedures yielded approximately the same d's (see Table 2.3).
7. If Weber's law were true for tone intensity, then the discriminability of tones differing by the same number of decibels would be constant, and the prediction that identification d' and discrimination d' are proportional would be equivalent to the prediction that identification d's for equally spaced stimuli are equal, or, in other words, that the curves in Figure 2.7 are flat. In fact, there is a "near miss" to Weber's law on this continuum (Rabinowitz, Lim, Braida, & Durlach, 1976) – discriminability of such stimulus pairs improves slightly with overall intensity. The curves in Figure 2.7 have been adjusted to take this into account. The values plotted are actually d' *ratios*, as required by equation (6).

References

Ades, A. E. (1977). Vowels, consonants, speech and nonspeech. *Psychological Review, 84*, 524–530.
Békésy, G. von (1960). *Experiments in hearing*. New York: McGraw-Hill.
Berliner, J. E., & Durlach, N. I. (1973). Intensity perception. IV. Resolution in roving-level discrimination. *Journal of the Acoustical Society of America, 53*, 1270–1287.
Berliner, J. E., Durlach, N. I., & Braida, L. D. (1977). Intensity perception. VII. Further data on roving-level discrimination and the resolution and bias edge effects. *Journal of the Acoustical Society of America, 61*, 1577–1585.
Berliner, J. E., Durlach, N. I., & Braida, L. D. (1978). Intensity perception. IX. Effect of a fixed standard on resolution in identification. *Journal of the Acoustical Society of America, 64*, 687–689.
Braida, L. D., & Durlach, N. I. (1972). Intensity perception. II. Resolution in one-interval paradigms. *Journal of the Acoustical Society of America, 51*, 483–502.
Braida, L. D., Durlach, N. I., Lim, J. S., Berliner, J. E., Rabinowitz, W. M., & Purks, S. R. (1984). Intensity perception. XIII. Perceptual anchor model of context coding. *Journal of the Acoustical Society of America, 76*, 722–731.
Carney, A. E., Widin, G. P., & Viemeister, N. F. (1977). Noncategorical perception of stop consonants differing in VOT. *Journal of the Acoustical Society of America, 62*, 961–970.

Creelman, C. D., & Macmillan, N. A. (1979). Auditory phase and frequency discrimination: A comparison of nine procedures. *Journal of Experimental Psychology: Human Perception and Performance, 5,* 146–156.

Cutting, J. E. (1982). Plucks and bows are categorically perceived, sometimes. *Perception & Psychophysics, 31,* 462–476.

Cutting, J. E., & Rosner, B. S. (1974). Categories and boundaries in speech and music. *Perception & Psychophysics, 16,* 564–570.

Cutting, J. E., & Rosner, B. S. (1976). Discrimination functions predicted from categories in speech and music. *Perception & Psychophysics, 20,* 87–88.

Durlach, N. I., & Braida, L. D. (1969). Intensity perception. I. Preliminary theory of intensity resolution. *Journal of the Acoustical Society of America, 46,* 372–383.

Fujisaki, H., & Kawashima, T. (1969). On the modes and mechanisms of speech perception. *Annual report of the Engineering Research Institute* (Vol. 28, pp. 67–73). Tokyo: University of Tokyo, Faculty of Engineering.

Fujisaki, H., & Kawashima, T. (1970). Some experiments on speech perception and a model for the perceptual mechanism. *Annual report of the Engineering Research Institute* (Vol. 29, pp. 207–214). Tokyo: University of Tokyo, Faculty of Engineering.

Green, D. M., & Swets, J. A. (1974). *Signal detection theory and psychophysics.* Huntington, New York: Krieger.

Hary, J. M., & Massaro, D. W. (1982). Categorical results do not imply categorical perception. *Perception and Psychophysics, 32,* 409–418.

Healy, A. F., & Repp, B. H. (1982). Context independence and phonetic mediation in categorical perception. *Journal of Experimental Psychology: Human Perception and Performance, 8,* 68–80.

Jesteadt, W., & Sims, S. L. (1975). Decision processes in frequency discrimination. *Journal of the Acoustical Society of America, 57,* 1161–1168.

Kaplan, H. L., Macmillan, N. A., & Creelman, C. D. (1978). Tables of d' for variable-standard discrimination paradigms. *Behavior Research Methods and Instrumentation, 10,* 796–813.

Liberman, A. M., Harris, K. S., Hoffman, H. S., & Griffith, B. C. (1957). The discrimination of speech sounds within and across phoneme boundaries. *Journal of Experimental Psychology, 54,* 358–368.

Luce, R. D. Detection and recognition. (1963a). In R. D. Luce, R. R. Bush, & E. Galanter (Eds.), *Handbook of Mathematical Psychology* (Vol. 1, pp. 103–189). New York: Wiley.

Luce, R. D. (1963b). A threshold theory for simple detection experiments. *Psychological Review, 70,* 61–79.

Macmillan, N. A. (1979). Categorical perception of musical sounds: The psychophysics of plucks and bows. *Bulletin of the Psychonomic Society, 11,* 241. (Abstract)

Macmillan, N. A. (1983). A psychophysical interpretation of a "categorical perception" experiment by Hary and Massaro. *Perception & Psychophysics, 34,* 494–498.

Macmillan, N. A., Braida, L. D., & Goldberg, R. F. (1987). Central and peripheral process in the perception of speech and nonspeech sounds. In M. E. H. Schouten (Ed.) *Psychophysics of speech perception.* Martinus Nijhof.

Macmillan, N. A., & Kaplan, H. L. (1985). Detection theory analysis of group data: Estimating sensitivity from average hit and false-alarm rates. *Psychological Bulletin, 98,* 185–199.

Macmillan, N. A., Kaplan, H. L., & Creelman, C. D. (1977). The psychophysics of categorical perception. *Psychological Review, 84,* 452–471.

Miller, G. A. (1956). The magical number seven, plus or minus two: Some limits on our capacity for processing information. *Psychological Review, 63,* 81–96.

Miller, J. D., Wier, C. C., Pastore, R. E., Kelly, W. J., & Dooling, R. J. (1976). Discrimination and labeling of noise-buzz sequences with varying noise-lead times: An example of categorical perception. *Journal of the Acoustical Society of America, 60,* 410–417.

Pastore, R. E., Ahroon, W. A., Baffuto, K. J., Friedman, C., Puleo, J. S., & Fink, E. A. (1977). Common-factor model of categorical perception. *Journal of Experimental Psychology: Human Perception and Performance, 3,* 686–696.

Perey, A. J., & Pisoni, D. B. (1977). Dual processing versus response-limitation accounts of categorical perception: A response to Macmillan, Kaplan, and Creelman. *Journal of the Acoustical Society of America, 62,* S60 (Abstract).

Pisoni, D. B. (1973). Auditory and phonetic memory codes in the discrimination of consonants and vowels. *Perception & Psychophysics, 13,* 253–260.
Pisoni, D. B. (1975). Auditory short-term memory and vowel perception. *Memory & Cognition, 3,* 7–18.
Pynn, C. T., Braida, L. D., & Durlach, N. I. (1972). Intensity perception. III. Resolution in small-range identification. *Journal of the Acoustical Society of America, 51,* 559–566.
Rabinowitz, W. M., Lim, J. S., Braida, L. D., & Durlach, N. I. (1976). Intensity perception. VI. Summary of recent data on deviations from Weber's Law for 1000-Hz tone pulses. *Journal of the Acoustical Society of America, 59,* 1506–1509.
Repp, B. H. (1981). Two strategies in fricative discrimination. *Perception & Psychophysics, 30,* 217–227.
Repp, B. H., Healy, A. F., & Crowder, R. G. (1979). Categories and context in the perception of isolated steady-state vowels. *Journal of Experimental Psychology: Human Perception and Performance, 5,* 129–145.
Rosen, S. M., & Howell, P. (1981). Plucks and bows are not categorically perceived. *Perception & Psychophysics, 30,* 156–168.
Rosner, B. S. (1984). Perception of voice-onset time: A signal detection analysis. *Journal of the Acoustical Society of America, 75,* 1231–1242.
Samuel, A. G. (1977). The effect of discrimination training on speech perception: Noncategorical perception. *Perception & Psychophysics, 22,* 321–330.
Sawusch, J. R., Nusbaum, H. C., & Schwab, E. C. (1980). Contextual effects in vowel perception II: Evidence for two processing mechanisms. *Perception and Psychophysics, 27,* 421–434.
Soli, S. D. (1983). The role of spectral cues in discrimination of voice onset time differences. *Journal of the Acoustical Society of America, 73,* 2150–2165.
Stevens, K. N. (1981). Constraints imposed by the auditory system on the properties used to classify speech sounds: Data from phonology, acoustics and psychoacoustics. In T. F. Myers, J. Laver, & J. Anderson (Eds.), *The cognitive representation of speech.* Amsterdam: North Holland.
Studdert-Kennedy, M., Liberman, A. M., Harris, K. S., & Cooper, F. S. (1970). Motor theory of speech perception: A reply to Lane's critical review. *Psychological Review, 77,* 234–249.
van Heuven, V. J. J. P., & van den Broecke, M. P. R. (1979). Auditory discrimination of rise and decay times in tone and noise bursts. *Journal of the Acoustical Society of America, 66,* 1308–1315.
Watson, C. S. (1980). Time course of auditory perceptual learning. *Annals of Otology, Rhinology, and Laryngology, 89* (Suppl. 74), 96–102.
Wood, C. C. (1976). Discriminability, response bias, and phoneme categories in discrimination of voice onset time. *Journal of the Acoustical Society of America, 60,* 1381–1389.

Part II

Categorical perception of speech

3 Phonetic category boundaries are flexible

Bruno H. Repp and Alvin M. Liberman

In this chapter we review the various factors that may influence the location of phonetic category boundaries on physical-stimulus continua of the kind widely used in speech-perception research. These factors range from the context provided by other stimuli in a test (which gives rise to effects such as sequential contrast, range-frequency shifts, and selective adaptation) to the internal structure of a single speech stimulus (effects of other cues or features present, of adjacent phonetic segments, of speaking rate and speaker characteristics) to the listener's linguistic experience and expectations (effects of semantic and syntactic structure, and of cross-language phonetic differences). We conclude that phonetic category boundaries are flexible in a way that suggests that speech perception is constrained by tacit knowledge of what a vocal tract does when it makes linguistically significant gestures.

In the grammatical domains of language we find no gradients, only categories. Thus, gradations of, for example, tense (present–past), form class (noun–verb), or even word (night–day) are everywhere absent. Indeed, they are impossible, for syntactic, morphologic, and phonologic devices do not permit continuous variation. At the surface of language, however, the situation is different. There, in the relation between phonetic structure and sound, the role of the segments is categorical – a segment is, for example, [d] or [g], not something in between – but the sound can vary continuously. That being so, at least in synthetic speech, we can ask whether the phonetic segments are categorical, not only in their linguistic function, but also in the way they are perceived. The answer is a qualified "yes." Other things being equal, stimuli belonging to the same phonetic category are more difficult to discriminate than stimuli on opposite sides of a phonetic boundary. This phenomenon has long been known as "categorical perception" (CP) (Studdert-Kennedy, Liberman, Harris, & Cooper, 1970). The research it has generated, which was recently reviewed by one of us (Repp, 1984), is largely concerned with the ability of listeners to detect stimulus differences within the categories – that is, with the degree to which perception is perfectly categorical – and with the conditions under which that ability can be made to vary. Our concern in this chapter is rather with the conditions under which the *locations* of the categories on a continuum can be shown to vary, and with the implications of that variation for a theory about the nature of the categories. More particularly, we will be concerned with the boundaries between

Preparation of this chapter (completed in June, 1984) was supported by NICHD Grant HD-01994 to Haskins Laboratories.

the categories (and with their movement), so before considering the relevance to theory, we should justify our concern with the boundaries.

We take the boundary to be the point along the appropriate (acoustic) stimulus continuum at which subjects classify stimuli into alternative categories with equal probability. In the typical case of two (adjacent) categories, this is simply the point corresponding to the 50% crossover of the response function. If more than one stimulus dimension is varied, category boundaries may be represented by contours in a multidimensional space (see, e.g., Oden & Massaro, 1978). The standard method of obtaining category boundaries is to present a set of stimuli repeatedly (and in random order) for identification as members of one class or another. Several alternative methods – for example, a method of adjustment – have been used, but all yield similar boundaries (Ganong & Zatorre, 1980).

Why do we take account only of the boundaries? After all, it is the categories themselves, rather than the boundaries between them, that play the important role in speech communication. Why not, then, deal with some appropriate exemplar – the prototype, as it were – of the category? A sufficient reason is that, until recently, no one had used methods designed to identify the prototypes. Worse yet, the application of such methods has so far failed to yield entirely satisfactory results (Samuel, 1979, 1982). The measurement of boundaries, on the other hand, has long been common in research on speech, so the data are plentiful. Moreover, the boundaries do inform us about the categories and, under some specifiable conditions, about their positions on the appropriate acoustic continua. And, finally, as we will argue in this chapter, it is the boundaries, not the prototypes, that are central to the assumptions underlying at least one of the important theories about the categories.

Still, it is important to keep in mind that the location of a category boundary is determined not only by the listeners' internal representations (the prototypes) of the categories, but also by the criterion they adopt for deciding between two competing categories, which makes the boundary vulnerable to biasing influences of various kinds. In principle, at least, a change in the location of a boundary may result either from a change in one or the other (or both) of the category prototypes, or from a criterion shift.

It is important to know whether, and under what conditions, the boundaries between phonetic categories are flexible, because the question bears on two very different hypotheses about the processes that underlie the categorization. According to one hypothesis, the perceived categories result from psychophysical discontinuities that directly reflect the characteristics of the auditory system. Thus, given an acoustic-stimulus continuum appropriate for some phonetic distinction, a category boundary is assumed to fall naturally at a point on the continuum where, owing to the way the ear works, differential sensitivity undergoes a sudden change. Perhaps the most general implication of this hypothesis is that auditory categories are the stuff of which phonetic categories are made. Put another way, the implication is that articulatory gestures are so governed as to produce sounds that fit within the categories that the auditory system happens to provide. Accordingly, we will refer to this as the "auditory" hypothesis. By any name, it is the hypothesis that deals directly with the boundaries of the categories rather than their ideal exemplars or prototypes. As to movement of category boundaries – this is allowed under this hypothesis, but only as a result of psychoacoustic factors that apply to auditory perception in general, and only to the extent that such factors can actually modify the patterns of differential sensitivity on which the auditory boundaries rest.

The other hypothesis is that the boundaries are determined by category prototypes that reflect typical *productions* of the relevant speech segments. Accordingly, the prototypes and the boundaries between them need not conform to boundaries set by discontinuities in the auditory system, but are instead free to be precisely as flexible as the acoustic consequences of the articulatory gestures require. Considerable flexibility may in fact be demanded. The efficiency of phonetic communication depends crucially on the ability of the several articulators to produce successive phonetic segments at the same time (or with considerable overlap), and also to accommodate in other ways to changes in phonetic context and rate. These maneuvers can produce systematic changes in the way a particular phonetic segment is represented in the sound. If the perceiving apparatus were not flexibly responsive to those changes, communication would break down, or so it seems. Moreover, the inventory of phones will itself change as language changes, and this, too, requires flexibility in the prototypes. Our hypothesis is that a link between perception and production (in most general terms) enables the category prototypes to respond appropriately to articulatory or coarticulatory adjustments, and so to mirror the speaker's phonetic intent. Needing a convenient name to refer to this hypothesis, and wishing to distinguish it from the "auditory" hypothesis we described first, we will call it "phonetic."[1]

Our aim in this chapter is to bring together the many data that demonstrate flexibility of a kind the phonetic hypothesis leads us to expect. These pertain to the influences on perceived phonetic boundaries of such factors as phonetic context, speaking rate, the mix of acoustic cues, and linguistic experience. There are other effects on the perceived boundaries, however, about which the auditory and phonetic theories are neutral. These include the consequences of varying the range, frequency, and order of the stimuli, as well as such phenomena as contrast and adaptation. Because effects of that kind need to be distinguished from those that are more directly relevant to the auditory and phonetic theories, we will consider them first. We will note, however, that even these "simple" effects sometimes follow patterns that seem difficult to reconcile with a purely auditory theory, and that suggest that speech-specific perceptual criteria may play a role in certain situations. Our review will be selective and focus especially on these instances.

Stimulus-sequence effects

Under the heading of stimulus-sequence effects we consider influences on the perception of speech stimuli exerted by other, similar stimuli preceding or following them in a sequence. These effects need to be distinguished from the "stimulus-structure effects" discussed in another section, which concern perceptual dependencies within a single coherent speech stimulus or influences entirely due to factors within the listener.[2]

It is generally agreed that vowel identification – of isolated steady-state vowels, at least – is highly susceptible to all sorts of stimulus-sequence effects. On the other hand, the identification of consonants, and of stop consonants in particular, is more stable and less sensitive to stimulus context. This difference parallels the well-known difference between these two stimulus classes in the extent of CP; indeed, the criterion of "absoluteness" (i.e., independence of surrounding stimuli) constituted part of the classical definition of CP (Studdert-Kennedy et al., 1970). "Context sensitivity" in a sequence may be distinguished on logical grounds, however, from the extent of the subject's reliance on category labels in discriminating between stimuli (Lane, 1965; Repp, Healy, & Crowder, 1979), and these two aspects of CP can, to some extent, be dissociated experimentally (Healy & Repp, 1982).

Local sequential effects

Local sequential effects – typically, influences of a preceding stimulus on the identification of a following stimulus – may occur in any random test sequence. These effects are pervasive in absolute identification, magnitude estimation, and other psychophysical tasks involving nonspeech stimuli. Surprisingly, there have been very few attempts to determine the extent of sequential effects in standard speech-identification tests, where stimuli are presented in random order. Of course, there is an indirect test in the shape of the labeling function, as it can be steep only if sequential effects are relatively small.

In several studies of speech-sound identification, however, the stimuli have been presented in balanced arrangements specifically designed for the assessment of sequential-context effects. In one of the earliest of these studies, Eimas (1963) called for identification of stimuli presented in ABX triads of the sort often used in discrimination tasks and found large context effects for isolated vowels (see also Fry, Abramson, Eimas, & Liberman, 1962) and smaller, but by no means negligible, effects for both the voicing and place dimensions of stop consonants. All effects were contrastive – that is, a stimulus tended to be classified into a category different from that of the stimulus it was paired with – and the magnitude of the effect increased with the acoustic distance between adjacent stimuli. Comparable results have been obtained more recently by, among others, Healy and Repp (1982).

Although sequential effects are generally considered to be common to speech and nonspeech stimuli, there are some intriguing differences. For example, it has been found in several studies that the magnitude of the contrast effect is greater for continua of isolated vowels than for nonspeech continua such as pitch or duration (Eimas, 1963; Healy & Repp, 1982; Fujisaki & Shigeno, 1979; Shigeno & Fujisaki, 1980). Although it is possible that the difference is to be accounted for by the more complex acoustic (and auditory) nature of the vowels (and there are also problems with comparing the magnitudes of contrast effects across different stimulus continua), it may, with equal plausibility, be taken to reflect a flexibility of categorization peculiar to the class of vowel sounds, a class that happens to carry the major burden of dialectal variation and language change.

If two or more stimuli in a sequence must be held in memory before a response is permitted, as in the procedure of Eimas (1963) described at the beginning of this section, the effects of the stimuli on each other are retroactive as well as proactive. Interestingly, retroactive effects tend to be larger than proactive effects for isolated vowels, while the opposite tends to be the case for all other types of stimuli examined, whether speech or nonspeech (Diehl, Elman, & McCusker, 1978; Healy & Repp, 1982; Shigeno & Fujisaki, 1980). This finding, like the one having to do with the magnitude of contrast, may be explicable by acoustic-stimulus properties alone, or it may reflect a specific tendency, derived perhaps from experience with fluent speech, to revise tentative decisions about vowel categories in the light of later information.

One reason we consider that even simple sequential effects may exhibit speech-specific patterns is that these effects almost certainly take place in two quite distinct ways, one reflecting a sensory effect, the other a judgmental effect (see Simon & Studdert-Kennedy, 1978). That is, there may be an effect of a preceding stimulus on the sensory representation of a following stimulus (as well as the reverse, if both are held in a precategorical memory store), but the judgment of a stimulus may also be affected by the response that was assigned to the preceding or following stimulus, usually in a contrastive fashion. Whereas the purely sensory effects are presumably shared by speech and nonspeech stimuli and are sensitive to factors like spectral similarity and temporal proximity (Crowder, 1981, 1982), the special structure and function of phonetic categories may produce criterion shifts in the response domain that are specific to speech. Although a clear separation of stimulus and response effects has rarely been achieved in speech experiments, separate studies provide evidence for each type. Thus, Crowder (1982) has shown that proactive-contrast effects for isolated vowels decrease with temporal separation over about 3 seconds in a manner that parallels the decay of auditory sensory storage in other paradigms. On the other hand, Sawusch and Jusczyk (1981) found that sequential contrast depended more on the perceived category of the preceding stimulus than on its acoustic structure. Judgmental effects may depend in part on whether or not a response to the contextual stimulus is required: A comparison of Crowder's (1982) data with those of Repp et al. (1979) for isolated vowels suggests that proactive-contrast effects are reduced when only the second stimulus in a pair requires a response. (It goes almost without saying that retroactive-contrast effects would be reduced or eliminated if only the first stimulus in a pair were responded to.)

The distinction between sensory and judgmental components of sequential effects is also familiar in nonspeech psychophysics (see, Petzold, 1981) and is compatible with Braida and Durlach's (1972) two-factor theory of perceptual coding (see Chapter 2 by Macmillan, this volume). Thus, Petzold (1981) has found that preceding stimuli exert a contrastive effect whereas preceding responses exert an assimilative effect. On the other hand, Shigeno and Fujisaki (1980) have proposed a two-factor model for sequential effects in speech and nonspeech that predicts precisely the opposite. The limited data available suggest, on the contrary, that for speech *both* components of sequential effects are contrastive in nature.

Global sequential (range-frequency) effects

Shifts in phonetic-category boundaries may occur as a consequence of variations in the overall composition of a stimulus sequence – that is, the range of stimuli used and the frequency of occurrence of the individual stimuli. In general, if the stimulus range is shifted or expanded in a certain direction, the boundary will shift in the same direction; and if one stimulus (typically one of the endpoints, the ''anchor'') occurs more frequently than other stimuli, the boundary will shift toward it. In other words, the effects are contrastive in nature, and in the case of speech sounds, they exhibit variations in magnitude similar to those observed for simple sequential effects: For stop consonants varying in place or voicing, the effects are small (Brady & Darwin, 1978; Rosen, 1979), whereas for isolated vowels (Sawusch & Nusbaum, 1979), certain other consonantal contrasts (Repp, 1980), and even for stop consonants in Polish (Keating, Mikos, & Ganong, 1981), they may be quite large.

An interesting asymmetry has been observed in the anchoring paradigm for isolated vowels (Sawusch, Nusbaum, & Schwab, 1980): An analysis of anchoring effects on an /i/-/I/ continuum has suggested that the effect of the /i/ anchor was due to sensory adaptation while that of the /I/ anchor represented a change in response criterion. In a recent and similar study in which the anchor always came first in a stimulus pair and only the second stimulus required a response, Crowder and Repp (1984) found an effect of /i/ but not of /I/. The explanation for this asymmetry may be found in the acoustics of the stimuli; alternatively, it may be owing to the special status of /i/ as one of the corners of the vowel space.

We should note, perhaps, that although range-frequency effects are usually considered to derive from stimulus context beyond the immediate local environment, they are often confounded with sequential probabilities: If a given endpoint stimulus (the anchor) occurs more often than other stimuli, the probability that a given stimulus is immediately preceded by the anchor will be increased relative to an equal-frequency (or a different anchoring) condition. Similarly, if the stimulus range is shifted or expanded in one direction, the likelihood that certain critical stimuli are preceded by other stimuli from that part of the continuum is increased. Therefore, range-frequency effects may in many cases be just local sequential effects in disguise. The extent to which nonlocal stimulus context makes any additional contribution has, to our knowledge, not been ascertained experimentally for speech stimuli. It is possible, however, that the frequent occurrence of a single stimulus has an additional adapting influence not evident in regular balanced stimulus sequences. In that sense, the anchoring paradigm approximates the selective-adaptation paradigm.

Selective adaptation

In selective-adaptation experiments, an adapting stimulus (frequently one or the other endpoint stimulus of a speech continuum) is presented repeatedly many times before responses to a few test stimuli are collected. The original motivation for using this paradigm in speech research was the assumption that the effects of the adapting stimulus might reveal the existence and nature of "phonetic feature detectors" (Eimas & Corbit, 1973; see Chapter 6 by Remez and Chapter 7 by Diehl & Kluender, this volume). Apart from the difficulty of conceiving that phonetic features (place, manner, voicing) could possibly be perceived by detectors that respond to such simple features as the auditory analogs of edges and angles in vision (see, e.g., Diehl, 1981; Studdert-Kennedy, 1981), a large number of experiments suggest that the effect of selective adaptation takes place primarily at the auditory, not the phonetic (judgmental) level. (However, see Elman, 1979.)

The most striking demonstrations of the auditory (as opposed to the phonetic) nature of selective adaptation were provided in two recent studies. In one of these, Roberts and Summerfield (1981) presented audiovisual adapting stimuli that, due to the overriding influence of a conflicting visual display, were never classified into the category normally associated with the auditory stimulus. Nevertheless, the audiovisual adaptors had exactly the same influence on the identification of auditory test stimuli as did purely auditory adaptors. Thus, the phonetic category assigned to the adaptors seemed to play no role in selective adaptation. A similar result was obtained by Sawusch and Jusczyk (1981), who used adaptors of the form /spa/, in which the stop consonant was classified phonetically as *p* but was acoustically identical with the initial *b* in /ba/. The adapting effects of /spa/ and /ba/ did not differ.[3] These studies, together with several earlier attempts to dissociate acoustic and phonetic stimulus properties (Blumstein, Stevens, & Nigro, 1977; Sawusch & Pisoni, 1976), suggest that selective adaptation with speech is an exclusively auditory phenomenon. Even though studies of interaural transfer of adaptation effects suggest more than one site at which adaptation takes place (Ganong, 1978; Sawusch, 1977), both of these sites appear to be auditory (nonphonetic) in nature.

There are two types of evidence, however, that do indicate some involvement of phonetic processing in selective adaptation. One has to do with the influence of the listeners' native language. The relevant finding is that selective-adaptation effects on the same stimulus continuum are different for American and Thai listeners, as independently demonstrated by Donald (1976) and Foreit (1977). The continuum was one of stop consonants varying in voice-onset time (VOT), ranging from prevoiced (voicing lead) to devoiced (0-ms VOT) to aspirated (voicing lag). For

American listeners, who do not distinguish prevoiced and devoiced stops, a −60-ms VOT and a 0-ms VOT adaptor had the same effect on the category boundary. For Thai listeners, on the other hand, who have three separate categories on the continuum, only the 0-ms adaptor affected the devoiced-aspirated boundary while the −60-ms adaptor was ineffective. This finding agrees with earlier results of Cooper (1974) showing that, on a place-of-articulation continuum divided into three categories, adapting stimuli affected only the adjacent but not the remote category boundary.

The other piece of evidence for a role of phonetic categorization in selective adaptation comes from studies that have revealed differences in the effectiveness of adaptors as a function of their distance from the category boundary. In general, the effectiveness of an adaptor increases with its distance from the boundary (Ainsworth, 1977; Cole & Cooper, 1977; Miller, 1977b) unless it crosses another phonetic boundary (Cooper, 1974; Donald, 1976; Foreit, 1977). Of course, this may be just another instance of the well-confirmed fact that the spectral similarity of adaptor and test stimuli is the major determinant of the size of the adaptation effect. In other words, the distance effect may have a purely auditory explanation. In a recent study, however, Miller, Connine, Schermer, and Kluender (1983) demonstrated that even if no other phonetic boundary intervenes, the adaptation effect does not increase indefinitely as the adaptor moves away from the boundary, but instead reaches a maximum and then declines (or, for some subjects, remains on a plateau). The adaptor that produces the maximum effect has characteristics that may reasonably be assumed to be optimal for its category, which led Miller et al. to conjecture that the size of the adaptation effect is related to the adaptor's distance from the listener's internal category prototype. Preliminary support for this hypothesis was obtained by Miller et al. in a condition in which the category boundary on a /ba/-/wa/ continuum, and with it the presumable location of the /wa/ prototype (see Miller & Baer, 1983), was made to shift by reducing the duration of the syllables. The peak in the function relating the size of the adaptation effect to the location of the adaptor on the continuum shifted accordingly, as predicted.

Even stronger support for a role of ''category goodness'' in selective adaptation comes from a study by Samuel (1982). He first asked his subjects to locate the optimal /ga/ on a /ga/-/ka/ VOT continuum. The subjects were then divided into two groups – those with short-VOT and those with long-VOT prototypes. Two adapting stimuli matching the two average prototypes were then selected. For each group of subjects, the adaptor matching the group's prototype produced the larger boundary shift. Because exactly the same adaptors were used for both groups, the listeners' internal category prototype seemed to be responsible for the magnitude of the adaptation obtained.

These recent results lead to the tentative conclusion that selective adaptation takes place at an auditory level that is *phonetically relevant*. Perhaps this should not come as a surprise. The adapting stimuli, after all, are speech, and therefore *are* phonetically relevant auditory patterns. Conversely, the internal standards or category prototypes against which listeners presumably compare stimuli in the process of categorization must entail detailed auditory specifications; otherwise, in the absence of a common metric, the comparison would be impossible. Selective adaptation may then be viewed as a temporary modification of the prototype itself – a weakening of the critical specifications that is proportional to the degree to which the auditory input meets those specifications. With this interpretation, the results reviewed in this section can be reconciled with the numerous earlier demonstrations of "purely auditory" effects in selective adaptation.

From this vantage point, the various "low-level" effects reviewed so far – sequential contrast, range-frequency effects, and selective adaptation – are relevant to the topic of our chapter, the flexibility of phonetic boundaries. In essence, the data seem to show that not even a psychophysical procedure like selective adaptation has its effects exclusively at a "general auditory level" of processing; rather, as long as the adapting stimuli are speech, their effects reflect the extent to which they engage the speech-processing apparatus. Because speech stimuli ordinarily engage the mechanisms of phonetic categorization (even in the absence of an overt or covert response), selective adaptation with speech is properly viewed as a speech-specific phenomenon – a modification of the frame of reference within which speech stimuli are interpreted. The same is true for range-frequency and sequential-contrast effects, except that overt responses to contextual stimuli may have additional effects at a judgmental level. In other words, although speech must pass through the auditory nerve, there may be no "general auditory" level of representation beyond the peripheral transduction. Speech perception takes place within a preestablished frame of reference, and the auditory representation of speech cannot be separated from the (equally "auditory") internal structures, due to cumulative experience in conjunction with biological predispositions, through which the incoming information is filtered. (See also Chapter 2 by Macmillan and Chapter 13 by Wilson, this volume.)

Stimulus-structure effects

Under this heading we consider perceptual dependencies that arise among different components of a single coherent speech stimulus. That stimulus may be as short as a single syllable or as long as a whole sentence. Stimulus-structure effects, even though they are most easily revealed in the laboratory, are closer to the real-life situation than the stimulus-sequence effects discussed in the preceding section, which represent or exploit artifacts of test-sequence construction. Although the experimental induction of selective adaptation or sequential contrast may be useful for the purpose of probing perceptual mechanisms, there is no reason to believe that these phenomena (as distinct from the mechanism they reveal) play any significant role in the perception of coherent speech. The various effects discussed in the present section, on the other hand, have more direct implications for normal speech perception, as they reflect the perceptual functions of integration and normalization that make speech perception so effortless and efficient.[4]

Cue-integration effects

Distinctions among phonetic segments are known to rest on a multiplicity of acoustic cues in the speech signal. Typically, these many cues are acoustically diverse, relatively widely distributed in time, and overlap with cues for other segments. Yet the perceiver somehow integrates these diverse and distributed aspects of the speech signal to recover the phonetic structure of the message (Liberman & Studdert-Kennedy, 1978; Repp, Liberman, Eccardt, & Pesetsky, 1978). Exactly how the individual acoustic cues are characterized depends to some extent on the methods of analysis and experimental manipulation and on the descriptive framework chosen by the investigator. From a purely acoustic point of view, however, they seem in most cases to be incoherent. From an articulatory point of view, on the other hand, they make sense – that is, they reflect a unitary event in the domain of articulatory planning.[5]

The statement that there are multiple cues for each phonetic contrast must be qualified by the fact that some cues are more important than others. That is, some cues are easily overridden by others. Listeners' sensitivity to the weaker cues can be demonstrated in the laboratory by eliminating the stronger ones or by setting them at ambiguous values. From the existing evidence it can indeed be concluded that, given the opportunity, listeners will make use of *any* cue for a given phonetic distinction (Bailey & Summerfield, 1980). This general observation suggests that, as Bailey and Summerfield have pointed out, the concept of cue has limited theoretical relevance. As a practical matter it is useful, even essential, in dealing with the acoustic basis of speech perception. But the sensitivity to the many and various cues for a phonetic segment suggests, as we have already implied, that listeners are perceiving just what all the cues have in common – namely, some economical representation of the coherent process underlying the peripheral articulation.

The relevance of cue integration to the topic of our chapter is evident when we consider that a phonetic category boundary is usually determined on a continuum of stimuli varying in only one important cue dimension. The flexibility of that phonetic boundary may then be assessed by introducing other, usually less important, cues that favor either one or the other response alternative. That boundaries are indeed flexible in this particular sense has been demonstrated in numerous studies. (For a recent review, see Repp, 1982.) By definition, phonetic boundaries are located at the point of maximal ambiguity, where weaker cues have their strongest effect. The perceptual-cue integration, or phonetic "trading relation," revealed by the boundary shift generally takes place without the listener's awareness. (The term "trading relation" refers to the fact that the physical settings of several cues to the same phonetic contrast can be played off against each other, so as to yield the same phonetic identification probabilities.) Perception tends to remain categorical even in the presence of multiple acoustic differences among stimuli (see, e.g., Fitch, Halwes, Erickson, & Liberman, 1980).

The ubiquity of trading relations among acoustically diverse cues provides one of the strongest arguments against theories that predict fixed boundary locations on any acoustic speech continuum. In many cases, cues are so disparate as to be extremely unlikely to engage in any direct psychoacoustic interaction. Rather, what seems to unite them is that they are common consequences of the articulatory gestures that differentiate phonetic segments; at the same time, they are members of the set of structural acoustic differences that characterize a particular phonetic contrast. To cite only one specific example, the primary cue for the prevocalic /s/-/ʃ/ distinction is the spectrum of the fricative noise, but a secondary cue is provided by the voiced formant transitions following the noise. The phonetic boundary on an /s/-/ʃ/ continuum, obtained by varying the spectral properties of the fricative noise, is at different locations depending on whether the formant transitions are appropriate for /s/ or for /ʃ/ (Mann & Repp, 1980). Considering that the fricative noise is of relatively long duration, produced by a different source, and of a spectral composition quite different from that of the following signal, there is little reason to expect any direct effect of the formant transitions on the auditory representation of the fricative noise. Indeed, when listeners are led to focus on the "pitch" of the fricative noise (rather than on the phonetic fricative category), there seems to be no influence of the following formant transitions on their judgments (Repp, 1981). Thus, the perceptual integration of the cues provided by fricative-noise-spectrum and formant transitions seems to be phonetically motivated; this is related to the fact that both cues are consistently correlated with different places of fricative production. Similar arguments may be applied to other phonetic trading relations, even including those that could, in principle, result from some psycho-acoustic interaction.

Feature-integration effects

The trading relations discussed in the preceding section (and reviewed by Repp, 1982) take place among cues to a single phonetic feature – for example, voicing or place of articulation. This is a consequence of the fact that the phonetic categories constituting the endpoints of a speech continuum nearly always differ only in a single feature. Here we consider a related class of effects that reveals perceptual dependencies among cues to different features of the same phonetic segment. The main reason for considering these effects separately is that they give the theorist an additional degree of freedom: Feature interactions may be hypothesized to occur after a process of "feature extraction" but before assembly of the features into a phonetic segment (see, e.g., Miller, 1977a; Sawusch & Pisoni, 1974). For theorists who instead postulate either direct psychoacoustic interactions among the cues or reference to phoneme- or syllable-sized prototypes, the effects considered here are further instances of cue integration (see Oden & Massaro, 1978; Massaro, Chapter 8, this volume).

The literature on genuine feature-integration effects is rather small, because it is difficult to vary cues for different features in a strictly orthogonal fashion. A well-known finding is that the voicing boundary on a VOT continuum is at increasingly larger voicing lags for labial, alveolar, and velar stop consonants (Lisker & Abramson, 1970). In most studies, however, the duration of the first-formant transition, which itself constitutes a voicing cue (as well as a weak cue for place of articulation) has covaried with place of articulation, so that the boundary shifts may be considered as arising from a simple trading relation among voicing cues. In one experiment, however, the $F1$ transition was held constant (with only the $F2$ and $F3$ transitions varying so as to cue differences in place of articulation), and a small but reliable voicing boundary shift as a function of place of articulation was obtained (Miller, 1977a). (See, however, Massaro & Oden, 1980, for a failure to replicate this result.) Subsequently, Miller (1977a) showed that the boundary on a labial-alveolar place of articulation continuum shifted depending on whether the stop consonants were synthesized as nasal, voiced, or voiceless. She interpreted these results as revealing processing dependencies among phonetic features. An alternative interpretation has been proposed in a model that builds feature dependencies into prespecified critical feature values and so avoids any processing interactions after the feature extraction stage (Oden & Massaro, 1978; Massaro & Oden, 1980). Because of the built-in dependencies, however, the model rests on the assumption of phoneme- or syllable-sized prototypes and merely pays lip service to phonetic features.

Feature interactions of the kind observed by Miller (1977a) presumably reflect the inherent nonorthogonality of articulatory features and their acoustic correlates. Clearly, the binary-feature matrix devised by phonologists is inadequate from a phonetic viewpoint. Because of their longer VOTs, initial velar stops, for example, simply are relatively "more voiceless" than labial stops. The possibility of psychoacoustic interactions among signal components must be considered, but there is no well-supported psychoacoustic explanation for the observed feature interactions.

One case in which a psychoacoustic interaction between feature dimensions can definitely be ruled out is the finding (Carden, Levitt, Jusczyk, & Walley, 1981) that, given a single continuum of formant transitions, listeners place the phonetic boundary at different locations depending on whether they are instructed to hear the stimuli as stops ([ba], [da]) or as fricatives ([fa], [θa]). This can only be accounted for as an adjustment – and apparently a perfectly automatic one – for the fact that the places of production are somewhat different for the two stops from what they are for the fricatives. Hence, it becomes yet another example of the rule that phonetic categorization is guided by internal criteria that reflect the prototypical acoustic and articulatory characteristics of speech.

Segmental-context effects

A third class of perceptual interactions taking place within a single utterance concerns perceptual dependencies among cues for different phonetic segments. Although the conceptual distinction from the two classes we have discussed (integration of cues to the same feature, or to different features of the same segment) is straightforward, practical distinctions are somewhat fuzzy because acoustic cues generally cannot be apportioned exclusively to one or the other phonetic segment. However, an experimental dissociation is usually possible between those signal aspects that provide weak (coarticulatory) cues to one segment and those that are strong and sufficient cues for a different segment, even when both very nearly coincide in time.

For example, take the effect of a following vowel on fricative perception, investigated – among others – by Mann and Repp (1980). The periodic signal portion following a fricative noise necessarily has formant transitions characteristic of the fricative's place of production, which contribute to the fricative percept, particularly when the fricative-noise spectrum carries little distinctive information (Carden et al., 1981; Mann & Repp, 1980). This effect therefore belongs under the heading of cue integration. The identity of the vowel itself, however, is quite independent of the preceding fricative and therefore cannot provide any direct cues to fricative place of production. Nevertheless, as Mann and Repp (1980) and others (Kunisaki & Fujisaki, 1977; Whalen, 1981) have shown, the vowel also exerts an influence on fricative perception: When the fricative noise is ambiguous between /s/ and /ʃ/, listeners report more instances of /s/ when the following vowel is rounded (/u/) than when it is not (/a/), resulting in a quite substantial boundary shift on an /s/-/ʃ/ fricative-noise continuum.

A number of other effects of this kind have been found in recent research. For example, a preceding fricative noise (/s/ versus /ʃ/) affects the perception of a following stop consonant (/t/ versus /k/): The /t/-/k/ boundary shifts in favor of /k/ when the precursor is /s/ (Mann & Repp, 1981). The effect is independent of coarticulatory cues to stop place of articulation in the fricative noise, and it occurs also when the fricative appears to belong to a preceding syllable (Repp & Mann, 1981). Yet another effect operating across a syllable boundary has been obtained by Mann (1980): The boundary on a /da/-/ga/ continuum shifts in favor of /g/ when the preceding syllable is /al/ rather than /ar/.

How are such segmental context effects to be accounted for? Psychoacoustic interactions between adjacent signal portions, although not impossible, become rather implausible. For example, there is little reason to expect that a fricative noise would "sound" different before different vowels. Indeed, when listeners are required to judge the "pitch" of the noise rather than the phonetic category of the fricative, effects of the following vowel disappear (Repp, 1981). The most plausible hypothesis is that segmental-context effects represent a perceptual compensation for coarticulatory interactions in speech production. For example, anticipatory lip rounding for rounded vowels is known to affect the noise spectrum of preceding fricatives (Fujisaki & Kunisaki, 1978; Mann & Repp, 1980), and there are indications that the formant transitions of stop consonants shift with the place of articulation of preceding fricatives (Repp & Mann, 1982) and liquids (Mann, 1980). The ability of listeners to compensate for these coarticulatory effects implies an internal representation of these dependencies, which may be conceptualized in dynamic or static terms.

Segmental-context effects have been demonstrated even among nonadjacent segments. Thus, shifts in the place-of-articulation boundaries for initial stop consonants have been found to occur as a function of the place of articulation of the final stop consonant in the same syllable (Alfonso, 1981). Perceptual interdependencies between two vowels separated by a consonant have also been reported (Kanamori, Kasuya, Arai, & Kido, 1971). These effects may reflect perceptual compensation for coarticulatory dependencies operating over wider time spans (see Martin & Bunnell, 1981, 1982; Öhman, 1966).

Speaking-rate effects

The perception of phonetic distinctions that rest on temporal cues may be affected by the temporal structure of surrounding signal portions. As these effects have been thoroughly reviewed by Miller (1981), we can be brief here.

It is useful to distinguish between experimental manipulations of the duration of selected (steady-state) acoustic segments and of time-varying spectral changes connected with actual (or simulated) changes in articulatory rate. Both temporal and spectrotemporal manipulations have been shown to affect the perception of certain temporal cues, but it is not clear whether their effects take place at the same level.

Some experiments on effects of "speaking rate" concern trading relations among cues for the same phonetic segment. When two temporal cues contribute to the same distinction, a change in one will necessarily require a compensatory change in the other to maintain perceptual constancy. An example of such a trading relation is that between (preceding) silence duration and fricative-noise duration as joint cues to the fricative-affricate distinction (Repp et al., 1978). Affricate percepts are favored by both long silences and short noises, so an increase in silence duration can be compensated for, within limits, by an increase in noise duration. But when this trading relation was examined in the context of a true rate manipulation – the critical cues were embedded in sentence frames produced at a fast or at a slow rate – relatively *more* silence was needed in the fast sentence frame to maintain the same level of affricate responses. One possible interpretation of this reliable effect (cf. Dorman, Raphael, & Liberman, 1979) is that, in the rapidly articulated context, the (constant) fricative noise sounded relatively longer and hence more fricative-like, so that a longer silence was required to restore the same level of affricate responses. This assumes that the perception of the silence cue was less affected by the rate manipulation. Why this should be so is not clear at present. We should also remark that the speaking-rate effect was probably mediated primarily by the immediately adjacent signal portions – the durations of the vocalic segments preceding the silence and following the fricative noise. If so, the speaking-rate effects observed may have been a special instance of a segmental-context effect or even a trading relation.

A good example of another "speaking-rate effect" that could just as well be put in the preceding section on segmental-context effects is the influence of the duration of a following vowel on the perception of the /b/-/w/ distinction cued by varying formant transition duration (Miller & Liberman, 1979): The longer the vowel, the longer the formant transition duration at the /b/-/w/ boundary. This finding was interpreted as a speaking-rate effect, and it is indeed consistent with observed changes in /w/ transition duration at different speeds of articulation (Miller & Baer, 1983). However, the effect has also been obtained with infants (Eimas & Miller, 1980) and with nonspeech stimuli (Pisoni, Carrell, & Gans, 1983), which suggests a possible psychoacoustic origin – in other words, a temporal normalization early in the perceptual process. It is indeed questionable whether changes in the duration of a (steady-state) synthetic vowel are sufficient to convey anything like "speaking rate." Within the context of cue-trading relations, both Fitch (1981) and Soli (1982) have been able to separate perceptual effects of vowel duration from effects due to vowel "structure," which are more complex spectral changes taking place over time. It is the latter that are more properly viewed as the carriers of information about rate of articulation.

The examples given in this section illustrate that true "speaking-rate effects" are not easy to distinguish from simpler temporal trading relations and local-context effects. Moreover, if speaking rate is varied, those changes that occur closest to the target segment will affect its perception most (Summerfield, 1981). In addition, Miller, Aibel, and Green (1984) have recently demonstrated that listeners' overt judgments of speaking rate do not predict the perceptual effects of rate manipulations. On the other hand, considering the extensive speech knowledge that listeners must possess, it seems reasonable to assume that they also have intrinsic knowledge of the acoustic changes that accompany changes in speaking rate and that they "know" how to apply this knowledge in perception. An example of this was also provided by Miller and Liberman (1979) in their study of the /b/-/w/ distinction. When the following vowel was extended by a nonstationary portion containing transitions appropriate for a syllable-final /d/, the effect on the /b/-/w/ boundary was equivalent to that of *shortening* the steady-state vowel. This paradoxical finding presumably reflects an increase in the perceived rate of articulation caused by the additional phonetic segment in the syllable.

Speaker-normalization effects

Phonetic boundaries along a spectral cue dimension may shift in accordance with the size of the vocal tract that is perceived to be the source of the utterance – that is the hypothesis, at least. As with speaking-rate effects, genuine speaker-normalization effects are not easy to distinguish from local-context effects and spectral trading relations. Moreover, a demonstration of true speaker normalization requires that the test utterance representing different sources be perceived as coming from a single source (speaker), which is possible only with target segments that are relatively ambiguous as to their source. For these reasons, there are few convincing demonstrations of speaker-normalization effects in the literature.

One of the earliest demonstrations was provided by Ladefoged and Broadbent (1957), who showed that synthetic vowel targets were perceived differently in sentence carriers simulating different speakers. This result was replicated with natural speech by Dechovitz (1977). More recently, May (1976) with synthetic speech and Mann and Repp (1980) with natural speech found a shift in the /ʃ/-/s/ boundary when the same fricative noises occurred in the context of vowels produced by different-sized vocal tracts. More experiments along these lines are needed to establish firmly listeners' sensitivity to the static aspects of the perceived speech source.

Semantic and syntactic effects

It is a commonplace observation that listeners tend to hear what they expect to hear. Effects of semantic context are ubiquitous in speech perception (Bagley, 1900–01; Cole & Rudnicky, 1983). However, these effects are generally obtained only when some acoustic information is missing and needs to be "filled in." Apparently, semantic factors can also influence the phonetic boundary on an acoustic continuum characterized by ambiguous (rather than missing) cues.

That such factors can influence the category boundary on a VOT continuum was demonstrated by Ganong (1980). He found that the boundary shifted in favor of word responses when one of the alternatives was a word and the other a nonword, even though the phonetic distinction was in the initial consonant. The pattern of the data suggested that the effect was not merely a response bias; rather, lexical status seemed to influence phonetic categorization directly. But this kind of direct interaction between "top-down" and "bottom-up" processes is a controversial notion (see, e.g., Swinney, 1982), and we do not wish to enter into a discussion of the matter here. Suffice it to point out that phonetic boundaries may be shifted by semantic biases. Such biases can be manipulated not only by changing the lexical status of the target word but also by inducing expectations through preceding sentence context (Garnes & Bond, 1977; Miller, Green, & Schermer, 1982). However, the phonetic-boundary shift obtained in that case may be eliminated by selective attention to the target word (Miller et al., 1982), suggesting that semantic processing can be consciously avoided in certain conditions (e.g., when the same materials are repeated over and over). Interestingly, the same study by Miller et al. (1982) also revealed that effects on segmental perception due to the speaking rate of a carrier sentence could not be voluntarily disengaged.

Effects of syntactic boundaries on certain phonetic distinctions have also been reported (Dechovitz, 1979; Price and Levitt, 1983): If the critical cue for the distinction is silence duration (as in the fricative-affricate contrast), more silence is needed if a syntactic boundary is made to coincide with the silence. Although claims have been advanced that this effect can be produced by syntactic structure per se (Dechovitz, 1979), no convincing evidence for such "pure syntax" effects exists so far. Rather, the effects of syntactic boundaries seem to be mediated by the prosodic changes that accompany them. The fricative-affricate boundary may shift depending on whether the preceding word has clause-final intonation and lengthening (Price & Levitt, 1983; see also Rakerd, Dechovitz, & Verbrugge, 1982). To what extent these effects should be considered merely local-context effects or temporal trading relations remains to be seen. In either case, they seem genuinely phonetic rather than psychoacoustic.

Cross-language effects

For the purpose of ruling out psychoacoustic factors and establishing that the location of a phonetic boundary is largely determined by factors internal to the listener, cross-language comparisons are most instructive. Languages do differ in their articulatory-acoustic patterns, frequently even for phonetic categories that seem phonemically identical (see Ladefoged, 1983). To the extent that these cross-linguistic differences are captured by a single acoustic speech continuum (and this is not always the case), we should want to know whether the phonetic boundaries in fact differ for speakers of different languages.

Unfortunately, cross-linguistic studies using the same stimuli and procedures are not very numerous. Among those that do exist, most have dealt with the voicing dimension, as cued by VOT, taking advantage of the fact that languages such as English, French, and Thai make their voicing contrasts in phonetically different ways. Whereas English distinguishes voiced (either prevoiced or voiceless unaspirated) and voiceless aspirated stops, French, Spanish, and Polish contrast prevoiced with voiceless unaspirated stops and Thai makes both distinctions. The single voicing boundary for English listeners is located in the short-lag values of VOT, between roughly 20 and 40 ms, depending on place of articulation (Lisker & Abramson, 1970). The single boundary for French, Spanish, and Polish listeners, on the other hand, is generally located at shorter lag times, close to zero, and is considerably more variable (Caramazza, Yeni-Komshian, Zurif, & Carbone, 1973; Keating et al., 1981; Williams, 1977). Thai listeners have two boundaries, one in the voicing-lead region (where none of the other languages mentioned exhibits any boundary), and the other at voicing lags somewhat longer than in English (Lisker & Abramson, 1970; Foreit, 1977). Thus, native language does seem to influence the location of comparable phonetic boundaries on a VOT continuum, and it certainly determines whether a boundary exists at all.

There is ample evidence that discrimination performance is best in the vicinity of a phonetic boundary. Thus, discrimination peaks shift with the phonetic boundaries across languages. Speakers of a language such as Thai have a discrimination peak in the voicing-lead region where English listeners' ability to detect differences is extremely poor (Abramson & Lisker, 1970). Another well-known example of such a cross-language difference is provided by the /r/-/l/ contrast, which is easily discriminated by English listeners but nearly indistinguishable for speakers of Japanese, a language that does not contain these phonetic segments (Miyawaki et al., 1975). For a review of these and related data, see Strange and Jenkins (1978) and Repp (1984).

In view of the flexibility of phonetic boundaries, demonstrations of a coincidence of category boundaries obtained for chinchillas or monkeys with those of English-speaking humans lose some of their impact. To the extent that these animal boundaries are stable at all (see Waters & Wilson, 1976, for a demonstration of large range effects), they may reveal certain psychoacoustic sensitivities that, however, seem to exert only a weak constraint on the possible locations of human boundaries. (See also Chapter 11 by Snowden and Chapter 12 by Kuhl, this volume.)

It is likely, of course, that the locations of phonetic boundaries in the languages of the world are not totally arbitrary. The structure of the speech-production apparatus imposes universal constraints on articulation that may be reflected in a limited number of preferred boundary locations. The hypothesis that human infants may possess some innate sensitivity to these universal *potential* phonetic boundaries (see Aslin & Pisoni, 1980) has recently gained momentum through the remarkable findings of Werker and Tees (1984), who showed that prelinguistic American infants are capable of distinguishing phonetic categories foreign to English, but lose that ability around ten months of age. It has not been conclusively established, however, that these prelinguistic category distinctions are truly phonetic, rather than psychoacoustic, in nature. Exposure to the phonetic distinctions of the native language may merely induce a "speech mode" of listening in the one-year-old infant and thereby lead it to ignore irrelevant acoustic detail. Similarly, several demonstrations of adults' ability to discriminate foreign phonetic categories in certain laboratory situations (MacKain, Best, & Strange, 1981; Pisoni, Aslin, Perey, & Hennessy, 1982) may, at least in part, reflect skills of deploying a nonphonetic mode of processing, and not the acquisition of a new phonetic distinction that can be generalized beyond the laboratory. On the other hand, mastery of a new language does imply the establishment of new phonetic categories, and it is primarily a matter of implementing all the necessary controls to permit the conclusion that this is indeed what has happened in any given laboratory experiment. Rigorous investigations of the process of phonetic learning, which may be a good deal slower than the time span of the typical speech experiment, are just beginning (e.g., Flege & Port, 1981).

Conclusion

Evidence from a variety of experiments on speech perception establishes that phonetic category boundaries are flexible in response to each of two quite different sets of conditions. One set is commonly created by the way utterances are arranged in experiments that require the presentation of sequences of test stimuli. Most of the effects of such conditions are found with nonspeech sounds as well, though, for reasons that are not yet clear, some may be peculiar to speech. The other conditions are the more interesting, at least for our purposes, because they seem to be integral parts of the processes by which utterances are perceived in any test sequence and so, presumably, in the real-life situation. Their effects are of several superficially different kinds, but, common to all, there is a (more or less) apparent correspondence between the shift in the perceived category boundary and the acoustic effects of an articulatory or coarticulatory maneuver. Thus, these boundary shifts imply a link between speech perception and speech production, much as if perception were constrained by tacit "knowledge" of what a vocal tract does when it makes linguistically significant gestures. Considerations of this kind, roughly similar to those that led originally to the (so-called) "motor theory of speech perception" (Liberman, Delattre, & Cooper, 1952), lead us to suppose that such boundary shifts as these are peculiar to speech.

Notes

1. We are uncertain where to place in the present framework another important class of hypotheses, that of acoustic invariance (Stevens & Blumstein, 1978; Kewley-Port, 1983; Lahiri, Gewirth, & Blumstein, 1984). Sometimes invariant properties are described in terms that suggest a boundary-oriented approach – for example, when a spectral shape is considered to be either rising or falling. On the other hand, the use of optimal "templates" (Stevens & Blumstein, 1978) suggests a prototype-oriented approach. Because the invariance hypothesis postulates invariant acoustic correlates for linguistically distinctive features, it would seem to permit little flexibility in category boundaries, particularly if the boundaries themselves are taken to be the invariant correlates.
2. Not all the studies we will cite actually examined boundary shifts. Some studies showed only that the perception of a single ambiguous stimulus could be influenced in one or the other direction. It is safe to infer, however, that had that stimulus been part of an acoustic continuum, the category boundary on that continuum would have shifted in precisely the same direction.
3. In the same study, however, sequential contrast was found to be contingent on the perceived phonetic category; in other words, the effect of /spa/ differed from that of /ba/ (Sawusch & Jusczyk, 1981). It is worth noting that in the selective-adaptation paradigm the adaptors are typically presented at a fast rate that may discourage even covert categorization. Phonetic (judgmental) effects may be contingent upon overt or covert labeling of contextual stimuli.
4. We call them perceptual *functions*, rather than perceptual *processes*, because we believe that these accomplishments of the perceptual system should not be viewed in process terms. In any case, whatever neural or cognitive processes may underlie these functions is totally unknown at present.
5. Although there have been persistent attempts to conceptualize single "invariant" acoustic properties for distinctive features in speech (see Stevens & Blumstein, 1978; Kewley-Port, 1983; Lahiri et al., 1984), these properties never fully capture the phonetically distinctive information. It seems to be a fact to be accepted that what may be a unitary event at the level of linguistic structure or articulatory planning emerges in a fractionated form at the level of acoustic description.

References

Abramson, A. S., & Lisker, L. (1970). Discriminability along the voicing continuum: Cross-language tests. *Proceedings of the Sixth International Congress of Phonetic Sciences* (pp. 569–573). Prague: Academia.

Ainsworth, W. A. (1977). Mechanisms of selective feature adaptation. *Perception & Psychophysics, 21,* 365–370.

Alfonso, P. (1981). Context effects on the perception of place of articulation. *Journal of the Acoustical Society of America, 69* (Suppl. 1), S93 (Abstract).

Aslin, R. N., & Pisoni, D. B. (1980). Some developmental processes in speech perception. In G. H. Yeni-Komshian, J. F. Kavanagh, & C. A. Ferguson (Eds.), *Child phonology* (Vol. 2, pp. 67–96). New York: Academic Press.

Bagley, W. C. (1900–01). The apperception of the spoken sentence: A study in the psychology of language. *American Journal of Psychology, 12,* 80–130.

Bailey, P. J., & Summerfield, Q. (1980). Information in speech: Observations on the perception of [s]-stop clusters. *Journal of Experimental Psychology: Human Perception and Performance, 6,* 536–563.

Blumstein, S. E., Stevens, K. N., & Nigro, G. N. (1977). Property detectors for bursts and transitions in speech perception. *Journal of the Acoustical Society of America, 61,* 1301–1313.

Brady, S. A., & Darwin, C. J. (1978). Range effect in the perception of voicing. *Journal of the Acoustical Society of America, 63,* 1556–1558.

Braida, L. D., & Durlach, N. I. (1972). Intensity resolution: II. Resolution in one-interval paradigms. *Journal of the Acoustical Society of America, 51,* 483–502.

Caramazza, A., Yeni-Komshian, G. H., Zurif, E. B., & Carbone, E. (1973). The acquisition of a new phonological contrast: The case of stop consonants in French-English bilinguals. *Journal of the Acoustical Society of America, 54,* 421–428.

Carden, G., Levitt, A., Jusczyk, P. W., & Walley, A. (1981). Evidence for phonetic processing of cues to place of articulation: Perceived manner affects perceived place. *Perception & Psychophysics, 29,* 26–36.

Cole, R. A., & Cooper, W. E. (1977). Properties of friction analyzers for /j/. *Journal of the Acoustical Society of America, 62,* 177–182.

Cole, R. A., & Rudnicky, A. I. (1983). What's new in speech perception? The research and ideas of William Chandler Bagley, 1874–1946. *Psychological Review, 90,* 94–101.

Cooper, W. E. (1974). Adaptation of phonetic feature analyzers for place of articulation. *Journal of the Acoustical Society of America, 56,* 617–627.

Crowder, R. G. (1981). The role of auditory memory in speech perception and discrimination. In T. Myers, J. Laver, & J. Anderson (Eds.), *The cognitive representation of speech.* Amsterdam: North-Holland.

Crowder, R. G. (1982). Decay of auditory memory in vowel discrimination. *Journal of Experimental Psychology: Learning, Memory, and Cognition, 8,* 153–162.

Crowder, R. G., & Repp, B. H. (1984). Single formant contrast in vowel identification. *Perception & Psychophysics, 35,* 372–378.

Dechovitz, D. (1977). Information conveyed by vowels: A confirmation. *Haskins Laboratories Status Report on Speech Research,* SR-51/52, 213–219.

Dechovitz, D. (1979). Effects of syntax on the perceptual integration of segmental features. In J. J. Wolf & D. H. Klatt (Eds.), *Speech communication papers presented at the 97th Meeting of the Acoustical Society of America* (pp. 319–322). New York: Acoustical Society of America.

Diehl, R. L. (1981). Feature detectors for speech: A critical reappraisal. *Psychological Bulletin, 89,* 1–18.

Diehl, R. L., Elman, J. L., & McCusker, S. B. (1978). Contrast effects on stop consonant identification. *Journal of Experimental Psychology: Human Perception and Performance, 4,* 599–609.

Donald, L. (1976). The effects of selective adaptation on voicing in Thai and English. *Haskins Laboratories Status Report on Speech Research,* SR-47, 129–136.

Dorman, M. F., Raphael, L. J., & Liberman, A. M. (1979). Some experiments on the sound of silence in phonetic perception. *Journal of the Acoustical Society of America, 65,* 1518–1532.

Eimas, P. D. (1963). The relation between identification and discrimination along speech and nonspeech continua. *Language and Speech, 6,* 206–217.

Eimas, P. D., & Corbit, J. D. (1973). Selective adaptation of linguistic feature detectors. *Cognitive Psychology, 4,* 99–109.

Eimas, P. D., & Miller, J. L. (1980). Contextual effects in infant speech perception. *Science, 209,* 1140–1141.
Elman, J. L. (1979). Perceptual origins of the phoneme boundary effect and selective adaptation of speech: A signal detection theory analysis. *Journal of the Acoustical Society of America, 65,* 190–207.
Fitch, H. L. (1981). Distinguishing temporal information for speaking rate from temporal information for intervocalic stop consonant voicing. *Haskins Laboratories Status Report on Speech Research,* SR-65, 1–32.
Fitch, H. L., Halwes, T., Erickson, D. M., & Liberman, A. M. (1980). Perceptual equivalence of two acoustic cues for stop consonant manner. *Perception & Psychophysics, 27,* 343–350.
Flege, J. E., & Port, R. Cross-language phonetic interference: Arabic to English. (1981). *Language and Speech, 24,* 125–146.
Foreit, K. G. (1977). Linguistic relativism and selective adaptation for speech: A comparative study of English and Thai. *Perception & Psychophyics, 21,* 347–351.
Fry, D. B., Abramson, A. S., Eimas, P. D., & Liberman, A. M. (1962). The identification and discrimination of synthetic vowels. *Language and Speech, 5,* 171–189.
Fujisaki, H., & Kunisaki, O. (1978). Analysis, recognition, and perception of voiceless fricative consonants in Japanese. *IEEE Transactions (ASSP), 26,* 21–27.
Fujisaki, H., & Shigeno, S. (1979). Context effects in the categorization of speech and non-speech stimuli. In J. J. Wolf & D. H. Klatt (Eds.), *Speech communication papers* (pp. 5–8). New York: Acoustical Society of America.
Ganong, W. F. III. (1978). The selective adaptation effects of burst-cued stops. *Perception & Psychophysics, 24,* 71–83.
Ganong, W. F. III. (1980). Phonetic categorization in auditory word perception. *Journal of Experimental Psychology: Human Perception and Performance, 6,* 110–125.
Ganong, W. F. III., & Zatorre, R. J. (1980). Measuring phoneme boundaries four ways. *Journal of the Acoustical Society of America, 68,* 431–439.
Garnes, S., & Bond, Z. S. (1977). The influence of semantics on speech perception. *Journal of the Acoustical Society of America, 61* (Suppl. 1), S65 (Abstract).
Healy, A. F., & Repp, B. H. (1982). Context sensitivity and phonetic mediation in categorical perception. *Journal of Experimental Psychology: Human Perception and Performance, 8,* 68–80.
Kanamori, Y., Kasuya, H., Arai, S., & Kido, K. (1971). Effect of context on vowel perception. *Proceedings of the Seventh International Congress on Acoustics,* Budapest: 37–40.
Keating, P. A., Mikos, M. J., & Ganong, W. F. III. (1981). A cross-language study of range of voice onset time in the perception of initial stop voicing. *Journal of the Acoustical Society of America, 70,* 1261–1271.
Kewley-Port, D. (1983). Time-varying features as correlates of place of articulation in stop consonants. *Journal of the Acoustical Society of America, 73,* 322–335.
Kunisaki, O., & Fujisaki, H. (1977). On the influence of context upon perception of voiceless fricative consonants. In *Annual Bulletin* (Vol. 11, pp. 85–91). Tokyo: University of Tokyo, Research Institute of Logopedics and Phoniatrics.
Ladefoged, P. (1983). Cross-linguistic studies of speech production. In P. F. MacNeilage (Ed.), *The production of speech* (pp. 177–188). New York: Springer.
Ladefoged, P., & Broadbent, D. E. (1957). Information conveyed by vowels. *Journal of the Acoustical Society of America, 29,* 98–104.
Lahiri, A., Gewirth, L., & Blumstein, S. E. (1984). A reconsideration of acoustic invariance for place of articulation in stop consonants: Evidence from a cross-language study. *Journal of the Acoustical Society of America, 76,* 391–404.
Lane, H. (1965). Motor theory of speech perception: A critical review. *Psychological Review, 72,* 275–309.
Liberman, A. M., Delattre, P. C., & Cooper, F. S. (1952). The role of selected stimulus-variables in the perception of the unvoiced stop consonants. *American Journal of Psychology, 65,* 497–516.
Liberman, A. M., & Studdert-Kennedy, M. (1978). Phonetic perception. In R. Held, H. W. Leibowitz,

& H.-L. Teuber (Eds.), *Handbook of sensory physiology, Vol. VIII: Perception* (pp. 143–178). New York: Springer.

Lisker, L., & Abramson, A. S. (1970). The voicing dimension: Some experiments in comparative phonetics. *Proceedings of the 6th International Congress of Phonetic Sciences* (pp. 563–567). Prague: Academia.

MacKain, K. S., Best, C. T., & Strange, W. (1981). Categorical perception of English /r/ and /l/ by Japanese bilinguals. *Applied Psycholinguistics, 2,* 369–390.

Mann, V. A. (1980). Influence of preceding liquid on stop consonant perception. *Perception & Psychophysics, 28,* 407–412.

Mann, V. A., & Repp, B. H. (1980). Influence of vocalic context on perception of the [ʃ]-[s] distinction. *Perception & Psychophysics, 28,* 213–228.

Mann, V. A., & Repp, B. H. (1981). Influence of preceding fricative on stop consonant perception. *Journal of the Acoustical Society of America, 69,* 548–558.

Martin, J. G., & Bunnell, H. T. (1981). Perception of anticipatory coarticulation effects. *Journal of the Acoustical Society of America, 69,* 559–567.

Martin, J. G., & Bunnell, H. T. (1982). Perception of anticipatory coarticulation effects in vowel-stop consonant-vowel sequences. *Journal of Experimental Psychology: Human Perception and Performance, 8,* 473–488.

May, J. Vocal tract normalization for /s/ and /š/. (1976). *Haskins Laboratories Status Report on Speech Research, SR-48,* 67–73.

Massaro, D. W., & Oden, G. C. (1980). Evaluation and integration of acoustic features in speech perception. *Journal of the Acoustical Society of America, 67,* 996–1013.

Miller, J. L. (1977a). Nonindependence of feature processing in initial consonants. *Journal of Speech and Hearing Research, 20,* 519–528.

Miller, J. L. (1977b). Properties of feature detectors for VOT: The voiceless channel of analysis. *Journal of the Acoustical Society of America, 62,* 641–648.

Miller, J. L. (1981). The effect of speaking rate on segmental distinctions: Acoustic variation and perceptual compensation. In P. D. Eimas & J. L. Miller (Eds.), *Perspectives on the study of speech.* Hillsdale, NJ: Erlbaum.

Miller, J. L., Aibel, I. L., & Green, K. (1984). On the nature of rate-dependent processing during phonetic perception. *Perception & Psychophysics, 35,* 5–15.

Miller, J. L., & Baer, T. (1983). Some effects of speaking rate on the production of /b/ and /w/. *Journal of the Acoustical Society of America, 73,* 1751–1755.

Miller, J. L., Connine, C. M., Schermer, T. M., & Kluender, K. R. (1983). A possible auditory basis for internal structure of phonetic categories. *Journal of the Acoustical Society of America, 73,* 2124–2133.

Miller, J. L., Green, K., & Schermer, T. (1982). On the distinction between prosodic and semantic factors in word identification. *Journal of the Acoustical Society of America, 71* (Suppl. 1), S95 (Abstract).

Miller, J. L., & Liberman, A. M. (1979). Some effects of later-occurring information on the perception of stop consonant and semivowel. *Perception & Psychophysics, 25,* 457–465.

Miyawaki, K., Strange, W., Verbrugge, R., Liberman, A. M., Jenkins, J. J., & Fujimura, O. (1975). An effect of linguistic experience: The discrimination of [r] and [l] by native speakers of Japanese and English. *Perception & Psychophysics, 18,* 331–340.

Oden, G. C., & Massaro, D. W. (1978). Integration of featural information in speech perception. *Psychological Review, 85,* 172–191.

Öhman, S. E. G. (1966). Coarticulation in VCV utterances: Spectrographic measurements. *Journal of the Acoustical Society of America, 39,* 151–168.

Petzold, P. (1981). Distance effects on sequential dependencies in categorical judgment. *Journal of Experimental Psychology: Human Perception and Performance, 7,* 1371–1385.

Pisoni, D. B., Aslin, R. N., Perey, A. J., & Hennessy, B. L. (1982). Some effects of laboratory training on identification and discrimination of voicing contrasts in stop consonants. *Journal of Experimental Psychology: Human Perception and Performance, 8,* 297–314.

Pisoni, D. B., Carrell, T. D., & Gans, S. J. (1983). Perception of the duration of rapid spectrum changes in speech and nonspeech signals. *Perception & Psychophysics, 34,* 314–322.
Price, P. J., & Levitt, A. G. (1983). The relative roles of syntax and prosody in the perception of the /š/-/č/ distinction. *Language and Speech, 26,* 291–304.
Rakerd, B., Dechovitz, D. R., & Verbrugge, R. R. (1982). An effect of sentence finality on the phonetic significance of silence. *Language and Speech, 25,* 267–282.
Repp, B. H. (1980). A range-frequency effect on perception of silence in speech. *Haskins Laboratories Status Report on Speech Research, SR-61,* 151–166.
Repp, B. H. (1981). Two strategies in fricative discrimination. *Perception & Psychophysics, 30,* 217–227.
Repp, B. H. (1982). Phonetic trading relations and context effects: New evidence for a phonetic mode of perception. *Psychological Bulletin, 92,* 81–110.
Repp, B. H. (1984). Categorical perception: Issues, methods, findings. In N. J. Lass (Ed.), *Speech and language: Advances in basic research and practice* (Vol. 10). New York: Academic Press.
Repp, B. H., Healy, A. F., & Crowder, R. G. (1979). Categories and context in the perception of isolated steady-state vowels. *Journal of Experimental Psychology: Human Perception and Performance, 5,* 129–145.
Repp, B. H., Liberman, A. M., Eccardt, T., & Pesetsky, D. (1978). Perceptual integration of acoustic cues for stop, fricative and affricate manner. *Journal of Experimental Psychology: Human Perception and Performance, 4,* 621–637.
Repp, B. H., & Mann, V. A. (1981). Perceptual assessment of fricative-stop coarticulation. *Journal of the Acoustical Society of America, 69,* 1154–1163.
Repp, B. H., & Mann, V. A. (1982). Fricative-stop coarticulation: Acoustic and perceptual evidence. *Journal of the Acoustical Society of America, 71,* 1562–1567.
Roberts, M., & Summerfield, Q. (1981). Audiovisual presentation demonstrates that selective adaptation in speech perception is purely auditory. *Perception & Psychophysics, 30,* 309–314.
Rosen, S. M. (1979). Range and frequency effects in consonant categorization. *Journal of Phonetics, 7,* 393–402.
Samuel, A. G. (1979). *Speech is specialized, not special.* Unpublished doctoral dissertation, University of California at San Diego.
Samuel, A. G. (1982). Phonetic prototypes. *Perception & Psychophysics, 31,* 307–314.
Sawusch, J. R. (1977). Peripheral and central processing in speech perception. *Journal of the Acoustical Society of America, 62,* 738–750.
Sawusch, J. R., & Jusczyk, P. (1981). Adaptation and contrast in the perception of voicing. *Journal of Experimental Psychology: Human Perception and Performance, 7,* 408–421.
Sawusch, J. R., & Nusbaum, H. C. (1979). Contextual effects in vowel perception I: Anchor-induced contrast effects. *Perception & Psychophysics, 25,* 292–302.
Sawusch, J. R., Nusbaum, H. C., & Schwab, E. C. (1980). Contextual effects in vowel perception II: Evidence for two processing mechanisms. *Perception & Psychophysics, 27,* 421–434.
Sawusch, J. R., & Pisoni, D. B. (1974). On the identification of place and voicing features in synthetic stop consonants. *Journal of Phonetics, 2,* 181–194.
Sawusch, J. R., & Pisoni, D. B. (1976). Response organization and selective adaptation to speech sounds. *Perception & Psychophysics, 20,* 413–418.
Shigeno, S., & Fujisaki, H. (1980). Context effects in phonetic and non-phonetic vowel judgments. *Annual Bulletin* (Vol. 14, pp. 217–224). Tokyo: University of Tokyo, Research Institute for Logopedics and Phoniatrics.
Simon, H. J., & Studdert-Kennedy, M. (1978). Selective anchoring and adaptation of phonetic and nonphonetic continua. *Journal of the Acoustical Society of America, 64,* 1338–1357.
Soli, S. D. (1982). Structure and duration of vowels together specify fricative voicing. *Journal of the Acoustical Society of America, 72,* 366–378.
Stevens, K. N., & Blumstein, S. E. (1978). Invariant cues for place of articulation in stop consonants. *Journal of the Acoustical Society of America, 64,* 1358–1368.
Strange, W., & Jenkins, J. J. (1978). Role of linguistic experience in the perception of speech. In R. D.

Walk & H. L. Pick, Jr. (Eds.), *Perception and experience* (pp. 125–169). New York: Plenum Press.

Studdert-Kennedy, M. (1981). Perceiving phonetic segments. In T. Myers, J. Laver, & J. Anderson (Eds.), *The cognitive representation of speech*. Amsterdam: North Holland.

Studdert-Kennedy, M., Liberman, A. M., Harris, K. S., & Cooper, F. S. (1970). Motor theory of speech perception: A reply to Lane's critical review. *Psychological Review, 77*, 234–249.

Summerfield, Q. (1981). Articulatory rate and perceptual constancy in phonetic perception. *Journal of Experimental Psychology: Human Perception and Performance, 7*, 1074–1095.

Swinney, D. A. (1982). The structure and time-course of information interaction during speech comprehension, lexical segmentation, access, and interpretation. In J. Mehler, E. C. T. Walker, & M. Garrett (Eds.), *Perspectives on mental representation* (pp. 151–167). Hillsdale, NJ: Erlbaum.

Waters, R. S., & Wilson, W. A., Jr. (1976). Speech perception by rhesus monkeys: The voicing distinction in synthesized labial and velar stop consonants. *Perception & Psychophysics, 19*, 285–289.

Werker, J. F. & Tees, R. C. (1984). Cross-language speech perception: Evidence for perceptual reorganization during the first year of life. *Infant Behavior and Development, 7*, 49–63.

Whalen, D. H. (1981). Effects of vocalic formant transitions and vowel quality on the English [s]-[š] boundary. *Journal of the Acoustical Society of America, 69*, 275–282.

Williams, L. (1977). The perception of stop consonant voicing by Spanish-English bilinguals. *Perception & Psychophysics, 21*, 289–297.

4 Auditory, articulatory, and learning explanations of categorical perception in speech

Stuart Rosen and Peter Howell

Categorical perception (CP) has been among the most extensively studied of phenomena in speech perception because it seems to indicate something about the nature of phonemic categories. Early explanations, based on the "motor theory," posited that the categorical nature of perception was a result of the categorical nature of the gestures used in production. More recently, it has been proposed that CP arises from natural sensitivities of the auditory system, with no reference to articulation, or, in fact, to any speech-specific mechanisms. A third point of view considers it to arise from the use of categories that are determined not by articulatory or auditory factors, but rather by learning. These three approaches are evaluated with regard to what is currently known about the perception of two segmental speech contrasts: the distinction between voiceless affricates and fricatives, and that between voiced and voiceless plosives. Data from adults, children, infants and nonhuman mammals perceiving speech are considered, along with results obtained from adults and infants listening to nonspeech sounds that have some acoustic features in common with speech. We conclude that none of the theories is completely adequate on its own, and discuss ways that they might be combined.

The ability to categorize speech is an essential requirement for the user of spoken language. Categorical perception (CP), a mode of perception that was claimed, at least originally, to be unique to certain speech sounds, is interesting because it may reflect important aspects of this process. The notion of CP was first established in experiments designed to determine how English plosive consonants (/b/, /d/, /g/, /p/, /t/, and /k/) are classified by listeners. The results exhibited certain unusual characteristics that seemed to distinguish the perception of these speech sounds from the perception of other stimuli, auditory or other. The observed pattern of results was termed "categorical" and can best be illustrated with an example – the perception of the English bilabial plosive voicing contrast, which distinguishes *ba* from *pa*.

There are several acoustic differences between a naturally spoken *ba* and *pa*, most of which are associated with the time of onset of laryngeal vibration relative to the release gesture for the plosive. For illustrative purposes, only one difference

First and special thanks to Quentin Summerfield for his comments on an earlier version of this paper. Our gratitude, also, to Heidi Wall, for help on issues of style, and to Adrian Fourcin, who provided helpful discussions. Both authors are supported by the Medical Research Council of the United Kingdom.

need concern us. In *ba*, laryngeal vibration causes quasiperiodic energy to excite the vocal tract near the start of the sound, and continues throughout. In *pa*, on the other hand, the sound is initially excited aperiodically (by air turbulence in the vocal tract) and quasiperiodic excitation from the larynx does not start until well after this.

For perceptual testing, a speech synthesizer can be used to create a continuum of sounds between *ba* and *pa*, in which the time of onset of the quasiperiodic excitation is varied directly. Such a continuum is known as a voice-onset time (VOT) continuum. VOT is specified in time units representing the onset of quasiperiodic excitation relative to the acoustic events reflecting the release of the plosive. Thus, 0-ms VOT would mean all formants are excited quasiperiodically at the release, a VOT of +10 ms that quasiperiodic excitation starts 10 ms after release, and so on. A typical continuum for examining English listeners' ability to distinguish voiced from voiceless bilabial plosives might consist of sounds varying in VOT from 0 to 80 ms in 10-ms steps.

If listeners are asked to categorize sounds drawn from this continuum as voiced or voiceless, they classify sounds with short VOTs as voiced (*ba*) and sounds with longer VOTs as voiceless (*pa*). The point on the continuum where each category is heard equally often is known as the phoneme boundary. Of equal interest is the abrupt way in which categorizations change across the continuum. These categorization curves are supposed to be steeper than those occurring with nonspeech (Liberman, Cooper, Shankweiler, & Studdert-Kennedy, 1967).

Another aspect of CP is the way in which the ability to discriminate sounds varies along the VOT continuum. Usually an *ABX* task is used. Each trial consists of a triplet of sounds (designated *A*, *B*, and *X*, respectively). The *A* and *B* sounds are always different and always have the same physical difference – for example, with VOTs differing by 10 ms. The third sound (*X*) is the same as either the first (*A*) or the second (*B*) sound, and listeners have to indicate which of the two they think the third sound matches. Performance with two sounds drawn from the same category is found to be almost at chance, but performance with sounds straddling the phoneme boundary is considerably better. In other words, two sounds given the same label are not discriminated very well, whereas two sounds given different labels are, resulting in peaks in discrimination performance at the phoneme boundary. Discrimination peaks like these had not been observed with nonspeech continua (see Miller's 1956 review of identification and discrimination experiments with continua other than speech, contemporary with the initial work on CP). There are, then, according to these early studies, three distinguishing characteristics of CP: a sharp identification function, poor discrimination within a phoneme category, and a peak in discrimination performance at the phoneme boundary.

The original interpretation of CP posited that the listener, because the sounds were speech, could only respond to them with phonemic labels. Categorization was sharp because sounds were only one thing or another, not a continuum of possibilities. Discrimination was poor for two stimuli in the same phoneme class because the first two sounds of an ABX triplet would be given the same label. A response as to the identity of X could then only be based on guessing. If, however, the A and B sounds were labeled differently (as happens when they straddle the phoneme boundary) the listener only has to ascertain the label of the third sound to make the discrimination correctly (Liberman et al., 1967). Thus all the distinguishing features of CP are accounted for.

This explanation of CP is consistent with two classes of theory: those in which the phoneme boundaries arise from a perceptual process that is linked to the way sounds are articulated (as in the motor theory of speech perception presented by Liberman et al., 1967), and those in which the phoneme categories are learned (Lane, 1965). The common factor in both these approaches is that perception is mediated by phonemic labels.

A third class of explanation, developed over recent years, proposes that the phenomena of CP derive from the inborn sensitivities of the auditory system (see Stevens, 1981). Hence no labeling is involved. Here it is supposed that, due to the processing imposed by the auditory system, discriminability in some regions of acoustic continua is inherently higher than in others. Hence equal physical differences need not imply equal perceptual differences. Sounds drawn from regions of the continua where discriminability is low will sound more alike than sounds drawn from regions where discriminability is high. Given such variations in discriminability, both sharp labeling, and appropriately peaked discrimination functions would arise. In these latter accounts, the auditory properties of the stimuli rather than the phonemic categories to which they belong (as in the motor and learning theories) are the critical factors in determining whether CP occurs.

Before we go on to detail and evaluate these three approaches, it will be useful to highlight some of the major differences among them and to outline the type of data we will use in their assessment.

One important distinction is that only the motor theory posits a necessary difference between the perception of speech and nonspeech sounds, as it holds that phonemic categories are perceived via reference to articulation. If CP arises from the use of learned labels, it need not be restricted to speech. Similarly, inbuilt sensitivities arising from sensory processing could likewise occur in other sensory continua, so in this case too, CP need not be speech- or even sound-specific. Thus the issue of whether CP occurs only with speech ("Is speech 'special'?") is vitally important. Many of the chapters in this volume speak to this issue, focusing on CP in modalities other than audition and on sounds other than speech. Our evaluation of the theories rests upon stimuli drawn only from the auditory modality (both speech and nonspeech). Although we recognize the importance of the nature of perception in other modalities, we leave these issues to those more competent to deal with them.

The theories also differ as to their predictions of how infants and animals will respond to continua that are known to be categorically perceived by adult humans (see Chapter 5 by Eimas, Miller, & Jusczyk; Chapter 9 by Bornstein; Chapter 10 by Ehret; Chapter 11 by Snowdon; Chapter 12 by Kuhl; Chapter 14 by Molfese).

Clearly, categorical perception of speech sounds by animals cannot be mediated either by an articulatory mode or by the use of learned labels (unless specific training is given). Hence, both the motor and learned-label theories predict that animal listeners should not categorically perceive such continua. Auditory sensitivities, on the other hand, might be common to the higher mammals.

Data from infant studies distinguish the theories in another way. Although infants might have auditory systems similar to those of adults or innate mechanisms to mediate perception via some reference to articulation (no matter how abstract), they are unlikely to have developed appropriate labels for speech sounds. Hence, categorical perception by infants (at least when they are young enough) may be taken as evidence against learned-label theories.

Another important issue in assessing theories of CP is the extent to which category boundaries are rigidly fixed (see Chapter 3, by Repp & Liberman). Liberman et al. (1967) note that the boundaries vary in situations where differences in articulation cause differences in the acoustic properties of the sound produced, for instance, when speech rate varies. If a speaker articulates at a faster rate, the duration of at least some of the sounds has to decrease. So voiceless plosive consonants might be reduced in overall duration and this could cause the phoneme boundary on a VOT continuum to shift to shorter values. Such context-induced alterations in phoneme boundary placement would be permitted in a motor or learning theory, but they would represent a serious challenge to auditory-sensitivity theories. In the latter case, it would have to be shown that phoneme-boundary shifts occur because changes in the acoustic structure of the sound cause a shift in the hypothesized primary auditory feature.

Experimental manipulations of a different sort can also alter phoneme boundaries. These are generally known as judgment effects, and are usually induced by varying the range of stimuli or the relative frequency with which they are presented (Parducci, 1965; see also Chapter 2 by Macmillan and Chapter 13 by Wilson, this volume). According to motor theory, range and frequency manipulations should not alter the placement of the boundary because they would not affect the way the sound is articulated (see Studdert-Kennedy, Liberman, Harris, & Cooper, 1970 for a discussion of the "context-free" nature of judgments of speech sounds perceived categorically). Similarly, little shift in phoneme boundary is permitted by natural auditory-sensitivity theories, as the boundaries are "hard-wired" into the auditory system. On the other hand, if the labels are learned, boundary shifts with range and frequency manipulations would simply reflect some update of the learned boundaries.

Three approaches to explaining CP

Now that the general nature of the three theories and the type of data we will use in their assessment have been discussed, we will proceed to a rather more detailed description. For simplicity, we will initially treat each of the three theories as if they were mutually exclusive. In the final section of the chapter, we discuss ways of jointly accommodating them.

Motor theory

The principal factor that led to the formulation of the motor theory is the well-known observation that there is a complex relation between a phoneme and its acoustic realization. For example, a noise burst centered on a frequency of 1440 Hz is heard as /p/ before /i/ or /u/ (*pee* or *poo* in everyday spelling) but /k/ before /ɑ/ (*kah* – see Liberman, Delattre, & Cooper, 1952). Another illustration is found in the acoustic structure of voiced plosive consonants, /b/, /d/, and /g/. One important cue to their identity is the pattern over time of the bands of energy (known as formants, and numbered ordinally with increasing frequency) that are typical of most speech sounds. This pattern differs, however, depending on the particular vowel that follows the plosive. Thus /d/ before /i/ (*dee*) has a rising second formant while /d/ before /u/ (*doo*) has a falling one (Liberman, Delattre, Cooper, & Gerstman, 1954). Such acoustic variability is more evident for certain classes of speech sounds (such as plosive consonants) than others (e.g., vowels). Although plosive consonants show marked acoustic variability, they differ less in the way they are produced.[1] Speakers seem to use discrete places of production for them. Vowels show the reverse pattern; less acoustic variability and apparently less limitation on where subjects can position their tongue, jaw, lips, and larynx.

The basic hypothesis of motor theory ("perception follows production") is that speech is perceived by referring the sounds to the way in which they are articulated. The hypothesized invariance in the motor commands of sounds that have different acoustic properties in different contexts would reveal that the different sounds are, in fact, the product of the same articulation. This hypothesis neatly explains the acoustic differences between the way /d/ is realized in /di/ and /du/. The argument, in simplified form, goes like this: At the beginning of making either sound, the tongue is pressed against the alveolar ridge behind the teeth, sealing the vocal tract. At the release of the plosive (as the tongue starts moving toward the position appropriate for the following vowel), the resonance properties of the vocal tract (and their acoustic reflection, the formants) are similar. Hence, the starting positions of the second formant ($F2$) are also similar. The differences in the movement of $F2$ occur because it has to move to a higher frequency for /i/, and to a lower frequency for /u/, compared with its starting frequency. In short, the same articulatory maneuver (closure of the vocal tract at a particular point) leads to varying acoustic patterns resolvable by referring the sound back to its method of production.

Motor theory attempts to explain much more than CP, and this is one of its appeals. The aspects of speech perception that it claims to explain are outlined most extensively by Liberman, Cooper, Shankweiler, and Studdert-Kennedy (1967). Although some of these claims have been abandoned in the light of later experimental work, the idea that articulatory knowledge is used in speech perception still persists (see Liberman & Studdert-Kennedy, 1978, and Chapter 3, this volume). We will be concerned with motor theory as formulated by Liberman et al. (1967) because later expositions are more limited in scope and are not as explicit about its underlying assumptions. Our assessment here is confined to motor theory as an explanation of CP, not as an account of other aspects of speech perception (see Howell & Harvey, 1983, for this).

The phenomena of CP were of interest to the motor theorists because they seemed to reflect the operation of a mechanism that categorized speech sounds using classes based on discrete productive gestures. One of the first studies to show CP involved the perception of a place-of-articulation continuum. Liberman, Harris, Hoffman, and Griffith (1957) synthesized a continuum ranging from /be/ through /de/ to /ge/. The distinction between the different places of articulation was carried by the starting frequencies of the transition of the second formant, which were spaced equally in frequency. Identification functions changed abruptly from one category to another. Discrimination (measured in the standard *ABX* task) was poor for pairs of stimuli drawn from within a phoneme category, but good for stimuli that straddled the phoneme boundary. Vowels, on the other hand, did not appear to be perceived categorically. Fry, Abramson, Eimas, and Liberman (1962) synthesized a two-formant vowel continuum, which ranged from /ɪ/ through /ɛ/ to /æ/ in acoustically equal steps. No discrimination peaks were observed with these stimuli and discrimination performance was uniformly better than that noted with plosive consonants. (See Liberman et al., 1967, for an extensive review of studies showing differences between the perception of plosives and vowels.)

Motor theory can account for these phenomena. Sharp identification functions would be expected with plosive consonants (but not vowels) because listeners can only refer their perception to discrete productive categories. Chance discrimination performance for two sounds drawn from the same phoneme category would occur because both would be mapped onto the same discrete articulatory gesture. Peaks would occur when the sounds straddled the boundary because each member of the stimulus pair would be associated with gestures appropriate for the production of two qualitatively different speech sounds. None of these phenomena would occur with vowels because they are not produced with discrete gestures. Hence, they are not categorically perceived.

It follows from this interpretation that CP should only occur with speech sounds (and then not all) because reference is made to *phonemic* categories. It was originally claimed that CP did not occur with nonspeech stimuli and this was accordingly taken as an indication of the special status of speech perception. For example, Mattingly, Liberman, Syrdal, and Halwes (1971) synthesized a /bæ/-/dæ/-/gæ/ continuum (as in *bat*), in which the different places of articulation were cued by the direction and rate of change of the second formant alone. Perception of these was categorical (as reported by Liberman et al. in 1957 for a comparable continuum). Discrimination of the isolated transitional portions of the second formants of the speech continuum used by Mattingly et al. was also assessed. These are not heard as speech and have been described as "chirps." The discrimination peaks were less apparent and did not coincide with those found with the speech sounds. In this case, CP occurs with a speech continuum but not with nonspeech sounds of similar acoustic structure.

One implication of motor theory is that identification and discrimination functions should not change with manipulations in stimulus range and relative frequency of presentation (Parducci, 1965; Chapter 2 by Macmillan and Chapter 13 by Wilson, this volume) because articulatory gestures inferred for the sounds would not change. It has in fact been claimed that such judgment effects do not occur with certain speech sounds (Strange & Broen, 1980). On the other hand, motor theory does account for adjustments by listeners to alterations in the speech signal that occur because speech is produced in different ways (e.g., at a faster rate than normal). Whatever ability speakers have to alter the way they produce speech is supposed to be automatically incorporated into perception because perception is referred to the mechanism that gives rise to these alterations. (See Chapter 3 by Repp & Liberman, this volume for a more extensive discussion of these points.)

Other articulatory-referential theories of speech perception have been proposed that do not depend on the mechanisms for production being accessed during perception as in motor theory (e.g., Shankweiler, Strange, & Verbrugge, 1977). Such accounts claim similarity with Gibson's (1966) theory of object perception. Gibson considers that objects are perceived "directly" rather than through an analysis of their components (e.g., a feature analysis). The pattern of visual stimulation from an object as it moves around in space has high-level invariant properties that allow this direct perception to occur. For example, the light pattern that reaches observers from the angled corners of a table as they move around it changes in characteristic ways because the object is a table. Low-level feature detectors could not determine that the angle included by the edges of the table was a table corner because the angle changes when the table is viewed from different positions. It is the way in which the pattern of stimulation remains invariant under the changes that determines by direct (nonanalytic) detection what the object is.

By the same token, speech sounds are supposed to show a systematic acoustic patterning because the articulators that produce the patterns are constrained in the movements they can make. Thus, according to a theory of direct perception, a listener perceives speech by using information about the way the auditory pattern changes over time to access information about articulatory movement.

The Gibsonian type of theory avoids certain problems encountered in motor theory. For one, perception of speech will have similarities with perception of other sounds and stimuli in other modalities (i.e., they are all hypothesized to be perceived "directly"), so CP could occur outside of speech (Remez, Cutting, & Studdert-Kennedy, 1980), a possibility not explicitly allowed by motor theory. There are points of continuity with motor theory too, in that the neoGibsonian view links the perception of sound patterns to articulatory movements. Although CP has not been cited in support of a theory of direct perception of speech, some of the data we discuss are relevant to its claims.

Natural auditory sensitivities

In motor theory, the phenomena of CP were considered to be evidence for a special speech-decoding mechanism. In the mid 1970s, several reports showed that CP could arise from variations in auditory sensitivity along some nonspeech acoustic continua. Some of these perceptual discontinuities seemed to be implicated in the separation of one phoneme class from another. Although convincing reports of categorical perception of auditory continua with no obvious relation to speech (and certain nonauditory continua as well) were reported at about the same time, because of our primary interest in the implications for speech perception, we will focus on the nonspeech continua that seem to have acoustic properties related to contrasts in speech.

There are several versions of a natural auditory sensitivities account and we will discuss two of them (Pastore, 1976; Pastore et al., 1977; Stevens, 1981; Chapter 1 by Pastore, this volume). Stevens claims that certain acoustic continua, because of the way the sounds comprising them are processed by the auditory system, contain regions where discrimination is poor and other regions where it is good. The difference in discriminability across the stimulus range may be used for the purpose of distinguishing one phoneme category from another. Speech sounds that fall within a region where discriminability is poor sound relatively alike and may be regarded as possessing the same acoustic property. Their discriminability would be at (or near) chance. Sounds that fall on opposite sides of a region where discriminability is relatively good can be discriminated easily and give peaks in the discrimination function. Sharp identification functions also arise from the clear dichotomy between the response classes.

CP should then occur for nonspeech continua that incorporate the same acoustic feature responsible for the categorical perception of the corresponding speech continua. Stevens (1981) cites the study by Cutting and Rosner (1974) of rise-time perception in support of his theory. (Rise time is defined here as the time a sound takes to reach full amplitude from its onset.) Cutting and Rosner showed that a nonspeech continuum varying in rise time (heard as a plucked or bowed string depending on whether the rises are short or long, respectively) is categorically perceived, as is a speech continuum varying in rise time (heard as an affricate /tʃ/ as in *ch*erry or fricative /ʃ/ as in *sh*erry). Furthermore, the category boundary occurs at about the same rise time (40 ms) in each case. This was taken by Stevens as evidence for a predisposition of the auditory system to separate sounds with fast rise times from sounds with more gradual rise times.

It is important to note that Stevens refers to regions of heightened sensitivity, which separate one phoneme class from another. This region of auditory sensitivity specifies the limits over which a discriminative response between two phonemes could occur. It is possible that listeners show some latitude in where they place the boundary within this region. Differences in boundaries brought about by manipulations in the range or relative frequency of presentation of the stimuli used could be incorporated into the theory if the effects only operate over the range of heightened discriminability (see Chapter 2 by Macmillan and Chapter 13 by Wilson, this volume). Even so, this would mean that something other than a purely auditory process was responsible for the position of phoneme boundaries.

Even this limited latitude of boundary movement is not permitted in the common-factor theory of Pastore and his colleagues unless ad hoc assumptions are made. They propose that a stable and relatively precisely defined internal or external limitation (the common factor) gives rise to CP. The stable limitation may be a constant physical factor present in the stimulus (for example, a reference or interfering stimulus) or an internal threshold. This model is very similar to that of Stevens in that the phenomena of CP are supposed to arise from nonuniform discriminability across a continuum.

There are three lines of evidence to support the idea that natural auditory sensitivities may be responsible for CP. First, CP has been reported with nonspeech continua in which the acoustic contrast seems to be related to an acoustic contrast used to distinguish phonemes, as in the previously cited example of rise time and the affricate-fricative contrast. Another important class of categorically perceived nonspeech continua are those in which the relative-onset time of two sounds is varied (Miller, Wier, Pastore, Kelly, & Dooling, 1976; Pisoni, 1977) as they may provide a basis for the categorical perception of voice-onset time continua. Second, mammals appear to perceive VOT continua categorically (see Chapter 10 by Ehret, Chapter 11 by Snowdon, Chapter 12 by Kuhl, this volume). Perhaps the animals are responding to the same auditory properties that humans respond to. Third, CP occurs in infants for certain speech and, moreover, analogous nonspeech continua (see Chapter 5 by Eimas, Miller, & Jusczyk; and Chapter 14 by Molfese, this volume). Eimas, Siqueland, Jusczyk, and Vigorito (1971) give evidence that babies perceive a voice-onset time continuum categorically. Jusczyk, Rosner, Cutting, Foard, and Smith (1977) showed similar results for a nonspeech rise-time continuum, as do Jusczyk, Pisoni, Walley, and Murray (1980) for a relative tone-onset time continuum. All this evidence indicates that CP may have an innate basis that arises from an auditory rather than a linguistic predisposition.

Learned labels

In both the motor and the auditory-sensitivity theories, there is a natural mapping between the stimuli and the categories used, via either an articulatory or an auditory constraint. An alternative point of view is that the categories are not predetermined and arise solely from learning which sounds belong together in a particular class. Hence, the category boundaries are fairly arbitrary. If subjects then came to rely on these learned labels in their responses to stimuli (especially in tasks that encourage their use), all the phenomena of CP would arise. Sharp labeling functions would follow naturally from well-learned labels. Stimuli put into the same class would tend to be not discriminated from one another, whereas stimuli from different classes would be discriminated well.

Lane (1965) was the first to promulgate such a view in relation to CP. He showed that CP could arise if subjects were trained to impose discrete categorizations on a set of objects. Lane did not consider the effects of range and frequency manipulations, but these are easily incorporated into a theory of this type. Such manipulations might serve simply to redefine the category boundaries (as in Helson, 1964; Parducci, 1965; and Chapter 13, by Wilson this volume).

The most convincing evidence that learned labels can give rise to CP comes from studies of the perception of musical pitch, a well-understood sensory continuum with no discontinuities in discriminability. Burns and Ward (1978) investigated the perception of melodic intervals between sequentially presented tones by trained musicians and obtained strong evidence for CP. Interval-identification functions were sharp, and discrimination was best at the (equal-tempered) semitone boundaries. That this was attributable to learning, and not to any special properties of the stimuli, was supported by the finding that non-musically-trained listeners showed discrimination functions that were flat across the continuum. The studies by Siegel and Siegel (1977a,b) of similar continua, although they do not contain an explicit test of CP, are also consistent with the notion that musicians (but not nonmusicians) perceive musical intervals categorically.[2]

Modern-day learned-label accounts of CP are couched in a dual-process memory model that assumes a quickly decaying but fairly literal sensory store (similar to "echoic" memory) in parallel with the more abstract, but longer lasting, memory for the applied labels. (See Chapter 2, this volume, by Macmillan for a particularly enlightening and detailed exposition of dual-process models.) Dual-process models were first introduced into speech research by Fujisaki and Kawashima (1969, 1971), who saw a listener's responses to speech stimuli as resulting from the interaction of an auditory and a phonemic (or labeling) process. The function of this labeling process is not completely specified, but it is not restricted to speech (hence, of course, it is not exclusively phonemic). Fujisaki and Kawashima (1971) explicitly deny the possibility that labeling is based in articulation and consider the phoneme labels to be formed by "linguistic experience." The auditory process is timbre-based, with no possibility of special sensitivities. Therefore, in this model, CP can *only* arise on the basis of the learned labels (phonemic ones in the case of speech). The real power of this formulation is not only that it offers an explanation of CP per se, but that it also offers a way to understand results that seem to be neither fish nor fowl: neither categorically perceived in the ideal sense nor continuously perceived, with features reminiscent of both.

The fact is that CP in its idealized form (with intracategory discrimination at chance) never occurs. The degree to which a continuum is categorically perceived depends on a number of task variables (e.g. interstimulus intervals, presentation paradigm) and the dual-process model accounts for these data well. We will not concern ourselves further with this area, as it is peripheral to our main topic, and Repp (1983) and Studdert-Kennedy (1976) have recently provided comprehensive reviews.

Ades (1977) has outlined a view that is similar to Fujisaki and Kawashima's but that is more open minded about the nature of the auditory process in allowing explicitly for auditory discontinuities. His approach is based on a dual-process model for intensity resolution developed by Durlach and Braida (1969), which is closely related in structure to Fujisaki and Kawashima's, but is much more extensively elaborated (see Chapter 2 by Macmillan, this volume, for a detailed description of both models, as well as an account of the important differences between them).

Again, two modes of memory are assumed: a sensory-trace mode (the short-term "echoic" store) and a context-coding mode (the labeling or "phonemic" process). The sensory trace is affected by any other sounds following the test sound, and is subject to decay over time. The context code is stable in time but is affected by the range of stimuli and the relative frequency with which they are presented. The memory noise in this mode is proportional to the range of stimuli presented. Larger stimulus ranges make for increased uncertainty in the context-coding mode. (There is a third source of noise in the transformation from stimulus to sensation that need not concern us here.) Durlach and Braida use this model to explain the classical discrepancy between the number of stimuli it is possible to discriminate (many) and the number it is possible to identify consistently (limited to 7 ± 2; Miller, 1956).

It is this discrepancy, typically found for unidimensional nonspeech continua, that has always been contrasted to the situation found for plosive consonants, where discrimination seemed equivalent to identification. Of particular relevance to this discussion, Durlach and Braida also predict an equivalence between identification and discrimination (or CP, in the sense proposed by Macmillan, Kaplan, & Creelman, 1977) when the range spanned by the stimuli is small, a prediction borne out for the case of intensity by Pynn, Braida, and Durlach (1972). Conversely, the larger the stimulus range, the greater the discrepancy between identification and discrimination.

Ades (1977) describes how the Durlach and Braida model might apply to the categorical perception of speech. Several studies (e.g., Sachs, 1969) indicate that vowels span a wider perceptual range than consonants. One would therefore expect a smaller discrepancy between identification and discrimination (in other words, that results would be more "categorical") for consonants than for vowels. This does not in itself account for discrimination peaks, which, Ades hypothesizes, can occur for two reasons. First, in a version of the natural-auditory-sensitivities theory, there might be discontinuities in the first transformation from stimulus to sensation. Discrimination peaks that arise from this process should be relatively fixed. Second, peaks could arise because the subject is making judgments on the basis of the context code. Discrimination peaks that occur on the basis of this process would depend on experience with the categories and be subject to judgment effects like those of range and frequency. Ades indicates that the peaks in speech discrimination result primarily from the imposed categorizations of the context-coding mode.

Assessing the evidence

There are many studies that address, directly or indirectly, the adequacy of the three different explanations of CP detailed in the previous section. We have chosen to evaluate the three theories with respect to what is known about two segmental contrasts: the voicing distinction in homorganic plosive consonants (those at the same place of articulation, as in "*b*an" versus "*p*an" or "*d*ill" versus "*t*ill" or "*g*ilt" versus "*k*ilt") and the voiceless affricate/fricative contrast (as in "*ch*ip" versus "*sh*ip"). There is little need to justify our choice of the former: Voicing is probably the most intensively studied of any phonetic feature, reflecting its phonemic role in the majority of the world's languages. The voiceless affricate/fricative distinction, on the other hand, is a rather more exotic beast.[3] It has been chosen for a number of reasons, not least of which is that we have personally been involved in some of the relevant investigations. Most important, it was at one time thought to provide, if not the first, certainly the strongest support for the natural-sensitivities point of view. Not only were the speech and analogous nonspeech continua thought to be categorically perceived, but it was also claimed that the category boundaries on the two types of continua were virtually identical. Place continua, which are categorically perceived, and are most often considered in connection with the motor theory, will not be considered here because they have not played such a prominent role in other theoretical accounts of CP. We begin our assessment, then, with the voiceless affricate/fricative distinction.

The voiceless affricate/fricative distinction

Although there were a few prior studies, Gerstman's (1957) thesis can be said to be the first major acoustic-phonetic investigation of the voiceless affricate/fricative contrast. In common with much of the early work, which sought to determine the acoustic correlates of phonemic categories, there is a judicious blend of experiments involving both production and perception, a mix that modern studies could profitably emulate. Gerstman also studied the voiced affricate/fricative pair, /dʒ/ as in *j*ump, and /ʒ/ as in plea*s*ure, but we are only concerned with his results for the voiceless pair, /tʃ/ as in *ch*op and /ʃ/ as in *sh*op. Although there is some controversy over the details of his results (which we discuss later), the general conclusion he reached remains firm: Affricates can be distinguished from fricatives by at least two aspects of the noisy, aperiodic fricative sounds (caused by air turbulence between two closely held articulators in the vocal tract), which are their main components. Both the overall duration of the fricative noise and the time it takes the noise to go from silence to its full amplitude (otherwise known as its "rise time") are distinctive. Affricates are relatively quick rising and short, whereas fricatives are slower rising and last longer.

The first demonstration of categorical perception for the affricate/fricative contrast. Gerstman himself did not address the issue of CP, but his study provided the requisite information for Cutting and Rosner (1974) to create the continuum of synthetic sounds necessary for such an experiment. They used two speech continua, one from /tʃɑ/ to /ʃɑ/ and one from /tʃæ/ to /ʃæ/. Both continua varied in the rise time and duration of the initial fricative noise, which were presumably identical for corresponding stimuli from the two continua. The rise times (0 to 80 ms in 10-ms steps) were based on Gerstman's measurements using the average amplitude display of a spectrograph. He showed the rise times in natural syllables of this type to range from about 5 ms (affricates) to about 100 ms (fricatives), with only 25% of the fricatives having rise times greater than 80 ms. Furthermore, nearly all affricates (94%) had rise times shorter than 40 ms, whereas all the fricatives had rise times longer than this.[4] The overall duration of Cutting and Rosner's fricative noise is not specified (nor is its amplitude contour from the finish of the rise to its termination indicated), but rough measurements on the wave forms of their Figure 1 show the duration of the nonrising part of the frication to be about 100 ms. As the rising portion of the noises was added to the base 100 ms of fricative noise (J. Cutting, personal communication), the duration of the frication covaried with the duration of the rises, from about 100 to about 180 ms. Thus, as in natural speech, the longer rises were associated with longer-duration fricative noises.

Having constructed these two speech continua, Cutting and Rosner applied the standard paradigm of labeling and *ABX* discrimination tasks. The results were not different for the two continua, and so are shown averaged together in Figure 4.1. The classic pattern for a categorically perceived continuum was found: a reasonably sharp labeling function and a discrimination function whose peak corresponds to the phoneme boundary, with troughs of performance within phoneme classes.

These results, in themselves, surprised no one. The motor theorists could point to the assumed "categorical nature" of the articulatory gestures used to produce affricates and fricatives. Those espousing an explanation invoking the use of learned labels could point to the long linguistic experience of differentially labeling what was, at least to these subjects, a phonemic contrast.

What was surprising, and the crucial factor in the encouragement of the auditory sensitivities theory, was that Cutting and Rosner were also able to demonstrate CP for nonspeech continua that varied in rise time (or "attack").

Categorical perception of a nonspeech analog of the affricate/fricative contrast. To demonstrate nonspeech CP, Cutting and Rosner created two sawtooth continua varying in rise time. Both were based on constant fundamental frequency waveforms from a Moog synthesizer, differing only in the particular frequency used (294

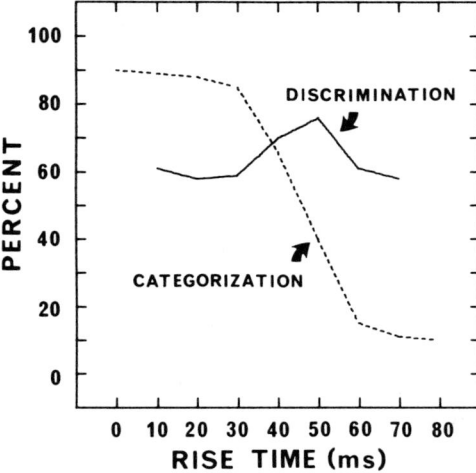

Figure 4.1. Categorization and discrimination functions obtained by Cutting and Rosner (1974) for a voiceless affricate/fricative distinction. The curves shown are the mean of two continua: In both, the consonantal distinction is cued by the duration and rise time of the initial frication noise, but two different vowels follow. For the categorization curve, ordinate values give the percentage of /tʃ/ response for each stimulus. For the discrimination curve, the values give percent correct in an *ABX* task. (Redrawn using Table 1 of Cutting & Rosner [1974] and Table 2 of Macmillan, Kaplan, & Creelman [1977].)

or 440 Hz). Each continuum consisted of nine sounds, differing primarily in rise time. As for the speech continua, rise times varied from 0 to 80 ms in 10-ms steps. After this rise, all stimuli decayed to zero amplitude in 1.02 s, making the total duration of the stimuli vary with rise time from 1.02 to 1.1 s. Listeners were instructed to regard the stimulus with the 0-ms rise time as coming from the plucking of a stringed instrument and the 80-ms stimulus as coming from the bowing of a stringed instrument. (Subjectively speaking, the plucks are rather more convincing than the bows.) Listeners were first asked to label the stimuli and then to discriminate them. The two continua did not give different results, so only the mean of the two is shown in Figure 4.2.

The "pluck-bow" continuum is seen to be categorically perceived. What is even more striking is the correspondence between the speech and nonspeech continua in the rise time at which peak discrimination is found, near 50 and 40 ms, respectively. It is this near equality that made us (and others) consider this experiment to have been the strongest support for the natural-auditory-sensitivities theory.

The three theories react. Motor theory, with its dependence on a reference to articulation, is flatly contradicted by this last result. Learned-label theorists still had an out: Perhaps the discrimination results were obtained because the subjects were mediating their responses with the verbal labels "pluck" and "bow" that they had learned in the previous identification task, or (given reasonably natural stimuli) from real-world experience of such sounds. These possibilities were explicitly considered and rejected by Cutting and Rosner on the basis of results from a further experiment. Here, all discrimination tasks preceded labeling tasks. In addition, another two nonspeech rise-time continua were generated, now of sinusoids at two frequencies (294 and 440 Hz as before) but having amplitude contours identical to

Auditory, articulatory, and learning explanations

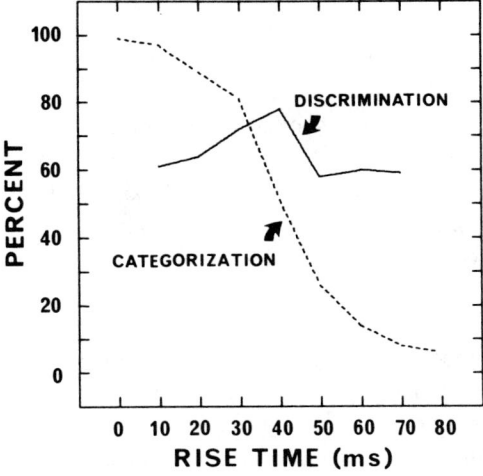

Figure 4.2. Categorization and discrimination functions obtained by Cutting and Rosner (1974) for two sawtooth pluck/bow continua. The curves shown are the mean of the two continua, which differed only in fundamental frequency. The pluck/bow distinction was cued by changes in the rise time or "attack" of the stimuli. The two curves are referred to the ordinate in a manner analogous to that described in Figure 4.1. (Redrawn using Table 1 of Cutting & Rosner [1974] and Table 1 of Macmillan, Kaplan, & Creelman [1977].)

those of the sawtooth stimuli. These sound less musiclike and are thus much less likely to call up previously learned categories. Discrimination and labeling tasks were run with both the sawtooth and sinusoidal stimuli. Again, results were categorical, impressively so for the sawtooth stimuli; less, but convincingly so, for the sinusoids.

The final blow to a learned-label explanation came from a study of two-month-old infants by Jusczyk et al. (1977). Using a high-amplitude sucking habituation technique, they measured the infants' ability to discriminate between pairs of stimuli drawn from the 440 Hz sawtooth rise-time continuum (see Chapter 5 by Eimas, Miller, & Jusczyk for details). Only stimuli labeled differently by adults (30 ms vs. 60 ms) were shown to be discriminated; stimuli from within the same adult categories (0 ms vs. 30 ms or 60 ms vs. 90 ms) were not.[5] It is rather farfetched, to say the least, to suppose that infants could somehow mediate their responses with a verbal label.

Although the original version of motor theory was helpless in the face of such data, not so its heirs apparent: theories of direct perception. Their first appearance in the pluck/bow saga was in a paper by Remez et al. (1980), who suggested that the categorical nature of rise-time perception might be directly related to the intrinsically categorical mechanical events of plucking and bowing. How such theories explain the perception of such unnatural stimuli as sinusoids (which are not very convincing as plucked and bowed strings, as noted by Cutting and Rosner) is not altogether clear, nor was an explanation attempted in that paper.

The importance of the claims made by Cutting and Rosner was immediately recognized and played an important role in the versions of the natural auditory sensitivities hypothesis put forward by Stevens (1981) and Pastore (1976). No progress in the understanding of the auditory basis of rise-time perception was made before Delgutte's (1980) attempts to find correlates for phonetic categories in the firing patterns of auditory nerve fibers. One possibility he suggested for the affricate/fricative distinction cued by rise time is based on the well-known rapid adaptation found in such fibers. When sounds with fast rises and sufficient amplitude are presented, the rate of nerve firing is highest at the start of the sound and decays quickly over 15 to 20 ms, and then more slowly (with a time constant of 30 to 45 ms) to a steady-state rate (Kiang, Watanabe, Thomas, & Clark, 1965). Delgutte compared the firing patterns for noise stimuli with rise times of 1 ms (said to be *CH*-like) and 40 ms (said to be *SH*-like). When presented at levels found in everyday speech, the fast initial decay was much more prominent to the *CH*-like stimulus than to the *SH*-like stimulus.

Because motor theory cannot accommodate Cutting and Rosner's findings, they have not been discussed extensively by its supporters (see Repp, Liberman, Eccardt, & Pesetsky, 1978, where the only reference to Cutting and Rosner's work concerns the general finding that rise time could be a cue in the affricate/fricative distinction; Dorman, Raphael, & Liberman, 1979, where Cutting and Rosner are not cited; although Dorman, Raphael, & Isenberg, 1980, do address the issue of whether rise time alone could serve to contrast affricates and fricatives, but not whether it is responsible for categorical perception of the continuum). This group of workers took an entirely different tack by attempting to show that the interaction of a number of different acoustic cues could only be explained by reference to articulation. Because those experiments do not directly address the problem of CP, we do not discuss them here (but see Chapter 1 by Pastore and Chapter 3 by Repp & Liberman, this volume). Two points are important, however. First, Delgutte (1982) provides a rationale for the interaction of two acoustically dissimilar cues on a purely *auditory* basis. Hence, complex-cue interaction need not necessarily involve articulatory reference. Second, none of the studies shows that the acoustic cues interact in production in exactly the same way they are shown to interact in perception (Howell & Rosen, 1983b). In fact, Howell and Rosen (1983c) have made acoustic measurements showing that the cue interaction necessary to account for some perceptual results is not the one actually found in production.

Some cause for doubt? So matters stood until 1979, when two reports hinted that things were not perhaps what they seemed with plucks and bows. Van Heuven and van den Broecke (1979) presented data indicating that the discriminability of rise times could be described by Weber's law. Sensitivity near 40 ms was not found to be significantly greater than at other rise times, as would be expected from Cutting and Rosner's results. They noted this discrepancy and attributed it to the latter's use of audio tape to record and present the stimuli. For a number of reasons, this paper had little impact vis-à-vis plucks and bows. First, the stimuli were sinusoids and white noise, not the sawtooths, which were shown to be the most strongly categorically perceived. Second, instead of the standard *ABX* format, a reproduction (analog) paradigm was used, in which listeners are required to adjust the rise time of

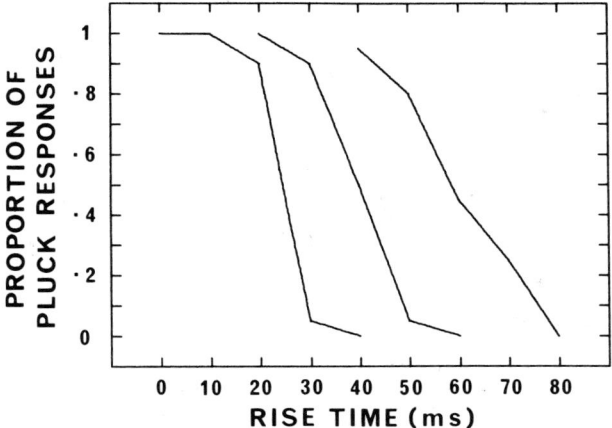

Figure 4.3. Categorization functions for three different subranges of a nonspeech rise-time continuum. (Redrawn from Figure 1 of Rosen [1981].)

one sound to match that of a test sound. Although the *ABX* task has its drawbacks, it has come to be the standard in investigations of CP. Even in psychophysical investigations, which van Heuven and van den Broecke's study resembled in spirit, the reproduction task is nowadays seldom used because discriminability can only be measured indirectly on the basis of the variability in the subjects' settings. Finally, the use of a reproduction paradigm introduced floor and ceiling effects in the results, as rise times cannot be shorter than 0 ms and were not longer than 103 ms. These limitations had a strong influence on the variability of the subjects' settings (and hence on the discriminability measure) at the short and long rise-time ends of the continuum. Thus, even accepting the assumptions underlying the use of subject variability as a discrimination measure, it is only in the middle range of rise times that this paradigm is reliable. Nevertheless, these results (at least in retrospect) provide some reason to reconsider Cutting and Rosner's (1974) results.

Work conducted in the same year pointed out that if a natural auditory sensitivity did underlie a sound contrast, category boundaries should not shift with a shift in the range of stimuli presented (Rosen, 1981). In fact, large differences in the categorization function were obtained when different subranges of sawtooth rise-time stimuli were used. Figure 4.3 shows that far from being a constant at about 40 ms, the boundary between plucks and bows is primarily determined by the range of stimuli presented, at approximately the middle of the continuum.

A direct failure to replicate. This last result sparked a series of investigations by us (Rosen & Howell, 1981). Our original aim was to see whether range manipulations would affect discrimination functions as dramatically as they affected categorization functions. Such a finding would strongly support a learned-label explanation for the categorical perception of plucks and bows, as unlikely as this seemed in the light of

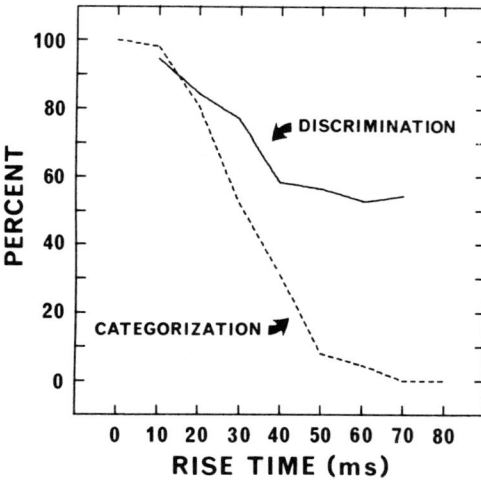

Figure 4.4. Categorization and discrimination functions for a rise-time continuum. The two curves are referred to the ordinate in a manner analogous to that described in Figure 4.1. (From Figure 1 of Rosen and Howell [1981].)

Cutting and Rosner's experiment in which discrimination preceded categorization. The obvious first step was to replicate Cutting and Rosner's basic result. We constructed a continuum of stimuli with rise times from 0 to 80 ms in 10-ms steps and ran the standard labeling and *ABX* discrimination tasks. There were some minor differences between our stimuli and those that Cutting and Rosner specified (see Rosen & Howell, 1981, for details), but nothing of the sort that would be likely to give "rise" to the unexpected results we obtained, shown in Figure 4.4.

No indication of CP is seen. Although the categorization function is steep, discrimination is best, not at the category boundary of about 30 ms, but at the shortest rise-time end of the continuum. As we have noted, van Heuven and van den Broecke (1979) had speculated that recording the stimuli, as Cutting and Rosner had done, would affect the results. We found, in fact, that tape recording had no effect on the shape of the discrimination function.

In view of the importance attached to Cutting and Rosner's results, we created another sawtooth rise-time continuum. These stimuli were much more closely modeled on the stimuli specified by Cutting and Rosner (1974). Categorization and discrimination tasks gave results similar to what we had obtained before: reasonably good categorization, and discrimination that was best at the short rise-time end of the continuum, worsening monotonically with increasing rise time.

Resolving the discrepancy. It seemed to us unlikely that the discrepancy between our results and those of Cutting and Rosner could be explained by any minor differences in stimulus construction, generation, or testing techniques. Cutting was as anxious as we were to clear up this mystery and so kindly loaned us the original experimental tapes. Using these, we were able to replicate the original result of a discrimination function peaked at 40 ms. This convinced us that our stimuli must have been significantly different from those used by Cutting and Rosner. We

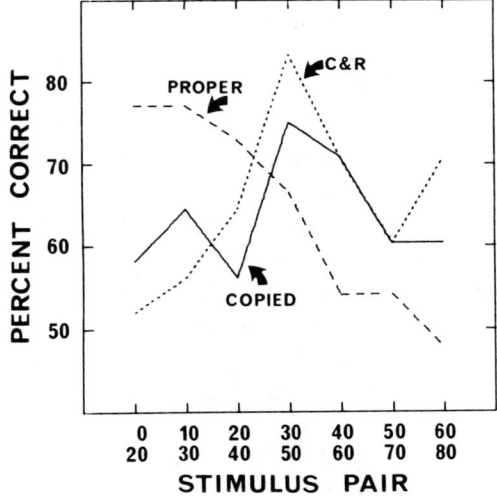

Figure 4.5. *ABX* discrimination results for three rise-time continua. The "PROPER" stimuli had the correct rise times, "C&R" stimuli were from the original tapes of Cutting and Rosner (1974), and the "COPIED" stimuli had the same rise times as those measured from the original Cutting and Rosner stimuli. (From Figure 6 of Rosen & Howell [1981].)

proceeded to make oscillograms of the original stimuli and to measure their rises. We found that the rise times of Cutting and Rosner's stimuli were not as specified. Instead of being equally spaced, the stimuli had the widest spacing at the point on the continuum where Cutting and Rosner found best discrimination.

We showed both theoretically and empirically that the rise times exhibited by Cutting and Rosner's original stimuli would lead to the results they obtained. Theoretically, we were able to describe the results obtained from our subjects and our stimuli (determined from oscillograms to have the correct rise times) with a simple model based on a Weber fraction that decreases with increasing rise time. This model, when applied to a continuum with the rise times we measured from Cutting and Rosner's stimuli, predicted a discrimination function peaked at 40 ms. Empirically, we were able to synthesize a continuum with the rise times of the original stimuli and to obtain from our subjects a discrimination function also peaked at 40 ms, as shown in Figure 4.5.

Our theoretical model also enabled us to explain the results obtained from infants by Jusczyk et al. (1977), who used Cutting and Rosner's stimuli plus one 90-ms rise-time stimulus not in the original set. Assuming the 90-ms stimulus to have approximately the proper rise time (as did the longer rise-time stimuli in the original set), we showed that the 30- to 60-ms pair was more discriminable than either the 0-30 ms or the 60- to 90-ms pair because of the unequal stimulus spacing. Thus the infants are "perceiving categorically" for the same reasons that the adults are.

For the sake of completeness we also synthesized a rise-time continuum of sinusoidal sounds (Rosen & Howell, 1983a). Perception was not categorical: Discrimination was best for stimuli with the shortest rise times, not for those straddling the category boundary.

In short, it is clear that nonspeech rise-time continua with a linear spacing of rise times are not categorically perceived, as has now been confirmed by Rosner (1981), Cutting (1982), Hary and Massaro (1982), and Kewley-Port and Pisoni (1984). Cutting (1982), however, has claimed that a sawtooth continuum with logarithmically spaced stimuli *is* categorically perceived. Such an effect of stimulus spacing is surprising and has not been reported before. Although it deserves further investigation, it can in no way be interpreted as a rescue of the natural-sensitivities hypothesis, as Kewley-Port and Pisoni measured discrimination using standard psychophysical techniques and found no indication of a midcontinuum peak in sensitivity. The Weber function they found was typical of that found for nearly all sensory continua. In any case, the effect of stimulus spacing is a side issue, as our interests are primarily in comparing results obtained from similar acoustic contrasts in speech and nonspeech (pluck/bow versus affricate/fricative) where it is only necessary to ensure that the stimulus spacing on all the continua compared be identical.

Reevaluating the three theories. These new findings clearly demand a reevaluation of the status of our three theories. Since the affricate/fricative distinction was found to be categorically perceived, and the pluck/bow continuum was not, the natural-sensitivities hypothesis is contradicted. It could be argued that such a sensitivity would only be found for stimuli more closely resembling fricative noises (e.g., white noise), although van Heuven and van den Broecke's (1979) results make this unlikely. Such tightly specified sensitivities also seem out of keeping with the general spirit of the theory in which general auditory processes are supposed. At best, then, this can only be considered a null result for such a theory.

Theories of direct perception are not supported either. Insofar as the stimuli are a good simulation of real-life plucks and bows, the discontinuous nature of the sound generating mechanism is not reflected at all in the perception of the sounds. Also, Remez (1978) synthesized a pluck-bow continuum with acoustic characteristics different from our rise-time continua and claimed it was categorically perceived. The existence of CP must therefore depend on the particular acoustic form of the stimuli, not on the imputed sound source.

A motor-theoretic explanation fares rather better. Its specific reference to an articulatory basis for perception gives it an advantage over its rather more general, but conceptually related direct-perception cousin in explaining why categorical perception of an acoustic contrast is dependent on its occurrence in a speech context.

Finally, learned-label explanations are also supported. We are presumably much more apt to use verbal labels for *cha*s and *sha*s than for "plucks" and "bows" due to our long experience with speech.

Taking another look at speech. Because the demonstration of CP for the voiceless affricate/fricative continuum is such a crucial factor in the evaluation of all the theories, we decided to reinvestigate this issue. Our initial attempts at synthesizing a continuum based on Cutting and Rosner's specifications foundered because stimuli

Auditory, articulatory, and learning explanations

with short rise times sounded unnatural. When we made some measurements of our own from oscillograms of the utterances of four speakers (samples of which can be found in Figure 4.6), we discovered two interesting things (Howell & Rosen, 1983a).

First, the rise times we measured were considerably longer than those reported by Gerstman. For sounds like the consonant-vowel (CV) pairs in isolation he used, affricates had a mean rise time of 56 ms whereas fricatives had a mean of 136 ms. The boundary of 40 ms proposed by Gerstman would have classified all but one of our utterances as fricatives. We were not able to determine the cause of this discrepancy, but we were able to replicate our own results with a number of different oscillographic techniques. Measurements from an average amplitude display of a spectrograph machine (the technique Gerstman used) were even longer than our original oscillographic measurements, as we expected (see Howell & Rosen, 1983a, for details), instead of shorter, as Gerstman found. In any case, we feel that oscillographic traces are a more accurate way to measure rise time, and furthermore, that using the rise times we determined led to much more natural-sounding stimuli. This means that the stimuli Delgutte (1980) used in his investigation of possible correlates of the voiceless affricate/fricative distinction in auditory-nerve-firing patterns (noises with rise times of 1 and 40 ms) were inappropriate. Sounds with more natural rise times would probably not lead to the highly discernible differences in the prominence of the fast initial decay in the firing patterns found with the unnatural stimuli.

Second, rise times for affricates and fricatives vary depending on the context in which they are spoken. Measurements from connected speech give rise times considerably shorter than those from nonsense syllables in isolation. For example, in word initial position, the mean rise time is 26 ms for affricates and 67 ms for fricatives. This means that a fixed auditory sensitivity, no matter what its value, could not serve to distinguish affricates from fricatives both in isolation and in running speech.

These measurements, in addition to their intrinsic interest, allowed us to synthesize a reasonably realistic voiceless affricate/fricative continuum. A natural /ʃɑ/ was recorded and stored digitally. Its rise time was 150 ms and its decay time was 46 ms. The continuum was created by contouring the fricative at various points in its initial rising phase to the point at which it reached its maximum. The 0-ms stimulus was created by removing all the frication before it reached its maximum. The stimulus with the 10-ms rise was created in two steps: First, the frication from the original onset of the stimulus to a point 10 ms before its maximum was excised. Then the frication of the first 10 ms of this new stimulus was contoured by multiplying it by a linear ramp that went from 0 to 1 over the 10 ms. The same technique of excising frication and ramping was applied a further 11 times to obtain stimuli with rises varying from 0 to 120 ms in 10-ms steps. Thus, the duration of the frication covaries with rise time as it does in natural speech and as it did in the synthetic continua used by Gerstman (1957) and Cutting and Rosner (1974). The only thing

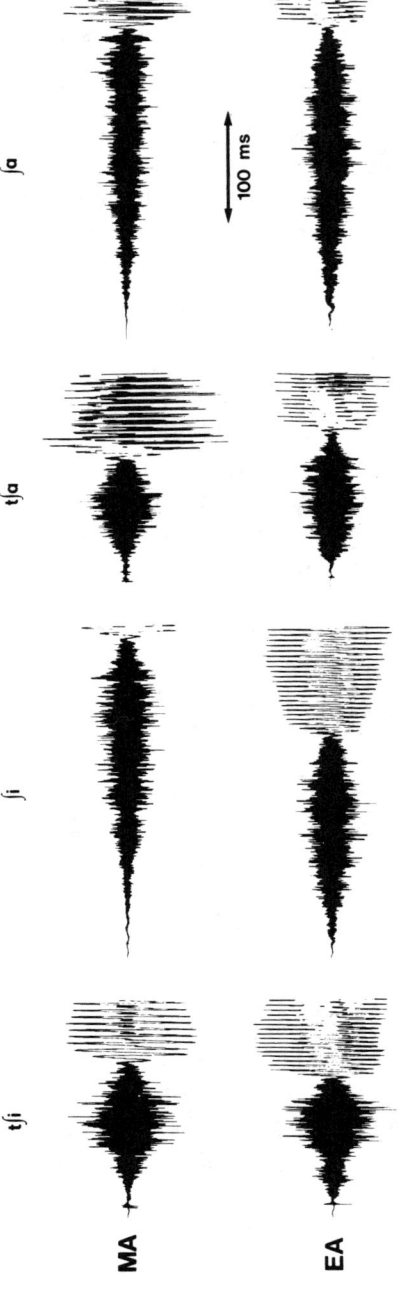

Figure 4.6. Oscillograms of four syllables (from left to right, *chee, she, chah, shah*) spoken by a man (MA) and a woman (EA). (From Figure 1 of Howell and Rosen [1983a].)

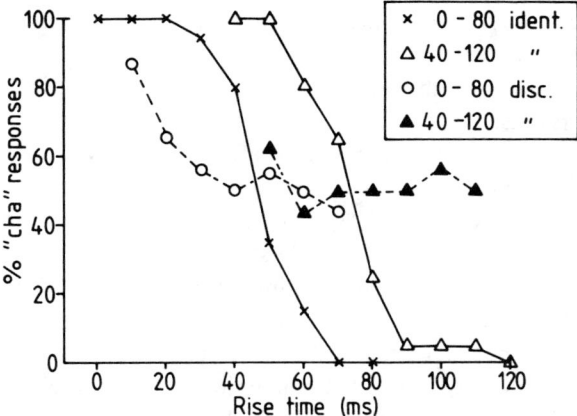

Figure 4.7. Categorization and discrimination functions (as identified in the inset) from two subranges of a /tʃa/ to /ʃa/ continuum cued by the rise time and duration of the initial frication. For the categorization functions, the ordinate gives the percentage of *cha* responses. For the discrimination function, the ordinate gives the percentage correct. (From Figure 12 of Howell & Rosen [1984].)

the continuum lacks in comparison to real speech is the presence of a release burst at the affricate end of the continuum. Even so, affricates are clearly heard for rise times around 40 ms. The total range of rise times was chosen to cover the unnatural range previously used by these other workers, as well as what we felt to be (and heard as) a more suitable range, 40 to 120 ms.

This continuum was used to investigate two of Cutting and Rosner's original claims (Howell & Rosen, 1984). First, our production measurements show that for isolated CVs, affricates are optimally distinguished from fricatives by a boundary anywhere between 74 and 83 ms in rise time. Why, then, should Cutting and Rosner have found a phoneme boundary of about 45 ms of rise time? Could it be that the phoneme boundary is determined by the subrange of stimuli used, as we found for the pluck/bow continuum? Second, is the affricate/fricative continuum categorically perceived for the range of rise times, 0 to 80 ms? Rosner (1981) already reported that a synthetic continuum with rise times from 5 to 65 ms in 10-ms steps was not categorically perceived, but we also wanted to know whether the continuum would be categorically perceived for the realistic range of rise times, 40 to 120 ms.

Standard identification and *ABX* discrimination tasks were performed separately on the two subranges, 0 to 80 ms and 40 to 120 ms. The mean results from two subjects are shown in Figure 4.7. The phoneme boundary is strongly influenced by the range of stimuli used, being placed roughly at the midpoint of the stimulus range. The boundary of 45 ms that Cutting and Rosner found is thus consistent with their 0- to 80-ms range. Furthermore, neither one of the ranges of stimuli is categorically perceived. For the 0- to 80-ms range, performance is best for the shortest rise times and decreases montonically with increasing rise time in a way similar to that found for the nonspeech pluck/bow continuum. For the 40- to 120-ms range, the discrimination function is quite flat. In neither case is there any evidence of a discrimination peak at the phoneme boundary.

With the benefit of hindsight, there are a number of reasons to suspect Cutting and Rosner's (1974) results. For one thing, there is the matter of the close correspondence between the phoneme boundary for the affricate/fricative continuum and the category boundary for plucks and bows. It is now clear that this is primarily due to range effects (see Howell & Rosen, 1983a, for a discussion of why they are not identical). But it was already known from Gerstman's work that affricates and fricatives could be distinguished both by rise time and by overall duration. (Van Heuven, 1983, has in fact made a strong case, based on Gerstman's data, that the overall duration cue is dominant.) Because the base duration of the frication was about 100 ms, the changes in the overall duration of the frication caused by the rises (up to 80 ms) would have been highly discriminable. Not so for the sawtooth stimuli, with their base duration of about 1 s. Thus, as the sawtooths were judged only by rise time, and the frication noises by a combination of rise time and duration, why should the outcome have been so similar in the two cases?

Also, a close examination of Figures 4.1 and 4.2 shows that the endpoint stimuli of the pluck/bow continua were categorized more accurately than the corresponding speech stimuli, in which no stimulus reached 100% identifications as affricate or fricative. One reason for this could be the inappropriate rise times, although our results in Figure 4.7 show that it is possible to get good categorization functions even with this range of rise times. What may be of greater importance in such synthetic sounds is the lack of sensible formant transitions between values appropriate for the fricative noise and the steady-state values of the vowel. When such transitions are missing, one hears, in addition to the appropriate fricative and vowel, an extra noise dissociated from the flow of speech. Such effects are common in the outputs of speech-synthesis-by-rule systems, and are sometimes termed "fricative splitting." The general phenomenon has been extensively studied in nonspeech (see Bregman & MacAdams, 1979, for a review) and is known as "stream segregation." Although it is possible to label such "streamed" sounds reasonably appropriately (especially when given exemplars), the percept is hardly natural. A technique based on modifications of natural syllables (as described above) would obviously not be subject to such difficulties, nor would syntheses that incorporated natural formant transitions between the fricative and the vowel.

Summing up. In summary, rise time is not perceived categorically, whether it is cueing a pluck/bow or an affricate/fricative distinction.[6] Because the categorical perception of the affricate/fricative continuum was taken as evidence in favor of motor and learning theories, it is perhaps too much to expect that noncategorical perception should be taken as evidence against them. In fact, motor theory could adequately explain the results if there were some way in which an independent determination of the extent to which articulation was categorical could be made. At present, the theory is completely retrospective in character: Continua that are categorically perceived must have discrete articulatory gestures; those that are not, must not. Intuition may be sufficient to suppose that the categorical perception of place continua arises from discrete articulatory gestures; it hardly seems adequate for the affricate/fricative distinction. (For a further discussion of this general issue, see our discussion of the motor-theoretic "explanation" in relation to voicing.)

Theories that posit that the learning of labels is responsible for CP need to explain its absence even in the presence of well-learned labels in speech.

Finally, as regards the natural-auditory-sensitivities hypothesis, these findings only weigh against claims that *all* phonemic contrasts are so mediated. A less extreme version of the theory, in which it is only supposed that *some* phonemic contrasts are based on auditory sensitivities, gets neither support nor refutation here. What is most striking is the similarity of results from the speech and nonspeech continua, implying that although auditory sensitivities may not be present, the perception of the speech sounds is strongly influenced by general auditory processes.

The voicing distinction in initial plosives

In contrast to the voiceless affricate/fricative distinction, with its rather unstable empirical base, we now come to consider plosive voicing, where at least some of the findings have remained secure after many years and many replications. In particular, there is no doubt that speech continua ranging from a phonemically voiced to a voiceless plosive are categorically perceived.

The $F1$-cutback continuum. Although most studies of the voicing contrast use variations in VOT (as described earlier in our chapter) to create a continuum, the first demonstration of CP for voicing in initial plosives (Liberman, Harris, Kinney, & Lane, 1961) used a different, but related, manipulation – $F1$ cutback. This acoustic feature is based on an interaction between the time of onset of voicing, its spectrum, and the spectrum of the aspiration noise that appears after the release of plosives with a positive VOT. Aspiration noise has relatively little energy at the low frequencies where $F1$ is found. Although the upper formants (excited by aspiration) are present from the release of the plosive, $F1$ does not appear strongly until voicing, with its strong low-frequency components, starts. It turns out that this acoustic cue is sufficient for the distinction and it is thus possible to synthesize voiced and voiceless plosives without using any aspiration, simply by varying the onset time of $F1$ relative to the upper formants. In English, sounds with simultaneous onsets of all formants are labeled *voiced*, while sounds with the onset of $F1$ significantly delayed are labeled *voiceless*.

Liberman, Harris, Kinney, and Lane demonstrated CP for a /do/ to /to/ continuum created by progressively delaying the onset of the first formant relative to the upper formants from 0 to 60 ms in 10-ms steps. A nonspeech control condition was also included in which the pattern playback schematic spectrograms (used to generate the sounds) were turned upside down and further modified before use. These were not heard as speech and resulted in a continuum in which the third and highest formant had its onset delayed relative to the two lower formants. Strictly speaking, it is not possible to say whether perception of the nonspeech stimuli was categorical or not, as they were not presented for labeling, only in the *ABX* discrimination paradigm. Discrimination performance for these stimuli was much inferior to that obtained for the speech stimuli, however, and it was concluded that (assuming the control to be fair) the performance obtained with speech could be interpreted as an example of distinctiveness acquired through learning.

Another nonspeech analog to F1 cutback – a reanalysis. Liberman, Harris, Kinney, and Lane also compared their results to those obtained by Hirsh (1959) with sounds that can also be considered a nonspeech control for the $F1$ cutback stimuli. Two claims were made by Liberman et al.: First, that the overall performance exhibited by Hirsh's subjects judging the nonspeech continuum was inferior to subjects judging the speech continuum in Liberman's tests, and second, that the speech-discrimination functions were peaked, unlike the discrimination functions from nonspeech.

Hirsh investigated the ability of subjects to tell which of two sinusoids of different frequencies started first for a range of relative onset times varying from -60 to $+60$ ms (i.e., from the low-frequency tone leading the high-frequency tone by 60 ms, to the high leading the low by 60 ms) in 10-ms steps. Figure 4.8 shows the average results from a set of five such continua.

Note that this curve is really nothing other than a labeling function. Liberman, Harris, Kinney, and Lane (1961) seemed to have misinterpreted it as a discrimination function. They compare Hirsh's finding of 75% correct performance with relative-onset times of about 17 ms with their own finding of 75% correct performance in an *ABX* task with less than 12 ms difference between the *AB* pair in time of onset on the $F1$ cutback continuum. Only the speech-categorization functions can be properly compared with Hirsh's results, a comparison that, in fact, leads to much stronger support for the assertion by Liberman's group of acquired distinctiveness for the speech sounds. They state that "in every case a change of 10 msec in the first-formant cutback is sufficient to shift the responses from 75% /d/ to 75% /t/," whereas Hirsh's data show that a change of about 35 ms in relative-onset time is necessary to shift the responses from 75% "low leads high" to 75% "high leads low."

A more complicated analysis is needed to address the second claim of Liberman, Harris, Kinney, and Lane: "One finds in Hirsh's results no indication of the sharp peaks so clearly evident in the discrimination functions of the present experiment." This is equivalent to looking for sharp peaks in the speech-labeling functions. We can, however, transform Hirsh's data into a form closer to Liberman et al.'s discrimination function under some simple and fairly reasonable assumptions (Rosen

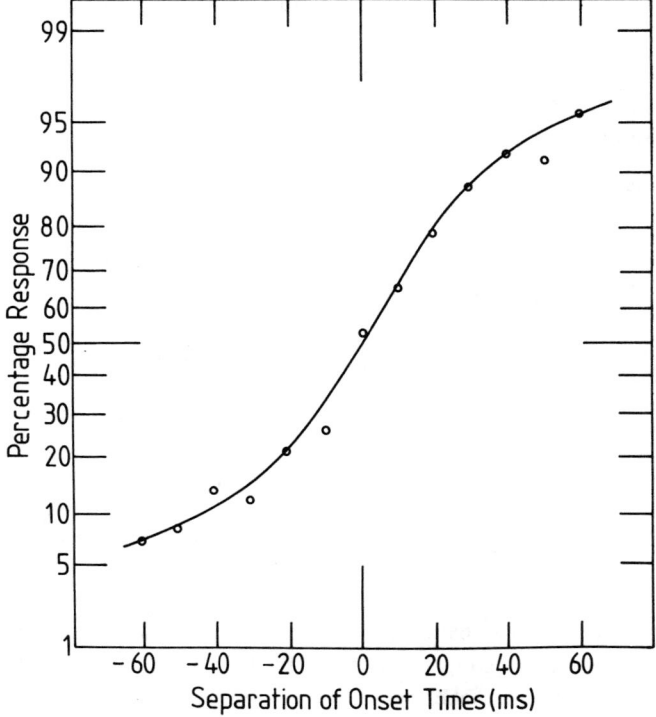

Figure 4.8. Mean results obtained by Hirsh (1959) from a task requiring the judgment of the relative order of onset of two tones. Points to the right of 0 on the abscissa indicate that the higher tone led the lower. Points to the left of 0 indicate that the lower tone led the higher. The ordinate indicates the percentage of times the subject reported that the high tone led the low. The smooth curve is fitted by eye to the original data points. (Selectively redrawn from Figure 4 of Hirsh [1959] to include only those points that deal with two-tone stimulus complexes.)

& Howell, 1983b).[7] Figure 4.9 shows the discrimination function predicted from Hirsh's data for a two-step (20-ms difference) *ABX* task.

Here we see another confirmation of Liberman, Harris, Kinney, and Lane's assertion that performance with the speech continuum is far superior to that obtained with nonspeech. For a 20-ms difference in relative-onset time, we predict that Hirsh's subjects would obtain, at best, 61% correct in an *ABX* discrimination task. Liberman et al.'s subjects, as noted, had about 75% correct with differences of slightly less than 12 ms. (Some of these differences may be attributable to differences in subject-selection procedures. Liberman et al. selected the best 11 of 20 subjects. Hirsh makes no explicit statement and seems to have used whatever subjects were available. As we shall see later, it is possible to obtain much better performances from listeners than Hirsh did.)

On the other hand, it is clear that the discrimination function is significantly peaked, contrary to the assertions by Liberman's group. Under the assumptions we

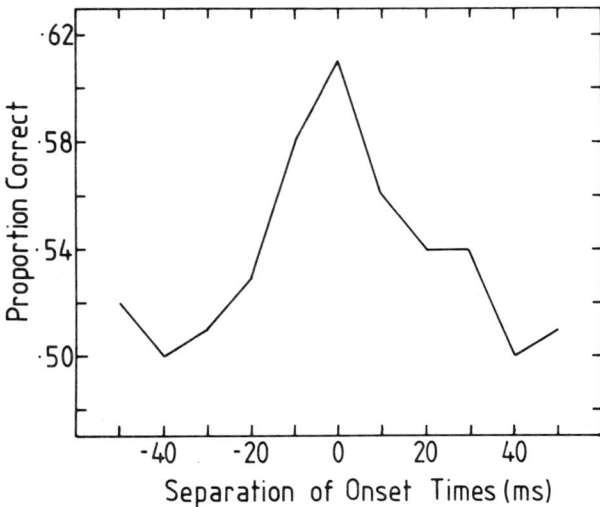

Figure 4.9. *ABX* discrimination results for stimuli varying in relative tone-onset time predicted from the data in Figure 4.8. See text and note 7 for details.

have made, predicted discrimination performance is simply a monotonic transformation of the derivative of the labeling curve. The discrimination peak is therefore a reflection of the fact that the labeling function is steepest at its center and visibly flattens towards its edges, as clearly seen in Figure 4.8.

This result might be expected if Weber's law described the discrimination of relative onset time. Remember that our predictions for discrimination were based on a fixed 20-ms difference between stimuli; if the difference limen for relative-onset time was proportional to the magnitude of the relative-onset time (as Weber's law states), then the constant 20-ms change should lead to best performance at the shortest relative-onset times (i.e., simultaneity), which decreases monotonically with increasing relative-onset time, just as we have shown. This also implies that the original labeling function (Figure 4.8) should be more linear under a logarithmic transformation of the relative-onset-time axis. We leave out consideration of 0-ms relative-onset time, as this value cannot be log-transformed. Taking advantage of the symmetry of Hirsh's results around 0 ms, we averaged the absolute values of the normal deviates corresponding to performance at each of the six onset times from 10 to 60 ms. (In other words, we average the performance at −10 ms with that of 10 ms, −20 ms with that of 20 ms, and so on.) These values are plotted as a function of linear and log relative-onset time in Figure 4.10.

With the linear scaling on the left of Figure 4.10, we see the curvature of the function already displayed in Figure 4.8: a decreasing slope with increasing onset time. When the stimuli are plotted on a logarithmic scale, however, the slope of the curve seems to remain constant out to the longest times measured. This is further support for the notion that Weber's law holds for these stimuli.

Auditory, articulatory, and learning explanations 141

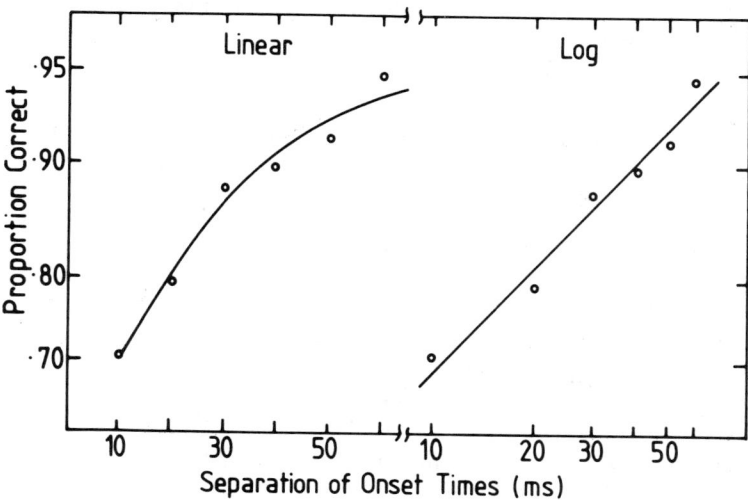

Figure 4.10. Linear and logarithmic scaling of the transformed data points of Figure 4.8 as a function of the absolute value of the separation of onset times. The value for a separation of 0 ms is not used because it cannot be logarithmically scaled. The smooth curve on the left is fitted by eye to the data points; that on the right is a least-squares straight-line fit. (See text for further details.)

Our reanalysis of Hirsh's data, although it has thrown up some surprises, in no way impugns the substance of what Liberman, Harris, Kinney, and Lane (1961) were saying. As we have noted, performance with the speech sounds is much better than that obtained for nonspeech. Furthermore, even though Hirsh's data may, contrary to the assertions by Liberman's group, indicate the possibility of discrimination peaks, they are not, at 0 ms, in the same place as the peaks for the speech continuum, at about 20 to 30 ms.

The motor-theoretic "explanation": What does it really mean? Originally brought to bear on the issue of innate versus learned phoneme boundaries, and of acquired distinctiveness versus similarity, the results with the $F1$ cutback continuum were soon subsumed into the data base purported to support the motor theory (Liberman, Cooper, Harris, & MacNeilage, 1963; Liberman et al., 1967). As Liberman et al. (1967) wrote:

The categorical perception of stop consonants also supports [the] . . . assumption [that] . . . the listener uses the inconstant sound as a basis for finding his way back to the articulatory gestures that produced it and thence, as it were, to the speaker's intent. . . . As described earlier in this paper, perception of these sounds is categorical, or discontinuous, even when the acoustic signal is varied continuously. Quite obviously, the required articulations would also be discontinuous. (P. 453)

It is just as "obvious," however, that the voiceless affricate/fricative distinction would require discontinuous articulations, and yet it is not, as we have seen, categorically perceived. It is interesting to note that in elaborations of the motor-theoretic explanation of CP, the intuitively appealing place continuum is always used as an example (see the discussion in the article by Liberman et al. following the paragraph quoted above). Never has there appeared an explanation of what is necessarily discontinuous about the plosive voicing distinction. Such an explanation may be possible, but no satisfactory definition of the "categorical nature" of production exists. In fact, we doubt that it is possible to construct a definition that will predict categorical perception of plosive voicing.

Let us consider some possibilities. We might take the view that continua are only categorically perceived when it is impossible for a speaker (of any language) to make articulations intermediate between those that are responsible for the endpoints of the acoustic continuum. This viewpoint might be considered consonant with comments by Liberman et al. (1963):

Consider the case of /b,d,g/. The appropriate acoustic cues occupy different positions along a single acoustic continuum (extent of second-formant transition), but they are produced by very different articulations. Thus /b/ is produced by a movement of the lips and /d/ by a movement of the tongue. Given the discontinuous articulation, we should expect, in spite of the continuous nature of the acoustic variations, that the perception would be discontinuous (i.e., categorical), and that a discrimination peak would appear at the phoneme boundary. There are no intermediate articulations between /b/ and /d/, and, as a consequence, no intermediate perceptions. (P. 4)

There is a serious problem in applying this idea to the initial-position plosive-voicing continuum. If we look across languages as Lisker and Abramson (1964) did, we see that human vocal tracts can produce intermediate articulations between, say, an English /b/ and /p/. Interestingly, their measurements of voice onset time (VOT), summed across a number of languages, show a relative scarcity of occurrences of VOTs in the range between about −25 and 0 ms. Therefore, under this definition of articulatory discontinuity, we should expect CP effects to be centered on a boundary somewhere in this region. This would be fine for speakers of Spanish and Tamil, but would be completely inappropriate for English speakers, whose boundary for production (and perception) lies above 0 ms. Also, unlike the /b/ versus /d/ contrast, the articulators responsible for these sounds are presumably identical across the entire VOT continuum.

Therefore, it cannot simply be a matter of what vocal tracts can and cannot do. Furthermore, it would perhaps be a caricature of motor theory to suppose that this is what its creators had in mind, especially given their early stand that the discrimination peaks evidenced for categorically perceived continua are a result of learning (Liberman et al., 1963). Perhaps we can only map sounds onto articulations that we actually produce or have heard? If so, we might expect to gain relevant data from bilinguals proficient in languages that use different boundaries on a VOT continuum for distinguishing voiced from voiceless plosives. Spanish and English provide a convenient pair as, for a bilabial continuum, the English phoneme boundary occurs at about 25 ms of VOT, considerably longer than the Spanish boundary of about −4 to −10 ms (Williams, 1977). If Spanish/English bilingual listeners can refer perceived sounds to all their available productions, we should expect them to evidence broad discrimination peaks covering the boundary regions appropriate for both languages.

Williams (1977) obtained quite a different result. She presented the Abramson and Lisker (1970, 1973) bilabial VOT continuum to eight Spanish/English bilinguals in both labeling and same-different discrimination paradigms. Most of the subjects showed little ability to discriminate between stimuli drawn from the prevoicing region. Of the three who are said by Williams to have broad discrimination functions covering the range between the Spanish and English boundaries, only one exhibits a discrimination ability at −20 ms as good as that shown by the Spanish monolinguals. This is especially telling in light of measurements of the same subjects' productions of both Spanish and English words. Spanish words had VOTs indistinguishable from those produced by Spanish monolinguals, as did the English words with voiceless plosives compared with those from English monolinguals. The only difference between the monolinguals and the bilinguals was in the production of English voiced plosives, where it was found that the bilinguals used more prevoicing than monolinguals. Thus, perception *did not* follow production.

Also, it would be wrong to think that by restricting consideration to only one language, measured VOTs would then group themselves into two nonoverlapping categories. Williams's (1977) measurements of English productions show a considerable overlapping of categories, as does Lisker and Abramson's (1967) analysis of plosives in sentence material. Therefore, even within a single language community, a range of VOTs is produced and heard.

Finally, we might consider a definition in which the relevant articulatory gestures must also be *phonemically* distinct (that is, must differentially signal meaning differences within a language). Support for the inclusion of some sort of phonemic component comes from the well-known cross-language studies (see Williams, 1977), which show both the phoneme boundaries of labeling functions and the peaks of discrimination functions to be strongly dependent on language experience. Other support comes from a study of Spanish/English bilinguals by Elman, Diehl, and Buchwald (1977), who (unlike Williams, the difference probably being attributable to methodological differences, see footnote 10 for further details) were able to show the effect of language set on the perception of a naturally produced labial VOT continuum. Although Elman et al. did not do a discrimination experiment, their results only make sense from a motor-theoretic point of view if the reference to articulation is through the phonemic system of the particular language the listener is set for, an easy choice for the monolingual. On the other hand, Pisoni, Aslin, Perey, and Hennessy (1982) have shown that monolingual English subjects readily and accurately label phonetic contrasts in the prevoicing region of a VOT continuum (an intraphonemic distinction for English listeners). This phoneme-based definition also leads to problems in the interpretation of an early study of the perception of the voicing of intervocalic labial plosives.

Liberman, Harris, Eimas, Lisker, and Bastian (1961) created a "rabid" to "rapid" continuum by varying from 20 to 130 ms the interval of silence between the two syllables. Relatively short periods of silence led to the perception of "rabid" while long periods led to the perception of "rapid." The stimuli were presented for labeling and *ABX* discrimination. Comparisons were made between the obtained discrimination performance and that predicted from identification under the assumption that discrimination is limited by the ability to identify (using the standard Haskins formula). The discrimination functions calculated from identification predicted successfully the occurrence of a peak in performance at about 70 ms, but failed to predict a secondary peak at about 100 ms. Liberman, Harris, Eimas, Lisker, and Bastian claimed that stimuli with the longest durations of silence did not sound like ordinary /p/s. "This was a strange and unnatural /p/ to American ears, but we thought it might nevertheless be heard *and articulated by our listeners almost as if it were a different speech entity*" (p. 186, emphasis ours). All of the subjects still available were recalled and asked to identify the stimuli once again, only this time using three labels: /b/, /p/, and */p/, the last being the "unnatural /p/."[8] Discrimination functions predicted from these data had both of the peaks actually obtained. In short, in order to explain their data, Liberman's group was forced to posit that their subjects could produce (and hence perceive) contrasts that were *nonphonemic* in their own language, in contradiction to the definition we have been considering. If English subjects can perceive nonphonemic distinctions in this case, why do they not do likewise for VOT continua, perceiving distinctions in the extreme lag or prevoicing region?

One way to maintain that only phonemic contrasts are perceived is by supposing that the unnatural [p]s were not heard as speech sounds at all, but as nonspeech. The peak in the discrimination function could then be considered as resulting from this speech/nonspeech boundary, with sounds to the left of the boundary being interpreted in articulatory terms and those to the right in purely auditory terms. This, however, leads to difficulties in accounting for the fact that obtained discrimination performance is superior to that predicted from labeling performance. Liberman, Harris, Eimas, Lisker, and Bastian suggest that this superiority might be the result of articulatory movements varying slightly (rather than remaining constant) within the range of stimuli on the continuum that constitute a phoneme class. This explanation may be adequate when the two sounds to be compared are heard as speech; it is not satisfactory when one of the sounds is interpreted as speech and one as nonspeech. It is presumably irrelevant what particular articulatory configuration is responsible for the speech sound if the other sound is nonspeech. Yet in this region (where one stimulus has a gap 110 ms or above and the other below) obtained discrimination is still better than predicted.[9]

There may be other approaches to the problem of defining articulatory discontinuity that we have not considered here. In any case, such considerations were not responsible for the motor theorists' abandonment of the facts of CP as a fruitful source of supportive data.

Categorical perception of nonspeech analogs to voicing continua. The real blow to the motor theory came from a series of studies showing CP for nonspeech continua. Only two of these need concern us here (Miller, Weir, Pastore, Kelly, & Dooling 1976; Pisoni, 1977), both of which used continua that had some acoustic feature in common with voicing continua.

Miller et al. used a bandpass noise (900 to 2700 Hz) and buzz (100 Hz train of 1-ms pulses bandpass filtered at 500 to 3000 Hz) and varied the onset of the noise relative to the onset of the constant-duration buzz. A continuum of sounds was created whose endpoints were the noise starting after the buzz by 10 ms and the noise leading the buzz by 80 ms. Labeling and discrimination experiments showed this continuum to be categorically perceived to the same extent as Abramson and Lisker's (1970) VOT continuum. Thus, CP was not restricted to speech and hence could not depend on an articulatory referent.

The nonspeech F1-cutback continuum revisited. Pisoni (1977) used a similar continuum, but one more closely modeled on Hirsh's (1959) stimuli. Here two tones were used, at 500 and 1500 Hz, and their relative-onset times varied from −50 to +50 ms. Again, labeling and discrimination results showed a pattern clearly indicative of CP. Surprisingly, given Hirsh's results, the category boundary obtained from the labeling task was not at simultaneity (0 ms relative-onset time), as discussed above, but rather in the region where the high tone led the low by about 20 ms.

There are a number of differences between Hirsh's and Pisoni's studies that may be responsible for this discrepancy. Some minor differences in the stimuli do not seem to account for the differences in results (see Rosen & Howell, 1983b, for the details). Likely to be of more importance are the differences in the task set the subjects, which may have caused them to attend to different aspects of the stimulus complex. Hirsh asked his listeners to identify which of the two tones came first, instructions that favor a category boundary at simultaneity. Pisoni trained his listeners to respond differentially to the endpoints of the continuum, and gave no verbal labels for the important stimulus characteristics. Differences in the nature of the feedback given to the listeners may also be important. Hirsh makes no explicit statement about feedback in the original paper, but informs us (personal communication) that none was ever given. Pisoni's subjects only received feedback in initial training with stimuli at relatively extreme positions on the continuum.

This training is probably responsible for Pisoni's subjects' evidencing much better performance than Hirsh's, although detailed comparisons are difficult to make, as Hirsh presents group data and Pisoni presents data for each subject individually. Even so, Hirsh's subjects never do better than a 95% correct labeling of the order of the tones, even when there is 60 ms between the two onsets, whereas all of Pisoni's subjects show perfect or nearly perfect performance for onset asynchronies of ±50 ms. In fact, Pisoni's best five (of eight) listeners show an accuracy in both labeling and discrimination at least roughly equivalent to that evidenced by those eleven listeners (of twenty) selected by Liberman, Harris, Kinney, & Lane (1961) to judge speech sounds.

It is important to resolve these serious discrepancies, especially in the light of common misinterpretations of what Hirsh's data actually show. We have already noted that these were taken to support a "speech is special" notion (Liberman, Harris, Kinney, & Lane, 1961); now we see them supporting the opposite view. The basic misinterpretation has to do with the nature of a psychometric function. Hirsh found performance in his experiments to vary smoothly with increasing onset separations, and, as is commonly done, chose the 75% correct point to summarize his data. Thus he concluded that 17 ms are needed to resolve the order of events. He could just as well have picked 60%, giving about 5 ms as the crucial time, or, perhaps more appropriately for linguistic use (to ensure more reliable reception), 90%, giving about 30 ms. None of these choices is preordained. There is, therefore, no reason to suppose that discriminability between stimuli will be better around 17 ms, and indeed, Hirsh's data show no sign of this.

This characterization is too crude to do justice to at least some of the arguments advanced as to why one might find discontinuities in the perception of a tone-onset time continuum. Miller et al. (1976), in a discussion of Hirsh's experiment, suppose that distinct percepts occur as one increases the separation of the two onsets: "Thus, as the amount by which the high tone precedes the low is increased, perceptual boundaries or thresholds are crossed corresponding to the perceptual effects of nonsimultaneity, Gestalt sequence with obvious ordering, and ordered onsets of two distinct percepts . . . one would expect to find perturbations in the Weber fraction at the perceptual boundaries'' (p. 415). However, Hirsh's data show a smooth increase in subjects' accuracy with increasing onset separation with no evidence of a discontinuity. Even Pisoni's data show only one main discrimination peak where three might be expected.

Further evidence for auditory sensitivities from animals. However these problems are eventually solved, both Miller et al.'s and Pisoni's data showed convincingly that CP was not unique to speech sounds. Furthermore, the only sensible interpretation of such demonstrations was that it resulted from natural sensitivities that were purely auditory. From this position, it was only a short hop to the claim that the categorical perception of *speech* sounds was underpinned by auditory discontinuities. Strong supporting evidence along these lines came from a series of studies investigating the perception of VOT continua by chinchillas, members of the rodent family. Kuhl and Miller (1975; 1978; Chapter 12 by Kuhl, this volume) trained these animals to respond differentially to the endpoints of synthetic VOT continua constructed for three places of articulation: bilabial, alveolar, and velar. All continua spanned VOTs of 0 to 80 ms in 10-ms steps, and each continuum was tested separately. After the animals reached a criterion performance of 96% correct for four consecutive days on the endpoint stimuli alone, generalization testing occurred in which all the possible stimuli on the particular continuum being tested occurred. This technique results in a labeling function for a VOT continuum that is completely analogous to the labeling functions obtained from human listeners.

A comparison between the functions obtained by the animal and adult human listeners showed only minor differences. In particular, those obtained from the humans were slightly, but statistically significantly, steeper than those obtained from the chinchillas. More important, no cross-species differences were found for the absolute values of the category boundaries. The position of the boundary varied with place of articulation for both human and chinchilla listeners in the way expected from results obtained by Lisker and Abramson (1970): highest for the velar continuum (about 42 ms), lowest for the bilabial continuum (about 25 ms), with the alveolar boundary in between (about 34 ms). It was thus concluded that the position of *human* phoneme boundaries on these continua was auditorily determined.

Such results, as striking as they are, still do not directly address the issue of CP, as no measure of discrimination performance was obtained. This was supplied in a further study by Kuhl (1981), who investigated chinchillas' abilities to discriminate stimuli from an alveolar VOT continuum presented in a same-different paradigm. The just-noticeable-difference (jnd) in VOT was smallest for stimuli near the previously determined boundary. Thus the complete complement of results indicative of CP had been obtained from a nonlinguistic species.

Range effects in animals and their interpretation. Waters and Wilson (1976) also investigated the perception of VOT continua by nonhuman mammals (rhesus monkeys), but obtained rather less clearcut results. Again, animals were trained to respond differentially to the endpoints of the continuum before presenting midcontinuum stimuli. Three important results were obtained. First, the category boundaries always occurred in the voicing-lag region of the continuum, in agreement with the findings of Kuhl and Miller. Second, the category boundaries were highly dependent on the range of stimuli presented. A labial continuum spanning -140 to 140 ms had a mean boundary of about 28 ms, whereas the same continuum spanning 0 to 140 ms had a mean boundary of about 66 ms. This is difficult to explain if, as Kuhl and Miller suppose, auditory discontinuities are responsible for the positions of the category boundaries. Finally, the velar continuum spanning 0 to 140 ms had a boundary at 56 ms, slightly less than that obtained for the labial continuum spanning the same range, in direct contradiction to what Kuhl and Miller found.

Kuhl (1979) argued that the boundary shift with a change in stimulus range obtained by Waters and Wilson might well be due only to sampling error. She did not address the discrepancy between their results and hers with regard to the relative positions of the boundaries on the velar and labial continua. Although sampling error may be a reasonable explanation here, the boundary shift in the previous case is some 37 ms, which makes sampling error an unlikely account. In fact, Waters and Wilson's findings are easily understood by looking at the details of their procedure. Let us take their Phase 1 as an example. The animal is first trained on the endpoints of the continuum, −140 ms and +140 ms VOT. The monkey must shuttle over a barrier when the "go" stimulus is presented (here with a VOT of +140 ms) and remain in the chamber of the two-compartment shuttlebox when the "no-go" stimulus is presented (here with a VOT of −140 ms). Failure to execute the correct behavior results in a brief shock applied to the grid floor.

After reaching criterion performance, "boundary testing" with intermediate stimuli commenced. Five stimuli were possible, having VOTs of +140, +70, 0, −70, and −140 ms. On each day of testing, subjects were retrained on the endpoint stimuli (−140 and 140) and then received 40 trials with one of the ten possible pairs of the five stimuli. The stimulus closer to +140-ms VOT was the "go" stimulus and the other was the "no-go." Interpreted in terms of a labeling task with human listeners, we require the subjects to redefine *ba* and *pa* each day. In other words, we force the subjects (through electric shocks!) to move their boundaries to a point between the particular pair of stimuli chosen. On average, of course, the boundary will be at the midpoint of the range. Such a procedure will clearly cause boundaries to shift dramatically with changes in the range of stimuli used, as Waters and Wilson found.

Kuhl and Miller used a procedure whereby only responses to the endpoint stimuli were maintained: Responses to intermediate stimuli were treated as correct no matter what the animal did. The chinchillas were thus relatively "free," as it were, to define their own boundaries in a way the monkeys were not. This explains why Waters and Wilson found the boundary for the labial continuum to occur at the nearly midcontinuum value of 66 ms (for a continuum spanning 0 to +140 ms) whereas Kuhl and Miller found a boundary of 23 ms (for the range 0 to 80 ms). When the "natural" boundary is not too far from the middle of the continuum, it is not shifted about excessively by Waters and Wilson's procedures. Hence, reasonable boundary values are obtained when a span of −140 to 140 ms of VOT is used. When the endpoints of the stimuli are brought closer, however, spanning −100 to 120 ms, the boundary is more tightly constrained to be near 0, and is thus found to be 11.5 ms instead of the 22 to 35 ms found with the −140 to 140 ms range. Such processes also explain why Waters and Wilson found no significant difference between the boundaries obtained from labial and velar continua. Their procedure forces the boundary to midcontinuum, nullifying any possible differences. Kuhl and Miller found the boundary to shift by nearly 20 ms across these two continua. A rough analog to what Waters and Wilson did can be found in a study by Carney, Widin, and Viemeister (1977), who showed that human subjects can assign consistent labels to arbitrary subsets of VOT when so instructed. In other words, they too evidence large boundary shifts under the appropriate conditions.

In summary, it is possible to demonstrate categorical perception both of non-speech sounds by human listeners, and of speech sounds by animal listeners. Therefore, it need not involve specifically linguistic behavior (as claimed by the motor theorists), nor the learning of appropriate labels. Purely auditory processes can be responsible.

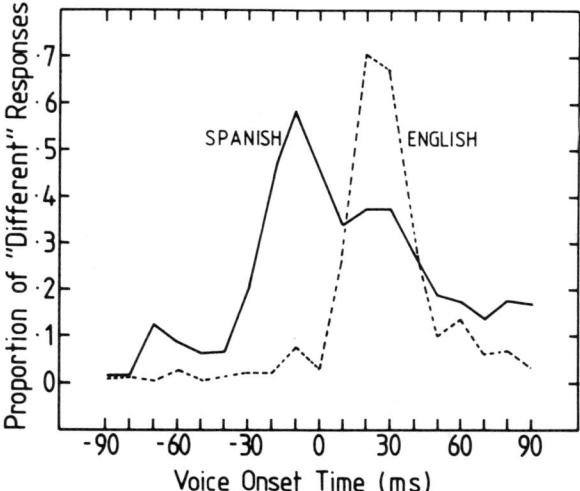

Figure 4.11. *AX* discrimination functions obtained by Williams (1977) for English and Spanish monolingual listeners judging the same labial VOT stimuli. A 20-ms step size was used. (Selectively redrawn from Figures 1 and 2 of Williams [1977].)

Is categorical perception of speech sounds always due to auditory sensitivities? Allowing for these facts, however, it is still a long jump to the claim that auditory processes are solely responsible for the categorical perception of speech sounds by human listeners. There is much evidence that bars this jump (Howell & Rosen, 1984); here we concern ourselves only with those areas in which CP experiments have figured importantly.

First, as we have seen, different languages partition the VOT continuum at different points. Can a case be made for a natural auditory sensitivity at every natural boundary encountered? Figure 4.11 shows the discrimination results Williams (1977) obtained from monolingual Spanish and English listeners in an *AX* (same–different) task. The positions of the main peaks in the discrimination functions differ across languages in the way expected from the results of labeling the stimuli and from production measurements in the same two groups. As we discussed above, the boundary for the Spanish voiced–voiceless contrast is in the prevoicing region, whereas that for English is in the voicing-lag region. What is striking is that the Spanish listeners exhibit a secondary discrimination peak coincident with the main peak shown by the English listeners. This is clear evidence that an auditory sensitivity exists at a place in the VOT continuum appropriate for English speakers. On the other hand, the peak is not nearly so high, reflecting the linguistic experience of the English listeners. Furthermore, the English listeners do not exhibit a secondary peak in the region appropriate for the Spanish voiced–voiceless distinction. There is therefore no natural auditory sensitivity at the Spanish boundary.[10]

This supposition is also supported by studies of the discrimination capabilities of infants (Eilers, Gavin, & Wilson, 1979). Both Spanish- and English-learning infants exhibit greatest sensitivity across the English VOT boundary, although at the same age (6 to 8 months) only the Spanish infants show evidence of discriminating stimuli across the Spanish boundary. Neither is there evidence from animal audition of a specific sensitivity in the prevoicing region. Finally, the psychophysical evidence for auditory discontinuities in the prevoicing region is sparse. Only Pisoni's (1977) study of a tone-onset-time continuum directly addresses the issue. His discrimination data from untrained subjects (Experiment II), when averaged, do show evidence of a secondary discrimination peak in the analogous "prevoicing" region, although it is considerably smaller than the peak in the "lag" region. Furthermore, of the eleven subjects who performed at levels above chance (one subject did not), only six show convincing discrimination peaks in the "prevoicing" region whereas all show peaks in the "lag" region. If phonemic contrasts are based on auditory sensitivities, such variable phenomena would not serve the needs of a listener well.

Second, Brady and Darwin (1978) show that the phoneme boundary for plosive VOT continua depends on the range of stimuli presented. Shifts in the range of stimuli cause shifts in the phoneme boundary. Although no discrimination tests were performed, this result implies that an auditory sensitivity alone cannot determine the position of the phoneme boundary, as the theory would suppose.

Third, there are many doubts about the adequacy of the psychophysical explanations of the perception of VOT, even when we only consider English-like contrasts. The boundaries obtained from nonspeech VOT analogs are usually at much shorter times than those obtained from true VOT continua. Although some of these discrepancies may be due to the differences in the detailed spectral structure of the stimuli, no convincing account of the relevant mechanisms is available. To be fair, of the two initial studies involving VOT analogs, only Pisoni has claimed explicitly that the acoustic contrast incorporated in his continuum is the primary acoustic contrast used by listeners in perceiving the VOT contrast. Both Soli (1983) and Summerfield (1982) have presented convincing evidence from adult listeners that perception of VOT continua cannot rely solely on temporal-order judgments. An infant study using two-tone stimuli whose components varied in relative-onset time (similar to those used by Pisoni, 1977, with adults) supports this view. Jusczyk et al. (1980) found that best discrimination for pairs of stimuli differing by 30 ms in tone-onset time occurred at a different place in the continuum than it did for adults, even though the peak discrimination for VOT stimuli does not differ between infants and at least English-speaking adults (Eimas et al., 1971).

Accounting for the auditory sensitivities that do seem to exist. Of course, there may be auditory processes underlying the perception of VOT continua other than those dependent on the determination of the relative onset of components in the stimulus complex. Soli (1983) has argued that the critical acoustic feature underlying VOT perception is spectral, expressed in differences in $F1$ onset frequency. As we noted earlier, the aspiration noise used to excite the supraglottal resonances when VOT is positive has little energy in the region of $F1$. $F1$, therefore, is relatively weak until the onset of quasiperiodic voicing excitation. As the shape of $F1$ does not vary across VOT continua and is normally undergoing a transition in frequency over the 30 to 60 ms following release, changes in VOT are necessarily correlated with changes in $F1$ onset frequency, at least for VOTs in the range where English phoneme boundaries are found. Well accounted for in this way are the variations in phoneme boundary with place of articulation, which are shown to be a result of changes in the time-patterning of $F1$.

Although Soli's claims may seem to buttress the auditory-sensitivities point of view, they in a sense presume no special auditory sensitivities at all. The non-uniform discriminability across the VOT continuum is seen to be a function of the acoustic structure of the stimuli and would occur with a wide variety of auditory systems, as long as they did some sort of frequency analysis. Properly speaking, then, this is a theory of natural acoustic discontinuity. In other words, the crucial perceptual feature here ($F1$ onset) does not change uniformly with the explicitly controlled one (here, VOT).

This hypothesis can explain effects of speaking rate on labeling VOT stimuli as long as the alterations in rate are reflected in the $F1$ transition of the syllable being judged, as in Summerfield's (1974) finding that phoneme boundaries shift to shorter VOTs with quicker formant transitions. The effects of the rate of the precursor alone that Summerfield found cannot be accounted for in this way, however. Also difficult to handle, as in any theory emphasizing auditory or acoustic factors, is the change in phoneme boundary caused by changes in the range of VOT stimuli presented (Brady & Darwin, 1978).

Soli's ideas account for the infant and animal data well. In particular, they are consistent with Eilers, Morse, Gavin, and Oller's (1981) finding that infants are relatively insensitive to changes in VOT in stimuli in which $F1$ only executes a small transition, or is entirely flat, as compared with stimuli in which $F1$ undergoes a large transition.

Simon and Fourcin (1978) claim to find a rather different developmental trend. British children of various ages were tested with continua of velar VOT stimuli with flat and normal $F1$ transitions. The youngest children (three-year-olds) showed little difference in their ability to label the two stimulus continua appropriately. The older children (eleven- to fourteen-year-olds) would only label the stimuli with the appropriately rising $F1$ contour as voiced. It is therefore the use of VOT per se, and not the spectral cues, that dominates first in perception. Simon and Fourcin's data are highly variable, however. Although there is a general trend toward progression in the use of $F1$ as the children get older, the four-year-olds show as big a difference in the judgement of stimuli between conditions as the oldest children do, and the ten-year-olds show rather smaller differences. Support for Simon and Fourcin's claims of clear progression in the use of $F1$ information, on the other hand, is found in the position of the phoneme boundary, which, for the changing $F1$ stimuli, decreases with age from about 33 ms to about 25 ms. Because the $F1$ transition only lasted 30 ms, it is only the older children who place the boundary in a region where there are $F1$ onset frequency differences, where Soli claims the boundary should be.

It is wrong to suppose, however, that if Simon and Fourcin's claims are correct, there is a contradiction between their data and the infant studies of Eilers et al. (1981). As Simon and Fourcin point out, the infants (and animals) are performing a discrimination task with little linguistic relevance. Any differences among the stimuli, even ones irrelevant for the phonemic contrast in general, will help performance. The children, on the other hand, are trying to extract a meaningful message from an acoustic signal: Irrelevant features must be ignored and only distinctive aspects attended to. This ability can only develop over time. Simon and Fourcin's study, taken together with Eilers et al.'s results, implies that the most distinctive auditory features are not the ones attended to at the beginning of development. This may seem counterintuitive, but as we have seen, many languages do not place their VOT boundaries at the place in the continuum where auditory discrimination is easiest.

Summing up. In summary, the use of continua with nonuniform discriminability (arising from properties of the stimuli, or the auditory system, or, more likely, both) can result in a pattern of results consistent with CP. This holds for adult human, infant, and animal listeners. Specifically linguistic processing is not necessary. On the other hand, auditory processes do not seem to be able to explain all occurrences of CP in speech, as studies with Spanish speakers show. Learning of appropriate phoneme categories must play a large part. The motor theory's predictions for performance in any nonlinguistic situation (animal listeners or nonspeech sounds) are clearly wrong. Although it may still be useful in explaining CP in speech, we have noted the difficulties of making unambiguously testable predictions. It is interesting to note that the phenomena of CP, initially considered strong support for the motor theory (see Liberman et al., 1967), are nowadays not even mentioned (see Liberman & Studdert-Kennedy, 1978).

Final remarks

Perhaps the safest remark to make is that none of the three theories of CP will serve to explain all the findings on its own. Some interplay among them is necessary. Throughout our assessment, we have treated the three approaches as if they were mutually exclusive. This was perhaps most unfair to the version of the learned-label theory developed by Ades (1977). As we noted above, Ades took explicit account of the possibility of natural auditory sensitivities in his modification of Durlach and Braida's (1969) dual-process theory by allowing the possibility of a nonuniform mapping from the stimulus to the sensation. The notion that learned labels can cause CP was easily accommodated by associating the use of learned labels with the context-coding mode. In this model, then, CP can arise from either a natural auditory sensitivity (or acoustic discontinuity) or the use of learned labels. We have seen much evidence in the previous section that purely auditory processes can lead to CP. In other instances (e.g., in the behavior of Spanish listeners perceiving VOT continua), auditory processes do not seem sufficient and there has to be some way to take account of experience.

The model as it stands, however, is not adequate to deal with the finding that the affricate-fricative continuum is apparently not categorically perceived. There is no reason to suppose that the labels for this pair of sounds are any less well developed than those for plosives that differ in voicing. Perhaps the sensory trace for affricates and fricatives is more stable than that for plosives, and thus less reliance is placed on the context-coding mode. Explanations of this sort have long been offered to account for the differences in the extent to which vowels and consonants are categorically perceived and for the finding that short-duration vowels are perceived more categorically than long-duration vowels (Fujisaki & Kawashima, 1968; Pisoni, 1973). On the other hand, there is no reason to expect that the sensory trace of the steady-state pitches used in demonstrations of musically related CP (see Burns & Ward, 1978) are any more ephemeral than those of affricates and fricatives.

It would also be possible to construct a dual-process motor-theoretic model by associating the context-coding mode with the speech-specific decoding via reference to articulation. This perhaps unlikely marriage preserves in a conceptually neat fashion the distinction between the speech mode (context coding) and the nonspeech mode (sensory trace) considered so important to the motor theorists. One drawback to such a model is that it would require a further parallel nonspeech context-coding branch to explain, say, the categorical perception of pitch continua by musicians (Burns & Ward, 1978; Siegel & Siegel, 1977a,b). Such a complication, however, does not seem inconsistent with at least some motor theorists' views (e.g., Liberman, 1982) on the "vertical" nature of language processes. The advantage of such a model is that it would give motor theory the ability to handle some rather uncomfortable data without denying its possible role in specifically linguistic situations.

Notes

1. Velar stops show rather more variability in their production than bilabial and alveolar stops, although still considerably less than that exhibited by vowels.
2. There are a number of other studies that have tried to assess the extent to which CP occurs for musically related sounds, but the data from these are rather more variable and difficult to interpret. All use stimuli in which multiple sinusoidal components are presented simultaneously in chords, with the continuum spanning the major/minor boundary (one semitone). The first such study, by Locke and Kellar (1973), is often cited as demonstrating CP for musicians, and continuous perception for nonmusicians. Under the standard criteria applied, this is indeed so, but there are some difficulties in further interpretation. Although the nonmusicians evidenced much less sharp identification functions than the musicians (using a procedure already criticized as inadequate by Pastore, 1976), both groups tended to show midcontinuum peaks in the discrimination function. Even granting that the musicians' peaks are higher and more consistent across conditions (nonmusicians have no midcontinuum peak when discriminating stimuli two steps apart), this indicates that the stimuli at some points of the continuum may be inherently more discriminable than they are at others. Thus, part of the categorical nature of these results

may arise from the properties of the stimuli, and not from the learned labeling, although the possible contribution of passive learning by extensive exposure to Western music even in nonmusicians should not be ignored.

The procedures and results of Zatorre and Halpern (1979) are rather cleaner (and intuitively more attractive) in this respect. Using slightly different stimuli (two component tones rather than the three used in Locke and Kellar's chords), they showed a clear difference between musicians and nonmusicians, the former perceiving the stimuli much more categorically, both from the point of view of sharp categorization and appropriately peaked discrimination. It is of interest that even the nonmusicians showed a slight peak in the discrimination function at the same point the musicians did, indicating that there may be something at least slightly special about certain frequency relationships between simultaneously presented tones, arising either from auditory processing, or, more likely, from passive listening experience with Western music.

Finally, Pastore, Schmuckler, Rosenblum, and Szczesiul (1983) tested CP in a set of eight listeners, all musically trained to some extent. They used a continuum of sinusoidal tones varying in frequency, either in isolation or with two other tones (at frequencies appropriate for all three tones again to form major or minor triads at the endpoints of the continuum) presented simultaneously in the contralateral ear. Six of the eight listeners perceived the chords but not the isolated tones categorically, the outcome predicted by the authors. Two subjects, however, did the opposite: CP for the tones but not the chords. The latter outcome is difficult to explain, unless, as Pastore et al. suggest, the two unusual listeners had perfect pitch.

In summary, there seems to be reasonably good evidence that tones in a chord can be categorically perceived, and that the primary cause of this is the use of learned labels. Part of the effect is probably due to the unchanging tones in the chord providing a stable reference (as proposed by Pastore et al.).

3. It should not be thought, however, that voiceless affricate/fricative pairs are rare occurrences in the languages of the world. The UCLA Phonological Segment Inventory Database (Maddieson, 1981) shows that of 317 languages catalogued, 122 (or 38%) have both a voiceless affricate and a voiceless fricative at the same place of articulation (considering only unaspirated affricates at the three most commonly occurring places, although one category – dental/alveolar – is not completely precise, indicating a dental or alveolar place of articulation). Taking the palatoalveolar case alone, 90 languages (or 28%), have a voiceless affricate and fricative.

4. The only affricates that had rise times longer than 40 ms were the so-called "inflected rise" /tʃ/s, which had significantly longer rises than the uninflected ones. Howell and Rosen (1983a) attribute this to the stop burst being merged with the following frication by a long time-constant on the average amplitude display.

5. It is interesting to note that these discrimination results are more "ideally categorical" than those from adults (ignoring the lack of labeling data) in that within-(adult) category discrimination was impossible. This probably results either from the less developed sensory abilities of the infants or from the insensitivity of the measuring technique. In any case, the crucial point for us is not the absolute level of performance but the fact that discrimination was better across the adult category boundary.

6. Ferrero, Pelamatti, and Vagges (1982) have shown that an affricate/fricative continuum cued by the duration of the frication alone is not categorically perceived either.

7. This predicted discrimination function is based upon a Thurstonian Case V analysis (assuming a unidimensional psychological continuum where stimulus-induced probability densities are normally distributed with equal variance; see Torgerson, 1958, for details). First we take the normal deviates of the proportion of "high precedes low" judgments (Figure 4.8) as the scale values for each of the stimuli. In order to predict performance in a discrimination task for two-step comparisons, the d' values between the appropriate stimuli are computed by taking the difference between the scale values. We can then convert these values into the proportion correct that might be expected in an *ABX* task, using a method based on signal-detection theory developed by Macmillan, Kaplan, and Creelman (1977) and the tables of Kaplan, Macmillan, & Creelman (1978). Because this transformation is monotonically increasing, it will preserve any peaks in the d' function, so for that purpose it is not crucial whether we examine d' or proportion correct: We use the latter for a more direct comparison to Liberman, Harris, Kinney, & Lane's (1961) results.

We are, of course, making the assumption that discrimination is predictable from identification or, in Macmillan et al.'s (1977) definition, that the continuum is categorically perceived! This is legitimate here because Pynn et al. (1972) show that in experiments where the signals span a small range, discrimination distances inferred from identification experiments are close to those estimated directly. That Hirsh's (1959) stimuli do indeed only span a small range is attested to by the fact that the subjects never do better than about 95% correct at the extremes of the range, even though only two categories are involved.

Also, for our current purposes, the absolute level of performance is less important than the shape of the curve, which would be preserved even if overall accuracy is underestimated.

8. This notation is rather unfortunate. Square brackets are more appropriate for this type of phonetic transcription as slanted lines are normally reserved for phonemic transcriptions. Liberman, Harris, Eimas, Lisker, & Bastian's (1961) use of /p/ and */p/ implies that this distinction is phonemic in English. It would be better to talk about subjects using the three labels [b], [p], and [*p]. This confusion regarding appropriate levels of description is not confined to notation. Liberman et al. state: "The fact that the peaks of the speech discrimination functions rose above the control may then be taken to indicate a learned increase in discrimination across *phoneme* boundaries" (emphasis ours). As we have already noted, there was a peak in discrimination in a region where no phonemic distinction is made.

9. There is a discrepancy between the results reported by Liberman, Harris, Eimas, Lisker, and Bastian (1961) for the nonspeech control condition and what would be expected on the basis of the more recent findings of Abel (1972). In the Liberman group's main control condition, the amplitude envelopes of the speech stimuli were used to modulate a white-noise source. Thus, the continuum consisted of noise stimuli (with some not-easily-reconstructable amplitude envelopes) with silent gaps varying in duration from 20 to 130 ms in 10-ms steps. Luckily for the possibility of closer comparisons with Abel's data, another control condition was constructed in which the noise stimuli had the same silent gaps in them but had equal-duration noise bursts (300 ms) with abrupt onsets and offsets defining the gap. Liberman, Harris, Eimas, Lisker, and Bastian claimed that these stimuli gave results very similar to those with the original control stimuli. In Abel's extensive study of gap discrimination, one of the conditions she used was identical to the latter control condition. She found, over the range of gap durations used by Liberman's group, that the 75% just-noticeable-difference (jnd) in gap-duration increases with increasing gap duration (a finding analogous to that found for nearly all sensory continua, related to Weber's law). This implies that the *ABX* discrimination functions of Liberman's group should show best performance at smallest-gap durations because a constant difference in gap duration is used across the continuum. There is no hint of such a trend, with performance fairly constant across the continuum for all step sizes, with, if anything, an indication of a very broad peak in its middle. This is perhaps all the more surprising because Abel's data give a relatively good prediction of the overall level of performance shown by the subjects in the study by Liberman's group. However, differences in intensity level between the two experiments (not specified by Liberman, Harris, Eimas, Lisker, & Bastian) may invalidate the last comparison, as Abel has shown this factor to be an important determinant of subject performance. (See the appendix of Rosen & Howell 1981 for a description of the method used to predict *ABX* discrimination functions from a measure of the jnd.)

10. Repp (1983) has also noted this asymmetry of results from the English and Spanish listeners of Williams (1977) and points out that Abramson and Lisker's (1973) data don't show a similar effect. He also notes that the Spanish-category boundaries reported by Abramson and Lisker are surprisingly close to the English boundaries, whereas Williams found a Spanish boundary quite different from the English one. These discrepancies are unexplained. They cannot be due to differences in the stimuli, for Williams's stimuli were constructed at the Haskins Laboratories to the specifications of Abramson and Lisker (1973). We will only discuss results from the bilabial continuum, as this was the only one used by Williams.

Abramson and Lisker obtained a labeling boundary of +14 ms VOT from 12 native Spanish speakers, close to the +25 ms they had previously found for English speakers (Lisker & Abramson, 1970). Williams found labeling boundaries of −4 ms for Spanish listeners and +25 ms for English listeners. This discrepancy in the boundary for Spanish listeners is almost certainly due to the differences in the subjects used. That Abramson and Lisker's subjects should show a boundary shifted towards a value appropriate for English is not surprising as they were all "more or less bilingual in Spanish and English, having studied English for some years" (p. 2). Williams's results come from monolinguals. Lisker and Abramson's attempts at putting their subjects (all tested in the United States) into a Spanish "mode" (with instructions in Spanish and responses in Spanish orthography) were obviously not totally successful. Williams's experiments with bilinguals confirm this: Using a procedure similar to theirs, she was unable to get differences in either labeling or discrimination performance with different language "sets." Elman, Diehl, and Buchwald (1977), however, with different techniques (a precursor phase before every trial and filler words scattered throughout the test, all in the appropriate language, and a naturally spoken VOT continuum) *were* able to show an effect of language set.

Considerable English interference is also present in the discrimination results obtained by Abramson and Lisker. Only two subjects completed the experiment. One has a labeling boundary of about 22 ms and shows a corresponding peak in his discrimination functions. This is reasonable for English but inappropriate for Spanish. The other shows a more reasonable (for Spanish) labeling boundary of −15 ms as well as a secondary discrimination peak there, but the biggest discrimination peak is at about +15 to +20 ms, near the English boundary. There is much variability in the data, however, and other secondary peaks: We have only discussed the robust peaks that occur for all three step sizes employed.

References

Abel, S. M. (1972). Discrimination of temporal gaps. *Journal of the Acoustical Society of America, 52*, 519–524.

Abramson, A. S., & Lisker, L. (1970). Discriminability along the voicing continuum: Cross-language tests. *Proceedings of the 6th International Congress of Phonetic Sciences* (pp. 569–573). Prague: Academia.

Abramson, A. S., & Lisker, L. (1973). Voice-timing perception in Spanish word-initial stops. *Journal of Phonetics, 1,* 1–8.

Ades, A. E. (1977). Vowels, consonants, speech and nonspeech. *Psychological Review, 84,* 524–530.

Bregman, A. S., & MacAdams, S. (1979). Hearing musical streams. *Computer Music Journal, 3,* 26–43.

Brady, S. A., & Darwin, C. J. (1978). Range effects in the perception of voicing. *Journal of the Acoustical Society of America, 63,* 1556–1558.

Burns, E. M., & Ward, W. D. (1978). Categorical perception – phenomenon or epiphenomenon: Evidence from experiments in the perception of melodic musical intervals. *Journal of the Acoustical Society of America, 63,* 456–468.

Carney, A. E., Widin, G. P., & Viemeister, N. F. (1977). Noncategorical perception of stop consonants differing in VOT. *Journal of the Acoustical Society of America, 62,* 961–970.

Cutting, J. E. (1982). Plucks and bows are categorically perceived, sometimes. *Perception & Psychophysics, 31,* 462–476.

Cutting, J. E., & Rosner, B. S. (1974). Categories and boundaries in speech and music. *Perception & Psychophysics, 16,* 564–570.

Delgutte, B. (1980). Representation of speech-like sounds in the discharge patterns of auditory-nerve fibers. *Journal of the Acoustical Society of America, 68,* 843–857.

Delgutte, B. (1982). Some correlates of phonetic distinctions at the level of the auditory nerve. In R. Carlson & B. Granstrom (Eds.), *The representation of speech in the peripheral auditory system.* Amsterdam: North-Holland.

Dorman, M. F., Raphael, L. J., & Isenberg, D. (1980). Acoustic cues for a fricative-affricate contrast in word-final position. *Journal of Phonetics, 8,* 397–405.

Dorman, M. F., Raphael, L. J., & Liberman, A. M. (1979). Some experiments on the sound of silence in phonetic perception. *Journal of the Acoustical Society of America, 65,* 1518–1532.

Durlach, N. I., & Braida, L. D. (1969). Intensity perception: I. Preliminary theory of intensity resolution. *Journal of the Acoustical Society of America, 46,* 372–383.

Eilers, R. E., Gavin, W., & Wilson, W. R. (1979). Linguistic experience and phonemic perception in infancy: A cross-linguistic study. *Child Development, 50,* 14–18.

Eilers, R. E., Morse, P. A., Gavin, W. J., & Oller, D. K. (1981). Discrimination of voice onset time in infancy. *Journal of the Acoustical Societ of America, 70*, 955–965.
Eimas, P. D., Siqueland, E. R., Jusczyk, P., & Vigorito, J. (1971). Speech perception in infants. *Science, 171*, 303–306.
Elman, J. L., Diehl, R. L., & Buchwald, S. E. (1977). Perceptual switching in bilinguals. *Journal of the Acoustical Society of America, 62*, 971–974.
Ferrero, F. E., Pelamatti, G. M., & Vagges, K. (1982). Continuous and categorical perception of a fricative-affricate continuum. *Journal of Phonetics, 10*, 231–244.
Fry, D. B., Abramson, A. S., Eimas, P. D., & Liberman, A. M. (1962). The identification and discrimination of synthetic vowels. *Language and Speech, 5*, 171–189.
Fujisaki, H., & Kawashima, T. (1968). The influence of various factors on the identification and discrimination of synthetic speech sounds. *Sixth International Conference on Acoustics*, Paper B-3-6: B-95–B-98.
Fujisaki, H., & Kawashima, T. (1969). On the modes and hearing mechanisms of speech perception. *Annual Report of the Engineering Research Institute* (Vol. 28, pp. 67–73). Tokyo: Faculty of Engineering, University of Tokyo.
Fukisaki, H., & Kawashima, T. (1971). A model for the mechanisms of speech perception: Quantitative analysis of categorical effects in discrimination (Vol. 30, pp. 59–68). Tokyo: Faculty of Engineering, University of Tokyo. *Annual Report of the Engineering Research Institute*.
Gerstman, L. J. (1957). *Perceptual dimensions for the friction portions of certain speech sounds*. Unpublished doctoral dissertation. New York University, New York.
Gibson, J. J. (1966). *The senses considered as perceptual systems*. Boston: Houghton Mifflin.
Hary, J. M., & Massaro, D. W. (1982). Categorical results do not imply categorical perception. *Perception & Psychophysics, 32*, 409–418.
Helson, H. (1964). *Adaptation-level theory*. New York: Harper & Row.
Hirsh, I. J. (1959). Auditory perception of temporal order. *Journal of the Acoustical Society of America, 31*, 759–767.
Howell, P., & Harvey, N. (1983). Perceptual equivalence and motor equivalence in speech. In B. Butterworth (Ed.), *Language Production* (Vol. 2, pp. 203–224). London: Academic Press.
Howell, P., & Rosen, S. (1983a). Production and perception of rise time in the voiceless affricate/fricative distinction. *Journal of the Acoustical Society of America, 73*, 976–984.
Howell, P., & Rosen, S. (1983b). Perception of rise time and explanations of the affricate/fricative contrast. *Speech Communication, 2*, 164–166.
Howell, P., & Rosen, S. (1983c). Closure and frication measurements and perceptual integration of temporal cues for the voiceless affricate/fricative contrast. *Speech, Hearing and Language* (Vol. 1, pp. 109–117). Progress Report of the Department of Phonetics & Linguistics, University College, London.
Howell, P., & Rosen, S. (1984). Natural auditory sensitivities as universal determiners of phonemic contrasts. In B. Butterworth, B. Comrie, & O. Dahl (Eds.), *Explanations for Language Universals* (pp. 205–235). The Hague: Mouton. Also in *Linguistics* (1984). *21*:205–235.
Jusczyk, P. W., Pisoni, D. B., Walley, A., & Murray, J. (1980). Discrimination of relative onset time of two-component tones by infants. *Journal of the Acoustical Society of America, 67*, 262–270.
Jusczyk, P. W., Rosner, B. S., Cutting, J. E., Foard, C. F., & Smith, L. B. (1977). Categorical perception of nonspeech sounds by 2-month old infants. *Perception & Psychophysics, 21*, 50–54.
Kaplan, H. L., Macmillan, N. A., & Creelman, C. D. (1978). Tables for d' for variable standard discrimination paradigms. *Behaviour Research Methods & Instrumentation, 10*, 796–813.
Kewley-Port, D., & Pisoni, D. B. (1984). Identification and discrimination of rise time: Is it categorical or noncategorical? *Journal of the Acoustical Society of America, 75*, 1168–1176.
Kiang, N. Y.-S., Watanabe, T., Thomas, E. C., & Clark, L. F. (1965). *Discharge patterns of single fibers in the cat's auditory nerve* (Research Monograph No. 35). Cambridge, MA: M.I.T. Press.
Kuhl, P. K. (1979). Models and mechanisms in speech perception: Species comparisons provide further contributions. *Brain, Behavior and Evolution, 16*, 374–408.
Kuhl, P. K. (1981). Discrimination of speech by nonhuman animals: Basic auditory sensitivities conducive to the perception of speech-sound categories. *Journal of the Acoustical Society of America, 70*, 340–349.

Kuhl, P. K., & Miller, J. D. (1975). Speech perception by the chinchilla: Voiced-voiceless distinction in alveolar plosive consonants. *Science, 190,* 69-72.
Kuhl, P. K., & Miller, J. D. (1978). Speech perception by the chinchilla: Identification functions for synthetic VOT stimuli. *Journal of the Acoustical Society of America, 63,* 905-917.
Lane, H. (1965). Motor theory of speech perception: A critical review. *Psychological Review, 72,* 275-309.
Liberman, A. M. (1982). On finding that speech is special. *American Psychologist, 37,* 148-167.
Liberman, A. M., Cooper, F. S., Harris, K. S., & MacNeilage, P. F. (1963). A motor theory of speech perception. *Proceedings of the Speech Communication Seminar, Volume II, Stockholm, 1962* (D3). Stockholm: Royal Institute of Technology.
Liberman, A. M., Cooper, F. S., Shankweiler, D. P., & Studdert-Kennedy, M. (1967). Perception of the speech code. *Psychological Review, 74,* 431-461.
Liberman, A. M., Delattre, P. C., & Cooper, F. S. (1952). The role of selected stimulus variables in the perception of the unvoiced stop consonants. *American Journal of Psychology, 65,* 497-516.
Liberman, A. M., Delattre, P. C., Cooper, F. S., & Gerstman, L. J. (1954). The role of consonant-vowel transitions in the perception of the stop and nasal consonants. *Psychological Monographs, 68*(8), Whole No. 379.
Liberman, A. M., Harris, K. S., Eimas, P. D., Lisker, L., & Bastian, J. (1961). An effect of learning on speech perception: The discrimination of durations of silence with and without phonemic significance. *Language and Speech, 4,* 175-195.
Liberman, A. M., Harris, K. S., Hoffman, H. S., & Griffith, B. C. (1957). The discrimination of speech sounds within and across phoneme boundaries. *Journal of Experimental Psychology, 54,* 358-368.
Liberman, A. M., Harris, K. S., Kinney, J. A., & Lane, H. (1961). The discrimination of relative onset time of the components of certain speech and nonspeech patterns. *Journal of Experimental Psychology, 61,* 379-388.
Liberman, A. M., & Studdert-Kennedy, M. (1978). Phonetic perception. In R. Held, H. W. Leibowitz, & H.-L. Teuber (Eds.), *Handbook of sensory physiology:* Vol. 8, *Perception,* (pp. 143-178). New York: Springer.
Lisker, L., & Abramson, A. S. (1964). A cross-language study of voicing in initial stops: Acoustical measurements. *Word, 20,* 384-422.
Lisker, L., & Abramson, A. S. (1967). Some effects of context on voice onset time in English stops. *Language and Speech, 10,* 1-28.
Lisker, L., & Abramson, A. S. (1970). The voicing dimension: Some experiments in comparative phonetics. *Proceedings of the 6th International Congress of Phonetic Sciences* (pp. 563-567). Prague: Academia.
Locke, S., & Kellar, L. (1973). Categorical perception in a non-linguistic mode. *Cortex, 9,* 355-369.
Maddieson, I. (1981). UPSID: Data and index. *UCLA working papers in phonetics* (No. 53). Los Angeles: The Phonetics Laboratory, Department of Linguistics, UCLA.
Macmillan, N. A., Kaplan, H. L., & Creelman, C. D. (1977). The psychophysics of categorical perception. *Psychological Review, 84,* 452-471.
Mattingley, I. G., Liberman, A. M., Syrdal, A. K., & Halwes, T. (1971). Discrimination in speech and nonspeech modes. *Cognitive Psychology, 2,* 131-137.
Miller, G. A. (1956). The magical number seven plus or minus two, or, some limits on our capacity for processing information. *Psychological Review, 63,* 81-96.
Miller, J. D., Wier, C. C., Pastore, R. E., Kelly, W. J., & Dooling, R. J. (1976). Discrimination and labeling of noise-buzz sequences with varying noise-lead times: An example of categorical perception. *Journal of the Acoustical Society of America, 60,* 410-417.
Parducci, A. (1965). Category judgment: A range-frequency model. *Psychological Review, 72,* 407-418.
Pastore, R. E. (1976). Categorical perception: A critical re-evaluation. In S. K. Hirsh, D. H. Eldredge, I. J. Hirsh, & S. R. Silverman (Eds.), *Hearing and Davis: Essays honoring Hallowell Davis* (pp. 253-264). St. Louis: Washington University Press.
Pastore, R. E., Ahroon, W. A., Baffuto, K. J., Friedman, C., Puleo, J. S., & Fink, E. A. (1977).

Common-factor model of categorical perception. *Journal of Experimental Psychology: Human Perception and Performance, 3,* 686–696.
Pastore, R. E., Schmuckler, M. A., Rosenblum, L., & Szczesiul, R. (1983). Duplex perception with musical stimuli. *Perception & Psychophysics, 33,* 469–474.
Pisoni, D. B. (1973). Auditory and phonetic memory codes in the discrimination of consonants and vowels. *Perception & Psychophysics, 13,* 253–260.
Pisoni, D. B. (1977). Identification and discrimination of the relative onset time of two-component tones: Implications for voicing perception in stops. *Journal of the Acoustical Society of America, 61,* 1352–1361.
Pisoni, D. B., Aslin, R. N., Perey, A. J., & Hennessy, B. L. (1982). Some effects of laboratory training on identification and discrimination of voicing contrasts in stop consonants. *Journal of Experimental Psychology: Human Perception and Performance, 8,* 297–314.
Pynn, C. T., Braida, L. D., & Durlach, N. I. (1972). Intensity perception: III. Resolution in small-range identification. *Journal of the Acoustical Society of America, 51,* 559–566.
Remez, R. E. (1978). *An hypothesis of event-sensitivity in the perception of speech and bass violins.* Unpublished Doctoral Dissertation, University of Connecticut.
Remez, R. E., Cutting, J. E., & Studdert-Kennedy, M. (1980). Cross-series adaptation using song and string. *Perception & Psychophysics, 27,* 524–530.
Repp, B. H. (1983). Categorical perception: Issues, methods, findings. In N. J. Lass (Ed.), *Speech and language: Advances in basic research and practice* (Vol. 10). New York: Academic Press.
Repp, B. H., Liberman, A. M., Eccardt, T., & Pesetsky, D. (1978). Perceptual integration of acoustic cues for stop, fricative and affricate manner. *Journal of Experimental Psychology: Human Perception and Performance, 4,* 621–637.
Rosen, S. (1981). Untitled contribution. In T. F. Myers, J. Laver, & J. Anderson (Eds.), *The Cognitive Representation of Speech* (pp. 93–94). Amsterdam: North-Holland.
Rosen, S., & Howell, P. (1981). Plucks and bows are not categorically perceived. *Perception & Psychophysics, 30,* 156–168.
Rosen, S., & Howell, P. (1983a). Sinusoidal plucks and bows are not categorically perceived, either. *Perception and Psychophysics, 34,* 233–236.
Rosen, S., & Howell, P. (1983b). Is there a natural sensitivity at 20 ms in relative tone-onset-time continua? A reanalysis of Hirsh's (1959) data. *Speech, Hearing and Language* (Vol. 1, pp. 145–149). Progress Report of the Department of Phonetics & Linguistics, University College London.
Rosner, B. S. (1981). *Rise time and the perception of transient sounds.* (Final Progress Report for Grant NS-13545 at the University of Pennsylvania, 1 December 1977 to 30 April 1981.)
Sachs, R. M. (1969). Vowel identification and discrimination in isolation vs. word context. *Quarterly Progress Report No. 93* (pp. 220–229). Cambridge, MA: MIT Research Laboratory of Electronics.
Shankweiler, D. P., Strange, W., & Verbrugge, R. R. (1977). Speech and the problem of perceptual constancy. In R. E. Shaw, & J. Bransford (Eds.), *Perceiving, Acting and Knowing: Toward an Ecological Psychology* (pp. 315–345). Hillsdale, NJ: Erlbaum.
Siegel, J. A., & Siegel, W. (1977a). Absolute identification of notes and intervals by musicians. *Perception and Psychophysics, 21,* 143–152.
Siegel, J. A., & Siegel, W. (1977b). Categorical perception of tonal intervals: Musicians can't tell *sharp* from *flat. Perception and Psychophysics, 21,* 399–407.
Simon, C., & Fourcin, A. J. (1978). A cross-language study of speech-pattern learning. *Journal of the Acoustical Society of America, 63,* 925–935.
Soli, S. D. (1983). The role of spectral cues in discrimination of voice onset time differences. *Journal of the Acoustical Society of America, 73,* 2150–2165.
Stevens, K. N. (1981). Constraints imposed by the auditory system on the properties used to classify speech sounds: Data from phonology, acoustics and psycho-acoustics. In T. F. Myers, J. Laver, & J. Anderson (Eds.), *The Cognitive Representation of Speech.* Amsterdam: North Holland.
Strange, W., & Broen, P. A. (1980). Perception and production of approximant consonants by three-year-olds. In G. Yemi-Komshian, J. F. Kavanagh, & C. A. Ferguson (Eds.), *Child phonology: Perception, production and deviation* (Vol. 2, pp. 117–124). New York: Academic Press.

Studdert-Kennedy, M. (1976). Speech perception. In N. J. Lass (Ed.), *Contemporary issues in experimental phonetics* (pp. 243–293). New York: Academic Press.

Studdert-Kennedy, M., Liberman, A. M., Harris, K. S., & Cooper, F. S. (1970). Motor theory of speech perception: A reply to Lane's critical review. *Psychological Review 77*, 234–249.

Summerfield, Q. (1974). Towards a detailed model for the perception of voicing contrasts. *Speech perception: Report of speech research in progress* (Series 2, No. 3, pp. 1–26). Belfast: Department of Psychology, Queen's University.

Summerfield, Q. (1982). Differences between spectral dependencies in auditory and phonetic temporal processing: Relevance to the perception of voicing in initial stops. *Journal of the Acoustical Society of America, 72*, 51–61.

Torgerson, W. S. (1958). *Theory and methods of scaling.* New York: Wiley.

van Heuven, V. J. (1983). Rise time and duration of friction noise as perceptual cues in the affricate-fricative contrast in English. In M. van den Broecke, V. van Heuven, & W. Zonneveld (Eds.), *Sound Structures.* Dordrecht, Holland: Foris.

van Heuven, V. J., & van den Broecke, M. P. R. (1979). Auditory discrimination of rise and decay times in tone and noise bursts. *Journal of the Acoustical Society of America, 66*, 1308–1315.

Waters, R. S., & Wilson, W. A. Jr. (1976). Speech perception by rhesus monkeys: The voicing distinction in synthesized labial and velar stop consonants. *Perception & Psychophysics, 19*, 285–289.

Williams, L. (1977). The perception of stop consonant voicing by Spanish-English bilinguals. *Perception & Psychophysics, 21*, 289–297.

Zatorre, R. J., & Halpern, A. R. (1979). Identification, discrimination and selective adaptation of simultaneous musical intervals. *Perception & Psychophysics, 26*, 384–395.

5 On infant speech perception and the acquisition of language

Peter D. Eimas, Joanne L. Miller, and Peter W. Jusczyk

In our discussion, we review the evidence on the abilities of prelinguistic infants to perceive speech and we begin to relate their perceptual abilities to the development of phonological and lexical systems. Young infants have a highly developed and sophisticated system for the perception of speech. In addition to being able to discriminate fine differences in the speech signal, they are able to form a categorical representation of speech that takes into account a number of contextual factors, including the rate of speech and the multiplicity of cues that signal a single phonetic contrast. A consideration of the infant data in conjunction with findings from adult listeners tested with a variety of experimental procedures leads to the hypothesis that the processing of speech in infants (and adults) is performed on a nonsegmented, continuous speech signal and that the categorical representations resulting from this processing have a syllabic structure. For the prelinguistic infant, this syllabic structure probably takes the form of a consonant-vowel sequence. These initial structures are modified by linguistic experience, however, and come to reflect the syllabic structures of the parental language and to provide a basis for the construction of phonological and lexical systems.

In the 16 years since the first published experiments describing the infant's ability to perceive speech (Eimas, Siqueland, Jusczyk, & Vigorito, 1971; Moffitt, 1971), it has become increasingly apparent that the very young, prelinguistic infant possesses highly developed perceptual mechanisms for the perception of speech.[1] The capacity of this perceptual system to provide a categorical representation of speech is the primary concern of our discussion. We examine the evidence for the categorization of speech: a representation that, we believe, serves as the basis for perception at a phonetic level and for the development of phonological and lexical rules and representations. We also consider very recent experimental evidence indicating that these categorization procedures are complex in their mode of operation. Indeed, they are able to accommodate sources of variation in the speech signal that might arise from variation in the rate of speech and from trading relations that exist among the many sources of information for most phonetic contrasts.

In addition, we discuss findings from experiments on the perception of visual patterns and nonspeech acoustic events by infants. These results likewise support

Preparation of this chapter was completed in March 1983 and was supported by a James McKeen Cattell Sabbatic Award and NICHHD Grant HD 05331 to PDE, by NINCDS Grant NS 14394, RCDA NS 00661, NIH BRSG Grant RR 07143 to JLM, and by NICHHD Grant HD 15795 to PWJ.

the existence of categorical representations and add to our belief that categorization processes are inherent to human perceptual systems and are functional very early in life without any apparent formal tuition.[2] We also discuss the possibility that the categorical representations of speech are structured entities, well described by prototypes (e.g., Oden & Massaro, 1978; Posner & Keele, 1968), and thus not unlike representations of visual categories found in adults and infants. In our final two sections, we consider first the nature of the units of processing and representing speech and then we provide some conjectures about how the infant's processing capabilities and representation of speech promote the acquisition of a phonological system and a lexicon.

The categorization of speech

When we listen to speech, we experience perceptual constancy; we hear the many acoustically different variants of the same segmental or syllabic units as instances of the same category. Thus, for example, the word-initial consonant /b/ in the word /bæt/ is heard as the same consonant as the final segment in the word /tæb/. The perception of the segmental unit /t/ is also phenomenally quite similar in both instances. This constancy of perception would hardly be of interest if each instantiation of a particular segment were physically identical, for then the necessary isomorphism between antecedent events and perceptual experiences would be present. But this is hardly the case in virtually all productions of the same units and certainly in the examples just cited.

There are a variety of conditions related to the production of the units of speech that alter considerably their spectral and temporal characteristics. For example, we find substantial differences in the acoustic structure of speech with different speakers, and even with the same speakers as changes occur in the rate of speech, stress pattern, and emotional state. Similarly, the consequences of coarticulation, that is, the alterations in production as a function of the preceding and following segmental units, cause changes in the acoustic signal, and these changes may even cross syllabic and morphemic boundaries. Furthermore, a single articulatory act has numerous, diverse acoustic consequences, each of which typically contributes to phonetic perception. For example Lisker (1978a) has listed 16 different cues for voicing in medial syllabic position, as in the contrast between /ræbId/ and /ræ pId/. It should also be noted that there are instances where a single acoustic feature can serve to signal quite different segmental percepts. A case in point is that differences in vowel length can be sufficient to signal both vowel quality (e.g., Ainsworth, 1972) and voicing of syllable-final consonants (e.g., Raphael, 1972).[3] Finally, there are moment-to-moment changes that occur in the articulatory apparatus of a single speaker, even when attempts are made to stabilize the conditions of production (Lisker & Abramson, 1964, for example). All of these factors that alter the mechanisms of speech production produce variation in the acoustic features that are sufficient sources of information for segmental and suprasegmental distinctions in the speech signal. (For reviews of this literature, the reader is referred to Liberman, Cooper, Shankweiler, & Studdert-Kennedy, 1967; Pisoni, 1978; Repp, 1983; see also Chapter 3 by Repp & Liberman and Chapter 7 by Diehl & Kluender, this volume).

Given the extent of acoustic variation, the constancy of our phonetic experiences is truly impressive. At issue is how we achieve this constancy, and how it develops.[4] It is obviously not possible to study perceptual constancy in young infants (and perhaps in any inarticulate organism). We simply do not have the experimental means to determine whether infants perceive two physically different instances of the same natural category as phenomenally identical or even similar events. We can, however, ask a simpler but closely related question of infants, namely, whether physically different occurrences of the same category are responded to as if they were equivalent experiences under any set of circumstances. In other words, we can ask whether infants form equivalence classes, that is, categorical representations, which are, without question, a necessary precondition for perceptual constancy; if the answer is yes, we can then set about determining the conditions under which equivalence of physical events is evident.

The study of the categorization of speech by infants has been concerned with two forms of acoustic variation. In one instance, the focus has been the infant's sensitivity to variation in category-defining acoustic characteristics that arise from moment-to-moment alterations in the articulatory mechanisms of speech. In the second instance, the variation of interest has been the one resulting from coarticulation and from speaker differences as well as from differences in patterns of intonation. Although studies with both forms of variation are ultimately concerned with the same issues, they have been given different names; the former have been labeled "studies of categorical perception," whereas the latter have been called "studies of equivalence class formation or perceptual constancy." For ease of explication, we shall keep this classificatory system and begin our discussion with the formation of equivalence classes.

Equivalence class formation

The first reported study of equivalence class formation was that of Fodor, Garrett, and Brill (1975). They showed that infants approximately four months of age were slightly better able to group together consonant-vowel syllables that shared the initial consonant than syllables that did not share this phonetic segment. Moreover, given their selection of syllables, there was no obvious acoustic feature that could serve as the basis for similarity (cf. Liberman, Delattre, & Cooper, 1952). In recent years, the problem of equivalence class formation in infants about six months of age has been actively pursued by Kuhl and her associates (Hillenbrand, 1980; Holmberg, Morgan, & Kuhl, 1977; Kuhl, 1979, 1980, 1983, 1985; Chapter 12 by Kuhl, this volume). They have used a discriminative head-turning response, as did Foder et al., but with the difference that only a single response was required of the infant, a turn to the source of the target stimulus. In one series of studies (Kuhl, 1979, 1983), the categories of concern were the vowels /a/ versus /i/ and /a/ versus /ɔ/, with the vowels in the latter pair being much more similar acoustically than those in the former pair. After initial training during which the infant learned to turn when the target stimulus /i/, for example, briefly interrupted the background sound, /a/, acoustic variants of both vowel categories were introduced gradually or all at once in a random order. With the gradual introduction of variation, all infants were able to classify the stimuli, although the criterion level of performance was attained more rapidly with /a/ and /i/ than with /a/ and /ɔ/. When the variation was rapidly introduced, seven of eight infants performed better than chance with the first pair, whereas only four of eight infants achieved this level with the latter pair. That equivalence classes can be formed does not seem to be in doubt, although the salience or discriminative difference of the contrast may be related in an important way to the ease of category formation, a point to which we return shortly. Moreover, recent findings suggest that four-day-old infants are able to form equivalence classes based on vowel quality (Jusczyk, Mehler, Bijeljac-Babic, & Bertoncini, in preparation). The latter findings speak not only to the biological determination of such processes, but also to the minimal experience that is necessary to activate this form of processing. It will be interesting to learn whether categorization can be found this early in life with other, perhaps less biologically significant stimuli.

In another series of studies by Kuhl and her associates it was found that infants were also able to categorize the fricative contrasts, /s/ versus /ʃ/ and /f/ versus /θ/, in both syllable-initial and syllable-final positions when they were produced with different vowels and by different speakers. Once again, there were differences in the level of performance, with the former contrast being acquired more quickly than the latter, perhaps again reflecting a discriminative difference between the two pairs (Holmberg et al., 1977; Kuhl, 1980). There were also quite marked individual differences, but, as in the vowel studies where the acoustic variants were introduced rapidly, we cannot be sure whether these differences are specific to the particular task or whether there are other aspects of speech processing that are correlated with the ability to form equivalence classes. There is also some suggestion that categorization occurs for stops versus nasals, as well as for place distinctions within nasal consonants (Hillenbrand, 1980) and within stop consonants (Katz & Jusczyk, 1980), although the evidence for the latter was not very strong. Furthermore, in accord with the findings of Katz and Jusczyk, Jusczyk and Derrah (in preparation) found no evidence of equivalence class formation in four-month-old infants when the categories were based on the acoustic information for place of articulation among stop consonants that varied as a consequence of differences in the following vowel. These stop-consonant data are interesting in that they indicate limitations on the ability of infants to form equivalence classes. However, whether these limitations arise from the possibly greater encoding of phonetic information in stop consonants, as has been claimed, for example, by Liberman, Mattingly, and Turvey (1972), remains to be determined.

In studies of this sort it is always possible to argue that there is no natural "proclivity" to discern some distinguishing feature for purposes of categorization, but rather that the infant slowly attains criterion by learning which individual sounds will be reinforced and which sounds will not be reinforced. This criticism has much less force when it can be demonstrated that the initial presentations of abruptly introduced variants are responded to correctly or at least at levels better than chance and with no increments in response latency. This was true for at least some infants in the studies of vowel categorization (Kuhl, 1979, 1983). Another way to meet this criticism, especially when there has been a gradual introduction of categorical variation, is to show that learning the reinforcement contingencies for individual sounds could not be the sole determinant of the final form of categorization. This has been attempted by experimentally defining the category members by random assignment of the stimuli for some infants and comparing their performance with that of infants for whom the stimuli provide a natural basis for categorization. In two such comparisons (Katz & Jusczyk, 1980; Kuhl, 1985), the evidence has favored the hypothesis that infants use some acoustic or phonetic similarity among the stimuli as the basis for response equivalence, that is, for categorization.

Kuhl and Hillenbrand (1979) have also investigated the formation of equivalence classes based on suprasegmental information. Using the stimuli of the vowel-categorization studies described above, they presented the stimuli such that the relevant categories were rising and falling intonation contours and the variable information was vowel category and speaker. Given that the /a/–/i/ contrast was easier to categorize than the /a/–/ɔ/ contrast, Kuhl and Hillenbrand quite reasonably predicted that the categorization of intonation would be more difficult when the irrelevant vowel information was more salient (and presumably more difficult to ignore), as would be true for the vowels /a/ and /i/. However, infants were able to categorize the stimuli in both situations and with equal facility. This unexpected failure to find an effect of salience (that is, discriminability in this instance) on the ease of equivalence class formation may have resulted from ceiling effects, as Kuhl (1983) has noted. Alternatively, one might turn to recent work in phonology for a possible explanation of these results. Proponents of autosegmental phonology have argued that information about prosodic and segmental features of speech may require independent levels of representation (see Goldsmith, 1976, 1979; Leben, 1976; and the papers in van der Hulst & Smith, 1982a). If such is the case, it is possible that an effect of salience might be found only within a level and not across levels, and hence the absence of a salience effect in Kuhl and Hillenbrand (1979). Finally, we should note that a number of acoustic parameters unrelated to phonetic distinctions have been the basis for the formation of equivalence classes; these include harmonic structure (Endman, 1984), the pitch of harmonic complexes (Clarkson & Clifton, 1984) and the complex of spectral differences arising from female as opposed to male voices (Miller, Younger, & Morse, 1982).

The range of acoustic information in the speech signal that may function as the source of categorization is impressive, as is, at times, the apparent ease with which infants are able to discover the basis of similarity among the relevant category members. It would be interesting to know the relative ease with which different information – for example, segmental versus suprasegmental – can be categorized, and it will be important to define the basis for the perceived similarity. Both tasks are formidable, requiring in the first instance complex designs in which the relative salience of the potential phonetic category-defining and nondefining information is systematically varied (cf. Carrell, Smith, & Pisoni, 1981) and in the second instance, similarly complex designs in which the nature of the category-defining information is systematically varied. Although the last set of studies may not provide the acoustic invariants that have been long sought (e.g., Searle, Jacobson, & Rayment, 1979; Stevens & Blumstein, 1981) it may help to limit our conception of what might serve as the information by which human listeners begin the task of acquiring the sound system of their parental languages.

Studies of categorical perception

Categorical perception (CP) experiments have typically used a high-amplitude sucking procedure with infants four months of age and less. In this procedure, the presentation of speech sounds, usually synthetically generated, is made contingent on the occurrence of a criterial sucking response. Infants generally show an increase in the rate of sucking with implementation of the contingency, followed by a diminution in sucking, presumably as a result of satiation. When the decrement in response rate has reached some fixed criterion or when a fixed time has elapsed, the stimulus is changed. Differences in sucking rate to this new stimulus, relative to appropriate control stimuli, are taken as the basis for inferring discrimination, and the pattern of discriminability along some category-defining continuum is in turn the basis for inferring the mode of perception.

This type of experiment is of course directly analogous to the experiments on CP with adult listeners. As is well known, adult listeners are known to be able to classify readily the continuously varying members along a vast number of acoustic dimensions with considerable consistency. More important, the discriminability data show that there are constraints on discrimination; essentially, discrimination is quite high when the stimuli are drawn from different categories, and quite poor, usually not much above chance levels, when the two tokens are acoustic variants of the same phonetic category. The discrimination functions are, in other words, nonmonotonic (unlike the stimulus dimension), with a marked peak in discrimination at the region of the category boundary – the phoneme boundary effect (Wood, 1976) that most investigators consider sufficient evidence for inferring a CP-like mode of perception (see Repp, 1983, for a review of this literature).

Discrimination can be said to be limited in some manner by the listener's ability to differentially categorize the sounds, although this limitation is not complete: The levels of within-category discrimination are rarely at the level of chance as one would expect if categorical assignments completely determined the ability to discriminate one speech pattern from another.[5] Indeed, there are a number of experimental demonstrations of listeners being able to differentiate within-category patterns with considerable accuracy (see Barclay, 1972; Carney, Widin, & Viemeister, 1977; Macmillan, Kaplan, & Creelman, 1977; and Macmillan in Chapter 2, this volume, for a theoretical treatment of CP; and Perey & Pisoni, 1977, for an opposing view). Our view is that these demonstrations do not weaken the basic concept of categorical perception of speech. Rather they force upon us the very interesting conclusion that when CP does occur, which is virtually always in natural listening situations, it is a result of further processing and not simply a result of an inability to discriminate. This additional processing serves, in effect, to permit listeners when perceiving the sounds of speech to listen through the acoustic characteristics of the speech signal and extract the significance of the message, which at this level of processing is the phonetic intent of the speaker. Of interest to those who undertook the study of CP in infants was whether similar processes occurred in young, prelinguistic infants, and if so, what was the relation of these early categorizations of the speech signal to the phonetic categories of mature language users.[6]

Establishing the presence or absence of a phoneme boundary effect is a relatively simple endeavor with adult observers, given that it is only necessary to obtain identification and discrimination functions from the same listeners. This is not the case with infant listeners, however, especially very young infants who cannot provide us with identification functions, that is, an independent means for assessing the boundary locations. Moreover, very young infants also cannot provide us with functions that are analogous to identification functions, as have been obtained with chinchillas (e.g., Kuhl & Miller, 1978). The demands of the presently available experimental procedures are simply more than can be reasonably and ethically imposed on infants. Given this, inferences concerning the mode of perception for infant listeners have had to rely solely on the nature of the discriminability functions, with nonmonotonic but orderly functions being taken as evidence of CP-like perception. It is not unreasonable, or so we believe, to assume that discriminative peaks reflect cross-category comparisons, whereas the troughs in the function reflect within-category levels of discrimination, and that the number of peaks reflects the number of categories minus one.

If one accepts this basis for the existence of categorical representation of speech in infants, then there is ample experimental evidence for CP-like perception for a variety of acoustic continua that signal phonetic contrasts in adult listeners (for more extensive reviews see Aslin, Pisoni, & Jusczyk, 1983; Jusczyk, 1981). For example, evidence of categorization has been found for small differences in voice-onset-time, a sufficient source of information for voicing distinctions in adult listeners (Eimas et al., 1971; Lasky, Syrdal-Lasky, & Klein, 1975; Miller & Eimas, 1983; Streeter, 1976). In addition, relatively small differences in the spectral composition of formant transitions, sufficient information for distinctions based on place of articulation, are also processed in a categorical manner by infants (Eimas, 1974; cf. Morse, 1972). Information for differences in manner of articulation are perceived approximately categorically for a stop consonant–semivowel distinction (Eimas & Miller, 1980a; Miller and Eimas, 1983) and for an oral–nasal distinction, although somewhat less categorically for the latter than is usually the case (Eimas & Miller, 1980b). Finally, the information for the distinction among the glides /r/ and /l/ is categorically represented (Eimas, 1975).

Recent investigations with adults have revealed that the processes of categorization are more complex than was originally presumed (e.g., Fitch et al., 1980; Miller & Liberman, 1979; Repp, Liberman, Eccardt, & Pesetsky, 1978; Summerfield & Haggard, 1977; to cite but a few studies; for a review of this literature, see Repp, 1982). What has been shown, essentially, is that the mapping of a range of acoustic variants onto a phonetic category – for example, the range of voice-onset-time values that signals a voiced bilabial stop – is not an invariant mapping. Rather, it is markedly affected by contextual factors such as rate of speech and phonetic environment. In addition, more than one acoustic property specifies any given phonetic segment, and the value of one of these properties affects the way stimuli varying along another of those properties are classified; that is, these multiple cues in effect enter into trading relations with each other (cf. Repp & Liberman, in Chapter 3, this volume).

Consider first the problem of contextual influences, in particular, the effects of rate of speech. Miller and Liberman (1979) have studied the effects of one acoustic correlate of rate of speech, namely, syllable duration, on the categorization of information sufficient to signal the stop-consonant–semivowel distinction, /b/ versus /w/, in this case. The critical acoustic feature was transition duration; relatively short transitions are classified as stop consonants, whereas longer transitions are heard as semivowels. However, when the rate of speech is slowed, there are relatively long transition durations that are perceived as stop consonants, and when the rate of speech is increased, there are relatively short transition durations that are heard as semivowels. In other words, there is a range of absolute values of transition duration classified sometimes as stop consonants and sometimes as semivowels. However, the perceptual experiences of listeners do not reflect this apparent ambiguity in the signal; their identification responses are orderly and do not evidence a large range of uncertainty. How listeners are able to disambiguate the signal appears to be rather straightforward. They simply do not process transition duration absolutely, but rather in relation to the duration of the syllable, which reflects the rate of speech. In effect, then, listeners are normalizing the signal for rate of speech. Eimas and Miller (1980a; Miller & Eimas, 1983) asked whether three- and four-month-old infants would use contextual information in the classification of transition duration. The answer was an unequivocal yes. When syllable durations were very short, the infants' category boundary was situated between 16 and 40 milliseconds of transition duration, whereas when the syllables were long, the boundary was situated between 40 and 64 milliseconds of transition duration – boundary values that closely mirrored those obtained for adult listeners by Miller and Liberman (1979) and by Miller (1981b). More recently, Jusczyk, Pisoni, Reed, Fernald, and Myers (1983) have shown that the same effects can be obtained with sine-wave analogs of speech, just as Pisoni, Carrell, and Gans (1983) were able to replicate the results of Miller and Liberman (1979) with these same stimuli in adult listeners. Inasmuch as the stimuli are not heard as speech (but see Best, Morrongiello, & Robson, 1981; and Remez, Rubin, Pisoni, & Carrell, 1981, for evidence that some sine-wave stimuli can be perceived as speech in some instances), the argument that has been proffered by Carrell et al. (1981; and see Aslin, Pisoni, & Jusczyk, 1983) is that these contextual effects cannot be the result of processing mechanisms that are specialized for speech. Nevertheless, the ability to use this form of contextual information provides infants and adults with a procedure for normalizing speech for rate of speech – a procedure that serves well the necessary function of categorization.[7]

A second example of contextual influences on the perception of speech has been reported by Jusczyk, Murray, Murphy, Levitt, and Carden (in preparation). They found, first, that two- to four-month-old infants were able to discriminate natural tokens of /fa/ and /θ/. However, when the initial frication was removed, there was no evidence of discrimination, despite differences in the formant transitions of the vocalic portions of the two syllables. However, when these same truncated syllables were preceded by a constant frication noise, that is, a pattern of frication that provided no differential cues for identification or discrimination, the infants discriminated them.

These findings correspond nicely with those obtained by Carden, Levitt, Jusczyk, and Walley (1981) with adult listeners. They constructed a series of synthetic speech patterns that varied in the starting frequency of the second- and third-formant transitions and were perceived as the stop consonants /b/ or /d/ plus the vowel /a/. A second series was made by adding an initial segment of an identical pattern of frication to each stimulus of the first series. These stimuli were now perceived as the fricatives /f/ or /θ/ plus the vowel /a/. Identification functions for the two series showed that the boundary for the fricative series fell within the stop-consonant category, /b/; that is, it was nearer to the beginning of the series than was the /b/–/d/ boundary. Moreover, stimuli that crossed the category boundary for fricatives but were not preceded by frication, and thus were perceived as instances of the category /b/, were considerably less discriminable than when they were preceded by the constant frication and perceived as different fricatives, /f/ and /θ/.

Thus, the infants' failure to discriminate the truncated patterns, which were not preceded by a constant frication pattern, may have come about because they, like adult listeners, perceived the stimuli to be members of the same category. However, when the truncated patterns were preceded by frication, the infants perceived the stimuli as members of different categories. The presence or absence of frication appeared to provide a frame of reference or context, signaling which boundary location is to be used for purposes of categorization: When frication is present the near boundary is appropriate and when there is no frication the far boundary is the criterion for categorization (see Carden et al., 1981, for a more complete description of the boundary locations).

Miller and Eimas (1983) investigated infant speech perception for the presence of trading relations that exist among the multiple sources of information for a phonetic contrast. More specifically, they studied the three- and four-month-old infant's categorization of the temporal aspects of voice-onset-time as a function of the value of a second cue for voicing, the frequency of the first-formant transition at the moment of onset (see Lisker, Liberman, Erickson, Dechovitz, & Mandler, 1977; and Summerfield & Haggard, 1977, for a full discussion of these cues). With adult listeners, the voicing boundary will be situated at a lower value of voice-onset-time when the first formant has a high-onset frequency than when it has a low-onset frequency. Again, if one considers only the absolute values of voice-onset-time, there are ambiguous values, that is, there is a range of values that is heard as both voiced and voiceless stops. However, when voice-onset-time is processed in conjunction with the spectral information for the first formant, this ambiguity no longer exists. Miller and Eimas found that this same trading relation exists in the perception of voicing information in infants. When the onset frequency of the first formant was high, the boundary value in milliseconds of voice-onset-time was between 5 and 30; when the frequency was low, the boundary value was situated between 30 and 55 milliseconds, values well in accord with the adult data. (For comments on the apparent contradiction between these findings and those discussed by Rosen & Howell, in Chapter 4, this volume, see Miller & Eimas, 1983.)

In summary, there is ample evidence for inferring the existence of categorization procedures in the processing system underlying the perception of speech by infants. Indeed, it seems to us that nature has generously endowed human infants with a sufficiently complex perceptual system so that their initial efforts at language acquisition can be directed toward discovering how the outputs of this system are to be used linguistically. This must certainly result in a faster acquisition process than if they also had to acquire the knowledge that speech must be represented by discrete categories as well as knowledge about which information should serve as the basis for categorization.

Relation of infant and adult categories

Examining the location of the infant's category boundaries allows one, in a number of instances, to infer close correspondences between the infant's presumably nonlinguistic categories and the phonetic categories of adult speakers of some languages. Thus, for example, categories that are based on the information for the three places of articulation among stop consonants found in English and some other languages show a markedly close correspondence in terms of boundary locations and category width (compare the results of Eimas, 1974, with infant listeners and those of Pisoni, 1973, with adult listeners). Infant–adult correspondences have also been found for the /r/-/l/ distinction and the stop consonant–semivowel contrast (compare Eimas, 1975, with Miyawaki, Strange, Verbrugge, Liberman, Jenkins, & Fujimura, 1975; and Eimas & Miller, 1980a, with Miller and Liberman, 1979, for the two contrasts, respectively). The information for voicing distinctions among the stop consonants, about which we know a great deal, presents an interesting picture of close correspondences as well as language-specific differences. The overall data (Aslin & Pisoni, 1980; Eimas et al., 1971; Lasky et al., 1975; Miller & Eimas, 1983; Streeter, 1976) indicate that infants divide the voice-onset-time continuum into three categories, with boundaries situated approximately at values that correspond to the voiced–voiceless boundary in English and other languages and to the prevoiced–voiced boundary of Thai, among other languages. However, many languages of the world do not divide this continuum in the same way that infants do. There are differences both in the number of categories and in the locations of boundary positions. Thus, for example, Thai has three categories, whereas English and Spanish have but two. Moreover, in the case of the latter two languages, the boundary location is markedly different (Abramson & Lisker, 1970, 1973; Lisker & Abramson, 1964; 1970; Williams, 1977a). Thus the initial categorical representations of infants must be malleable with respect to both category number and boundary location, so that with linguistic experience they can come to mirror the manner of categorization demanded by the parental language.

From this brief description it would seem that the infant comes to the world biologically endowed with the ability to distinguish and categorize virtually all of the information that is relevant to the phonetic categorization in natural languages. Experience with the parental language serves to maintain and perhaps enhance those categorizations for which there is an early correspondence (cf. Aslin & Pisoni, 1980; Strange & Broen, 1980). On the other hand, experience will eliminate a category or alter the boundary location between categories in situations where the correspondence is quite disparate (cf. Eimas, 1975; Lasky et al., 1975; Miyawaki et al., 1975 for evidence relating to these forms of alteration). Of course, we would also like to identify the factors that, in the course of the evolution of human languages, determined which of the inherent processing abilities of infants with respect to categorization were exploited (maintained) for a given language. That story, however, will be a difficult one to detail, for obvious reasons; we must be satisfied for now with attempting to describe the role of linguistic experience in speech processing as well as how this processing influences the acquisition of phonological competence.

Concerning the role of experience with the parental language, it is worth noting that its influence is evident at quite an early age. Werker and Tees (1984) found that two contrasts not present in the parental language, English in this case, which could be discriminated at 6 months of age, failed to be discriminated by virtually all of the infants who were tested at 12 months. What has been responsible for this dramatic change in capacity cannot be specified at present, but achieving some understanding of the processes that permit change in our capacity to discriminate and categorize speech is certainly central to an understanding of language acquisition. A critical and closely related issue is the nature of this loss of capacity: Is the loss permanent and thus presumably a reflection of some structural modification of the perceptual system during a critical period, or is it reversible and thereby a reflection of cognitive processes such as attention that can be altered again, even quite late in development? The issue is vigorously debated, and until recent experiments by Pisoni and his colleagues (McClasky, Pisoni, & Carrell, 1980; Pisoni, Aslin, Perey, & Hennessy, 1982), the weight of evidence seemed to favor permanent loss (see Strange & Jenkins, 1978). However, Pisoni et al. (1982) and McClasky et al. (1980) have shown the rather minimal amounts of training that directed listeners toward the relevant acoustic information to be sufficient to reestablish the absent prevoiced–voiced distinction in American–English-speaking listeners. Moreover, this capacity transferred across place of articulation. Whether this limited training is sufficient to permit a listener to function effectively in a natural listening situation where this distinction is phonemically relevant remains to be determined, however. A positive outcome would be most encouraging for those who are concerned with the remediation of language disabilities that seem to have at least part of their etiology in an inability to process the sounds of speech in an efficient manner (e.g., Tallal & Stark, 1980; Eimas & Clarkson, 1986).

The categorization of nonspeech sounds and visual patterns

The study of infant speech perception has revealed a number of impressive processing abilities, especially those that support the categorization of inherently variable signals. But the categorization of information is not restricted to the domain of speech; it is also evident in the infant's perception of some nonspeech auditory patterns as well as in the perception of some visual patterns (see Chapter 9 by Bornstein, this volume). Indeed, it would seem that the processes of categorization are a basic, biologically determined component of all perceptual systems; but then how could they be otherwise if we, and other species that rely on similar sensory systems for information, are to survive in environments that provide such an array of variation?

Nonspeech auditory patterns

With regard to the perception of nonspeech acoustic events that have phonetic significance in speech contexts, the perception of transition duration has, as we noted, been found to be CP-like in patterns that are not heard as speech. Moreover, the way that individual values of transition duration are mapped onto categorical representations is sensitive to the duration of the acoustic patterns as it is with speech signals (see Jusczyk et al., 1983, for results with infants, and Pisoni et al., 1983, for data with adults). In a similar vein, the perception of tone-onset-time, which is the temporal order of two tones and can be considered a nonspeech analog of the temporal aspects of voice-onset-time, has also been found to be perceived in a CP-like fashion by infants and adults (Jusczyk, Pisoni, Walley, & Murray, 1980; and Pisoni, 1977, respectively). And virtually the same effects have been obtained for rise time in both adults and infant listeners (Cutting & Rosner, 1974; and Jusczyk, Rosner, Cutting, Foard, & Smith, 1977, respectively), although the CP-like perception of rise time may have been a function of inadvertent discontinuities in the stimulus continuum (Rosen & Howell, 1981 and Chapter 4 by Rosen & Howell, this volume; but see Cutting, 1982). Finally, we should note that not all acoustic information that has significance in the context of speech is perceived categorically in nonspeech environments, whether by infants (Eimas, 1974, 1975) or by adults (Mattingly, Liberman, Syrdal, & Halwes, 1971; Miyawaki et al., 1975).[8] However, this absence of CP may be due to inappropriate definitions of the critical information for speech (cf. Jusczyk, Smith, & Murphy, 1981; Pastore, 1981).

Findings of CP-like perception of nonspeech acoustic events have been the basis of arguments against the existence of specialized mechanisms for the perception of speech (e.g., Cutting, 1978; Pisoni, 1977, among others). The issue of domain specificity in the earliest levels of speech perception has had a long history, and continues with renewed vigor as new evidence is found (e.g., Liberman, 1970, 1982; Liberman et al., 1967). Sufficient space is not available for a complete discussion of this issue; however, we do wish to note that the data cited above can be logically, if not parsimoniously, accommodated by assuming both specialized processors for speech and general auditory mechanisms that also subserve categorization. The latter would presumably not be unique to human beings and thus would be responsible for the categorization of speech by nonhuman organisms, chinchillas, for example (Kuhl & Miller, 1978), and for the categorization of nonspeech signals by all organisms. The possibility of a dual-processing system in human listeners finds support in recent experiments of Summerfield (1982), who showed that the perception of tone-onset-time was not influenced by spectral manipulations that markedly alter the categorization of voice-onset-time, and in the discrepancy between the boundary locations for tone-onset-time and voice-onset-time (Jusczyk et al., 1980; but see Jusczyk, Rosner, Reed, & Kennedy, in preparation).

Visual patterns

In an early study of the categorization of visual information, McGurk (1972) found that infants as young as six months were able to categorize instances of the same form that varied in orientation. In what is the experimental procedure corresponding to the equivalence-class-formation paradigm in infant speech perception, McGurk presented a simple configural pattern in a number of different orientations during a familiarization period. Immediately thereafter, the infant's attention was assessed by the time spent looking toward one of two test patterns: a pattern that varied once more in orientation with no change in form or one that varied only in form. Increased attention relative to the last familiarization trial period (i.e., dishabituation of attention) occurred with the new pattern but not with the old pattern in a new orientation. McGurk also demonstrated that the orientational difference could be discriminated; hence the results can be explained by assuming that the infants formed an equivalence class for the single configural pattern regardless of orientation.

In a very similar experiment, Cohen and Strauss (1979) showed that seven-month-old infants could form categorical representations of "a specific female face regardless of orientation," and, most impressively, of "female faces in general." Again, it was shown that the basis for the equivalence in responding was not a failure to discriminate, in that these same-aged infants (and even younger infants who could apparently not form these equivalence classes) could discriminate changes in orientation after they had been familiarized with a single female face in a single orientation. The latter finding also indicates, of course, that the abstraction of categorical representations requires experience with more than a single instance of the category. This is, of course, quite reasonable in that the number of potential categories to which a single entity, complex or simple, may belong is unbounded (see Chapter 19 by Harnad, this volume). Only by encountering variations with respect to the category in question is there a reasonable probability, all other things being equal, that the intended category will match that which is abstracted by the infant.

Further evidence of equivalence-class formation has been obtained with a variety of categories, including stimulus configurations per se, in three-month-old infants (Milewski, 1979), natural categories such as animals and foods in twelve-month-old infants (Ross, 1980), characteristics of human faces, age and sex, for example, in five-month-old infants (Fagan, 1976; Fagan & Singer, 1979) and number in seven-month-old infants (Starkey, Spelke & Gelman, 1983). Representations of this kind are also possible in ten-month-old infants even when the criterial features are ill-defined or fuzzy (Husaim & Cohen, 1981).

Strauss (1979) and Bomba and Siqueland (1983) have also attempted to determine whether the infant's categorical abstractions of visual information can be described by prototypic structures, that is, by some central or average categorical value that is also the best exemplar of the category. In both studies, evidence of prototypic structuring was obtained. Indeed, in the Bomba and Siqueland experiments, the infants, who were only three and four months old never actually experienced the prototypic patterns and yet recognized them as more familiar than other categorical exemplars that had been experienced during the familiarization period (see Chapter 16 by Medin & Barsalou, this volume).[9]

Finally, we should mention that there are two series of studies that have assessed the categorical nature of infant visual perception by comparing the discriminability of within- and between-category differences along the dimensions of wavelength and orientation (Bornstein, Kessen, & Weiskopf, 1976; Chapter 9 by Bornstein, this volume; and Bomba, 1982; respectively). Bornstein et al. showed not only that four-month-old infants tend to perceive the continuum of wave length in terms of categories, but also that their "color categories" are highly similar to those of normal, trichromatic adult observers. Bomba, on the other hand, showed that whereas orientational differences in square-wave gratings were perceived in a CP-like manner by three-month-old infants, four-month-old infants showed equivalently high levels of discrimination for both within-category and between-category differences in orientation. Perhaps with smaller stimulus differences or with greater demands on processing, older infants would also show CP-like perception, although it is always possible that our increasing abilities to differentiate stimuli with overshadow inherent categorization procedures for at least some forms of environmental information (see also Chapter 18 by Bialystock & Olson, this volume).

In brief, the abundant evidence for categorization in infants as young as four days in one instance and in several sensory domains attests to the prevalence of this form of processing as well as to its existence very early in the course of our interactions with the environment. These findings support assumptions that the mechanisms underlying the categorization of information are to a large degree biologically determined and organized, although certainly not immutably so. We shall consider further characteristics of the processing system for speech after a discussion of the possibility that the categories of speech, like those of vision, are structured entities, describable by prototypes.

The structure of the categories of speech

In discussing the issue of category structure, we shall focus on categorization of stimuli that vary in properties that define phonetic categories, as virtually all the relevant research to date has dealt with this type of variation. Consider a typical speech series that varies along a linguistically relevant acoustic dimension and that ranges from one category to another. An example is a /ba-pa/ series that varies in voice-onset-time from a value low enough to specify the voiced consonant, /b/, to a value high enough to specify the voiceless consonant, /p/. The CP literature reveals, as noted above, that if such stimuli are presented for identification, listeners readily classify them into two categories, corresponding to /ba/ and /pa/, with a rather sharp boundary between categories. Furthermore, although discrimination of stimuli within a category is considerably more difficult than discrimination of members of two different categories, discrimination is possible, and at times quite good, given appropriate task conditions (see Repp, 1983). The issue of the internal structure of these phonetic categories concerns whether the members of a given category are differentiated in terms of their relative goodness as category members. That is, are some tokens of /ba/ perceived as better /ba/s than others, and similarly for tokens of the /pa/ category? (Cf. Chapter 7 by Diehl & Kluender, this volume.)

The informal answer to this question is certainly yes. As anyone who has had experience synthesizing speech continua can attest, stimuli within a category are not equally representative. More specifically, as one synthesizes stimuli that vary from a value near the category boundary to a more extreme value, they are heard as increasingly better exemplars of the category in question. However, as the values along the dimension become too extreme, the stimuli begin to be heard as less good exemplars of the category. This is true even when there is no adjacent third phonetic category along the dimension. For the typical CP experiment that includes two categories, the experimenter preselects one good exemplar of each category to serve as an endpoint stimulus, and only stimuli that range between these two endpoints are included in the stimulus set – more extreme stimuli are simply omitted.

It is interesting that published data bearing directly on the issue of the relative goodness of stimuli as category members are virtually nonexistent. In particular, we know of no studies in which stimuli from a continuum have been presented to listeners for judgments of goodness, where the stimuli varied from a value near the category boundary to one well beyond what would be considered informally as a good exemplar of the category (see Chapter 8 by Massaro, this volume).[10] Perhaps this is due partly to a long history of focusing on the listener's relative *inability* to distinguish within-category members: If stimuli are assumed to be indiscriminable, there is no reason to believe they might differ in perceived category goodness. Recently, however, Samuel (1982) addressed the issue of relative category goodness. As part of a larger experiment, he investigated whether there are stimuli within a phonetic category that listeners consider to be the best exemplars, or prototypical members, of the category. Focusing on a /ga-ka/ series that varied in voice-onset-time, he asked listeners to choose which stimulus from the /ga/ category was the "best," or prototypical /ga/. The stimuli varied from a value near the average /ga-ka/ boundary to a value beyond one judged informally to be the best /ga/. Samuel reported that listeners could indeed perform the task. We should point out, however, that because data on the reliability of the listeners' choices were not presented, it is not clear whether each listener actually considered only a very narrowly defined region of stimulus values to be prototypic or, alternatively, whether a relatively wide range of values was considered to be equally representative of the category. Clearly, more extended investigations of the differential perception of within-category members are needed. It will be important to determine not only the range of stimuli along any given series that listeners treat as instances of the "best exemplar" of the category, but also the relative degree to which members on either side of these critical values are perceived as reasonable category members.[11]

Let us assume that the appropriate experiments will indeed confirm our informal impression that stimuli within a category vary in their relative representativeness or typicality as category members; that is, phonetic categories have internal structure. One issue concerning internal structure that is particularly relevant from the point of view of infant speech categories is the level of processing at which the structure arises. Two possibilities can be distinguished. The first is that the structure arises at an early prephonetic level of processing; hence the initial representations generated by early analytic routines would not only be CP-like, but also structured. The second possibility is that the internal structure derives from subsequent processes that map the prephonetic representation onto a linguistic representation; that is, the internal structure depends on linguistic processes. Of course, for this to happen, there must be information at the prephonetic level about the actual values of stimuli that would permit subsequent processes to provide the structure, perhaps by differentially weighting these stimulus values. If the second possibility obtains, then we might expect that the infant's categories, which are prephonetic, have no internal structure. Rather, this structure would arise over the course of language acquisition, when the prelinguistic perceptual categories begin to take on linguistic significance. However, if there *is* a prephonetic basis for internal-category structure for the adult, then it may well be that the infant's perceptual categories also have internal structure. In this case, one important role of linguistic experience would be to modify this structure appropriately in accordance with the parental language.

It is thus of considerable interest to determine the level at which the internal structure of adult phonetic categories arises. Recently, Miller, Connine, Schermer, and Kluender (1983) addressed this issue using a selective-adaptation procedure, which has been shown to tap processing at a prephonetic level (Roberts & Summerfield, 1981; Sawusch & Jusczyk, 1981). In a typical adaptation experiment, identification of the stimuli along a continuum, such as one that ranges from /ba/ to /pa/, is assessed before and after repeated exposure to a member of the continuum called the adaptor. One effect of this exposure is to alter identification, such that fewer stimuli from the category of the adaptor are now labeled as members of that category. Miller et al. (1983) investigated the issue of internal-category structure by assessing the relative effectiveness of members of a category as adaptors, using adaptors that ranged from boundary stimuli to stimuli well beyond those judged to be reasonable category members. For example, one test used a /ba-pa/ series, with adaptors ranging from a /pa/ with a voice-onset-time value low enough to place it near the /ba-pa/ boundary to a /pa/ with such a high voice-onset-time value that it was perceived as a very poor exemplar of the /pa/ category. The underlying assumption was that relative differences in category exemplariness would be reflected in differences in stimulus effectiveness as adaptors. For three different phonetic contrasts, (/ba-pa/, /dæ-gæ/, and /bæ-wæ/), Miller et al. (1983) found that as the adaptor varied from a value near the boundary to one informally perceived to be a good exemplar of the category, the magnitude of adaptation increased; however, as the adaptor became more extreme, it began to lose its effectiveness. Thus, the adaptation functions had an inverted U-shape, with a rather narrow range of stimuli producing the maximal adaptation effect.

Miller et al. (1983) interpreted the nonmonotonic adaptation functions as evidence that at the prephonetic level of processing tapped by the selective adaptation technique, stimuli are effectively grouped into categories and, moreover, that stimuli within these categories vary in effectiveness as category members. On this interpretation, the structure of adult phonetic categories finds its roots at prephonetic levels of processing. As to how the structure may arise at a prephonetic level, one possibility is that there are certain stimuli that serve as defining stimuli or prototypes for categories because of some as yet unknown psychoacoustic properties. Other stimuli are ordered relative to the prototype to which they most closely correspond, with the boundary between categories approximately equidistant from the two adjacent prototypes. As a stimulus varies from the prototype in either direction along the continuum, it loses its effectiveness as a category member.[12]

The findings of Miller and her associates support the proposition that there exist structured speech categories at a prephonetic level of processing; they are also consistent with the view that these categories are defined in terms of prototypical values. This raises the intriguing possibility that the speech categories of the prelinguistic infant also have internal structure that is based on category prototypes. If this is true (and there is some recent affirmative evidence for vowel categories; Grieser & Kuhl, 1983), then given the evidence we reviewed earlier for a prototype-based structure of infant categories in the visual domain, we might conjecture that not only is the human infant well-endowed with domain-specific procedures for categorizing an inherently variable world, but also that these procedures yield similar prototypically structured categories, regardless of modality.

The units of processing and perception

In theoretical descriptions of perceptual systems it is often assumed that the initial level of processing operates on units of physical information or their neural transforms consisting of temporal and structural characteristics of the stimulus rather than the objects, scenes, and events that actually populate our environments and are the contents of perception. To explain that our perceptions correspond to things in the world and not to the initial units of processing, investigators have further assumed that the outputs of the initial level of processing are integrated, if only in terms of sequential order, and compared to stored representations of environmental entities. Perception occurs when there is an acceptable correspondence between representations generated by the processing system and representations of the world that have been previously acquired and stored.[13]

Theories of this general sort must ultimately define precisely the stimulus units that serve as inputs to the processing system as well as the stored representations that correspond to the basic units of perception (see Chapter 19 by Harnad, this volume). Theories of speech perception have often conformed to this metatheoretical framework that is at the heart of modern cognitive psychology. For example, Klatt (1979) defined the units of processing in terms of time, each overlapping unit being approximately 26 milliseconds in duration, and the units of stored representation in terms of lexical items, at least in one version of the model. Other theoretical models of speech processing have typically been less explicit about the initial units of processing, while assuming quite different units of representation. The latter units have included syllables (e.g., Mehler, Segui, & Frauenfelder, 1981; Savin & Bever, 1970), context-conditioned allophones (Wickelgren, 1969), diphones (Klatt, 1979), and phones that are defined in terms of discrete features (e.g., Liberman, 1970; Liberman & Studdert-Kennedy, 1978).

In our view of speech perception, we assume that the first level of processing operates in a continuous manner on an unsegmented speech signal in both infants and adults. There are, in effect, no processing units per se. Processing at this level may be construed as simply passing the signal, transformed by the peripheral auditory system, through an array of analytic processes. These processes yield CP-like decisions about the acoustic correlates of phonetic categories for comparison with stored representations of these same categories. Each individual decision, of which there are many for each representational unit, is arrived at as soon as the relevant information has been received, and consequently the time for different decisions may vary substantially. The processes are, in effect, intelligent (cf. Runeson, 1977); they possess "knowledge" about the informational requirements for the many categorizations of acoustic information that are relevant to perception at the phonetic level. Moreover, given the processing capabilities of infants already described, much of this information is probably an innate part of the perceptual system.

We hypothesize a system that does continuous processing largely because we know of no principled way to justify an initial segmentation of the speech signal on a purely temporal basis, such that the resulting segments provide sufficient information for the initial categorical decisions.[14] For example, Stevens and Blumstein (1981) have shown that decisions regarding the correlates of place of articulation may occur with extremely brief speech signals, often less than 30 milliseconds in duration, whereas Miller (1981b; Miller & Eimas, 1983; Miller & Liberman, 1979) has shown that much longer inputs are necessary for decisions relevant to the distinction between a stop consonant and a semivowel. The latter, as we have noted, is true for adult and infant listeners. Moreover, the information that is relevant to certain other phonetic decisions may be spread over hundreds of milliseconds and may even cross morphemic boundaries (e.g., Repp et al., 1978). Given findings of this sort, there is certainly no readily apparent temporal basis for segmentation. Furthermore, an early segmentation of the speech signal on the basis of structural properties of speech, for example, the stretch of speech bounded by two periods of silence or two peaks in intensity, cannot be accomplished in a principled manner; these acoustic segments simply do not correspond to linguistic units, whether segmental or syllabic (cf. Fant, 1960).

We turn now to the basic representations of speech. The evidence from studies of adult speech processing strongly supports the inference that there is a representation of speech that is prelexical in nature (see Foss & Blank, 1980; Mehler, Segui, & Frauenfelder, 1981; Segui, Frauenfelder, & Mehler, 1981). However, the data do not dictate an unequivocal decision as to whether these prelexical representations are segmental or syllabic in nature. Arguments can be made for either unit of representation, as well as for the possibility that both units exist.

There are numerous demonstrations of faster decision times for syllabic targets than for phonemic targets (e.g., Savin & Bever, 1970), which have been taken as inferential evidence that syllabic codes form the basic representations of speech and that phonemic codes are derived from an analysis of syllabic representations. However, the data are, in fact, questionable, as must be the inference as to which code is basic and which is derived. Swinney and Prather (1980; cf. Mills, 1980) have shown that the difference in decision times favoring monitoring for syllables as opposed to phonemes can be eliminated, although not reversed, by presenting the consonantal phonemic targets in carrier items with a constant following vowel. This creates a situation comparable to what occurs with syllable targets, when by definition all the segmental information is known to the listener. Given such data, Mills (1980) has argued that the original findings of faster monitoring times with syllables may have resulted from mismatches between listeners' expectations of the targets and their actual physical instantiations rather than from the additional time required to perform the necessary decomposition of syllabic representations to arrive at phonemic information. Although these data argue against the idea that syllabic representations are the more basic form of representation, they do not, of course, indicate that phonemic representations are more basic. Indeed, the data do not permit a choice, and consequently present the possibility that both phonemes and syllables are initially represented.

More recently, Mehler and his associates (Cutler, Mehler, Norris, & Segui, 1983, 1986; Mehler, Dommergues, Frauenfelder, & Segui, 1981) have provided intriguing experimental results that are relevant not only to the issue of the basic level of representation but also to the possible effects that linguistic experience may have on the representation of speech. In the first experiments, with French-speaking listeners, Mehler et al. (1981) showed that the decision times with syllable targets were faster when the targets corresponded to the initial syllables of the carrier words than when they did not. Moreover, this effect was independent of the length of the target syllable. Thus, for example, the times for the targets /pa/ and /pal/ were faster (and, importantly, equal) when the carrier words were *pa-lace* and *pal-mier*, respectively, than when the carrier words were reversed. This kind of evidence is comfortably accommodated by assuming that the units of representation are syllables, and not individual phonemes. However, in later studies with English-speaking listeners, Cutler et al. (1986) did not find the same pattern of results. Rather, their findings were generally consistent with a representational format that was either segmental or syllabic, provided that in the latter case the syllable structures were limited to consonant–vowel sequences. Inasmuch as the syllabic structure of English is much more ambiguous than that of French, the failure of English-speaking listeners to use complex, or perhaps any, syllabic representations in monitoring tasks is not unreasonable. It would appear from these results, then, that linguistic experience helps to determine the unit of representation.

A question naturally arises about how speech is represented before the acquisition of language. There are two studies of speech processing with infants that bear on this issue. In the first, Bertoncini and Mehler (1981) showed that infants less than two months of age were better able to discriminate speech patterns when these contained a consonant–vowel–consonant sequence than when they contained only consonantal sequences – results that are consistent with the assumption that the outputs of the initial level of processing are integrated into holistic units that correspond to syllabic structures. In the second study, Miller and Eimas (1979) demonstrated that three- and four-month-old infants were able to recognize the recombinations of segmental constituents of consonant-vowel syllables. Whereas the latter finding can be interpreted as recognizing the ordering of segmental units, it is equally likely that the infants were recognizing changes in syllable-like structures.

Up to this point, we have claimed only that the outputs of processing – that is, the infant's categorical representations of the linguistically relevant acoustic information – are integrated, and that the infant's discriminative decisions may be based on these integrated units. If one takes these integrated units in infants to have syllable-like structure, then a consideration of the extensive variation in syllabic structures both within and across languages supports the contention that these units must be relatively simple, as would be the case if they were limited at least initially to consonant–vowel sequences. What is perhaps most notable about the variation in syllabic form is the range in the number of segmental units that may constitute a syllable as well as the number of ways that the same string of phonemes may be segmented into syllables in different lexical contexts. Moreover, in that there are no well-documented acoustic cues for syllable boundaries, considerable linguistic knowledge must be required for the segmentation of speech into the possible syllables of any language – knowledge that we would prefer to attribute to experience rather than to the biology of the infant. One inference from recent developments in autosegmental phonology is that attention to prosodic information might be helpful in providing a rough syllabic segmentation of continuous speech. In particular, it has been suggested that syllables are tone-bearing units (Goldsmith, 1981; van der Hulst & Smith, 1982b). Hence, attention to the tonal patterning of speech could serve as a basis for defining units of representation such as the syllable. Given that infants appear to be highly attentive to the prosody of speech (see Fernald, 1984), it is possible that syllabic segmentation occurs, or at least begins, in this way.

Finally, there is no reason to believe that the actual representations of speech stored during early infancy, whether innately given or acquired through experience, differ in structure from the integrated representations that are generated by the processing routines and that, we believe, have a simple syllabic structure. Exactly what information is stored in this syllable-like auditory structure remains to be determined empirically, and indeed this is one focus of our research and that of Mehler and his associates. In addition, we believe that the existence of a single structural representation of speech during early infancy can be reconciled with the strong possibility that more than one form of representation exists at the phonetic and phonological levels in mature listeners, both within a single language and across different languages. One needs to assume, however, that different languages and varying forms of experience with language may generate different forms of stored speech representation. Thus, for example, languages that are characterized by well-defined syllabic structures may foster complex syllabic representations, whereas the demands of becoming literate may encourage the development of phonemic (segmental) codes (Morais, Cary, Alegria, & Bertelson, 1979).

Acquisition of a phonological system and a lexicon

Given our assumption that the prelinguistic infant's initial representation of speech takes the form of simple syllables, what can we say about the role of speech-perception capacities in language acquisition? As a first step in this direction, we should consider the nature of the task that confronts the infant. Among the fundamental prerequisites for acquiring a spoken language is the ability to discriminate the different words of the language from each other and to identify words as important units. In other words, the infant must begin by acquiring some sort of vocabulary in the language. To be sure, the infant will also have to learn the rules for lawfully relating the words of the language to one another in complex utterances, but the first step probably involves learning to recognize the vocabulary items themselves. Another consideration is the speed with which the words can be recognized. The skilled listener is normally able to understand speech spoken at rates of three or four words per second. Thus, a constraint on language learners is that they must arrive at some organization of the lexicon that makes it possible to understand speech produced at such rates. Presumably, a process for recognizing speech that involved exhaustively comparing the incoming signal individually to all elements in some mental lexicon would not be a plausible one, given the time constraints. Hence, one would expect a pressure to organize the items to be learned so as to facilitate the rapid recognition of words. The nature of the basic speech-perception capacities will certainly be a critical factor in determining what that organization is. It is also reasonable to assume that the sound properties of the language being learned will constrain the form of the organization that the listener will use. Indeed, it may be that the attempt to find the optimal organization for processing words in a particular language is ultimately responsible for the cross-language differences in perceptual boundaries that we noted earlier. Finally, within a given language, words often take on multiple forms, and the relationships between these forms are generally lawful (e.g., the relationship between singular and plural forms of the same word). For the average listener such variations apparently pose no great difficulty even on the first hearing of a new variant of some familiar lexical item (provided that the context is appropriate). Thus, the underlying structure for the word-recognition process should permit these generalizations naturally.

With these considerations in mind, let us speculate about the role of infant speech-perception capacities in the acquisition of a particular language. From the point of view of the perception of language, when learning a particular word, the infant must store some form of representation of that word that can be used to check against information available from the analysis of incoming utterances. When there is a satisfactory match between the output of the analysis and the stored representation for a given word, then that particular word will be recognized. There are three important points to be made here. First, it should be obvious that the analysis of utterances goes on even before the infant has "learned" a word. This type of analysis is available for all the utterances that the infant hears. In fact, it is this analysis that is the source of the infant's discrimination and categorization of speech sounds in the typical speech-perception experiments. Second, the analysis of the speech signal is neither open-ended nor arbitrary. It is *not* a discovery procedure. Rather, the analysis is constrained by the innately structured processing system, and hence there is only a limited set of dimensions along which the speech signal might be analyzed. Third, the information that is stored as a representation of a word is only an approximation of that available from the auditory analysis (cf., Chapter 19, this volume). Thus, from the limited set of dimensions furnished by the auditory analysis routines, the infant might begin by storing only a few highly salient properties of the word. Later the stored representation of the word would be elaborated by the addition of other information (available from the analysis routines) that would help to distinguish it from other words with similar sound properties. In effect, this process of selecting a particular subset of dimensions from an innately available set to represent the words of the language would be an example in phonology of what Chomsky (1980) has described as "parameter setting." In the end, the particular information contained in the representation of a given word would amount to a prototype of the sound properties of the word.

Thus, the analytic processing yields a description of the incoming acoustic signal, which forms the basis for any representation of a word that the infant might develop and store. At first, new words might be stored as separate entities with no particular organization relating them, other than that they are language items. Consequently, whenever the infant attempts to identify a particular word, it would be necessary to search exhaustively through the set of stored items until a match was obtained. Whereas such a procedure might be workable as long as the number of items to be searched remained relatively small, it would soon become unwieldy as the number of items greatly increased. At this point, some sort of systematic organization of the representations of the vocabulary items would be required. It is reasonable to suppose that this organization is based on characteristics of the information available in the CP-like representations derived from the processing. One suggestion (cf. Jusczyk, 1984; Klatt, 1979) is that information about the spectral characteristics of the onsets of words could provide the original basis for the organization. According to this view, words with similar spectral-onset characteristics would occupy positions relatively close to one another. The obvious reason for choosing an organization on the basis of onset characteristics is that this matches the temporal sequence of the input string and would allow the perceiver to begin processing the incoming utterance before it had been completed. An organization of this sort – one whereby processing can begin immediately – is important for the listener to be able to cope with the speed with which successive words are presented under normal speaking conditions. By organizing things along these lines, the perceiver narrows the size of the set of the items to be searched during word recognition to a smaller set with similar onset characteristics. Given our original assumption of a perceptual unit on the order of a syllable, it would follow that syllables having similar onset characteristics would be grouped together, and especially that multisyllabic words having the same initial syllable would occupy adjacent locations. For multisyllabic words, the onset characteristics of noninitial syllables would further constrain the location of these words in the growing recognition network.

At this point it is worth considering in more detail the nature of the representations used in the network. As noted earlier, the initial representations are likely to be quite global, incorporating a limited number of salient features of the acoustic form of the world. In this respect, our view is similar to the position taken by a number of investigators studying the acquisition of phonology who have suggested that the initial phonological distinctions occur between global features of whole words, with a gradual progression toward more fine-grained units such as phonemes (see Ferguson, 1978; Menyuk & Menn, 1979; Moskowitz, 1973; Waterson, 1971). In our view, as the size of the infant's vocabulary grows, there will be increasing pressure to make the form of the representation more specific in order to differentiate it more readily from other similar words that the infant has learned. It is at this point that the specific nature of the sound structure of the language being learned begins to have an impact on the relationship between the acoustic characteristics of a word and its representation by the infant. Specifically, the task of the language-learner is to devise a representation for a particular word so that it has the greatest number of properties in common with the various tokens of that word, yet the smallest number in common with utterances of different words. This is to say that the language-learner's representation will take the form of a prototype (Hyman & Frost, 1975; Posner & Keele, 1968; Rosch & Mervis, 1975). Hence, from the information available about a word through the application of the analytic processes, the infant would be inclined to select what is most germane for distinguishing between the possible words in that language. This is apt to be a gradual process, dependent on experience with the language. Hence, the prototype associated with a particular word would undergo continual refinement as the infant mastered the phonological structure of the language.

What might be involved in refining a prototype in this way? One possibility is that the infant learns to weight the information available through the analytic processes in specific ways. That is, certain types of information will be deemed as more important indicators of distinctions between words in the language than others. In effect, the perceiver orders which sources of information are to be checked in word recognition and the relative importance of each. In some cases, it is possible that the analytic processes themselves undergo some modification (e.g., the criterion value used to determine which of the possible output messages the processes will return would be reset from some initial default value to another one given the language context). Thus, in order to refine the prototype in an appropriate way, the infant develops a scheme or prescription for weighting the information to be used in recognizing the words in the language. This scheme, which is specific to the language being learned, will be directly reflected as constraints that guide the formation of the prototypes to be used in recognition.

Let us consider a possible example of the way in which the phonological structure of a given language could influence the weighting scheme the infant develops. Voicing differences are used to signal contrasts between words in many languages. However, as Lisker (1978a) has noted, there are many different acoustic correlates of voicing information. It would not be unreasonable to assume that languages differ in the exact way in which these correlates are used to signal voicing changes. A case in point is voicing changes in English and Spanish. In Spanish, the determination of voicing contrasts between words is largely dependent on whether voicing is present at the onset of a segment, whereas in English, many so-called voicing contrasts are cued by differences in the amount of aspiration (voiced sounds being unaspirated and voiceless ones generally aspirated, as Ladefoged [1971] has noted). Furthermore, Macken (1980) has reported that Spanish speakers substitute a stop-spirant distinction for voicing contrasts in utterance-initial positions 30 to 40% of the time and that Spanish-learning children initially use the stop-spirant distinction for this purpose in their early productions as well. Therefore, given the present view, one would anticipate that English and Spanish speakers have developed different ways of weighting information relating to voicing contrasts. The available perceptual evidence is certainly consistent with this view, because, as we noted earlier, it is known that the category boundary for voiced–voiceless contrasts differs for the two languages (Abramson & Lisker, 1973; Williams, 1977a,b). A further implication is that bilingual speakers would develop different weighting schemes for each language (and there is some evidence that this is true; see Elman, Diehl, & Buchwald, 1977).[15]

Having considered some aspects of the way the structure of the representations of the individual words develop, we now turn to a further examination of the word-recognition network and its relation to phonological development. One important question is how the ability to analyze words into component phonemes arises. Recall that the perceptual units we postulated are of syllable length. Again, the organization of the word-recognition network helps to explain how the ability for phonemic segmentation might arise. Words that share common initial segments would tend to be located near each other because of similarities in their acoustic characteristics at onset. The pressure to implement some further segmentation of the perceptual units could lead in the direction of looking for commonalities between items in the same general vicinity in the network. Common characteristics shared by a large number of nearby items and not shared by more distant ones might serve as an initial basis for developing representations corresponding to phonemic units. Once again, this would amount to developing a prototype, only in this instance a prototype for a phonemic segment, one that would be used to match against the output from the analytic processing in the case of new words to be analyzed or against the information encoded in the prototype for the whole word in the case of decisions about previously stored items. One important caveat is necessary here. Although phonemic segmentation might arise as a result of operations performed on the word-recognition network, it would not necessarily follow that the network would be reorganized so as to provide a segment-by-segment analysis of words during the course of on-line processing. Instead, a segment-by-segment analysis might constitute an entirely independent process occurring only in special circumstances (e.g., when encountering a nonword or an unfamiliar word).

It is difficult to say exactly when the child begins to engage in phonemic segmentation. This is not the type of process infants would be likely to use. There is some suggestion that the ability to perform phonemic segmentation arises in conjunction with learning how to read (see Liberman, Shankweiler, Fisher, & Carter, 1974; Walley, Smith, & Jusczyk, 1980). In fact, Morais et al. (1979) found that illiterate adults were unable to learn a task that involved segmentation into phonemes even though they were able to master the same task when it involved manipulating syllables.

A second issue is the role assigned to rules in descriptions of the child's behavior. Historically, there was a tendency to provide a description of the child's behavior in terms of the rules that the child was using and to discuss those rules in relation to the ones in descriptions of adult-based phonologies. More recently, there has been a recognition of the need to separate rules that relate to output constraints on what the child is able to articulate from those that relate to generalizations about the sound structure of language (see Ingram, 1974; Kiparsky & Menn, 1977; Menn, 1980). Much of the early behavior of the child is best viewed as the acquisition of rules for pronunciation, rather than as acquiring generalizations about structural properties of the language. In this respect, it is interesting to note that changes in pronunciation tend to occur first for individual words; only later does there appear to be an attempt to generalize the potential rule to other words in the child's vocabulary (Ferguson, 1978). The latter tendency is apparently responsible for the instances of overgeneralization and regression in pronunciation that have often been observed (see Kiparsky & Menn, 1977; Smith, 1973). Again, the notion is that there is a tendency for words to undergo an increasing phonological organization during the course of development.

It is quite likely that that development of pronunciation rules will have consequences for the word-recognition network we proposed. For example, the effort to generalize rules for pronunciation may lead to the search for commonalities between different words that result in representations for individual phonemic segments. More important, knowledge gained about phonological regularities in the language could be directly incorporated into the network in ways that might help facilitate word recognition (e.g., by providing shortcuts or alternative routes as Klatt [1979] has suggested). One consequence of reorganizing the network in this fashion would be that during on-line processing it would not be necessary to postulate the explicit application of phonological rules. Instead, the application of such rules would be a byproduct of the way in which the recognition system was structured – for example, if the rules were "precompiled" into the network. The effort to organize the network in this way might be considerable, yet the payoff would be the increase in speed it would permit in on-line speech processing.

In conclusion, we have attempted to describe how the earliest capacities of the infant to perceive speech relate to the development of phonological competence and the acquisition of a lexicon. Although much of the theoretical discussion is highly speculative, we believe that the account we have offered is a useful way to view the transition from the prelinguistic processing of speech to the beginnings of linguistic competence. Of course, full competence with a human language involves more than acquiring a phonology and a lexicon; it requires learning syntactic structures and semantic interpretative schemes as well as the pragmatics of communication. What we have tried to do is provide a theoretical foundation for those later acquisitions.

Notes

1. This is not to say that the mechanisms underlying the perception of speech at the earliest levels of analysis are domain specific. It may well be the case that speech and other acoustic events are processed by a general auditory-processing system. We will consider one aspect of this controversy in our later discussion of the perception of nonspeech events.

2. We do not wish to imply that categorization procedures or their inherent nature are properties of only human perceptual systems (see Chapter 10 by Ehret and Chapter 11 by Snowdon, this volume). There is evidence that nonhuman organisms impose categorical representations on arrays of information (e.g., Herrnstein & Loveland, 1964), and even on the sounds of speech (e.g., Kuhl & Miller, 1978; Chapter 12 by Kuhl, this volume). We do not know of any studies with infant animals describing their categorizing abilities, but given that their world, like ours, comes with infinite variety, and given the general similarity of nonhuman sensory systems to human sensory systems, it is reasonable to assume that such procedures are available very early in their lives.

3. It is of interest to note that vowel length is also a cue for rate of speech (see Miller, 1981a) as well as phrase-final position (Cooper, Paccia & Lapointe, 1978). But just how the perceptual system correctly determines the one or more functions that vowel length may be serving remains a deep mystery.

4. That is to say, we have no substantial evidence that perceptual constancy arises as a result of some as yet unspecified acoustic invariants (see Kewley-Port, 1982; Searle, Jacobson, & Rayment, 1979; Stevens & Blumstein, 1981, for attempts to find these invariants; but see Chapin, Tseng, & Lieberman, 1982, for recent contradictory evidence). At the same time we have no compelling explanations based on the operating characteristics of perceptual systems for perceptual constancy (for preliminary versions of this form of explanation see Eimas & Corbit [1973], Liberman et al. [1967], and Stevens & House [1972]). Finally, learning in some sense, such as assumed by the principle of acquired similarity (Dollard & Miller, 1950), seems an inadequate explanation given both the sheer number of instances that one encounters and the ability of infants to form equivalence classes with great rapidity (e.g., Kuhl, 1980; and see our discussion above as well as Eimas [1982], for some consideration of why such abilities should be considered inherent properties of perceptual systems).

5. For analogous findings with infants, see Eimas (1975) and Miller and Eimas (1983).

6. We should note that even if invariant properties that determine our perception are discovered, we would still need to account for the facts of CP-like perception by infants and adults. This is true inasmuch as invariant properties cannot always exist in the speech signal as single ideal values, as is often implied. That is to say, although there may theoretically be a single-valued invariant property, the inherent variability of the articulatory system will actually produce variation in it. Thus, for example, the

templates of Stevens and Blumstein (1981) that are used to define place of articulation are really standards, and we need some explanation of how listeners are able to categorize individual instances in terms of these standards.

7. Note that this ability to use later-occurring information, that is, information about syllable duration, when processing transition duration, indicates processing mechanisms in infants that operate "in other than a temporally defined, linear fashion" (Eimas & Miller, 1980a, p. 1141). As we shall see, this has important implications for determining the units of speech processing.

8. We know of no evidence bearing on how infants perceive other acoustic features, for example, frequency of pure tones and intensity, or whether these can serve as the basis for equivalence classes. For a review of the literature on the perception of acoustic properties of this nature, see Aslin et al. (1983).

9. Our reading of the literature is that there is no compelling evidence as yet as to the nature of prototypes. They may take the form of feature lists (Rosch & Mervis, 1975), or template-like structures (e.g., Smith & Medin, 1981) or a location in multidimensional space (Repp, 1977). Whereas a resolution of this issue would be theoretically interesting, the failure to pinpoint the specific nature of the representation at this time does not detract from the fact that prototype structures may constitute the categorical representations of infants and adults.

10. There have been a few studies in which listeners have been asked to assign ratings – typically confidence ratings – to stimuli along a continuum that varied from a boundary stimulus to the preselected endpoint stimulus of the series. The data generally indicate that, at least for those stimuli near the boundary region, listeners can effectively differentiate category members, assigning better ratings to stimuli further from the boundary. For a review of these and related studies, the reader is referred to Repp (1983) and to Chapter 8 by Massaro, this volume.

11. It is important to note that although few data exist on the perceived goodness of stimuli as category members, the idea that phonetic categories are internally structured and, specifically, that they are structured in terms of prototypical exemplars, has played a role in theories of speech perception. Theories proposed by both Repp (1977) and Oden and Massaro (1978) assume that the identification of a speech sound involves a comparison of the incoming stimulus (or its auditory transform) with an ideal representation of the sound – the category prototype – stored in long-term memory. The prototype that gives the best match determines category identity of the stimulus. Eimas and Corbit's (1973) feature detector model assumes that each detector is maximally tuned to the prototypic value of the acoustic correlate of the feature category. Identification, at the feature level, is determined by which of the opposing detectors of a set is activated more – that is, which ideal value the stimulus value is closest to. Although clearly different from one another, these models share the critical assumption that the categories of speech are defined, in some manner, in terms of prototypical values. (Cf. Chapter 6 by Remez, this volume.)

12. We should point out that this account of category structure is essentially the same as that offered by Samuel (1982), except that he appears to place the prototypes at a phonetic, rather than a prephonetic level of processing. For an alternative account of category structure and adaptation based on category boundary locations, rather than category prototypes, see Miller et al. (1983).

13. A very different description of perception is found in the writings of Gibson (1979) and his adherents (e.g., Shaw, Turvey, & Mace, 1983; Turvey, Shaw, Reed, & Mace, 1981). They argue that perception is direct, being the immediate consequence of the registration of invariant information and transformations that are present in the physical signal. Perception, in this view, does not involve processes that rely on internally represented knowledge.

14. A possible alternative to our view of continuous processing is one in which the speech signal is arbitrarily segmented on the basis of time and the processing routines for the various categorical decisions have information about the number of segments that must be considered for each decision (cf. Klatt, 1979). Our preference for a continuous model of processing rests on its apparently greater parsimony; it does not require the additional segmentation process.

15. Not only does the present view account for cross-language differences in speech perception, but it could also help to account for differences that occur in speech and nonspeech processing, given the assumption that the analytic processing routines are not speech specific. Because the information available through such processing will be weighted specially in speech contexts, some differences might be expected to occur for the way in which the same acoustic information is perceived in speech and

nonspeech contexts. Thus, results such as those of Best et al. (1981) or Bailey, Summerfield, and Dorman (1977), which demonstrate that the same acoustic information is categorized differently depending on one's set to hear it as speech or nonspeech, are explicable as a consequence of using different weightings in the two settings. In effect, the specialized phonetic processing of speech that has been observed in various experimental settings (e.g., Liberman, 1982) is the natural outcome of developing a weighting scheme for recognizing words in a particular language.

References

Abramson, A. S., & Lisker, L. (1970). Discriminability along the voicing continuum: Cross-language tests. In *Proceedings of the Sixth International Congress of Phonetic Sciences* (Prague 1967). Prague: Academia.

Abramson, A. S., & Lisker, L. (1973). Voice-timing perception in Spanish word-initial stops. *Journal of Phonetics, 1*, 1–8.

Ainsworth, W. A. (1972). Duration as a cue in the recognition of synthetic vowels. *Journal of the Acoustical Society of America, 51*, 648–651.

Aslin, R. N., & Pisoni, D. B. (1980). Some developmental processes in speech perception. In G. H. Yeni-Komshian, J. F. Kavanagh, & C. F. Ferguson (Eds.), *Child phonology, Vol. 2: Perception.* New York: Academic Press.

Aslin, R. N., Pisoni, D. B., & Jusczyk, P. W. (1983). Auditory development and speech perception in infancy. In M. M. Haith & J. J. Campos (Eds.), *Infancy and the biology of development.* Vol. 2 of *Carmichael's manual of child psychology* (4th ed.). New York: Wiley.

Bailey, P. J., Summerfield, Q., & Dorman, M. (1977). On the identification of sinewave analogues of certain speech sounds. In *Status report on speech research* (SR-51/52). New Haven, CT: Haskins Laboratories.

Barclay, J. R. (1972). Noncategorical perception of a voiced stop: A replication. *Perception & Psychophysics, 11*, 269–273.

Bertoncini, J., & Mehler, J. (1981). Syllables as units in infant perception. *Infant Behavior & Development, 4*, 246–260.

Best, C. T., Morrongiello, B., & Robson, R. (1981). Perceptual equivalence of acoustic cues in speech and nonspeech perception. *Perception & Psychophysics, 29*, 191–211.

Bomba, P. C. (1982). *Categorization of orientation in 2–4-month-old infants.* Unpublished Doctoral Dissertation, Brown University, Providence, RI.

Bomba, P. C., & Siqueland, E. R. (1983). The nature and structure of infant form categories. *Journal of Experimental Child Psychology, 35*, 294–328.

Bornstein, M. H., Kessen, W., & Weiskopf, S. (1976). Color vision and hue categorization in young infants. *Journal of Experimental Psychology: Human Perception and Performance, 2*, 115–129.

Carden, G., Levitt, A., Jusczyk, P. W., & Walley, A. (1981). Evidence for phonetic processing of cues to place of articulation: Perceived manner affects perceived place. *Perception & Psychophysics, 29*, 26–36.

Carney, A. E., Widin, G. P., & Viemeister, N. F. (1977). Noncategorical perception of stop consonants differing in VOT. *Journal of the Acoustical Society of America, 62*, 961–970.

Carrell, T. D., Smith, L. B., & Pisoni, D. B. (1981). Some perceptual dependencies in speeded classification of vowel color and pitch. *Perception & Psychophysics, 29*, 1–10.

Chapin, C., Tseng, C., & Lieberman, P. (1982). Short-term release cues to stop-consonant place of articulation in child speech. *Journal of the Acoustical Society of America, 71*, 179–186.

Chomsky, N. (1980). *Rules and representations.* New York: Columbia University Press.

Clarkson, M. G., & Clifton, R. E. (1984, April). *Pitch extraction and categorization by 7 month olds.* Paper presented at the Fourth International Conference on Infant Studies, New York.

Cohen, L. B., & Strauss, M. S. (1979). Concept acquisition in the human infant. *Child Development, 50*, 419–424.

Cooper, W. E., Paccia, J. M., & Lapointe, S. G. (1978). Hierarchical coding in speech timing. *Cognitive Psychology, 9*, 154–177.

Cutler, A., Mehler, J., Norris, D., & Segui, J. (1983). A language-specific comprehension strategy. *Nature, 304,* 159–160.
Cutler, A., Mehler, J., Norris, D., & Segui, J. (1986). The syllable's differing role in the segmentation of French and English. *Journal of Memory and Language, 25,* 385–400.
Cutting, J. E. (1978). There may be nothing peculiar to perceiving in a speech mode. In J. Requin (Ed.), *Attention and performance VII.* Hillsdale, NJ: Erlbaum.
Cutting, J. E. (1982). Plucks and bows are categorically perceived, sometimes. *Perception & Psychophysics, 31,* 462–476.
Cutting, J. E., & Rosner, B. S. (1974). Categories and boundaries in speech and music. *Perception & Psychophysics, 16,* 564–570.
Dollard, J., & Miller, N. E. (1950). *Personality and psychotherapy.* New York: McGraw-Hill.
Eimas, P. D. (1974). Auditory and linguistic processing of cues for place of articulation by infants. *Perception & Psychophysics, 16,* 513–521.
Eimas, P. D. (1975). Auditory and phonetic coding of the cues for speech: Discrimination of the [r-l] distinction by young infants. *Perception & Psychophysics, 18,* 341–347.
Eimas, P. D. (1982). Speech perception: A view of the initial state and perceptual mechanisms. In J. Mehler, E. C. T. Walker, & M. Garrett (Eds.), *Perspectives on mental representation.* Hillsdale, NJ: Erlbaum.
Eimas, P. D., & Clarkson, R. L. (1986). Speech perception in children: Are there effects of otitis media? In J. F. Kavanagh (Ed.), *Otitis media and child development.* Parkton, MD: York Press.
Eimas, P. D., & Corbit, J. D. (1973). Selective adaptation of linguistic feature detectors. *Cognitive Psychology, 4,* 99–109.
Eimas, P. D., & Miller, J. L. (1980a). Contextual effects in infant speech perception. *Science, 209,* 1140–1141.
Eimas, P. D., & Miller, J. L. (1980b). Discrimination of the information for manner of articulation. *Infant Behavior & Development, 3,* 367–375.
Eimas, P. D., Siqueland, E. R., Jusczyk, P., & Vigorito, J. (1971). Speech perception in infants. *Science, 171,* 303–306.
Elman, J. L., Diehl, R. L., & Buchwald, S. E. (1977). Perceptual switching in bilinguals. *Journal of the Acoustical Society of America, 62,* 971–974.
Endman, M. (1984, April). *Perceptual constancy for nonspeech stimuli.* Paper presented at the Fourth International Conference on Infant Studies, New York.
Fagan, J. F., III. (1976). Infants' recognition of invariant features of faces. *Child Development, 47,* 627–638.
Fagan, J. F., III, & Singer, L. T. (1979). The role of simple feature differences in infant's recognition of faces. *Infant Behavior & Development, 2,* 39–45.
Fant, G. (1960). *Acoustic theory of speech production.* The Hague: Mouton.
Ferguson, C. A. (1978). Learning to pronounce: The earliest stages of phonological development in the child. In F. D. Minifie & L. L. Lloyd (Eds.), *Communicative and cognitive abilities: Early behavioral assessment.* Baltimore, MD: University Park Press.
Fernald, A. (1984). The perceptual and affective salience of mothers' speech to infants. In L. Geagaus, C. Garvey, & R. Golinkoff (Eds.), *The origins and growth of communication.* Norwood, NJ: Ablex.
Fitch, H. L., Halwes, T., Erickson, D. M., & Liberman, A. M. (1980). Perceptual equivalence of two acoustic cues for stop-consonant manner. *Perception & Psychophysics, 27,* 343–350.
Fodor, J. A., Garrett, M. F., & Brill, S. L. (1975). Pi Ka Pu. The perception of speech sounds by prelinguistic infants. *Perception & Psychophysics, 18,* 74–78.
Foss, D. J., & Blank, M. A. (1980). Identifying the speech codes. *Cognitive Psychology, 12,* 1–31.
Gibson, J. J. (1979). *The ecological approach to visual perception.* Boston, MA: Houghton Mifflin.
Goldsmith, J. (1976). An overview of autosegmental phonology. *Linguistic Analysis, 2,* 23–68.
Goldsmith, J. (1979). The aims of autosegmental phonology. In D. Dinnsen (Ed.), *Current approaches to phonological theory.* Bloomington, IN: Indiana University Press.

Goldsmith, J. (1981). English as a tone language. In D. Goyvaerts (Ed.), *Phonology, in the 1980's*. Ghent: Story-Scientia.
Grieser, D. L., & Kuhl, P. K. (1983). The internal structure of vowel categories in infancy: Effects of stimulus "goodness." *Journal of the Acoustical Society of America, 74* (Suppl. 1), S102(A).
Herrnstein, R. J., & Loveland, D. H. (1964). Complex visual concepts in the pigeon. *Science, 146*, 549–551.
Hillenbrand, J. M. (1980). *Perceptual organization of speech sounds by young infants*. Unpublished doctoral dissertation, University of Washington.
Holmberg, T. L., Morgan, K. A., & Kuhl, P. K. (1977). Speech perception in early infancy: Discrimination of fricative consonants. *Paper presented at the 94th meeting of the Acoustical Society of America*, Miami Beach.
Husaim, J. S., & Cohen, L. B. (1981). Infant learning of ill-defined categories. *Merrill-Palmer Quarterly, 27*, 443–456.
Hyman, R., & Frost, N. (1975). Gradients and schema in pattern recognition. In P. M. A. Rabbitt and S. Dornic (Eds.), *Attention and Performance V*. New York: Academic Press.
Ingram, D. (1974). Phonological rules in young children. *Journal of Child Language, 1*, 46–64.
Jusczyk, P. W. (1981). Infant speech perception: A critical appraisal. In P. D. Eimas and J. L. Miller (Eds.), *Perspectives on the study of speech*. Hillsdale, NJ: Erlbaum.
Jusczyk, P. W. (1984). On characterizing the development of speech perception. In J. Mehler and R. Fox (Eds.), *Neonate cognition: Beyond the blooming, buzzing confusion*. Hillsdale, NJ: Erlbaum.
Jusczyk, P. W., Pisoni, D. B., Walley, A., & Murray, J. (1980). Discrimination of relative onset time of two-component tones by infants. *Journal of the Acoustical Society of America, 67*, 262–270.
Jusczyk, P. W., Pisoni, D. P., Reed, M. A., Fernald, A., & Myers, M. (1983). Infants' discrimination of the duration of a rapid spectrum change in nonspeech signals. *Science, 222*, 175–177.
Jusczyk, P. W., Rosner, B. S., Cutting, J. E., Foard, C. F., & Smith, L. B. (1977). Categorical perception of nonspeech sounds by 2-month-old infants. *Perception & Psychophysics, 21*, 50–54.
Jusczyk, P. W., Smith, L. B., & Murphy, C. (1981). The perceptual classification of speech. *Perception & Psychophysics, 30*, 10–23.
Katz, J., & Jusczyk, P. W. (1980, April). *Do six-month-olds have perceptual constancy for phonetic segments?* Paper presented at the International Conference on Infant Studies, New Haven, CT.
Kewley-Port, D. (1982). Measurement of formant transitions in naturally produced stop consonant-vowel syllables. *Journal of the Acoustical Society of America, 72*, 379–389.
Kiparsky, P., & Menn, L. (1977). On the acquisition of phonology. In J. Macnamara (Ed.), *Language, learning and thought*. New York: Academic Press.
Klatt, D. H. (1979). Speech perception: A model of acoustic-phonetic analysis and lexical access. *Journal of Phonetics, 7*, 279–312.
Kuhl, P. K. (1979). Speech perception in early infancy: Perceptual constancy for spectrally dissimilar vowel categories. *Journal of the Acoustical Society of America, 66*, 1668–1679.
Kuhl, P. K. (1980). Perceptual constancy for speech-sound categories in early infancy. In G. H. Yeni-Komshian, J. F. Kavanagh, & C. A. Ferguson (Eds.), *Child phonology, Vol. 2: Perception*. New York: Academic Press.
Kuhl, P. K. (1983). Perception of auditory equivalence classes for speech in early infancy. *Infant Behavior & Development, 6*, 263–285.
Kuhl, P. K. (1985). Constancy, categorization, and perceptual organization for speech and sound in early infancy. In J. Mehler and R. Rox (Eds.), *Neonate cognition: Beyond the blooming, buzzing confusion*. Hillsdale, NJ: Erlbaum.
Kuhl, P. K., & Hillenbrand, J. (1979). *Speech perception by young infants: Perceptual constancy for categories based on pitch contour*. Paper presented at the biennial meeting of the Society for Research in Child Development, San Francisco.
Kuhl, P. K., & Miller, J. D. (1978). Speech perception by the chinchilla: Identification functions for synthetic VOT stimuli. *Journal of the Acoustical Society of America, 63*, 905–917.
Ladefoged, P. (1971). *Preliminaries to linguistic phonetics*. Chicago: University of Chicago Press.

Lasky, R. E., Syrdal-Lasky, A., & Klein, R. E. (1975). VOT discrimination by four-to-six-and-a-half-month-old infants from Spanish environments. *Journal of Experimental Child Psychology, 20*, 215–225.
Leben, W. (1976). The tones of English intonation. *Linguistic Analysis, 2*, 69–107.
Liberman, A. M. (1970). The grammars of speech and language. *Cognitive Psychology, 1*, 301–323.
Liberman, A. M. (1982). On finding that speech is special. *American Psychologist, 37*, 148–167.
Liberman, A. M., Cooper, F. S., Shankweiler, D. S., & Studdert-Kennedy, M. (1967). Perception of the speech code. *Psychological Review, 74*, 431–461.
Liberman, A. M., Delattre, P., & Cooper, F. S. (1952). The role of selected stimulus-variables in the perception of the unvoiced stop consonants. *American Journal of Psychology, 65*, 497–516.
Liberman, A. M., Mattingly, I. G., & Turvey, M. T. (1972). Language codes and memory codes. In A. W. Melton & E. Martin (Eds.), *Coding processes in human memory*. Washington, DC: H. V. Winston and Sons.
Liberman, A. M., & Studdert-Kennedy, M. (1978). Phonetic perception. In R. Held, H. W. Leibowitz, and H.-L. Teuber (Eds.), *Handbook of sensory physiology, Vol. VII: Perception*. New York: Springer.
Liberman, A. M., Shankweiler, D., Fisher, F. W., & Carter, B. (1974). Explicit syllable and phoneme segmentation in the young child. *Journal of Experimental Child Psychology, 18*, 201–212.
Lisker, L. (1978a). Rapid vs. rabid: A catalogue of acoustic features that may cue the distinction. In *Status report on speech research* (SR/54). New Haven, CT: Haskins Laboratories.
Lisker, L., & Abramson, A. S. (1964). A cross-language study of voicing in initial stops: Acoustical measurements. *Word, 20*, 384–422.
Lisker, L., & Abramson, A. S. (1970). The voicing dimension: Some experiments in comparative phonetics. In *Proceedings of the Sixth International Congress of Phonetic Sciences* (Prague 1967). Prague: Academia.
Lisker, L., Liberman, A. M., Erickson, D. M., Dechovitz, D., & Mandler, R. (1977). On pushing the voice-onset-time (VOT) boundary about. *Language and Speech, 20*, 209–216.
Macken, M. A. (1980). Aspects of the acquisition of stop systems: A cross linguistic perspective. In G. Yeni-Komshian, J. F. Kavanagh, & C. A. Ferguson (Eds.), *Child Phonology, Vol. I: Production*. New York: Academic Press.
Macmillan, N. A., Kaplan, H. L., & Creelman, C. D. (1977). The psychophysics of categorical perception. *Psychological Review, 84*, 452–471.
Mattingly, I. G., Liberman, A. M., Syrdal, A. K., & Halwes, T. (1979). Discrimination in speech and nonspeech modes. *Cognitive Psychology, 2*, 131–157.
McClasky, C. L., Pisoni, D. B., & Carrell, T. D. (1980). Effects of transfer of training on identification of a new linguistic contrast in voicing. In *Research on speech perception* (Progress Report No. 6). Bloomington, IN: Department of Psychology, Indiana University.
McGurk, H. (1972). Infant discrimination of orientation. *Journal of Experimental Child Psychology, 14*, 151–164.
Mehler, J., Dommergues, J. V., Frauenfelder, U., & Segui, J. (1981). The syllable's role in speech segmentation. *Journal of Verbal Learning and Verbal Behavior, 20*, 298–305.
Mehler, J., Segui, J., & Frauenfelder, U. (1981). The role of the syllable in language acquisition and perception. In T. Myers, J. Laver, & J. Anderson (Eds.), *The cognitive representation of speech*. Amsterdam: North Holland.
Menn, L. (1980). Phonological theory and child phonology. In G. A. Yeni-Komshian, J. F. Kavanagh, & C. A. Ferguson, (Eds.), *Child Phonology, Vol. I, Production*. New York: Academic Press.
Menyuk, P., & Menn, L. (1979). Early strategies for the perception and production of words. In P. Fletcher & M. Garman (Eds.), *Studies in language acquisition*. NY: Cambridge University Press.
Milewski, A. E. (1979). Visual discrimination and detection of configurational invariance in 3-month infants. *Developmental Psychology, 15*, 357–363.
Miller, C. L., Younger, B. A., & Morse, P. A. (1982). The categorization of male and female voices in infancy. *Infant Behavior & Development, 5*, 144–159.

Miller, J. L. (1981a). The effects of speaking rate on segmental distinctions. In P. D. Eimas & J. L. Miller (Eds.), *Perspectives on the study of speech*, Hillsdale, NJ: Erlbaum.
Miller, J. L. (1981b). Some effects of speaking rate on phonetic perception. *Phonetica, 38,* 159–180.
Miller, J. L., Connine, C. M., Schermer, T. M., & Kluender, K. R. (1983). A possible auditory basis for internal structure of phonetic categories. *Journal of the Acoustical Society of America, 73,* 2124–2133.
Miller, J. L., & Eimas, P. D. (1979). Organization in infant speech perception. *Canadian Journal of Psychology, 33,* 353–367.
Miller, J. L., & Eimas, P. D. (1983). Studies on the categorization of speech by infants. *Cognition, 13,* 135–165.
Miller, J. L., & Liberman, A. M. (1979). Some effects of later-occurring information on the perception of stop consonant and semivowel. *Perception & Psychophysics, 25,* 457–465.
Mills, C. B. (1980). Effects of the match between listener expectancies and coarticulatory cues on the perception of speech. *Journal of Experimental Psychology: Human Perception and Performance, 6,* 528–535.
Miyawaki, K., Strange, W., Verbrugge, R., Liberman, A. M., Jenkins, J. J., & Fujimura, O. (1975). An effect of linguistic experience: The discrimination of [r] and [l] by native speakers of Japanese and English. *Perception & Psychophysics, 18,* 331–340.
Moffitt, A. R. (1971). Consonant cue perception by twenty- to twenty-four week old infants. *Child Development, 42,* 717–731.
Morais, J., Cary, L., Alegria, J., & Bertelson, P. (1979). Does awareness of speech as a sequence of phones arise spontaneously? *Cognition, 7,* 323–331.
Morse, P. A. (1972). The discrimination of speech and nonspeech stimuli in early infancy. *Journal of Experimental Child Psychology, 14,* 477–492.
Moskowitz, A. I. (1973). Acquisition of phonology and syntax: A preliminary study. In G. Hintikka, J. Moravesik, and P. Suppes (Eds.), *Approaches to natural language*. Dordrecht: Reidel.
Oden, G. C., & Massaro, D. W. (1978). Integration of featural information in speech perception. *Psychological Review, 85,* 172–191.
Pastore, R. E. (1981). Possible psychoacoustic factors in speech perception. In P. D. Eimas and J. L. Miller (Eds.), Perspectives on the study of speech. Hillsdale, NJ: Erlbaum.
Perey, A. J., & Pisoni, D. B. (1977, December). *Dual processing vs. response-limitation accounts of categorical perception: A reply to Macmillan, Kaplan, and Creelman.* Paper presented at the 94th meeting of the Acoustical Society of America, Miami Beach.
Pisoni, D. B. (1973). Auditory and phonetic memory codes in the discrimination of consonants and vowels. *Perception & Psychophysics, 13,* 253–260.
Pisoni, D. B. (1977). Identification and discrimination of the relative onset time of two component tones: Implications for voicing perception in stops. *Journal of the Acoustical Society of America, 61,* 1352–1361.
Pisoni, D. B. (1978). Speech perception. In W. K. Estes (Ed.), *Handbook of learning and cognitive processes* (Vol. 6). Hillsdale, NJ: Erlbaum.
Pisoni, D. B., Aslin, R. N., Perey, A. J., & Hennessy, B. L. (1982). Some effects of laboratory training on identification and discrimination of voicing contrasts in stop consonants. *Journal of Experimental Psychology: Human Perception and Performance, 8,* 297–314.
Pisoni, D. B., Carrell, T. D., & Gans, S. J. (1983). Perception of the duration of rapid spectrum changes in speech and nonspeech signals. *Perception & Psychophysics, 34,* 314–322.
Posner, M. I., & Keele, S. W. (1968). On the genesis of abstract ideas. *Journal of Experimental Psychology, 77,* 353–363.
Raphael, L. J. (1972). Preceding vowel duration as a cue to the perception of the voicing characteristic of word-final consonants in American English. *Journal of the Acoustical Society of America, 51,* 1296–1303.
Remez, R. E., Rubin, P. E., Pisoni, D. B., & Carrell, T. D. (1981). Speech perception without traditional speech cues. *Science, 212,* 947–950.

Repp, B. H. (1977). Dichotic competition of speech sounds: The role of acoustic stimulus structure. *Journal of Experimental Psychology: Human Perception and Performance, 3,* 37–50.
Repp, B. H. (1982). Phonetic trading relations and context effects: New experimental evidence for a speech mode of perception. *Psychological Bulletin, 92,* 81–110.
Repp, B. H. (1983). Categorical perception: Issues, methods, findings. In N. J. Lass (Ed.), *Speech and language: Advances in basic research and practice* (Vol. 10). New York: Academic Press.
Repp, B. H., Liberman, A. M., Eccardt, T., & Pesetsky, D. (1978). Perceptual integration of acoustic cues for stop, fricative, and affricate manner. *Journal of Experimental Psychology: Human Perception and Performance, 4,* 621–637.
Roberts, M., & Summerfield, Q. (1981). Audiovisual presentation demonstrates that selective adaptation in speech perception is purely auditory. *Perception & Psychophysics, 30,* 309–314.
Rosch, E., & Mervis, C. B. (1975). Family resemblances: Studies in the internal structure of categories. *Cognitive Psychology, 7,* 573–605.
Rosen, S. M., & Howell, P. (1981). Plucks and bows are not categorically perceived. *Perception & Psychophysics, 30,* 156–168.
Ross, G. S. (1980). Categorization in 1- to 2-year-olds. *Developmental Psychology, 16,* 391–396.
Runeson, S. (1977). On the possibility of 'smart' perceptual mechanisms. *Scandinavian Journal of Psychology, 18,* 172–179.
Samuel, A. G. (1982). Phonetic prototypes. *Perception & Psychophysics, 31,* 307–314.
Savin, H. B., & Bever, T. G. (1970). The nonperceptual reality of the phoneme. *Journal of Verbal Learning and Verbal Behavior, 9,* 295–302.
Sawusch, J. R., & Jusczyk, P. (1981). Adaptation and contrast in the perception of voicing. *Journal of Experimental Psychology: Human Perception and Performance, 7,* 408–422.
Searle, C. L., Jacobson, J. Z., & Rayment, S. G. (1979). Stop consonant discrimination based on human audition. *Journal of the Acoustical Society of America, 65,* 799–809.
Segui, J., Frauenfelder, U., & Mehler, J. (1981). Phoneme monitoring, syllable monitoring and lexical access. *British Journal of Psychology, 72,* 471–477.
Shaw, R. E., Turvey, M. T., & Mace, W. (1983). Ecological psychology: The consequences of a commitment to realism. In W. Weimer & D. Palermo (Eds.), *Cognition and the symbolic processes. II.* Hillsdale, NJ: Erlbaum.
Smith, E. E., & Medin, D. L. (1981). *Categories and concepts.* Cambridge, MA: Harvard University Press.
Smith, N. V. (1973). *The acquisition of phonology.* Cambridge: Cambridge University Press.
Starkey, P., Spelke, E. S., & Gelman, R. (1983). Detection of intermodal numerical correspondences by human infants. *Science, 222,* 179–181.
Stevens, K. N., & Blumstein, S. E. (1981). The search for invariant acoustic correlates of phonetic features. In P. D. Eimas & J. L. Miller (Eds.), *Perspectives on the study of speech.* Hillsdale, NJ: Erlbaum.
Stevens, K. N., & House, A. S. (1972). Speech perception. In J. Tobias (Ed.), *Foundations of modern auditory theory* (Vol. 2). New York: Academic Press.
Strange, W., & Broen, P. A. (1980). Perception and production of approximate consonants by 3-year-olds: A first study. In G. H. Yeni-Komshian, J. F. Kavanagh, & C. A. Ferguson (Eds.), *Child phonology, Vol. 2: Perception.* New York: Academic Press.
Strange, W., & Jenkins, J. J. (1978). Role of linguistic experience in the perception of speech. In R. D. Walk and H. L. Pick (Eds.), *Perception and experience.* New York: Plenum Press.
Strauss, M. S. (1979). Abstraction of prototypical information by adults and 10-month-old infants. *Journal of Experimental Psychology: Human Perception and Performance, 5,* 618–632.
Streeter, L. A. (1976). Language perception of 2-month-old infants shows effects of both innate mechanisms and experience. *Nature, 259,* 38–41.
Summerfield, Q. (1982). Differences between spectral dependencies in auditory and phonetic temporal processing: Relevance to the perception of voicing in initial stops. *Journal of the Acoustical Society of America, 72,* 51–61.
Summerfield, Q., & Haggard, M. (1977). On the dissociation of spectral and temporal cues to the

voicing distinction in initial stop consonants. *Journal of the Acoustical Society of America, 62,* 435–448.
Swinney, D. A., & Prather, P. (1980). Phonemic identification in a phoneme monitoring experiment: The variable role of uncertainty about vowel contexts. *Perception & Psychophysics, 27,* 104–110.
Tallal, P., & Stark, R. E. (1980). Speech perception of language-delayed children. In G. H. Yeni-Komshian, J. F. Kavanagh, & C. A. Ferguson (Eds.), *Child phonology,* Vol. 2: *Perception.* New York: Academic Press.
Turvey, M. T., Shaw, R. E., Reed, E. S., & Mace, W. H. (1981). Ecological laws of perceiving and acting: In reply to Fodor and Pylyshyn. *Cognition, 9,* 236–304.
van der Hulst, H., & Smith, N. (1982a). *The structure of phonological representations,* (Part 1). Cinnaminson, NJ: Foris.
van der Hulst, H., & Smith, N. (1982b). An overview of autosegmental and metrical phonology. In H. van der Hulst and N. Smith (Eds.), *The structure of phonological representations.* Cinnaminson, NJ: Floris.
Walley, A. C., Smith, L. B., & Jusczyk, P. W. (1980). Classification of CV syllables by readers and pre-readers. *Research on speech perception* (Progress Report No. 6). Bloomington, IN: Indiana University.
Waterson, N. (1971). Child phonology: A prosodic view. *Journal of Linguistics, 7,* 179–211.
Werker, J. F., & Tees, R. C. (1984). Cross-language speech perception: Evidence for perceptual reorganization during the first year of life. *Infant Behavior & Development, 7,* 49–63.
Wickelgren, W. A. (1969). Context-sensitive coding, associative memory, and serial order in (speech) behavior. *Psychological Review, 76,* 1–15.
Williams, L. (1977a). The perception of stop consonant voicing by Spanish-English bilinguals. *Perception & Psychophysics, 21,* 289–297.
Williams, L. (1977b). Voicing contrasts in Spanish. *Journal of Phonetics, 5,* 169–184.
Wood, C. C. (1976). Discriminability, response bias, and phoneme categories in discrimination of voice onset time. *Journal of the Acoustical Society of America, 60,* 1381–1389.

Part III

Models for speech categorical perception

6 Neural models of speech perception: A case history

Robert E. Remez

Speech perception has commonly been described as the process by which acoustic stimulation is transformed by the listener into the consonants and vowels spoken by the speaker. Among other properties of the speech chain linking speaker and listener, the robustness and efficiency of speech transmission has been said to inhere in specialized perceptual functions, often including categorical perception of the sounds in the phoneme repertoires of many languages. The assumption of the unique nature of the perceptual process serving speech encouraged a specific characterization of speech perception set in neural terms appropriated from descriptions of the visual system that were then emerging. This conceptualization of speech perception postulated an anatomically discrete ensemble of neural feature detectors arrayed in hierarchical fashion, itself a portrait of the linguistic structure of sound patterns. The first echelon of feature detectors analyzed auditory attributes and fed the results to the next, at which phonetic attributes were determined. Individual consonant and vowel segments were identified at the ultimate level by detectors that collected distinctive phoneme features represented at the preceding stage. Noninvasive perceptual tests were used to evaluate the model. Although initial findings were not unfavorable, the model ultimately proved to be inadequate warranting the abandonment of this deliberately physiological hypothesis about speech perception.

This chapter performs a postmortem examination of the phonetic-feature detector. A part of the neural conduit spanning the auditory periphery and the cortical speech centers, this hypothetical element has been probed, fatigued, nurtured, cloned, and ultimately discarded to wither over the past ten years. The fact that it has been abandoned as an explanatory device in theories of speech perception does not by itself provide evidence of its demise, nor could it. The real cause was that the experimental test of the model revealed its failure to predict perceptual results and its inability to grow to accommodate them. However, the mixture of psychology, neurophysiology, and linguistics that the model intended to achieve possesses a kind of prima facie validity, and the dismissal of the feature-detector hypothesis would be misconstrued if taken to demonstrate unbridgeable rifts among the disciplines that inform research on speech. The model simply failed. Although the need for a unifying concept is still great, we may be confident that the phonetic-feature

> The author gratefully acknowledges support from the National Institute of Neurological and Communicative Disorders and Stroke, Grant NS-22096; and, the timely hagiographical comments of David Pisoni.

detector is an unlikely candidate. This conclusion is not readily apparent in the abstract, and without a detailed consideration of the experimental results, my verdict may even be judged too hasty, entailing the premature disposal of the theory. After all, we are just beginning to discover the logic of neural information processing, and the neurons composing the sensory pathways may actually possess trigger features specially appropriate for speech.

On the contrary, the point of this review is that the neural mechanism for speech, however it is structured, could not be a feature-detector hierarchy. In order to make the case, a number of findings in speech perception are described here, along with the hints about the neural correlates of perceptual functions contributed by physiological studies. The review of the phonetic-detector literature is selective, compiled to reflect the appeal of the neural model as it was originally constituted, the problems that developed as it stretched to incorporate the diverse data generated in its wake, and the derelict status of the model at the present time. Because the treatment is oriented toward these topics, it does not provide a comprehensive chronicle. Other reviews of the experiments pertaining to the feature-detector model will be helpful to those readers seeking an exhaustive treatment (Cooper, 1979; Diehl, 1981; Diehl & Kluender, Chapter 7, this volume; Eimas & Miller, 1978).

Pandemonium and distinctive features

Feature detectors for phonetic perception integrate two concurrent lines of thought, the *pandemonium* model of pattern analysis (Selfridge, 1959) and the concept of the *distinctive feature* of phonemic variation (Jakobson, Fant, & Halle, 1963). The juxtaposition of these ideas gave vitality to the phonetic-feature-detector notion when each alone would have mattered much less, psycholinguistically. Pandemonium is actually a very old technique, representing the distribution of criterial properties across a range of items by using a hierarchical taxonomy (see Cassirer, 1923). Its neurophysiological version portrayed the recognition of complex forms as a matter of analysis, and the analytic activity was represented as a process of successive decomposition and integration of the stimulus by a nested set of filters. A key aspect of each analyzer was its manner of responding, which was proportional to the closeness of the match between the parameters of its preference (its filter characteristics, in other words) and those of the stimulus it examined.

In the primary stage of analysis by pandemonium, the extrinsic stimulation is simply impressed upon a set of analyzers, each responding to the extent that it encounters its preferred attribute, a discrete physical property of the transduced signal. These are the *image* demons, for an image of the proximal stimulus inheres in the selective response of the analyzers, presumably only some of which find the element they prefer (see Figure 6.1.) This image is then analyzed by a set of feature-sensitive filters, each of which responds essentially to the activity of just those demons in the prior level that present a property of the stimulus that is criterial for identifying an object. A criterial property or stimulus feature of this kind might be a

Neural models of speech perception

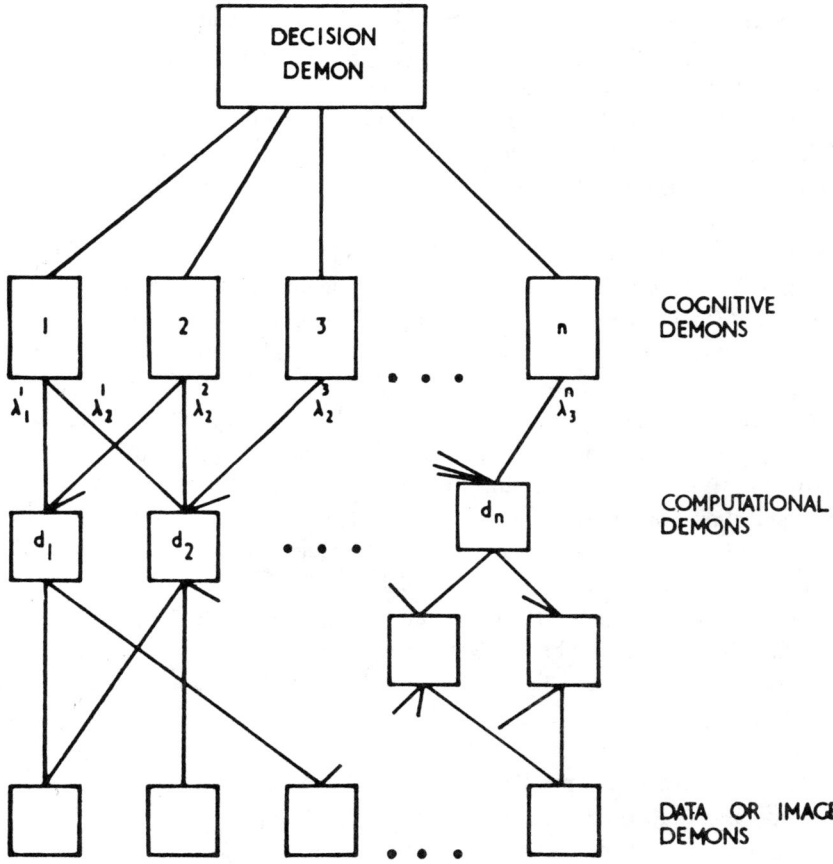

Figure 6.1. The pandemonium model. This diagram describes the connections among demons of various orders of selectivity, from Selfridge's model (1959). The primary structural revision that phonetic detectors necessitated was the formation of opponent demons within levels, to match the binary nature of phonetic contrasts.

particular contour at a given orientation in a visual case, or a specific pattern of frequency variation within a band of the spectrum in an auditory case. This echelon of analyzers is designated to consist of the *computational* demons.

The final tier of analyzers is composed of *cognitive* demons, each of which is responsible for noting a pattern in the responses of the computational demons. A cognitive demon responds to the extent that the feature detectors for its favorite object are active in the preceding detector tier. (A related model consisting of iconic, categorical, and symbolic representations is proposed by Harnad in Chapter 19 of this volume.)

The amusing name given by Selfridge to this kind of hierarchical analyzer derives from the premise that all of the analytic units are active at once. Thus, at any instant, there will be some units whose response is great because the stimulus matches the preferences closely, and there will be other units exhibiting less activity due to the relative discrepancy of stimulus properties and their analytic dimensions. The response of each unit is metaphorically cast as a "yell," and, in consequence, the analytic mechanism rings constantly with the yelling of units. It is pandemonium, with each unit a "demon," and only the demons yelling loudest are "heard" above the din by the demons at the next level. The cognitive demon with the loudest yell determines the percept.

The problem of identifying the criterial properties that the computational demons detect turns out to be crucial for the success of pandemonium schemes. Because these are often difficult to establish, whether by experiment or rational analysis, this problem is consequently the most serious weakness of pandemonium as a model of perception. In consequence, a stage of cognitive interpretation is often alleged to finish the process of perceptual identification upon the failure of demonic filtration of criterial properties, for example, in ambiguous or otherwise indeterminate cases (Weisstein, 1973). Likewise, a seemingly endless proliferation of criterial attributes of objects and their correlated stimuli is needed to accommodate learning (not to mention new inventions), which weighs against pandemonium as a neuropsychological model of object perception. In fact, the attrition of neurons throughout life suggests that perceptual differentiation continues despite the dwindling reserve of neurons, other things equal. To be fair, various forms of pandemonium have at least been tolerably effective in suitably restricted engineering applications (see Hyde, 1972; Klatt, 1977).

Regardless of the weakness of pandemonium as a general psychological theory, in the specific circumstance of phonetic perception the model was potentially appropriate simply by virtue of the natural constraints on variation of the sounds of language. Initially, there may seem to be wide variation in the sounds that speakers use to form utterances, but the dimensions of variation are in fact few in number. No more than 50 types suffice to characterize the sound patterns of thousands of human languages (see Table 6.1). Of course, the explanation for this apparently infinite use of finite means is controversial (described by Halle, 1981; Ladefoged, 1980). However, the linguistic data suggest that the indefinite proliferation of criterial features necessary to describe distal objects in general is unnecessary in the case of speech sounds in particular. This has been taken to encourage the premise of feature-detector studies: Distinctive feature properties in language take hold universally by virtue of innately established dimensions of sensitivity of feature detectors. The combination of these two principles, pandemonium and distinctive features, justified the phonetic-feature-detector program, making it immune to more general conceptual criticisms of pandemonium (for a detailed exposition, see Anderson, 1974; Neisser, 1967; Pribram, 1971; Rock, 1970; Wilson, Chapter 13, this volume). But granting this qualification, there were additional attractions to the notion that speech is perceived by a hierarchy of detectors.

Table 6.1. *The consonants and vowels of English as bundles of binary distinctions*

Distinctive feature	Consonants																					
	p	b	m	f	v	k	g	t	d	θ	ð	n	s	z	č	ǯ	š	ž
Vocalic	−	−	−	−	−	−	−	−	−	−	−	−	−	−	−	−	−	−
Consonantal	+	+	+	+	+	+	+	+	+	+	+	+	+	+	+	+	+	+
Compact	−	−	−	−	−	+	+	−	−	−	−	−	−	−	+	+	+	+
Tense	+	−	−	+	−	+	−	+	−	+	−	−	+	−	+	−	+	−
Voiced	−	+	+	−	+	−	+	−	+	−	+	+	−	+	−	+	−	+
Nasal	−	−	+	−	−	−	−	−	−	−	−	+	−	−	−	−	−	−
Continuant	−	−	−	+	+	−	−	−	−	+	+	−	+	+	−	−	+	+
Strident	−	−	−	+	+	−	−	−	−	−	−	−	+	+	+	+	+	+
Grave	+	+	+	+	+	+	+	−	−	−	−	−	−	−	−	−	−	−

Distinctive feature	Vowels and glides												
	i	ɪ	e	ɛ	æ	ɨ	ə	ʌ	a	u	ʊ	o	ɔ	y	w	h
Vocalic	+	+	+	+	+	+	+	+	+	+	+	+	+	−	−	−
Consonantal	−	−	−	−	−	−	−	−	−	−	−	−	−	−	−	−
High	+	+	−	−	−	+	−	−	−	+	+	−	−	+	+	−
Back	−	−	−	−	−	+	+	+	+	+	+	+	+	−	+	−
Low	−	−	−	+	+	−	−	−	+	−	−	−	+	−	−	+
Round	−	−	−	−	−	−	−	−	−	+	+	+	+	−	+	−
Tense	+	−	+	−	+	−	−	−	+	+	−	+	−	−	−	−

Note: Although the feature assignments were motivated by intuitions about linguistically significant sound contrasts, they were taken to reflect the underlying perceptual physiology.
Source: After Pisoni, 1978.

Acoustic variation and invariant cues

The phonetic-feature-detector model of speech perception was proposed not only as a timely fusion of the important accomplishments of descriptive linguistics and electrophysiology. It also proposed a solution to a long-standing problem in explaining speech perception. Since the inception of studies in acoustic phonetics, research had sought to identify the acoustic correlates of phonetic segments in order to establish the properties of auditory stimulation relevant to speech perception. Starting with the inventory of linguistic contrasts (the elements that compose the messages that people comprehend), investigators implicated a variety of acoustic patterns that distinguish between phones in many languages (Cooper, Delattre, Liberman, Borst, & Gerstman, 1952; Fant, 1962; Halle, Hughes, & Radley, 1957; Heinz & Stevens, 1961; Peterson & Barney, 1952). In English, for example, the contrast between *bag* and *wag* may be signaled by the rate of frequency transition of the resonant peaks, or formants, over the initial 100 msec of the syllable. The difference between *sop* and *shop* may be carried by the center frequencies of noise-filled fricative formants occurring at the beginning of the syllable. The words *heat* and *eat* may be distinguished by the respective presence or absence of low-amplitude noise in the oral formants before the start of the vowel.

Although the original objective of research in speech perception was to isolate the acoustic attributes *unique* to particular phones, it soon became obvious that the identity of a segment could be signaled in any number of different ways, and by a variety of acoustic cues. There is typically some variety in the acoustic correlates of each phonetic segment, and a fairly limited subset of these is often capable of evoking an unequivocal percept of the segment. This point is well illustrated with the closely examined instance of *voicing* (Lisker & Abramson, 1964). The articulatory combinations of laryngeal buzzing and oral gesture occur in two kinds in English: coincident or lagged voicing. Stop consonants are among the segments that display this contrast: *b*ox and *p*ox, *d*ire and *t*ire, *g*ill and *k*ill in initial position; ra*b*id and ra*p*id, o*dd*er and o*tt*er, bi*gg*er and bi*ck*er in intervocalic position; bo*b* and bo*p*, men*d* and mean*t*, ta*g* and ta*ck* in final position. These consonant pairs differ analogously, in that the former members all are the articulated with simultaneous laryngeal buzzing and oral gesture, whereas the latter members all exhibit delay or interruption of laryngeal activity during oral articulation.

Consider the enormous variation in the acoustic elements that signal the voicing distinction (Lisker, 1978; Lisker & Abramson, 1964; Stevens & Klatt, 1974). On particular occasions, the perception of voicing may be affected by (1) the presence or absence of aspiration noise, (2) the duration of the first formant transition, (3) the frequency of the fundamental period, (4) the starting frequency of the first formant at onset, (5) the duration of the syllable, overall, (6) the amplitude of the noise burst at the beginning of the syllable, (7) the duration of silence preceding the vocalic portion of the syllable in intervocalic position, or (8) the relative temporal patterning of the onsets of low- and mid-frequency energy. Although some of these acoustic elements are more potent than others in evoking the voicing contrast, all are able to affect the perceptual process of segment identification. The wide range of potential realizations of this contrast has been attributed to the mechanics of vocal sound production (Lisker & Abramson, 1964); the alternative temporal combinations of laryngeal and oral gestures happen to produce multiple acoustic events correlated with each. A particular acoustic element thereby attains its ability to elicit the perception of its complementary phonetic value.

Perceptual accounts of these and related phenomena must explain the correspondences of many acoustic patterns to individual phonetic segments. The solution to this problem is further complicated, however, by the *parallel transmission* of segment information in the acoustic signal (Liberman, Cooper, Shankweiler, & Studdert-Kennedy, 1967). Not only may several acoustically isolable cues contribute to a single percept, as in the case of voicing, but a single acoustic cue may contribute simultaneously to the perception of several phonetic segments. The competent listener, we must suppose, finds relevant acoustic patterns and integrates these cues in a phonetic manner, although the perceptual details of the processes of analysis and integration are quite obscure. The scope of this problem can be estimated by considering a few typical cases. An experiment conducted by Dorman, Studdert-Kennedy, & Raphael (1977) examined the use of multiple acoustic cues for consonant identity. Listeners were evidently capable of implicitly evaluating concurrent and successive acoustic correlates of a single segment, even when the elements were improbably arrayed through strategic manipulation of the waveforms. In another case, listeners were shown to integrate acoustic ingredients arrayed throughout a syllable, thereby recognizing a single phonetic segment (Strange, Jenkins, & Edman, 1977). The effect of any single cue therefore seems to depend as much on the acoustic pattern within which it occurs as it does on its particular physical details. (A bracing essay on the perceptual status of the "acoustic cue" occurs at the conclusion of a research report by Bailey & Summerfield, 1980.)

Finally, however the mechanism of perception works, the general consensus is that any regime for projecting the acoustic structure of the stimulus onto a sequence of phonetic elements must segment the physically continuous waveform. In other words, the perceptual impression that speech contains concatenated consonants and vowels is not brought about by literally isomorphic segmental properties of the acoustic signal (Fant, 1962). Most discussions of speech perception agree that this problem of segmentation is fundamental for the theory of phonetic perception (see, for example, Liberman & Studdert-Kennedy, 1978; Pisoni, 1978; Stevens & Blumstein, 1981; a contrary view is expressed by Klatt, 1979). The model of speech perception cast in terms of feature detectors proposed that individual neural elements, tuned to specific acoustic or phonetic properties, act as if they filtered phonetic segments from the continuous acoustic waveform. The mutual influences among these neural elements were further hypothesized to account for the general and specific phenomena of phonetic perception, phonetic development in infancy, and general specializations for linguistic abilities in humans. Within this program, it would seemingly be a manageable empirical matter to determine how the demons were tuned and arranged. The concern with this ensemble of issues placed feature-detector theories squarely in the mainstream of explanatory speculation in cognitive science over the past decade. Nonetheless, the notable aspects of the appeal of feature detectors include its radical differences with past and enduring perspectives on the problems of speech perception.

The appeal of feature detectors

Although some accounts of speech perception have considered the syllable to be the basic unit of perceptual analysis (for example, Bondarko, 1969; Savin & Bever, 1970; Wickelgren, 1969), and others have considered the phonetic segment to be basic (for example, Pisoni, 1978; Stevens & Blumstein, 1981; Studdert-Kennedy, 1976), the primitives in phonetic-feature-detector explanations are the distinctive features determined through linguistic analysis. The essential argument for this approach was that the assortment of distinctive features yielded from the analysis of linguistic sound contrasts (Chomsky & Halle, 1968; Jakobson, Fant, & Halle, 1963) could be assumed to provide specifications for the physiological mechanisms of perception. The inventory of phonetic-feature detectors, then, was hypothesized to be exactly the inventory of phonetic features used by linguistics to label distinctions among utterances (for example, voiced or voiceless, oral or nasal, stop or continuant, etc.). Although the psychological legitimacy of the distinctive-feature notion had been generally well defended by studies of the psychophysics of detection, memory, and speech production (among them, respectively, Fromkin, 1971; Miller & Nicely, 1955; Wickelgren, 1966), the contribution made by feature-detector theorists was a hypothetical mechanism that operated feature by feature. The psychological use of distinctive features could then be explained as a natural consequence of the ensemble of phonetically sensitive units composing the perceptual mechanism.

  The feature-detector model of speech perception was also based quite deliberately on physiological mechanisms, principally on findings in electrophysiology of sensory processes (Hubel & Wiesel, 1965). Although other accounts of speech perception have betrayed an occasional interest in speculative physiology (Lenneberg, 1967; Studdert-Kennedy & Shankweiler, 1970; see also Chomsky, 1965, p. 205: note 27), the feature-detector approach was actually modeled structurally on the apparent neural connections in the visual system, which at the time offered a kind of confirmation of pandemonium (but see Barlow, 1982; Maffei, Fiorentini, & Bisti, 1973). Specifically, a neuron exhibits a restricted "preference" for particular patterns of stimulation within its receptive field. The feature-detector notion in speech, in complementary fashion, assumed that a portion of the auditory system contains specialized neurons that exhibit phonetic preferences. By definition, then, this model for speech perception assumed a physiologically plausible mechanism. Each of a set of phonetic neurons would have a preference for a feature of the physical speech signal, and each would respond when its feature was present in the acoustic waveform. Moreover, the binary nature of distinctive features (Chomsky & Halle, 1968) was easily embodied in an opponent-process arrangement of phonetic neurons, again on the analogy to retinal ganglion and thalamic cells (for example, DeValois & DeValois, 1975; Hurvitch & Jameson, 1957). Complementary features, then, were detected by the net activity of phonetic-feature opponents. This model gained its credibility from the direct analogy with visual processes, a kind of independent validation supplementing the customary metatheoretical virtues that models should be logical and economical.

A perceptual process composed of mechanisms *devoted* to speech is inherently distinct from a general perceptual capacity *applied* to speech stimuli. By the phonetic-detector view, speech perception could only be accomplished through the activity of a restricted set of cells with established, stable phonetic preferences. Two types of experiments independently supported the plausibility of specialized modules in perception. On the one hand, various animals, examined electrophysiologically, seemed to possess higher-order sensory neurons whose activity was correlated specifically with ecological factors of the investigated species. The most celebrated of these special processors is the class-2 retinal-ganglion cell of the frog, which gave its maximal response to the introduction of a convex shape, a "fly," into its receptive field (Lettvin, Maturana, McCulloch, & Pitts, 1959). There are also mammalian and specifically primate examples of ecologically correlated neural-trigger features (for example, Gross, Rocha-Miranda, & Bender, 1972; Winter & Funkenstein, 1973; Wollberg & Newman, 1972; see Figure 6.2). Behavioral studies even suggested a functional parallel to speech perception in macaques, inasmuch as a right-ear advantage for recognition of a species-typical vocalization was observed (Petersen, Beecher, Zoloth, Moody, & Stebbins, 1978). At the time that the feature-detector model was introduced, there also appeared to be converging behavioral evidence about human newborn infants, specifically, that the perceptual capacity for identifying speech sounds was "prepared" for functioning considerably before the potentially entraining linguistic experience could have occurred, and well in advance of any possible utility in the development of articulatory finesse (Eimas, Siqueland, Jusczyk, & Vigorito, 1971). Although other perceptual explanations have differed in the extent to which they absolutely rely on specialization or innateness of the machinery of speech perception, the feature-detector account made the very specific claim of ecologically relevant pretuning of the perception mechanism for speech by analogy with the animal studies, thus also making sense of the otherwise unexplained precociousness of human infants.

One final distinction between the detector model and the more customary conceptualizations of speech perception was the relative detail with which experimental tests of the feature-detector activity could be devised. In other words, it was a model of the process of speech perception, rather than simply a characterization of the existence of particular processing stages, or of the particular transformations occurring during the flow of information along the nervous system. Tests could easily

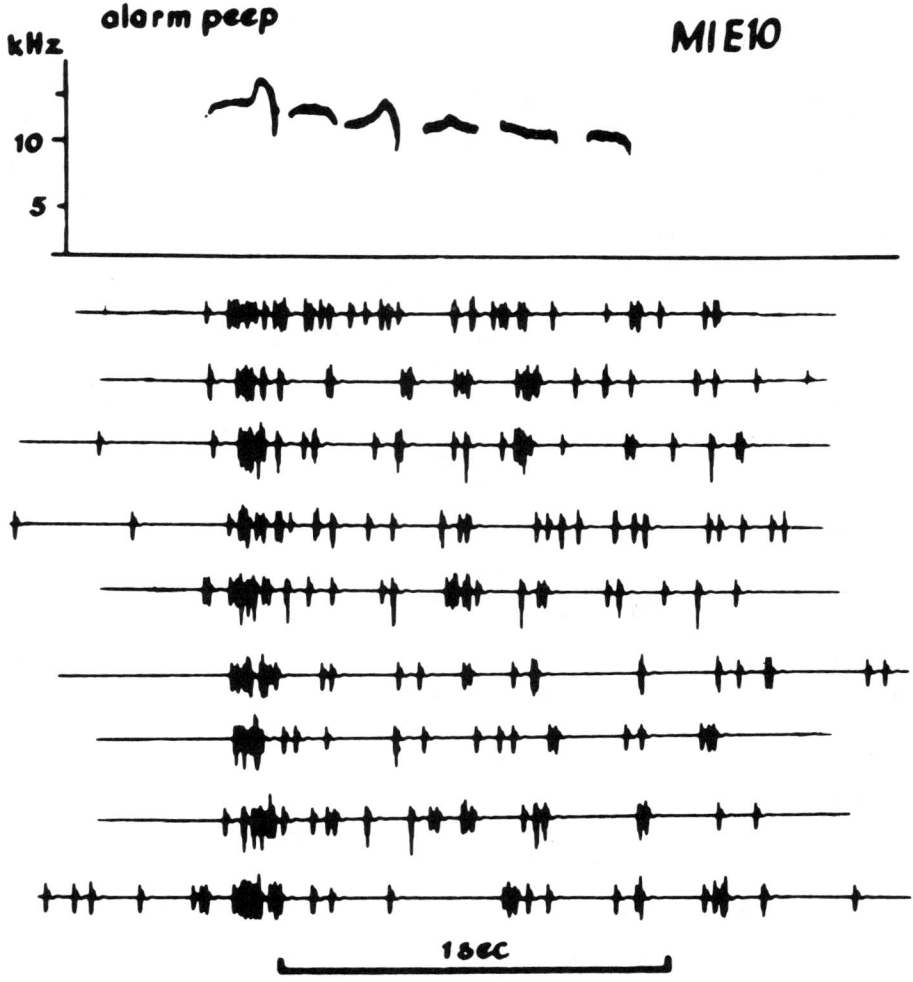

Figure 6.2. The response of auditory cortical units of the squirrel monkey to species-typical calls. In this figure from Winter and Funkenstein (1973) a spectrographic representation of the acoustic signal is shown at the top and the record of single-unit responses at the bottom. Such data were taken to suggest that single cells mediate the perception of ecologically significant events.

follow the rationale of McCulloch (1965) and Weisstein (1969) that the output of a set of property detectors is the sum of the individual detectors within the set. The tuning parameters of any individual feature detector could then be measured perceptually as a property-selective change in the perceiver's sensitivity to a series of complex stimuli, each of which has a slightly different value of the property in question. In the instance of speech sounds, the rationale predicted that the perceptual response should be altered by selective fatigue along the dimensions of the

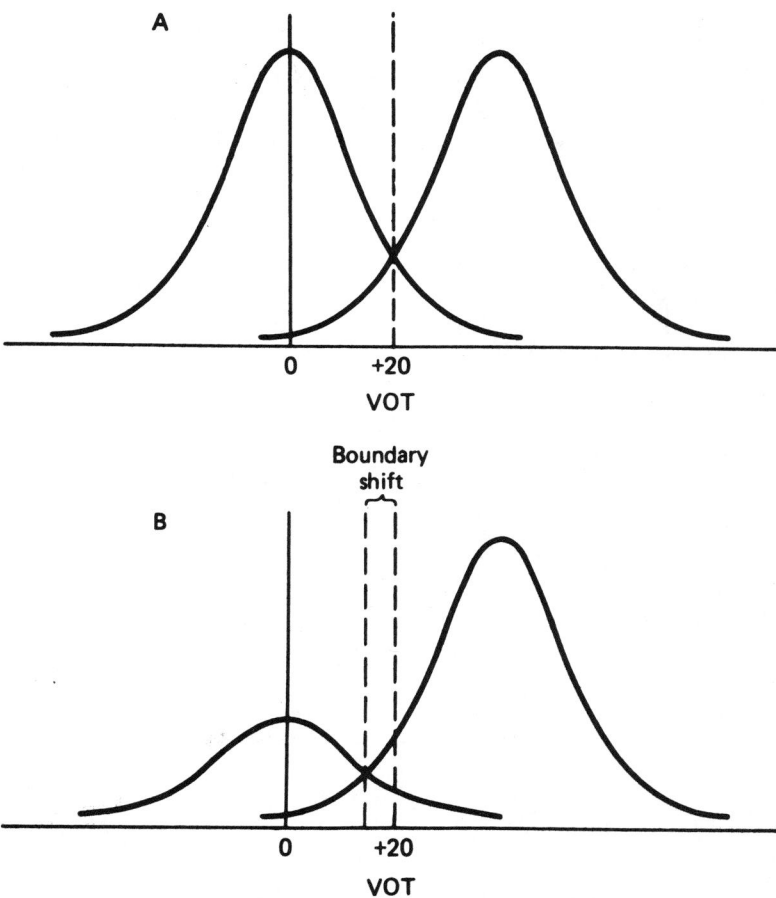

Figure 6.3. Fatigue effects on voicing detectors. Panel A describes the unfatigued responsiveness of hypothetical paired voicing detectors. "VOT" refers to voicing-onset time, a principal acoustic correlate of voicing alternations in many languages. When VOT approaches 0 msec, the voiced detector responds more vigorously than the voiceless detector; when VOT is relatively great, the voiceless detector responds more vigorously. At 20 msec, the responses of the two detectors are equivalent, indicating the basis for the unfatigued point of subjective equality, the perceptual-category boundary. Panel B shows the hypothetical effect of fatiguing the voicing detector. Note that the point of equivalent responsiveness is shifted, now closer to 0 msec of VOT. (Reproduced from Foss & Hakes, 1978.)

detectors, which, of course, happen to be the distinctions derived by linguistic analysis (see Figures 6.3 and 6.4.) This is because the distinctive features of linguistic analysis were conceived in this nativist theory to stand in one-to-one correspondence with the units of the perceptual mechanism, the feature detectors themselves. The feature-detector model of phonetic perception suggested a technique for improving and evaluating its adequacy: *selective adaptation*. It also made unambiguous predictions about the experimental outcomes, *adaptation-induced*

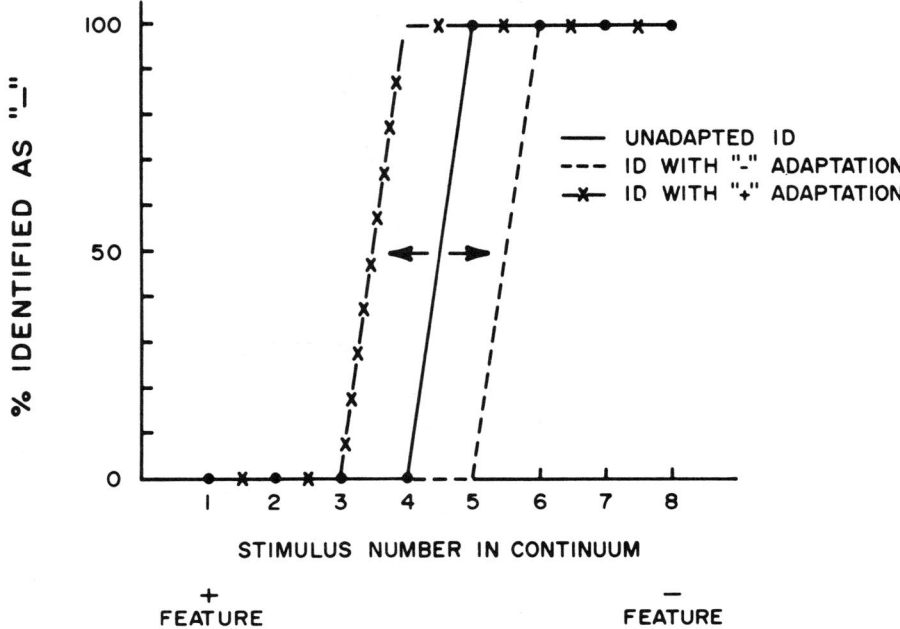

Figure 6.4. Adaptation effects in identification. The solid line plots ideal unadapted identification of a generic (+feature) to (−feature) phonetic test series. As the result of detector fatigue, the category boundary of the identification function is displaced toward the end of the series possessing the same feature value as the adaptor.

change in perceptual sensitivity along the dimensions of linguistic analysis (see also Chapter 3 by Repp & Liberman, Chapter 9 by Bornstein, and Chapter 13 by Wilson, this volume; also Moncrieff [1966], for a similar perspective in olfactory perception). In comparison to the specificity of hypotheses that could be generated for the feature-detector theory of speech perception, other contemporary theories appeared to be much more abstract and preliminary in nature (see Studdert-Kennedy, 1976), offering heuristic rather than explanatory value in the description of perceptual processes. These other approaches concentrated on particular aspects of speech perception, such as the independent constraints on acoustic variation imposed by the articulatory apparatus (Liberman, Cooper, Harris, & MacNeilage, 1962), the differential effects of representing certain speech sounds in short-term memory (Massaro, 1974; Pisoni, 1975), the deployment of general linguistic knowledge (Stevens & House, 1972), or the pragmatic considerations of the speaker's identity or conversational topic (Morton, 1969). Such emphases, however self-evidently valid they may be, do not account in detail for the chain of events between sensory transduction and the apprehension of the message. Overall, then, the many issues in speech perception were simply and specifically delineated in the case of the phonetic-feature-detector approach.

Phonetic feature detectors and selective adaptation

The original experiment establishing the adaptation test as the measure of feature-detector activity used the voicing distinction (Eimas & Corbit, 1973). Synthetic syllables composed the test series, which varied in the lag of voicing onset after the initial turbulent excitation of the formants. The resulting syllables were heard as [ba] (with coincident voicing) or [pa] (with lagged voicing). A standard identification test determined the categorization of these syllables according to their initial consonants, locating the category boundary, or point of subjective equality, between coincident and lagged voicing. Following that test, subjects listened to one of the series-endpoint syllables presented repetitively in blocks of numerous repetitions interpolated throughout a second identification test. When subjects had been presented with [ba] repetitively, the position of the category boundaries in their identifications changed – a smaller portion of the series was identified as *b*, overall. When subjects had heard [pa] as the repetitive item, their categorization of the series changed in the complementary fashion – there was a reduction in the range of items in the series identified as *p*.

Alone, this phenomenon of perceptual adaptation of phonetic categories might not have seemed remarkable, given the evidence of contrast phenomena in psychophysics (Helson, 1964). But Eimas and Corbit used repetitive stimuli in a subsequent test that presented the same voicing contrast in a different consonantal place. These syllables were [da] (coincident voicing) and [ta] (lagged voicing), and their effectiveness as adaptors was measured with the original voicing-test series. Relative to unadapted categorization of the stimulus series, the effect of the [da] adaptor resembled the effect of [ba], and the effect of [ta] resembled [pa]. The results of adaptation with [da] and [ta] (syllables with a coronal-place feature) tested on the [ba–pa] series (syllables with a labial-place feature) suggested that selective adaptation was specific for the phonetic feature of voicing. In turn, it implied that adaptation of the categories to repetitive stimulation was evidence for analytic devices, albeit fatigable ones, tuned to detect the presence of phonetic features in the speech signal independent of the contexts of occurrence. The model of categorization and adaptation of phonetic stimuli basically extended this finding: For every phonetic distinction there was a pair of detectors, set in opposition, mediating the perception of the distinction (Miller, 1975).

Almost immediately, the use of the selective-adaptation technique to verify phonetic dimensions of analysis was troubled by findings that simpler general auditory mechanisms were involved, to the possible exclusion of a role for phonetic detectors (Ades, 1974; Bailey, 1975; Pisoni & Tash, 1975; Tartter & Eimas, 1975; see also Roberts & Summerfield, 1981). The study reported by Tartter and Eimas illustrates this problem for phonetic-feature detectors. In that case, adaptation on a [ba]-[da] test series was produced by acoustic patterns that were not themselves perceived phonetically. The adaptors were "chirps," brief snippets of the initial formant-frequency transitions of the endpoint syllables. These formant transitions in a phonetic context are known to provide "minimal acoustic cues" to the identity of the place-of-articulation feature of the stop consonants in question (Delattre, Liberman, & Cooper, 1955), and among the test syllables, the formant transitions varied with the identity of the syllables in the series. Because perceptual adaptation of phonetic categories resulted from repetitive presentation of these nonspeech "chirps," the authors presumed that lower-level general auditory processes common to both speech and nonspeech perception were implicated in the effect. Of course, specifically phonetic processes are excluded in the perception of sounds other than speech.

Although a number of other studies also described adaptation effects that required no appeal to a phonetic-feature-detector mechanism, the role of auditory processes in adaptation was nonetheless cast in terms of feature detectors (for example, Darwin, 1976), as if the mechanism of perceptual analysis was necessarily composed of demons of one kind or another. Like the phonetic-feature detector, an auditory-feature detector was considered to respond less well following fatigue by a stimulus that contained the detector's critical property. The auditory detectors were presumably sensitive to acoustic cues, such as the patterns of formant-frequency variation that signal place of articulation. Auditory-pattern detectors might prefer particular starting or ending frequencies, or durations, or rates of change, as the studies of Whitfield and Evans (1965) encouraged. In these experiments, the existence of frequency-transition preferences of auditory cortical neurons was noted. It seemed, therefore, that adaptation of phonetic perceptual categories could be attributed to nonphonetic auditory fatigue when the adapting stimulus was acoustically similar to the phonetic stimuli of the test series, however different in perceptual quality each type of stimulus was.

The emphasis on auditory analyzing mechanisms made it seem as though adaptation would ultimately be explicable in sensory terms, arguably at the auditory-feature-detector level of the phonetic-detector hierarchy, and perhaps without resort to a phonetic level of detectors at all. Nonetheless, there remained several empirical cases supporting the existence of a phonetic level of analysis, therefore offering counterevidence to the emerging explanation of adaptation exclusively in terms of lower-order pattern analyzers (Cooper, 1975; Cooper & Blumstein, 1974; Diehl, 1975, 1976; Ganong, 1975; Hall & Blumstein, 1978; Sawusch, 1977; Sawusch & Jusczyk, 1981; Wolf, 1978). In Ganong's study, to take an illustrative example, the items of the test series varied in the feature place of articulation, from [bæ] (labial) to [dæ] (apical). This series was composed by manipulating the rise and fall of formant frequency, from their onsets through their transitions to the steady-state vowel configuration, within synthetic syllables. The [d] endpoint had second- and third-formant transitions falling in frequency, while the [b] endpoint formant transitions all rose in frequency. Two versions of the syllable [sæ], containing the fricative consonant [s] with apical place, were used as adapting stimuli. The first [sæ] adaptor had formant transitions identical to those of the [dæ] endpoint, which should have been sufficient to produce adaptation by the auditory-detector rationale. Recall that the auditory principle says that the extent of adaptation is determined by the spectral similarity of test item and adaptor: The more similar, the greater the adaptation effect. The second [sæ] adaptor was synthesized simply by joining a steady-state aperiodic segment to a steady-state vowel, in the proper temporal arrangement. By the auditory rationale, no adaptation should have occurred with this second [sæ], because the consonantal portions of the adaptor, on the one hand, and the test items, on the other, were quite dissimilar: The adaptor was aperiodic and relatively high frequency in the concentration of its acoustic energy, and the test items were periodic and relatively midrange on the frequency scale. Both adaptor syllables were subjectively identified as [sæ], and *both* produced adaptation, as if each shared a feature with the [d] side of the test series.

Only the adaptation produced by the [sæ] adaptor with formant transitions could be ascribed to fatigue of auditory detectors. The adaptation caused by the other [sæ] was attributed to its phonetic properties, namely, that it shared the apical-place feature with items at the [dæ] end of the test series. It was tempting to conclude that a distinctly phonetic process had undergone a change, indicated in the identification performance. Whether the transitionless adaptor had its effect by fatiguing the apical-feature detector or not, the phenomenon required an explanation at a stage beyond the representation of auditory features of the stimulus.

Confronted with one set of adaptation effects explainable by phonetic-feature detectors and another set that implicated only auditory-pattern detectors, several authors argued that the underlying perceptual mechanism was composed of two kinds of detectors, a modification of the original model (Blumstein, Stevens, & Nigro, 1977; Cooper, 1975; Diehl, 1976; Eimas & Miller, 1978; Ganong, 1975; Sawusch, 1977). In addition to the phonetic-feature detectors that operate in advance of segmental (cognitive) demons, the modified hierarchy included auditory-pattern detectors. These could be thought of as hypercomplex image demons whose responses are indifferent to the correspondence of acoustic pattern and phonetic identity, but which reflect the patterns within the stimulus nevertheless. The benefit of including this level in the perceptual process was clear: In cases of auditory-detector fatigue, adaptation occurs because the higher-level detectors receive degraded information from the lower-level detectors. Because the response of any detector is bound to the particular activity in the preceding level to which it attends, the biasing of the auditory registration of stimulus patterns indirectly biases the verdicts of the phonetic detectors. The higher-level process can also be directly altered in cases of phonetic-detector fatigue, when the auditory similarity of adaptor and test stimuli is either slight or nil.

The emerging hypothesis could accommodate one theoretically important development in particular. When speech and nonspeech sounds contain acoustically identical components, it stands to reason that those components activate the same auditory detectors along the path to recognition. Quite obviously, such speech and nonspeech sounds need not also share the higher-order detectors whose activity indicates perceptual categorization. This concept of a common stock of auditory analyzers, within which there exists a phonetically appropriate subset, was bolstered by adaptation studies with nonspeech test series. Several reports (Cutting, Rosner, & Foard, 1976; Diehl, 1976; Samuel & Newport, 1979) described adaptation effects with nonspeech sounds, including those in which plucked and bowed string tones affected phonetic judgments. In those instances of crossed adaptation of speech and nonspeech sounds, the acoustic structure of one end of the adapted speech series could be likened to the structure of the nonspeech adaptor (but see Remez, Cutting, & Studdert-Kennedy, 1980). As a result of these studies, the connections between auditory and phonetic analyzers subserving speech perception seemed nonexclusive. Although the phonetic level of analysis was fed by the auditory level, auditory detectors also contributed to the perception of nonphonetic sounds. But the putative categoricity of the distinction between plucked-and-bowed strings (Cutting & Rosner, 1974; since invalidated by Rosen & Howell, 1981, and Chapter 4, this volume) implied that all of the perceptually significant processing, of which categoricity was taken as an emblem, occurred at the lower auditory level.

The rejection of the detector model

As the model was revised, incorporating phonetic and auditory detectors, the phenomena to be explained by its use changed. Instead of simply being to account for the physiological reflection of distinctive-feature theory (see Cooper & Blumstein, 1974), the goal became one of outlining the connections between auditory-feature detectors and phonetic-feature detectors (Eimas & Miller, 1978). Multiple tunings were invoked to represent the use (and the fatigability) of particular auditory patterns in the service of several different phonetic features (as in Pisoni & Tash, 1975), although the opponent process structure was retained to accommodate the studies that showed adaptation without specific auditory similarity (for example, Diehl, 1976; Sawusch, 1977). The opponent pairs in this extended version of the model were the hierarchical-detector ensembles themselves. The justification for supposing that any single auditory-pattern analyzer was part of the causal chain of phonetic recognition was provided by the demonstration that the pattern was, in fact, a cue, or that it affected the value of other cues. In other words, the hierarchy of detectors, with the phonetic-feature detector at the pinnacle, was essentially recast as a kind of probability distribution of auditory patterns correlated with the presence of the phonetic feature in the acoustic signal. Because the criteria that the demons were originally held to apply seemed inadequate to organize the phenomena of adaptation, this improved model attempted to be comprehensive by increasing the number of contingencies encompassed by the detector arrangements, although the cost was becoming apparent: The phonetic demon in this modification must be a little homunculus, capable of identifying the *meaning* of the auditory image rather than simply its structure.

Two clear questions developed in response to this complication of the original, simple, and elegant (though inadequate) detector model: (1) Is adaptation predicted exclusively by phonetic features or their auditory counterparts? (2) Is adaptation the result of detector fatigue? The answers to these questions seem at this point to be negative, and as a result, the perplexities of this field of study have forced the abandonment of the detector model for immediately explaining adaptation, and for ultimately explaining the preception of speech.

To take the questions in order, first, a variety of counterevidence now exists to the assumption that adaptation is predicted exclusively by phonetic or auditory similarity, as dictated by the model. For one, adaptation of the categories along a [ba] to [da] to [ga] place series only occurred when adaptors and test syllables shared suprasyllabic organization (Hall & Blumstein, 1978). In this study, adaptors were drawn directly from the test series, but were presented both in isolation (for example, [ba]) and in two-syllable combinations (for example, [baga]), some of which were modified slightly to create an impression of stress on one of the two syllables. Although the monosyllable adaptors were effective, as expected, none of the two-syllable adaptors were, save one containing [ga] as a stressed final syllable that was marginal in its effect. Evidently, adaptation was sensitive to the context provided by the syllable structure of the adaptor, overriding phonetic and acoustic similarity that should otherwise be sufficient to produce adaptation.

A parallel finding was reported by Bryant (1978), who simply varied the manner of presenting identification-and-adaptation trials in an otherwise standard adaptation test. The adaptors, drawn from a [bæ] to [dæ] test series of 250-msec syllables and shortened to 70 msec, were presented at different rates of repetition, either at 75 msec or 225 msec of stimulus-onset asynchrony. Identification trials from the test series were also presented in two forms: in the original 250-msec durations with an intertrial interval of 2 sec, or in a train of five repeated presentations in which each test item was shortened to a duration of 70 msec, with an intertrain interval of 2 sec. The requirement of phonetic and acoustic similarity between adaptor and test-series items was met inasmuch as the adaptors were produced by shortening the vowel portion of the syllable and leaving the formant transitions alone. Consequently, adaptation should have occurred, whether by auditory or by phonetic fatigue, regardless of the rate of repetition, although a fatigue model might have predicted that adaptation would be greater for high rates of adaptor repetition; in that case, the effect should have been proportional to the rate of presentation of the adapting items. However, adaptation was *contingent* on rate of repetition, surprisingly. When the adaptors were presented at 2-sec intervals, greater adaptation was measured with the identification trials presented slowly than with the train-type trial. The reverse occurred with adaptors presented at the fast rate. When the train-type identification trial was used to measure the categories, the adaptation effect was greater than when the slow-rate identification trial was used. This shows, first, that phonetic and auditory similarity is insufficient to explain the incidence of adaptation. Second, it raises the absurd possibility that the detectors supposedly mediating the effect are sensitive to the rate of syllable repetition – although it is difficult to recall any phonetic distinction that operates by this principle. This study therefore produced counterevidence to the claim that adaptation (hence perception) is explained by postulating a detector hierarchy whose preferences are determined by the utility of auditory patterns in evoking phonetic percepts.

Even if it were supposed that neurons were recruited or entrained during linguistic development to monitor auditory patterns that were occasionally effective for perceiving speech sounds, the evidence would rule out that speculation about the assortment of auditory detectors and their arrangements. In an experiment presenting this conclusion (Remez, 1980), a test series was created ranging from [ba] to a nonspeech buzz by iteratively broadening the bandwidths of the formants of the syllable. Listeners judged the items in the series to be either [ba], a *speech* sound, or buzz, a *nonspeech* sound. When the [ba] endpoint was used as the adaptor, the portion of the series perceived to consist of speech sounds diminished, and, conversely, when the buzz endpoint was the adaptor, the portion perceived to be nonspeech diminished. Feature detectors were eliminated from consideration in explaining the observed adaptation for two reasons. First, the inventory of detectors is supposedly given by linguistic analysis, and no language uses contrasts among phonetic segments that oppose sounds that are [+speech] from those that are [−speech]. It would therefore be nonsensical to admit a property detector of this type within the restricted specialized-speech processor, even one that is trainable by linguistic experience. Second, according to principle, the variety of auditory-pattern detectors attached to phonetic-feature detectors should be limited, by inheritance or linguistic experience, to those relevant to phonetic-feature assignment. But the buzz pattern is broadband (see Figure 6.5), and clearly nonphonetic. To suppose that a detector for it belongs in the speech-perception ensemble implausibly admits that the "specialized" phonetic hierarchies may incorporate auditory detectors responsive to *any* pattern exciting the auditory system. Because there is no known dependency of phonetic-feature assignment, either direct or contextual (Summerfield, 1981: Experiment 7) on nonspeech sounds, the buzz "detector" should not be part of any phonetic-feature hierarchy.

These adaptation findings (Bryant, 1978; Hall & Blumstein, 1978; Remez, 1980) together suggest that the changes in categorization occasioned by repetitive stimulation need not be interpreted as the effects of a fixed set of detectors, whether auditory or phonetic in preference. This naturally casts doubt on the claim that adaptation tests ever revealed the action of phonetically motivated ensembles of detectors. The dimensions of adaptation are simply arbitrary, and more numerous than those of acoustic-phonetic correspondences.

If the answer to the first question, pertaining to the usefulness of the detector assumption for predicting the incidence of adaptation, was negative, its consequences were limited. Whereas it seemed implausible that every subtle, adaptable dimension of auditory contrast was specially included in the linguistic detector ensemble, it was not unimaginable – it was merely unimaginably complex, and obviously contrary to the independent evidence favoring a limited, devoted neural process with a restricted anatomical substrate (for example, Penfield & Roberts, 1959; more recently, Ojemann & Mateer, 1979). To reject the detector model

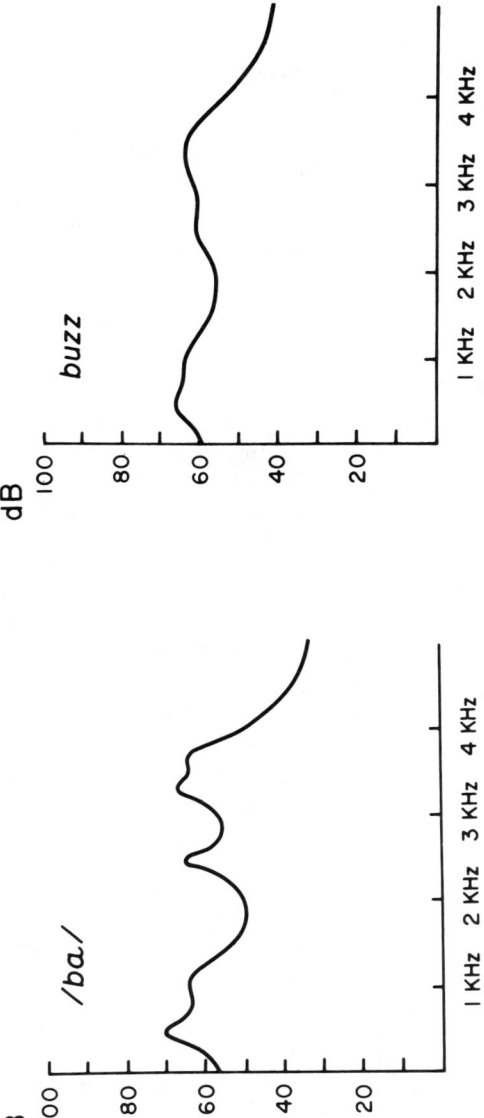

Figure 6.5. A comparison of the acoustic spectrum at onset (initial 20 msec) of the syllable /ba/ and the nonspeech buzz derived from it. The buzz spectrum is not characteristic of any speech sound, and should therefore not be present in the auditory detector level of the phonetic detector cascade. Although logically the buzz should not cause adaptation of a speech signal, or vice versa, adaptation does occur (Remez, 1980).

finally, evidence was brought against its hypothetical mode of function because the feature-detector mechanism was as much a model of the process of detecting linguistic properties as it was a description of the result of the process. The crucial premise in this regard, that selective adaptation occurred because the sensitivity or responsiveness of detectors was reduced by fatigue, was challenged from several perspectives.

First, experiments by Sawusch (1976) showed that adaptation not only affected the balance between opponent detectors (or detector systems), but it also affected the subjective quality of test items that were never ambiguously identified (see also Miller, 1975). By using a rating procedure rather than an absolute identification forced-choice task, Sawusch determined that the best example of an adapted category became a less "good" example after undergoing adaptation. However, the fatigue of an opponent cell should only be detectable when stimuli are marginal examples of the category it mediates. In other words, a detector "yells" to win the attention of a cognitive demon, successfully or not. Competition between detectors should only be close for intermediate acoustic values, those that are similar to the preferences of several detectors and that consequently present poor examples of a conceptual category. Therefore, the graded responses of Sawusch's subjects exemplified a process that at least included something other than pandemonium. If a mechanism were required to supplement pandemonium to explain the judgments within categories, it seemed as though the supplementary process might just as well supplant the detectors.

Second, a variety of experiments began to demonstrate adaptation with very few fatiguing trials (Diehl, Elman, & McCusker, 1978; Diehl, Lang, & Parker, 1980; Simon & Studdert-Kennedy, 1978; cf. Bailey, 1975), hinting that adaptation effects were not fatigue effects. In the study by Diehl et al. (1978), listeners identified items from a labial voicing test series presented in isolation as well as in combination with contrast-inducing items. The latter were either the two endpoints of the test series, or two midrange items from the series, or two velar consonants that also differed in the voicing feature. The identification performance, with and without the contrasting item, resembled data obtained before and after adaptation, including the crossed case. It is noteworthy that an effect of contrast was observed whether the item to be identified preceded *or* followed the contrasting item, indicating again that the creation of fatigue through adaptation was not the only way to displace the identification function. If this had been an instance of one-trial fatigue, we would have expected the effect to appear only when the adaptor preceded the identification item, thereby producing the fatigue that alters the response to the lagging syllable.

Ultimately, the argument that in this case adaptation and contrast were mediated by the same process rested on the similarity of the data that each technique generated. As such, the argument made on the basis of these data was indirect, appealing to parsimony for the verdict (see Diehl & Kluender, Chapter 7 of this volume). The detector model was not capable of explaining the pattern of results in both paradigms, but the response contrast principle was.

Finally, the direct test of the fatigue premise was recently performed by Harris and Pastore (1983), who measured recognition thresholds as well as the identification boundary for a [bi]-[di] test series with and without adaptation. Both endpoint items were used as adaptors, and both altered the placement of the boundary along the series, as is typically observed. However, the adaptors also *lowered* the thresholds for identifying test items presented in noise. The labial adaptor lowered thresholds for the apical-category items, and the apical adaptor lowered thresholds for the entire series. If adaptation had been caused by the fatigue of detectors, then the reduction of sensitivity should have corresponded to an elevation of the recognition thresholds due to the sluggish response of the units. In addition to producing a kind of terminal counterevidence for the fatigue principle, this finding is also a problem for the response-contrast accounts of adaptation effects (Diehl, 1981; Elman, 1979), which have assumed that there is no sensory role in these phenomena. However the effects are explained, fatigue of detectors was finally eliminated as a candidate by this psychoacoustic study.

Epilogue

The inadequacy of the phonetic-feature-detector concept was established as a matter of evidence, independent of the premises that led to its invention. Thus, the possibility remains that speech is represented in linguistic features or in prototypical auditory patterns in the nervous system. Linguistic messages may even be perceived by an activity that explicitly derives complex auditory patterns from the waveform and determines linguistic features in turn from them. The form of representation and derivation, though, is necessarily more diffuse or complex than pandemonium allows (for example, see the neurophysiological speculations of Anderson, Silverstein, Ritz, & Jones, 1977 and the representational model of Harnad in Chapter 19, this volume). Yet despite the enduring temptation to fuse neurophysiology, psychology, and linguistics, the precipitating causes for the pandemonium model have also lost the force they had in 1973.

First, the structural hypotheses about the visual processes that so greatly influenced the feature-detector concept in speech are apparently no longer valid. In a recent review, Barlow (1982) explains that the neural arrangements proposed by Hubel and Wiesel for explaining the progressive refinement of trigger features in visual units (a specific application of pandemonium) have not fared well in experimental tests. Selectivity is apparently not caused by privileged connections between lower- and higher-order units. Evidence now indicates that inhibitory interactions produce selectivity in cortical units, much as inhibition determines selectivity in the retina. Some complex cells are directly excited by thalamic units, bypassing the cortical simple cells, in contrast to a strictly hierarchical scheme. Patterns of retinal stimulation that are effective for complex cells also are often ineffective for the simple cells that were initially held to mediate their activity. In the absence of a demonstrated visual example of pandemonium on which to model a linguistic

Figure 6.6. Saint Anthony tormented by demons, an engraving by Schongauer (c. 1475) offers an appropriate connotation of pandemonium, given the outcome of phonetic-detector research. Compare this to Selfridge's abstract version (Figure 6.1). (Metropolitan Museum of Art.)

version, there is little justification a priori for supposing that detector hierarchies mediate speech perception (see Figure 6.6).

Second, the precocious abilities of human infants seem less specially phonetic now than they did in 1971. Although the neonate can discriminate an impressive variety of acoustic patterns correlated with phonetic alternations, similar discrimination performance is elicited with patterns containing phonetically criterial acoustic variation within nonspeech sounds. Prior to linguistic experience, it seems that the discrimination of speech sounds is subserved by general auditory abilities (Aslin, Pisoni, & Jusczyk, 1984), although this argument is an indirect one, once again, based on the similarity of the judgments in speech and nonspeech cases, and on an appeal to parsimony. But, if the precocious sensitivity is less distinctly phonetic than originally supposed, the need for an innately installed phonetic-detector ensemble is considerably reduced.

Third, recent perceptual research on acoustically reconstructed speech signals undermines the explanations of perception that are grounded in the elaboration of particular acoustic cues, and, by implication, the specific auditory-feature detectors that perform that function. There seems to be no special set of sound elements that evoke phonetic percepts (Liberman & Cooper, 1972). Instead, listeners may perceive speech by attending to the phonetically significant patterns of acoustic change, regardless of the momentary ingredients that compose the signal. This is the conclusion suggested by studies with sine-wave replicas of utterances (Remez & Rubin, 1983, 1984; Remez, Rubin, Pisoni, & Carrell, 1981), in which listeners detected the linguistic message of acoustic patterns that simultaneously preserved the time-varying structure of speech and discarded the characteristically vocal short-time spectrum elements. In view of these findings, it seems unlikely that the perceiver identifies speech sounds by detecting particular momentary acoustic elements that are typical of each consonant and vowel, as the phonetic-feature-detector model assumed.

Through hindsight, we see that the rise and fall of the phonetic-feature-detector occurred rapidly owing both to the nature of its appeal and to the virtues of the model itself. It unified a set of broad concerns, and borrowed physiological plausibility for a psychological model (as it loaned psychological plausibility to the physiological model, the more difficult exchange to make). It was uncomplicated to test, and, fortunately, the results were ultimately clear, although often problematic. Presently, there is no single coherent rationale for predicting adaptation, contrast, and assimilation effects with phonetic materials, although the rejection of the detector model is occasioned logically by its falsification, not by the advent of its replacement. Just as we cannot ignore the privileged status that adaptation effects had for evaluating the model, we should recognize that much of the urgency to identify the causes and meaning of adaptation effects has been lost with the relegation of that theory to the status of a curious and unsuccessful comingling of neurophysiology, psychology, and linguistics.

References

Ades, A. E. (1974). How phonetic is selective adaptation? Experiments on syllable position and vowel environment. *Perception & Psychophysics, 16,* 61–66.

Anderson, J. A., Silverstein, J. W., Ritz, S. A., & Jones, R. S. (1977). Distinctive features, categorical perception, and probability learning: Some applications of a neural model. *Psychological Review, 84,* 413–451.

Anderson, R. M., Jr. (1974). Wholistic and particulate approaches in neuropsychology. In W. B. Weimer & D. S. Palermo (Eds.), *Cognition and the Symbolic Processes* (pp. 389–396). Hillsdale, NJ: Erlbaum.

Aslin, R. N., Pisoni, D. B., & Jusczyk, P. W. (1984). Auditory development and speech perception in infancy. In M. M. Haith & J. J. Campos (Eds.), *Infancy and the biology of development*. New York: Wiley.

Bailey, P. J. (1975). *Perceptual adaptation in speech*. Unpublished dissertation, Cambridge University, Cambridge, U.K.

Bailey, P. J., & Summerfield, Q. (1980). Information in speech: Observations on the perception of [s]-stop clusters. *Journal of Experimental Psychology: Human Perception and Performance, 6,* 536–563.

Barlow, H. B. (1982). David Hubel and Torsten Wiesel: Their contributions towards understanding the primary visual cortex. *Trends in NeuroSciences, 5,* 145–152.

Blumstein, S. E., Stevens, K. N., & Nigro, G. N. (1977). Property detectors for bursts and transitions in speech perception. *Journal of the Acoustical Society of America, 61,* 1301–1313.

Bondarko, L. V. (1969). The syllable structure of speech and distinctive features of phonemes. *Phonetica, 20,* 1–40.

Bryant, J. S. (1978). Feature detection process in speech perception. *Journal of Experimental Psychology: Human Perception and Performance, 4,* 610–620.

Cassirer, E. (1923). *Substance and function & Einstein's theory of relativity*. Chicago: Open Court.

Chomsky, N. (1965). *Aspects of a theory of syntax*. Cambridge, MA: M.I.T. Press.

Chomsky, N., & Halle, M. (1968). *The sound pattern of English*. New York: Harper & Row.

Cooper, F. S., Delattre, P. C., Liberman, A. M., Borst, J. M., & Gerstman, L. J. (1952). Some experiments on the perception of synthetic speech sounds. *Journal of the Acoustical Society of America, 24,* 597–608.

Cooper, W. E. (1975). Selective adaptation to speech. In F. Restle, R. M. Shiffrin, N. J. Castellan, H. R. Lindman, & D. B. Pisoni (Eds.), *Cognitive theory* (Vol. 1, pp. 23–54). Hillsdale, NJ: Erlbaum.

Cooper, W. E. (1979). *Speech perception and production*. Norwood, NJ: Ablex.

Cooper, W. E., & Blumstein, S. E. (1974). A ''labial'' feature analyzer in speech perception. *Perception & Psychophysics, 15,* 591–600.

Cutting, J. E., & Rosner, B. S. (1974). Categories and boundaries in speech and music. *Perception & Psychophysics, 16,* 564–570.

Cutting, J. E., Rosner, B. S., & Foard, C. F. (1976). Perceptual categories for musiclike sounds: Implications for theories of speech perception. *Quarterly Journal of Experimental Psychology, 28,* 361–378.

Darwin, C. J. (1976). The perception of speech. In E. C. Carterette & M. P. Friedman (Eds.), *Handbook of perception* (Vol. 1, pp. 175–226). New York: Academic Press.

Delattre, P. C., Liberman, A. M., & Cooper, F. S. (1955). Acoustic loci and transitional cues for consonants. *Journal of the Acoustical Society of America, 27,* 769–773.

DeValois, R. L., & DeValois, K. K. (1975). Neural coding of color. In E. C. Carterette and M. P. Friedman (Eds.), *Handbook of perception: Vol. 5; Seeing* (pp. 117–166). New York: Academic Press.

Diehl, R. L. (1975). The effect of selective adaptation on the identification of speech sounds. *Perception & Psychophysics, 17,* 48–52.

Diehl, R. L. (1976). Feature analyzers for the phonetic dimension *stop vs. continuant*. *Perception & Psychophysics, 19,* 267–272.

Diehl, R. L. (1981). Feature detectors for speech: A critical reappraisal. *Psychological Bulletin, 89,* 1–18.

Diehl, R. L., Elman, J. L., & McCusker, S. B. (1978). Contrast effects on stop consonant identification. *Journal of Experimental Psychology: Human Perception and Performance, 4,* 599–609.

Diehl, R. L., Lang, M., & Parker, E. M. (1980). A further parallel between selective adaptation and contrast. *Journal of Experimental Psychology: Human Perception and Performance, 6,* 22–44.

Dorman, M. F., Studdert-Kennedy, M., & Raphael, L. J. (1977). Stop-consonant recognition: Release bursts and formant transitions as functionally equivalent context-dependent cues. *Perception & Psychophysics, 22,* 109–122.

Eimas, P. D., & Corbit, J. D. (1973). Selective adaptation of linguistic feature detectors. *Cognitive Psychology, 4,* 99–109.

Eimas, P. D., & Miller, J. L. (1978). Effects of selective adaptation on the perception of speech and visual patterns: Evidence for feature detectors. In R. D. Walk & H. L. Pick (Eds.), *Perception and experience* (pp. 307–345). New York: Plenum Press.

Eimas, P. D., Siqueland, E. P., Jusczyk, P., & Vigorito, J. (1971). Speech perception in infants. *Science, 171,* 303–306.

Elman, J. L. (1979). Perceptual origins of the phoneme boundary effect and selective adaptation to speech: A signal detection theory analysis. *Journal of the Acoustical Society of America, 65,* 190–207.

Fant, C. G. M. (1962). Descriptive analysis of the acoustic aspects of speech. *Logos, 5,* 3–17.

Foss, D. J., & Hakes, D. T. (1978). *Psycholinguistics.* Englewood Cliffs, NJ: Prentice-Hall.

Fromkin, V. (1971). The non-anomalous nature of anomalous utterances. *Language, 47,* 27–52.

Ganong, W. F., III. (1975). An experiment on "phonetic adaptation." *Progress Report, Research Laboratory of Electronics, Massachusetts Institute of Technology, 116,* 206–210.

Gross, C. G., Rocha-Miranda, C. E., & Bender, D. B. (1972). Visual properties of neurons in inferotemporal cortex of the macaque. *Journal of Neurophysiology, 35,* 96–111.

Hall, L. L., & Blumstein, S. E. (1978). The effect of syllabic stress and syllabic organization on the identification of speech sounds. *Perception & Psychophysics, 24,* 137–144.

Halle, M. (1981). On the relationship of phonological features to phonetic parameters. In A. S. House (Ed.), *Acoustic phonetics and speech modeling* (pp. F7:1–22). Princeton, JN: Communications Research Division, Institute for Defense Analyses.

Halle, M., Hughes, G. W., & Radley, J.-P. A. (1957). Acoustic properties of stop consonants. *Journal of the Acoustical Society of America, 29,* 107–116.

Harris, L. B., & Pastore, R. E. (1983). Recognition thresholds for a speech continuum following selective adaptation. *Perception & Psychophysics, 34,* 268–272.

Heinz, J. M., & Stevens, K. N. (1961). On the properties of voiceless fricative consonants. *Journal of the Acoustical Society of America, 33,* 589–596.

Helson, H. (1964). *Adaptation-level theory.* New York: Harper.

Hubel, D. H., & Wiesel, T. N. (1965). Receptive fields and functional architecture in two nonstriate visual areas (18 and 19) of the cat. *Journal of Neurophysiology, 28,* 229–289.

Hurvitch, L. M., & Jameson, D. (1957). An opponent-process theory of color vision. *Psychological Review, 64,* 384–404.

Hyde, S. R. (1972). Automatic speech recognition: A critical survey and discussion of the literature. In E. E. David and P. B. Denes (Eds.), *Human communication: A unified view* (pp. 399–438). New York: McGraw-Hill.

Jakobson, R., Fant, G., & Halle, M. (1963). *Preliminaries to speech analysis.* Cambridge, MA: M.I.T. Press.

Klatt, D. H. (1977). A review of the ARPA speech understanding project. *Journal of the Acoustical Society of America, 62,* 1345–1366.

Klatt, D. H. (1979). Speech perception: A model of acoustic-phonetic analysis and lexical access. *Journal of Phonetics, 7,* 279–312.

Ladefoged, P. (1980). What are linguistic sounds made of? *Language, 56,* 485–502.

Lenneberg, E. H. (1967). *Biological foundations of language.* New York: Wiley.

Lettvin, J. Y., Maturana, H. R., McCulloch, W. S., & Pitts, W. H. (1959). What the frog's eye tells the frog's brain. *Proceedings of the IRE, 47,* 1040–1059.

Liberman, A. M., & Cooper, F. S. (1972). In search of the acoustic cues. In A. Valdman (Ed.), *Papers in linguistics and phonetics to the memory of Pierre Delattre* (pp. 329–338). The Hague: Mouton.

Liberman, A. M., Cooper, F. S., Harris, K. S., & MacNeilage, P. F. (1962). A motor theory of speech perception. In *Proceedings of the Speech Communication Seminar* (Vol. 2). Stockholm: Royal Institute of Technology.

Liberman, A. M., Cooper, F. S., Shankweiler, D. P., & Studdert-Kennedy, M. (1967). Perception of the speech code. *Psychological Review, 74*, 421–461.

Liberman, A. M., & Studdert-Kennedy, M. (1978). Phonetic perception. In R. Held, H. Leibowitz, & H.-L. Teuber (Eds.), *Handbook of sensory physiology:* Vol. 8, *Perception* (pp. 143–178). New York: Springer.

Lisker, L. (1978). *Rapid vs. Rabid:* A catalog of acoustic features that may cue the distinction. *Haskins Laboratories Status Report on Speech Research, SR-54*, 127–132.

Lisker, L., & Abramson, A. S. (1964). A cross-language study of voicing in initial stops: Acoustical measurements. *Word, 20*, 384–422.

Maffei, L., Fiorentini, A., & Bisti, S. (1973). Neural correlate of perceptual adaptation to gratings. *Science, 183*, 1036–1038.

McCulloch, C. (1965). Color adaptation of edge-detectors in the human visual system. *Science, 149*, 1115–1116.

Massaro, D. W. (1974). Perceptual units in speech recognition. *Journal of Experimental Psychology, 102*, 199–208.

Miller, G. A., & Nicely, P. E. (1955). An analysis of perceptual confusions among some English consonants. *Journal of the Acoustical Society of America, 27*, 338–352.

Miller, J. L. (1975). Properties of feature detectors for speech: Evidence from the effects of selective adaptation and dichotic listening. *Perception & Psychophysics, 18*, 389–397.

Moncrieff, R. W. (1966). *Odour Preferences.* New York: Wiley.

Morton, J. (1969). Interaction of information in word recognition. *Psychological Review, 76*, 165–178.

Neisser, U. (1967). *Cognitive Psychology.* Englewood Cliffs, NJ: Prentice-Hall.

Ojemann, G., & Mateer, C. (1979). Human language cortex: Localization of memory, syntax and sequential motor-phoneme identification systems. *Science, 205*, 1401–1403.

Penfield, W., & Roberts, L. (1959). *Speech and brain mechanisms.* Princeton, NJ: Princeton University Press.

Petersen, M. R., Beecher, M. D., Zoloth, S. R., Moody, D. B., & Stebbins, W. C. (1978). Neural lateralization of species-specific vocalizations by Japanese macaques (*Macaca fuscata*). *Science, 202*, 324–327.

Peterson, G. E., & Barney, H. L. (1952). Control methods used in a study of the vowels. *Journal of the Acoustical Society of America, 24*, 175–184.

Pisoni, D. B. (1975). Auditory short-term memory and vowel perception. *Memory & Cognition, 3*, 7–18.

Pisoni, D. B. (1978). Speech perception. In W. K. Estes (Ed.), *Handbook of learning and cognitive processes, Vol. 6: Linguistic functions in cognitive theory* (pp. 167–233). Hillsdale, NJ: Erlbaum.

Pisoni, D. B., & Tash, J. (1975). Auditory property detectors and processing place features in stop consonants. *Perception & Psychophysics, 18*, 401–408.

Pribram, K. H. (1971). *Languages of the brain.* Englewood Cliffs, NJ: Prentice-Hall.

Remez, R. E. (1980). Susceptibility of a stop consonant to adaptation on a speech-nonspeech continuum: Further evidence against feature detectors in speech perception. *Perception & Psychophysics, 27*, 17–23.

Remez, R. E., Cutting, J. E., & Studdert-Kennedy, M. (1980). Cross-adaptation using song and string. *Perception & Psychophysics, 27*, 524–530.

Remez, R. E., & Rubin, P. E. (1983). The stream of speech. *Scandinavian Journal of Psychology, 24*, 63–66.

Remez, R. E., & Rubin, P. E. (1984). On the perception of intonation from sinusoidal sentences. *Perception & Psychophysics, 35*, 429–440.

Remez, R. E., Rubin, P. E., Pisoni, D. B., & Carrell, T. D. (1981). Speech perception without traditional speech cues. *Science, 212*, 947–950.

Roberts, M., & Summerfield, Q. (1981). Audiovisual presentation demonstrates that selective adaptation is purely auditory. *Perception & Psychophysics, 30*, 309–314.

Rock, I. (1970). Perception from the standpoint of psychology. In D. A. Hamburg (Ed.), *Perception and its disorders* (pp. 1–11). Baltimore: Williams & Wilkins.
Rosen, S. M., & Howell, P. (1981). Plucks and bows are not categorically perceived. *Perception & Psychophysics, 30,* 156–168.
Samuel, A. G., & Newport, E. L. (1979). Adaptation of speech by nonspeech: Evidence of complex acoustic cue detectors. *Journal of Experimental Psychology: Human Perception and Performance, 5,* 563–578.
Savin, H., & Bever, T. G. (1970). The nonperceptual reality of the phoneme. *Journal of Verbal Learning and Verbal Behavior, 3,* 295–302.
Sawusch, J. R. (1976). Selective adaptation effects on end-point stimuli in a speech series. *Perception & Psychophysics, 20,* 61–65.
Sawusch, J. R. (1977). Peripheral and central processes in selective adaptation of place of articulation in stop consonants. *Journal of the Acoustical Society of America, 62,* 738–750.
Sawusch, J. R., & Jusczyk, P. W. (1981). Adaptation and contrast in the perception of voicing. *Journal of Experimental Psychology: Human Perception and Performance, 7,* 408–421.
Selfridge, O. G. (1959). Pandemonium: A paradigm for learning. In *Mechanisation of thought processes* (pp. 511–531). London: H. M. Stationery Office.
Simon, H. J., & Studdert-Kennedy, M. (1978). Selective anchoring and adaptation of phonetic and nonphonetic continua. *Journal of the Acoustical Society of America, 64,* 1338–1357.
Stevens, K. N., & Blumstein, S. E. (1981). The search for invariant acoustic correlates of phonetic features. In P. D. Eimas & J. L. Miller (Eds.), *Perspectives in the study of speech* (pp. 1–38). Hillsdale, NJ: Erlbaum.
Stevens, K. N., & House, A. S. (1972). Speech perception. In J. V. Tobias (Ed.), *Foundations of modern auditory theory,* Vol. 2 (pp. 1–62). New York: Academic Press.
Stevens, K. N., & Klatt, D. H. (1974). Role of formant transitions in the voiced-voiceless distinction for stops. *Journal of the Acoustical Society of America, 55,* 653–659.
Strange, W., Jenkins, J. J., & Edman, T. R. (1977). Identification of vowels in "vowel-less" syllables. *Journal of the Acoustical Society of America, 61,* S39.
Studdert-Kennedy, M. (1976). Speech perception. In N. J. Lass (Ed.), *Contemporary Issues in Experimental Phonetics* (pp. 243–293). New York: Academic Press.
Studdert-Kennedy, M., & Shankweiler, D. (1970). Hemispheric specialization for speech perception. *Journal of the Acoustical Society of America, 48,* 570–594.
Summerfield, Q. (1981). Articulatory rate and perceptual constancy in phonetic perception. *Journal of Experimental Psychology: Human Perception and Performance, 7,* 1074–1095.
Tartter, V. C., & Eimas, P. D. (1975). The role of auditory feature detectors in the perception of speech. *Perception & Psychophysics, 18,* 293–298.
Weisstein, N. (1969). What the frog's eye tells the human brain: Single cell analyzers in the human visual system. *Psychological Bulletin, 72,* 157–176.
Weisstein, N. (1973). Beyond the yellow-Volkswagen detector and the grandmother cell: A general strategy for the exploration of operations in human pattern recognition. In R. L. Solso (Ed.), *Contemporary issues in cognitive psychology* (pp. 17–51). Washington, D.C.: V. H. Winston.
Whitfield, I. C., & Evans, E. F. (1965). Responses of auditory cortical neurones to stimuli of changing frequency. *Journal of Neurophysiology, 28,* 655–672.
Wickelgren, W. A. (1966). Distinctive features and error in short-term memory for English consonants. *Journal of the Acoustical Society of America, 39,* 388–398.
Wickelgren, W. A. (1969). Auditory or articulatory coding in verbal short-term memory. *Psychological Review, 76,* 232–235.
Winter, P., & Funkenstein, H. H. (1973). The effect of species-specific vocalization on the discharge of auditory cortical cells in the awake squirrel monkey (*Saimiri sciureus*). *Experimental Brain Research, 18,* 489–504.
Wolf, C. G. (1978). Perceptual invariance for stop consonants in different positions. *Perception & Psychophysics, 24,* 315–326.
Wollberg, Z., & Newman, J. D. (1972). Auditory cortex of squirrel monkey: Response patterns of single cells to species-specific vocalization. *Science, 175,* 212–214.

7 On the categorization of speech sounds

Randy L. Diehl and Keith R. Kluender

We begin by defending the following claims about the correspondence between speech signals and phonetic categories:

1. Within certain limits of time and frequency, there is almost no significant aspect of acoustic structure that is irrelevant to phonetic categorization.
2. Experienced listeners make use of *all* potentially relevant cues for phonetic categories, provided these cues are detectable.
3. Relatively localized (e.g., syllable-sized) portions of the acoustic signal generally do not contain sufficient information to specify phonetic categories unambiguously.

If these claims are approximately correct, then an important class of speech-perception models – those based on the notion of feature detectors – can be shown to be inadequate in crucial respects. In addition, template-matching models of speech recognition (e.g., the LAFS model of Dennis Klatt) are criticized on the grounds that significant perceptual facts (in particular, certain kinds of phonetic-similarity judgments) cannot be explained in a principled manner.

We outline an alternative approach to speech recognition that depends on considerably greater computational power and more sophisticated knowledge structures than those of many existing models. In our view, phonetic categorization requires deployment of the full range of the listener's tacit knowledge of speech: knowledge of the acoustic consequences of biomechanical, aerodynamic, physiological, phonological, dialectal, and other factors influencing speech production. Finally, we consider how an understanding of general auditory processing may place important constraints on speech-recognition models and provide a partial account of the phenomenon of categorical perception.

The aims of this chapter are three: First, to defend some general claims about the correspondence between speech signals and phonetic categories; second, to explore implications of these claims for several current hypotheses about human speech recognition; and finally, to consider (in vague outline) an alternative approach to speech recognition that relies on significantly greater computational power than most existing models.

The correspondence between speech signals and phonetic categories

In this section, we wish to argue for the following propositions:

1. Within certain time and frequency limits, there is almost no significant aspect of the acoustic structure of speech signals that is irrelevant to phonetic categorization.

2. Experienced listeners make use of *all* potentially relevant cues for phonetic categories, provided these cues are detectable.
3. It is generally not the case that relatively localized (e.g., syllable-sized) portions of the acoustic signal contain sufficient information to specify phonetic categories unambiguously.

Good scientific strategy almost always involves some form of simplification or idealization. For example, in modeling aspects of speech production, theorists have found it convenient to assume a degree of independence among component sound-producing and filtering mechanisms. Classical phonetics treated vocal-tract resonances or formants as the products of individual cavities, the first formant typically being assigned to the back (pharyngeal) cavity, and the second formant to the front (mouth) cavity. More recently, the laryngeal sound source and the vocal-tract resonators were modeled as contributing independently to the acoustic output (Fant, 1960). Consistent with these kinds of simplifying assumptions, various versions of distinctive-feature theory (Chomsky & Halle, 1968; Jakobson, Fant, & Halle, 1963) were formulated such that the presumed articulatory correlates of different feature dimensions are approximately orthogonal.

If one supposes that component mechanisms of speech production are independently regulated then it is also natural to assume that the acoustic signal can be partitioned into orthogonal substructures each corresponding to the independent production states or features. The latter assumption was made explicitly in distinctive-feature theory (Chomsky & Halle, 1968; Jakobson et al., 1963) and has also been implicit in recent theories of human speech recognition (Eimas & Corbit, 1973; Stevens & Blumstein, 1981).

Whether a particular simplifying assumption is warranted depends in part on our theoretical aims. In the domain of speech production and distinctive-feature theory, some version of the orthogonality principle is clearly useful and even necessary for certain purposes. However, generalizing this principle to the domain of acoustic outputs may be an inappropriate simplification if one's theoretical task is to understand the normal complexities of human speech recognition.

Strictly speaking, the orthogonality principle is incorrect as a description of both speech-production states and acoustic outputs. Despite its own simplifying assumptions, Fant's (1960) fundamental work on the acoustic theory of speech production was largely devoted to overturning the classic view of the vocal tract as a set of independent Helmholtz resonators each producing a single formant. In place of the classical notions, Fant used compound tube or horn models that explicitly allow *all* parts of the vocal tract to contribute in varying degrees to the determination of *all* formants. Only in the case of the "point" vowels /i/, /a/, and /u/ and in certain cases of consonantal occlusion are the front and back cavities even approximately decoupled acoustically (Stevens, 1972). For the most part, the vocal-tract resonators form a single, highly interactive system.

Even the assumed independence between the laryngeal sound source and the vocal-tract resonators (Fant, 1960) is a rather crude first approximation. More recent theoretical models (Fant, 1979, 1981; Flanagan & Ishizaka, 1978) acknowledge various forms of interaction between glottal (source) and supralaryngeal (filter) parameters. Not surprisingly, empirical studies have demonstrated a number of clear instances of mechanical and aerodynamic coupling between source and filter. Vocal-fold vibration requires that the folds be positioned reasonably close together and that there be sufficiently greater air pressure below the glottis than above. The frequency of vibration depends on, among other things, the magnitude of this pressure drop across the glottis and the tension of the vocal folds (Atkinson, 1978). However, both of these factors depend in turn on the state of the supralaryngeal vocal tract. For example, oral closure during voicing (vocal-fold vibration) creates an increased air pressure above the glottis that tends to equalize the transglottal pressures and thus terminate voicing (Rothenberg, 1968). Also, high vowels (e.g., /i/ and /u/) are known to be associated with a higher frequency of vocal-fold vibration than low vowels (e.g., /æ/ and /a/). The most likely explanation of this relation is in terms of a mechanical coupling between the larynx and supralaryngeal structures. Higher vowels presumably place greater tension on the vocal folds (Ewan, 1979; Lubker, McAllister, & Lindblom, 1977; Ohala, 1973).

Source/filter interaction also occurs in the opposite direction. When the vocal folds are positioned far enough apart to prevent spontaneous vibration, the primary sound source is produced by turbulent airflow through the open glottis. But in this state, the system no longer consists merely of a laryngeal source and a supralaryngeal filter. The *sub*laryngeal cavities (which produce both resonances and antiresonances) are now acoustically coupled to the vocal tract, and the filter characteristics are thereby changed (Fant, 1960, 1973). Typically, an open glottis results in a greatly attenuated first formant and an increase in bandwidth for the higher formants.

The existence of interactions among the component sound-producing and filtering mechanisms of the vocal tract is well documented and uncontroversial. However, the implications of such interactions have not always been fully appreciated. Given the direct mapping between articulatory/phonatory configurations and acoustic outputs (Fant, 1960), any interactions in the former should be reflected in the latter. This serves as the basis for proposition 1 listed at the beginning of this section. We are claiming that (within certain time and frequency limits) the production of a given phonetic segment or feature will in varying degrees affect virtually all aspects of the acoustic signal. What is more, these effects on the signal are systematic (although not necessarily invariant) and therefore serve as potential information to the listener about the identity of the segment or feature. Proposition 2 goes further and asserts that listeners actually make use of all this potential information in the process of phonetic categorization. Together, these propositions suggest that it is a serious theoretical oversimplification to attempt to partition the acoustic signal into orthogonal substructures each corresponding to, say, separate distinctive features.

For three decades, a favorite strategy among speech researchers has been to examine waveform and spectrographic representations of minimal pairs of natural utterances (i.e., pairs differing by one phoneme or feature), to make guesses as to the critical acoustic cues that distinguish the utterance categories, and to test these guesses by asking listeners to identify synthetic-speech samples whose acoustic parameters are well controlled. A review of the early synthetic-speech work (Liberman, 1957; Liberman, Cooper, Shankweiler, & Studdert-Kennedy, 1967; Liberman, Delattre, & Cooper, 1952; Liberman, Delattre, & Cooper, 1958; Liberman, Delattre, Cooper, & Gerstman, 1954; Liberman, Delattre, Gerstman, & Cooper, 1956; Liberman, Ingemann, Lisker, Delattre, & Cooper, 1959) encourages the belief that acoustic cues for phonetic categories are fundamentally isolable and orthogonal, although this was perhaps not the intention of the authors. A recurrent diagram in this early work shows nine synthetic consonant–vowel syllables arranged in a two-dimensional matrix of *place of articulation* (labial-alveolar-velar) versus "*manner*" *of articulation* (voiced-voiceless-nasal). Place of articulation is shown to be specified by the slope and direction of the second-formant transition, and for each place value this cue is invariant across the different manner categories. Similarly, the cues for each of the three manner categories are displayed as being invariant across the three values of place. (Voiced-stop consonants have a low frequency "voice bar" and periodically excited formant transitions; voiceless stops have a delayed onset of the first formant and an aperiodically excited second-formant transition; nasals have several low-amplitude steady-state resonances prior to the formant transitions.) As a description of minimal rules for consonant–vowel synthesis, this diagram is quite useful. However, in adhering strictly to the orthogonality principle, it grossly oversimplifies the relation between cues and categories.

More recent synthetic-speech research at Haskins Laboratories and elsewhere has yielded a much more complex picture of cue/category relations, one that tends to support propositions 1 and 2. Consider, for example, that judgments about the voicing category of initial stops (/b/ versus /p/, /d/ versus /t/, /g/ versus /k/) depend on all of the following acoustic parameters: voice-onset time (VOT), the interval between the release burst and the onset of waveform periodicity associated with voicing (Lisker & Abramson, 1970; Lisker, Liberman, Erickson, Dechovitz, & Mandler, 1977); duration of voiced-formant transitions (Lisker et al., 1977; Stevens & Klatt, 1974; Summerfield & Haggard, 1974); first-formant onset frequency (Lisker, 1975; Summerfield & Haggard, 1977); onset frequencies and directions of second- and third-formant transitions (Miller, 1977; Repp, 1977a, 1977b); spectral characteristics of the following vowel (Summerfield, 1974); duration of the following vowel (Summerfield 1978; Summerfield & Haggard, 1972); duration of aspiration (Winitz, LaRiviere, & Herriman, 1975); intensity of aspiration (Repp, 1979); and fundamental frequency at voicing onset (Fujimura, 1971; Haggard, Ambler, & Callow, 1970; Haggard, Summerfield, & Roberts, 1981). Lisker (1978) has described an even longer list of acoustic parameters that may affect voicing judgments for stops in word-medial position. These include presence or absence of low-frequency buzz during the closure interval; duration of closure; first-formant offset frequency before closure; first-formant offset transition duration; first-formant onset frequency following closure; first-formant onset transition duration; preceding-vowel duration; amount of first-formant "cutback" before and after closure; VOT after closure; amplitude of the following vowel relative to the preceding vowel; decay time of the glottal signal preceding closure; and burst intensity following closure.

In short, there appear to be very few (if any) significant aspects of the acoustic signal that are irrelevant to phonetic categorization. The lists cited in the previous paragraph included only cues that occur in the immediate locale of the segment in question. As we shall see, phonetic categorization also depends on acoustic information outside this immediate locale.

It is worthwhile to examine in more detail the articulatory/phonatory rationale for some of these cues. As we argued earlier, the production of a phonetic segment involves the entire vocal apparatus as an interactive system. Inasmuch as any aspects of acoustic output depend systematically on segment- or feature-specific characteristics of the vocal-tract configuration, such aspects serve as potential cues to segment or feature identity. Let us consider how this might work in the case of voicing category judgments for initial stops. In the phonetics literature, the term *voiced* as it is applied to stop consonants refers to the presence of vocal-fold vibration during stop closure, whereas *voiceless* refers to the absence of vocal-fold vibration during closure. In initial position, English stops are usually voiceless in this technical phonetic sense. However, at the more abstract phonological level of description, we usually say that the stops /b/, /d/, and /g/ are *voiced* (even in initial position) and /p/, /t/, /k/ are *voiceless*. Our use of terms here will reflect this phonological sense.

If vocal-fold vibration during closure does not reliably distinguish voiced from voiceless stops in initial position, what does? The most common answer, based on the important work of Lisker and Abramson (1964, 1971), is that the critical distinguishing property is the temporal difference between the initial release of the articulators and the onset of voicing or, briefly, voice-onset time (VOT). Voiced stops in English occur either with voicing lead, simultaneous release and voicing, or a short voicing lag, usually no greater than 10 to 30 msec. Voiceless stops, on the other hand, are produced with a voicing lag of between 30 and 90 msec. These relations indicate clearly why VOT, acoustically defined as the interval between the release burst and the onset of waveform periodicity, is such an important voicing cue. They also help to account for most of the other voicing cues in initial stops, as these cues tend to be natural acoustic correlates of VOT. All other things being equal, a longer voicing lag following release will result in a shorter interval of voiced transitions; a higher first-formant onset frequency (because an open glottis introduces an antiresonance, which effectively cancels out the low-frequency part of the first-formant transition); and a longer and more intense aspiration interval. In addition, several production studies (Haggard et al., 1981; House & Fairbanks, 1953; Klatt, 1975; Lehiste & Peterson, 1961) have found a systematically lower fundamental frequency at the onset of periodicity in voiced stops than in voiceless ones, thus explaining the cue value of onset pitch. (The physiological basis of this voicing correlate is not entirely clear, although it is sometimes explained in terms of greater transglottal pressure and greater vocal-fold stiffness at voicing onset for a voiceless stop [Halle & Stevens, 1971].)

Apart from being sensitive to the full range of acoustic correlates of the voiced–voiceless distinction, the listener also compensates perceptually for a variety of production interactions. The VOT values of naturally produced initial stops vary systematically as a function of both the place value of the stop (Lisker & Abramson, 1964) and the height of the following vowel (Klatt, 1975). These effects appear to have straightforward mechanical and aerodynamic explanations. As already noted, the onset of voicing requires a sufficient air-pressure drop across the glottis. Oral closure tends to equalize transglottal pressures, delaying voicing onset, whereas articulatory release allows the oral air pressure to dissipate, yielding favorable conditions for voicing. Two factors that influence the time required to produce a suitable transglottal-pressure drop after release are (1) the inertia of the articulators being released and (2) the openness of the vocal tract following release. The tongue body, used in the articulation of velar stops, is more massive (hence slower to accelerate) than are either the tongue tip or lips, used in the production of alveolar and labial stops, respectively. This would explain the greater VOT values for velars. Moreover, the production of high vowels, with relatively narrow oral openings, retards the dissipation of oral air pressure longer than does the production of low vowels, accounting for the typically greater VOT values of stops preceding high vowels. What is of considerable interest is that listeners adjust their VOT-category boundaries in accordance with both of these production interactions (Cooper, 1974; Diehl, Lang, & Parker, 1980; Lisker & Abramson, 1970).

Our discussion has focused mainly on voicing cues in initial stops, but the same points can be made with respect to virtually any other phonetic categories that have been studied. For example, Lindblom and Studdert-Kennedy (1967) showed that listeners shift their acoustic boundaries separating vowel categories according to the consonantal context, and that this shift effectively compensates for vowel-target undershoot effects that occur in normal vowel production (Lindblom, 1963).

Similarly, Mann and Repp (1980) found an effect of the following vowel on the identification of a noise segment that was intermediate between /s/ and /ʃ/. This segment was more likely to be labeled s before /u/ than before /a/. Such a context effect may be explained in terms of the listener's tacit knowledge of the acoustic consequences of fricative-vowel coarticulation. Lip rounding appropriate for /u/ occurs during the preceding fricative segment, causing the fricative to be lowered in frequency. To compensate perceptually for this, listeners more readily accept a lower frequency noise as /s/ (rather than /ʃ/) before a rounded vowel.

To take a final example from the early speech literature, Liberman, Delattre, and Cooper (1952) found that a particular filtered-noise burst was variously identified as /p/ or /k/ depending on whether the following vowel was /i/, /a/, or /u/. Again, this amounts to a perceptual compensation for normal coarticulatory effects of the vowel on the preceding consonant. (For other examples of such compensatory effects, see Repp & Liberman in Chapter 3, this volume.)

We have been using the term "interaction" in two different senses: first, to denote the dependence of all significant aspects of an acoustic output on the *entire* articulatory/phonatory configuration, and second, to refer to the articulatory and acoustic influences that exist between adjacent phonetic segments. There is a third kind of interaction to which we now turn, namely, extrasyllabic influences on phonetic categorization. Such influences form the basis of proposition 3: Relatively localized (e.g., syllable-sized) portions of the acoustic signal generally do not contain sufficient information to specify phonetic categories unambiguously. At first glance, this proposition seems to be at odds with propositions 1 and 2, which emphasize the richness or redundancy of within-syllable cues for phonetic categories. In fact, however, there is no contradiction. Within-syllable cues are indeed plentiful and collectively quite reliable, provided the more global acoustic context is taken into account. (This proviso holds both for syllables within longer utterances and for syllables produced in isolation, where the acoustic context is silence.)

Phonetic categorization of target syllables has been shown to be significantly influenced by global properties of the carrier sentence such as utterance rate (Ainsworth, 1972, 1974; Diehl, Souther, & Convis, 1980; Miller & Grosjean, 1981; Minifie, Kuhl, & Stecher, 1976; Port, 1978; Repp, Liberman, Eccardt, & Pesetsky, 1978; Summerfield, 1974, 1975a,b, 1976), implied vocal-tract size of the talker (Ladefoged & Broadbent, 1957), and, for bilingual listeners, the language (e.g., English versus Spanish) of the carrier sentence (Elman, Diehl, & Buchwald, 1977). In addition, phonetic categorization is typically altered if the target syllable is removed from its original speech context and placed in an "inappropriate" context. For example, a syllable excised from a rapidly articulated utterance and presented either in isolation or in a slowly articulated speech context is often mislabeled in the direction of an intrinsically shorter vowel category, as in /pæp/ → /pɛp/ (Verbrugge & Shankweiler, 1977).

Each of these effects, like those of the segmental voicing cues listed earlier, is consistent with the view that listeners have detailed tacit knowledge of normal speaker-imposed constraints on the acoustic structure of utterances. For example, when an utterance is rapidly articulated, most acoustic segments, including VOT intervals, are shortened (Summerfield, 1975b). Listeners compensate for this by shifting the voicing boundary toward smaller VOT values (Summerfield, 1974, 1975a,b, 1976). Thus, a syllable categorized as /ba/ after a slowly spoken precursor phrase may be labeled /pa/ when the precursor is more rapid. Moreover, this "rate normalization" effect can be reduced or eliminated by introducing a sharp change in vocal-tract parameters at the juncture between the precursor phrase and the target syllable (Diehl et al., 1980). In other words, listeners appear to follow the quite reasonable perceptual strategy of disregarding prior rate information given sufficient cues signaling a change in speaker.

The feature-detector hypothesis

If, as we have argued, propositions 1 to 3 are correct, what are the implications for models of human speech recognition? We suggest that these propositions are fundamentally at odds with an important class of speech-perception models – those based on the notion of feature detectors. In this secton, we will try to make explicit why this is so.

The first formal proposals that feature detectors subserve speech perception appeared in the early 1970s. Such detectors were characterized by Abbs and Sussman (1971) as sensorineural configurations that are selectively sensitive to certain complex acoustic properties of speech sounds, especially properties that are "trademarks" of distinctive features:

For example, the voicing feature possesses the distinguishing characteristics of (1) a formant structure, (2) a negative slope of the voice spectrum, and (3) greater intensity of lower formants. These physical qualities could be recognized by an appropriate spatial array of receptive fields innately sensitive to temporal characteristics of this acoustic signal. (p. 29)

Similar proposals were made by Lieberman (1970) and Stevens (1971).

Over the past decade, the feature-detector hypothesis has been extended and refined in two principal ways. First, there have been a great many empirical studies designed to uncover the detailed operational characteristics of the putative detectors. Almost all of these studies have used variations of the selective-adaptation technique. Second, there have been significant attempts, primarily by Blumstein and Stevens (1979), to characterize invariant acoustic properties that correspond to each of the distinctive-feature categories and that purportedly serve as the adequate stimuli for feature detectors.

Eimas and Corbit (1973) developed the first explicit model of feature detectors for speech. It was designed to apply specifically to the categorical perception of voicing contrasts in word-initial stop consonants, but was later generalized to other features and contexts. The model posits two detectors with partially overlapping ranges of sensitivity along the VOT dimension. Each detector is most sensitive to the modal production value of one voicing category. All else being equal, the VOT value to which both detectors are equally sensitive corresponds to the perceptual boundary between voiced and voiceless stops. Moreover, a detector may be fatigued, that is, reduced in sensitivity, by continuous repeated exposure to its adequate stimulus. This last assumption provides the theoretical motivation for the use of the selective-adaptation technique.

Eimas and Corbit (1973) found that after repeated presentation of (say) a voiced stop the listener's perceived voicing boundary was shifted along the VOT dimension toward the voiced category, confirming the predictions of the model. (If the voiced detector is reduced in sensitivity across the entire range of stimulus values to which it normally responds then the VOT value at which the voiced and voiceless detectors are equally sensitive should be displaced toward the voiced category.) Apart from Eimas and Corbit, many other investigators seized upon the selective-adaptation technique to attempt to answer various questions: Could the detector model be generalized to dimensions other than VOT? Were the detectors peripherally or centrally located in the auditory system? Were the detectors responsive to purely acoustic properties of speech stimuli or to more abstract phonetic or phonological features? (For reviews of much of this work, see Ades, 1976; Cooper, 1975, 1979; Diehl, 1981; Eimas & Miller, 1978; Miller & Eimas, 1982.)

Recently, the detector-fatigue account of adaptation effects has been challenged on various grounds (Diehl, 1981; Diehl, Elman, & McCusker, 1978; Diehl, Lang, & Parker, 1980; Elman, 1979; Rosen, 1979; Sawusch & Nusbaum, 1979; Simon & Studdert-Kennedy, 1978). Diehl and his colleagues, for example, have reported experiments showing a close similarity between adaptation results and results of a simple contrast procedure. In the latter procedure, the long adaptation sequence is replaced by a single-context stimulus that is preceded or followed by a single test item. As in adaptation, the context stimulus typically has a contrastive effect on test-stimulus identification. With the contrast procedure, we have found rather striking parallels to a variety of adaptation effects reported in the literature. The principle of parsimony suggests that common processes underlie both adaptation and contrast effects.[1] Because detector fatigue is not a plausible factor in contrast experiments, we have opted for an account based on Helson's (1964) adaptation-level theory. If we are right, adaptation results should no longer be viewed as evidence for feature detectors. (For an extended version of this argument, see Diehl, 1981. See also Wilson, Chapter 13 of this volume. For other arguments against feature detectors, see Remez in Chapter 6 of this volume.)

Arguments against feature detectors

Advocates of the feature-detector hypothesis appear to agree that detector inputs are fairly direct neural transforms of the speech signal, or in other words, transforms that preserve most of the spectral and temporal information (Ades, 1976; Eimas & Miller, 1978; Pisoni & Sawusch, 1975). However, there are at least two different views about the nature of detector outputs. It is quite natural to suppose (in view of the name *feature detector*) that detectors yield phonetic or phonological features (e.g., *voiced* or *voiceless*) as direct output. Such an assumption is implicit in early versions of the feature-detector hypothesis (Abbs & Sussman, 1971; Lieberman, 1970; Stevens, 1971). In contrast, some more recent versions of the hypothesis claim that decisions about phonetic or phonological features are reserved for processing stages beyond that of feature detectors. For example, Eimas and Miller (1978) suggested that the role of detector outputs is to "provide sufficient information for the assignment of distinctive phonetic values by some higher, more abstract level of processing" (p. 317). (See Eimas, Miller, & Jusczyk in Chapter 5, this volume.)

The view that detector outputs consist of phonetic or phonological features encounters serious difficulties, as we will show. But at least this view assigns feature detectors a recognizable function. In the more recent versions of the feature-detector hypothesis, it is by no means clear what the detectors are supposed to accomplish. To claim that detectors provide sufficient information for later feature decisions is hardly adequate because the same information and more is presumably already available in the initial neural transform of the acoustic signal. It is, of course, conceivable that there is a need for specialized information processing (e.g., data reduction) between the "neural spectrogram" and the stage at which phonetic decisions are made. However, arguments detailing such a need have never, to our knowledge, been offered in the speech-perception literature. Although feature decisions are an obvious form of data reduction, it is not evident that significant data reduction prior to the decision-making stage would serve any useful function. Indeed, propositions 1 and 2 state that the decision-making stage uses most of the fine-grained acoustic information preserved in the neural spectrogram. Therefore, if our arguments in favor of propositions 1 and 2 are valid, we can think of no motivation for including a stage of feature detectors between the neural spectrogram and the higher decision-making stage.

Next consider the view, implicit in earlier versions of the feature-detector hypothesis, that detectors yield phonetic or phonological features as direct output. This view appears to presuppose that relatively localized (e.g., syllable-sized) portions of the acoustic signal contain sufficient information to specify phonetic or phonological features uniquely. However, in our argument for proposition 3, we cited a number of important ways in which this assumption of "local determinacy" is violated. In general, aspects of the more global acoustic context, specifying utterance rate, vocal-tract characteristics, and so forth, are required along with intrinsic syllabic information to determine phonetic categories unambiguously.

One way to rescue the feature-detector hypothesis is simply to avoid the assumption of local determinacy. It might be proposed, for example, that the transfer function of a detector is modifiable "on line" by earlier feature decisions or by acoustic properties of the context. By this account, utterance rate and other variables would be continuously monitored and the information would be used to "retune" detectors of segmental features. But such an approach fundamentally alters the "bottom-up" processing mode of detectors (which is almost a defining characteristic) and thus eliminates their principal theoretical advantage, namely, simplicity of function.

A related approach is to assume that feature-detector outputs are determined entirely by local segmental cues but that these feature decisions may be overridden at higher decision-making levels that have access to more global information. Such an approach, which is similar to the recognition model of Pisoni and Sawusch (1975), avoids the inordinate complexity of continuous "top down" regulation of feature detectors. But it faces a problem analogous to that associated with models in which *all* feature decisions are reserved for some higher, postdetector stage. To the extent that detectors make feature decisions, however tentative, a good deal of acoustic information presumably becomes unavailable to the higher processing stage at which phonetic category decisions are made. Such data reduction is, of course, contrary to propositions 1 and 2.

In short, the versions of the feature-detector hypothesis considered here fail to assign detectors a clear and necessary function, impose unacceptable limits on the availability of acoustic information to the ultimate stage of phonetic categorization, or require an assumption of local determinacy that is clearly incorrect.

The search for invariant acoustic correlates of distinctive features

Earlier we noted that, in addition to the empirical studies concerned with feature detectors per se, there have also been attempts, mainly by Blumstein and Stevens (1979), to describe invariant acoustic correlates of feature categories. The link between these two lines of inquiry was indicated explicitly in their article on place cues:

> We will argue that there are different integrated acoustic properties which manifest acoustic invariance for different places of articulation. These properties reflect the configuration of acoustic events occurring at the release of the stop consonant, and reside in the short-term spectrum sampled at the moment of consonantal release. The existence of such invariance suggests that the perception of speech makes use of property-detecting mechanisms which can extract the necessary information for perceiving place of articulation directly from the acoustic signal. As a consequence, abstract theories of recoding (Liberman et al., 1967; Studdert-Kennedy, Liberman, Harris, & Cooper, 1970) contextual dependencies (Liberman et al., 1967) and analysis by synthesis (Halle & Stevens, 1972; Stevens & Halle, 1967) are not required to account for the ability of the listener to categorize the sounds of speech. (p. 1002)

In short, if invariant acoustic correlates of features exist, then successful speech recognition is simply a matter of detecting those correlates. Categorization schemes based on elaborate use of tacit knowledge are rendered unnecessary.

On grounds of parsimony, this approach is obviously appealing. We see little likelihood, however, that it will ultimately prove to be correct. Blumstein and Stevens favored a particularly strong version of the assumption of local determinacy. Invariant-feature correlates were assumed to be defined over a temporal domain of only a few tens of milliseconds. For example, in analyzing place information, a window length of 26 msec was used to measure the gross shape of the onset spectrum, and only one such sample was assumed to be needed to yield cues that are both invariant and distinctive. Apparently, similar temporal domains were deemed sufficient for other types of features as well (Stevens & Blumstein, 1981). The problem, as we have seen, is that the assumption of local determinacy is very typically wrong. The same syllable in different contexts is often categorized differently. Moreover, such context effects are quite systematic and suggest that the listener uses sophisticated decision rules based on extensive tacit knowledge of both segmental and suprasegmental aspects of speech.

If the extrasyllabic context is held constant, is there any evidence for invariant and distinctive acoustic correlates of features? Blumstein and Stevens (1979) argued that the place value of initial stops is invariantly specified by the gross spectral shape in the moments just following consonantal release. Labials were assumed to have a diffuse falling spectrum, alveolars a diffuse rising spectrum, and velars a compact spectrum with most energy in the mid-frequency range (1200-3500 Hz). To test these assumptions, Blumstein and Stevens devised templates corresponding to the gross spectral shapes. A total of 1,800 consonant–vowel and vowel–consonant syllables were matched against each template. The syllables contained the stops /p t k b d g/ in a variety of vowel contexts. Overall, the templates correctly accepted about 85% of the initial stops and correctly rejected about the same percentage. The corresponding percentages for final stops were considerably lower. From these results, Blumstein and Stevens concluded that "acoustic invariance for place of articulation is directly derivable from the acoustic signal" (p. 1014).

However, in our view, the template error rates were not low enough to justify the claim of acoustic invariance. The most informative measure of template performance is the proportion of utterances that were correctly classified (i.e., accepted by the appropriate template and rejected by both the other templates). Although Blumstein and Stevens (1979) did not report this proportion, it may have been as low as 65% for initial stops if the rates of correct acceptance and correct rejection of the three templates correlated weakly across tokens.[2] Thus, even in the best of conditions (fixed extrasyllabic context, syllable-initial position), spectral place cues are far from invariant.

In promoting the claim of acoustic invariance, Blumstein and Stevens did not deny that many acoustic properties of segments vary with context. They acknowledged, for example, that particular formant frequencies are context dependent and that listeners actually use such context-dependent cues in phonetic categorization. They suggested, however, that the invariant cues are "primary" in the sense that they can be detected by innate biological mechanisms (i.e., feature detectors), whereas the context-dependent cues are "secondary" in the sense they are defined relative to adjacent segments and must be learned. Despite the abundance of data from studies of infant speech perception (for recent reviews, see Aslin, Pisoni, & Jusczyk, in press; Jusczyk, 1981; Eimas, Miller, & Jusczyk in Chapter 5, this volume), there appears to be no evidence specifically favorable to this claim.

Given proposition 3 alone, we strongly doubt that there exist any phonetic category cues that are temporally localized, distinctive, *and invariant in the strict sense*. All acoustic properties of segments or features must apparently be judged relative to their context. Nevertheless, it is very likely that some acoustic cues are more stable or reliable than others, and that experienced listeners know not only what the cues are, but also how to weight them in relative importance. The "primary–secondary" distinction of Blumstein and Stevens might, therefore, appropriately be replaced by a continuous weighting function.

Steps toward an alternative approach

In the first section of this chapter, we reviewed some of the empirical evidence supporting propositions 1, 2, and 3. Here, we will consider these claims, particularly proposition 2, from a somewhat more theoretical perspective. As we have seen, the high level of redundancy in the acoustic specification of phonetic categories follows directly from the interactive nature of vocal-tract components. Virtually every aspect of the acoustic output is affected by the entire articulatory/phonatory configuration. But the claim that experienced listeners make use of *all* this potential information in phonetic categorization may strike some as theoretically implausible, despite the weight of the empirical evidence.

In designing a practical speech-recognition device, one attempts to maximize accuracy and speed of performance within the limits imposed by the available computational resources. Because these limits are usually quite severe, a reasonable strategy might be to process only a few of the most robust cues for each category and to disregard all the rest. In the case of the human listener, limits on attentional capacity might well dictate this kind of strategy. Why then do listeners seem to use all cues, even those of presumably marginal importance (e.g., onset pitch for initial voicing judgments)?

The most likely answer is that a high level of redundancy is required to ensure accuracy of recognition in the general case where aspects of the communication situation are nonoptimal. In natural settings, listeners have to contend with noise and reverberation, while in more artificial situations the speech signal may be degraded by a variety of kinds of filtering and distortion. The vocal apparatus, and especially the auditory system, may have defective components that reduce the quality of speech communication. Wide variation in vocal-tract characteristics and dialect make the listener's task even more difficult. A strategy of making full use of redundant cues may be the only way to overcome the impressive odds against successful speech recognition. There are certainly situations where the entire array of cues may not be needed, but a recognition device that works well only in those situations would not be a suitable model of the human listener.

Furthermore, there appear to be no convincing theoretical reasons to assume that a strategy of processing all available speech information is beyond the attentional capacity of experienced listeners. A number of theorists (e.g., Shiffrin & Schneider, 1977; Schneider & Shiffrin, 1977) have distinguished between "automatic" and "controlled" processes in cognition. Automatic processes are assumed to be integrated, well-learned processes that may operate in parallel with other activities and that do not require attention. Controlled processes, on the other hand, are assumed to demand attention and to be executed in a strictly sequential manner, with attention being directed first to one phase of activity and then to another. Controlled processes may become automatic but generally only after rather extensive training. Pattern-recognition processes that are highly overlearned (e.g., letter recognition or phoneme recognition) are exactly the kinds of cognitive activities that Shiffrin and Schneider view as automatic. From this perspective, processing multiply redundant speech cues does not waste cognitive resources, because the cues can be extracted in parallel and with no demands on attention.

When the full implications of propositions 1, 2, and 3 are drawn out, it becomes clear that relatively simple devices such as feature detectors are computationally inadequate to handle the normal complexities of human speech. We are led to the view that phonetic classification, like virtually all other forms of high-level cognitive activity, is regulated by an extensive store of knowledge. This knowledge is largely tacit, and it encompasses most of the regular acoustic consequences of speech production, including the full range of acoustic correlates of phonetic categories and the myriad ways in which phonetic coarticulation, utterance rate, and other prosodic and contextual variables affect those correlates.

We have already reviewed a variety of normal production effects that listeners exploit or at least compensate for in making phonetic decisions.[3] It is worthwhile to emphasize the diversity of levels at which these and other production effects occur. First, as we indicated repeatedly, acoustic correlates of phonetic categories are conditioned by various biomechanical and aerodynamic processes and constraints, many of which are only poorly understood at present. VOT variation as a function of place value and following vowel height is one prominent example that we described.

Second, the speech output is affected by physiological control processes such as those governing articulatory (hence formant) trajectories during vowel production. The effect of a consonantal environment is to shift vowel-formant trajectories away from their target frequencies and toward frequencies corresponding to the consonantal vocal-tract resonances (Broad & Fertig, 1970; Stevens & House, 1963). A natural way of describing this undershoot of vowel targets is in terms of a trade-off between the listener-oriented goal of vowel identification and the speaker-oriented goal of articulatory economy or "least effort." The former goal would motivate the speaker at least to approximate the target-formant values, whereas the latter goal would constrain him to do so with as little articulatory displacement as possible. The compromise result would be some degree of undershoot that tends to increase in proportion to the articulatory distance between the consonant and vowel configurations. In fact, just this result has been observed (Stevens & House, 1963). That listeners have tacit knowledge of these undershoot effects and compensate for them is indicated by the results of Lindblom and Studdert-Kennedy (1967) described earlier.

A third level of constraint on the speech output involves language- or dialect-specific phonological processes. For obvious reasons, these tend not to be reducible either to physical constraints on the vocal tract or to physiological processes for optimizing motor control. Consider, for example, vowel-duration differences that are contingent on the voicing characteristic of the following consonant. In most languages, vowels are slightly longer in front of voiced than in front of voiceless stops or fricatives (Chen, 1970), presumably owing to mechanical or physiological factors. (See Lisker, 1974, for a critical review of various explanatory hypotheses.) In English, however, these durational differences have become substantially larger than would be expected on the basis of physical or physiological factors alone (Chen, 1970). In the terminology of Hyman (1975) and others, vowel-duration differences in English have become "phonologized." It is no surprise, therefore, that vowel duration is one of the principal cues for final voicing in English (Denes, 1955; Krause, 1982; Raphael, 1972).

Finally, one can point to a wide range of idiolectal or vocal-tract-specific properties of the speech signal that listeners must take into account in order to make correct phonetic decisions. In the classic study by Ladefoged and Broadbent (1957) referred to earlier, listeners identified the same test syllables differently depending on the vocal-tract size implied by the formant values of a precursor sentence. Furthermore, these perceptual adjustments were almost always in the appropriate direction as determined by natural size/frequency relations. Although perceptual data are generally lacking, it seems likely that listeners also have knowledge of, and actively adjust for, certain transitory modifications of the speech signal such as those induced by smiling, yawning, gum chewing, or pipe smoking.

On the basis of these examples, one might be tempted to assume that listeners organize their tacit knowledge of speech according to different levels of constraint on production: physical, physiological, phonological, and so on. We can think of no convincing reasons why this should be so, however, unless one subscribes to some version of motor theory in which the listener is assumed to "make reference" to a level of production in addition to the acoustic signal itself (e.g., Liberman et al., 1967). In our view, it is theoretically unnecessary to posit any such reference to production. The listener's task is to map acoustic information onto abstract phonetic or phonological categories, and we assume that this mapping, however complex, can be made directly. Speech recognition requires extensive knowledge of the regularities of acoustic outputs, but knowledge of the underlying physical or physiological factors that give rise to these regularities seems quite gratuitous.

The point of our discussion so far is that even if higher-order aspects of language processing, for example, syntactic parsing, lexical access, and semantic integration, are disregarded, speech recognition demands an enormously sophisticated, knowledge-based algorithm.

Aside from feature-detector models, there have been several recent attempts to model speech recognition with devices of rather limited computational power. Two such models that have received a good deal of attention are HARPY (Lowerre, 1976; Lowerre & Reddy, 1980; Reddy, 1980) and LAFS (Klatt, 1979; 1980). These models embody a number of interesting and innovative computational techniques. Our focus, however, will be limited to the manner in which acoustic-phonetic knowledge is brought to bear on the problem of recognition. In this respect, both models are abstractly similar, but we will here refer only to LAFS because it represents a considerably more refined solution to the problem.

The central feature of LAFS ("Lexical Access From Spectra") is a decoding structure consisting of a finite-state network of spectral templates. Word recognition is accomplished by finding the best matching sequence of templates for each input utterance. In the network, the termination of each template sequence corresponding to a word is connected to the beginning of every other such sequence, so that inputs may be of any length and either grammatical or ungrammatical. Each template appears only once in the network and may be used in any number of different word representations.

Acoustic-phonetic knowledge, including coarticulatory effects on the speech signal, phonological constraints on permissible phonetic sequences, and cross-word-boundary phonological phenomena, is "precompiled" directly into the decoding network. For example, allophonic variations of a stop consonant due to coarticulation with the following vowel are represented as distinct spectral templates, hence as distinct pathways through the network. The principal advantage of this kind of precompilation is efficiency. By storing each of the particular instances of an abstract phonological rule directly in the network, much computation is eliminated.

If LAFS is viewed merely as an engineering solution to the problem of speech recognition, its strategy of precompilation may be considered a virtue. However, the model is, in fact, offered as a hypothesis about how humans perceive speech, and thus it must be judged not only by the usual engineering criteria (e.g., sufficiency and efficiency) but also in terms of psychological plausibility and theoretical economy. By the latter criteria, the strategy of precompilation seems to us less than satisfactory. A speech-recognition model that purports to be "psychologically real" must assign utterances to the correct linguistic categories (words or word strings in the case of LAFS) and moreover it must do this in such a way that genuine perceptual commonalities among utterances are accounted for naturally. By requiring separate network pathways for every spectrally distinct instance of a phonological process, LAFS fails to capture the perceptual commonalities of the various instances. In English, for example, phonologically voiceless stops are aspirated in word-initial position but unaspirated following /s/. To precompile this phonological constraint into the LAFS network, the /s/ template or templates would first be connected to a "silence" template (corresponding to articulatory closure), which would in turn be linked to a set of templates each corresponding to the onset spectrum of an unaspirated stop. Separate templates would be required for each of the principal allophonic variants of /p/, /t/, and /k/, so this set would be spectrally quite diverse. (An analogous collection of templates would probably be needed for the various aspirated stops occurring word initially, because aspirated and unaspirated homorganic stops differ considerably in the low-frequency region of their spectra.) Notice that this proliferation of spectral instances and pathways, although necessary for the system to work at all, completely obscures the underlying perceptual uniformity of the phonological process in question.

It is true that outside the LAFS decoding network proper, a set of phonological rules is stored as part of the listener's overall linguistic competence. These rules presumably have an important role in guiding the initial elaboration of the decoding network. However, they appear to have no direct role in the process of perception itself, so they cannot serve as a basis for explaining the *perceptual* commonalities and regularities that are important correlates of phonological rules. Thus, in attempting to satisfy the engineering criteria of sufficiency and efficiency, LAFS trades away psychological plausibility.

Our argument here is abstractly analogous to Chomsky's (1957) critique of phrase-structure grammars (and a fortiori finite-state grammars) as possible models of linguistic competence. Without the power of unrestricted rewrite rules or transformations, basic co-occurrence restrictions among lexical categories must be restated for each variation in constituent structure, and therefore the psychological uniformity of these restrictions cannot be expressed by the grammar. We think that the inability of LAFS to account naturally for certain important perceptual generalizations is similarly due to the computational limits of a finite-state device.

Antecedent to both HARPY and LAFS are the speech-recognition systems known as HEARSAY (Erman & Lesser, 1978; Reddy, 1980; Reddy, Erman, Fennel, & Neely, 1973). Although computationally more cumbersome, HEARSAY (especially version II) strikes us as a far more plausible psychological model than either of the later systems. Instead of a finite-state network, HEARSAY II incorporates a "blackboard" on which hypotheses are elaborated by various knowledge sources operating in parallel. Each knowledge source corresponds to a different level of analysis (e.g., acoustic parameters, segments, syllables, and words), and the hypotheses generated by a given source are accessible on the blackboard to all other sources. The highly interactive nature of HEARSAY should not obscure the fact that items of knowledge such as phonological rules need only be stored once, at least in principle.

In advocating a more powerful computational approach to speech recognition, we recognize that a serious new problem must be dealt with, one that has arisen repeatedly in every branch of cognitive science. The move toward greater computational power allows certain classes of phenomena to be explained more simply or revealingly, but in the process models often become *too* powerful, generating potentially all manner of outcomes, whether consistent with the psychological facts or not. In linguistics, for example, the great extension in computational power implied by the use of grammatical transformations forced theorists to devote much effort to the task of constraining grammars so as to prevent the output of unacceptable word strings. Although psychologists (e.g., those attempting to model semantic knowledge) have generally been less attentive to this problem, it is there nonetheless.

We suggest, however, that the problem of excessive computational power may be rather more tractable in modeling speech recognition than in other domains. First, the knowledge base that must be represented in order to categorize speech sounds is much more restricted and well understood by theorists than the kinds of knowledge required for such higher-order tasks as sentence comprehension. In the typical semantic-network theory, the choice between alternative knowledge representations is largely arbitrary, because investigators have so little relevant empirical information. In contrast, much is already known about the acoustic regularities of speech and about how listeners exploit these regularities, and this knowledge will obviously help constrain theoretical choices in modeling recognition.

Second, a potentially very useful way to impose constraints on recognition models is to take into account what is known about human psychoacoustics. In the next section, we briefly review some ways in which factors of auditory processing may be brought to bear on the problem of speech categorization.

Psychoacoustic constraints

Those who are willing, as we are, to ascribe rather prodigious amounts of stored knowledge and computational complexity to the human speech-recognition system are obligated to consider carefully the role of the auditory periphery. It is desirable to know as much as possible about the "neural spectrogram" that serves as the direct input to the recognition system, simply because the form of this input will determine in a general way the form of the recognition algorithm.

More specifically, auditory constraints may help to explain perceptual similarities and groupings that serve as the basis for phonetic categories as well as certain perceptual discontinuities that enhance category boundaries. Although we have argued that much of what listeners do in recognizing speech depends on tacit knowledge, we admit that for any particular case this must always be an explanation of last resort. To the extent that general psychoacoustic principles can account for the location of category boundaries, it becomes unnecessary to posit a role for tacit knowledge.

There have been several recent attempts to derive an auditory representation of speech sounds from psychoacoustic principles (e.g., Bladon & Lindblom, 1981; Klatt, 1979; Miller, 1982). Bladon and Lindblom (1981), for example, modeled listeners' judgments of vowel quality differences using (1) a theory of peripheral auditory processing based on work by Zwicker (1961, 1970) and implemented algorithmically by Schroeder, Atal, and Hall (1979), and (2) a perceptual-distance metric devised by Plomp (1970). The auditory theory used incorporates nonlinear transformations underlying the loudness and pitch scales as well as properties associated with frequency resolution and masking such as critical bands. Despite the fact that the model of Bladon and Lindblom is far from complete, it achieved a correlation of .89 between predicted and obtained values for listeners' judgments of quality differences between two- and four-formant synthetic vowel stimuli. This theoretical framework has recently been expanded to account for perceptual relations among consonant–vowel syllables (Lindblom, MacNeilage, & Studdert-Kennedy, 1983).

A somewhat different strategy has been to invoke psychoacoustic principles to account for particular phonetic contrasts, especially those that are perceived categorically. Listeners are said to perceive a dimension categorically if they divide the items along the dimension into discrete labeling categories and discriminate only between items from separate categories. Early studies at Haskins Laboratories (reviewed in Liberman et al., 1967) suggested that, among auditory stimuli, categorical perception (CP) was limited to speech, supporting claims about a special "speech mode" of perception. However, more recent demonstrations of CP for nonspeech stimuli (e.g., Miller, Wier, Pastore, Kelly, & Dooling, 1976; Pisoni,

1977) have been accompanied by serious efforts to explain categorical perception of *both* speech and nonspeech in general psychophysical terms. In the studies by Miller et al. and Pisoni, nonspeech analogs to VOT stimuli were created by varying the relative temporal onset of noise and buzz segments or of two tones. Significantly, in both cases the perceived category-boundaries and the corresponding peaks in discriminability were located at relative-onset values roughly comparable to those for VOT stimuli. On the basis of their findings, Miller et al. suggested that the enhanced discriminability typically observed at the VOT category-boundary occurs because that region of the VOT dimension corresponds to a natural psychophysical boundary. A VOT smaller than the boundary value is below the listener's threshold for judging successive events (in this case, the release burst and voicing onset) as nonsimultaneous (see Hirsch, 1959; Hirsh & Sherrick, 1961). Above the boundary value, VOT discriminability decreases according to Weber's law.

This psychophysical model accounts not only for adult data but also for data from human infants (Eimas, Siqueland, Jusczyk, & Vigorito, 1971) and animals (Kuhl, 1981; Kuhl & Miller, 1975, 1978). The animal work is especially important, because the perceptual outcomes can reasonably be attributed only to general psychophysical factors. Kuhl and her colleagues trained chinchillas to respond differently to two endpoint stimuli of a synthetic VOT series (/d/, 0 msec VOT; and /ta/, 80 msec VOT) and then tested them with stimuli at intermediate values. "Identification" corresponded almost exactly to that of adult English-speaking listeners. Further generalization tests with bilabial (/ba/-/pa/) and velar (/ga/-/ka/) VOT stimuli, as well as tests of VOT discriminability, also showed close agreement with the performance of English-speaking adults. Analogous perceptual results were recently obtained with macaque monkeys (Kuhl & Padden, 1982). It is natural to conclude from these data that, among English-speaking listeners at least, categorical perception of VOT stimuli derives more from general mammalian auditory constraints than from a special "speech mode" of perception.

One of the most intriguing findings of the chinchilla studies is the fact that the VOT category-boundary shifts according to place value in a manner nearly identical to that of English-speaking listeners (Lisker & Abramson, 1970). Earlier, we interpreted this effect in humans as a knowledge-based perceptual compensation for mechanical and aerodynamic constraints on speech production. The animal results strongly suggest, however, that a tacit-knowledge account is unwarranted in this instance and that a psychophysical explanation should be sought. As we noted earlier, two correlated acoustic factors that are known to influence the location of the VOT category-boundary are the duration of voiced-formant transitions (Lisker et al., 1977; Stevens & Klatt, 1974) and the first-formant onset frequency (Lisker, 1975; Summerfield & Haggard, 1977). Each of these acoustic factors varied with place value in the VOT stimuli used in both the human (Lisker & Abramson, 1970) and the chinchilla studies. (The stimulus sets in those studies were in fact identical.) The assumption that at least one of these factors has a purely psychophysical effect on the location of the VOT category-boundary would help to explain the otherwise puzzling similarities between the chinchilla and human data. Although variation of onset frequency in nonspeech analogs of VOT stimuli does not appear to affect the category boundary (Hillenbrand, 1984; Summerfield, 1982), changes in the transition duration do produce boundary shifts for nonspeech comparable to those found for VOT stimuli (Hillenbrand, 1984). This suggests that the effect of transition duration on VOT categorization is largely psychoacoustic.

Macmillan (Chapter 2, this volume) distinguishes between two types of psychophysical explanation of CP. The category boundary (and the accompanying peak in discriminability) may correspond to a natural sensory threshold or discontinuity such as that proposed by Miller et al. (1976). Alternatively, it may correspond to the location of an anchor or reference stimulus (e.g., Pastore et al., 1977). Following the theoretical work of Durlach and Braida, Macmillan argues that these two possibilities can be evaluated by comparing listeners' performance in identification, fixed-level discrimination, and roving-level discrimination. We think Macmillan's approach is quite important both because of its generality and because of the high level of conceptual rigor it brings to the subject of CP. Of course, its ultimate value must be judged by how well it predicts the clear cases. We suggest that the chinchilla studies provide convincing evidence that the English VOT boundary occurs at a natural sensory boundary and that perceptual anchors have, if anything, a secondary role. In psychophysical experiments, a perceptual anchor may correspond inter alia to an endpoint of the stimulus range, a fixed-standard stimulus, a frequently occurring stimulus, or a gap in the stimulus distribution. Even if such anchors are not experimentally induced, human listeners may acquire them naturally through previous exposure to speech sounds, so it may be difficult to control for their effects. In the chinchilla studies, on the other hand, the possibility that CP resulted from anchors, whether naturally or artificially induced, seems extremely remote. None of the conditions that might plausibly contribute to the formation of an interior anchor were present in either the identification or the discrimination tasks.

A lesson from the chinchilla and the nonspeech work is that tacit-knowledge accounts of speech categorization, even when plausible, should not be accepted until general psychophysical explanations have been carefully tested and ruled out. This caveat notwithstanding, we should anticipate that a relatively small part of the problem of speech recognition will be resolvable in terms of psychoacoustic principles alone. Although a language community may position its phonetic categories so as to exploit preexisting auditory discontinuities, cross-language studies (Lotz, Abramson, Gerstman, Ingemann, & Nemser, 1960; Miyawaki et al., 1975; Williams, 1977) indicate a wide range of variation in the number and placement of phonetic-category boundaries along continua such as VOT. Moreover, as we noted, the category boundary of an individual bilingual listener may be shifted according to his linguistic "set" (Elman et al., 1977). Such effects call for a tacit-knowledge explanation.

In this chapter we have reviewed a diverse set of production effects and their acoustic correlates and we have seen that in virtually every instance listeners adjust their perceptual boundaries in accordance with these effects. Despite the example of the place/VOT boundary interaction, it seems unlikely that most of these compensatory effects in perception will turn out to be derivable from principles of psychoacoustics. Many of the underlying production effects are rooted in the laws of physics and articulatory physiology, and it would be a bizarre coincidence indeed if for each such effect there happened to exist a corresponding psychophysical effect that produced just the appropriate direction and degree of perceptual adjustment. To deal effectively with the multiplicity of speech cues and their various interactions and context dependencies, one requires much more than the common components of mammalian auditory systems. One requires a flexible, knowledge-driven, and computationally powerful recognition device.

It is interesting to compare human speech recognition with the perception of species-relevant communication signals by various kinds of animals. Ehret (Chapter 10, this volume) reviews evidence that categorical perception of species-relevant sounds is not unique to humans: It definitely occurs in mice and probably occurs in crickets and frogs as well, although some critical data are lacking. As Ehret points out, the use of CP across a broad range of species is not surprising, inasmuch as it helps to reduce the disturbing effects of signal variation and to enhance the contrast between distinct signal types.

This apparent convergence between aspects of human and nonhuman perceptual capabilities must be interpreted cautiously, however. In the early 1970s, proponents of the feature-detector hypothesis cited various electrophysiological findings from animals as analogical support for their views about human speech perception. Recordings of single-neuron activity in the visual and auditory pathways of certain animals indicated selective sensitivity to complex, biologically significant stimuli (Frishkopf & Goldstein, 1963; Konishi, 1970; Lettvin, Maturana, McCulloch, & Pitts, 1959; Mudry, 1978; Roeder, 1971; Wollberg & Newman, 1972). Diehl (1981) argued that, although this work points to the existence of feature detectors in the sensory systems of certain animals, one should avoid drawing any simple parallel between such detectors and the mechanisms of human speech perception. Consider some of the differences between human utterances and animal vocalizations such as those of bullfrogs and squirrel monkeys. First, the number of functionally distinct human utterances is almost limitless, whereas the number of call types used by most animal species is apparently quite restricted, for example, fewer than 10 for the bullfrog (Bogert, 1960) and fewer than 30 for the squirrel monkey (Winter, Ploog, & Latta, 1966). Second, human utterances consist of elaborately arranged sets of phonological, morphological, and syntactic units. Animal calls, for the most part, appear to function as discrete unanalyzable units. Third, as we have seen, acoustic correlates of phonological units vary substantially with context, utterance rate, and stress level. Animal calls tend to be far more stereotyped in form. Although different tokens of, for example, the bullfrog mating call vary in certain respects, other properties (e.g., fundamental frequency) are virtually invariant (Capranica, 1965).

In view of the striking differences between human speech and animal vocalizations, one should be wary of analogical inferences about speech perception based on animal work. The fact that both humans and nonhumans perceive species-relevant signals categorically indicates that there are selection pressures common to a diverse set of naturally evolved communication systems. However, one has little reason to suppose that, between humans and other species, there are significant commonalities in the *means* by which CP is achieved.

Concluding remarks

In important respects our views about speech recognition are similar to the theoretical approach long advocated by investigators at Haskins Laboratories (Liberman et al., 1967; Liberman, 1982; Repp, 1982; Repp & Liberman in Chapter 3, this volume). We share a general skepticism that purely psychophysical explanations will suffice for most of the interesting phenomena of phonetic categorization, and we agree that listeners' recognition performance depends on detailed tacit knowledge of acoustic correlates of regular production effects.

However, we are not inclined to accept the traditional Haskins argument that there are two distinct "modes" of perception: auditory and phonetic. It is tautological that speech and nonspeech stimuli involve different classification schemes, but this does not seem sufficient to warrant the "two modes" hypothesis. Traffic noises, music, and the sound of rain also involve different classification schemes, yet no one supposes that fundamentally different modes or mechanisms of perception are required in these cases. For listeners to interpret the auditory concomitants of environmental events, whether speech or nonspeech, tacit knowledge appropriate to those events must invariably be applied. The specific content of this knowledge will obviously vary from case to case, and decision algorithms will vary accordingly. But it is a mistake, we think, to insist on a basic distinction between speech and all other forms of auditory stimulation and on a corresponding distinction between modes of perception.

Notes

1. Sawusch and Jusczyk (1981) reported a dissociation between selective adaptation and contrast and concluded that the two effects are "unrelated and independent." Specifically, they found that a VOT test stimulus near the /b/-/p/ boundary was more likely to be labeled *b* following adaptation with /pa/ and more likely to be labeled *p* following adaptation with /ba/ or /spa/ (the latter consisting of /ba/ preceded by /s/ noise). In the contrast session, the /ba/ and /pa/ contexts had contrastive effects similar to those of the /ba/ and /pa/ adaptors, but the /spa/ context produced an increase in *b* responses to the test stimulus, an effect opposite to that of the /spa/ adaptor. One interpretation of this difference is that rapid repetitive presentation of the /spa/ adaptor gave rise to "streaming" (Bregman & Campbell, 1971), whereby the /s/ was perceptually segregated from the lower-frequency /ba/ component. Diehl, Kluender, and Parker (1984) recently obtained evidence supporting this interpretation. First, they replicated the results of Sawusch and Jusczyk using procedures similar to theirs. Next, they substantially increased the interadaptor interval to remove the likelihood of stream segregation and found that the adaptation and contrast effects converged.

2. This represents an average percentage for each of the six stop consonants. The percentage of correctly identified tokens of a particular stop category was computed by multiplying the rate of correct acceptance by the appropriate template by the rates of correct rejection by the two inappropriate templates (Blumstein & Stevens, 1979; Table 1). The overall rate of correct identification may, of course, be higher than 65% if the performance of the three templates is positively correlated across tokens.
3. Notions such as "perceptual compensation" and "normalization" usually imply some canonical representation or template to which the input stimulus is matched by means of various transformations. We have no commitment to this kind of perceptual model, and we use the terms "compensation," "normalization," and "adjustment" in a more or less descriptive way to refer to certain shifts in perceptual judgment that correspond appropriately to underlying regularities of production.

References

Abbs, J. H., & Sussman, H. M. (1971). Neurophysiological feature detectors and speech perception: A discussion of theoretical implications. *Journal of Speech and Hearing Research, 14,* 23–36.

Ades, A. E. (1976). Adapting the property detectors for speech perception. In R. J. Wales & E. Walker (Eds.), *New approaches to language mechanisms*. Amsterdam: North-Holland.

Ainsworth, W. A. (1972). Duration as a cue in the recognition of synthetic vowels. *Journal of the Acoustical Society of America, 51,* 648–651.

Ainsworth, W. A. (1974). The influence of percursive sequences on the perception of synthesized vowels. *Language and Speech, 17,* 103–109.

Aslin, R. N., Pisoni, D. B., & Jusczyk, P. W. (in press). Auditory development and speech perception in infancy. In M. M. Haith & J. J. Campos (Eds.), *Infancy and the biology of development*. New York: Wiley.

Atkinson, J. E. (1978). Correlation analysis of the physiological factors controlling fundamental voice frequency. *Journal of the Acoustical Society of America, 63,* 211–222.

Bladon, R. A. W., & Lindblom, B. (1981). Modeling the judgment of vowel quality differences. *Journal of the Acoustical Society of America, 69,* 1414–1422.

Blumstein, S. E., & Stevens, K. N. (1979). Acoustic invariance in speech production: Evidence from measurements of the spectral characteristics of stop consonants. *Journal of the Acoustical Society of America, 66,* 1001–1017.

Bogert, C. M. (1960). The influences of sound on the behavior of amphibians and reptiles. In W. E. Lanyon & W. N. Tavolga (Eds.), *Animal sound and communication*. Washington, D.C.: American Institute of Biological Sciences.

Bregman, A. S., & Campbell, J. (1971). Primary auditory stream segregation and perception of order in rapid sequences of tones. *Journal of Experimental Psychology, 89,* 244–249.

Broad, D. J., & Fertig, R. H. (1970). Formant-frequency trajectories in selected CVC-syllable nuclei. *Journal of the Acoustical Society of America, 47,* 1572–1582.

Capranica, R. R. (1965). *The evoked vocal response of the bullfrog*. Cambridge, MA: M.I.T. Press.

Chen, M. (1970). Vowel length variation as a function of the voicing of the consonant environment. *Phonetica, 22,* 129–159.

Chomsky, N. (1957). *Syntactic structures*. The Hague: Mouton.

Chomsky, N., & Halle, M. (1968). *The sound pattern of English*. New York: Harper & Row.

Cooper, W. E. (1974). Contingent feature analysis in speech perception. *Perception & Psychophysics, 15,* 201–204.

Cooper, W. E. (1975). Selective adaptation to speech. In F. Restle, R. M. Schiffrin, N. J. Castellan, H. R. Lindman, & D. B. Pisoni (Eds.), *Cognitive theory* (Vol. 1). Hillsdale, NJ: Erlbaum.

Cooper, W. E. (1979). *Speech perception and production*. Norwood, NJ: Ablex.

Denes, P. (1955). Effect of duration on the perception of voicing. *Journal of the Acoustical Society of America, 27,* 761–764.

Diehl, R. L. (1981). Feature detectors for speech: A critical reappraisal. *Psychological Bulletin, 89*, 1–18.
Diehl, R. L., Elman, J. L., & McCusker, S. B. (1978). Contrast effects on stop consonant identification. *Journal of Experimental Psychology: Human Perception and Performance, 4*, 599–609.
Diehl, R. L., Kluender, K. R., & Parker, E. M. (1984, May 9). *Are selective adaptation and contrast effects really distinct?* Paper presented at the 107th meeting of the Acoustical Society of America, Norfolk, VA.
Diehl, R. L., Lang, M., & Parker, E. M. (1980). A further parallel between selective adaptation and contrast. *Journal of Experimental Psychology: Human Perception and Performance, 6*, 24–44.
Diehl, R. L., Souther, A. F., & Convis, C. L. (1980). Conditions on rate normalization in speech perception. *Perception & Psychophysics, 27*, 435–443.
Eimas, P. D., & Corbit, J. D. (1973). Selective adaptation of linguistic feature detectors. *Cognitive Psychology, 4*, 99–109.
Eimas, P., & Miller, J. L. (1978). Effects of selective adaptation on the perception of speech and visual patterns: Evidence for feature detectors. In H. Pick & R. Walk (Eds.), *Perception & Experience.* New York: Plenum Press.
Eimas, P. D., Siqueland, E. R., Jusczyk, P., & Vigorito, J. (1971). Speech perception in infants. *Science, 171*, 303–306.
Elman, J. L. (1979). Perceptual origins of the phoneme boundary effect and selective adaptation to speech: A signal detection theory analysis. *Journal of the Acoustical Society of America, 65*, 190–207.
Elman, J. L., Diehl, R. L., & Buchwald, S. E. (1977). Perceptual switching in bilinguals. *Journal of the Acoustical Society of America, 62*, 971–974.
Erman, L. D., & Lesser, V. R. (1980). The HEARSAY-II speech understanding system. In W. A. Lea (Ed.), *Trends in speech recognition.* Englewood Cliffs, NJ: Prentice-Hall.
Ewan, W. G. (1979). Can intrinsic vowel F0 be explained by source/tract coupling? *Journal of the Acoustical Society of America, 66*, 358–362.
Fant, G. (1960). *Acoustic theory of speech production.* The Hague: Mouton.
Fant, G. (1973). *Speech sounds and features.* Cambridge, MA: M.I.T. Press.
Fant, G. (1979). *Vocal source analysis: A progress report.* (Quarterly Progress and Status Report, pp. 3–4). Speech Transmission Laboratory, Royal Institute of Technology, Stockholm, Sweden.
Fant, G. (1981). The source filter concept in voice production. (Quarterly Progress and Status Report, p. 1). Speech Transmission Laboratory, Royal Institute of Technology, Stockholm, Sweden.
Flanagan, J. L., & Ishizaka, K. (1978). Computer model to characterize the air volume displaced by the vibrating vocal cords. *Journal of the Acoustical Society of America, 63*, 1559–1565.
Frishkopf, L. S., & Goldstein, M. H. (1963). Responses to acoustic stimuli from single units in the eighth nerve of the bullfrog. *Journal of the Acoustical Society of America, 35*, 1219–1228.
Fujimura, O. (1971). Remarks on stop consonants: Synthesis experiments and acoustic cues. In *Form and substance: Phonetic and linguistic papers presented to Eli Fischer-Jorgenson, 11th February, 1971.* Akademisk Forlag.
Haggard, M., Ambler, S., & Callow, M. (1970). Pitch as a voicing cue. *Journal of the Acoustical Society of America, 47*, 613–617.
Haggard, M. P., Summerfield, A. Q., & Roberts, M. (1981). Psychoacoustical and cultural determinants of phoneme boundaries: Evidence from trading F0 cues in the voiced-voiceless distinction. *Journal of Phonetics, 9*, 49–62.
Halle, M., & Stevens, K. N. (1971). A note on laryngeal features. *Research Laboratory of Electronics Quarterly Progress Report No. 101* (pp. 198–213). Cambridge, MA: M.I.T. Press.
Halle, M., & Stevens, K. N. (1972). Speech recognition: A model and a program for research. In J. A. Fodor & J. J. Katz (Eds.), *The structure of language.* Englewood Cliffs, NJ: Prentice-Hall.
Helson, H. (1964). *Adaptation-level theory.* New York: Harper & Row.
Hillenbrand, J. (1984). Perception of sine-wave analogs of voice onset time stimuli. *Journal of the Acoustical Society of America, 75*, 231–240.

Hirsh, I. J. (1959). Auditory perception of temporal order. *Journal of the Acoustical Society of America, 31,* 757–767.

Hirsh, I. J., & Sherrick, C. E. (1961). Perceived order in different sense modalities. *Journal of Experimental Psychology, 62,* 423–432.

House, A. S., & Fairbanks, G. (1953). The influence of consonant environment upon the secondary acoustical characteristics of vowels. *Journal of the Acoustical Society of America, 25,* 105–113.

Hyman, L. M. (1975). *Phonology: Theory and analysis.* New York: Holt, Rinehart, & Winston.

Jakobson, R., Fant, G., & Halle, M. (1963). *Preliminaries to speech analysis.* Cambridge, MA: M.I.T. Press.

Jusczyk, P. W. (1981). Infant speech perception: A critical appraisal. In P. D. Eimas & J. L. Miller (Eds.), *Perspectives on the study of speech.* Hillsdale, NJ: Erlbaum.

Klatt, D. H. (1975). Voice onset time, frication, and aspiration in word-initial consonant clusters. *Journal of Speech and Hearing Research, 18,* 686–706.

Klatt, D. H. (1979). Speech perception: A model of acoustic-phonetic analysis and lexical access. *Journal of Phonetics, 7,* 279–312.

Klatt, D. H. (1980). SCRIBER and LAFS: Two approaches to speech analysis. In W. A. Lea (Ed.), *Trends in speech recognition.* Englewood Cliffs, NJ: Prentice-Hall.

Konishi, M. (1970). Comparative neurophysiological studies of hearing and vocalizations in songbirds. *Zeitschrift fur vergleichende Physiologie, 66,* 257–272.

Krause, S. E. (1982). Vowel duration as a perceptual cue to postvocalic consonant voicing in young children and adults. *Journal of the Acoustical Society of America, 71,* 990–995.

Kuhl, P. K. (1981). Discrimination of speech by nonhuman animals: Basic auditory sensitivities conducive to the perception of speech-sound categories. *Journal of the Acoustical Society of America, 70,* 340–349.

Kuhl, P. K., & Miller, J. D. (1975). Speech perception by the chinchilla: The voiced-voiceless distinction in alveolar plosive consonants. *Science, 190,* 69–72.

Kuhl, P. K., & Miller, J. D. (1978). Speech perception by the chinchilla: Identification functions for synthetic VOT stimuli. *Journal of the Acoustical Society of America, 63,* 905–917.

Kuhl, P. K., & Padden, D. M. (1982). Enhanced discriminability at the phonetic boundaries for the voicing feature in Macaques. *Perception & Psychophysics, 32,* 542–550.

Ladefoged, P., & Broadbent, D. E. (1957). Information conveyed by vowels. *Journal of the Acoustical Society of America, 29,* 98–104.

Lehiste, I., & Peterson, G. E. (1961). Some basic considerations in the analysis of intonation. *Journal of the Acoustical Society of America, 33,* 419–425.

Lettvin, J. Y., Maturana, H. R., McCulloch, W. S., & Pitts, W. H. (1959). What the frog's eye tells the frog's brain. *Proceedings of the Institute of Radio Engineers, 47,* 1940–1951.

Liberman, A. M. (1957). Some results of research on speech perception. *Journal of the Acoustical Society of America, 29,* 117–123.

Liberman, A. M. (1982). On finding that speech is special. *American Psychologist, 37,* 148–167.

Liberman, A. M., Cooper, F. S., Shankweiler, D. P., & Studdert-Kennedy, M. (1967). Perception of the speech code. *Psychological Review, 24,* 431–461.

Liberman, A. M., Delattre, P., & Cooper, F. S. (1952). The role of selected stimulus-variables in the perception of the unvoiced stop consonants. *The American Journal of Psychology, 65,* 497–516.

Liberman, A. M., Delattre, P. C., & Cooper, F. S. (1958). Some cues for the distinction between voiced and voiceless stops in initial position. *Language and Speech, 1,* 153–167.

Liberman, A. M., Delattre, P. C., Cooper, F. S., & Gerstman, L. J. (1954). The role of consonant-vowel transitions in the perception of the stop and nasal consonants. *Psychological Monographs, 68* (Whole No. 379), 1–13.

Liberman, A. M., Delattre, P. C., Gerstman, L. J., & Cooper, F. S. (1956). Tempo of frequency chance as a cue for distinguishing classes of speech sounds. *Journal of Experimental Psychology, 52,* 127–137.

Liberman, A. M., Ingemann, F., Lisker, L., Delattre, P., & Cooper, F. S. (1959). Minimal rules for synthesizing speech. *Journal of the Acoustical Society of America, 31,* 1490–1499.

Lieberman, P. (1970). Towards a unified phonetic theory. *Linguistics Inquiry, 1,* 307–332.
Lindblom, B. (1963). Spectrographic study of vowel reduction. *Journal of the Acoustical Society of American, 35,* 1773–1781.
Lindblom, B., MacNeilage, P., & Studdert-Kennedy, M. (1983). Self-organizing processes and the explanation of phonological universals. In B. Butterworth, B. Comrie, & O. Dahl (Eds.), *Explanations of linguistic universals.* The Hague: Mouton.
Lindblom, B., & Studdert-Kennedy, M. (1967). On the role of formant transitions in vowel recognition. *Journal of the Acoustical Society of America, 42,* 830–843.
Lisker, L. (1974). On "explaining" vowel duration variation. *Glossa, 8,* 233–246.
Lisker, L. (1975). Is it VOT or a first-formant transition detector? *Journal of the Acoustical Society of America, 57,* 1547–1551.
Lisker, L. (1978). *Rapid vs. rabid: A catalogue of acoustic features that may cue the distinction* (Status Report on Speech Research SR-54). New Haven, CT: Haskins Laboratories.
Lisker, L., & Abramson, A. S. (1964). A cross-language study of voicing in initial stops: Acoustic measurements. *Word, 20,* 384–422.
Lisker, L., & Abramson, A. S. (1970). The voicing dimension: Some experiments in comparative phonetics. *Proceedings of the 6th International Congress of Phonetic Sciences, Prague, 1967* (pp. 563–567). Prague: Academia.
Lisker, L., & Abramson, A. S. (1971). Distinctive features and laryngeal control. *Language, 47,* 767–785.
Lisker, L., Liberman, A. M., Erickson, D. M., Dechovitz, D., & Mandler, R. (1977). On pushing the voice-onset-time (VOT) boundary about. *Language and Speech, 20,* 209–216.
Lotz, J., Abramson, A. S., Gerstman, L. J., Ingemann, F., & Nemser, W. J. (1960). The perception of English stops by speakers of English, Spanish, Hungarian and Thai: A tape-cutting experiment. *Language and Speech, 3,* 71–77.
Lowerre, B. T. (1976). *The HARPY speech recognition system.* Unpublished doctoral dissertation, Carnegie-Mellon University.
Lowerre, B. T., & Reddy, D. R. (1980). The HARPY speech understanding system. In W. A. Lea (Ed.), *Trends in speech recognition.* Englewood Cliffs, NJ: Prentice-Hall.
Lubker, J., McAllister, R., & Lindblom, B. (1977). Vowel fundamental frequency and tongue height. *Journal of the Acoustical Society of America, 62* (Abstract), S16–17.
Mann, V. A., & Repp, B. H. (1980). Influence of vocalic context on perception of the /ʃ/-/s/ distinction. *Perception & Psychophysics, 28,* 213–228.
Miller, J. D. (1982, September). *Implications of the auditory-perceptual theory of phonetic perception for speech recognition by the hearing impaired.* Paper presented at the Workshop on Speech Recognition by the Hearing Impaired (NINCDS), Bethesda, MD.
Miller, J. D., Wier, C. C., Pastore, R. E., Kelly, W. J., & Dooling, R. J. (1976). Discrimination and labeling of noise-buzz sequences with varying noise-lead times: An example of categorical perception. *Journal of the Acoustical Society of America, 60,* 410–417.
Miller, J. L. (1977). The perception of voicing and place of articulation in initial consonants: Evidence for the non-independence of feature processing. *Journal of Speech and Hearing Research, 20,* 519–528.
Miller, J. L., & Eimas, P. D. (1982). Feature detectors and speech perception: A critical evaluation. In D. G. Albrecht (Ed.), *Recognition of pattern and form.* New York: Springer.
Miller, J. L., & Grosjean, F. (1981). How the components of speaking rate influence perception of phonetic segments. *Journal of Experimental Psychology: Human Perception and Performance, 7,* 208–215.
Minifie, F., Kuhl, P., & Stecher, B. (1976). Categorical perception of /b/ and /w/ during changes in rate of utterance. *Journal of the Acoustical Society of America, 62,* (Abstract), S79.
Miyawaki, K., Strange, W., Verbrugge, R., Liberman, A. M., Jenkins, J. J., & Fujimura, O. (1975). An effect of linguistic experience: The discrimination of /r/ and /l/ by native speakers of Japanese and English. *Perception & Psychophysics, 18,* 331–340.
Mudry, K. M. (1978). A comparative study of the response properties of higher auditory nuclei in

anurans: Correlation with species-specific vocalizations (Doctoral dissertation, Cornell University, 1978). *Dissertation Abstracts International, 39,* 1650B–1651B. (University Microfilms No. 78-17, 839)

Ohala, J. (1973, January). *Explanations for the intrinsic pitch of vowels.* Monthly Internal Memorandum, Phonology Laboratory, University of California, Berkeley. 9-26.

Pastore, R. E., Ahroon, W. A., Baffuto, K. J., Friedman, C., Puleo, J. S., & Fink, E. A. (1977). Common-factor model of categorical perception. *Journal of Experimental Psychology: Human Perception and Performance, 3,* 686–696.

Pisoni, D. B. (1977). Identification and discrimination of the relative onset time of two component tones: Implications for voicing perception in stops. *Journal of the Acoustical Society of America, 61,* 1352–1361.

Pisoni, D. B., & Sawusch, J. R. (1975). Some stages of processing in speech perception. In A. Cohen & S. G. Nooteboom (Eds.), *Structure and process in speech perception.* New York: Springer.

Plomp, R. (1970). Timbre as a multidimensional attribute to complex tones. In R. Plomp & G. F. Smoorenburg (Eds.), *Frequency analysis and periodicity detection in hearing.* Leiden: Sijthoff.

Port, R. F. (1978). Effects of word-internal versus word-external tempo on the voicing boundary for medial stop closure. *Journal of the Acoustical Society of America, 63* (Abstract), S20.

Raphael, L. J. (1972). Preceding vowel duration as a cue to the perception of the voicing characteristic of word-final consonants in American English. *Journal of the Acoustical Society of America, 51,* 1296–1303.

Reddy, D. R. (1980). Machine models of speech perception. In R. A. Cole (Ed.), *Perception and production of fluent speech.* Hillsdale, NJ: Erlbaum.

Reddy, D. R., Erman, L. D., Fennell, R. D., & Neely, R. B. (1973). The HEARSAY speech understanding system: An example of the recognition process. *Proceedings of the International Joint Conference on Artificial Intelligence* (pp. 180–194). Stanford, CA.

Repp, B. H. (1977a). Further observations on the function relating the voicing boundary to change along a place continuum. *Journal of the Acoustical Society of America, 61* (Abstract), S47.

Repp, B. H. (1977b). "Cross-talk" between voicing and place cues in initial stops. *Journal of the Acoustical Society of America, 62,* (Abstract), S79.

Repp, B. H. (1979). Relative amplitude of aspiration noise as a voicing cue for syllable-initial stop consonants. *Language and Speech, 22,* 173–189.

Repp, B. H. (1982). Phonetic trading relations and context effects: New experimental evidence for a speech mode of perception. *Psychological Bulletin, 92,* 81–110.

Repp, B. H., Liberman, A. M., Eccardt, T., & Pesetsky, D. (1978). Perceptual integration of acoustic cues for stop, fricative, and affricate manner. *Journal of Experimental Psychology: Human Perception and Performance, 4,* 621–637.

Roeder, K. D. Acoustic alerting mechanisms in insects. (1971). *Annals of the New York Academy of Sciences, 188,* 63–79.

Rosen, S. M. (1979). Range and frequency effects in consonant categorization. *Journal of Phonetics, 7,* 393–402.

Rothenberg, M. (1968). *The breath-stream dynamics of the simple-release plosive production.* Basel: Karger.

Sawusch, J. R., & Jusczyk, P. (1981). Adaptation and contrast in the perception of voicing. *Journal of Experimental Psychology: Human Perceptive and Performance, 7,* 408–421.

Sawusch, J. R., & Nusbaum, H. C. (1979). Contextual effects in vowel perception I: Anchor-induced contrast effects. *Perception & Psychophysics, 25,* 292–302.

Schneider, W., & Shiffrin, R. M. (1977). Controlled and automatic human information processing: I. Detection, speech, and attention. *Psychological Review, 84,* 1–66.

Schroeder, M. R., Atal, B. S., & Hall, J. L. (1979). Objective measure of certain speech signal degradations based on masking properties of human auditory perception. In B. Lindblom & S. Ohman (Eds.), *Frontiers of speech communication research.* London: Academic Press.

Shiffrin, R. M., & Schneider, W. (1977). Controlled and automatic human information processing: II. Perceptual learning, automatic attending, and a general theory. *Psychological Review, 84,* 127–190.

Simon, H. J., & Studdert-Kennedy, M. (1978). Selective anchoring and adaptation of phonetic and nonphonetic continua. *Journal of the Acoustical Society of America, 64*, 1338-1357.
Stevens, K. N. (1971). Perception of phonetic segments: Evidence from phonology, acoustics, and psychoacoustics. In D. L. Horton, & J. J. Jenkins (Eds.), *The perception of language*. Columbus, OH: Merrill.
Stevens, K. N. (1972). The quantal nature of speech: Evidence from articulatory-acoustic data. In E. E. David & P. B. Denes (Eds.), *Human communication: A unified view*. New York: McGraw-Hill.
Stevens, K. N., & Blumstein, S. E. (1981). The search for invariant acoustic correlates of phonetic features. In P. D. Eimas & J. L. Miller (Eds.), *Perspectives on the study of speech*. Hillsdale, NJ: Erlbaum.
Stevens, K. N., & Halle, M. (1967). Remarks on analysis by synthesis and distinctive features. In W. Wathen-Dunn (Ed.), *Models for the perception of speech and visual form*. Cambridge, MA: M.I.T. Press.
Stevens, K. N., & House, A. S. (1963). Perturbation of vowel articulations by consonantal context: An acoustical study. *Journal of Speech and Hearing Research, 6*, 111-128.
Stevens, K. N., & Klatt, D. H. (1974). Role of formant transitions in the voiced-voiceless distinction for stops. *Journal of the Acoustical Society of America, 55*, 653-659.
Studdert-Kennedy, M., Liberman, A. M., Harris, K. S., & Cooper, F. S. (1970). Motor theory of speech perception: A reply to Lane's critical review. *Psychological Review, 77*, 234-249.
Summerfield, A. Q. (1974). Towards a detailed model for the perception of voicing contrasts. *Speech Perception* (No. 3). Department of Psychology, Queen's University of Belfast.
Summerfield, A. Q. (1975a). Cues, contexts, and complications in the perception of voicing contrasts. *Speech Perception* (No. 4). Department of Psychology, Queen's University of Belfast.
Summerfield, A. Q. (1975b). How a full account of segmental perception depends on prosody and vice versa. In A. Cohen & S. G. Nooteboom (Eds.), *Structure and process in speech perception*. New York: Springer.
Summerfield, A. Q. (1976, April). *Speech rate influences on the perception of stop voicing*. Paper presented at the meeting of the Acoustical Society of America, Washington, D.C.
Summerfield, A. Q. (1978). *On articulatory rate and perceptual constancy in phonetic perception*. Unpublished manuscript.
Summerfield, A. Q. (1982). Differences between spectral dependencies in auditory and phonetic temporal processing: Relevance to the perception of voicing in initial stops. *Journal of the Acoustical Society of America, 72*, 51-61.
Summerfield, A. Q., & Haggard, M. P. (1972). Speech rate effects in the perception of voicing. *Speech synthesis and perception* (No. 6). Psychology Laboratory, University of Cambridge.
Summerfield, A. Q., & Haggard, M. P. (1974). Perceptual processing of multiple cues and contexts: Effects of following vowel upon stop consonant voicing. *Journal of Phonetics, 2*, 279-295.
Summerfield, A. Q., & Haggard, M. P. (1977). On the dissociation of spectral and temporal cues to the voicing distinction in initial stop consonants. *Journal of the Acoustical Society of America, 62*, 435-448.
Verbrugge, R. R., & Shankweiler, D. (1977). Prosodic information for vowel identity. *Journal of the Acoustical Society of America, 61* (Abstract), S39.
Williams, L. (1977). The voicing contrast in Spanish. *Journal of Phonetics, 5*, 169-184.
Winitz, H., LaRiviere, C., & Herriman, E. (1975). Variations in VOT for English initial stops. *Journal of Phonetics, 3*, 41-52.
Winter, P., Ploog, D., & Latta, J. (1966). Vocal repertoire of the squirrel monkey (*Saimiri sciureus*), its analysis and significance. *Experimental Brain Research, 1*, 359-384.
Wollberg, Z., & Newman, J. D. (1972). Auditory cortex of squirrel monkey: Response patterns of single cells to species-specific vocalizations. *Science, 175*, 212-214.
Zwicker, E. (1961). Subdivision of the audible frequency range into critical bands (Frequenzgruppen). *Journal of the Acoustical Society of America, 33*, 248.
Zwicker, E. (1970). Masking and psychological excitation as consequence of the ear's frequency analysis. In R. Plomp & G. F. Smoorenburg (Eds.), *Frequency analysis and periodicity detection in hearing*. Leiden: Sijthoff.

8 Categorical partition: A fuzzy-logical model of categorization behavior

Dominic W. Massaro

The phenomenon of categorical perception (CP) is assessed by drawing upon a broad range of methodological, theoretical, and experimental issues. It is argued that the identification/discrimination task provides no support for the existence of CP. The categorical model usually provides an inadequate description of the results, and it has not been shown to provide a better description than alternative models. Even if the results in the task provided unequivocal support for the categorical model, alternative explanations are possible. It is necessary to distinguish between sensory and decision processes in the categorization task. Decision processes can transform continuous sensory information into results usually taken to reflect CP; and finding relatively categorical partitioning of a set of stimuli in no way implies that these stimuli were perceived categorically. Three new results are relevant to the issue of categorical versus continuous perception. First, subjects are asked to make repeated ratings of the degree to which a stimulus represents a given category. The distribution of the rating judgments to a given stimulus is more adequately described by a continuous than a categorical model of perception. Second, subjects asked to classify speech events independently varying along two dimensions produce identification results consistent with the assumption of continuous information along each of the two dimensions. A model based on categorical information along each dimension gives a very poor description of the identification judgments. Third, the reaction times of identification judgments illustrate that members within a speech category vary in ambiguity or the degree to which they represent the category. The best conclusion is to reject all reference to categorical perception of speech and to concentrate instead on the structures and processes responsible for categorizing the world of speech.

The goal of this chapter is to clarify the issues involved in the study of categorical perception (CP) and to offer an alternative view of the phenomenon. Although most of our actions reflect a categorical partitioning of the environment, perception of the instances within a category is not necessarily categorical. In fact, many of our actions depend on making highly accurate within-category discrimination or identification. Leaving work for home, we accurately choose our car among many in the parking lot and drive to the appropriate house in our neighborhood. These within-category discriminations are made simultaneously with the superordinate categorization of cars, neighborhoods, and houses. What is necessary is a theory that

---

The research reported in this paper was supported in part by grants from the National Institute of Mental Health and the National Institute of Neurological and Communicative Disorders and Stroke. I would like to thank Michael Cohen for help at all stages of the projects and Neil Macmillan and Bruno Repp for comments on this chapter.

accounts for the categorization of our stimulus world, while also accounting for our parallel ability to perform fine within-category discrimination or identification.

Categorical perception

In this chapter, I evaluate categorization processes in the domain of auditory-information processing, asking whether certain auditory continua are perceived categorically or in a continuous manner. Continuous perception refers to a relatively continuous relationship between changes in a stimulus and changes in the perceptual experience of that stimulus. In contrast, categorical perception refers to a mode of perception in which changes along a stimulus continuum are not perceived continuously, but in a discrete manner (Studdert-Kennedy, Liberman, Harris, & Cooper, 1970). For example, listeners might be limited in their ability to discriminate differences between different speech sounds that belong to the same phoneme category. The sounds within a category can only be identified absolutely, and discrimination is possible for only those sounds that are identified as belonging to different categories.

Seminal study

In a seminal study, Liberman, Harris, Hoffman, and Griffith (1957) used synthetic speech to generate a series of 14 consonant–vowel syllables going from /be/ to /de/ to /ge/ (/e/ as in *gate*). The onset frequency of the second-formant transition of the initial consonant was changed in equal steps to produce the continuum. In the identification task, observers identified random presentations of the sounds as /b/, /d/, or /g/. The discrimination task used the *ABX* paradigm. Three stimuli were presented in the order *ABX; A* and *B* always differed and *X* was identical to either *A* or *B*. Observers were instructed to indicate whether *X* was the same as *A* or *B*. This judgment was supposedly based on auditory discrimination in that observers were instructed to use whatever auditory differences they could perceive.

The experiment by Liberman et al. (1957) was designed to test the hypothesis that listeners can discriminate stimuli only to the extent that they can recognize them as different phoneme categories. The hypothesis was quantified in order to predict discrimination performance from identification judgments. According to this formalization, stimuli can be discriminated only to the extent that they are identified as different. Figure 8.1 gives the results of a single subject for identification and discrimination reprinted from the article by Liberman et al. (1957). The authors concluded that the discrimination results were fairly well described by the predictions based on the identification judgments. This rough correspondence between identification and discrimination has provided the major source of support for the CP concept. In the most recent review of categorical-speech perception, the conclusion from this same study was that "the perception of these syllable-initial stops was invariably quite categorical" (Repp, 1984, p. 282). As Macmillan pointed out

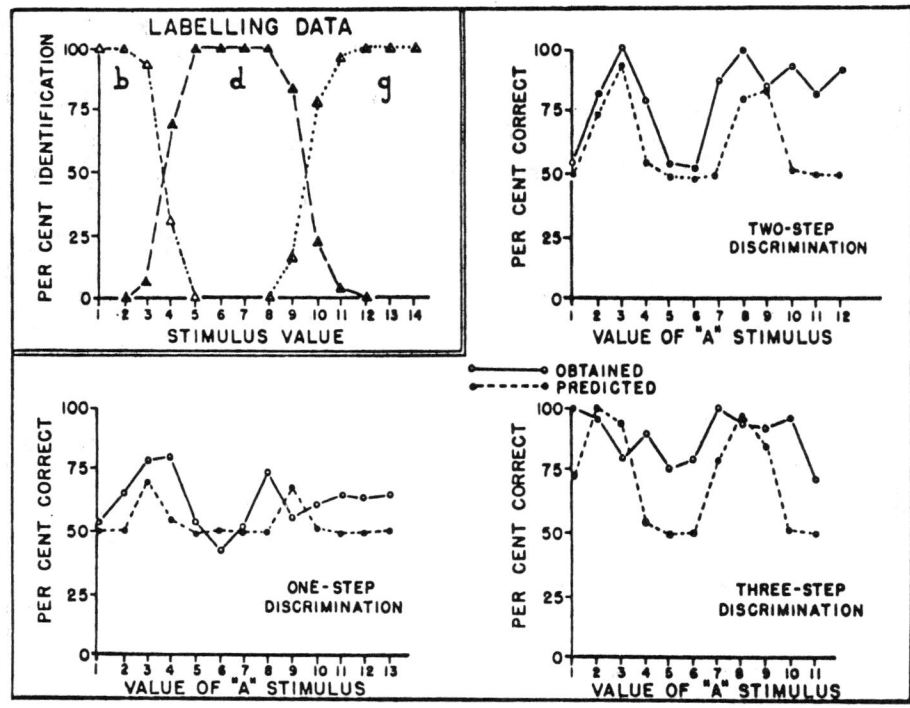

Figure 8.1. Probability of identification in the labeling task as a function of the 14 levels along the speech continuum (top left panel). The other three panels give the obtained and predicted probability of discrimination in the *ABX* task. The three panels correspond to different numbers of steps, between the *A* and *B* stimulus. (After Liberman et al., 1957.)

(see Chapter 2, this volume), however, observed discrimination is usually better than that predicted by identification. For some reason, the discrepancy has never been a deterrent for advocates of CP, or a central result for the alternative view.

To provide a proper assessment of the CP model, it is necessary to determine how closely the predicted discrimination matches the observed and to compare this prediction with other possible predictions. The most direct goodness-of-fit measure is the root-mean-squared deviation (RMSD), which is the square root of the average squared difference between the predicted and observed points. The RMSD can take on values between zero and one if the predicted and observed values lie between zero and one. Hence, a rough measure of goodness of fit is simply how close to zero or one a given RMSD value is. In reality, the RMSD value cannot get too close to one if the observations cover the range of values between zero and one. The results in Figure 8.1 give RMSD values of 0.128, 0.249, and 0.253 for the one-, two-, and three-step discrimination tasks, respectively. ("Steps" refers to the number of equal increments along a continuum between the test-stimuli.) What is striking is just how poorly the categorical model predicts discrimination. Because the discrimination values are between 0.5 and 1 given the two-alternative task, a model predicting 75% correct discrimination across all conditions would have to give RMSD values of less than 0.25. With hindsight, we see that quantitative tests of the categorical model and just about any alternative model would have precluded the authors and others from finding support for the existence of CP.

Although performance in the identification/discrimination task already appears to be inadequately described by CP, the arguments that I support in this chapter disqualify the identification/discrimination task as diagnostic of CP. It is necessary to distinguish between the phenomenon of "categorical perception" and "categorical-perception results" in the identification/discrimination task. "Categorical perception" is defined in terms of whether the sensory system makes available continuous or categorical information, whereas "categorical-perception results" refer to the accuracy with which identification predicts discrimination. There are alternative explanations of CP results that do not depend on CP. I now turn to three possible explanations of this kind.

Auditory-memory limitations

The well-known contribution of memory limitations in the discrimination task can lead to CP results (Fujisaki & Kawashima, 1969; Massaro, 1975a,b; Paap, 1975; Pisoni & Lazarus, 1974). The failure to discriminate two sounds may simply reflect a limitation in short-term auditory memory for the sounds. Given the good evidence for the important role of auditory memory in the discrimination task (Papp, 1975; Pisoni, 1973; Pisoni & Lazarus, 1974), I will not discuss this evidence here. To the extent that short-term auditory memory is not available in the discrimination task, it is impossible for discrimination performance to exceed that predicted from identification.

I would emphasize that the present description of the role of auditory and verbal memory in the discrimination task differs from the dual-coding model first proposed by Fujisaki and Kawashima (1969). In the dual-coding model, verbal codes are primary and auditory memory is secondary in that it is only used if the stimuli to be discriminated are given the same verbal code. As nicely demonstrated by Macmillan (Chapter 2, this volume), the dual-coding model fails to predict discrimination performance. In my view (Massaro, 1976), however, subjects use auditory information in the discrimination task to the extent that it is present, and they may rely on verbal codes when the auditory information is insufficient. This interpretation of discrimination performance is not easy to test quantitatively, as the contribution of auditory memory cannot be measured in the traditional identification/discrimination task. Demonstrating the accuracy of the interpretation, however, is not as important as realizing that the ability of identification to predict discrimination performance may simply be due to poor auditory memory and the use of verbal codes in the discrimination task.

Qualitative dimensions

Results consistent with CP might also occur whenever a single acoustic continuum gives rise to both quantitative and qualitative perceptual dimensions. For example, Pastore et al. (1977) asked subjects to identify and discriminate loudness differences. When test tones of different amplitudes were presented in silence, the relationship between identification and discrimination was not consistent with the predictions of CP. With a reference tone present, however, the test tones could be perceived as small increases or decreases in amplitude relative to the reference tone. The reference tone caused a sharp boundary in the identification function and a corresponding peak in the discrimination function, as predicted by CP. Listeners were able to discriminate whether the test tone was louder or softer than the reference tone, but they were not able to discriminate the magnitude of the difference. Accordingly, sounds perceived as continuous in silence produced CP results in the context of a reference tone. Discriminating the direction of loudness change with respect to the reference tone overshadowed the continuous discrimination of absolute loudness. Hence, a qualitative dimension might be responsible for the apparent categorical perception of a quantitative dimension.

Context influences

Even without auditory-memory limitations and the contribution of qualitative dimensions in the identification/discrimination task, a correspondence between identification and discrimination is not sufficient evidence for CP. Contextual variables can always serve to encourage CP results, even though perception is continuous. The major goal of the experiments reported by Hary and Massaro (1982) was to demonstrate that a stimulus continuum can appear to be categorically perceived even though the sounds within each category along the continuum are noticeably different from one another. Achieving this goal would demonstrate that CP results in the identification/discrimination task do not necessarily mean that perception is categorical. If CP results can be found with a continuum of sounds shown to be perceived continuously, the identification/discrimination task must be rejected as a valid measure of CP.

By varying the amplitude rise time of tones, it is possible to generate a continuum of musical sounds that vary in their pluckish/bowish quality (Cutting & Rosner, 1974). The pluckish quality resembles a stringed instrument that is plucked, whereas the bowish quality resembles a stringed instrument that is bowed. Hary and Massaro (1982) studied the pluck/bow distinction but with the rise-time continuum extended in positive and negative directions. In the standard continuum, the rise times were varied in just the positive direction. In the bipolar continuum, the rise times varied in both negative and positive directions. Figure 8.2 illustrates the first 100 msec of the nine sounds along the bipolar continuum. The standard continuum consisted of the same five stimuli with positive rise times and four additional stimuli

Categorical partition 259

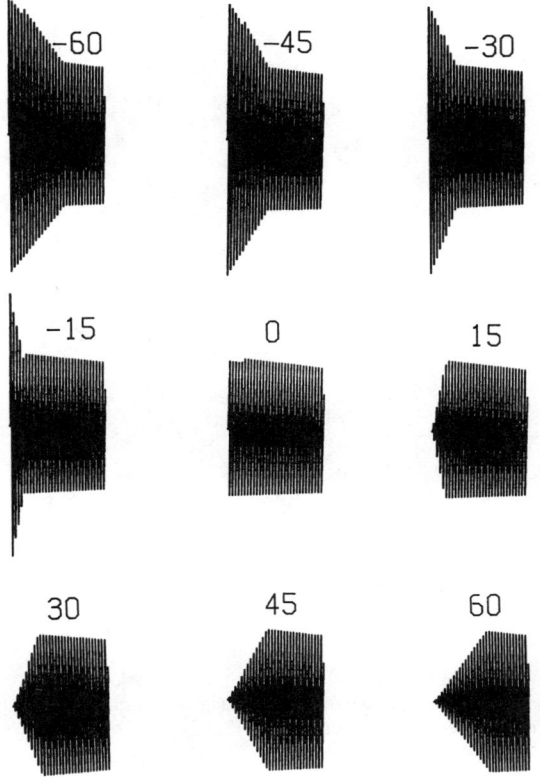

Figure 8.2. Illustration of the waveform of the first 100 msec of each of the nine sounds along the bipolar rise-time continuum. The rise time is given at the top of each of the sounds. Negative numbers refer to negative rise times and positive numbers to positive rise times. The rise times of the nine sounds along the standard continuum ranged between 0 and 120 msec in steps of 15 msec.

with positive rise times. All subjects were tested with both the bipolar and the standard continuum. Given that five of the sounds were identical in the two continua, it was possible to evaluate discrimination and identification of the same stimuli when tested within both types of continua. Based on the earlier results of Rosen and Howell (1981), Hary and Massaro (1982) predicted that the standard continuum would not produce categorical results. In addition, the presence of the positive and negative rise times along the bipolar continuum should lead to categorical results. Given continuous results along the standard continuum of rise times, the categorical results along the bipolar continuum would support the hypothesis that traditional CP results can be found along a continuum of sounds that is perceived continuously.

Figure 8.3 gives the average identification, percentage correct discrimination,

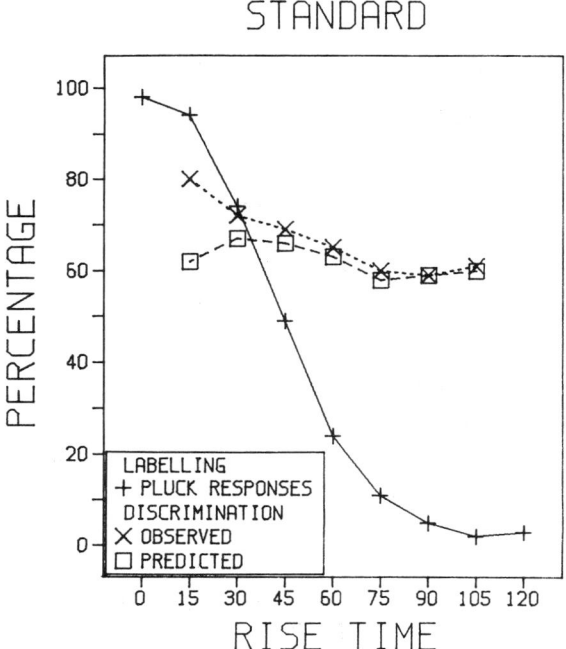

Figure 8.3. Percentage of "pluck" responses in the identification task as a function of the rise time of the test sound. Observed versus predicted percentage of correct discriminations in the AX discrimination task for the standard continuum. (After Hary & Massaro, 1982.)

and predicted discrimination functions for the standard condition. These functions are very similar to those obtained earlier by Rosen and Howell (1981). Both the identification and discrimination functions indicate that the subjects perceived the sounds along the continuum in a continuous manner. The identification function reveals a relatively gradual change in the percentage of "pluck" responses with increases in rise time. The discrimination function shows that subjects discriminated the 0- to 30-msec comparison most accurately, with accurate performance falling off continuously as rise time increased. These results from the standard continuum seem to be most consistent with continuous perception and the applicability of Weber's law to the rise-time continuum (Cutting, 1982; Rosen & Howell, 1981).

Figure 8.4 presents the average identification, discrimination, and predicted discrimination functions for the bipolar condition. The identification function shows a very sharp drop in the percentage of pluck responses between the 0- and 15-msec rise times. In addition, discrimination was best near the category boundary and relatively poor within the categories. Figure 8.4 shows that discrimination seems to be accurately predicted by identification performance. Normally these results would be taken as evidence of CP for these stimuli. However, the same subjects were able to discriminate the stimuli within a category more accurately when they were tested within the context of the standard continuum. It is clear that subjects could perceive

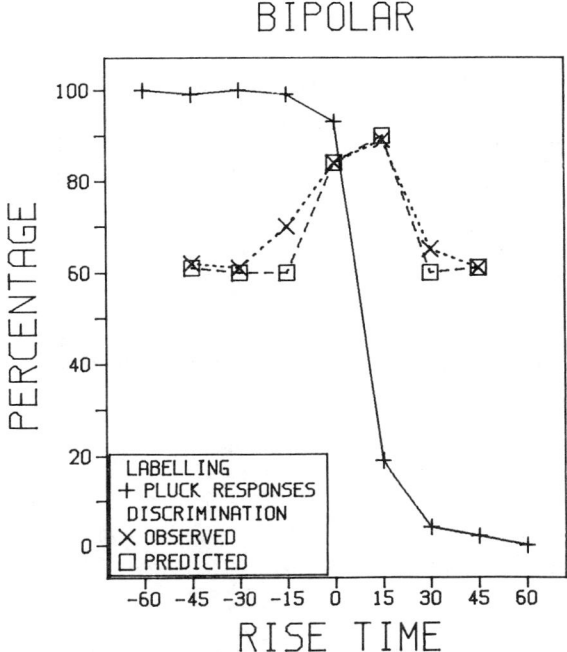

Figure 8.4. Percentage of "pluck" responses in the identification task as a function of the rise time of the test sound. Observed versus predicted percentage of correct discriminations in the AX discrimination task for the bipolar continuum. (After Hary & Massaro, 1982.)

within-category differences even though the bipolar results, considered alone, would traditionally lead to the conclusion of CP.

Summary

Previous studies taken as evidence for CP have failed to demonstrate that the categorical model gave a good description of the results or a significantly better one than alternative models. In addition, categorical results in the identification/discrimination task can occur because of short-term auditory memory limitations, the presence of qualitative dimensions, and context influences. Thus, finding relatively good discrimination between categories and poor discrimination within a category or an agreement between identification and discrimination performance cannot be taken as evidence for CP. I now turn to a new framework and test of categorical versus continuous speech perception.

Sensory and decision processes in categorization

The issue of categorical perception might be clarified by using a model of performance derived from the field of psychophysics. It is now generally accepted that a

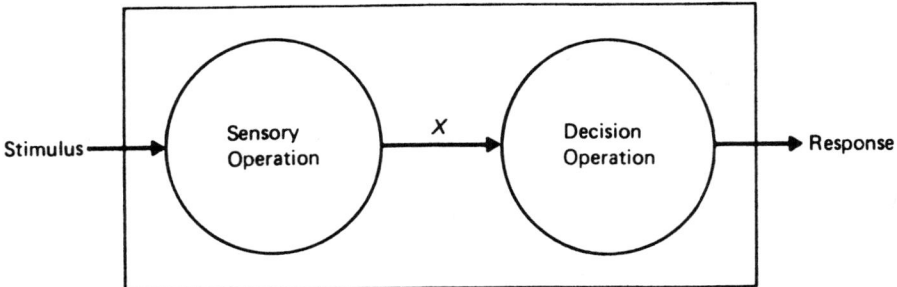

Figure 8.5. A flow diagram of two operations that occur between stimulus and response in an identification or categorization task. The sensory operation transmits some information, X, to the decision operation.

psychophysical task contains both sensory and decision stages of processing. Figure 8.5, taken from Massaro (1975a), illustrates the sequence of processing in a psychophysical task. Applying this model to the domain of CP, we can ask whether the output of the sensory stage before the decision stage is categorical. If it is, we call it CP. If it is only the output of the decision stage that is categorical, then we say that perception is continuous. Performance in the latter case might be described as "categorical partitioning" because the decision stage is usually required to make categorical responses. (Compare the pandemonium model in Chapter 6, by Remez and analog/digital filtering in Chapter 19, by Harnad, both in this volume.)

Continuous sensory information

A continuous model assumes that the sensory information is continuous, with the understanding that the meaning of a message is usually conveyed by discrete alternatives. The perceiver has continuous information about the degree to which a given alternative was presented, but must decide which pattern category was presented. Accordingly, the perceiver requires a decision algorithm to map continuous information into a discrete choice. It seems reasonable to assume that the listener establishes a criterion value of information and responds as a function of the observed value of information relative to the criterion value. This assumption is a direct application of the decision mechanisms given by the theory of signal detectability (Green & Swets, 1966).

Strong evidence for continuous perception of acoustic features comes from a training study carried out by Pisoni, Aslin, Perey, and Hennessey (1982). They taught native English speakers to categorize three rather than two categories across the voice-onset-time continuum. That subjects were able to learn the new category in just a short training session validates the assumption of continuous-feature information. This experiment is similar in some respects to an experiment carried out a decade earlier by Barclay (1972) in which subjects were required to partition a

Categorical partition 263

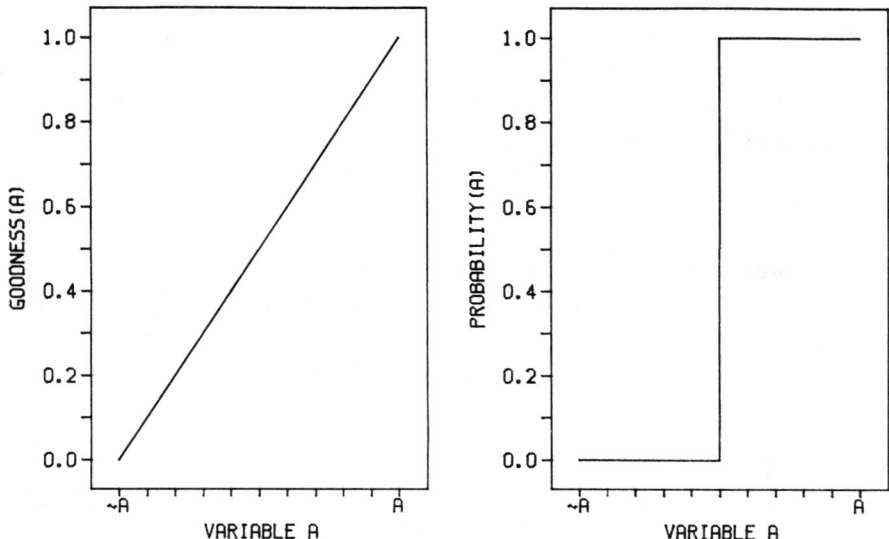

Figure 8.6. *Left panel:* Hypothetical category – "goodness," Goodness(A), values as a function of the continuous changes in stimulus-variable A. *Right panel:* The probability of an A response, probability(A), as a function of the continuous changes in stimulus-variable A.

/b/-/d/-/g/ continuum into just two categories, /b/ and /g/. The categorization of a stimulus usually identified as /d/ was related to its similarity to the /b/ and /g/ stimuli. That is, subjects were more likely to identify a /d/ stimulus as /b/ to the extent it was similar to /b/. In both types of studies, subjects are able to modify their categorization of a stimulus continuum, and this categorization behavior must result from the differential partitioning of the continuous information along the speech dimension of interest.

Molfese (Chapter 14, this volume) reviews a series of experiments that recorded auditory-evoked responses (AER) to temporal cues in speech and nonspeech stimuli. Various components of the AER recorded from different sites proved to be sensitive to changes in the temporal-onset asynchrony between components of stop consonants and complex tones. The major finding relevant to our concerns is that the AER components consistently reflect stimulus differences within a category just about as well as, if not better than, stimulus differences between categories. This physiological evidence complements the behavioral evidence for continuous rather than categorical sensory information in both speech and nonspeech domains.

Discrete decision rule

Assume a stimulus continuum, A, that is perceived continuously. The value, $G(A)$, is defined as the goodness of A and is an index of the degree to which the information represents a given category. The left panel of Figure 8.6 presents a hypothetical function of the relative goodness of A, defined $G(A)$, as a linear function of variable A. What is the most reasonable decision rule? An optimal decision rule would set the criterion value at 0.5 and classify the pattern as A for any value greater than this. Otherwise, the pattern is classified as non-A. In this case, the probability of an A response, $P(A)$, would take the step-function form shown in the right panel of Figure 8.6. That is, with a fixed criterion value and no variability, the decision operation changes the continuous linear function given by the operation into a step function. A step function occurs as long as the observer holds a fixed-criterion value, regardless of the actual value held. It is worth noting that this function is also identical to the idealized form of CP in a speech-identification task (Studdert-Kennedy et al., 1970). Thus, a step function cannot be taken as evidence for CP because it can occur given continuous featural information.

Noise

A step function is rarely observed in identification, for what seem to be good reasons. If there is noise in the perceptual operation, a given level of variable A cannot be expected to produce the same $G(A)$ on each presentation. If the noise is assumed to have equal variance across the stimulus continuum, then the noise near the criterion value will have a much larger consequence than the noise away from the criterion value. Figure 8.7 illustrates the outcome of pattern classification for two types of noise given a criterion value of 0.5. A safe assumption is that the noise is symmetrical at the mean, the mean is equal across the continuum, and the variance is equal across the continuum. A stimulus whose mean goodness, $G(A)$, is at the criterion value will produce random classifications if the noise is symmetrical. With symmetrical noise, the value of $G(A)$ will be above the criterion on half of the trials and below the criterion on the other half. As the mean perception moves away from the criterion value, the noise will have a diminishing effect on the classification response. Noise has a larger consequence at the middle of the range of $G(A)$ values than at the extremes because variability goes in both directions in the middle and only inward at the extremes. If the noise is also normal, the resulting identification function will be ogival in form.

This decision algorithm allows categorical decisions to be made on the basis of continuous information. In addition, the model can predict classification functions with sharp boundaries, previously taken to represent CP. Some investigators (Siegel & Siegel, 1977a,b) have interpreted a sharp boundary along the identification function as evidence for CP. However, as I made clear in my formalization of a continuous-perception model, a decision operation intervenes between the percept and an identification response. The rules of the decision operation and the noise that it introduces can lead to a range of identification functions, given the same underlying perceptual function. Thus, unless the decision stage is accounted for, the identification function cannot address the issue of CP.

Categorical partition 265

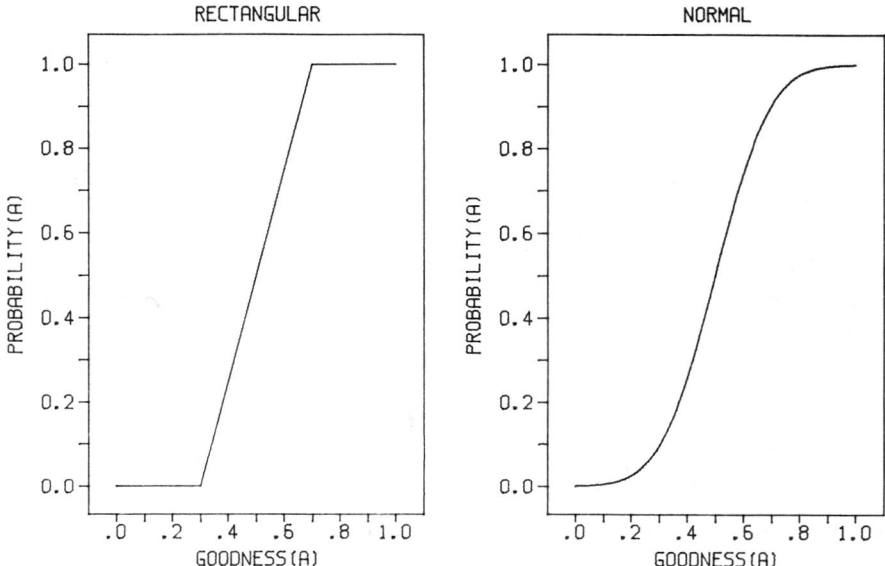

Figure 8.7. The predicted outcome of pattern classification given continuous perception of some variable, A, and two types of noise during the perceptual operation. The probability of an A identification is plotted as a function of the degree to which variable A is perceived as representing the category A, Goodness(A). The left panel assumes rectangular noise and the right panel, normal noise present during the perceptual operation.

New views of current explanations

This representation of the problem equates CP with threshold models and continuous perception with the theory of signal detectability. Because threshold models are currently out of favor, I might be accused of setting up a straw man rather than providing a fair representation of CP. However, one of the most attractive properties for supporters of CP has been that it stands in marked contrast to how perception usually works. In the domain of speech perception, some supporters have argued that CP was one characteristic that provided evidence for the qualitative difference between speech and nonspeech perception (Liberman, Cooper, Shankweiler, & Studdert-Kennedy, 1967).

The two-stage model illustrated in Figure 8.5 also clarifies alternative explanations of CP. Explanations either in terms of auditory discontinuities (Pastore et al., 1977) or acoustic invariance (Stevens & Blumstein, 1978) are clearly statements about the output of the sensory stage. These views represent instances of threshold models of the sensory system.

The explanation of CP results in terms of speech-specific phonetic processing might be viewed as a decision phenomenon. For example, Repp and Liberman

(Chapter 3, this volume) state that "the link between perception and production (in most general terms) enables the category prototypes to respond appropriately to articulatory or co-articulatory adjustments." However, an intelligent categorization at the decision stage, such as the one proposed by Repp and Liberman, is not sufficient to qualify speech as special because it occurs in so many other domains of categorization (Massaro, 1984; Oden, 1981).

Repp and Liberman interpret flexible boundaries in categorization as evidence for a phonetic mode rather than a pure auditory mode in speech perception. However, they fail to address the important issue of the relationship between flexible boundaries and categorical versus continuous information. I claim that flexible boundaries are more compatible with continuous than with categorical sensory information.

A new test

Given the distinction between sensory and decision processes, Massaro and Cohen (1983a) offered a new approach to the question of CP. The distinguishing feature of this approach is the use of continuous rather than discrete perceptual judgments (Watson, Rilling, & Bourbon, 1964). Although rating judgments have been used in a number of previous studies (Elman, 1979; Sawusch, 1977), they have not been analyzed so as to test between categorical and continuous models of speech perception. Relative to discrete judgments, continuous judgments may provide a more direct measure of the listener's perceptual experience. For example, McNabb (1974) found that a binary response proved insensitive to the manipulation of an independent variable whereas confidence ratings revealed significant effects of this variable. In the Massaro and Cohen (1983a) study, subjects were asked to rate the degree to which they felt that the speech stimulus represented one alternative or the other, rather than simply indicating which alternative was present. Categorical and continuous models of speech perception were formalized and evaluated against the distribution of repeated rating responses to each test stimulus along a speech continuum.

Categorical model

Consider the assumptions of the CP model illustrated in Figure 8.8. One is that the listener has only two perceptual stages, a or b, along a sound continuum of five levels. Referring to Figure 8.5, the output x from the sensory stage can take on only the values a or b. At stimulus level 1, the likelihood of an a percept is very high whereas the likelihood of a b percept is very low. As the levels increase, the relative likelihood of the two percepts changes so that at level 5, b is the most likely percept. However, in all cases, the sound is heard as either a or b. If perception is truly categorical, any sound along the continuum can be heard only as a or b and nothing in between. What does a CP subject do when asked to make continuous rating judgments? He might note the foolishness of the request, but most probably would

Categorical partition

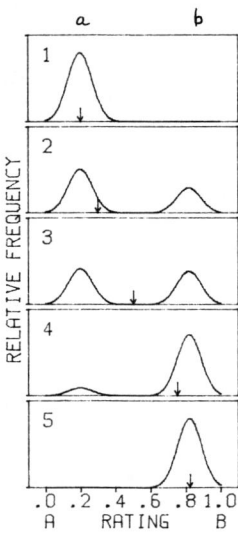

Figure 8.8. Illustration of the categorical-perception-rating model. The sizes of the *a* and *b* distributions depict the likelihood of an *a* or *b* percept given each of five levels (1 through 5) along a hypothetical-stimulus continuum. The location and range of each distribution gives the rating responses that will be observed. The downward-pointing arrows give the mean ratings across the five levels of the stimulus continuum.

attempt to comply in a reasonable manner. The subject would choose a rating toward the *A* end of the response scale for the perception of *a* and toward the *B* end for the perception of *b*. If there is variability in memory and response, however, the subject would generate a distribution of rating responses for each of the two percepts. That is, subjects may not remember where they last rated the *a* category and they may also only approximate the intended rating because of response variability. Furthermore, given the demand characteristics of the task, subjects might actually generate additional variability in their ratings if their percepts were categorical and they were expected to make a range of rating responses. A safe assumption is that the rating responses to the percept *a* would be normally distributed, with a mean Xa and a variance Sa and in a similar manner for the *b* percept.

The important question is how the mean rating responses are expected to differ as a function of the different stimulus levels along the speech continuum. Consider the speech continuum of five levels as illustrated in Figure 8.8. Although perception is categorical, a stimulus is more likely to produce the percept *a* to the extent that it is away from the category boundary and toward the *A* end of the continuum. Variation in the category boundary, the perceptual system, or both allows the percept to have only a probabilistic relation to a given stimulus. A given stimulus produces the percept *a* with probability Pa and the percept *b* with probability $1-Pa$. Hence, the distribution of rating responses to a given stimulus will actually be a mixture of ratings generated by the two percepts. The proportion of ratings generated from the percept *a* will increase with increases in Pa, the likelihood of the percept *a*. Similarly, the proportion of ratings generated from the percept *b* will decrease with increases in Pa. The arrows in Figure 8.8 give the mean rating responses resulting from the mixture of the two distributions over trials. Figure 8.9 gives the mean

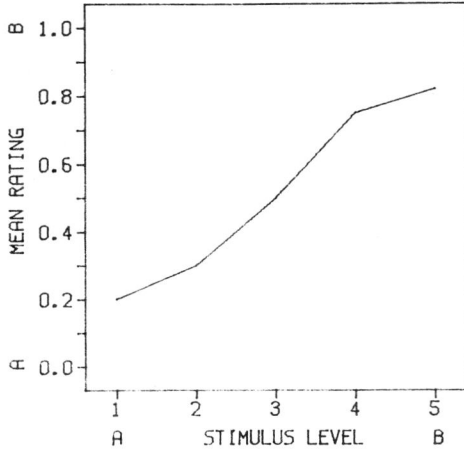

Figure 8.9. Hypothetical-mean-rating responses predicted by both the categorical and continuous models based on the representations in Figures 8.8 and 8.10.

ratings based on the analysis in Figure 8.8 and illustrates that continuous changes in the mean rating response with changes in stimulus level can be predicted by the categorical model.

Continuous model

The continuous model is illustrated in Figure 8.10. In this model, the rating given to a stimulus is a direct function of the percept generated by that stimulus. This model is similar to Thurstone's (1927) law of comparative judgment in which each stimulus is seen as giving rise to a normal distribution of percepts along an internal dimension. In the continuous model, the percepts of two adjacent stimuli will usually differ from each other and the rating responses will reflect this fact (as described in the section entitled "A new test"). In terms of the model in Figure 8.5, the value of x given by the sensory stage will differ for each level along the stimulus continuum. The percept of a stimulus toward the A end of the continuum will be more A-like than that of a neighboring stimulus towards the B side of the continuum. Random variability in the perceptual, memory, or response systems will also result in a distribution of rating responses to any given stimulus. Figure 8.9 shows how the continuous model predicts a systematic and continuous change in mean rating responses with changes in stimulus level. The continuous model, therefore, makes the same predictions as the categorical model with respect to the mean rating responses.

Given that the categorical and continuous perception models make similar predictions about the mean rating judgments, they are not capable of distinguishing between the two models. The models might, however, be distinguished on the basis of the actual distribution of rating responses. The final distribution of rating responses is predicted to differ for the two models. Figures 8.8 and 8.10 illustrate the

Categorical partition

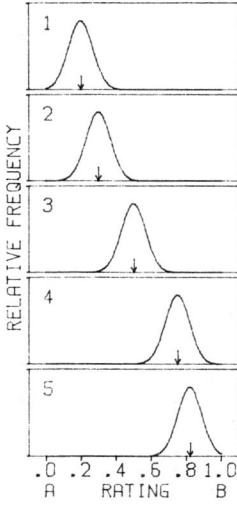

Figure 8.10. Illustration of the continuous-perception-rating model. The distributions depict the likelihood of a percept given each of the five levels (1 through 5) along a hypothetical-stimulus continuum. The location and range of each distribution gives the rating responses that will be observed. The downward-pointing arrows give the mean ratings across the five levels of the stimulus continuum.

overall form of the predicted distribution of rating responses for each of the two models. As can be seen in the figures, although the average rating function (indicated by the arrows) is identical for the two models, the distribution of rating responses is not. For example, at level 3 on the stimulus continuum, the continuous model would predict a single, central distribution, while the categorical model would predict a bimodal distribution with a central trough.

Experimental test

To gather data for the model tests, Massaro and Cohen (1983a) had three groups of subjects rate continua of synthetic-speech stimuli. One group rated consonants differing in place of articulation from /bae/ (as in *bat*) to /dae/, a second group rated consonants differing in voicing from /bae/ to /pae/, and a third group rated vowels on a continuum from /i/ (as in *heat*) to /I/ (as in *hit*). In all cases, the subject rated the degree to which each stimulus represented one category or the other on a continuous scale between the two categories. Because the three continua gave similar results, I will discuss only the voicing data. The stimulus continuum consisted of seven stops, with voice-onset times varying from 0 to 60 msec in steps of 10 msec. As expected from both models, the mean ratings changed relatively continuously as a function of the stimulus level.

The critical feature of our analysis is not the examination of the mean ratings but rather the exact nature of their distribution of occurrence. In order to determine whether the observed distributions of ratings were best fitted by the continuous or the categorical models, the computer program STEPIT (1969) was used. A model is represented to the analysis program STEPIT as a set of prediction equations that

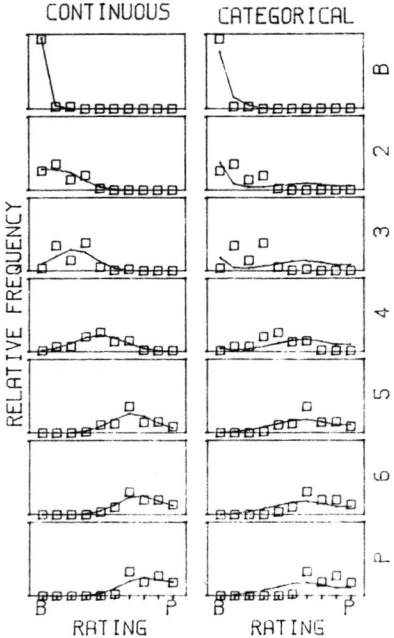

Figure 8.11. Observed and predicted distributions of rating responses for a typical subject as a function of the seven levels along a /b/-/p/ stimulus continuum. (After Massaro & Cohen, 1983a.)

contain a set of unknown parameters. By iteratively adjusting the parameters of the model, STEPIT minimizes the chi-square deviations between the observed and predicted values. Thus, what STEPIT does is to find a set of parameter values that, when put in a model, come closest to describing the observed data. We can discriminate between competing models on the basis of the overall goodness of fit. The categorical model required 11 parameters, which included two means and two standard deviations for the two normal distributions and seven sampling probabilities for the seven stimulus levels. For the continuous model there were 14 parameters, which included seven means and seven standard deviations for the seven normal distributions corresponding to the seven stimuli.

Figure 8.11 gives the results for a typical subject, along with the predictions of the continuous and categorical models and demonstrates that the continuous model does a better job of fitting the observed data. What is most noticeable in the figure is how much better the continuous model does for the intermediate-stimulus level. Its superiority stems from the observed data appearing to result from a single, central distribution rather than from a mixture of two distant distributions. The figure also illustrates how much better the continuous model does for the other levels of the distributions. The continuous model much more accurately captures and reproduces the different number of observations occurring in the tails of the endpoint stimuli.

The continuous model also gave a better description of the results when contrasted with a categorical model that included a guessing state. This model is the same as the categorical model, but with the additional feature that for each level of the stimulus there is a certain probability that the response is based on a neutral "guessing" distribution. One way of viewing the guessing model would be in terms of a threshold or criterion for making a particular response. If the evidence for one or the other alternative does not exceed the criterion level, then a guessing response is made. Naturally, it would be expected that the guessing response would occur most frequently for the more central, ambiguous levels of the stimulus dimension. This model has 20 parameters: three means and three standard deviations for the /bae/, /pae/, and the guessing distribution, and two sampling probabilities for each of the seven levels along the continuum. Each of the seven stimulus levels needs only two probability parameters to compute because the three probabilities must sum to one. The continuous model was the better descriptor of the results, even with the disadvantage of having six fewer free parameters than the guessing model.

Summary

Building on the developments in psychophysics, it is important to distinguish between sensory and decision stages of processing. Categorical and continuous models of perception made different predictions about the output of the sensory stages. The two theories make different predictions about the distribution of repeated rating judgments to a stimulus along some speech continuum. The results of such a study (Massaro and Cohen, 1983a) provide conclusive evidence that there is continuous information available to the listener in speech perception. The important question, therefore, is how the continuous information is evaluated and integrated in speech perception. In the next section, a fuzzy logical model of perception is developed to provide a comprehensive account of perceptual recognition of speech based on continuous information available to the listener.

Fuzzy logical model of perception

The fuzzy logical model of perception (FLMP) allows a quantitative formulation of the view of continuous-speech perception. Faced with continuous sources of information, the perceiver must evaluate and integrate the sources and then categorize the input. To carry out these functions, the sources must be assigned values that can be easily compared to one another. To achieve this common metric, it is assumed that each of the sources is assigned a fuzzy-truth value based on the degree to which the source supports a given category. It is, therefore, necessary to discuss the concept of fuzzy logic before describing the operations assumed by the model.

Fuzzy logic

In nature it is often the case that things are neither entirely true nor false but rather take on continuous-truth values. For example, we might say that a president is doing a "very bad" job or that a meal is not too spicy. Ordinary logical quantification would require that the president be performing well or not and that the meal be either spicy or not. Fuzzy-logic theory (Goguen, 1969; Zadeh, 1965), on the other hand, allows us to represent the continuous nature of things. In fuzzy logic we can construct a membership function, for example, *short(x)*, which is true to the extent that item x is a member of the set *short*. It should be noted that fuzzy truth is different from probability. If we say that a whale is a fish to degree 0.2, this does not mean that there is a 0.2 probability that a particular whale is a fish. Rather, it is true that the whale is a fish to degree 0.2.

An important part of fuzzy logical theory concerns the realization of the standard logical operations of conjunction, negation, and disjunction. The range of truth values, $t(x)$, in fuzzy logic goes from 0 for perfectly false to 1 for perfectly true. Thus, a reasonable definition for negation is the additive complement:

$$t(\bar{x}) = 1 - t(x),$$

where $t(\bar{x})$ is the truth of *not x*. Goguen (1969) has suggested two possibilities for the conjunction of two events, a and b:

$$t(a \wedge b) = t(a) * t(b),$$

and

$$t(a \wedge b) = \min[t(a), t(b)].$$

With the help of DeMorgan's Law we can derive the two corresponding disjunction operations:

$$t(a \vee b) = t(a) + t(b) - t(a)*t(b)$$

and

$$t(a \vee b) = \max[t(a), t(b)].$$

We should note that either of these definitions reduces to ordinary logic if we restrict truth values to 0 and 1.

Fuzzy logic has been successful in describing logical conjunction and disjunction. In a typical experiment, Oden (1977) investigated which set of definitions of fuzzy logical conjunction and disjunction best fit subjects' judgments about logical combinations of pairs of statements about class-membership functions (e.g., a bat is a bird and a refrigerator is furniture). A large set of such compounds was created by factorially varying the truthfulness of each component. The data from the experiment were best explained by the multiplicative-based rules proposed by Goguen (1969). That does not mean that humans actually carry out the process of multiplication, just that multiplication closely represents the processes involved in information integration (Lopes, 1981; Rumelhart & Norman, 1983). (For further discussion of some of the issues of fuzzy logical representation, see Oden, 1979; Smith and Osherson, 1984; and Massaro, in press.)

Feature evaluation

According to the FLMP (Massaro & Oden, 1980a,b), recognition is carried out in three stages. The first stage is feature evaluation, during which the information is transduced by the sensory systems and various features are derived. The features are assumed to be independent of one another and provide continuous information about the degree to which each feature is represented in the speech sound. The outcome of feature evaluation is a truth value, $t(x)$, associated with the presence of each relevant feature.

Feature integration

The second stage of recognition involves the integration of the feature information from the independent sources. During this stage the feature information is compared with perceptual-unit definitions, or prototypes, to determine to what degree each prototype is realized in the speech sound. Prototypes define a perceptual unit in terms of arbitrarily complex fuzzy logical propositions. The outcome of feature integration and prototype matching determines to what degree the stimulus pattern matches each of the candidate prototypes in memory. An important consequence of this process in the model is that one feature has its greatest effect when the second is at its most ambiguous level. Thus, the most informative cue has the greatest impact on the judgments.

Pattern classification

The third stage is pattern classification. During this stage the merit of each potential prototype is evaluated relative to the summed merits of the other potential prototypes. The relative goodness of a perceptual unit gives the proportion of its selection or its judged magnitude. This is similar to Luce's (1959) choice rule. In pandemonium-like terms we might say that it is not how loud some demon is calling that counts, but rather the relative loudness of that demon in the relevant crowd of demons. (See also Remez, Chapter 6, and Harnad, Chapter 19, this volume.)

Another new test

It might be asked why another new test is needed given our rejection of the categorical model in favor of a continuous model. There are many reasons. First, no test should be limited to a single domain, and therefore it is important to address other tasks in addition to the rating task. Second, the current test involves identification performance, which is central to speech perception and categorization. Third, the test will allow the formalization and testing of what might be considered to be more general models of categorical and continuous perception. As Conant (1947, p. 36) states, "A theory is only overthrown by a better theory, never by contradictory facts," and the present test provides both fact and theory.

Very few identification experiments have explicitly contrasted formal models of categorical and continuous perception because application of the categorical model has been limited primarily to predicting the relationship between identification and discrimination. In addition, until the Oden and Massaro (1978) model (see also Massaro & Cohen, 1976, 1977), a formal model of continuous perception had not been tested in the context of speech-perception experiments. Another reason has been methodological, as Massaro (1978, 1979) has pointed out. Almost all speech-perception experiments assessed the psychophysical relationship between a single-stimulus property and categorization. This functional relationship is not diagnostic of the question of categorical versus continuous perception and does not have the power to test formal models of categorization performance.

Massaro and Cohen (1983b) used the methods of information-integration theory (Anderson, 1981, 1982) to test between categorical and continuous models of speech perception. The primary feature of this approach is to manipulate two or more properties of speech events in a factorial design. The results of such an experiment are much more informative than single-factor experiments. The experiment independently manipulated the audible and visible properties of speech syllables perceivers used in an identification task (see also Chapter 12 by Kuhl, this volume). Using videotape and a speech synthesizer, the authors were able to vary independently the visual and auditory properties of the syllables /ba/ and /da/. The visual property corresponded to the type of visual articulation that was present (in an image of a mouth making a sound). The auditory property corresponded to the values of the second- and third-formant transitions of the syllables. The design involved a visual /ba/, visual /da/, or no visual articulation crossed with nine synthesized speech sounds equally spaced along a /ba/-/da/ continuum. Subjects watched and listened to videotaped presentations of the 27 aural–visual events and identified the event presented on each trial as /ba/ or /da/.

With the single modification of increasing a single-factor to a two-factor design, it is now possible to contrast categorical and continuous models of performance in the task. Following the logic of previous views of CP, it is reasonable to assume that each dimension of the speech event is categorically perceived. There have been many conclusions that the auditory-place continuum between /b/ and /d/ is perceived categorically (Eimas, 1963; Liberman et al. 1957). A similar logic should apply to the visual information (MacDonald & McGurk, 1978). According to a categorical model based on this logic, the listener has only categorical information representing the auditory and visual dimensions of the speech event. This model implies that separate categorical (phonetic) decisions are made to the auditory and visual sources (MacDonald and McGurk, 1978).

In the identification task, subjects identified the aural–visual syllables as /ba/ or /da/. According to the formalization of the categorical model, each of the two modalities would be categorized independently of one another. Thus, separate covert /da/ or /ba/ decisions would be made to both the auditory and visual sources. The identification of the bimodal syllable would necessarily be based on these separate decisions. Given categorical information from each dimension, there are only four possible outcomes for a particular combination of auditory and visual information: /da/-/da/, /da/-/ba/, /ba/-/da/, or /ba/-/ba/. If the two covert categorizations of the auditory and visual dimensions of a given speech syllable

Categorical partition

agree, the identification response given the bimodal syllable can follow either source. If the two decisions disagree, it is reasonable to assume that the subject will respond with the decision of the auditory source on some proportion p of the trials, and with the decision of the visual source on the remainder $(1 - p)$ of the trials. In this conceptualization, the magnitude of p relative to $(1 - p)$ reflects the relative dominance of the auditory source.

The probability of a /da/ identification response, $P(D)$, given a particular auditory/visual speech event, A_iV_j, would be:

$$P(D : A_iV_j) = \{1 a_i v_j\} + \{p a_i (1 - v_j)\}$$
$$+ \{(1 - p)(1 - a_i) v_j\} + \{0(1 - a_i)(1 - v_j)\}$$
$$= p a_i + (1 - p) v_j,$$

where i and j index the levels of the auditory and visual stimuli, respectively. The a_i value represents the probability of a /da/ decision, given the auditory level, i, and v_j is the probability of a /da/ decision, given the visual level, j. Each of the four terms in the equation represents the likelihood of one of the four possible outcomes of the separate decisions multiplied by the probability of a /da/ identification response, given that outcome. In the experiment, nine auditory levels are factorially combined with three visual levels. In this model, each unique level of the auditory stimulus would require a unique parameter a_i, and analogously for v_j. Because p reflects a decision variable, its value also requires a unique parameter that would be constant across all stimulus conditions. Thus, a total of $9 + 3 + 1 = 13$ parameters must be estimated for the 27 independent conditions.

Continuous model

The continuous model will be formulated in terms of the FLMP. Applying the model to the present task, using auditory and visual speech, both sources are assumed to provide independent evidence for the alternatives /ba/ and /da/. Defining the important auditory cue as the onsets of the second and third formants and the important visual cue as the degree of initial opening of the lips, the prototypes are

/da/ : slightly falling $F2-F3$ & open lips

/ba/ : rising $F2-F3$ & closed lips,

where $F2-F3$ represent the onsets of the second and third formants. Given a prototype's *independent* specifications for the auditory and visual sources, the value of one source cannot change the value of the other source at the prototype-matching stage. In addition, the negation of a feature is defined as the additive complement. That is, we can represent rising $F2-F3$ as $(1 -$ slightly falling $F2-F3)$ and closed lips as $(1 -$ open lips),

/da/ : slightly falling $F2-F3$ & open lips

/ba/ : $(1 -$ slightly falling $F2-F3) \& (1 -$ open lips).

The integration of the features defining each prototype is evaluated according to the product of the feature values. If a_i represents the degree to which the auditory stimulus, A_i, has slightly falling $F2$–$F3$ and v_j represents the degree to which the visual stimulus, V_j, has open lips, the outcome of prototype matching would be:

/da/ : $a_i v_j$

/ba/ : $(1 - a_i)(1 - v_j)$.

If these two prototypes are the only valid response alternatives, the pattern-classification operation would determine their relative merit leading to the prediction that

$$P(D : A_i V_j) = \frac{a_i v_j}{a_i v_j + [(1 - a_i)(1 - v_j)]}.$$

Given nine levels of A_i and three levels of V_j in the present task, the predictions of the model require $9 + 3 = 12$ parameters, one fewer than the categorical model.

Experimental test

Each point in Figure 8.12 represents the proportion of /da/ identifications as a function of the auditory level; the curve parameter is the visual condition. Both the auditory and visual sources influenced identification, with the contribution of the visual source larger at the middle range of the auditory continuum. The lines in the left panel of Figure 8.12 give the average predictions of the continuous model applied to the individual results of each of seven subjects. The right panel gives the predictions for the categorical model. As the figure shows, the continuous model gave a significantly better account of the identification judgments with a RMSD of less than half the RMSD of the categorical model (Massaro & Cohen, 1983b).

Identification-reaction times

Reaction times of identification responses might also be used to assess continuous and categorical models of speech perception. The most direct interpretation of the CP assumption is that the reaction times of a given identification response should not vary with changes in the speech stimulus. If subjects cannot discriminate differences within a category then there is no basis for differences in reaction times to the different stimuli. A continuous-perception model predicts that the reaction time for identification would depend on the degree to which the sensory information provided unambiguous support for a given category (Norman & Wickelgren, 1969). If different within-category stimuli required different amounts of time for identification then these time differences would provide a source of information for discriminating within-category stimuli. Previous studies have revealed increases in identification reaction times near the category boundary between two speech items (Pisoni & Tash, 1974; Repp, 1981). In spite of these results, reaction times for identification have not played an important role in the study of the nature of the speech-

Categorical partition

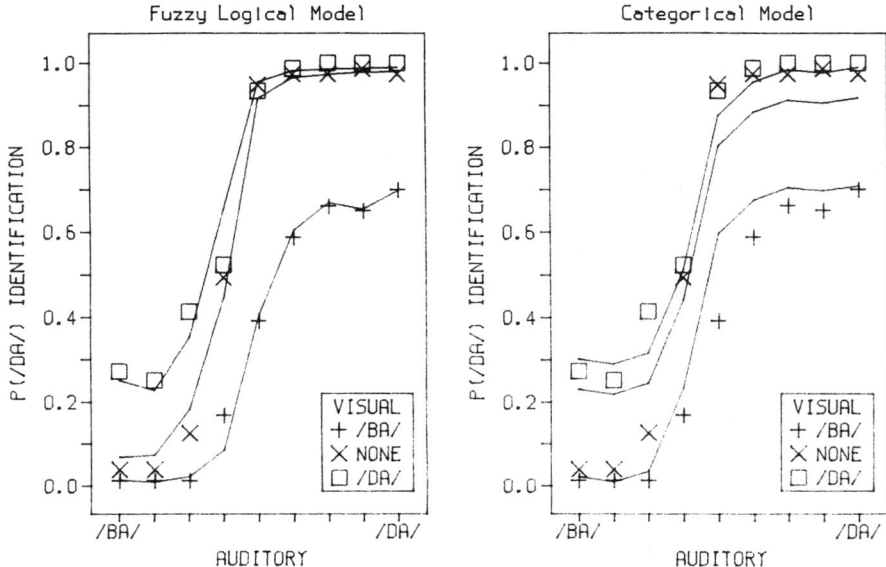

Figure 8.12. Proportion of observed (points) and predicted (lines) /da/ identifications as a function of the auditory and visual levels of the speech event. (After Massaro & Cohen, 1983b.) The predictions of the continuous fuzzy logical model are given in the left panel and the predictions of the categorical model are given in the right panel.

identification process. Analogous to the study of information processing in other domains, reaction times have the potential for making perceptual recognition processes transparent and for addressing the issue of categorical versus continuous speech perception.

Experimental test

We have evaluated reaction times to assess whether a source of information is continuous or categorical in feature evaluation. By independently varying two sources of information in the visual/auditory experiment, it was possible to provide quantitative tests of the continuous and categorical views of feature evaluation. For the analysis, the reaction times of the identification judgments were pooled across /ba/ and /da/ responses before the average reaction times were computed. Figure 8.13 gives the average identification-reaction times as a function of the auditory and visual levels of the speech event. The reaction times varied significantly with the auditory level, decreasing about 100 msec as the auditory level went from /ba/ to /da/ probably because the auditory continuum was biased toward the sound /da/. The overall response probability for /da/ was higher than for /ba/. Reaction times are known to decrease with increases in response probability (Sternberg, 1969; Theios & Walter, 1974).

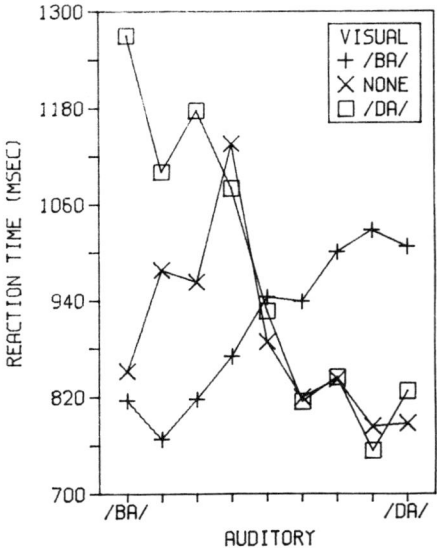

Figure 8.13. Identification-reaction times as a function of the auditory and visual levels of a speech event. (After Massaro & Cohen, 1983b.)

The significant interaction shown in Figure 8.13 shows that reaction times given a visual /ba/ articulation tend to increase with changes from /ba/ to /da/ along the auditory continuum. An analogous result occurred for the visual /da/ in that reaction times tend to decrease with auditory changes from /ba/ to /da/. There are two possible explanations for these results. First, subjects were significantly faster when the auditory and visual information agreed than when they conflicted. Second, the reaction time is positively related to the ambiguity of the speech event.

Ambiguity versus conflict

Although these two explanations make similar predictions for some of the speech events, conflicting auditory and visual information is not always correlated with the ambiguity of a speech event. Ambiguity can be defined in terms of the degree to which the probability of a /da/ identification differs from 0.5; and a given probability of a /da/ identification could result from a variety of levels of conflicting information. A very /da/-like sound paired with a good /ba/ articulation could give the same proportion of /da/ identifications as a very ambiguous sound paired with a relatively ambiguous /da/ articulation. The first case would have greater conflicting information than the second and yet both would be represented by the same amount of ambiguity.

The fuzzy logical model of perception is consistent with the result that reaction times increase with increases in ambiguity of the speech event. To the extent that listeners have ambiguous information, it should take longer to decide on one of the discrete-response alternatives at the pattern-classification stage (Thomas & Myers,

1972; Norman & Wickelgren, 1969; Smith, 1968). On the other hand, the increase in reaction times with increases in conflict of the visual and auditory sources is not necessarily consistent with the fuzzy logical model. Given independent sources of information and a multiplicative integration, the time for feature evaluation and prototype matching should not necessarily change with the degree of visual and auditory conflict. Accordingly, determining which explanation best accounts for the reaction times provides a new test of the fuzzy logical model of perception.

The categorical model has no mechanism to account for an effect of ambiguity, but would seem to predict some effect of conflict. We might expect that different decisions to the auditory and visual sources would lead to longer identification times than the same decision to the two sources. Accordingly, conflict should be related to the likelihood that the two sources give different decisions. To quantify the idea of conflicting information, we used the parameter values for the auditory and visual sources of information given by the fuzzy logical model. The degree of conflict was taken to be the absolute difference between the parameter values specifying the auditory and visual sources of information:

$$C_{ij} = |\text{visual } D_i - \text{auditory } D_j|,$$

where C_{ij} is the conflict given by the ith level of visual articulation and the jth level along the auditory continuum.

Ambiguity A was defined as the absolute difference between $P(/\text{da}/)$, the probability of a /da/ identification, and 0.5

$$A_{ij} = |P(/\text{da}/) - 0.5|.$$

In this conceptualization, the lowest ambiguity value possible would be 0.5 while the highest would be 0.

Results

To evaluate the conflict and ambiguity explanations, a critical result is the performance on neutral trials in which no articulation is given. In this case, the ambiguity of the auditory source of information will vary without a concomitant variation in the conflict between it and the visual source. If reaction times increase with increases in ambiguity along the auditory dimension, the result cannot be accounted for by conflict. In fact, the reaction times to neutral trials increased toward the middle of the auditory continuum. This result replicates previous studies that evaluated identification times as a function of only a single source of information (Pisoni & Tash, 1974; Repp, 1981; Studdert-Kennedy, Liberman, & Stevens, 1963). Accordingly, reaction times increased with increases in the ambiguity of the auditory stimulus even though there was no change in conflict between the auditory and visual sources.

For a complete comparison of the conflict explanation with the ambiguity explanation, correlations between conflict and ambiguity with reaction time were carried out on the results of individual subjects in the study by Massaro and Cohen (1983b, Experiment 2). Multiple-regression analyses across the seven subjects revealed that ambiguity accounted for 26% of the reaction time variance that could not be accounted for by conflict. Conflict accounted for only 3% of the variance that could not be accounted for by ambiguity. This result seems to resolve the question in favor of continuous perception of the auditory and visual sources of information, with identification time a direct function of the ambiguity of the speech event.

Conclusion

I have tried to refute the theory of CP, drawing on a broad range of methodological, theoretical, and experimental issues. At the methodological level, we have learned that the identification/discrimination task provides no support for CP. First, the categorical model usually provides an inadequate description of the results, and it has not been shown to provide a better description than alternative models. Second, even if the results in the task provided unequivocal support for the categorical model, explanations other than CP are possible.

At the theoretical level, it is necessary to distinguish between sensory and decision processes in the categorization task. What is central for our purposes is that decision processes can transform continuous sensory information into results usually taken to reflect CP. Thus, finding relatively categorical partitioning of a set of stimuli in no manner implies that these stimuli were perceived categorically.

The most convincing evidence against CP comes from direct experimental tests between categorical and continuous models of perception. Three new results were brought to bear on the issue of categorical versus continuous perception. First, subjects were asked to make repeated ratings of the degree to which a stimulus represents a given category. The distribution of the rating judgments to a given stimulus is more adequately described by a continuous than a categorical model of perception. Second, subjects asked to classify speech events independently varying along two dimensions produce identification results consistent with the assumption of continuous information along each of the two dimensions. A model based on categorical information along each dimension gives a very poor description of the identification judgments. Third, the reaction times of identification judgments illustrate that members within a speech category vary in ambiguity or the degree to which they represent the category. The best conclusion is to reject all reference to categorical perception of speech and to concentrate instead on the structures and processes responsible for categorizing the world of speech.

References

Anderson, N. H. (1981). *Foundations of information integration theory.* New York: Academic Press.
Anderson, N. H. (1982). *Methods of information integration theory.* New York: Academic Press.

Barclay, J. R. (1972). Noncategorical perception of a voiced stop: A replication. *Perception & Psychophysics, 11*, 269–273.
Conant, J. B. (1947). *On understanding science.* New Haven, CT: Yale University Press.
Cutting, J. E. (1982). Plucks and bows are categorically perceived, sometimes. *Perception & Psychophysics, 31*, 462–476.
Cutting, J. E., & Rosner, B. S. (1974). Categories and boundaries in speech and music. *Perception & Psychophysics, 16*, 564–570.
Eimas, P. D. (1963). The relation between identification and discrimination along speech and non-speech continua. *Language and Speech, 6*, 206–217.
Elman, J. L. (1979). Perceptual origins of the phoneme boundary effect and selective adaptation to speech: A signal detection theory analysis. *Journal of the Acoustical Society of America, 65*, 190–207.
Fujisaki, H., & Kawashima, T. (1969). On the modes and mechanisms of speech perception. *Annual Report of the Engineering Research Institute, Faculty of Engineering, University of Tokyo, 28*, 67–73.
Goguen, J. A. (1969). The logic of inexact concepts, *Synthese, 19*, 325–373.
Green, D. M., & Swets, J. A. (1966). *Signal detection theory and psychophysics.* New York: Wiley.
Hary, J. M., & Massaro, D. W. (1982). Categorical results do not imply categorical perception. *Perception & Psychophysics, 32*, 409–418.
Liberman, A. M., Cooper, F. S., Shankweiler, D. P., & Studdert-Kennedy, M. (1967). Perception of the speech code, *Psychological Review, 74*, 431–461.
Liberman, A. M., Harris, K. S., Hoffman, H. S., & Griffith, B. C. (1957). The discrimination of speech sounds within and across phoneme boundaries. *Journal of Experimental Psychology, 54*, 358–368.
Lopes, L. (1981). Decision making in the short run. *Journal of Experimental Psychology: Human Learning and Memory, 7*, 377–385.
Luce, R. D. (1959). *Individual choice behavior.* New York: Wiley.
MacDonald, J., & McGurk, H. (1978). Visual influences on speech perception processes. *Perception & Psychophysics, 24*, 253–257.
Massaro, D. W. (1975a). *Experimental psychology and information processing.* Chicago: Rand-McNally.
Massaro, D. W. (Ed.) (1975b). *Understanding language: An information processing analysis of speech perception, reading and psycholinguistics.* New York: Academic Press.
Massaro, D. W. (1976). Auditory information processing. In W. K. Estes (Ed.), *Handbook of learning and cognitive processes Vol. 4: Attention and memory.* Hillsdale, NJ: Erlbaum.
Massaro, D. W. (1978). A stage model of reading and listening. *Visible Language, 12*, 3–26.
Massaro, D. W. (1979). Reading and listening (Tutorial paper). In P. A. Kolers, M. Wrolstad, & H. Bouma (Eds.), *Processing of visible language (Vol. 1*, pp. 331–354). New York: Plenum Press.
Massaro, D. W. (1984). Building and testing models of reading processes: Examples from word recognition. In P. D. Pearson (Ed.), *Handbook of reading research.* New York: Longman.
Massaro, D. W. (In press). *Speech perception by ear and eye: A paradigm for psychological inquiry.* Hillsdale, NJ: Erlbaum.
Massaro, D. W., & Cohen, M. M. (1976). The contribution of fundamental frequency and voice onset time to the /zi/-/si/ distinction. *Journal of the Acoustical Society of America, 60*, 704–717.
Massaro, D. W., & Cohen, M. M. (1977). The contribution of voice-onset time and fundamental frequency as cues to the /zi/-/si/ distinction. *Perception & Psychophysics, 22*, 373–382.
Massaro, D. W., & Cohen, M. M. (1983a). Categorical or continuous speech perception: A new test. *Speech Communication, 2*, 15–35.
Massaro, D. W., & Cohen, M. M. (1983b). Evaluation and integration of visual and auditory information in speech perception. *Journal of Experimental Psychology: Human Perception and Performance, 9*, 753–771.
Massaro, D. W., & Oden, G. C. (1980a). Evaluation and integration of acoustic features in speech perception. *Journal of the Acoustical Society of America, 67*, 996–1013.
Massaro, D. W., & Oden, G. C. (1980b). Speech perception: A framework for research and theory. In

N. J. Lass (Ed.), *Speech and language: Advances in basic research and practice* (Vol. 3). New York: Academic Press.

McNabb, S. D. (1974). Must the output of the phonetic feature detector be binary? *Research in Speech Perception Progress Report* (Vol. 2). Bloomington, IN: Department of Psychology, Indiana University.

Norman, D. A., & Wickelgren, W. (1969). Strength theory of decision rules and latency in retrieval from short term memory. *Journal of Mathematical Psychology, 6*, 192–208.

Oden, G. C. (1977). Integration of fuzzy logical information, *Journal of Experimental Psychology: Human Perception and Performance, 3*, 565–575.

Oden, G. C. (1979). A fuzzy logical model of letter identification. *Journal of Experimental Psychology: Human Perception and Performance, 5*, 336–352.

Oden, G. C. (1981). Fuzzy propositional model of concept structure and use: A case study in object identification. In G. W. Lasker (Ed.), *Applied systems research and cybernetics*. Elmsford, NY: Pergamon Press.

Oden, G. C., & Massaro, D. W. (1978). Integration of featural formation in speech perception, *Psychological Review, 85*, 172–191.

Paap, K. R. (1975). Theories of speech perception. In D. W. Massaro (Ed.), *Understanding language*. New York: Academic Press.

Pastore, R. E., Ahroon, W. A., Baffuto, K. J., Friedman, C., Puleo, J. S., & Fink, E. A. (1977). Common-factor model of categorical perception. *Journal of Experimental Psychology: Human Perception and Performance, 3*, 686–696.

Pisoni, D. B. (1973). Auditory and phonetic codes in the discrimination of consonants and vowels. *Perception and Psychophysics, 13*, 253–260.

Pisoni, D. B., Aslin, R. N., Perey, A. J., & Hennessy, B. L. (1982). Some effects of laboratory training on identification and discrimination of voicing contrasts in stop consonants. *Journal of Experimental Psychology: Human Perception and Performance, 8*, 297–314.

Pisoni, D. B., & Lazarus, J. H. (1974). Categorical and noncategorical modes of speech perception along the voicing continuum. *Journal of the Acoustical Society of America, 55*, 328–334.

Pisoni, D. B., & Tash, J. (1974). Reaction times to comparisons within and across phonetic categories, *Perception & Psychophysics, 15*, 285–290.

Repp, B. H. (1981). Perceptual equivalence of two kinds of ambiguous speech stimuli. *Bulletin of the Psychonomic Society, 18*, 12–14.

Repp, B. H. (1984). Categorical perception: Issues, methods, findings. In N. J. Lass (Ed.), *Speech and language: Advances in basic research and practice*. (Vol. 10). New York: Academic Press.

Rosen, S. M., & Howell, P. (1981). Plucks and bows are not categorically perceived. *Perception & Psychophysics, 30*, 156–168.

Rumelhart, D. E., & Norman, D. A. (1983). Representation in memory, *Center for Human Information Processing, 116*, 1–117.

Sawusch, J. R. (1977). Peripheral and central processes in selective adaptation of place of articulation in stop consonants. *Journal of the Acoustical Society of America, 62*, 738–750.

Siegel, J. A., & Siegel, W. (1977a). Absolute identification of notes and intervals by musicians. *Perception & Psychophysics, 21*, 143–152.

Siegel, J. A., & Siegel, W. (1977b). Categorical perception of tonal intervals: Musicians can't tell *sharp* from *flat*. *Perception and Psychophysics, 21*, 399–407.

Smith, E. E., & Osherson, D. N. (1984). Conceptual combination with prototype concepts. *Cognitive Science, 5*, 337–361.

Smith, P. T. (1968). Cost, discriminability and response bias. *British Journal of Mathematical and Statistical Psychology, 21*, 35–60.

Sternberg, S. (1969). The discovery of processing stages: Extensions of Donder's method. *Acta Psychologica, 30*, 276–315.

Stevens, K. N., & Blumstein, S. E. (1978). Invariant cues for place of articulation in stop consonants. *Journal of the Acoustical Society of America, 64*, 1358–1368.

Studdert-Kennedy, M., Liberman, A. M., Harris, K. S., & Cooper, F. S. (1970). The motor theory of speech perception: A reply to Lane's critical review. *Psychological Review, 77,* 234–249.

Studdert-Kennedy, M., Liberman, A. M., & Stevens, K. N. (1963). Reaction times to synthetic stops and vowels at phoneme centers and at phoneme boundaries. *Journal of the Acoustical Society of America, 35,* 1900.

Theios, J., & Walter, D. G. (1974). Stimulus and response frequency and sequential effects in memory scanning reaction times. *Journal of Experimental Psychology, 102,* 1092–1099.

Thomas, E. A. C., & Myers, J. L. (1972). Implications of latency data for threshold and nonthreshold models of signal detection. *Journal of Mathematical Psychology, 9,* 253–285.

Thurstone, L. L. (1927). A law of comparative judgment. *Psychological Review, 34,* 273–286.

Watson, C. S., Rilling, M. E., & Bourbon, W. T. (1964). Receiver-operating characteristics determined by a mechanical analog to the rating scale. *Journal of the Acoustical Society of America, 36,* 283–288.

Zadeh, L. A. (1965). Fuzzy sets. *Information and Control, 8,* 338–353.

Part IV

Categorical perception in other modalities and other species

9 Perceptual categories in vision and audition

Marc H. Bornstein

This chapter has two objectives: The first is to review evidence that colors are perceived categorically, and the second is to overview some parallel lines of inquiry on categorization in vision and audition. Categorization may be defined for our purposes as treating a set of indiscriminable or discriminable stimuli as equivalent in some way (for example, by giving all of them the same name); this is the many-to-one reduction characteristic of categorization. Often categories also have an intrinsic qualitative distinctiveness. Several studies from different areas of psychology now document convincingly that hues are perceived categorically – categorical perception (CP) involves enhanced between-category discrimination relative to within-category discrimination of physical differences of equal magnitude – and that many rules and processes for categorizing hues in vision and phonemes of voicing in audition are similar. The major lines of study in color categorization are briefly summarized in the first part of this chapter and in the second part representative corresponding studies of hue and phoneme categories are compared so as to reveal deep parallels. The evidence comes from perceptual-cognitive, developmental, comparative, and physiological research. This analysis attempts to demonstrate the validity of the CP phenomenon and the value of cross-modal comparisons of categorization.

Visual categorization of hues

Of the radiant spectrum, only a small portion of electromagnetic energy – between approximately 400 and 700 nanometers – is visible. Visible light's principal quality is its chromaticity, as Isaac Newton (1671–1672) observed. Gazing at a spectrum today we are as impressed as Newton was three centuries ago by the separable color qualities of lesser or greater purity that dominate broad spectral ranges. We call these *hue categories*.

This apparent perceptual segmentation of the chromatic spectrum can also be inferred from the data of classic color-scaling experiments (such as those reviewed by Boynton, 1975). For example, Boynton and Gordon (1965) asked observers to describe single wavelengths using only four basic color terms – *blue, green, yellow,* and *red* or their combinations. The results lend quantitative support to our everyday

---

This chapter was written with the support of a Research Career Development Award from the National Institute of Child Health and Human Development (K04 HD00521) and a Guggenheim Foundation Fellowship.

impressions about the appearance of the chromatic spectrum. Boynton's observers could name all the wavelengths they could see using only one or at most two of the four basic color terms, with high agreement among observers. When permitted to use other color terms (such as *orange* or *violet*), observers were less reliable; all the wavelengths were more easily described using just the four primary terms. In short, the four color cohyponyms constitute a mutually contrastive set and can jointly be used to describe the color space exhaustively.

Most interesting about the color domain is the fact that the physics of color, the psychophysics of color discrimination, and the psychology of color naming are not isomorphic. Physically, the wavelength spectrum varies continuously – one wavelength differs from another by simple quantitative change. Psychophysically, human observers can discriminate many wavelengths – our powers to discern are keen. Psychologically, however, hues vary in a categorical fashion – our perceptions cross more or less discretely from one wavelength region to another. Considering hue, brightness, and saturation together, we can tell literally thousands of color nuances apart, but we still partition the color space into relatively few distinct qualitative sensations.

The difference between discrimination and categorization is crucial and warrants some additional explication. Questions about perceptual categorization and differentiation address different levels of analysis. The *discrimination question* concerns how many different wavelengths observers can tell apart. To address this question, an experimenter might juxtapose two spectral fields (either monochromatic lights or any other colors that yield relatively homogeneous energy distributions of a given wavelength) and alter one relative to the other systematically across the spectrum to derive a *jnd* (or $\Delta\lambda$) function, that is, the degree of wavelength change required to elicit a "just noticeable difference" in color as a function of the reference wavelength. With brightness and saturation controlled under the experimental conditions just described, adult color-normal trichromats discriminate approximately 120 to 150 *jnd*s across the visible spectrum.

The *category question* concerns whether observers perceive qualitative similarities of hue among spectral wavelengths. To address this question, an experimenter might expose observers to spectral fields that vary systematically in wavelength, asking them to name (or to identify or to group) the spectral fields to derive *color-naming* functions, that is, the percentage of times basic color names are applied to different wavelengths. Although a large number of wavelengths is discriminated, as we have learned, many are categorized together: Trichromats regularly and satisfactorily partition the spectrum into four basic hue categories, labeled blue, green, yellow, and red. Of course, the exact form that color-naming functions take depends on the way the category question is asked. For example, if observers are restricted to the four basic terms alone, they will generate rather discrete color-naming functions with broad plateaus and steep slopes (see Beare, 1963). If, alternatively, observers are permitted to use the four basic terms *and* combinations of them as descriptors, they will generate peaked color-naming functions with relatively shallow overlapping slopes (see Boynton & Gordon, 1965). These two types of color-naming functions are comparable, and both legitimately represent the relation between hue and wavelength; the type of function generated reflects the kind of instruction the observer is provided.

In brief, hue categorization subsumes groups of physically different wavelengths, some of which are discriminable and others of which are indiscriminable from one another. Discriminable wavelengths seem to be categorized together because they appear perceptually similar, probably because they share a dominant (hue) quality.

Relativism and universalism

The fact that a continuous physical dimension is perceived categorically provokes interesting questions about existing relations among the world, the brain, and the mind. Why do we categorize colors so regularly? One view, historically associated with the philosophical position of cultural relativism, is that we do so on account of a uniformity in experiences and in language as we grow up. A different view is universalist, and suggests that we categorize regularly because we innately see discrete regions of the color spectrum in a mostly uniform way.

Although founded by the German polymath Humboldt, and fostered by the American anthropologist Boas, relativism in language and perception is perhaps most widely identified with the anthropologist-linguist Whorf (1950, 1964). Whorf hypothesized that language organizes attributes of the world and that linguistic organization in turn influences perception. Whorf himself used color to exemplify his views (if only infrequently), but other anthropologists of the Whorfian school (e.g., Ray, 1953) have applied his hypothesis to the color domain in clear terms: "Each culture has taken the spectral continuum and divided it upon a basis which is quite arbitrary except for pragmatic considerations" (p. 102). Cultural relativism dominated anthropological, linguistic, philosophical, and even psychological thought on color (and related issues) for most of this century.

In the past decade, however, the competing universalist view has been supplanting relativism. Four separate lines of evidence have encouraged this new view: psychophysical studies with adults from different cultures, infancy studies, studies of infrahuman species, and studies of the physiological sensitivity of the visual system. Systematic research spanning cross-cultural, developmental, and animal comparisons constitutes the broadest kind of converging psychological inquiry (Bornstein, 1980). In the balance of this section I shall sketch these lines of investigation and summarize the findings (for a more detailed developmental exposition, see Bornstein, 1984).

Cross-cultural color categories

One major line of evidence that supports the universalist position derives from psychophysical and perceptual studies of color identification with adults from diverse linguistic and cultural communities (Table 9.1: section 1A). An impressive, though incomplete, uniformity obtains in basic color categorization, one that transcends English (e.g., Beare, 1963; Boynton & Gordon, 1965; Smith, 1971) and even related Indo-European languages such as Swedish (e.g., Ekman, 1963). The most comprehensive cross-cultural investigation has been conducted by Berlin and Kay (1969). These two anthropologists asked bilingual observers from 20 different language communities to identify the best examples of a small set of basic color terms from an array of 320 colors (40 hues by eight brightness levels). Despite the vast linguistic differences among them, observers rather uniformly identified color exemplars from relatively small and distinct areas of the color array. These areas match wavelength regions Boynton and others have identified as predominantly one or another of the basic hues. Berlin and Kay's findings on the uniformity of color identification leave aside the issue of linguistic or cultural differences in color naming; I will return to this point later.

Infants' color categories

The second major line of evidence that supports a universalist view of basic color categorization derives from developmental studies. Human infants – long before the acquisition of language or the inculcation even of the rudiments of culture – regularly partition the spectral continuum into categories of hue (Table 9.1: section 2A). The pertinent infant color data derive from a two-phase study conducted by Bornstein, Kessen, and Weiskopf (1976). In the first phase of one representative condition of their experiment, 4-month-old infants were familiarized with one wavelength that adults agreed was mostly blue. In the second phase, babies looked very little at that same wavelength and equally little at a new wavelength that adults also agreed was blue, but they looked significantly longer at another new wavelength that adults agreed was green. Comparing those wavelength ranges that the infants treated as similar and those they distinguished, Bornstein and his coworkers concluded that infants partition the spectral continuum into categories of hue and that infants' categories are very similar to those of adults. That is, the visible spectrum is organized into the basic psychological hues long before experience, language training, or formal tuition could influence categorization. Because the infants in this study were so young, these findings support the view that the categories these babies have may be universal; however, in the absence of cross-cultural studies of infancy it is not possible to confirm such a claim.

Animal color categories

The third major line of evidence for a universalist view shows that infrahuman species that perceive color but have no possibility of language or culture likewise partition the spectral continuum into "hue" categories (Table 9.1: section 3). At least one invertebrate and two vertebrate species (other than humans) have provided evidence of basic hue categorizations. Data from the European honeybee (von Frisch, 1964), from the pigeon (Wright, 1972; Wright & Cumming, 1971), and from the monkey (Sandell, Gross, & Bornstein, 1979) indicate that visual categorization of color is common across species. Although the ranges of the radiant spectrum that are visible to different species differ (e.g., humans see red but not ultraviolet as bees do), although different species partition the spectrum in different locations (e.g., the boundary positions for pigeons differ from those for humans), and although the number of categories varies across species (e.g., pigeons may have three categories and humans four), all color-sensitive species studied so far categorize the spectrum in some way. It is especially noteworthy that the data on trichromatic primates reveal hue-categorization functions very similar to the English-language color-naming system. Overall, this comparative approach clearly indicates that language, culture, and experience are not prerequisites for visual categorization of color. Together these data lend strong support to a universalist view of color categorization.

Physiology of color categories

The fourth major line of evidence that supports a universalist view focuses on the contribution of neural substrates to perceptual categorization (Table 9.1: section 4). For example, DeValois and his associates (e.g., DeValois & DeValois, 1975) have identified four classes of color-sensitive cells in the lateral geniculate nuclei of the monkey. These cells respond maximally to stimulation in the blue-, green-, yellow-, and red-appearing regions of the spectrum, respectively, and in a complementary fashion, their spontaneous levels of activity are inhibited by yellow-, red-, blue-, and green-appearing stimuli, respectively. The mechanism of action of these cells has been invoked to account directly for color categorization. DeValois has argued that the hue quality "green" is signaled by the excitation of $+G-R$ cells, "green-yellow" by the activity levels of $+G-R$ and $+Y-B$ cells, and so on. DeValois, Abramov, and Jacobs (1966) proposed that there is a simple "isomorphic relationship between the relative activity rates of the various cell types and the hue of a given light" (p. 976). Zeki (1980) has since contributed closely matching work on the primate visual system, but at the level of the cortex.

In the heyday of cultural relativism, the anthropologist Ray (1952) believed: "[T]he color patterning of man's world is not psychological, anatomical or physiological; there exist no natural divisions of the spectrum. Cultures divide it arbitrarily" (p. 43). On the basis of the more recent and programmatic cross-cultural, developmental, comparative, and physiological research we now know that the first parts of this relativist pronouncement are not accurate. Psychology, anatomy, and physiology help to construct and to pattern basic categorizations of color, and there do exist natural divisions of the spectrum.

Category-tuning and modifiability

The current results still allow the possibility, however, that in naming colors adults in different cultures could divide the spectrum into different categorical systems: They apparently do (e.g., Berlin & Kay, 1969; Bornstein, 1973). Why? It is certainly possible that different peoples have visual systems that are differentially sensitive to subtle differences in wavelength. This might be true from infancy, or it might be that, on account of what people are exposed to, what they eat, or what they see, their visual sensitivities develop differentially. Alternatively, it could be that different peoples have the same visual systems and sensitivities, even from infancy, but that they eventually categorize colors differently. If so, how might humans develop from perceptual uniformity in infancy to linguistic diversity in adult categorization? That is, in what ways could development proceed to overlay heterogeneity of categorization on homogeneity? Aslin (1981) has discussed various logical routes perceptual development might follow and the possible roles experience could play in interacting with the biological status of the developing organism. In general, he reasons, ordinary experience serves either to maintain or to attune structures or behaviors that are partially or fully developed at the time experience begins; this might describe the case of color categorization. Unusual experience may result in the loss of structure(s) or behavior(s). These principles can be applied directly to the question of hue categorization.

If color categories are functional at or near birth, if they have an identifiable neurological substrate, and if this is "hard wired," then human infants will be expected to partition the spectrum in uniform ways before they have experience with language or with culture, as indeed seems to occur. Afterward, development may follow different courses. In the simplest case of developmental continuity in the context of normative experience, the basic categories of hue in infancy would be maintained during ontogeny, projecting directly to the adult form of basic categorization. This continuity seems adequate to describe the development of humans born into most Indo-European linguistic communities. However, in societies where color-naming systems differ from the basic fourfold categorization, special linguistic or cultural experience may have influenced the structure of naming, or even of category perception, in particular ways during development. As a consequence, the "universal" categories of infancy may be differentiated or lost, or new categories may be induced.

Close analysis shows that category structures can change naturally or be altered artificially even in English (Table 9.1: section 2B). Normal development in color categorization entails a kind of fine-tuning: Boundary regions between hues narrow, and, in a complementary way, hue-category plateaus broaden (Bornstein, 1979; Raskin, Maital, & Bornstein, 1983). Whether these tuning processes reflect maturation, experience, or their interaction, is not yet well understood, however. Moreover, boundary locations in adult categorization are somewhat susceptible to instructional manipulation (Bornstein, 1976).

Perceiving categorically in vision and in audition: Major parallels

Like hue, which is the principal feature of color, voicing, which is one of the principal features of speech, is perceived categorically. Several potential parallels between these two classes of psychological categorization are known formally and a few are recognized informally, whereas others have not yet been noted. The aim of the second part of this chapter is to organize in one place the evidence for the major parallels between visual and auditory CP and to argue that comparing CP in different modalities may supply perceptual theory with some general principles.

In making comparisons between two percepts as phenomenally distinct as hue and voicing, I do not intend to imply that visual and auditory processes are identical, or even that CP mechanisms in the two modalities are identical. It is clear that the two are different on many dimensions of comparison: The physical correlates of these two perceptions – wavelength (λ) for hues and voice-onset time (VOT) for phonemes – differ from one another both in their absolute nature and in the complexity of their structure. Furthermore, speech has an analog motor-production medium in parallel with the perceptual medium that color does not. Nevertheless, it is possible to identify and catalog meaningful parallels between the two, and making such connections can promote further investigation and clarify the nature, ubiquity, and significance of categories in perception.

Table 9.1 summarizes representative studies of color and speech CP. Several major parallels are evident. First, in absolute-identification tasks, adults tend regularly and consistently to partition the VOT continuum into phoneme categories just as they partition the wavelength continuum into hue categories; that is, in both domains adults exhibit a high degree of equivalence within classes and equally high contrast between classes (Table 9.1: section 1). Second, preverbal human infants perceive both phonemes and hues categorically (section 2). Third, various infrahuman species also perceive "phonemes" and "hues" categorically (section 3). Finally, categorization appears to reflect special underlying (peripheral or central) neurological substrates (section 4). In brief, there is substantial evidence of significant parallels between visual and auditory CP.[1]

The fact that categorical modes of perceiving operate in such systematically similar ways in two sensory modalities encourages the conjecture that a more than superficial kinship exists between the two. Indeed, CP in these two modalities is not only comparable in broad outline, as the studies in sections 1, 2, 3, and 4 of Table 9.1 attest, but processes underlying the two may be alike in significant details. Studies in 1B, C, and D of Table 9.1 document that discrimination, reaction time, and adaptation subprocesses of adult categorization in the two domains parallel one another. For example, with both hue and voicing, adult relative discrimination along the physical continuum involved is much more acute than absolute identification (cf. Miller, 1956); relative discrimination is nonmonotonic and related to identification in a loosely reciprocal way, that is, it tends to be good at the boundaries between categories and poor in regions of generalization. Furthermore, the

Table 9.1. *Major aspects of categorization and parallels in vision and in audition*

Color perception	Speech perception
1. Basic categorization processes in adult humans	
A. Identification	
Beare (1963)	Lisker & Abramson (1964)
Ekman (1963)	Liberman, Cooper, Shankweiler, &
Boynton & Gordon (1965)	Studdert-Kennedy (1967)
Berlin & Kay (1969)	Abramson & Lisker (1970)
Smith (1971)	Liberman (1970)
Boynton (1975)	Cooper (1974)
Bornstein & Monroe (1980)	Pisoni & Tash (1975)
Bornstein & Korda (1984, 1985)	Tartter & Eimas (1975)
B. Discrimination	
Wright (1947)	Liberman, Cooper, Shankweiler, &
Ekman (1963)	Studdert-Kennedy (1967)
Graham (1965)	Pisoni & Tash (1974)
Smith (1971)	Hanson (1977)
Graham, Turner, & Hurst (1973)	
Bornstein & Korda (1984, 1985)	
C. Reaction time	
Beare (1963)	Studdert-Kennedy, Liberman, & Stevens
Bornstein & Monroe (1980)	(1963)
Bornstein & Korda (1984, 1985)	Pisoni & Tash (1974)
D. Adaptation	
von Kries (1878)	Eimas & Corbit (1973)
Wright (1934)	Cooper (1974)
MacAdam (1956)	Diehl (1975)
Jameson & Hurvich (1972)	Miller (1975)
Bornstein & Korda (1985)	Pisoni & Tash (1975)
	Eimas & Miller (1978)
	Eimas & Tartter (1979)
	Sawusch & Jusczyk (1981)
	Repp & Liberman (this volume)
Adaptor intensity	
Bornstein & Korda (1985)	Sawusch (1976)
Adaptor quality	
Bornstein & Korda (1985)	Ades (1974a)
	Sawusch (1976)
	Sawusch & Pisoni (1976)
	Miller (1977)
Recovery time	
Bornstein & Korda (1985)	Eimas & Corbit (1973)
E. Neurological locus	
Delabarre (1888)	Eimas, Cooper, & Corbit (1973)
Boynton (1971)	Ades (1974b)

Table 9.1. (*Continued*)

Color perception	Speech perception
Bornstein & Korda (1985)	Miller (1975)
	Sawusch (1977)
2. Ontogeny of categorization processes in humans	
A. Infancy	
Bornstein, Kessen, & Weiskopf (1976)	Eimas, Siqueland, Jusczyk, & Vigorito
Bornstein (1978, 1981b)	(1971)
	Eimas (1975)
	Lasky, Syrdal-Lasky, & Klein (1975)
	Streeter (1976)
	Eilers (1980)
	Eimas, Miller, & Jusczyk (this volume)
B. Childhood	
Mervis, Catlin, & Rosch (1975)	Wolf (1973)
Bornstein (1979)	Zlatin & Koeningsknecht (1975)
Raskin, Maital, & Bornstein (1983)	Streeter & Landauer (1976)
3. Categorization processes in infrahumans	
von Frisch (1964)	Kuhl & Miller (1975, 1978)
Wright & Cumming (1971)	Waters & Wilson (1976)
Wright (1972)	Sinnott, Beecher, Moody, & Stebbins
DeValois & DeValois (1975)	(1976)
Sandell, Gross, & Bornstein (1979)	Kuhl (1979)
	Ehret (this volume)
4. Physiological substrates of categorization	
DeValois, Abramov, & Jacobs (1966)	Eimas & Corbit (1973)
Cerf-Beare (1973)	Eimas, Cooper, & Corbit (1973)
DeValois & DeValois (1975)	Wilson (this volume)
Werner & Wooten (1979)	Molfese (this volume)
Zeki (1980)	Remez (this volume)
Regan (this volume)	

Note: The papers referred to in this table are representative; the table is not intended to be exhaustive. References are listed chronologically.

studies in section 2B of Table 9.1 document the fact that developmental changes in the two domains are also similar.

One of the benefits of formally tabulating such a comparison between hue and voicing CP is that it calls attention to studies not yet performed in one field that have already been undertaken in the parallel field. The potential of this approach is affirmed when hypotheses generated on the basis of findings in one modality are tested in the other and are found to be supported. This logic may suggest specific individual studies or even a systematic program of research in the visual domain to parallel the findings in the auditory domain, or vice versa. For example, cross-cultural studies of speech CP in infants have pinpointed which voicing categories may be universal and present near birth, and which may be particular and learned. Comparable studies in color have yet to be performed.

In a reciprocal fashion, because so much is precisely known about the physics, neurophysiology, and psychophysics of color vision, it would be surprising if additional color research or theory could not enhance our basic understanding of CP in speech. Consider, for example, the following connected series of findings on the internal structure of hue categories (and contemplate the speech-category experiments they might suggest):

First, Berlin and Kay (1969) identified certain colors as universally "focal" in human color naming. Focal colors are typically clear, simple, central representatives of hue categories. Shortly thereafter, the psychological salience and prototypical status of focal colors was confirmed by cross-cultural, developmental, physiological, and comparative experiments. Heider (1972) found distinct advantages for focal colors over nonfocal ones among adults asked to identify and remember different colors, and Bornstein and Monroe (1980) found that adults who learn to sort focal and nonfocal colors equally well still classify focal colors faster than nonfocal ones. Heider and Olivier (1972) also found that both Americans and the Dugum Dani (a Stone Age people from New Guinea) name focal colors more readily and recall them more accurately than nonfocal ones from both short- and long-term memory. Later, Bornstein (1975) found that young adults rate the group of focal colors as more pleasant than the group of nonfocal colors. These findings confirm and update research of the 1930s and 1940s by Dimmick and Hubbard (1939) and by Guilford (1940).

Second, Heider (1971) found that three- to four-year-olds pay more attention to focal colors, match them more accurately, and choose them more frequently as representative of specific basic color names. Mervis et al. (1975) and Raskin et al. (1983) found structural advantages for focal colors in young children's color naming. In addition, Bornstein (1975, 1981a,b) has shown that there is a consistent series of parallel advantages for focal over nonfocal colors even earlier in childhood, specifically in infants' preferences, encoding, and memory for color.

Finally, a physiological basis for focality in color exists in the primate visual system (Bornstein, 1973). Wright and Cumming (1971) even found that pigeons learn to match focal colors from their species-specific "color-naming" system faster than nonfocal colors.

The coherence of these findings in color CP strongly suggests that investigators who look may discover, first, that auditory categories possess a similar internal structure, consisting of better and poorer examples of voicing, and, second, that good exemplars (selected, perhaps, at or near the centers of phoneme categories) generally hold preferential, attentional, mnemonic, and learning advantages over poorer examples of categories (selected at or near boundaries between phonemes) both for humans of different ages and for infrahumans.

Conclusions

The phenomena of CP in vision and in audition are normally considered quite separately, and as a consequence the two have engendered segregated traditions in the psychological literature. However, as I have summarized, both general and specific parallels in categorizing exist between the two modalities. Modality comparisons like these may help us to formulate general principles of CP. Perhaps switching back and forth between eye and ear in this way will enable investigators of vision to see what researchers in hearing are saying, as they will encourage auditory investigators to lend a more sympathetic ear to the insights of visual researchers.

Note

1. Hues and phonemes are not the only categorical percepts in vision or in audition: See McGuirk and Herbert (1973), Pastore et al. (1977), and other chapters in this volume for further examples. CP may also be found in other sensory modalities; see Bornstein (1981a) and Wilson (Chapter 13, this volume).

References

Abramson, A. S., & Lisker, L. (1970). Discriminability along the voicing continuum: Cross-language tests. In *Proceedings of the Sixth International Congress of Phonetic Science*. Prague: Academia.
Ades, A. E. (1974a). How phonetic is selective adaptation? Experiments on syllable position and vowel environment. *Perception & Psychophysics, 16*, 61–67.
Ades, A. E. (1974b). Bilateral component in speech perception? *Journal of the Acoustical Society of America, 56*, 610–616.
Aslin, R. N. (1981). Experiential influences and sensitive periods in perceptual development: A unified model. In R. N. Aslin, J. R. Alberts, & M. R. Petersen (Eds.), *Development of perception: Psychobiological perspectives (Vol. 2). The visual system*. New York: Academic Press.
Beare, A. C. (1963). Color-name as a function of wave-length. *American Journal of Psychology, 76*, 248–256.
Berlin, B., & Kay, P. (1969). *Basic color terms: Their universality and evolution*. Berkeley: University of California Press.
Bornstein, M. H. (1973). Color vision and color naming: A psychophysiological hypothesis of cultural difference. *Psychological Bulletin, 80*, 257–285.
Bornstein, M. H. (1975). Qualities of color vision in infancy. *Journal of Experimental Child Psychology, 19*, 401–419.
Bornstein, M. H. (1976). Name codes and color memory. *American Journal of Psychology, 89*, 269–279.
Bornstein, M. H. (1978). Chromatic vision in infancy. In H. W. Reese & L. P. Lipsitt (Eds.), *Advances in child development and behavior* (Vol. 12). New York: Academic Press.
Bornstein, M. H. (1979). Perceptual development: Stability and change in feature perception. In M. H. Bornstein & W. Kessen (Eds.), *Psychological development from infancy*. Hillsdale, NJ: Erlbaum.
Bornstein, M. H. (Ed.). (1980). *Comparative methods in psychology*. Hillsdale, NJ: Erlbaum.
Bornstein, M. H. (1981a). Two kinds of perceptual organization near the beginning of life. In W. A. Collins (Ed.), *Minnesota symposia on child psychology* (Vol. 14). Hillsdale, NJ: Erlbaum.
Bornstein, M. H. (1981b). Psychological studies of color perception in human infants: Habituation, discrimination and categorization, recognition, and conceptualization. In L. P. Lipsitt (Ed.), *Advances in infancy research* (Vol. 1). Norwood, NJ: Ablex.
Bornstein, M. H. (1984). Infant into adult: Unity to diversity in visual categorization. In J. Mehler & R. Fox (Eds.), *Neonatal and infant cognition: Beyond the blooming, buzzing confusion*. Hillsdale, NJ: Erlbaum.
Bornstein, M. H., Kessen, W., & Weiskopf, S. (1976). Color vision and hue categorization in young human infants. *Journal of Experimental Psychology: Human Perception and Performance, 2*, 115–129.

Bornstein, M. H., & Korda, N. O. (1984). Discrimination and matching within and between hues measured by reaction times: Some implications for categorical perception and levels of information processing. *Psychological Research, 46*, 207–222.

Bornstein, M. H., & Korda, N. O. (1985). Identification and adaptation of hue: Parallels in the operation of mechanisms that underlie categorical perception in vision and audition. *Psychological Research, 47*, 1–17.

Bornstein, M. H., & Monroe, M. D. (1980). Chromatic information processing: Rate depends on stimulus location in the category and psychological complexity. *Psychological Research, 42*, 213–225.

Boynton, R. M. (1971). Color vision. In L. A. Riggs & J. Kling (Eds.), *Woodworth and Scholsberg's experimental psychology*. New York: Holt, Rinehart, & Winston.

Boynton, R. M. (1975). Color, hue, and wavelength. In E. C. Carterette & M. P. Friedman (Eds.), *Handbook of perception* (Vol. 5). New York: Academic Press.

Boynton, R. M., & Gordon, J. (1965). Bezold-Brücke hue shift measured by color-naming technique. *Journal of the Optical Society of America, 55*, 78–86.

Cerf-Beare, A. (1973). Regions of response transition of color-coded retinal units and attempted analogy to behavioral response transition. *Perception & Psychophysics, 13*, 541–547.

Cooper, W. E. (1974). Adaptation of phonetic feature analyzers for place of articulation. *Journal of the Acoustical Society of America, 56*, 617–627.

Delabarre, E. B. (1888). On the seat of optical after-images. *American Journal of Psychology, 2*, 326–328.

DeValois, R. L., Abramov, I., & Jacobs, G. H. (1966). Analysis of response patterns in LGN cells. *Journal of the Optical Society of America, 56*, 966–977.

DeValois, R. L., & DeValois, K. K. (1975). Neural coding of color. In E. C. Carterette & M. P. Friedman (Eds.), *Handbook of perception* (Vol. 5). New York: Academic Press.

Diehl, R. L. (1975). The effect of selective adaptation on the identification of speech sounds. *Perception & Psychophysics, 17*, 48–52.

Dimmick, F. L., & Hubbard, M. R. (1939). The spectral location of psychologically unique yellow, green, and blue. *American Journal of Psychology, 52*, 242–254.

Eilers, R. E. (1980). Infant speech perception: History and mystery. *Child Phonology, 2*, 23–39.

Eimas, P. D. (1975). Speech perception in early infancy. In L. Cohen & P. Salapatek (Eds.), *Infant perception: From sensation to cognition* (Vol. 2). New York: Academic Press.

Eimas, P. D., Cooper, W. E., & Corbit, J. D. (1973). Some properties of linguistic feature detectors. *Perception & Psychophysics, 13*, 247–252.

Eimas, P. D., & Corbit, J. D. (1973). Selective adaptation of linguistic feature detectors. *Cognitive Psychology, 4*, 99–109.

Eimas, P. D., & Miller, J. L. (1978). Effects of selective adaptation on the perception of speech and visual patterns: Evidence for feature detectors. In R. D. Walk & H. L. Pick, Jr. (Eds.), *Perception and experience*. New York: Plenum Press.

Eimas, P. D., Siqueland, E. R., Jusczyk, P., & Vigorito, J. (1971). Speech perception in infants. *Science, 171*, 303–306.

Eimas, P. D., & Tartter, V. C. (1979). On the development of speech perception: Mechanisms and analogies. *Advances in Child Development and Behavior, 13*, 155–193.

Ekman, G. (1963). Contributions to the psychophysics of color vision. *Studium Generale, 16*, 54–64.

Graham, B. V., Turner, M. E., & Hurst, D. C. (1973). Derivation of wavelength discrimination from color naming. *Journal of the Optical Society of America, 63*, 109–111.

Graham, C. H. (1965). Discriminations that depend on wavelength. In C. H. Graham (Ed.), *Vision and visual perception*. New York: Wiley.

Guilford, J. P. (1940). There is a system of color preferences. *Journal of the Optical Society of America, 30*, 455–459.

Hanson, V. L. (1977). Within-category discriminations in speech perception. *Perception & Psychophysics, 21*, 423–430.

Heider, E. R. (1971). "Focal" color areas and the development of color names. *Developmental Psychology, 4*, 446–455.

Heider, E. R. (1972). Universals in color naming and memory. *Journal of Experimental Psychology, 93*, 10–20.
Heider, E. R., & Olivier, D. C. (1972). The structure of the color space in naming and memory for two languages. *Cognitive Psychology, 3*, 337–354.
Jameson, D., & Hurvich, L. M. (1972). Color adaptation, sensitivity, contrast, and afterimages. In D. Jameson & L. M. Hurvich (Eds.), *Visual psychophysics.* Berlin: Springer.
Kuhl, P. K. (1979). Models and mechanisms in speech perception: Species comparisons provide further contributions. *Brain, Behavior and Evolution, 16*, 374–408.
Kuhl, P. K., & Miller, J. D. (1975). Speech perception by the chinchilla: Voiced-voiceless distinction in alveolar plosive consonants. *Science, 190*, 69–72.
Kuhl, P. K., & Miller, J. D. (1978). Speech perception by the chinchilla: Identification functions for synthetic VOT stimuli. *Journal of the Acoustical Society of America, 63*, 905–917.
Lasky, R. E., Syrdal-Lasky, A., & Klein, R. E. (1975). VOT discrimination by four to six and a half month old infants from Spanish environments. *Journal of Experimental Child Psychology, 20*, 215–225.
Liberman, A. M. (1970). The grammars of speech and language. *Cognitive Psychology, 1*, 301–323.
Liberman, A. M., Cooper, F. S., Shankweiler, D. S., & Studdert-Kennedy, M. (1967). Perception of speech code. *Psychological Review, 74*, 431–461.
Lisker, L., & Abramson, A. S. (1964). A cross-language study of voicing in initial stops: Acoustical measurements. *Word, 20*, 384–422.
MacAdam, D. L. (1956). Chromatic adaptation. *Journal of the Optical Society of America, 46*, 500–513.
McGuirk, F. D., & Herbert, J. A. (1973). Latency pattern in category judgments. *Bulletin of the Psychonomic Society, 1*, 457–459.
Mervis, C. B., Catlin, J., & Rosch, E. (1975). Development of the structure of color categories. *Developmental Psychology, 11*, 54–60.
Miller, G. A. (1956). The magical number seven, plus or minus two: Some limits on our capacity for processing information. *Psychological Review, 63*, 81–97.
Miller, J. L. (1975). Properties of feature detectors for speech: Evidence from the effects of selective adaptation on dichotic listening. *Perception & Psychophysics, 18*, 389–397.
Miller, J. W. (1977). Properties of feature detectors for VOT: The voiceless channel of analysis. *Journal of the Acoustical Society of America, 62*, 641–648.
Newton, I. (1671–1672). New theory about light and colors. *Philosophical Transactions of the Royal Society, 80*, 3075–3087.
Pastore, R. E., Ahroon, W. A., Baffuto, K. J., Friedman, C., Puleo, J. S., & Fink, E. A. (1977). Common factor model of categorical perception. *Journal of Experimental Psychology: Human Perception and Performance, 3*, 686–696.
Pisoni, D. B., & Tash, J. (1974). Reaction times to comparisons within and across phonetic categories. *Perception & Psychophysics, 15*, 285–290.
Pisoni, D. B., & Tash, J. (1975). Auditory property detectors and processing place features in stop consonants. *Perception & Psychophysics, 18*, 401–408.
Raskin, L. A., Maital, S., & Bornstein, M. H. (1983). Perceptual categorization of color: A life-span study. *Psychological Research, 45*, 135–145.
Ray, V. F. (1952). Techniques and problems in the study of human color perception. *Southwestern Journal of Anthropology, 8*, 251–259.
Ray, V. F. (1953). Human color perception and behavioral response. *Transactions of the New York Academy of Sciences, 16*, 98–104.
Sandell, J. H., Gross, C. G., & Bornstein, M. H. (1979). Color categories in Macaques. *Journal of Comparative and Physiological Psychology, 93*, 626–635.
Sawusch, J. R. (1976). Selective adaptation effects on end-point stimuli in a speech series. *Perception & Psychophysics, 20*, 61–65.
Sawusch, J. R. (1977). Peripheral and central processes in selective adaptation of place of articulation in stop consonants. *Journal of the Acoustical Society of America, 62*, 738–750.

Sawusch, J. R., & Jusczyk, P. (1981). Adaptation and contrast in the perception of voicing. *Journal of Experimental Psychology: Human Perception and Performance, 7,* 408–422.

Sawusch, J. R., & Pisoni, D. B. (1976). Response organization in selective adaptation to speech sounds. *Perception & Psychophysics, 20,* 413–418.

Sinnott, J. M., Beecher, M. D., Moody, D. B., & Stebbins, W. C. (1976). Speech sound discrimination by monkeys and humans. *Journal of the Acoustical Society of America, 60,* 687–695.

Smith, D. P. (1971). Derivation of wavelength discrimination from colour-naming data. *Vision Research, 11,* 739–742.

Streeter, L. A. (1976). Language perception of two-month-old infants shows effects of both innate mechanism and experience. *Nature, 259,* 39–41.

Streeter, L. A., & Landauer, T. K. (1976). Effects of learning English as a second language on the acquisition of a new phonemic contrast. *Journal of the Acoustical Society of America, 59,* 448–451.

Studdert-Kennedy, M., Liberman, A. M., & Stevens, K. N. (1963). Reaction time to synthetic stop consonants and vowels at phoneme centers and at phoneme boundaries. *Journal of the Acoustical Society of America, 35,* 1900 (Abstract).

Tartter, V. C., & Eimas, P. D. (1975). The role of auditory and phonetic feature detectors in the perception of speech. *Perception and Psychophysics, 15,* 293–298.

von Frisch, K. (1964). *Bees: Their vision, chemical senses, and language.* Ithaca, NY: Cornell University Press.

von Kries, J. (1878). Beitrag zur Physiologie der Gesichtsempfindungen. *Archives für Anatomie und Physiologie, 2,* 505–524.

Waters, R. S., & Wilson, W. A. (1976). Speech perception by rhesus monkeys: The voicing distinction in synthesized labial and velar stop consonants. *Perception & Psychophysics, 19,* 285–289.

Werner, J. S., & Wooten, B. R. (1979). Opponent chromatic mechanisms: Relation to photopigments and hue naming. *Journal of the Optical Society of America, 69,* 422–434.

Whorf, B. L. (1950). *Four articles on metalinguistics.* Washington, DC: Foreign Service Institute.

Whorf, B. L. (1964). *Language, thought and reality.* Cambridge, MA: M.I.T. Press.

Wolf, C. G. (1973). The perception of stop consonants by children. *Journal of Experimental Child Psychology, 16,* 318–333.

Wright, A. A. (1972). Psychometric and psychophysical hue discrimination functions for the pigeon. *Vision Research, 12,* 1447–1464.

Wright, A. A., & Cumming, W. W. (1971). Color-naming functions for the pigeon. *Journal of the Experimental Analysis of Behavior, 15,* 7–17.

Wright, W. D. (1934). The measurement and analysis of color adaptation phenomena. *Proceedings of the Royal Society* (London), *115B,* 49–87.

Wright, W. D. (1947). *Researches on normal and defective colour vision.* St. Louis, MO: Mosby.

Zeki, S. (1980). The representation of colours in the cerebral cortex. *Nature, 284,* 412–418.

Zlatin, M. A., & Koenigsknecht, R. A. (1975). Development of the voicing contrast: Perception of stop consonants. *Journal of Speech and Hearing Research, 18,* 541–553.

10 Categorical perception of sound signals: Facts and hypotheses from animal studies

Günter Ehret

Experimental evidence for categorical perception (CP) of sound signals in animals (insects, anurans, birds, mammals) is reviewed. Except for human speech perception, CP, in a strict sense with both labeling (identification) and discrimination functions indicating a sharp boundary between two perceptual classes of stimuli, has only been demonstrated for ultrasound perception in house mice. However, a variety of data from other animals shows at least categorical labeling of sounds that vary continuously along certain physical parameters. CP in animals is closely linked to the recognition of key- (sign-) stimuli and may be expected in cases in which recognition is based on only one or a few critical-sound parameters: those that carry the "meaning" of the sound. Thus CP is an important process, which helps to structure and classify the world of acoustic-communication signals. CP as an experimental concept provides a useful approach for systematic and quantitative studies of acoustic key-stimulus patterns. Mechanisms of CP related to learned and innate categorizations and to temporal and spectral sound analysis are proposed.

We perceive a number of speech sounds categorically. How do animals perceive their communicative sounds? Is categorical perception (CP) unique to human speech, where this phenomenon has received most attention (see Part II of this volume), or does it represent a more general perceptual mode; if so, what are the advantages and mechanisms of perceiving a physical continuum of acoustic variation in a categorical manner? A major goal of my chapter is to answer these questions on the basis of available data from various groups of animals (from insects to mammals).

Before discussing the results from the literature, it is necessary to clarify the CP concept, which in turn requires a definition that is, on the one hand, consistent with definitions derived from the considerable body of human-speech research, and on the other, applicable to the much less elaborate data from animal studies. Auditory CP can be said to exist (Liberman, Harris, Hoffman, & Griffith, 1957; reviews by Kuhl, 1979, and Chapter 12, this volume; Pisoni, 1979; Studdert-Kennedy, Liberman, Harris, & Cooper, 1970) if (1) stimuli from an acoustic continuum are labeled

---

Original studies by the author which contributed material to this work were supported by the Deutsche Forschungsgemeinschaft, Eh 53/1-5. I wish to thank R. Freeman, S. Harnad, H. Markl, P. Marler, and J. Tautz for their helpful comments on an earlier version of the manuscript and B. Haack for cooperation during the course of this study.

(or identified) as belonging to different classes, and (2) stimuli labeled differently are very well discriminated, whereas others labeled the same are less well discriminated. If both conditions are fulfilled the classes will be called categories. This definition of CP requires that there be a sharp perceptual boundary between stimuli from two different categories and that this boundary occur at the same place on the acoustic continuum in both labeling and discrimination tests.

One might suppose that the occurrence of a sharp boundary between perceptual classes in labeling tests would predict the outcome of discrimination tests and thus the existence of CP (Liberman et al., 1957; Studdert-Kennedy et al., 1970). This prediction does not hold in general, however, and depends on the detection theory proposed for explaining the data (see Macmillan, Kaplan, & Creelman, 1977, and Chapter 2 by Macmillan, this volume). It seems to be true only under the assumption that a listener can discriminate between two stimuli to the extent that they are labeled as different on an absolute basis, as demonstrated in the case of speech-phoneme boundaries (Pisoni, 1979). Because we do not know whether animals perceive their communication sounds the same way that we perceive phonemes in speech, we should be careful in applying the term "categorical perception" to animal sound perception. Strictly speaking, both labeling and discrimination tests must demonstrate a sharp boundary on a sound continuum to count as CP. Defined in this way, CP corresponds to the "phoneme boundary effect" defined by Wood (1976).

As we shall see later, compared with the work on human speech perception, relatively few studies are devoted directly to the question of CP in animal communication. To give the discussion a broader basis, I shall include studies on call type and individual recognition where CP appears to be a promising strategy for the interpretation of the data even when it has not yet been tested directly.

Another experimental requirement implicit in my definition of CP is the adequate control of the sound continuum. In speech-perception tests it is often only a single sound parameter, the decisive one for the perception of different phonemes, that is varied systematically by means of electronic devices. Thus, in order to test CP in animals, we have to know (1) the critical acoustic parameters leading to perceptual differences and (2) the variability of these parameters in natural calls (so as to determine a meaningful continuum); we also have to have (3) a behavior suitable for detecting and measuring perceptual differences. Thus, a starting point for designing a test of CP in animals requires an easily quantifiable behavior released by an acoustic key- or sign-stimulus (Lorenz, 1981; Manning, 1972) with only one or a few parameters critical for recognition. These parameters can be continuously varied and the ability of the stimuli from a specified continuum to release the behavior can be tested. Such labeling or identification tests must then be supplemented by appropriate discrimination tests. In spite of many descriptions of animal sounds capable of releasing specified behavior, there are only a few in the literature for which the parameters for recognition and response release have been well enough studied to allow CP to be tested. Most ethologists are interested in the key-stimulus configuration as an optimum releaser of behavior and in the organization of behavioral and social patterns through key-stimuli. They are much less interested in the perceptual side of key-stimuli (although the clarification of perceptual mechanisms could contribute to our understanding of the evolution of certain key-stimulus patterns, whether they are categorically perceived or not).

Questions about methods

When can categorical perception be expected to occur?

Categorical perception of communicative sounds can be expected when there is selective pressure for dividing a natural pool of variability or a continuum of sounds into discrete classes, or when a repertoire of discrete call types must be kept discrete during perception and recognition processes (see Marler 1976, 1977, 1982). For example, in breeding congregations of insects, frogs, and birds, discrete signal classes may serve to identify either a species or a certain individual. They can provide a basis for discriminating conspecific mates or family members from members of other species or from conspecific strangers. CP may play a significant role in the process of recognizing species-specific or individual-specific features by discrimination and abstraction, thereby facilitating clearcut decisions and adaptative behavior (see also Snowdon in Chapter 11, this volume).

CP could also be useful for individual recognition in well-organized social groups. Here CP would provide a means of structuring the acoustic surroundings and making the recognition of relevant senders easy and nearly error free. A necessary condition, however, would be that the senders divide the pool of variability (the acoustic continua) into individual-specific combinations of features that remain constant across time. Ideally the range of variability of a sender should not overlap with that of any other sender in the critical dimensions. In that case, the receiver could easily disregard individual variability and discriminate each individual from the others, resulting in reliable identification. To result in individual recognition, CP entails learning the critical parameters along a natural continuum of a call type in the repertoire of a species that will reliably identify and discriminate individuals.

If a discrete call repertoire already exists, reflecting well-defined internal states or a certain behavioral context of the sender, then innate mechanisms seem to be enough to keep calls discrete during sound processing to release adequate behavior (although learning and memory could also become important). Here the receiver ignores (or may learn to ignore) the variability caused by different senders and abstracts the decisive pattern to form a concept of the call type and thus of the "message." When discrete calls are perceived categorically, unimportant details (inherent "noise") as well as intervening background noise from the environment can effectively be suppressed so that CP facilitates recognition and adaptive responding.

What sound parameters are suitable for categorical perception?

Because total sound intensity, relative intensity variation, total frequency range, and upper frequency limits are heavily dependent on the distance between sender and receiver, the structure of the environment, and the presence of disturbing noise, these parameters cannot play the decisive role in categorization (at least with long-distance calls). Other parameters are more independent of the environment and better controlled by the sender. These include temporal patterns (e.g., duration, repetition frequency) and spectral patterns (e.g., carrier frequency, frequency shifts, modulations, noise components) and are more likely to provide a suitable substrate for categorization. Examples of the use of different parameters in CP are speech sounds differing in voice-onset time (e.g., Eimas, Siqueland, Jusczyk, & Vigorito, 1971; Kuhl, 1981; Kuhl & Miller, 1975, 1978; Pisoni, 1977; Pisoni & Lazarus, 1974; Waters & Wilson, 1976) and in formant transitions (for example, Eimas, 1974; Liberman et al., 1957; Mattingly, Liberman, Syrdal, & Halwes, 1971; Miyawaki et al., 1975; Morse & Snowdon, 1975; Sinnott, Beecher, Moody, & Stebbins, 1976). Categorization of nonspeech sounds has been found in cases in which the critical parameter was rise time (Cutting & Rosner, 1974; Hary & Massaro, 1982), frequency pattern (Locke & Kellar, 1973), noise-lead time (Miller, Wier, Pastore, Kelly, & Dooling, 1976), and sound-energy concentration in a certain small-frequency bandwidth (Ehret & Haack, 1981, 1982).

How to measure categorical perception

The experimental design for specifically testing CP with speech sounds seems to be crucial for demonstrating categorical as opposed to continuous perception in general (e.g., Kuhl, 1979, 1981; Pisoni, 1973; Pisoni & Lazarus, 1974; Repp & Liberman in Chapter 3, this volume). This unsatisfactory situation requires some interpretation.

Labeling tests with human subjects are normally done on an absolute basis, that is, listeners are asked to identify a given stimulus from a continuum as *A* or *B*, with *A* and *B* being endpoints or midpoints of the continuum presented. A prerequisite for such labeling tests is that the listener possess a concept of *A* and *B*, either innately or through learning. *A* and *B* have to be stored in memory and serve as a basis for classifying the test stimuli. Usually the decision has to be made within a few seconds after presentation of the stimulus. Every decision is itself categorical at the instant it is made, as only two categories tend to be provided as alternatives. By multiple repetition of the same task with many stimuli from the continuum between *A* and *B*, a distribution of the probability of being labeled *A* or *B* for each stimulus is obtained; this forms the basis for plotting labeling functions. These functions may show a more or less sharp inflection between neighboring stimuli in the transition region from *A* to *B*. Figure 10.1 (A & B) shows two sets of hypothetical labeling functions demonstrating continua from very sharp to continuous transitions between

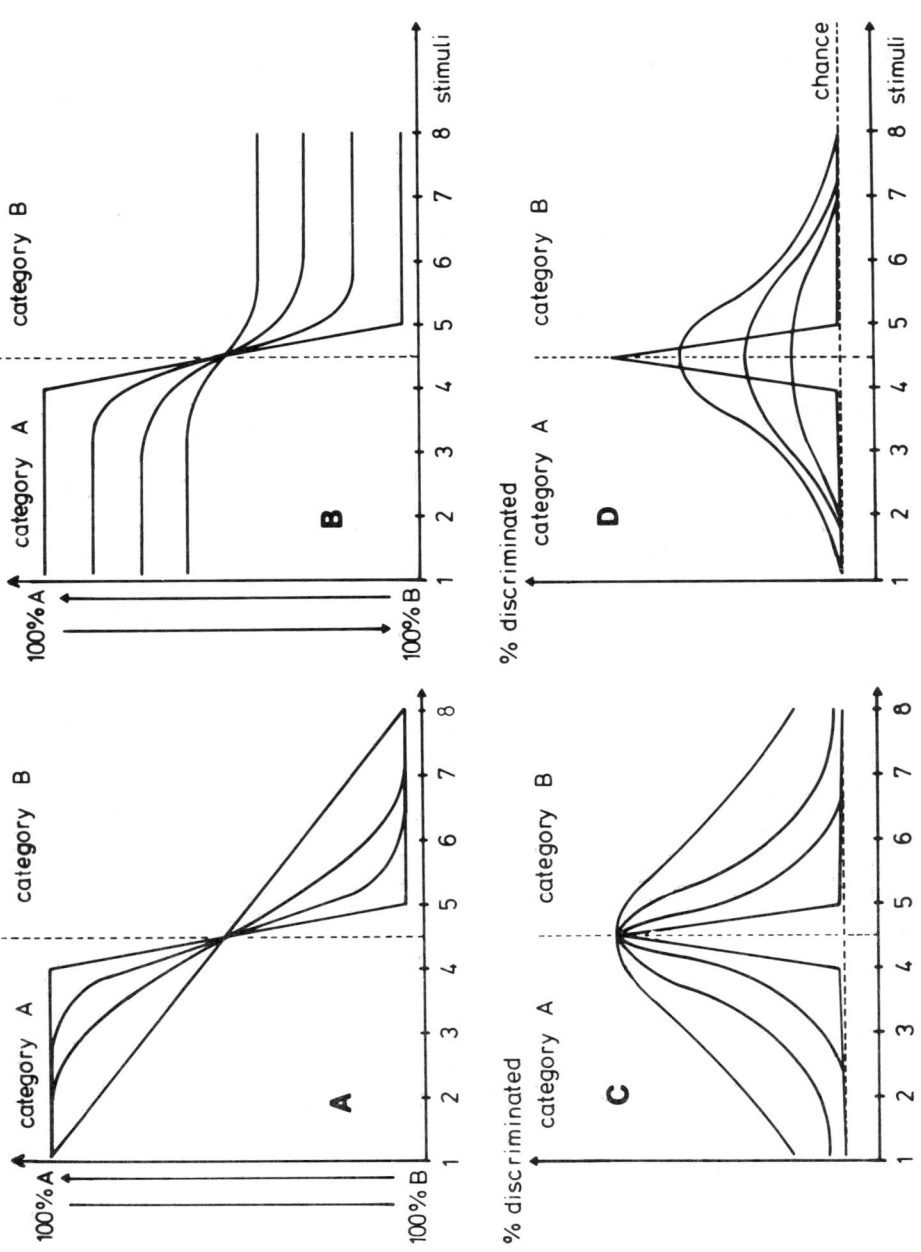

Figure 10.1. Some hypothetical labeling (A,B) and discrimination (C,D) functions. The eight stimuli on the abscissa vary systematically on a continuum of a given sound parameter. The ordinate shows the degree (in percent) to which a stimulus is labeled A or B (labeling functions) or neighboring stimuli are discriminated (discrimination functions). In the ideal case the boundary (vertical dashed lines) in the labeling functions is at the same place (between stimuli 4 and 5 in this example) as the peak of the discrimination functions. Functions in A and C demonstrate the transition from a sharp category boundary between stimuli 4 and 5 to continuous labeling and discrimination between all stimuli. The functions in B and D demonstrate that perceived category levels can be well separated (100% difference) or rather close together.

A and *B*. It obviously depends on the interpretation of the experimenter which kind of labeling function should be taken as evidence for CP. Clearly, labeling functions alone are not sufficient. More decisive are tests in which stimuli from the continuum must be discriminated.

Several methods of stimulus presentation have been used in speech-sound discrimination tests (Macmillan et al., 1977), for example, the *ABX* or a similar oddity design with normal training (e.g., Cutting & Rosner, 1974; Liberman et al., 1957; Mattingly et al., 1971; Miyawaki et al., 1975; Pisoni, 1977) or extensive training (Samuel, 1977), or a kind of same–different procedure (*AX*) in which either a pair of stimuli must be judged the same or different (e.g., Carney, Widin, & Viemeister, 1977; Hary & Massaro, 1982; Locke & Kellar, 1973; Miller et al., 1976), or a test stimulus (*X*) embedded in a series of repeating standards (*A*) must be identified as homogeneous or not (see Sinnott et al., 1976). These designs can be varied by randomly or systematically selecting stimuli from the relevant continuum, as well as by giving the listeners feedback about their performance.

A comparison of methods and results shows that the greater the dependence of discrimination on memory (*ABX*, oddity $>$ *AX* $>$ repeating standard), the higher the uncertainty of stimulus presentation; and the shorter the decision time, the greater the likelihood that discrimination will be categorical. In addition, extensive training in discrimination tasks makes CP less probable, whereas information indicating that the stimuli to be discriminated are speech sounds increases the probability of CP. From all this it is evident that CP as defined at the beginning of the chapter cannot be unambiguously assumed from discrimination tests alone. Figure 10.1 (C & D) shows two sets of hypothetical discrimination functions that demonstrate continua from very sharp to relatively continuous transitions, from a maximum to a chance level of discrimination. Which kind of discrimination function should be taken as sufficient evidence for inferring CP again depends on the interpretation of the experimenter. It is clear that CP will often depend on the interpretation of statistical significance levels. And, even more embarrassing, some authors reported *continuous* perception with practically the same stimuli for which others found CP when they applied different conditions of experience, training, and stimulus presentation (Carney et al., 1977; Cutting, 1982; Hary & Massaro, 1982; Miyawaki et al., 1975; Pisoni & Lazarus, 1974; Rosen & Howell, 1981). One can therefore ask: Is CP a useful concept at all? As I will show later in the chapter, CP can indeed be a useful working hypothesis for designing experiments and a helpful concept for critically interpreting the results.

Testing human subjects is of course relatively simple compared with testing animals, because direct communication is possible. With animals, in addition to the foregoing problems, which they share with human studies, we face additional difficulties: We must transform our questions so that animals can "understand" them and can respond in a meaningful way, and we must control their behavior and performance in order to obtain comprehensible results. Three basically different methods have been used:

1. *Operant conditioning.* This method has been applied in most tests of animal perception of human speech where speech sounds had either to be labeled (chinchilla: Kuhl & Miller, 1975, 1978; rhesus monkey: Waters & Wilson, 1976) or discriminated (blackbirds and pigeons: Hienz, Sachs, & Sinnott, 1981; chinchilla: Burdick & Miller, 1975; Kuhl, 1981; cat: Dewson, 1964; Warfield, Ruben, & Glackin, 1966; old-world monkeys: Sinnott et al., 1976; Waters & Wilson, 1976). The animals must learn to respond differently to different training stimuli and then to label or discriminate new stimuli by using one or the other learned response. This procedure can be expected to produce discrimination close to absolute difference thresholds. It is doubtful, however, whether such discrimination ability is actually used under natural conditions and in more normal behavioral contexts.
2. *Habituation and dishabituation of an unconditioned response.* Morse and Snowdon (1975) used a heart-rate orienting response to test speech discrimination by rhesus monkeys. With the same response, Miller and Morse (1976) demonstrated CP in young human infants. In these tests the performance of the listener is less controlled and factors like arousal, attention, and overall habituation to the test situation may influence the results. The whole situation can be designed to be more similar to natural conditions, however, so that the results of such tests can yield a better impression of the abilities actually used in normal behavioral contexts.
3. *Natural behavioral responses to species-specific calls.* CP in the strict sense has been tested with female green treefrogs (Gerhardt, 1978a,b) and female house mice (Ehret & Haack, 1981, 1982). These studies and others, which tested labeling of natural and synthesized calls in various animals, will be discussed in detail in section 3. Provided that the response to the test stimulus is an obvious and easily measured behavior that can repeatedly be elicited, this is the method of choice for testing CP. In a socially and ecologically relevant situation CP can show its full significance by structuring the acoustic world and making sound recognition easier. Thus, natural behavioral responses to sound might bias CP tests to yield categorization of stimuli that would have been well discriminated if conditioning procedures had been used (Snowdon, 1979, and Chapter 11, this volume).

Facts from animals

Evidence for categorical perception of species-specific sounds

Insects. To my knowledge there are no studies directly devoted to CP in insects. However, crickets, for example, are known to be highly vocal, at least during their breeding seasons and to show selective phonotaxis to certain calls of the species-specific repertoire (e.g., Elsner & Popov, 1978; Huber, 1977). Calling songs of males that are able to attract conspecific females over considerable distances are of special interest. The males produce sound elements called syllables, which are sequentially arranged forming a chirp, and chirps are repeated forming a song. These well-structured sequences of sound elements have species-specific characteristics for both the carrier frequency within the syllables and the temporal structure of the song (number of syllables in a chirp, duration of syllables, temporal arrangement of syllables and syllable repetition rate, duration of the whole song). It has been shown (see Pollack & Hoy, 1979, 1981; Popov and Shuvalov, 1977) that among the different characteristics of the song of a certain species, only one or two

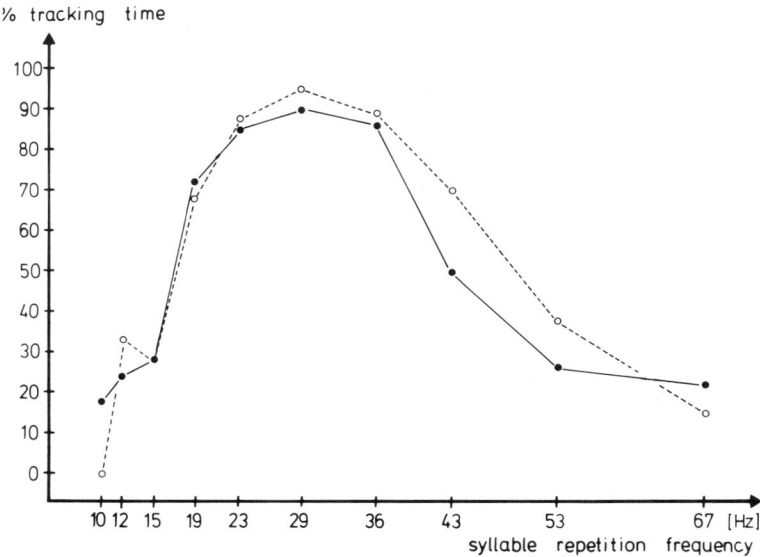

Figure 10.2. Labeling functions of female field-crickets for a conspecific calling song, which varies on a continuum of syllable-repetition frequency. On the ordinate the percent tracking time of a speaker playing the different songs is plotted. The abscissa shows syllable-repetition frequency. Closed symbols are means from 22 animals. Open symbols are from a single animal. (After data of Thorson et al., 1982.)

are really decisive for the song to be recognized and phonotactically responded to by conspecific females. As I outlined in the section on when CP can be expected, this can be a case of CP with two categories: Either the decisive pattern of the mating call is present (category A) or it is absent (category B). Category A would release an orienting response toward the sender, category B, either no response or an orientation away from the sender.

Recently Weber, Thorson, and Huber (1981) and Thorson, Weber, and Huber (1982) conducted the critical experiments from which CP for the calling song of the field cricket (*Gryllus campestris*) can be inferred. For this species the decisive parameter for recognition is the syllable-repetition rate. Thorson et al. (1982) synthesized a continuum of syllable-repetition rates between 10 and 67 Hz and tested the orienting response of the females by measuring their tracking of the speaker on a Kramer treadmill. The result is shown in Figure 10.2, where percent tracking time is plotted against syllable-repetition frequency. Frequencies of 15 Hz and below elicited very little tracking, those of 19 to 36 Hz, intensive tracking, and those of 43 Hz and above, again very little tracking. There are obviously two classes of songs, one that is hardly attractive at all and the other that is highly attractive. The lower boundary is especially sharp and the mean values on both sides of the boundaries (between 15 and 19 Hz and between 36 and 43 Hz) are significantly different from each other ($p < .001$). In addition to these labeling tests, two discrimination tests

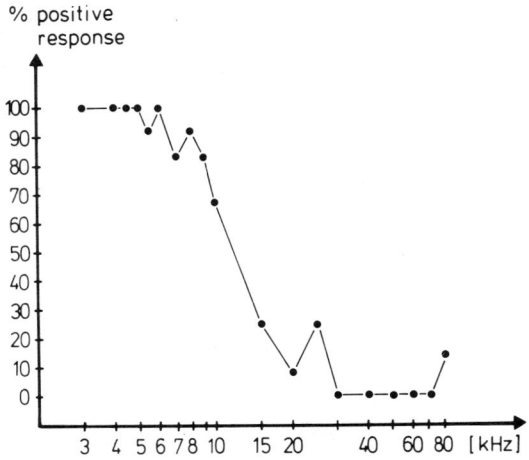

Figure 10.3. Percentages of positive responses (turning toward a speaker) of Australian crickets to models of conspecific calling song varying in carrier frequency (abscissa). The curve represents means of up to 12 animals. (After data of Moiseff et al., 1978.)

were performed (Weber et al., 1981). When a single syllable (no repetition) and a syllable repetition frequency of 50 Hz had to be discriminated from a repetition frequency of 33 Hz, 33 Hz was highly preferred. Unfortunately, no discrimination tests of within-class stimuli are reported, so that CP in the strict sense cannot be assumed. The available evidence, however, suggests that *Gryllus campestris* females perceive the syllable-repetition frequency in the calling song of their males in a manner better described as categorical than as continuous.

Another case that should be mentioned here is the steering response of flying crickets (*Teleogryllus oceanicus*). Moiseff, Pollack, and Hoy (1978) have shown that the crickets orient toward synthetic-tone bursts with carrier frequencies below 10 kHz (positive response to species-specific calling song, which has a carrier frequency between 3 and 6 kHz) and away from bursts with carrier frequencies above 15 kHz (negative response, possibly to avoid echolocating bats). In Figure 10.3 the percent positive response is plotted against carrier frequency. A relatively sharp boundary between 10 and 15 kHz, where the response shifts from more positive to more negative, is evident. The response rates at 10 and 15 kHz are significantly different from each other ($p < .05$). Can such a labeling function be taken as evidence for CP? On the one hand, there is a transition from 100% positive to 0% positive response; on the other hand, however, several points measured within the transition zone indicate that the boundary is a relative one. Because no discrimination tests were done, the question remains open. Accepting CP as a working hypothesis, discrimination tests could now be efficiently planned.

These two examples demonstrate that CP of species-specific sounds cannot be excluded at the evolutionary level of insects.

Anurans. Like crickets, frogs and toads use sound signals for communicating in various behavioral contexts. The most prominent sounds are the mating calls of

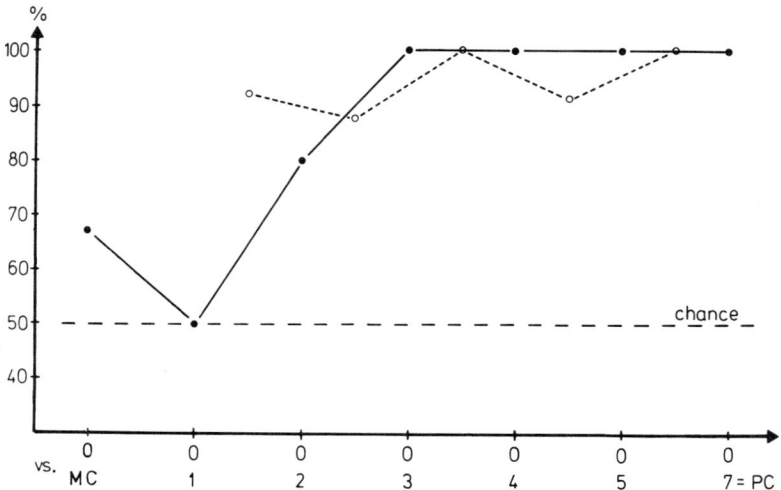

Figure 10.4. Labeling (closed symbols) and discrimination (open symbols) functions for calls lying on a continuum between a natural mating call and a pulsed call (PC, with seven pulses) of the green treefrog. The number of pulses in the synthesized calls increases from one to seven. All calls were labeled against a synthesized standard (unmodulated mating call, 0). The discrimination function is related to the discrimination of neighboring stimuli. The percentage of responses to one of the two alternatives (in each test) is plotted on the ordinate. (After data of Gerhardt, 1978a,b.)

males, which attract females during the breeding season. The females discriminate the species-specific mating call from that of other species and on that basis direct their choice toward conspecific mates, so that mating calls represent a significant species-isolation mechanism (see Blair, 1964; Gerhardt, 1982; Littlejohn, 1977). Most important for discrimination and species recognition are the spectral composition and fine temporal structure of the mating calls (see Gerhardt, 1974, 1978a, 1981). The fact that the females respond to synthetic mating calls having only the critical structural features indicates that they can generalize across the individual variability of the senders and abstract the key-stimulus configuration for recognition. With the concept of CP in mind, we may expect that females divide synthesized calls into two classes: those resembling the natural mating-call structure in the decisive elements (these release phonotaxis), and others differing substantially from it.

There are no studies in which CP of mating calls of different frog or toad species has been tested. Gerhardt (1978b), however, investigated whether females of the green treefrog (*Hyla cinerea*) can discriminate in a categorical way between conspecific mating calls and conspecific pulsed calls. The pulsed calls have the same fine temporal structure as mating calls and similar total duration, but they differ in their pulsatile structure. Although mating calls may begin with a single pulse, they are continuous thereafter, whereas pulsed calls are more than 75% amplitude modulated throughout, so they appear to be composed of seven pulses. Figure 10.4 presents a labeling and a discrimination function for the continuum between a natural mating call (MC), a synthesized unmodulated call (0), and calls with one,

Categorical perception of sound signals in animals

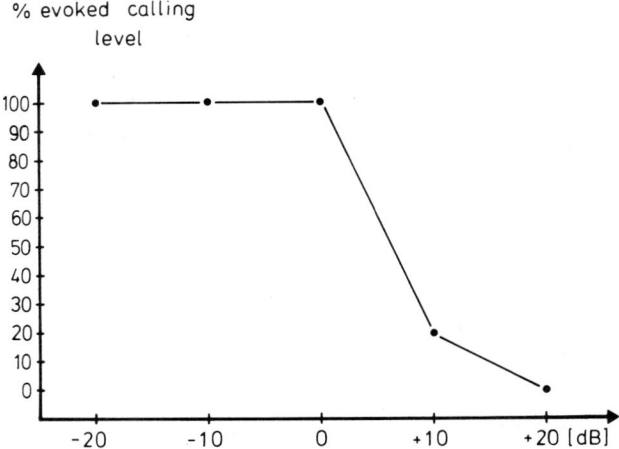

Figure 10.5. Percentage of evoked calling responses of male bullfrogs to models of conspecific mating calls into which an additional frequency component of 500 Hz is introduced. The abscissa shows the relative sound-pressure level of the 500-Hz component compared with the decisive 200 Hz component of the call. (After data of Capranica, 1966.)

two, three, four, five, and seven bursts, the seven-burst call representing the pulsed call (PC). Here labeling was not performed on an absolute basis as in speech-phoneme perception, but by means of a comparison with a fixed standard (the call 0). The labeling function can be interpreted as implying a boundary near calls with two pulses. Calls with two and more pulses are labeled as different from the unmodulated standard; the call with one pulse and the natural call are labeled the same. There is no boundary in the discrimination function, however, where calls with one pulse are discriminated against those with two, calls with two pulses are discriminated against those with three, and so on. Thus calls labeled the same in comparison with the standard are well discriminated, and therefore we have to conclude that the acoustic continuum between the mating call and the pulsed call is perceived rather more continuously than categorically. One reason for this finding may be that, when presented alone, pulsed calls can also attract females, albeit less strongly than mating calls (Gerhardt, 1978b). Thus both calls seem to elicit the same behavior (phonotaxis) on a graded scale of motivation, which inherently excludes CP.

Capranica (1966) tested synthetic mating calls of male bullfrogs (*Rana catesbeiana*) for their ability to evoke calling in other males. Evoked calling responses are important to initiate and maintain choruses of calling frogs. The mating call of adult bullfrogs has two spectral peaks, one near 200 Hz, the other near 1400 Hz. Both peaks, with similar amplitudes (or the higher-frequency peak with somewhat lower amplitude) are decisive for evoking a 100% calling response. If a third frequency is introduced near 500 Hz the evoked calling response is suppressed, depending on the amplitude at 500 Hz relative to that at 200 Hz. Figure 10.5 shows the evoked calling level at different relative amplitudes of the 500-Hz tone. The curve is equivalent to a labeling function and reveals a rather sharp boundary between 0-dB and +10-dB amplitudes, which separates 100% evoked calling from a very low level of evoked calling. Although one may infer a case of CP here, the question of whether male adult bullfrogs discriminate between mating calls from adults and subadults (small bullfrogs have a dominant frequency peak near 500 Hz) categorically remains open as no discrimination tests have yet been performed.

The two studies mentioned are related to labeling and discrimination of intraspecific call types, and CP could not be demonstrated. I can suggest, however, that CP would be a helpful means whereby females could reach a rapid and reliable decision on whether to approach conspecific males emitting mating calls in the presence of calling males from other species.

Birds. Categorical perception in the strict sense has not been tested in a bird species. There are numerous studies on call or song repertoires, specific behavioral responses to songs or parts of them, and on species and individual recognition based on distinct song or call elements; however, no attempt has been made to investigate whether the call elements decisive for recognition are perceived categorically. I have located two studies in which systematic variation of a single-sound parameter along the continuum showed effects on the kind of perception.

Beletsky, Chao, and Smith (1980) investigated song-based species recognition in red-winged blackbirds (*Agelaius phoeniceus*). They found that one part of the advertisement song, the trill, and especially trill duration, was decisive for species recognition. The response used to measure recognition was aggressive behavior of a territorial male to playbacks of natural and altered song under natural conditions. The aggressive behavior was scored on a hybrid scale, and a mean score of the aggressive tendency elicited by a certain song component was obtained. Figure 10.6 shows mean scores of aggressive tendencies plotted against the duration of the trill component (up to 700 msec) or of the whole three-syllable song (1200 msec). It is evident that the whole song and single-trill components of 350- and 700-msec duration release the full aggressive behavior whereas trills of 90- and 175-msec duration do not. The labeling function shown demonstrates a boundary between 175 and 350 msec where the behavior changes from very little to full aggression. Stimuli within the transition region have not been tested and this region seems rather wide to be taken as evidence for CP. In addition, discrimination tests are lacking, so that categorization of the trill duration continuum cannot be assumed.

Another case has been reported by Gottlieb (1980, 1982), who investigated the imprinting of mallard-duck embryos by embryonic contact-contentment calls. Such imprinting allows the ducklings to respond later with the species-specific preference for the maternal call. The contact-contentment call has a repetition rate of 4 notes per sec; the maternal call normally has a rate of 3.7 notes per sec. When the repetition rate of the contact-contentment call is artificially changed to either 2.1 or 5.8 notes per sec, it loses its imprinting capacity and the ducklings thus stimulated

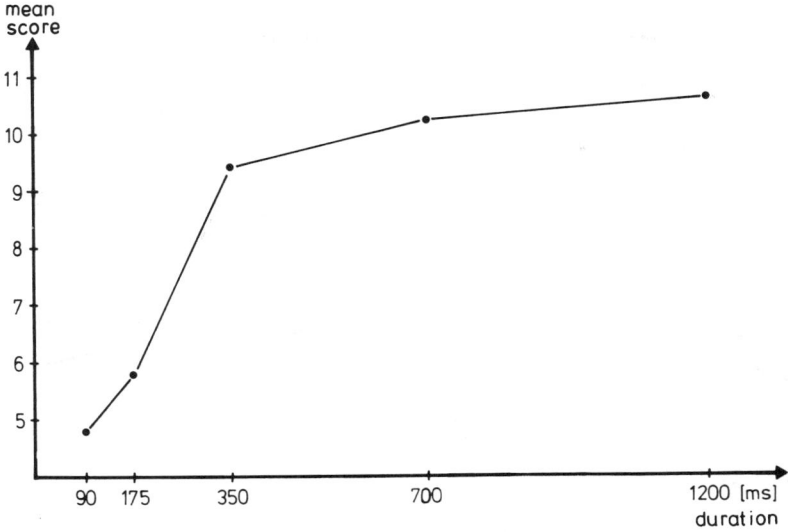

Figure 10.6. Labeling functions for a continuum of trill durations of the advertisement song of the red-winged blackbird. The ordinate presents a mean score of aggressive responses to the different stimuli. (After data of Beletsky et al., 1980.)

do not react to the maternal call. There seem to be only two alternatives separated by rather sharp boundaries: (a) being imprinted with calls of nearly 4 notes per sec, which leads to responses to maternal calls; or (b) exposure to repetition rates lower or higher than 4 notes per sec, which makes the natural response impossible. The sharp boundary suggests that the decision as to whether or not a call is accepted as an adequate imprinting stimulus may involve forming categories. Because too few labeling tests have been conducted and discrimination tests are lacking, we cannot yet decide whether the imprinting stimulus is in fact perceived categorically.

In conclusion, studies with birds are too few and inconclusive to demonstrate a clear case of CP. Imprinting by acoustic stimuli might be categorical because imprinting itself seems to be an either/or process with a very small transition zone, as well as a process that makes distinctions neither within the class of stimuli effective in normal imprinting nor within the class of nonimprinting stimuli.

Mammals. Only three mammalian species have been tested for whether they categorize species-specific calls: house mice (*Mus musculus*), pygmy marmosets (*Cebuella pygmaea*), and Goeldi's monkeys (*Callimico goeldi*).

House mouse. The perception of ultrasound vocalizations from mouse pups by their mothers has been shown to be categorical (Ehret & Haack 1981, 1982). To my knowledge, this is the first and, until now, the only demonstration of CP in the strict sense of a call from a species repertoire. Ultrasonic calls resemble pure tones

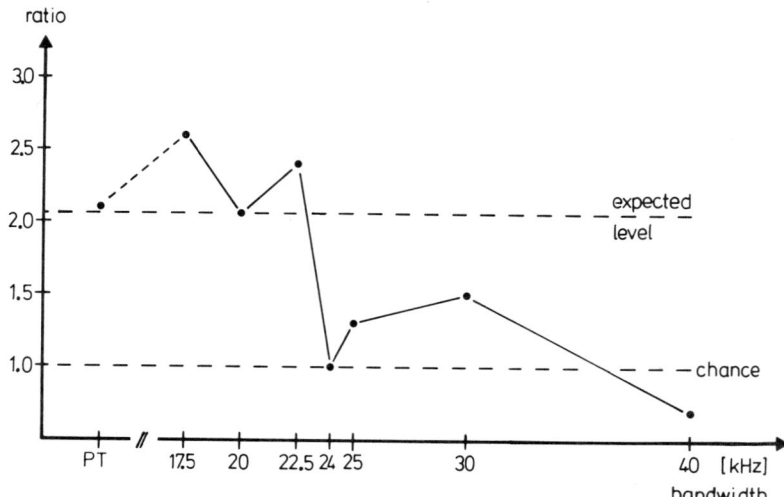

Figure 10.7. Labeling functions for a continuum of noise bandwidths (synthesized models of ultrasonic calls of mouse pups) centered at 50-kHz. PT is a pure tone of 60-kHz. All bandwidths were labeled against a standard comparison stimulus of 20-kHz tone bursts. The ordinate shows the ratio of responses to the ultrasound models and the 20-kHz tone bursts. The expected level was obtained from tests of playbacks of natural ultrasounds versus 20-kHz tone bursts. (Data from Ehret & Haack, 1981, 1982.)

with frequency sweeps and intensity variations in the frequency range between about 40 and 90 kHz (Sales & Smith, 1978). The duration can vary between about 20 and 120 msec. These calls are very variable in their parameters and there is no evidence for either individual-specific call structures or for individual recognition by sound. The calls are readily produced by pups (less than 10 days old) in situations of distress (such as becoming cold, being displaced from the nest or from littermates, or being handled; review in Smith & Sales, 1980; Haack, Markl, & Ehret, 1983). Ultrasounds reliably release maternal behavior in the mothers; sounds originating outside the nest elicit maternal-searching behavior and retrieval of the lost pup to the nest. This kind of maternal behavior in response to pup ultrasound does not seem to habituate (Zippelius & Schleidt, 1956).

We modeled the natural ultrasounds by using constant-frequency pure tones and band-passed white noise centered around 50 kHz with sharp cutoffs (96 dB/octave) at different frequencies. Then we tested the synthetic ultrasounds for their ability to release and guide maternal pup-searching behavior in the direction of the sound source. Labeling and discrimination tests were conducted in a two-alternative choice situation in which the females had to decide whether to move from a central nest area in one or the other direction (speaker) within 10 minutes of stimulus onset. The different sound signals were played alternately from the speakers until the females made a response. Tests were carried out in almost total darkness. Before the tests a female with her litter was allowed at least 6 hours to accept the running board

Categorical perception of sound signals in animals 315

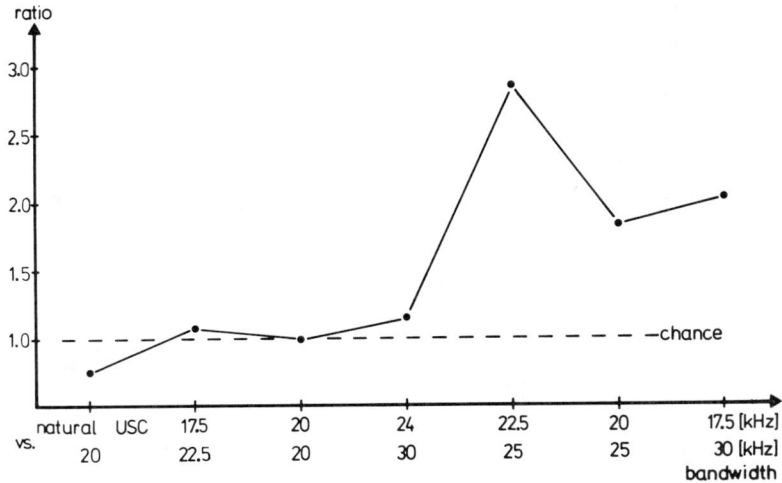

Figure 10.8. Discrimination function for ultrasound models labeled in Figure 10.7. The abscissa shows the stimuli in the discrimination tests; the ratio of responses is plotted on the ordinate. The cross-boundary discriminations (22.5 vs. 25, 20 vs. 25, 17.5 vs. 30 kHz bandwidths) are all significantly above chance level. (Data from Ehret & Haack, 1981, 1982.)

as her home range. Because we used a natural behavior, training was avoided and thus we were able to test the ability to label and discriminate ultrasound models under conditions approaching natural undisturbed ones.

Labeling was performed as in Gerhardt's (1978b) frog study by comparing responses to the test stimuli with those to a fixed standard (20-kHz tone bursts), which is not recognized as a preferred stimulus for releasing pup-searching behavior. We tested this beforehand by presenting the choice between playbacks of natural ultrasounds and 20-kHz tone bursts. The ratio of runs toward the natural ultrasound and toward the 20-kHz tone bursts could then serve as the expected level of preference that has to be reached or crossed if synthesized ultrasound models are adequate releasers. Otherwise, if the ultrasound models are not accepted as adequate releasers, a near chance level can be expected. Figure 10.7 shows the labeling function. The ratio of preference for the ultrasound models over the 20-kHz tone bursts is plotted against the frequency bandwidth of the models. A sharp boundary between 22.5- and 24-kHz bandwidth is evident. Ultrasound models with bandwidths smaller than 23 kHz are significantly preferred compared with the 20-kHz tones, whereas those with bandwidths broader than 23 kHz are not. This classification into preferred and nonpreferred ultrasound models was tested for categorization in discrimination tests, where stimuli across the boundary between the two classes and within each class were tested against each other. Figure 10.8 shows the ratios obtained when the stimulus pairs indicated on the abscissa are compared. Clearly, stimuli drawn from within a class are not discriminated, and stimuli from different

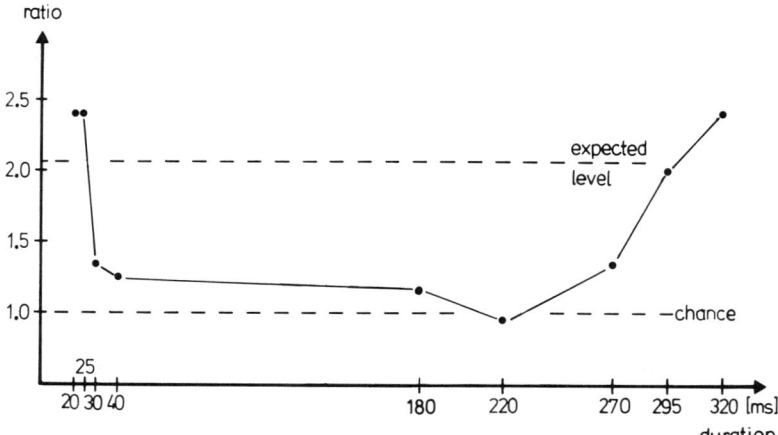

Figure 10.9. Labeling functions for a duration continuum of ultrasound models (rise-and-fall times included). The ratio of responses to a standard (100-msec duration, rise-and-fall times included) versus a test stimulus is indicated on the ordinate. The expected level is related to the test of natural ultrasounds versus 20-kHz tone bursts. (Data from Ehret & Haack, 1982.)

classes are well discriminated. The largest ratio (best discrimination) occurred for the two stimuli closest to the boundary.

When we take labeling and discrimination tests together, clear evidence for CP in the strict sense is obtained for the mouse. The boundary divided a continuum of energy bandwidths in the high ultrasonic range into two categories, one representing preferred ultrasound models, which can release pup-searching and retrieving behavior just as natural ultrasounds do, and another representing nonpreferred ultrasound models; these are able to increase the arousal level of the females (Ehret & Haack, 1984), but are significantly less attractive than the preferred ultrasound models in the choice situation.

In addition to the tests in the bandwidth dimension of natural ultrasounds, we obtained labeling functions for the duration continuum (Ehret & Haack, 1982). Labeling was done as before but the comparison stimulus (fixed standard) was a preferred ultrasound model (60-kHz tone bursts of 80 msec duration and 10 msec rise-and-fall times). The test stimuli were also 60-kHz tone bursts the duration of which (rise-and-fall times included) ranged from 20 to 320 msec. The labeling function is shown in Figure 10.9, where the ratios of standard against test stimulus are plotted against the durations of the test stimuli. A very sharp boundary is evident between 25 and 30 msec duration and a somewhat less sharp one between 270 and 295 msec. The boundary at the short durations clearly suggests CP of a duration continuum in addition to that of the bandwidth continuum; however, because we did not test for discrimination in this case, the question of whether the duration continuum is perceived categorically in the strict sense is still open.

In our tests we used a natural behavior of unrestrained mice under seminatural conditions; we could thus study how short-term motivation of the females might have influenced their decision as to which stimulus alternative to approach. We found that the preresponse behavior (the behavior in the nest immediately preceding the approaching response to one of the speakers) influences the perception (or recognition) process (Ehret & Haack, 1984). If the females were already occupied with a kind of maternal behavior (e.g., licking, warming, or nursing the pups in the nest) and thus had to switch only to another kind of maternal behavior (searching and retrieving pups) after stimulus onset, they discriminated the two categories significantly ($p < .005$) better than if they were involved in a nonmaterial behavior in the nest (e.g., orientation, self-directed behavior). The discrimination ratio after maternal activities was 2.8; after nonmaternal ones, only 1.7. The 1.7 ratio, however, is still significantly above chance, so that the categories and the sharpness of the boundary between them remained present in any case; only the distance between the category levels depended on the preresponse behavior (a short-term motivational tendency). It appears, then, that when a natural behavior under close-to-natural conditions is used in CP tests, short-term motivation of the animals may influence not so much the categorization of the stimuli per se as the accuracy of observable categorization.

Pygmy marmoset. Pygmy marmosets have five types of contact/location calls. These are trills differing in sound parameters like duration, center frequency, and frequency bandwidth (Pola & Snowdon, 1975; Snowdon & Pola, 1978). The closed-mouth trill is the most common one; when emitted, it is generally responded to antiphonally by other animals. The open-mouth trill differs significantly from the closed-mouth trill only in duration and does not elicit antiphonal vocal responses. Snowdon and Pola (1978) tested the responses to trills varying in the duration continuum under seminatural conditions. Their labeling function is shown in Figure 10.10. A sharp boundary between 249 and 257 msec is evident. Stimuli of 249 msec and shorter are labeled as the closed-mouth trill; longer stimuli are responded to only at a low spontaneous level, which is equivalent to responses to the open-mouth trill. The sharp boundary suggests CP. However, because discrimination was not tested, the question of whether pygmy marmosets categorize between closed and open-mouth trills on a duration continuum remains open. Labeling functions were also obtained for continua of center frequency, frequency bandwidth, and modulation frequency, but boundaries between classes suggesting CP were not found.

Goeldi's monkey. Masataka (1983) found five forms of alarm calls in these monkeys that typically elicited either of two response behaviors: freezing or antiphonal calling. In a series of tests with synthetic warning calls he obtained labeling functions that suggest CP for alarm calls on the basis of the frequency range of the calls. Antiphonal calling was released by calls with a frequency range between 1.6 and 2.4 kHz, whereas freezing occurred after calls with a larger frequency range (for further details see Snowdon in Chapter 11, this volume). As discrimination

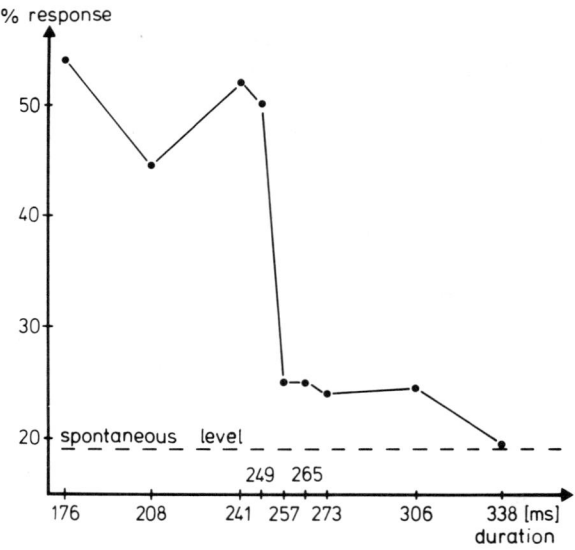

Figure 10.10. Labeling function for a duration continuum of trills of pygmy marmoset monkeys. The ordinate shows the percentage of trills responded to. (Replotted after data from Snowdon & Pola, 1978.)

tests have not been reported, we cannot yet decide whether Goeldi's monkeys perceive their alarm calls categorically in the strict sense.

Recognition of species, individuals, and call types: Cases of categorical perception?

The examples in the preceding section of species-specific sound perception in animals can be classified in terms of species, individual, and call-type recognition. If we consider only the cases in which CP has been demonstrated at least by labeling functions, we find: (a) CP of species-specific sounds (species recognition) in the field crickets and less convincingly in red-winged blackbirds and mallard ducklings; (b) CP of call types in bullfrogs, house mice, pygmy marmosets, and Goeldi's monkeys; (c) no CP of individual-specific sounds (individual recognition). Because one should think of individuals forming separate perceptual classes per se, it is remarkable that until now no case of individual recognition through CP (either in labeling or in discrimination tests) has been reported. Some speculations about possible reasons will be presented below.

Categorization of human speech by animals

Because humans can perceive nonspeech sounds categorically (Cutting & Rosner, 1974; Locke & Kellar, 1973; Mattingly et al., 1971; Miller et al., 1976), one might expect animals to be able to categorize sounds, including human speech, that do not belong to their own repertoires. CP (in the strict sense) of phonemes differing in voice-onset time has been demonstrated for chinchillas (Kuhl, 1981; Kuhl & Miller, 1978) and rhesus monkeys (Waters & Wilson, 1976). Interesting and certainly not predictable is the fact that the boundary on the /ba/-/pa/ continuum of voice-onset time was similar in humans (about 27 msec – see Kuhl & Miller, 1978; Pisoni & Lazarus, 1974), rhesus monkey (31 msec), and chinchilla (23 msec). In addition, the boundary on the /da/-/ta/ continuum of voice-onset time was almost equal in humans and chincilla (humans: 35 msec; chinchilla: 33 msec – see Kuhl & Miller, 1978; and Kuhl's Chapter 12, this volume). It seems that categorizing a voice-onset time continuum between two phonemes is based on very similar perceptual mechanisms in humans and the animals tested. It may be worth remembering that the lower boundary of labeling ultrasounds of mice on the duration continuum (Figure 10.9) was also between 25 and 30 msec, comparable to the boundary on the /ba/-/pa/ continuum. Whether this is more than just coincidence will be discussed in the next section, "Hypotheses, problems, and mechanisms."

Discussion of hypotheses, problems, and mechanisms

Hypotheses concerning the relation between CP and key-stimuli

Calls of a species in an ecological setting can be acoustically distinct from calls of other species (potentially emitted at the same place at the same time) or they can more or less overlap in some or many parameters. Similarly, a sound repertoire can consist of acoustically discrete call types, continuous gradations from one type to another, or some intermediate form between the two extremes. Also, different individuals may produce acoustically discrete calls of a given type and may thus be unambiguously characterized by the way they produce a call, or there can be so much interindividual variability that a call of one type cannot be labeled as having been produced by a particular sender.

One could argue that, if calls are acoustically discrete, a receiver only has to categorize discrete or slightly overlapping signals in order to recognize their "message," whereas calls varying along a continuum should be perceived continuously, with corresponding continuous changes in the perceived "message" (e.g., Maier, 1982). Categorical versus continuous perception as a function of the discreteness or continuity of call repertoires would fit the data from the numerous cases in which the recognition of species, call types, or individuals has been found. CP could be related to the recognition of discrete message elements, whereas continuous perception could be associated with the message of motivation, which is inherently graded and requires recognition of gradations.

Such a system, however, does not fit with the concept of CP derived from speech-perception studies. A test of CP has always been related to the physical continuum of a signal sound parameter, and not to a sound or an animal call as a whole. We can only test CP of one physical dimension of a call after the other, and we may find that one or more are perceived categorically. When we spoke of CP of species-specific calls or of calls from a repertoire of a species, it was implicit that one parameter of the calls was perceived categorically. The knowledge of that parameter may be more helpful for those interested in physiological mechanisms of CP than for others, mainly ethologists, who seek to describe the physical configuration of the whole call that is necessary and sufficient for recognition. CP of one call dimension is certainly part of the recognition process and sets one boundary at which recognition of the message changes through shifts in perception. What we mean by recognition of a stimulus includes more, however. If a stimulus is to be characterized and recognized as a key-stimulus, we must include the knowledge of boundaries in several physical dimensions of the sound within which the parameter values must be located. The key-stimulus concept, with simultaneous and additive perception of multidimensional ranges of a behavior-releasing stimulus, is an ethological one (Lorenz, 1981). It is related to instinctive behavior, releasing mechanisms, and ecology. The goal of key-stimulus identification is to find the (often multidimensional) perceptual space (the stimulus "niche") in the physical domain of a stimulus that is an effective releaser of a certain behavior. Studies of key-stimulus configurations thus involve research on the releasing abilities of stimuli rather than testing systematically the boundaries within which the parameters can vary and still be within an acceptable range. The concept of CP, on the other hand, is initially unidimensional and aims to describe the boundary between two perceptual alternatives on a single continuum. This is rather mechanistic and analytical and the background questions are mostly related to the perceptual mechanism and not, for example, to the adaptedness of an animal to the environment. This is a possible explanation for the rarity of studies of CP in animal calls.

The following approaches to research on CP of animal calls would seem reasonable:

1. Inspect the call repertoire of a species together with behaviorally important sounds. Determine the discreteness between, gradations among, and overlap (along acoustic dimensions) of the acoustic stimuli.
2. Determine whether calls are species-, context- or individual-specific, or whether they reflect motivational levels.
3. Describe natural response patterns to calls of an established specificity.
4. Conduct tests for CP of a sound parameter with a known contribution to the specificity of a call.

The following three existing examples would seem to be promising, as only step (4) is missing:

a. The lower spectral peaks of the mating calls of the sympatric treefrogs (*Hyla cinerea, H. gratiosa, H. squirella*), which are well separated, and the pulse-repetition rates of the mating calls of the sympatric treefrogs *H. versicolor* and *H. chrysoscelis*, which are also separate (Gerhardt, 1982). In the first case, the lower spectral peak, in the second, the pulse repetition rate are the most essential parameters for species recognition. Some labeling tests have already been conducted in

Categorical perception of sound signals in animals   321

   H. cinerea (Gerhardt, 1974), which suggest sharp boundaries around the optimum frequency of 900 Hz.
   b. Brooks and Falls (1975a,b) studied individual recognition in white-throated sparrows (*Zonotricha albicollis*). These birds discriminate in situ the songs of their territorial neighbors from those of strangers. The prominent frequency component of the first and the second note seems to be decisive for the individual recognition of neighbors and for discrimination of strangers. Frequency changes of about 10% and more change a neighbor to a stranger; that is, such a change abolishes the recognition of a learned song pattern. A 10% change of a 3.5-kHz tone (prominent frequency) is relatively small and there might be a boundary between recognition and nonrecognition, which is perceived categorically.
   c. Vervet monkeys (*Cercopithecus aethiops*) produce three acoustically distinct types of predator alarm calls (Seyfarth, Cheney, & Marler, 1980). One is emitted in response to large mammalian carnivores, the other to eagles, and the third to snakes. Eagle and snake calls consist of a series of short noise bursts and differ mainly in the repetition frequency of the bursts and their bandwidth. Because the animals respond differently to eagle and snake alarms, the two sound parameters mentioned could be tested for categorization through the use of synthesized playbacks under natural conditions.

Notice that quite a lot of information about the calls and the response pattern must be known before it is advisable to plan an investigation of CP. At the level of step 4 we are able to use the CP design to investigate systematically one or the other acoustical dimension of the key-stimulus configuration. Whether we actually find CP is less important than the analytical starting position and the rules introduced to analyze the key-stimulus. We may find the CP design helpful for separating parameters that express motivational levels (continuous perception expected) from others that are related to discrete elements of meaning (categorical perception expected). The CP design can thus contribute to a better understanding of coding principles and the relations among the coding of the sound structure, the message of a call, and the context in which the sound occurs.

Some authors who have investigated the recognition of species (e.g., Emlen, 1972) and individuals (e.g., Beer, 1970; Berger & Ligon, 1977; Espmark, 1975; Hutchison, Stevenson, & Thorpe, 1968) report that recognition is based on a specified combination of several sound parameters that together form the configuration of the releaser of a response behavior. In cases where recognition seems to be based neither on a single parameter nor even on a few, CP along any single dimension would appear unlikely. This may be the reason why CP of individual-specific sounds has not yet been demonstrated. If many individuals in a group have to be recognized, one or a few parameters (within the boundaries of a call type) may not be sufficient for giving different labels to all members of the group.

Problems with learning, motivation, and selective attention

As outlined in the section on questions and methods, learning plays a role in the outcome of CP tests. Under natural conditions learning can take place only if both the physical structure of the stimuli from a pool of variability and the behavioral context of call emission remain constant during the time necessary for learning. CP of individual-specific calls would be restricted to cases where the learning of call parameters is possible. Such learning has not yet been demonstrated for insects and frogs; we may therefore expect CP in these animals only for species and call-type recognition by innate mechanisms. In addition, CP in birds and mammals during ontogenetic development does not seem very probable unless the physical structure of a call remains constant in the critical dimensions. It might therefore be predicted that, if individuals are recognized by their sounds, infants will categorize the calls of their parents, but parents will perceive their infants' calls continuously during the period of call-structure development. The exception would be CP after imprinting, where a short-term exposure to a certain sound stimulus is sufficient for permanent recognition.

Short-term motivational tendencies in unconditioned and unrestrained mice have been shown to influence the decision about how to categorize a species-specific call (Ehret & Haack, 1984). When the behavior of the mice before a test belonged to the same class as the behavior in response to the test stimuli, then categorization was found to become sharper than when pretest and response behavior belonged to different behavioral classes (e.g., maternal behavior, orientation, self-directed behavior). A shift from one behavioral class to another apparently introduces interference with stimulus perception, so that the stimuli may be less clearly perceived and the category levels in discrimination functions may be less discrete.

The observation that motivational shifts can influence the separation of category levels, but not CP or the boundary itself, suggests that higher-order processes in the central nervous system are involved in the perception (recognition) mechanism. It also seems clear that the perceptual boundary is independent of motivational influences, suggesting that it is set at a different, probably more peripheral level, before the decision to respond to one or the other stimulus (in a discrimination test) is made. Motivational influences on CP could thus provide some hints about two separate processes in CP, one responsible for setting the boundary at a certain place on a continuum of a sound parameter, the other for recognizing the "labels" on each side of the boundary and for ordering the stimuli.

Selective attention has been shown to influence the perception of tonal patterns and especially knowledge and experience concerning the pattern to which attention has to be directed (Spiegel & Watson, 1981). It has also been suggested that, for example, the peak of a discrimination function of voice-onset time (in speech-phoneme perception) might be the result of an overlearned attentional focus to the specific region of the boundary occurring in labeling tests. It seems that learning which difference to perceive as different automatically directs the attention to such differences; these are then discriminated (cross-boundary discrimination), while others of the same magnitude receiving no attention are not discriminated (within-boundary non-discrimination). If the listeners are extensively trained to treat all differences equally, however, they can voluntarily pay the same attention to all differences and discriminate on a basis close to absolute-difference thresholds. CP disappears under such conditions (Samuel, 1977). Thus, selective attention appears to be a very critical factor in CP tests of speech phonemes.

There is evidence from Japanese macaques (*Macaca fuscata*) that selective attention plays a considerable role in the perception of animal calls as well (Beecher, Petersen, Zoloth, Moody, & Stebbins, 1979; Zoloth et al., 1979; see also Marler, 1982). Japanese macaques show selective attention to a communication-relevant parameter of a conspecific call (the "coo"). Coo-calls can have more small up-down frequency shifts in the first or second half of the call. These early or late frequency peaks require very little training to be very well discriminated by *M. fuscata*, but they require extensive training to be discriminated by related species (*M. nemestrina* and *M. radiata*). Either by learning or innate bias *M. fuscata* monkeys recognize the position of the frequency peak as most important when listening to a coo-call and pay selective attention to that feature. The other two species have had no such experience or no innate bias and discriminate pitch differences very well among the coo-calls, which are more general features of sound. The discrimination of pitch differences, however, is hard for *M. fuscata* to learn (when placed in opposition to peak differences), as they are biased to pay more attention to differences in peak position rather than pitch.

From these examples we can conclude that whenever animals categorize a continuum of stimuli that they have learned are important, they might do it by automatically directing their attention to the important features. This may also be true for the perception of human speech. In other cases, however, where learning does not play a role because innate responsiveness is efficient, selective attention may be part of the innate mechanism or seems to be of minor importance. Instead, the overall arousal or alertness level may come into play as a potentially influential factor (compare Ehret & Haack, 1984).

Possible mechanisms of categorical perception

Several possible mechanisms have to be considered in order to explain the different cases of CP that have been discussed. Some are closely connected with the sound parameters that are categorically perceived, others are related to the demonstrable innate and learned categorizations (discussion of further mechanisms based on adaptation level and selective adaptation can be found in Chapter 3 by Repp & Liberman, Chapter 9 by Bornstein, and Chapter 13 by Wilson, this volume).

Selective attention. Selective attention is one factor, as discussed in the preceding section, critically influencing the perception of sound. Selective attention may be even more than that, namely, a descriptive term for an unknown mechanism in those cases in which categorization of certain stimuli has to be learned (e.g., certain phoneme discriminations in human speech, imprinting, individual recognition). If, through experience with human language or with animal calls, phonemes and call elements that differ only in the position of a parameter on a single physical continuum are perceived again and again, it is conceivable that their relative position on the continuum is learned. If only a few alternatives occur, their positions receive specific labels. In a test of CP, new stimuli could be assigned to the existing labels on the basis of proximity to the learned position on the continuum. This may be accomplished by selective attention, with certain learned features suppressing other features of the sounds (or becoming relatively enhanced over other features) thus preventing unlearned features from being included in the discrimination.

This kind of mechanism would imply that CP was tuned to the structural elements of a sound or a call that characterized it, or to physical differences between two sounds (calls). This mechanism of learning to perceive what is important and afterward paying attention only to that is clearly an adaptive strategy, especially for the young animal growing up in a social group. The sounds or calls that are the substrate for learning can originate either from an innate repertoire or from one that is transmitted as a tradition, or from other sources (outside a species), which have proven to be of importance.

Temporal mechanisms. Two temporal parameters have been labeled categorically: (syllable) repetition rate and duration. Two possible neural mechanisms are proposed for categorization of repetition rates:

1. Neurons follow syllable onsets in a medium range of repetition rates. The upper boundary for following may be determined by the failure of a neuron to follow increasing repetition rates due to the restrictions of the refractory period or postexcitatory inhibition, which must decline before the next syllable can regain an excitatory effect. The lower boundary may be set by time constants of temporal summation.
2. Repetition rates of syllables are coupled to internal neural rhythms in order to be recognized by higher-order neurons. This coupling may be possible only within a certain range of repetition rates.

Categorical labeling of call durations could be accomplished in the nervous system by a simple positive feedforward system with tonically active elements. A schematic diagram is shown in Figure 10.11. An excitatory input into the system (sound onset) is passed through channel A and with a time delay (Δt) through channel B in a summation device, which produces an output only if both channels A and B are active. If the sound duration is shorter than Δt, the system produces no output; if the sound duration is longer than Δt, an output occurs. A number (n) of boundaries could easily be placed on a duration continuum by a serial coupling of n such circuits each with a different Δt with $\Delta t_1 < \Delta t_2 < \Delta t_3 \ldots < \Delta t_n$.

Such a model would be even more attractive if the time constants could be modified by learning and selective attention because it could be used for categorization on all duration continua, including voice-onset time. A special processor of differences in voice-onset time of speech phonemes would therefore not be necessary. There could exist a minimum Δt in the proposed circuit, which fixes one boundary at a relatively short duration. We have seen that the shortest boundary for voice-onset time perception was near 25 msec in man, monkey, and chinchilla. A

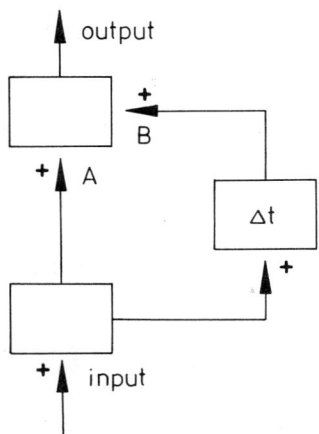

Figure 10.11. Diagram of a positive feedforward delay circuit with which stimulus durations could be categorically labeled and discriminated (see text for further explanation).

boundary was found at the same duration in the perception of ultrasounds by house mice. There is also a boundary (threshold) for the perception of temporal order near 20 msec (Hirsh, 1959). It seems that in tasks in which duration plays a decisive role for CP, the minimum time constant in the perception process is about 20 msec. According to the model in Figure 10.11, the minimum possible delay Δt would then be about 20 msec.

Spectral mechanisms. The examples presented in the section on facts from animals included categorical labeling of carrier frequency, energy peaks in a spectrum, and frequency bandwidths (which were also categorically discriminated). Because only one mechanism, the critical band, is known to be inherent in the auditory systems of all animals tested so far, from crickets to frogs, mammals, and man (e.g., Ehret, 1977; Ehret & Gerhardt, 1980; Ehret, Moffat, & Tautz, 1982; Scharf, 1970; Zwicker & Feldtkeller, 1967), and to be directly related to CP, it will be given special attention here. Critical bands (frequency bandwidths within which sound energy is summed and processed as a whole) are basic units of sound perception; sound energy within a critical band is perceived differently from that outside the band. The perceived sound quality of a broad-band spectrum changes with changes of the amount of sound energy falling in any of the array of critical bands that can be formed in the frequency range of hearing. These properties of critical bands make them ideal candidates for a CP of frequency bandwidths. We can predict that as long as the sound bandwidths are within the boundaries of a critical band, they are treated as one perceptual category, and if the boundaries of a critical band are crossed, the sound would belong to a different perceptual category.

Ehret and Haack (1982) have shown that critical bands explain the CP of ultrasounds in mice. The mean critical bandwidth of the mouse at a center frequency of 50 kHz has been found to be 22 kHz (Ehret, 1976). As Figure 10.7 demonstrates, a bandwidth of 22.5 kHz belongs to one category and 24 kHz to another. Critical

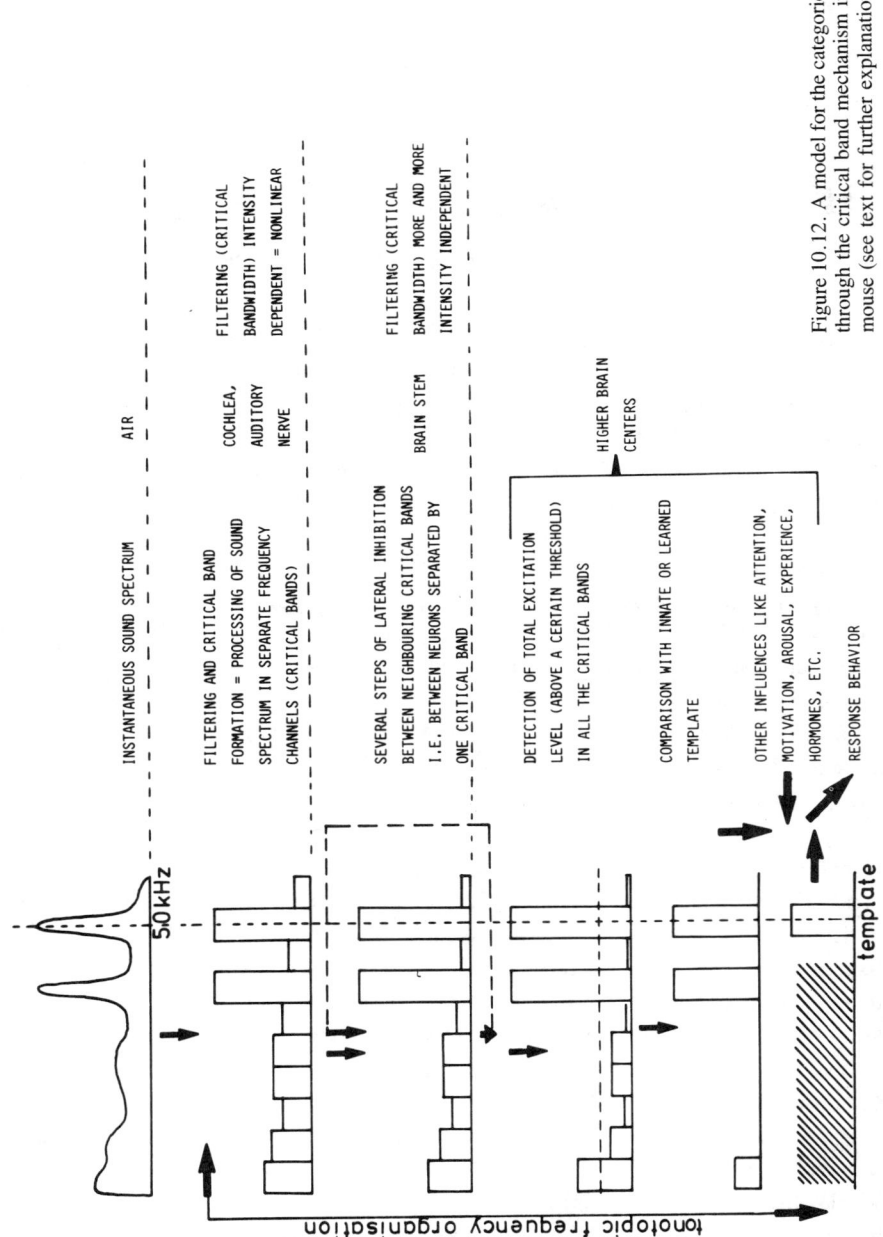

Figure 10.12. A model for the categorical perception of ultrasounds through the critical band mechanism in the auditory system of the mouse (see text for further explanation). (From Ehret, 1983.)

bands applied to CP in this case means that a 22.5-kHz bandwidth of a stimulus just fits into a single critical band at 50-kHz center frequency, while a 24-kHz stimulus and those of broader bandwidths do not. It is evident that the critical bandwidth of hearing is practically identical with the boundary bandwidth of categorization. We can conclude that ultrasound is responded to as a key-stimulus for eliciting maternal behavior if the sound spectrum does not exceed the bandwidth limits of a single critical band of hearing. We have also found that energy peaks in a sound spectrum containing mouse-pup ultrasound should be separated by at least one critical band, so that the ultrasound can be recognized as a key-stimulus.

Ehret (1983) has offered a model of critical-band processing and recognition of ultrasound in the auditory system of the mouse. This model is shown in Figure 10.12. It is based on the psychophysics of critical bands (e.g., Ehret, 1976; Scharf, 1970), the data of ultrasound perception by the mouse (Ehret & Haack, 1982), and data about the physiology of critical bands at the level of single neurons in the auditory pathway of the mouse (Ehret & Moffat, 1984; Ehret & Merzenich, 1985). The instantaneous sound spectrum shown has two energy peaks, one at 50 kHz mimicking mouse-pup ultrasound, and another at 25 kHz, which represents a disturbance from the environment, and some energy at lower frequencies. The sound spectrum is divided in the cochlea of the inner ear into tonotopically arranged frequency channels (auditory-nerve fibers). One column represents the total excitatory output of a number of neurons that respond to frequencies within one critical band. The psychophysical critical bandwidth is defined at a higher brain level as the frequency band over which excitation of many units is integrated. Several steps of lateral inhibition between neighboring critical bands are effective in rejecting noise during the processing of the input spectrum. After the excitation level within the array of the critical bands has been detected, the excitation pattern (excitation at 50 kHz, 25 kHz, and at the lower frequency end of hearing) is compared with an innate (or learned) template. The template pattern we found (Ehret & Haack, 1982) is energy (excitation) in a critical band in the ultrasonic range (e.g., around 50 kHz) and significantly less energy in neighboring critical bands, whereas energy in the lower frequency range (more than one critical band off the decisive one) is irrelevant for the perception and recognition of the key-stimulus.

The model demonstrates how boundaries for categorization in the frequency domain can be set. The influence of factors like short-term motivation on the actual release of response patterns is included in the model after boundary formation at the level of the comparison with the template.

Conclusions

The evidence from animals summarized in this chapter clearly indicates that categorical perception is neither restricted to human-speech perception nor to special perceptual abilities of man. CP can be seen as part of the problem of multidimensional key-stimulus recognition, which is reduced in CP to the recognition of only one stimulus dimension. The concept of CP (including the methods of testing and the experimental design) is useful for the systematic investigation of the different parameters of key-stimulus configurations. Parameters reflecting motivational levels can be separated from those encoding discrete elements of "meaning." CP is helpful for bringing structure and contrast into the acoustic world of communication signals; it reduces the effect of disturbing noise during the perception process and ensures recognition of sounds of importance. Predictions have been made about animal sounds most suitable for CP tests. Categorical perception is not bound to a single mechanism. Different mechanisms related to learned and innate categorizations and to categorization of different sound parameters have been proposed. One of these mechanisms, selective attention, seems to be of special importance when learned signals are to be categorized.

References

Beecher, M. D., Petersen, M. R., Zoloth, S. R., Moody, D. B., & Stebbins, W. C. (1979). Perception of conspecific vocalizations by Japanese macaques. Evidence for selective attention and neural lateralization. *Brain Behavior and Evolution, 16*, 443–460.

Beer, C. G. (1970). Individual recognition of voice in the social behavior of birds. *Advances in the Study of Behavior, 3*, 27–74.

Beletsky, L. D., Chao, S., & Smith, D. G. (1980). An investigation of sound-based species recognition in the red-winged blackbird (*Agelaius phoeniceus*). *Behavior, 73*, 189–203.

Berger, L. R., & Ligon, D. (1977). Vocal communication and individual recognition in the pinon jay, *Gymnorhinus cyanocephalus*. *Animal Behaviour, 25*, 567–584.

Blair, W. F. (1964). Isolation mechanisms and interspecies interactions in anuran amphibians. *Quarterly Review of Biology, 39*, 333–344.

Brooks, R. J., & Falls, J. B. (1975a). Individual recognition by song in white-throated sparrows. I. Discrimination of songs of neighbors and strangers. *Canadian Journal of Zoology, 53*, 879–888.

Brooks, R. J., & Falls, J. B. (1975b). Individual recognition by song in white-throated sparrows. III. Song features used in individual recognition. *Canadian Journal of Zoology, 53*, 1749–1761.

Burdick, C. K., & Miller, J. D. (1975). Speech perception by the chinchilla: Discrimination of sustained /a/ and /i/. *Journal of the Acoustical Society of America, 58*, 415–427.

Capranica, R. R. (1966). Vocal response of the bullfrog to natural and synthetic mating calls. *Journal of the Acoustical Society of America, 40*, 1131–1139.

Carney, A. E., Widin, G. P., & Viemeister, N. F. (1977). Noncategorical perception of stop consonants differing in VOT. *Journal of the Acoustical Society of America, 62*, 961–970.

Cutting, J. E. (1982). Plucks and bows are categorically perceived, sometimes. *Perception and Psychophysics, 31*, 462–476.

Cutting, J. E., & Rosner, B. (1974). Categories and boundaries in speech and music. *Perception and Psychophysics, 16*, 546–570.

Dewson, J. H. (1964). Speech sound discrimination by cats. *Science, 144*, 555–556.

Ehret, G. (1976). Critical bands and filter characteristics in the ear of the house mouse (*Mus musculus*). *Biological Cybernetics, 24*, 35–42.

Ehret, G. (1977). Comparative psychoacoustics: Perspectives of peripheral sound analysis in mammals. *Naturwissenschaften, 64*, 461–470.

Ehret, G. (1983). Auditory processing and perception of ultrasound in house mice. In J.-P. Ewert, R. R. Capranica, & D. J. Ingle (Eds.), *Advances in vertebrate neuroethology* (pp. 911–918). London: Plenum Press.

Ehret, G., & Gerhardt, H. C. (1980). Auditory masking and effects of noise on responses of the green treefrog (*Hyla cinerea*) to synthetic mating calls. *Journal of Comparative Physiology, 141*, 13–18.

Ehret, G., & Haack, B. (1981). Categorical perception of mouse pup ultrasounds by lactating females. *Naturwissenschaften, 68,* 208.
Ehret, G., & Haack, B. (1982). Ultrasound recognition in house mice: Key-stimulus configuration and recognition mechanism. *Journal of Comparative Phsyiology, 148,* 245–251.
Ehret, G., & Haack, B. (1984). Motivation and arousal influence sound-induced maternal pup-retrieving behavior in lactating house mice. *Zeitschrift für Tierpsychologie, 65,* 25–39.
Ehret, G., & Merzenich, M. M. (1985). Auditory midbrain responses parallel spectral integration phenomena. *Science, 227,* 1245–1247.
Ehret, G., & Moffat, A. J. M. (1984). Noise masking of tone responses and critical ratios in single units of the mouse cochlear nerve and cochlear nucleus. *Hearing Research, 14,* 45–57.
Ehret, G., Moffat, A. J. M., & Tautz, J. (1982). Behavioral determination of frequency resolution in the ear of the cricket, *Teleogryllus oceanicus*. *Journal of Comparative Physiology, 148,* 237–244.
Eimas, P. D. (1974). Auditory and linguistic processing of cues for place of articulation by infants. *Perception and Psychophysics, 16,* 513–521.
Eimas, P. D., Siqueland, E. R., Jusczyk, P., & Vigorito, J. (1971). Speech perception in infants. *Science, 171,* 303–306.
Elsner, N., & Popov, A. V. (1978). Neuroethology of acoustic communication. *Advances of Insect Physiology, 13,* 229–355.
Emlen, S. T. (1972). An experimental analysis of the parameters of bird song eliciting species recognition. *Behavior, 41,* 130–171.
Espmark, Y. (1975). Individual characteristics in the calls of reindeer calves. *Behaviour, 54,* 50–59.
Gerhardt, H. C. (1974). The significance of some spectral features in mating call recognition in the green treefrog *(Hyla cinerea)*. *Journal of Experimental Biology, 61,* 229–241.
Gerhardt, H. C. (1978a). Mating call recognition in the green treefrog *(Hyla cinerea)*: The significance of some fine-temporal properties. *Journal of Experimental Biology, 74,* 59–73.
Gerhardt, H. C. (1978b). Discrimination of intermediate sounds in a synthetic call continuum by female green treefrogs. *Science, 199,* 1089–1091.
Gerhardt, H. C. (1981). Mating call recognition in the barking treefrog *(Hyla gratiosa)*: Responses to synthetic calls and comparisons with the green treefrog *(Hyla cinerea)*. *Journal of Comparative Physiology, 144,* 17–25.
Gerhardt, H. C. (1982). Sound pattern recognition in some North American treefrogs (Anura: Hylidae): Implications for male choice. *American Zoologist, 22,* 581–595.
Gottlieb, G. (1980). Development of species identification in ducklings: VI. Specific embryonic experience required to maintain species-typical perception in Peking ducklings. *Journal of Comparative and Physiological Psychology, 94,* 579–587.
Gottlieb, G. (1982). Development of species identification in ducklings: IX. The necessity of experiencing normal variations in embryonic auditory stimulation. *Developmental Psychobiology, 15,* 507–517.
Haack, B., Markl, H., & Ehret, G. (1983). Sound communication between parents and offspring. In J. F. Willott (Ed.), *The auditory psychobiology of the mouse* (pp. 57–97). Springfield, IL: Charles C Thomas.
Hary, J. M., & Massaro, D. W. (1982). Categorical results do not imply categorical perception. *Perception and Psychophysics, 32,* 409–418.
Hienz, R. D., Sachs, M. B., & Sinnott, J. M. (1981). Discrimination of steady-state vowels by blackbirds and pigeons. *Journal of the Acoustical Society of America, 70,* 699–706.
Hirsh, I. J. (1959). Auditory perception of temporal order. *Journal of the Acoustical Society of America, 31,* 759–767.
Huber, F. (1977). Lautäusserungen and Lauterkennung bei Insekten (Grillen). *Rheinisch-Westfälische Akademie der Wissenschaften, Vorträge N 265,* 15–61.
Hutchison, R. E., Stevenson, J. G., & Thorpe, W. H. (1968). The basis for individual recognition by voice in the sandwich tern *(Sterna sandvicensis)*. *Behaviour, 32,* 150–157.
Kuhl, P. K. (1979). Models and mechanisms in speech perception. Species comparisons provide further contributions. *Brain Behavior and Evolution, 16,* 374–408.

Kuhl, P. K. (1981). Discrimination of speech by nonhuman animals: Basic auditory sensitivities conducive to the perception of speech-sound categories. *Journal of the Acoustical Society of America, 70,* 340–349.

Kuhl, P. K., & Miller, J. D. (1975). Speech perception by the chinchilla: Voiced-voiceless distinction in alveolar plosive consonants. *Science, 190,* 69–72.

Kuhl, P. K., & Miller, J. D. (1978). Speech perception by the chinchilla: Identification functions for synthetic VOT stimuli. *Journal of the Acoustical Society of America, 63,* 905–917.

Liberman, A. M., Harris, K. S., Hoffman, H., & Griffith, B. C. (1957). The discrimination of speech sounds within and across phoneme boundaries. *Journal of Experimental Psychology, 54,* 358–368.

Littlejohn, M. J. (1977). Long-range acoustic communication in anurans: An integrated and evolutionary approach. In D. H. Taylor & S. I. Guttman (Eds.), *The reproductive biology of amphibians* (pp. 263–294). New York: Plenum Press.

Locke, S., & Kellar, L. (1973). Categorical perception in a non-linguistic mode. *Cortex, 9,* 355–369.

Lorenz, K. Z. (1981). *The foundations of ethology.* New York: Springer.

Macmillan, N. A., Kaplan, H. L., & Creelman, C. D. (1977). The psychophysics of categorical perception. *Psychological Review, 84,* 452–471.

Maier, V. (1982). Acoustic communication in the Guinea fowl (*Numida meleagris*): Structure and use of vocalizations, and the principle of message coding. *Zeitschrift für Tierpsychologie, 59,* 29–83.

Manning, A. (1972). *An introduction to animal behavior* (2nd ed.). Reading, MA: Addison-Wesley.

Marler, P. (1976). Social organization, communication and graded signals: The chimpanzee and the gorilla. In P. P. Bateson & R. A. Hind (Eds.), *Growing points in ethology* (pp. 239–280). Cambridge: Cambridge University Press.

Marler, P. (1977). The structure of animal communication sounds. In T. H. Bullock (Ed.) *Recognition of complex acoustic signals* (pp. 17–35). Berlin: Abakon Verlagsgesellschaft.

Marler, P. (1982). Avian and primate communication: The problem of natural categories. *Neuroscience and Biobehavioral Reviews, 6,* 87–94.

Masataka, N. (1983). Categorical responses to natural and synthesized alarm calls in Goeldi's monkeys (*Callimico goeldi*). *Primates, 24,* 40–51.

Mattingly, J. G., Liberman, A. M., Syrdal, A. K., & Halwes, T. (1971). Discrimination in speech and nonspeech modes. *Cognitive Psychology, 2,* 131–157.

Miller, C. L., & Morse, P. A. (1976). The "heart" of categorical speech discrimination in young infants. *Journal of Speech and Hearing Research, 19,* 578–589.

Miller, J. D., Wier, C. C., Pastore, R. E., Kelly, W. J., & Dooling, R. J. (1976). Discrimination and labelling of noise-buzz sequences with varying noise-lead times: An example of categorical perception. *Journal of the Acoustical Society of America, 60,* 410–417.

Miyawaki, K., Strange, W., Verbrugge, R., Liberman, A. M., Jenkins, J. J., & Fujimura, O. (1975). An effect of linguistic experience: The discrimination of [r] and [l] by native speakers of Japanese and English. *Perception and Psychophysics, 18,* 331–340.

Moiseff, A., Pollack, G. S., & Hoy, R. R. (1978). Steering responses of flying crickets to sound and ultrasound: Mate attraction and predator avoidance. *Proceedings of the National Academy of Sciences, USA, 75,* 4052–4056.

Morse, P. A., & Snowdon, C. T. (1975). An investigation of categorical speech discrimination by rhesus monkeys. *Perception and Psychophysics, 17,* 9–16.

Pisoni, D. B. (1973). Auditory and phonetic memory codes in the discrimination of consonants and vowels. *Perception and Psychophysics, 13,* 253–260.

Pisoni, D. B. (1977). Identification and discrimination of the relative onset time of two component tones: Implications for voicing perception in stops. *Journal of the Acoustical Society of America, 61,* 1352–1361.

Pisoni, D. B. (1979). On the perception of speech sounds as biologically significant signals. *Brain Behavior and Evolution, 16,* 330–350.

Pisoni, D. B., & Lazarus, J. H. (1974). Categorical and noncategorical modes of speech perception along a voicing continuum. *Journal of the Acoustical Society of America, 55,* 328–333.

Pola, Y. V., & Snowdon, C. T. (1975). The vocalizations of pygmy marmosets (*Cebuella pygmaea*). *Animal Behaviour, 23,* 826–842.

Pollack, G. S., & Hoy, R. R. (1979). Temporal pattern as a cue for species-specific calling song recognition in crickets. *Science, 204,* 429–432.
Pollack, G. S., & Hoy, R. R. (1981). Phonotaxis to individual rhythmic components of a complex cricket calling song. *Journal of Comparative Physiology, 144,* 367–377.
Popov, A. V., & Shuvalov, V. F. (1977). Phonotactic behavior of crickets. *Journal of Comparative Physiology, 119,* 111–126.
Rosen, S. M., & Howell, P. (1981). Plucks and bows are not categorically perceived. *Perception and Psychophysics, 30,* 156–168.
Sales, G. D., & Smith, J. C. (1978). Comparative studies of the ultrasonic calls of infant murid rodents. *Developmental Psychobiology, 11,* 595–619.
Samuel, A. G. (1977). The effect of discrimination training on speech perception: Noncategorical perception. *Perception and Psychophysics, 22,* 321–330.
Scharf, B. (1970). Critical bands. In J. V. Tobias (Ed.), *Foundations of modern auditory theory* (Vol. 1, pp. 159–202). New York: Academic Press.
Seyfarth, R. M., Cheney, D. L., & Marler, P. (1980). Vervet monkey alarm calls: Semantic communication in a free-ranging primate. *Animal Behaviour, 28,* 1070–1094.
Sinnott, J. M., Beecher, M. D., Moody, D. B., & Stebbins, W. C. (1976). Speech sound discrimination by monkeys and humans. *Journal of the Acoustical Society of America, 60,* 687–695.
Smith, J. C., & Sales, G. D. (1980). Ultrasonic behavior and mother-infant interactions in rodents. In R. W. Bell and W. P. Smotherman (Eds.), *Maternal influences and early behavior* (pp. 105–133). New York: Spectrum.
Snowdon, C. T. (1979). Response of nonhuman animals to speech and to species-specific sounds. *Brain Behavior and Evolution, 16,* 409–429.
Snowdon, C. T., & Pola, Y. V. (1978). Interspecific and intraspecific responses to synthesized pygmy marmoset vocalizations. *Animal Behaviour, 26,* 192–206.
Spiegel, M. F., & Watson, C. S. (1981). Factors in the discrimination of tonal patterns. III. Frequency discrimination with components of well-learned patterns. *Journal of the Acoustical Society of America, 69,* 223–230.
Studdert-Kennedy, M., Liberman, A. M., Harris, K. S., & Cooper, F. S. (1970). Motor theory of speech perception: A reply to Lane's critical review. *Psychological Review, 77,* 234–249.
Thorson, J., Weber, T., & Huber, F. (1982). Auditory behavior of the cricket. II. Simplicity of calling-song recognition in *Gryllus,* and anomalous phonotaxis at abnormal carrier frequency. *Journal of Comparative Physiology, 146,* 361–378.
Warfield, D., Ruben, R. J., & Glackin, R. (1966). Word discrimination in cats. *Journal of Auditory Research, 6,* 97–120.
Waters, R. S., & Wilson, A. (1976). Speech perception by rhesus monkeys: The voicing distinction in synthesized labial and velar stop consonants. *Perception and Psychophysics, 19,* 285–289.
Weber, T., Thorson, J., & Huber, F. (1981). Auditory behavior of the cricket. I. Dynamics of compensated walking and discrimination paradigms on the Kramer treadmill. *Journal of Comparative Physiology, 141,* 215–232.
Wood, C. C. (1976). Discriminability, response bias, and phoneme categories in discrimination of voice onset time. *Journal of the Acoustical Society of America, 60,* 1381–1389.
Zippelius, H. M., & Schleidt, W. M. (1956). Ultraschall-Laute bei jungen Mäusen. *Naturwissenschaften, 43,* 502.
Zoloth, S. R., Petersen, M. R., Beecher, M. D., Green, S., Marler, P., Moody, D. M., & Stebbins, W. C. (1979). Species-specific perceptual processing of vocal sounds by monkeys. *Science, 204,* 870–873.
Zwicker, E., & Feldtkeller, R. (1967). *Das Ohr als Nachrichtenempfänger.* Stuttgart: Hirzel.

11 A naturalistic view of categorical perception

Charles T. Snowdon

This naturalistic view of categorical perception (CP) assumes an evolutionary continuity between nonhuman and human animals and uses a naturalistic methodology to illuminate the natural utility of CP. The function of CP in speech and vocal communication is similar to that of perceptual categories in other modalities and of linguistic and cognitive categories: It provides cognitive economy. Other forms of categorization lack the isomorphism of labeling and discrimination functions that some believe are essential to CP. This belief may have arisen from the use of artificial stimuli and testing conditions and an overly restrictive view of CP. A functional argument can be made that, even with speech and species-specific vocalizations, a recipient should differentiate "phonetic" categories while still making within-category distinctions too. Two experiments with pygmy marmosets are described. The first shows the presence of CP when the stimuli consist of synthesized sounds representing the average stimulus parameters for a population and the experimental task requires only "phonetic" labeling. The second experiment demonstrates within-category discrimination when the synthesized stimuli match the parameters of calls of familiar individuals and the experimental task requires individual discrimination. Both between- and within-category discrimination can be demonstrated with the same stimulus type depending on the methodology used. These results imply that at least some aspects of category boundaries must be acquired through individual experience rather than being hard-wired. CP in speech and nonlinguistic vocalization may be no different from perceptual processing in other modalities.

The naturalistic approaches

Before discussing the phenomenon of categorical perception (CP), I will outline some of the general characteristics of a naturalistic approach that make it different from a formal experimental or theoretical approach. There are three distinguishing characteristics of the naturalistic approach: (1) An interest in the utility of the phenomenon of interest in the natural world of the organisms displaying it. (2) An evolutionary assumption of continuity among phenomena and mechanisms across species, human beings included. (3) A concern that the methods for studying a phenomenon be adapted to the natural conditions of the organism under study or at least be oriented toward illuminating the natural function of the phenomenon. Let me briefly consider each of these points.

The research described and the preparation of the chapter were supported by USPHS grant, MH 29,775, and a Research Scientist Development Award, MH 00,177. I thank Jola Jakimik and Gregg Oden for their helpful comments on the manuscript.

It is generally assumed by biologists that many or most phenomena have some utility for the organism. According to the theory of natural selection, those behaviors, morphological structures, or physiological mechanisms that appear in an organism are by and large functioning to ensure the survival and reproduction of that organism. It is not true that every behavior, morphological feature, or physiological mechanism is adaptive – with imperfect sampling one could be studying a phenomenon that had no adaptive value or was even maladaptive. The naturalist would ascertain whether and how the particular phenomenon might be adaptive and then formulate tests of inferences about adaptiveness. As a general rule, the naturalist's initial working hypothesis would be that a phenomenon is adaptive to the organism under natural conditions.

Naturalists would expect to find general continuities among different species in behavior, in morphological structures, and in physiological mechanisms, although there might be species-specific or even individual-specific differences in the fine details of behavior, morphology, or physiology. For example, a naturalist would not be surprised to find that the vocal communication for each species consisted of a unique set of sounds used for communication. Thus, the vocal sounds of human beings would be different from those of chimpanzees, which would in turn differ from those of pygmy marmosets. Nonetheless, the naturalist would expect to find certain continuities in the general principles of communication, in the various phenomena of communication, and in the general mechanisms underlying communication across these different species. In terms of general principles and mechanisms there would be nothing "special," although the actual details of production and reception might be species specific.

The naturalist would expect to find similarities according to two evolutionary models. The first is the well-known model of divergent evolution. Species with a similar phylogenetic history can be expected to resemble each other in many, if not most, of their morphological, physiological, and behavioral characters. On this divergent model, the species of greatest interest to compare with human beings would be the great apes – chimpanzees, gorillas, and orangutans – our closest relatives. The other evolutionary model is that of convergent evolution. This model is less commonly known: It argues that species with diverse phylogenetic histories, but with similar ecologies and problems to solve, might be expected to have evolved similar solutions. Thus, we know that color vision has appeared independently several times in phylogeny: in insects, fishes, birds, and mammals. Whereas some of the details and mechanisms differ, there are several basic principles of color vision common to each of these diverse lines. Likewise, with respect to vocal communication Marler (1970) has argued that birds are useful models for studying certain human speech processes because they are highly vocal animals with a long period of vocal learning. I will argue that certain forest-living monkeys are better models for the vocal aspects of communication than our closer relatives, the apes, because the forest monkeys have a much more extensive and sophisticated vocal communication system than do the apes. (See also Ehret's chapter, this volume.)

A naturalist would be concerned that the methods used to learn about a phenomenon should be sensitive to the natural usage or occurrence of that phenomenon. The naturalist will generally avoid study in an unnatural context because the unnatural context can destroy the phenomenon. Some examples from studies of how animals perceive their own vocalizations will illustrate this point.

Beecher, Petersen, Zoloth, Moody, and Stebbings (1979) and Zoloth et al. (1979) demonstrated that Japanese macaques (*Macaca fuscata*) could learn to discriminate between two different variants of the "coo" vocalization. They used an operant testing procedure in which the monkey had to release its hold of a tube whenever it detected a change in the stimulus. Neither of these papers presents the total number of trials necessary to reach a criterion level of discrimination; they instead report the results in terms of sessions. Generally 20 to 30 sessions were provided to establish that the monkeys could discriminate between two forms of their own vocalizations. A later publication (Petersen et al., 1984) reported that 150 sessions of approximately 200 trials each (30,000 total trials) were needed to establish a discrimination between seven tokens of one type and eight of the other type. In contrast, Bauers and Snowdon (in preparation) have completed a study testing whether cotton-top tamarins (*Saguinus oedipus*) could discriminate between two brief chirp vocalizations (50 to 70 ms) that differed only in the amount of frequency modulation. Although each animal was tested four times with each stimulus type, statistically significant discriminations could also be obtained using only the first stimulus presentation to each animal. Furthermore, the behavior in response to the playback stimulus was identical to that expected from observations of animals' natural responses to spontaneous calls of the same types. Thus the animals indicated that they not only discriminated between stimuli, but that they also understood the meaning of the stimuli. Several other studies involving playback experiments with natural social groups have been able to demonstrate reliable discrimination between vocalizations in a small number of trials. Seyfarth, Cheney, and Marler (1980) showed that vervet monkeys (*Cercopithecus aethiops*) discriminated different forms of alarm calls after only a small number of trials using each stimulus type. Cheney and Seyfarth (1982) demonstrated that vervets discriminated between subtle variants of "grunt" vocalizations, again with very few trials. Snowdon, Cleveland, and French (1983) have shown that the cotton-top tamarin (*Saguinus oedipus*) can discriminate between two variants of their Long Calls. In their study they presented five trials of each stimulus type to each of five pairs of monkeys.

The results of the playback studies with natural social groups of monkeys are quite impressive, especially when compared with the traditional testing methods of animal experimental psychology. Undoubtedly the results obtained to date with the operant techniques used with birds and Japanese macaques are valid in the sense that they represent true discriminations by the animals. However, there is a danger that the use of highly controlled experimental techniques could lead to the conclusion that animals can discriminate more subtle differences than they would normally make. One could also conclude that it is extremely difficult for animals to learn to make discriminations between their natural vocal signals because the training process is so lengthy. Thus, one could be misled about the relative ease with which such discriminations are made in a natural context.

There are several features of the operant testing situation that make it inappropriate for understanding the natural capacities of animals. First, animals are tested in a nonsocial context using stimuli that are an integral part of social interactions. The context of stimulus presentation is highly abnormal to an animal that is in social isolation in an uncomfortable testing apparatus listening to a disembodied social signal coming from a speaker or an earphone. Furthermore, the animal is required to make a response that is quite different from the normal social response to the vocal signal – releasing a tube or pecking at a key. Finally, the consequences of responding are highly abnormal. An animal receives food, not the normal consequence of responding to the affiliative coos or territorial song. Perhaps with so many obstacles for the monkeys and birds to overcome we should marvel more that they can learn to make a discrimination at all. The entire situation of operant training to respond to natural vocal signals is a situation for which animals are "unprepared" or even "contraprepared," to use Seligman's (1970) terminology.

The playback technique, which is used by naturalistically oriented investigators, involves a lesser degree of control than the laboratory experiment, but control is sufficient to allow precise statements to be made about the discriminations of animals. The objective of the playback experiment, as in the laboratory study, is to test the response to an acoustic stimulus in the absence of other contextual features. Thus, stimuli are presented in the absence of the visual, chemical, and social contexts that normally accompany the signal, and if animals respond appropriately (that is, as they would to the spontaneous utterance of that call), then it can be inferred that the vocalization alone carries sufficient information for animals to perform a discrimination. The stimulus preparation and presentation can be arranged to have as much precision and fidelity as the presentation of any stimulus in an operant setting. Both natural and synthesized stimuli can and have been used.

It may appear that the playback study does not provide as much control over response measures as the formal laboratory experiment, but that is not true. If the investigator has observed the animals in a social situation and has been careful to record the range of normal responses given upon spontaneous emission of the calls in question, then a series of response measures can be constructed that are as reliable as any laboratory response. Thus, the visual orientations of animals toward or away from the stimulus and the latency of response can be filmed so that these measures can be assessed with precision (Cheney & Seyfarth, 1982). Or, with a stimulus that is generally followed by a vocal response, the session can be tape recorded and the number, type, and latency of vocalizations after the stimulus presentation can be recorded with accuracy. It is not possible to compare precisely the operant and playback techniques, but I suspect that animals make more errors in discriminating stimuli presented in the operant situation than they do in the playback test and that motivational problems are greater in operant settings where animals must make nonsocial responses to social stimuli. Thus, the playback technique used in naturalistic studies can be as precise and controlled as the laboratory operant test. In addition, the playback technique allows the observation of natural, semantically appropriate behavioral responses rather than imposing unusual responses on animals tested in social isolation. (See Ehret in Chapter 10, this volume, for further support of this point.)

Functional significance of categorical perception

Naturalistic principles can be applied to the topic of CP. I shall define CP as occurring when stimuli that vary along a physical continuum are perceptually segregated into a relatively small number of discrete units, which are clearly separable one from the other. The classic definition of CP was that members from within a category were indiscriminable from each other. However, the discriminability of within-category stimuli will, I shall argue, depend upon the testing methods used, the questions asked of the subject, and the significance to the subject of within-category subdivisions.

First, what might be the functional significance of categorization? Why should human beings and other animals have the capacity to form perceptual categories? The best functional explanation comes from Rosch (1978), who argued that categories are a means of attaining cognitive economy (see also Harnad in Chapter 19, this volume). It is more efficient to organize the world into a small number of superordinate units than to deal with each individual exemplar. Presumably, perceptual processing, memory storage, and memory-retrieval processes are all aided by the creation of superordinate categories (see also Miller, 1956). If categories are to function properly, they should be characterized by sharp boundaries to attain a precise separation of different categories.

The principle of economy can be applied to notions of motor and perceptual economy. For example, as organisms evolved into increasingly complex social organizations, presumably a greater expansion of communicative repertoire was needed. To produce more signals there are two options: (1) One can create an additional number of signals by developing new production mechanisms and corresponding perceptual mechanisms to produce and process totally new signals; (2) one can create divisions in existing motor capacities with corresponding divisions in existing perceptual capacities. In English there are six consonants that we can produce simply by varying two production parameters: voice-onset time and place of articulation. From varying these two parameters we can produce /b/, /d/, /g/, /p/, /t/, and /k/. Our ability to categorize each of these consonants perceptually provides us with more economy of both production and perception than if we had six sounds produced by totally different parameters to represent these six consonants. However, the economy resulting from dividing existing production continua will exist only if there is some precision in category boundaries, allowing for the accurate perception of categories.

It should be clear that dividing existing communicative continua into discrete categories is possible not only for human beings but for other species as well. Categorization can be adaptive for any species with a need for more vocal signals. Marler (1975) has suggested a phylogenetic progression toward categorization of communication signals. He argued that primitive animals tended to have signals that were each uniquely determined by a discrete set of acoustic parameters. At the next stage, species have continuous communication where a single state such as fear or aggression might be coded in intensity by the variation of a call along an acoustic continuum. Finally, at the highest level of phylogeny, the division of acoustic continua into discrete categories occurs. Although the details of his phylogenetic classification have been subsequently shown to be wrong (he argued that human beings were the only species to divide continua into categories), the general thrust of his argument is probably correct. The development of discrete categories along acoustic continua represents a sophisticated stage in the evolution of vocal communication.

One of the basic ideas in the classical descriptions of CP for speech sounds has been that discrimination and labeling functions should be isomorphic. That is, where there is a boundary in the labeling of categories there should be enhanced discrimination capacity and where there is none, discrimination between adjacent tokens should be difficult or impossible. As Pisoni (1977), Pisoni and Lazarus (1974), and others (see Chapter 1 by Pastore and Chapter 2 by Macmillan, this volume) document with studies on human beings, discrimination of within-category stimuli is possible. Some within-category discrimination is clearly demonstrable in studies of categorization in other dimensions as well.

Many writers on linguistic (as opposed to phonetic) categories have argued that, although natural categories exist at a superordinate level, some discriminations can be made at a subordinate level. Berlin (1978) and Newport and Bellugi (1978) argued that the basic category level has linguistically simpler labels, more common in word frequency, and more readily produced as spontaneous labels. However, the linguistic primacy of category labels does not prevent the use of within-category subordinate terms. Which categories have subordinate terms and how extensive these terms are varies from culture to culture and depends upon the particular needs of the culture. For example, Berlin (1978) noted that the Aguaruna Indians of Peru have 30 subordinate categories of manioc, 21 subcategories of bananas and plantains, and 9 subcategories of ginger. When I lived in the same region of the Amazon for a few months, I learned to distinguish 6 varieties of bananas and plantains and 4 varieties of chiles, but made no distinctions of manioc and ginger, which were not as important in my diet. Other botanicals in the Aguaruna Indian culture have an identity only at the basic category level, not at the subcategory level. As a primatologist, I have a relatively good understanding of genus identification of Old World monkeys and apes; I can identify the New World primate family that I study at the species level and can differentiate the genus I study to the level of subspecies. My knowledge of botanicals, on the other hand, is little more sophisticated than grasses, shrubs, and trees. When we deal with the world of objects, it is obvious that we have different degrees of sophistication in category formation and creating and discriminating subcategories that depend on our particular needs. It seems to me that speech and species-specific vocalizations should be subject to the same principles. That is, under appropriate circumstances, within-category discriminations should be not only possible but also relatively easy. Table 11.1 illustrates examples of categories and subcategories in color vision, speech, and animal vocalizations.

Within-category distinctions might have functional significance for speech. We can discriminate speech sounds between dialects, ages, genders, and different individuals. We can ignore those features and concentrate merely on the phonetic discrimination, but we can just as easily attend to both the phonetic discriminations and paralinguistic differences. We can pay attention to these differences or not as the situation requires. For example, if we are sitting in a dark theater and hear a voice shouting "Fire!", it is important that we respond immediately, regardless of any incidental demographic information that might be encoded. If in the same theater we hear, on the other hand, a voice saying, "Kiss me, I love you," it is extremely important that we identify the age, sex, and perhaps individual identity (or at least familiarity) of the speaker before we take action. Thus, the nature of the situation can determine the nature of our response and whether we should make within-category discrimination of subordinate features or simply attend to the phonetic information.

A parallel has been shown for at least one species of monkey. Snowdon, Coe, and Hodun (1985) did a playback study with squirrel monkeys, presenting them with recorded infant-distress vocalizations ("isolation peeps"). The animals came from one of three places: Peru, Bolivia, or Guyana, and there was a dialect difference in the structure of the isolation peep. The Guyanese monkeys had a call structure different from that of the monkeys from Peru and Bolivia. In our playback tests we found that all Peruvian and Bolivian monkeys responded equally to the calls of isolated Peruvian or Bolivian infants, regardless of whether those infants were related or even familiar. However, those monkeys failed to be aroused by the calls of infant Guyanese squirrel monkeys. The Guyanese adults behaved in the opposite way, responding only to the infant cries of Guyanese monkeys and ignoring the cries of Peruvian and Bolivian monkeys. Here is a discrimination of calls based on dialect differences, but all infants of a particular dialect were responded to by all adults of the same dialect, regardless of the adults' familiarity with those particular infants.

In another study on the same species, Kaplan, Winship-Ball, and Sim (1978) demonstrated that mothers would respond specifically to the isolation-peep vocalizations of their own infants. Thus, with infant-isolation calls there are at least two levels of discrimination: (1) *between-category discrimination*, in which the animals appear to make a categorical distinction between members of their own population (whether or not they are related or familiar) and members of a different population or dialect group, and (2) *within-category discrimination*, whereby a

Table 11.1. *Examples of categories and subcategories in color vision, speech, and animal vocalizations*

Modality	Vision		Audition
Dimension	Color	Human speech	Species-specific primate vocalizations
Basic level	Red, green, blue, yellow	Voice-onset time /ba/, /pa/ /da/, /ta/ /ga/, /ka/	Closed-Mouth, Open-Mouth Trills (Pygmy marmoset) F-Chirp, G-Chirp (Cotton-top tamarin) Smooth Early High; Smooth Late High (Japanese macaque)
Subordinate levels	Scarlet, magenta, pink	New Yorker vs. Texan Male vs. female Familiar vs. unfamiliar Sally vs. Susan Question vs. command	Peruvian vs. Columbian Male vs. female Familiar vs. unfamiliar Lana vs. Sally

mother can discriminate and selectively respond to her own infant. The presence and sensitivity of within-category vocal discrimination varies with the contextual situation in monkeys as it does with human beings.

In summary, categorization appears to serve a function of cognitive economy. In the case of speech and species-specific vocalizations, categorization also functions to produce an economy of motor and perceptual specialization, allowing an organism to produce and respond to a greater array of sounds with minimal additional mechanisms. At the same time, many categories, both cognitive and perceptual, are characterized by subordinate categories that may or may not be discriminated, according to the context in which discrimination occurs. Thus, for certain very important calls, such as distress or warning calls in animals or words uttered in similar contexts by human beings, the accurate and rapid perception of the phonetic features signaling a stressful or dangerous situation is critical. On the other hand, with affiliative vocalizations (and affiliative speech) it is important to know not just the phonetic structure, but also additional information about the speaker. Both phonetic category data and within-category paralinguistic information must be processed in evaluating the response to an affiliative utterance. Finally, there are utterances in both animals and human beings where the principal information extracted might simply be phonetic, but where a processing of information about within-category, paralinguistic information might proceed in parallel. Whether one finds strict categorical processing or clear within-category discrimination does not depend only on the use of different methods (see Chapter 1 by Pastore and Chapter 2 by Macmillan, this volume, for further discussion), but also on the functional significance of a particular utterance, which may be processed categorically or simultaneously categorically and subcategorically.

Categorical perception in nonhuman animals

Another point made in early writings on categorical perception of speech was that CP was a uniquely human phenomenon. Just as the notion of CP as special to speech has been discarded (Cutting, Rosner, & Foard, 1976; Miller, Wier, Pastore, Kelly, & Dooling, 1976), it is now clear that CP cannot be regarded as unique to human beings (see Chapter 10 by Ehret and Chapter 12 by Kuhl, this volume). There have been two types of attacks on this form of the "CP is special" argument. First, there have been studies in which nonhuman animals were tested with the same stimuli used in establishing CP with human beings. In three out of four of these studies, the evidence supported the notion that nonhumans can also process speech sounds in a categorical fashion. Morse and Snowdon (1975) and Waters and Wilson (1976) showed that rhesus macaques (*Macaca mulatta*) were able to discriminate consonants categorically on the place-of-articulation continuum or the voice-onset-time continuum. In the Morse and Snowdon (1975) study monkeys also appeared to make significant within-category discriminations, but these were not as great as the between-category discriminations. Kuhl and Miller (1975) showed that chinchillas could also display categorization of a voice-onset time continuum. Sinnott, Beecher, Moody, and Stebbins (1976) tested several Old World primate species and found that human beings were more adept than monkeys in discriminating within-category stimuli; however, response latency data showed that humans discriminated with shorter latencies between categories than within categories, whereas the monkeys showed no such categorization effects in their latency data. These authors concluded that human beings did have a special processing mechanism for speech sounds that monkeys did not have. Nonetheless, the general impression gleaned from this series of papers is that nonhuman animals are capable of showing categorical responses to human speech sounds.

Kuhl (1979 and in Chapter 12, this volume) has suggested that these categorization data might indicate some universal psychophysical specializations that are common to several species. Human beings may have evolved to show their speech-sound contrasts at some psychophysically ideal boundary, which also exists in other species. Indeed, there is some evidence that other species might have similar boundaries in their phonetic contrasts. For example, Green (1975) has shown that Japanese macaques have several "coo" variants, which are correlated with different situations. One of these variants is a double "coo," which is spectrographically similar to delayed voicing in human speech. Lillehei and Snowdon (1978) found a similar vocing delay in one of the "coos" of a related species, the stumptail macaque (*Macaca arctoides*). Differences in the initial slopes of different calls of the rhesus macaque (Rowell & Hinde, 1962) resemble changes in slope found in the second-formant transitions of human speech consonants. To date we do not have information on the natural sounds of chinchillas, and we thus do not know whether there is something similar to a voicing contrast in their species-specific vocalization, but it is clear that some features in monkeys' vocalizations are similar to features of human speech sounds. It is not surprising to find some similarities in perceptual processing between human and nonhuman animals.

A recent study on color perception in cotton-top tamarins (Savage, Droczek, & Snowdon, in preparation) has provided a parallel to the CP of speech sounds. The tamarins were reinforced for responding to Munsell color chips of varying brightness and saturation of the hue chosen as the "best" example of a color category: red, yellow, green, or blue. The test hue was systematically paired with color chips of various brightness and saturations representing each of the ten values in the Munsell system on either side of the training color. The tamarins were able to discriminate the test hues from the training hues at levels significantly better than chance for almost all pairs of hues, in some cases displaying better performance than human subjects tested in the same way. However, discrimination was nearly 100% correct only for those hues labeled as different by the human subjects. Thus, tamarins could discriminate perfectly between a red training stimulus and test hues labeled as yellow or purple by human subjects, and they also discriminated at better than chance levels, but not perfectly, those hues that human subjects labeled as being red. This result closely parallels the Morse and Snowdon (1975) results with discrimination of human speech sounds, showing that both between- and within-category stimuli were discriminated but between-category stimuli were discriminated with greater precision. (See also Chapter 9 by Bornstein, this volume.)

The other approach to the refutation of the idea that CP is unique to human beings is to test for categorization in the species-specific vocalizations of other species. The basic approach is to analyze the structure of a naturally occurring sound and then develop a means of synthesizing the sound and its systematic variations. If an animal categorizes its own communication sounds, then there should be a range of variation around the natural sound to which an animal will respond as though the same sound were being heard. There should be a sharp discrimination or response differentiation when the parameters of variation are moved a slight distance further from the natural sound. To date, there have been three demonstrations of categorization in nonhuman animals using this technique of synthesizing sounds, varying the parameters of the sound in a systematic way and showing a broad area of equivalence around the natural stimulus with a sharp categorical boundary on at least one parameter.

Ehret and Haack (1981) described CP for mouse-pup ultrasonic vocalizations by lactating females (see Ehret in Chapter 10, this volume). When mouse pups are in discomfort, they emit ultrasonic whistles that elicit searching and retrieving behavior by the mother. (No individual-specific cues were observed that would allow the mother to respond only to her own infant.) Ehret and Haack tested mothers by playing sounds through two speakers and observing toward which speaker the mother would orient and approach. In the first study, a natural ultrasonic pup vocalization was tested against a 20-kHz pure tone outside the frequency range of the normal vocalization. The mice made a significantly greater number of approaches toward the natural call. Then they were tested with a variety of ultrasonic-noise bands ranging from 17.5 to 40 kHz in bandwidth. Each of these models was tested against a 20-kHz pure tone. When the bandwidth was varied across a 5-kHz range from 17.5 to 22.5 kHz the mice showed equally significant selection of the noise burst rather than the 20-kHz pure tone. However, when the bandwidth was increased by 1.5 kHz to 24 kHz, the mice no longer discriminated between the synthesized call and the 20-kHz tone. All subsequent increases in bandwidth led to equal responses to the synthesized call and the pure tone. Thus, a variation of 5 kHz in bandwidth within the frequency range of a normal call had no effect on responding, but adding only 1.5 kHz more to the frequency range eliminated the specific response to the synthetic call. In a final series of studies, Ehret and Haack showed that mice could discriminate between noise bands of 22.5 kHz in preference to a noise band of 25 kHz but could not discriminate between a noise band of 17.5 kHz and one of 22.5 kHz. They also showed that the response to a 20-kHz noise band was equivalent to the response to a natural pup vocalization. Thus, Ehret and Haack have shown that mouse-pup ultrasonic vocalizations are categorized by lactating mice and that the principal dimension for perception is the frequency range of the noise band.

A second demonstration of CP for species-specific vocalizations was made by Masataka (1983), who studied the responses to alarm calls in Goeldi's monkeys (*Callimico goeldi*). Masataka first showed that there were five forms of alarm call in Goeldi's monkeys, which elicited two forms of typical responses. Three forms of call elicited freezing responses when heard by monkeys; the other two elicited antiphonal alarm calls. The two forms of responses were incompatible with one another. Determining the response of an animal was easy. Masataka selected two forms of the alarm call that were each specific to one typical response. These forms were both trill-like calls and differed on several dimensions (duration, center frequency, and frequency range) while being similar in the frequency range of a noise burst within the call. Masataka created synthetic calls that varied systematically on each of these four dimensions and he played them back to five individual Goeldi's monkeys. When he varied the frequency range of the call while holding other variables constant, he found a typical categorical labeling function. Calls with a frequency range between 1.6 and 2.4 kHz were responded to with antiphonal warning calls and calls with 2.6 kHz or greater frequency modulation were responded to with freezing responses. Subsequently the mean frequency range of the two spontaneous alarm calls (1.6 kHz and 3.0 kHz, respectively) was used while each of the other parameters was varied. None of the remaining parameters – duration, center frequency, or width of the noise band – had any effect on the responses of the monkeys to the synthesized alarm calls. Regardless of other parametric variations, the call with a frequency range of 1.6 kHz was responded to with antiphonal warning calls and the call with a frequency range of 3.0 kHz was responded to with freezing. Masataka's study shows quite clearly a categorical labeling of alarm calls; by systematically varying all the parameters of a call, it demonstrates the critical continuum (frequency range) on which the categorical discrimination occurs.

The third example of CP for species-specific vocalizations comes from the pygmy marmoset (*Cebuella pygmaea*), which is, like the Goeldi's monkey, a small New World monkey with an elaborate vocal repertoire. Pola and Snowdon (1975) described the vocal repertoire of the species and found four variations of a trill vocalization. Each of these variations could be acoustically differentiated from the other. The most commonly heard trill was the Closed-Mouth Trill, which appeared to be given as a contact call in quiet, undisturbed conditions. A related call was similar in all parameters except that it had a significantly smaller frequency range and a much lower amplitude. It was called the Quiet Trill and was generally heard between animals in close proximity. A third form of trill differed in many ways. It had an interrupted form – only the upsweep of the frequency modulation of the trill was present – thus it appeared on a spectrogram as a series of "j-like" patterns and was labeled the J-call. It was also significantly longer in duration and greater in frequency range than the Closed-Mouth Trill. However, despite all the structural differences between the J-call and the Closed-Mouth Trill, they appeared to be given in similar circumstances, that is, in a calm, contact-seeking context. Subsequent study of these vocalizations in a natural group of animals in the Peruvian Amazon indicated that one function of these call variants might be to provide differing cues for sound localization. In the wild, Quiet Trills tended to be made between animals in very close proximity, J-calls by animals who were quite far apart from each other, and Closed-Mouth Trills at intermediate distances between animals (Snowdon & Hodun, 1981).

The fourth-trill variant differed more subtly from the Closed-Mouth Trill than did the other variants. It was called the Open-Mouth Trill because it was given with the mouth open. It differed structurally only in having a longer duration than the Closed-Mouth Trill (mean 334 msec versus 176 msec). However, the context in which it appeared was quite different from those in which the other three forms occurred. We showed (Pola & Snowdon, 1975) that Open-Mouth Trills were followed with great probability by some form of aggressive or fearful behavior. Whereas each of the first three trill variants was followed by antiphonal vocal calling, there was rarely a vocal response to the Open-Mouth Trill. Thus, the Open-Mouth Trill appeared to have a communicative significance for pygmy marmosets different from that of the other trill forms, and its emission elicited different responses.

Because there appeared to be a clear functional distinction between these two trills differing only in duration we decided to test pygmy marmosets with a variety of synthesized variants of trills (Snowdon & Pola, 1978). We developed a synthesizer that could mimic natural Open-Mouth and Closed-Mouth Trills and we systematically varied the four parameters of the trill vocalization: duration, center frequency, frequency range, and rate of modulation. The calls were played back to monkeys through hidden speakers. The presence or absence of an antiphonal call within 5 seconds of the playback of a stimulus served as an index of response to a Closed-Mouth Trill (i.e., this was a labeling task). The results indicated a large range over which the stimuli could be varied and still be responded to as a Closed-Mouth Trill. For example, center frequencies ranging from 9 to 12 kHz were responded to equally (mean for natural Closed-Mouth Trills = 9.4 kHz); modulating frequencies between 20 and 36 kHz were responded to equally (mean for natural Closed-Mouth Trills = 36); frequency ranges of 1.0 kHz and from 3.6 to 4.8 kHz were responded to equally (mean for natural Closed-Mouth Trill = 4.0 kHz). It was interesting that the animals treated the frequency range of the Quiet Trill (1.0 kHz) as equivalent to the frequency ranges around the Closed-Mouth Trill, but they did not respond to an intermediate frequency range of 2.8 kHz. In our sample of Quiet and Closed-Mouth Trills we never found trills that were produced with this frequency range. Finally, trills varying in duration from 176 to 248 msec were responded to equally, but trills longer than 248 msec were not responded to (the average duration of natural Closed-Mouth Trills was 176 msec) (see Figure 11.1). In our sample of naturally produced Closed-Mouth and Open-Mouth Trills, classifying calls strictly on the basis of whether the mouth of the caller was open or closed, we had found that the distributions of durations of the two calls did not overlap and that the

A naturalistic view of categorical perception

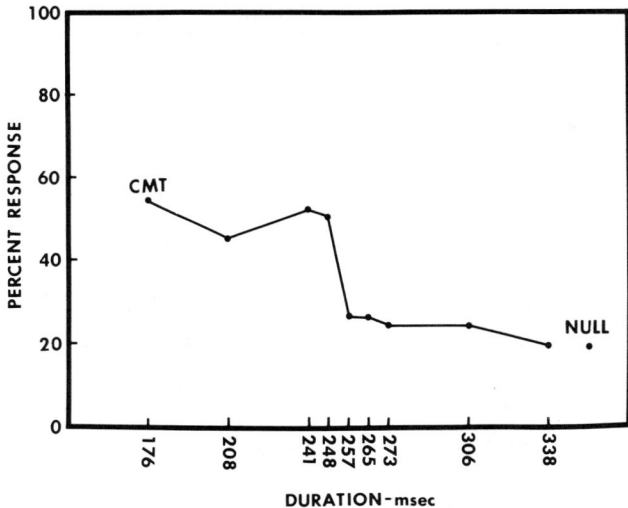

Figure 11.1. The responses of pygmy marmosets to playback presentations of synthesized trills. CMT refers to the duration of the average Closed-Mouth Trill; NULL refers to the baseline call rate in the absence of a playback stimulus. Percent response is the percentage of trials eliciting antiphonal calling within 5 sec of stimulus presentation. (Modified from Snowdon & Pola, 1978.)

production boundary between the two calls was at 250 msec. In our playback study we found a clear response differentiation between calls less than 250 msec and calls greater than 250 msec, a perceptual boundary that corresponded exactly to the production boundary between the call types. Simply increasing the call duration by 9 msec at the boundary produced a very different response pattern, while varying the stimulus duration from 176 to 248 msec (a range of 72 msec) produced no differences in response. This also appears to be a clear demonstration of categorization of species-specific vocalization in a nonhuman animal.

We tested human subjects with the same vocalizations and found a very different response pattern. Human beings were able to make very precise discriminations between stimuli on each of the acoustic dimensions except rate of frequency modulation. On the duration and frequency-range dimensions they did not show the categorical responding of the monkeys. Rather, they were able to make continuous discriminations. This is not unexpected because the human beings did not have any prior experience with pygmy-marmoset vocalizations and their functional separation, nor do the humans have any known perceptual contrasts that match the dimensions and values used by the pygmy marmosets for their trills.

Nonetheless, these results might appear somewhat odd. Why should human beings appear to have a better discrimination capacity for pygmy-marmoset vocalizations than pygmy marmosets? The answer, I think, is that human beings do not have a better discrimination capacity than pygmy marmosets. Rather, the procedures for testing biased the pygmy-marmoset results toward categorization and the human results toward continuous discrimination. All the pygmy marmosets were asked to do was to label a call type. If they gave an antiphonal trill, we assumed that they perceived the call as a Closed-Mouth Trill. We did not require them to make any finer discrimination nor did we measure any responses that would allow us to detect a finer discrimination. On the other hand, we tested the human subjects using a traditional *ABX* paradigm with some modifications to aid their memory for the standard trill stimulus. We did not ask them to label the calls, but to discriminate them.

Under what natural conditions might pygmy marmosets make within-category discriminations? As argued in the section on the functional significance of categorization, differences in age, sex, dialect, and individual identity might be encoded by variations of parameters within phonetic categories. Some studies have shown that separate parameters are used to distinguish "phonetic" variables from variables that encode individual differences. Lillehei and Snowdon (1978) measured 17 variables in the "coo" calls of infant stumptail macaques. They found that the features differentiating between call variants given in varying contexts were not the same as the acoustic features that differentiated between individuals. Newman, Smith, and Talmage-Riggs (1983) have suggested a similar distinction for the "chuck" calls of squirrel monkeys. However, analyses of individual differences for pygmy-marmoset Closed-Mouth Trills indicated that all acoustic parameters of trills, including the duration dimension on which the "phonetic" distinction was made, were used to encode individual-specific information (Snowdon & Cleveland, 1980). We have shown that animals do respond to each other on the basis of hearing playbacks of individual calls. If pygmy marmosets were to be tested for their response to individual differences in typical duration of Closed-Mouth Trills and if they showed individual-specific responses, there would be evidence that under appropriate test conditions pygmy marmosets could show within-category discrimination as well as CP on the same acoustic dimension.

To test this idea Ann Vertovec and I have completed a study in which we created synthesized versions of individual pygmy-marmoset Closed-Mouth Trills. We measured the parameters of Closed-Mouth Trills of five pygmy marmosets whose rate of trill emissions were frequent enough that we could collect a sufficient sample. Among these five were two mated pairs of animals, and within each of the mated pairs there were no statistical differences between the calls of the pair members. The average parameters of the pairs were used for purposes of synthesizing calls. This gave us three sets of Closed-Mouth Trills to synthesize. The mean values used for synthesis are shown in Table 11.2, and sonagrams of natural and synthesized calls are presented in Figure 11.2. Val/Marco represents one mated pair and Lana/Donald represents the other pair. Notice that each of the four parameters differs among the three groupings of animals. Also notice that the upper limit of the duration range varies for each of the three sets. Sally rarely gave trills longer than 350 msec,

Table 11.2. *Closed-Mouth Trill parameters of individual pygmy marmosets*

	Animal(s)		
Parameter	Sally	Val/Marco	Lana/Donald
Mean center frequency (kHz)	9.1	10.7	11.1
Mean frequency range (kHz)	4.6	1.9	2.9
Mean modulation rate (Hz)	41.5	32.8	38.3
Duration range (msec) (83% of calls)	200–350	150–400	150–500

Val/Marco rarely gave trills longer than 400 msec, and Lana/Donald had trills as long as 500 msec.[1]

We created syntheses of each of the three call types using the parameter values given in Table 11.2 for center frequency, frequency range, and modulation rates (Figure 11.2). We systematically varied the duration of the trill over a range of 100 to 600 msec. The duration intervals tested were 100, 200, 300, 325, 350, 375, 400, 425, 450, 475, 500, and 600 msec. We had discovered previously (Snowdon & Cleveland, 1980) that pygmy marmosets responded antiphonally to the playback of a familiar individual's call only when that call was played back through a speaker located in that individual's cage. For example, if Sally's trill was played back through a speaker in her own cage, other animals in the colony would give antiphonal trills. If her trill was played back through a speaker in a different cage, the other animals would not respond to her. This response differential can serve as an index of individual recognition. If a synthesized trill is perceived as Sally's, for example, it will be responded to more frequently when played back through a speaker in her cage than when played back through a speaker in another location. If the trill is not perceived as Sally's, then there should be no differential response to the call played back in her cage versus in another cage.

The colony was presented with 10 trials of each type of call at each of the durations from the normal cage location of the animal(s) whose call was synthesized and 10 trials of each type at each duration from a location different from that of the animal(s) whose call was being synthesized. The order of presentation of trial type, speaker location, and duration were randomized within each of the 10 replications. All trills occurring within 10 sec of the presentation of the synthesized stimulus were recorded as responses and identified by caller.

The results showed that there was a pattern of response corresponding to the average distribution of call durations (Figure 11.3). Calls ranging in duration from 200 to 450 msec were responded to with antiphonal calls when played back through the individual's own speaker more than they were when played back through a different speaker. This response distribution corresponded to the average distribution of call durations given by the five animals. It appeared to show a precise

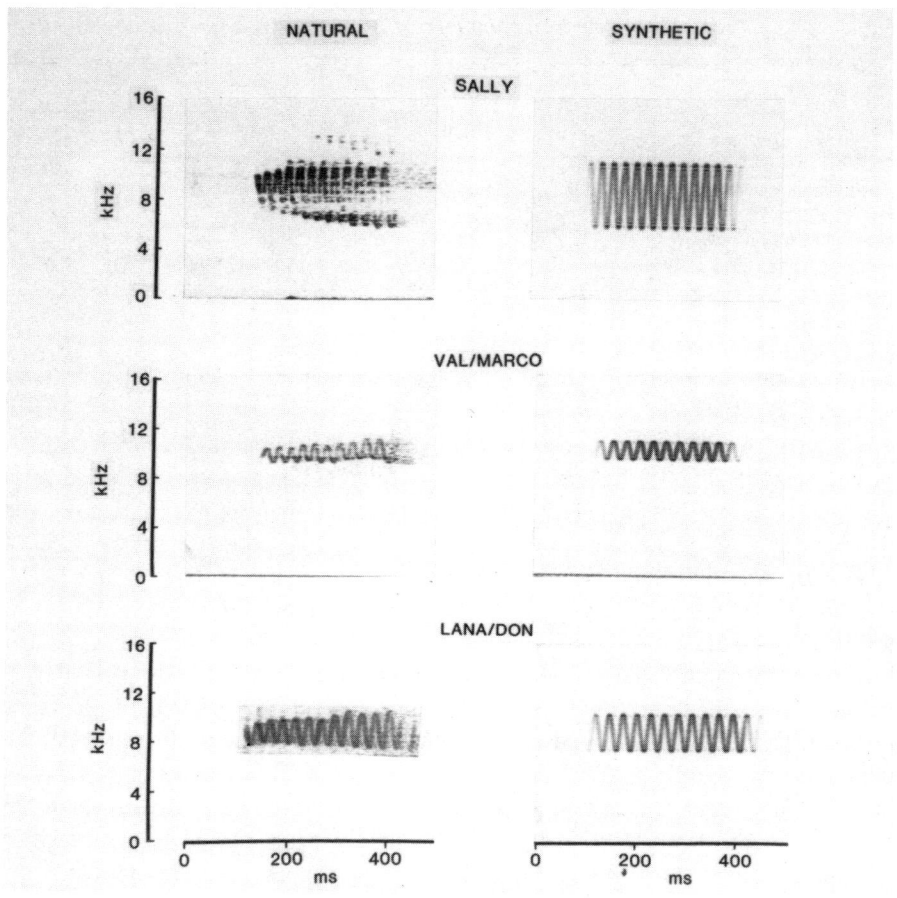

Figure 11.2. Sound spectrograms of natural and synthesized Closed-Mouth Trills from each of the subject individuals or pairs.

category boundary similar to that found in our previous study. However, when the response data to the calls of individual animals were analyzed separately, it appeared that the duration boundary differed as a function of the individual animal whose call was being tested. Thus, Sally's natural trills were rarely shorter than 200 msec or longer than 350 msec and the other animals responded to her specific trills only over the range of 250 to 350 msec (Figure 11.4). Val/Marco's natural trills ranged from 150 to 400 msec and their synthesized trills were responded to only over the range of 250 to 400 msec (Figure 11.5). Thus the category boundary for a Closed-Mouth-Trill duration is variable and depends on the unique structure of an individual's trill and on the respondent's previous experience with those individuals.

Parallels to these results can be found in the human-speech-perception literature

A naturalistic view of categorical perception

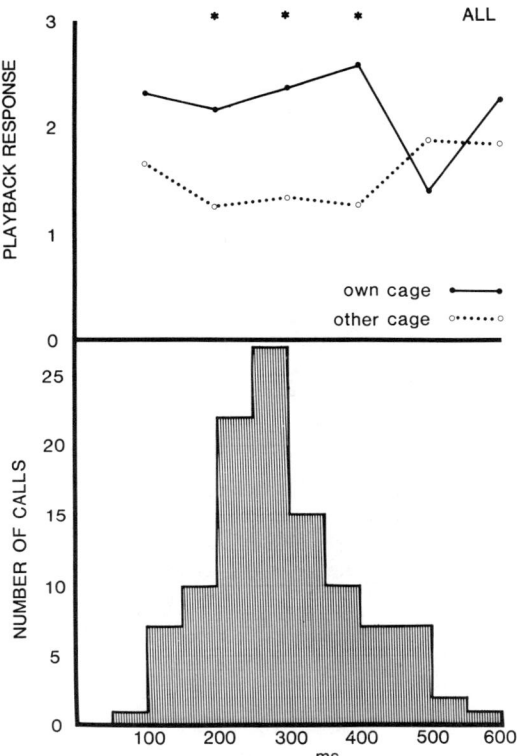

Figure 11.3. *Top:* The mean number of antiphonal calls given within 10 seconds of a playback presentation averaged over all stimulus types. The responses to calls played back from the stimulus animal's home cage are shown in solid lines. Responses to calls played back from another location are shown in dotted lines. (*indicates statistically significant difference, $p < .05$.) *Bottom:* Frequency distributions of Closed-Mouth Trills by duration for all stimulus animals.

but were not stressed in the classical formulation of CP. Lisker and Abramson (1970) have shown that the category boundary for voice-onset time varies with different languages (see also Pastore in Chapter 1, this volume). Eimas, Miller, and Jusczyk (Chapter 5, this volume) note that bilingual speakers are able to adopt two different processing modes for voice-onset time according to their expectations about which language they are going to hear. This has a direct parallel with pygmy marmosets, who appear to use different duration criteria for Closed-Mouth Trills as a function of their expectations about which animal is calling (the location of the playback speaker). Wilson (Chapter 13, this volume) discusses adaptation-level theory as a basis for understanding CP. Basic to this theory is the notion that different individuals will construct different boundaries based on their past perceptual history. She notes that identification and perception are history-dependent functions. Again, the data from the pygmy marmosets appear to supply a nonhuman parallel to this point.

Several further points can be made on the basis of this experiment. First, if an average stimulus is synthesized and the respondents are asked to label variations, one is likely to find a categorical labeling pattern. However, if the variant stimuli used are specific to familiar individuals and the experiment is designed to ask

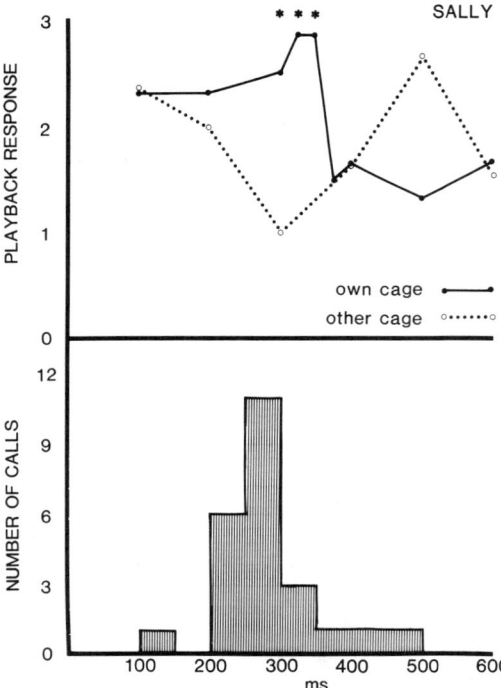

Figure 11.4. *Top:* The mean number of antiphonal calls given within 10 sec of a playback presentation of Sally's calls. (*indicates statistically significant difference, $p < .05$.) *Bottom:* Frequency distribution of Closed-Mouth Trills from Sally.

questions about individual differences, then, as we have shown above, the apparent category boundaries fluctuate to correspond to the expectations of the respondents concerning those familiar individuals. This experiment has shown that the same dimension used for a phonetic distinction (between Closed-Mouth and Open-Mouth Trills) can also be used with different boundaries to identify familiar individuals. In the context of individual recognition then, within-category discrimination can be demonstrated.

Second, several authors (Eimas & Corbit, 1973; Stevens, 1973) have argued for the existence of hard-wired feature detectors for speech contrasts. On the basis of our original study of categorization in pygmy marmosets, we also argued for hard-wired feature detectors (Snowdon & Pola, 1978). However, it should now be clear that these feature detectors are not fixed in the sense of being hard-wired. Lisker and Abramson (1970) had shown for the voicing contrast that the boundary varied as a function of the language used. We have now shown that the perceptual boundary can vary as a function of experience with the individual caller. Such a flexible category boundary cannot have been hard-wired, but must only have been acquired through experience with particular individuals. Thus, the species-specific vocalization-perception system of pygmy marmosets is learned and not innate and does not fit the key stimulus-releasing mechanism model proposed by Ehret (Chapter 10, this

A naturalistic view of categorical perception

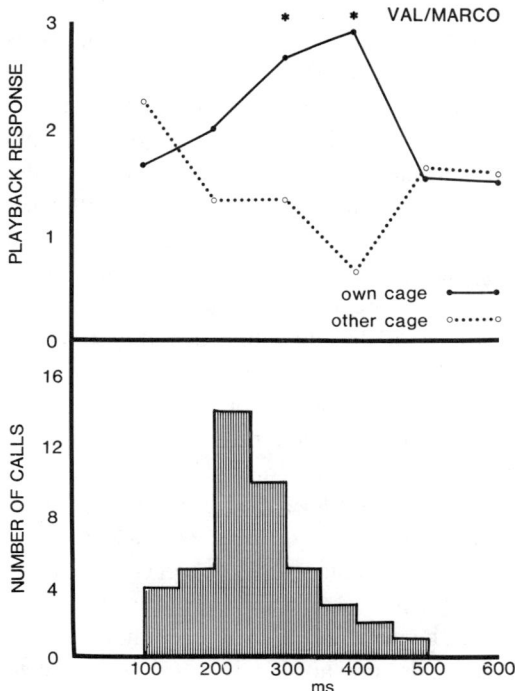

Figure 11.5. *Top:* The mean number of antiphonal calls given within 10 seconds of a playback presentation of Val/Marco's calls. (*indicates significant difference, $p < .05$.) *Bottom:* Frequency distribution of Closed-Mouth Trills given by Val/Marco.

volume). At least part of the vocal-perception system in human beings must also be learned.

I have previously proposed a two-stage model for processing species-specific sounds (Snowdon, 1979). I argued that there was a phonetic-categorization system that identified whether a signal was a species-specific signal and, if so, assigned it to the appropriate phonetic bin. Either simultaneously or subsequently a paralinguistic discrimination system analyzes such factors as gender, age, dialect, individual specificity, and intonation – the range of paralinguistic variables that could be encoded in an incoming signal. I do not know whether both of these systems operate in parallel or whether the phonetic-processing system has priority. One might naturally expect phonetic processing to have priority. However, in the study of whether Japanese macaques could perceive differences between two of their call variants (Zoloth et al., 1979), one pair of stimuli proved particularly difficult for the monkeys to discriminate on the basis of phonetic differences. It was subsequently discovered that these two tokens had been produced by the same individual (S. R. Zoloth, personal communication). Perhaps for monkeys individual identity is even more salient than the phonetic distinction. The role of social variables in the perception of vocal-communication signals is an area that greatly needs further study.

I have suggested that these two systems might be tapped with different techniques. The categorization system is most likely to be tapped in testing situations that impose memory constraints on subjects, that have instructional or task demands focusing the subject's attention on phonetic categories, and that use synthetic sounds to provide "pure" phonetic information while eliminating paralinguistic variables. The subcategorical system is more likely to be tapped by tests that minimize memory constraints on subjects, allowing them to discriminate subtler differences (Pisoni & Lazarus, 1974), by tasks that focus the subject's attention away from phonetic categories and onto other variables in the signal, and by natural vocal signals that include the paralinguistic variables of age, gender, individual specificity, and so on. Various investigators are likely to find evidence for or against CP in the strict sense of having poor discrimination of within-category tokens depending upon the research methods they use (see also discussions by Pastore in Chapter 1 and by Macmillan in Chapter 2, this volume). The fact that the demonstration of CP in this strict sense is dependent upon the use of some research techniques, but not on others, limits its usefulness as a concept.

In the context of the naturalistic approach I have developed, it appears from the data on human beings and monkeys that the perception of speech and species-specific sounds does not differ fundamentally from other types of perception. Under certain testing conditions and ecological demands, organisms may display a "pure" categorization and appear to fail or at least be inattentive in making within-category distinctions. Under other ecological demands, organisms will not only appear to have perceptual categories, but will also display a sophisticated system of subcategories that can readily be discriminated from each other. It is most likely that at least the subcategory system, if not the categories as well, are acquired through experience and not hard-wired. Both categorizing and subcategorizing are adaptive to highly social, actively communicating animals, human and nonhuman.

Note

1. All these trills are considerably longer than the 250-msec upper limit for Closed-Mouth Trills found in the Snowdon and Pola (1978) study. In that first study all the animals had come from Colombia and all had a short Closed-Mouth-Trill duration. Each of the animals in the present study came from Peru and, based on our observations both in the wild and of these captive animals, the Peruvian animals typically have a longer duration of Closed-Mouth Trills.

References

Bauers, K., & Snowdon, C. T. (In preparation). Perceptual discrimination of chirp vocalizations in the cotton-top tamarin.
Beecher, M. D., Petersen, M. R., Zoloth, S. R., Moody, D. B., & Stebbins, W. C. (1979). Perception of conspecific vocalizations by Japanese macaques. *Brain Behavior and Evolution, 16,* 433–460.
Berlin, B. (1978). Ethnobiological classification. In E. Rosch and B. B. Lloyd (Eds.), *Cognition and Categorization* (pp. 9–26). Hillsdale, NJ: Erlbaum.
Cheney, D. L., & Seyfarth, R. M. (1982). How vervet monkeys perceive their grunts: Field playback experiments. *Animal Behaviour, 30,* 739–751.

Cutting, J. E., Rosner, B. S., & Foard, C. F. (1976). Perceptual categories for music-like sounds: Implications for theories of speech perception. *Quarterly Journal of Experimental Psychology, 28,* 361–378.

Ehret, G., & Haack, B. (1981). Categorical perception of mouse pup ultrasound by lactating females. *Naturwissenschaften, 68,* 208.

Eimas, P., & Corbit, J. D. (1973). Selective adaptation of linguistic feature detectors. *Cognitive Psychology, 4,* 99–109.

Green, S. (1975). Variations of vocal pattern with social situation in Japanese monkey (*Macaca fuscata*): A field study. In L. A. Rosenblum (Ed.), *Primate Behavior* (Vol. 4, pp. 1–102). New York: Academic Press.

Kaplan, J. N., Winship-Ball, A., & Sim, L. (1978). Maternal discrimination of infant vocalizations in squirrel monkeys. *Primates, 19,* 187–193.

Kuhl, P. K. (1979). Models and mechanisms of speech perception. *Brain Behavior and Evolution, 16,* 374–408.

Kuhl, P. K., & Miller, J. D. (1975). Speech perception in the chinchilla: Voiced-voiceless distinction in alveolar plosive consonants. *Science, 190,* 69–72.

Lillehei, R. A., & Snowdon, C. T. (1978). Individual and situational differences in the vocalizations of young stump-tail macaques (*Macaca arctoides*). *Behaviour, 65,* 270–281.

Lisker, L., & Abramson, A. S. (1970). The voicing dimension: Some experiments in comparative phonetics. *Proceedings of the 6th International Congress of Phonetic Science*, Prague.

Marler, P. (1970). Birdsong and speech development: Could there be parallels? *American Scientist, 58,* 669–673.

Marler, P. (1975). On the origin of speech from animal sounds. In J. F. Kavanaugh & J. E. Cutting (Eds.), *The Role of Speech in Language* (pp. 11–37). Cambridge, MA: MIT Press.

Masataka, N. (1983). Categorical responses to natural and synthesized alarm calls in Goeldi's monkeys (*Callimico goeldi*). *Primates, 24,* 40–51.

Miller, G. A. (1956). On the magical number seven plus or minus two. Some limits on our capacity for processing information. *Psychological Review, 77,* 257–273.

Miller, J. D., Wier, C. C., Pastore, R. E., Kelly, W. J., & Dooling, R. J. (1976). Discrimination and labeling of noise-buzz sequences with varying noise-lead times: An example of categorical perception. *Journal of the Acoustical Society of America, 60,* 410–417.

Morse, P. A., & Snowdon, C. T. (1975). An investigation of categorical speech discrimination by rhesus monkeys. *Perception and Psychophysics, 17,* 9–16.

Newman, J. D., Smith, H. J., & Talmage-Riggs, G. (1983). Structural variability in primate vocalizations and its functional significance: An analysis of squirrel monkey chuck calls. *Folia Primatologica. 40,* 114–124.

Newport, E. L., & Bellugi, U. (1978). Linguistic expression of category levels in a visual-gestural language: A flower is a flower is a flower. In E. Rosch & B. B. Lloyd (Eds.), *Cognition and Categorization* (pp. 49–71). Hillsdale, NJ: Erlbaum.

Petersen, M. R., Beecher, M. D., Zoloth, S. R., Green, S., Marler, P. R., Moody, D. B., & Stebbins, W. C. (1984). Neural lateralization of vocalizations by Japanese macaques: Communicative significance is more important than acoustic structure. *Behavioral Neuroscience, 98,* 779–790.

Pisoni, D. B. (1977). Identification and discrimination of the relative onset of two component tones: Implications for the perception of voicing in stops. *Journal of the Acoustic Society of America, 61,* 1352–1361.

Pisoni, D. B., & Lazarus, J. H. (1974). Categorical and noncategorical modes of speech perception along the voicing continuum. *Journal of the Acoustical Society of America, 55,* 328–333.

Pola, Y. V., & Snowdon, C. T. (1975). The vocalizations of pygmy marmosets (*Cebuella pygmaea*). *Animal Behaviour, 23,* 826–842.

Rosch, E. (1978). Principles of categorization. In E. Rosch and B. B. Lloyd (Eds.), *Cognition and Categorization* (pp. 27–48). Hillsdale, NJ: Erlbaum.

Rowell, T. E., & Hinde, R. A. (1962). Vocal communication by the rhesus monkey (*Macaca mulatta*). *Proceedings of the Zoological Society of London, 138,* 279–294.

Savage, A., Droczek, L. A., & Snowdon, C. T. (In preparation). Color discrimination as it relates to the feeding ecology of the cotton-top tamarin.

Seligman, M. E. B. (1970). On the generality of the laws of learning. *Psychological Review, 77,* 406–418.

Seyfarth, R. M., Cheney, D. L., & Marler, P. (1980). Vervet monkey alarm calls: Semantic communication in a free-ranging primate. *Animal Behaviour, 28,* 1070–1094.

Sinnott, J. M., Beecher, M. D., Moody, D. B., & Stebbins, W. C. (1976). Speech sound discrimination by monkeys and humans. *Journal of the Acoustical Society of America, 60,* 687–695.

Snowdon, C. T. (1979). Response of nonhuman animals to speech and to species-specific sounds. *Brain, Behavior and Evolution, 16,* 409–429.

Snowdon, C. T., & Cleveland, J. (1980). Individual recognition of contact calls by pygmy marmosets. *Animal Behaviour, 28,* 717–727.

Snowdon, C. T., Cleveland, J., & French, J. A. (1983). Responses to context- and individual-specific cues in cotton-top tamarin long calls. *Animal Behaviour, 31,* 99–101.

Snowdon, C. T., Coe, C. L., & Hodun, A. (1985). Population recognition of infant isolation peeps in the squirrel monkey. *Animal Behaviour, 33,* 1145–1151.

Snowdon, C. T., & Hodun, A. (1981). Acoustic adaptation in pygmy marmoset contact calls: Locational cues vary with distance between conspecifics. *Behavioral Ecology and Socibiology, 9,* 295–300.

Snowdon, C. T., & Pola, Y.V. (1978). Interspectific and intraspecific responses to synthesized marmoset vocalizations. *Animal Behaviour, 26,* 192–206.

Stevens, K. N. (1973). Speech perception. In D. B. Tower (Ed.), *The Nervous System* (Vol. 3, pp. 163–171). *Human Communication and its Disorders.* New York: Raven Press.

Symmes, D., & Newman, J. D. (1974). Discrimination of isolation peep variants by squirrel monkeys. *Experimental Brain Research, 19,* 365–376.

Waters, R. S., & Wilson, W. A., Jr. (1976). Speech perception by rhesus monkeys: The voicing distinction in synthesized labial and velar stop consonants. *Perception and Psychophysics, 19,* 285–289.

Zoloth, S. R., Petersen, M. R., Beecher, M. D., Green, S., Marler, P., Moody, D. B., & Stebbins, W. (1979). Species-specific perceptual processing of vocal sounds by monkeys. *Science, 204,* 870–873.

12 The special-mechanisms debate in speech research: Categorization tests on animals and infants

Patricia K. Kuhl

The processing of natural language is assumed to involve specially evolved mechanisms at some stage during the conversion of an auditory waveform to a perceived message. Theories of speech perception suggest that even the phonetic level of language requires such special mechanisms because of the extreme complexity of the mapping between sound and percept. Phenomena such as categorical perception (CP) have also been attributed to mechanisms specially evolved to process speech sounds. This chapter analyzes the contribution of animal studies of CP to the special-mechanisms debate. Animals exhibit auditory-level processing without phonetic-level processing; this represents a natural test of whether a phenomenon like CP requires specialized mechanisms. The animal findings are compared with human CP effects using nonspeech stimuli. A review of the evidence shows that animals exhibit CP for the voicing and place features. These findings show that special mechanisms are not required for CP, and hence that they should not be imputed to human infants solely on the basis of CP. Human infants perceive phonetic equivalence classes that include both unimodal and cross-modal variants. Comparisons between human infants and animals should go beyond CP to focus on such tests that call for more sophisticated categorization and representational abilities.

No one seriously doubts the idea that the processing of language involves specialized mechanisms. The question is: At what "level" of language does specialization occur? Is it only syntax that requires the specialized linguistic machinery, or do all levels, including the phonetic one, have specialized mechanisms?

This question originated with the earliest psychological studies of language. At the phonetic level, the problem was cast as the "auditory versus phonetic" distinction. The distinction served to point out a commonly held expectation that at some stage in the processing of speech, purely auditory processes gave way to more specialized linguistic ones. The question was: Where did the more general auditory processes end and the more specialized phonetic processes take over? Was only the initial registration of frequency, intensity, and duration attributable to the auditory level, with the rest processed by more specialized phonetic mechanisms? What aspects of speech perception required a higher, special kind of processing?

There were two compelling reasons to accept the claim that the phonetic level of speech required special mechanisms. First, when the earliest studies tried to un-

The work discussed here was supported by grants to the author from NSF (BNS 8316318 and BNS 8103581) and NIH (HD-18286). The author thanks Andrew N. Meltzoff for helpful comments on an earlier draft of the chapter.

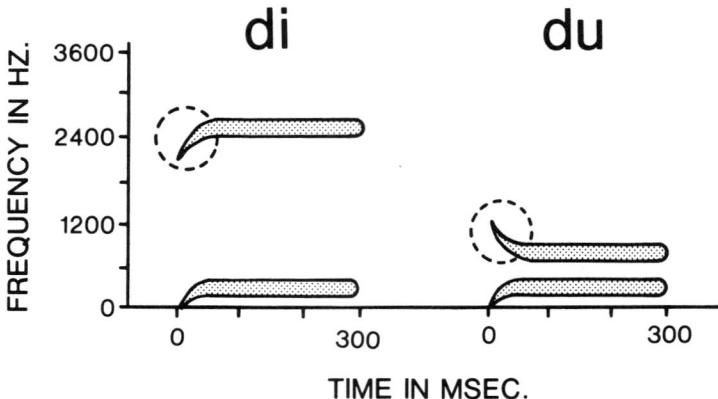

Figure 12.1. Computer-simulated syllables showing that the acoustic information corresponding to the consonant /d/ depends on vowel context. In /di/ the formant transition rises; in /du/ it falls. (From Liberman et al., 1967.)

cover what was expected to be a comparatively simple set of rules relating the acoustic properties of speech to its perception, an enormously complex mapping between sound and percept was found (Liberman, Cooper, Shankweiler, & Studdert-Kennedy, 1967). The transformation of physical sound to phonetic percept (the consonants and vowels we perceive in speech) did not appear to be straightforward. To be sure, specific acoustic events ("cues") were shown to underlie the perception of sound – as witnessed by our eventual ability to artificially create ("synthesize") intelligible speech – but rather than finding the expected one-to-one relationship between acoustic events and phonetic perception, researchers verified time and again that the rules relating the two were extremely complex.

One telling indication of the complexity of the phonetic level of speech is the fact that we still do not have a machine that understands speech. Given that many psychologists, engineers, and linguists are working on this problem, and that the solution is worth millions of dollars to industry, it is likely that if a solution were readily available we would have it today. In fact, because phoneme recognition is the major stumbling block in speech recognition, some machine solutions bypass the phonetic level of speech and try to recognize whole words (e.g., Klatt, 1977).

Why is it so difficult to categorize the sounds of human speech into phonetic categories correctly and reliably? Figure 12.1 shows one reason why computers fail, using a demonstration from early studies on speech (Liberman et al., 1967): The acoustic "cue" for the consonant /d/ varies a great deal depending on the vowel that accompanies it. When /d/ occurs in the /i/ vowel context, the critical acoustic cue (the direction of the second-formant transition) must rise for us to hear /d/, whereas in the /u/ vowel context, the second-formant transition must fall for /d/ to be heard. In addition, the cues change when the speaker changes, when the rate of speech changes, and when the phoneme occurs in different positions in a word. Nevertheless, even human infants categorize speech sounds correctly under these

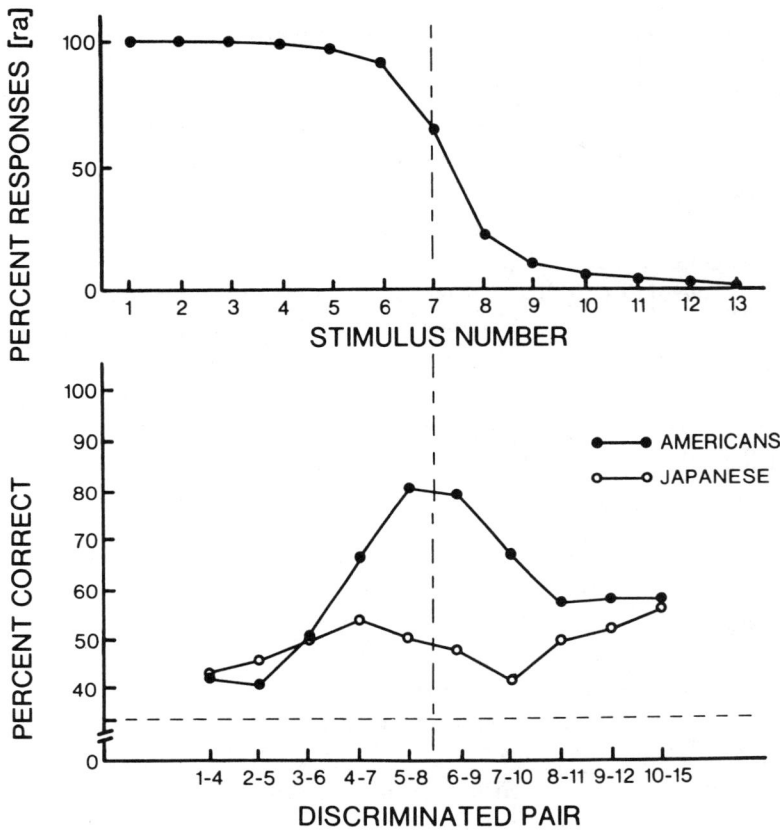

Figure 12.2. Test of the categorical perception of /ra/ and /la/ by American and Japanese adults. American listeners show the characteristic peak in discrimination at the phonetic boundary; Japanese listeners do not. (From Miyawaki et al., 1975.)

conditions (Kuhl 1979a, 1980, 1983, 1985a). The many-to-one relationship between sound and percept, resolved by babies but not by machines, has added face validity to the argument that phonetic processing is accomplished by "specialized mechanisms," perhaps ones that evolved especially for speech (Mattingly, 1972).

The second finding that has added strength to arguments for the existence of special mechanisms at the phonetic level came from the discovery in the 1950s of "categorical perception" (Liberman, 1957; Liberman, Harris, Hoffman, & Griffith, 1957). The phenomenon involved the following demonstration: A continuum of sounds was generated by computer along which an acoustic dimension was altered in small physically equal steps. In the present example the acoustic dimension under manipulation is the extent and direction of frequency change in the third-formant transition. This acoustic event distinguishes the two syllables /ra/ and /la/. Tests showed that although the acoustic dimension changed continuously along the continuum in a stepwise fashion, perception was discontinuous. The stimuli were heard as a series of /ra/s that shifted abruptly to a series of /la/s at some point on the continuum (Figure 12.2, top). This was true even though no obvious physical discontinuity occurred at the place on the continuum where perception abruptly changed. Moreover, the ability to discriminate between sounds taken from the series was constrained in a curious way. Adults appeared to be capable of discriminating only between sounds that fell in different categories (Figure 12.2, bottom). Two /ra/s on the continuum were not discriminable, but a /ra/ and a /la/, no further apart than the two /ra/s, were quite discriminable (Miyawaki et al., 1975).

Thus, the ability to discriminate small differences in the underlying dimension varied along the continuum in a nonmonotonic fashion. Enhanced discriminability occurred at the "boundaries" between phonetic categories, whereas reduced discriminability occurred within phonetic categories. As such, categorical perception (CP) defied one of the oldest principles of auditory psychophysics, Weber's law, which predicts a monotonic relationship for discrimination along a simple physical continuum, holding for the discrimination of auditory frequency, intensity, and duration. Moreover, CP defied a classic principle of cognitive psychology concerning categorization: Normally, many more stimuli are discriminable than are absolutely identifiable (Miller, 1956). CP differs in that the ability to discriminate is severely restricted unless the stimuli are identified as belonging to different categories. So how is it that the perception of speech is "categorical" (discriminable across but not within categories) when principles of psychophysics and cognitive psychology predict otherwise? How could it be done if not by "special mechanisms"?

Two other findings fueled the special-mechanisms argument. First, perception was categorical only for contrasts that were phonemic in the adult's language. Japanese adults, for whom the /ra-la/ distinction is not phonemic, did not produce the characteristic peak in the discrimination function for /ra-la/ stimuli (Figure 12.2, bottom) (Miyawaki et al., 1975). Their ability to discriminate the /ra-la/ stimuli hovered near the level of chance. These cross-language differences between adults from different language-speaking environments supported a second notion that was closely tied to the special-mechanisms claim. This was that the specialized mechanisms rely on an articulatory representation of sounds that mediates the relation between sound and percept (Liberman et al., 1967). According to this "motor theory," Japanese adults did not distinguish the /ra/ and /la/ sounds in perception because they did not distinguish them in their production of speech. This led to inquiries about infants' perception of these sounds. Was CP learned through experience with a specific language, perhaps through its production?

The question was answered by Eimas, Siqueland, Jusczyk, and Vigorito's (1971) work on 1-month-old infants' perception of speech. Their data supported the "special-mechanisms" view while dissociating it from the idea that the special mechanism relied on the ability to produce the sounds (see Chapter 5 by Eimas, Miller, & Jusczyk, this volume). Eimas showed that infants could discriminate computer-generated sounds that straddled the adult-defined phonetic boundary, but failed to discriminate within-category stimuli (Eimas, 1974, 1975; Eimas et al., 1971). Their ability to do this in the absence of a protracted period of experience in producing or listening to speech suggested that the phenomenon was not learned. Infants appeared to partition the stimulus continuum just as adults did, right from the start. Further evidence against the learning account came from the finding that infants demonstrated the effect for all phonemic contrasts, whether native to the language environment in which they were raised or not (Streeter, 1976).

What emerged, therefore, was a very strong theoretical claim, which, in its most general form, was that the processing of natural language involved specialized mechanisms. No one refuted this claim. However, the research on speech perception resulted in an extension of the claim to lower levels of language. It stated that even the phonetic level of processing required specialized mechanisms. As I have already indicated, there are good reasons to accept this claim as well. It is likely that at some level the conversion of sound to phonetic percepts requires specialized mechanisms. If we accept this, the important questions become, Which specific phenomena require these specialized mechanisms? Should we hypothesize specialized mechanisms to account for CP?

These questions motivated the research program I discuss here. In this chapter I describe tests of animals' perception of speech-sound categories and show how they bear on the special-mechanisms debate. I am motivated to do so in part because, although it is now a decade since the first study (Kuhl & Miller, 1975) appeared, the contribution of animal studies to the special-mechanisms debate is still often misunderstood.

The program of research began 10 years ago with the publication of a surprising finding. Miller and I discovered that the chinchilla appeared to perceive speech sounds "categorically." Needless to say, investigators' reactions to the result were complex. Some argued that an animal's perception of speech could not, in principle, teach us anything about humans' perception of speech. These individuals disregarded the finding. Others, less enthralled by the original CP effects in humans, embraced the finding. They argued that if a chinchilla exhibited CP one could surely abandon interest in the CP phenomenon and the special-mechanisms hypothesis. It was no longer interesting that 1-month-old human infants demonstrated the hallmark of speech perception because chinchillas did too.

Unfortunately, both the critics' and supporters' opinions were equally misguided. The critics were wrong to dismiss tests of animals' perception of speech; I will show that tests on animals allow a very specific and strong conclusion about CP. But the supporters were wrong to use the finding to dismiss CP as uninteresting. CP is, to this day, an auditory phenomenon that cannot be explained by known psychophysical principles, and interest in it will probably remain high at least as long as the anomaly persists.

This chapter is organized in three parts. In the first, I lay out the logic behind tests of speech perception in animals. Specifically, the first section attempts to answer the questions: What issues do the animal studies address? What is the hypothesis? An integral part of the answer involves distinguishing CP tests with animals from human tests of CP using nonspeech signals. Many equate the hypotheses under test in these two kinds of experiments. I will distinguish them.

The second part of the chapter is devoted to a review of the animal data. Five experimental studies have been completed and published during the past decade. Each serves to advance the enterprise one step further toward its eventual goal, which is to find out where the parallels between human and animal speech perception break down and to identify the phenomena that may require the hypothesis of special mechanisms. The chapter closes by considering the most important questions: What do we do with these findings? What do they mean?

Animals' perception of speech

What is the hypothesis under test?

When humans respond to speech stimuli we believe that they use both auditory and phonetic levels of processing. It is difficult to tease the two "levels" apart theoretically and experimentally, however. We do not know which effects to attribute to the auditory level and which to the phonetic. An animal model is valuable because it resolves this. If the animal species is chosen properly (Kuhl, 1979b), it can provide a good model of man's auditory level of processing in the absence of any higher-order (phonetic) processing. The advantage is fairly straightforward: The animal reflects what is natural for the auditory-processing system when phonetic-level influences have been stripped away and only auditory-level influences remain.

Stated simply, the hypothesis under test in animal experiments involving speech is this: Is auditory-level processing sufficient to account for CP? Or is phonetic-level processing necessary? If the experiment demonstrates a match between animals and humans then we can conclude that the auditory level is sufficient – CP can exist in the absence of specialized mechanisms.

Animal studies and their relation to nonspeech tests

Things become more complicated when one tries to relate animal experiments to human CP experiments with nonspeech signals. Although often equated, the two examine different hypotheses and contribute to the special-mechanisms debate in different ways. In what follows, I will distinguish the two.

Experiments using nonspeech have a long history in speech perception. Initial attempts to replicate CP effects using nonspeech signals failed (Liberman, Harris, Eimas, Lisker, & Bastian, 1961; Liberman, Harris, Kinney, & Lane, 1961; Mattingly et al., 1971), leading to the strong claim that the processing of speech required a specialized mechanism. Because the discrimination of speech did not conform to more traditional psychoacoustic discrimination results such as those predicted by Weber's law, it was not particularly surprising when nonspeech signals behaved differently from speech. Because only speech signals failed to conform, the absence of nonspeech CP was strongly tied to the claim that "speech was special."

In the middle 1970s, the situation changed. Further studies were conducted on nonspeech signals and these did yield CP effects (Miller, Wier, Pastore, Kelly, & Dooling, 1976; Pisoni, 1977). This led investigators to conclude that CP did not involve specialized mechanisms and should instead be attributed to general auditory processing mechanisms. But their conclusion does not necessarily follow. The problem is this: Although the "speech-specific" characteristic can be equated with the "specially evolved for speech" argument, the reverse is not necessarily true. That is, although a "speech-specific" mechanism must have evolved "especially for speech," mechanisms could, in principle, have evolved "especially for speech" without being "speech specific." As such, experiments with nonspeech signals do not provide a critical test for or against the existence of mechanisms evolved especially for speech. Nonspeech experiments test a different hypothesis.

Tests using nonspeech examine the "tuning" of the mechanisms underlying speech perception. In other words, they ask whether the mechanisms responsible for speech perception are so narrowly tuned as to exclude nonspeech signals that mimic the critical features in speech. The importance of replicating speech effects with nonspeech signals is that such a result ties the two signals, speech and nonspeech, to a common mechanism. The result provides no information concerning the origins of the mechanism. It simply addresses its selectivity. This means that if feature detecting or other "dedicated" mechanisms exist, they may not be so narrowly tuned that nonspeech sounds are excluded; nonspeech sounds that mimic the critical features in speech may "fool" them (Kuhl, 1978, 1986a).

The more narrowly tuned the underlying mechanisms, the more likely it is that they evolved specifically for speech. That is why when speech and nonspeech findings completely diverged, as they did in the early studies, the hypothesis that speech perception required "special mechanisms" was suggested (Liberman, Harris, Eimas, Lisker, & Bastian, 1961; Liberman, Harris, Kinney, & Lane, 1961). Now the results of speech and nonspeech tests show convergence, but the results do not lead to the opposite claim – that speech does *not* require special mechanisms. The nonspeech results can be equally accommodated by either alternative – by saying that specially evolved mechanisms exist and are "fooled" by signals carefully mimicking speech, or by the general auditory-mechanism account.

Animal studies contribute to the debate in a different way. They define what is "natural" in audition in the absence of phonetic processing. The successful demonstration of CP effects in animals shows that the phenomenon can exist in the absence of mechanisms that evolved specifically for speech. Although tests on animals do not rule out the possibility of specially evolved mechanisms in humans, they show that their existence is not a necessity, a claim that cannot be unambiguously supported by the results of studies using nonspeech signals.

In summary, this first section has distinguished between the hypotheses tested in animal and human studies involving nonspeech stimuli. I have argued that it is useful to clarify the different ways the two types of study contribute to the special-mechanisms debate. Tests with nonspeech examine the "tuning" of the mechanisms underlying speech perception. When speech and nonspeech studies converge, the main theoretical implication is that the two signals are tied to a common mechanism. Either account ("special mechanism" or "general auditory") can accommodate such findings. In contrast, animal tests do not address the tuning issue. Rather, they address the fundamental claim underlying the "special-mechanism" account, which is, that certain speech-perception phenomena cannot exist in the absence of special mechanisms. If successful, the tests enable one to entertain the notion that these phenomena are not due to a special mechanism but to "something else."

Studies on animals' perception of speech

Voice-onset-time generalization by chinchillas

Our first experiment (Kuhl & Miller, 1975) mimicked an adult-categorization experiment with animals. Adults are typically asked to identify stimuli drawn randomly from a continuum as either an example of stimulus category A or stimulus category B. In speech experiments, the two categories are syllables that differ phonetically, such as /da/ and /ta/. The test stimuli are computer generated and form a continuum in which the value of a particular acoustic dimension is altered in a stepwise fashion from one end of the continuum to the other. The resulting data produce a psychometric function showing the percentage of time each stimulus was categorized as /da/ as a function of changes in the underlying acoustic dimension. The 50% point on the psychometric function is termed the "phonetic boundary" between the two categories.

Our question was simple. Where would an animal place the boundary on a phonetic continuum? In our first experiment we used chinchillas, because they are mammals whose basic auditory abilities are similar to those of humans (Kuhl, 1979b). They were trained, using an avoidance-conditioning procedure, to distinguish computer-synthesized versions of the syllables /da/ and /ta/. These two syllables are distinguished by a number of acoustic cues (Lisker, 1975), the most prominent of which is a timing difference between the onset of laryngeal voicing and the onset of the "burst" in energy that occurs when a stop consonant like /d/ or /t/ is released. The timing difference, termed the "voice-onset-time" (VOT) and expressed in msec, is the amount of time by which the onset of voicing lags the onset of the burst. In voiced English stops such as /d/, /b/, or /g/, the two events occur nearly simultaneously; voicing follows the burst within 5 to 40 msec, the exact amount depending on the place of articulation of the stop. In voiceless stops such as /p/, /t/, or /k/, the onset of voicing is delayed; it typically occurs between 40 and 150 msec after the release of the burst. (See Klatt, 1975, and Lisker &

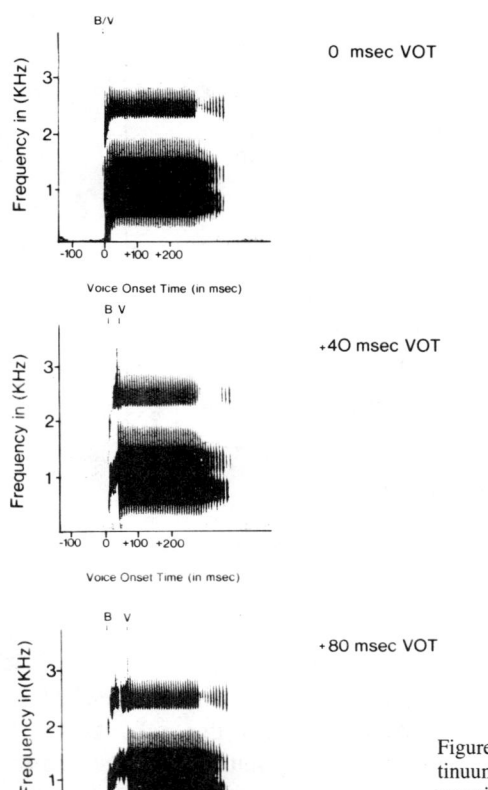

Figure 12.3. Stimuli from a voiced–voiceless continuum varying in voice onset time (VOT). Humans perceive the 0-msec VOT stimulus as /da/, whereas the +40-msec VOT and +80-msec VOT stimuli are perceived as /ta/. The onset of voicing (V) and the onset of the burst (B) are marked.

Abramson, 1964, for further discussion.) The timing difference can be seen in the computer-generated stimuli shown in Figure 12.3.

The animals were trained to discriminate the two endpoint stimuli on a VOT continuum. However, they were given no exposure to the rest of the test continuum. The test continuum ranged from 0 msec VOT (as a good instance of /da/) to +80 msec VOT (perceived by humans as a good instance of /ta/). In response to one of the endpoint stimuli (the positive stimulus, either 0 or +80 depending upon random assignment), animals were trained to cross a midline barrier in a cage to avoid a mild shock and the sounding of a buzzer. To the other stimulus, the animal was trained to inhibit the crossing response. Correct inhibition of the response was rewarded by the presentation of water from a drinking tube. When performance on these endpoint stimuli was near perfect, a generalization paradigm was used to test the stimuli between /da/ and /ta/ on the continuum (those theoretically critical stimuli between 0 msec VOT and +80 msec VOT, in 10-msec steps). The design of the experiment was that during generalization testing, half the trials would involve the endpoint stimuli. On the endpoint trials, the appropriate feedback (shock and

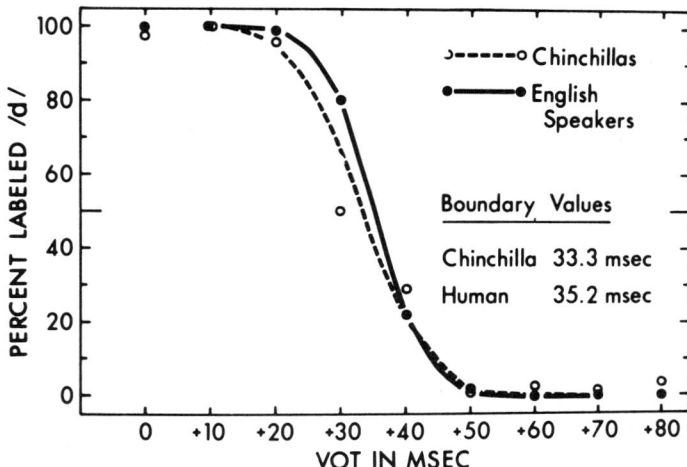

Figure 12.4. Mean percentage of "/d/" responses by chinchillas and humans for stimuli on a continuum ranging from /da/ to /ta/. The "phonetic boundaries" do not differ significantly. (From Kuhl & Miller, 1978.)

buzzer on incorrect positive trials; water on correct negative trials) was given, just as it had been during the training phase. On the other half of the trials, the novel stimuli (+10 to +70 msec VOT) were presented. The stimuli were presented in random order, eliminating any effects due to the ordered presentation of stimuli. On these trials, the feedback was arranged to indicate that the animal was always right, no matter what the response. The feedback was arranged to reinforce whatever the animal did naturally.

The experiment allowed us to ask where the perceptual boundary between /da/ and /ta/ was located for the animal. The data are shown in Figure 12.4. The mean percentage of /da/ responses to each stimulus on the continuum is plotted for four chinchillas and four human adults. The curves were generated by a least-squares method. The resulting phonetic boundaries, located at 35.2-msec VOT for humans and 33.3-msec VOT for animals, did not differ significantly.

The extremely good match between the two functions suggested that animals heard an abrupt qualitative change at precisely the location where human adults separate the /da/ and /ta/ categories. Our hypothesis was given tentative support. Animals had demonstrated the first component of the two-part CP requirement, which is a tendency to partition the continuum, placing the boundary between the two categories precisely where English speakers (and the speakers of some other languages) separate the two categories phonetically. On the basis of these findings, we speculated that the boundaries for other phonemic categories might coincide with animals' natural perceptual boundaries and argued that additional experiments should test this (Kuhl & Miller, 1975).

Interactions between voice onset time and place of articulation

We had demonstrated in one experiment that an animal's natural auditory boundary coincided with a phonetic one for humans. It was important to extend our initial results to other phonetic contrasts in order to test the notion that other natural boundaries would coincide with phonetic ones. The most logical extensions involved additional tests of the voicing feature because of another intriguing fact about phonetic boundaries in speech: They are not absolutely fixed but are altered by a number of factors. For example, the perceptual boundary dividing voiced and voiceless stimuli moves with the place of articulation of the voiced–voiceless pair. This perceptual effect is mirrored in peoples' production of speech as well (Lisker & Abramson, 1964). Results like these led to the suggestion that the perceptual mechanism functions to take articulatory factors into account; the original "motor theory" of speech perception embodied this idea (Liberman et al., 1967).

The perceptual data show that for human listeners the boundary on a voiced–voiceless continuum ranging from /ba/ to /pa/ is located at a VOT different from that of the boundary on a /da-ta/ continuum. Moreover, the locations of these boundaries differ from the one for a continuum ranging from /ga/ to /ka/. The approximate boundary values for bilabial (/ba-pa/), alveolar (/da-ta/), and velar (/ga-ka/) sounds are +25, +35, and +45 msec VOT, respectively (Abramson & Lisker, 1970). No acoustic or auditory explanation for the change in the location of the boundary can as yet be put forward. What we know about the processing of temporal-order information suggests that the boundary should be located in the vicinity of a 20-msec separation between two events; this was verified experimentally using nonspeech stimuli that mimic speech (Pisoni, 1977). But the temporal-order hypothesis does not explain why the boundary varies with place of articulation, even though considerable effort has been invested in attempting to explain it (Divenyi & Danner, 1977; Divenyi & Sachs, 1978). We simply do not know why the boundary "moves."

The fact that it does, however, makes an interesting test for animals, particularly if the VOT values of the endpoints on the continua are held constant across the tests. If the endpoints remain the same on all three continua (0 and +80 msec VOT), and yet the boundary values change with corresponding changes in the place of articulation, then this would affirm an additional fact; namely, that animals are not dividing the continuum in a fixed location, such as "in the middle." Our next experiment (Kuhl & Miller, 1978), then, was to test these same animals on two other sets of stimuli, a /ba-pa/ series and a /ga-ka/ series.

These tests were run exactly as the previous ones were. When the experiment involving the /da-ta/ stimuli was complete, we introduced the "endpoints" of the bilabial /ba-pa/ series. The endpoint VOT values were again 0 and +80 msec VOT. For the first few trials, the new endpoints were introduced without any feedback. We were curious to see whether the new /ba/ and /pa/ stimuli would be categorized appropriately as voiced and voiceless stimuli. Once the first trials indicated that they

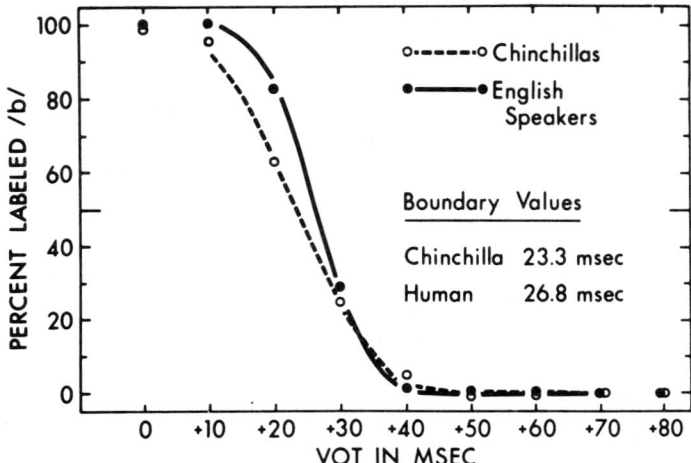

Figure 12.5. Mean percentage of "/b/" responses by chinchillas and humans for stimuli on a continuum ranging from /ba/ to /pa/. "Phonetic boundaries" do not differ significantly. (From Kuhl & Miller, 1978.)

were, we instituted the appropriate feedback conditions for these new endpoints, which again occurred on half the trials, and we replicated our test with the new stimuli. As in the previous test, the stimuli between the endpoints (+10 to +70 msec VOT, in 10-msec steps) were presented in random order as generalization stimuli. For these trials, all feedback was arranged to indicate that the animal had responded correctly, no matter what he did.

The results, shown in Figure 12.5, again showed good agreement between the human and animal categorization data. The boundary values were 26.8 msec VOT for humans and 23.3 msec VOT for animals, which are not significantly different. Because the animal and human subjects tested in the previous experiment were the same as those tested here, it was possible to compare boundary data for each individual subject to see whether it had "moved," and if so, whether it was in the predicted direction. The data indicated that each animal and human subject showed a decrease in the VOT value of the boundary between experiments one and two.

After tests involving the bilabial feature were completed, we tested the velar (/ga-ka/) stimuli. Here again, we were interested in whether the boundary would shift for animals as it does for humans. Figure 12.6 shows these results. As before, the data demonstrate a remarkable correspondence. The two categorization functions were virtually identical. The boundary value for human listeners was 42.3 msec VOT and for chinchilla, 42.5 msec VOT. Examination of the individual subjects' data showed that all human and animal subjects had shifted their boundary values in the positive direction.

Taking all three experiments into account, we examined individual categorization functions for the three places of articulation and verified that all human and animal

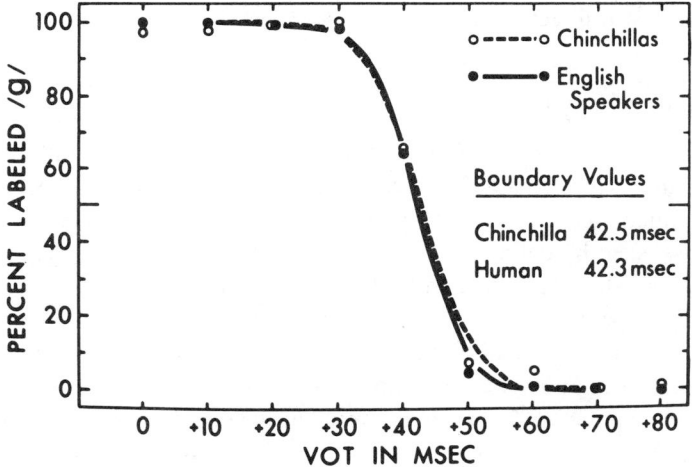

Figure 12.6. Mean percentage of "/g/" responses by chinchillas and humans for stimuli on a continuum ranging from /ga/ to /ka/. No significant difference exists between "phonetic boundaries." (From Kuhl & Miller, 1978.)

subjects had ordered their boundary values similarly. For every subject, the lowest boundary value was for the bilabial series; the highest boundary value occurred for the velar stimuli, with the alveolar boundary between these two.

The most obvious implication of these results was that they dispelled the possibility that animals were responding to a fixed VOT threshold located in the middle of the continuum. In all three experiments the contingencies were identical, and the endpoint stimuli were identical in VOT. Yet animals' boundaries appropriately shifted with the place of articulation of the voiced–voiceless pair. This shift was substantial; the mean boundary value changed from 23.3 msec VOT for bilabials to a mean of 42.5 msec VOT for velars.

With the completion of these experiments we felt confident that animals' categorization functions for speech were very similar to those of adult humans. We had demonstrated in three experiments that animals' natural boundaries coincided with humans' phonetic ones; these findings raised the intriguing possibility that phonetic boundaries in human language were designed to exploit auditorily natural ones in the first place (Kuhl, 1978, 1979b; Kuhl & Miller, 1975, 1978).

But whereas these possibilities had been newly raised by the data, more detailed questions about animals' abilities still remained. We had examined animals' categorization functions, but had not yet looked at animals' discrimination of specific pairs of stimuli from the continuum. Because it is the enhanced discriminability at the locations of phonetic boundaries and poor discriminability within categories – the "phoneme boundary effect" – that sets speech apart from other phenomena in psychophysics and in cognitive psychology, and because infants appear to demonstrate this effect without learning or experience (Eimas et al., 1971), we were motivated to test it directly.

Discrimination of just noticeable differences in voice-onset time by chinchillas

Our first discrimination study on animals (Kuhl, 1981) was unlike the discrimination procedures typically used in speech experiments. In typical speech experiments, discrimination is tested using a same–different, oddity, or *ABX* task. Pairs of stimuli are selected by defining a "step-size" or distance between two stimuli on the continuum. All pairs separated by this distance are tested. For example, if a VOT continuum varies in 10-msec steps, and a "two-step" discrimination test is conducted, all pairs of stimuli that differ by 20 msec on the continuum are tested. Pairs of stimuli such as 0 versus +20 msec VOT, and +10 versus +30 msec VOT, +20 versus +40 msec VOT, and so on, would be included. Under these conditions, the phoneme-boundary effect is demonstrated when the stimuli straddling the phonetic boundary are discriminable, whereas pairs in which both stimuli fall on the same side of the boundary are not.

Thus, CP demonstrates that listeners are more sensitive to a stimulus change at the phonetic boundary than they are at any other place on the continuum. This way of stating the effect suggests another approach to testing discrimination, one quite common in other areas of psychophysics. The approach is to test acuity directly – that is, to identify the exact amount of change that can be detected at various points along the continuum. In experiments on auditory psychophysics, for example, it is common to identify the "just noticeable difference" (*jnd*) at various values along a continuous dimension such as frequency or intensity. The results of experiments like these are lawful enough to have been described as Weber's law (Baird & Noma, 1978). Weber's law states that the *jnd* in a stimulus dimension is proportional to the amount of the dimension present in the base stimulus under test. Thus, the *jnd* for frequency increases proportionately with frequency (Wier, Jesteadt, & Green, 1977) such that the *jnd* is larger for higher frequencies. The same is true for intensity (Jesteadt, Wier, & Green, 1977) and duration (Abel, 1972).

To cast our speech example in this format, one would have to measure the *jnd* in VOT, at various VOTs along the continuum. Weber's law predicts that the resulting function will be monotonic – a linear function with the *jnd* in VOT being proportional to the VOT under test. This means that the smallest *jnd* would occur at 0 msec VOT and the largest *jnd* at +80 msec VOT. But the CP model predicts a very different function – one that is nonmonotonic, with the best acuity (smallest *jnd*) occurring at the location of the phonetic boundary.

The experiment we ran in 1981 was designed to test which of these two alternatives held for animals. The basic idea was to identify the smallest change in VOT an animal could detect at various VOT values along the continuum. Each VOT separated by 10 msec on the /da-ta/ continuum served as a "standard." A staircase procedure was used, whereby a given standard stimulus (e.g., +80 msec VOT) was

Categorization by animals and infants

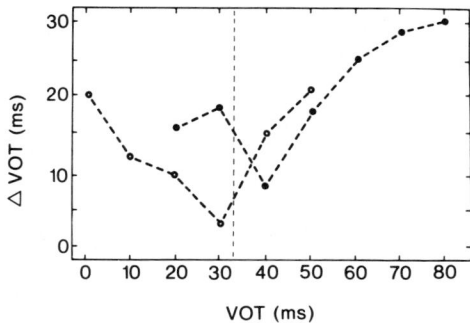

Figure 12.7. The average "just noticeable difference" (*jnd*) in VOT at various values of VOT along the voicing continuum. The open circles represent data obtained when the comparison stimulus was changed in a descending direction; closed circles were obtained when the comparison stimulus was changed in an ascending direction. Lower *jnds* indicate better discrimination performance. The human phonetic boundary, where best performance was obtained, is marked by a vertical dashed line. (From Kuhl, 1981.)

initially contrasted with a stimulus that was very different from it (e.g., +10 msec VOT). If this pair was successfully discriminated, the comparison stimulus was changed (e.g., to +20 msec VOT) to decrease the difference between the standard stimulus and the comparison stimulus and therefore make the task more difficult. If this difference was again discriminated, the comparison stimulus was again changed (e.g., to +30 msec VOT). This procedure continued until the animal failed to discriminate the standard stimulus from the comparison. After a failure occurred, the difference between the two stimuli was increased until the animal could once again demonstrate the ability to discriminate it. This up-down cycle was repeated until the *jnd* in VOT was identified.

This procedure is a modified "method of limits." It is frequently referred to an as "up-down" or "staircase" procedure because the test gradually narrows in on the animal's threshold for detecting a change in the stimulus (the *jnd*). There were rules that dictated the exact amount by which the comparison stimulus was changed on each trial and the number of times the animal had to succeed or fail before a reversal in the direction of change occurred. Moreover, control trials in which the stimulus was not changed occurred on half the trials on a random schedule. These procedures eliminate any effects of order that might otherwise influence the data (Kuhl, 1981).

Other than this, the animals were tested just as they had been in previous experiments. The animal had to cross the barrier when a stimulus change was detected and inhibit the crossing response when no change in the stimulus was detected. During the training phase of the experiment the animals listened to pairs of stimuli that were very different from one another, with all the feedback contingencies in effect (shock and buzzer for failing to detect a difference, water for correctly inhibiting the response for a no-change pair). During testing with the VOT stimuli, however, the feedback was arranged to indicate a correct response as soon as the animal was within 20 msec VOT of the standard under test. This was done to ensure that the animal was not given any training to produce *jnds* under 20 msec.

The results of the experiment are shown in Figure 12.7, where the *jnd* in VOT is plotted at nine different VOTs along the continuum. The most important result is that the functions are nonmonotonic, and that the smallest *jnd*, located at 30 msec

VOT, occurred at the VOT value nearest the phonetic boundary (shown as the dotted line). At this 30-msec VOT standard the *jnd* is about 3 msec, which means that a 30-msec VOT stimulus can be discriminated from a +33-msec stimulus. At +80 msec VOT, it takes a 30-msec change in VOT to detect a difference.

There are two functions shown, indicating the direction of stimulus change. The filled circles represent data obtained when the value of the comparison stimulus changed in an ascending direction from 0 msec VOT to higher VOT values. The open circles represent data obtained when the value of the comparison stimulus changed in a descending direction from +80 msec VOT to lower VOT values. Some standard stimuli were tested with comparison stimuli that approached the standard from both directions. An example will illustrate. For the +30-msec standard, one test run used comparison stimuli that ascended from the 0-msec endpoint. On another test run the comparison stimuli descended from the +80-msec endpoint. The direction from which the comparison stimulus approaches the standard is predicted to make a difference if the CP model holds because if the animal truly perceives a category boundary then stimuli approaching from *within the category* will be very difficult to discriminate, whereas stimuli approaching from *outside the category* will be very easy to discriminate. This directional difference will be largest for standards very near the boundary.

The effect is best illustrated with the +30-msec VOT standard. First, look at the *jnd* at +30 msec VOT when the comparison ascends from the 0-VOT endpoint. In this direction, the comparison stimuli (i.e., 0, +10, +20 VOT) are in the same category as the +30-msec stimulus and are all perceived as /da/ by adults. It therefore seems reasonable that it takes a large change in VOT, about 16 msec, to detect a difference. However, when this same standard stimulus located at +30 msec is approached in descending fashion from the +80-msec endpoint, the *jnd* decreases dramatically. Now the comparison stimuli belong to another category and are perceived as /ta/ by adults. It takes only a 3-msec change in VOT (from +30 msec to +33 msec) to be reliably detected.

Although somewhat complicated, the experiment demonstrates very dramatically the effect of the perceived shift in stimulus quality at the location of the phonetic boundary, reinforcing the notion that a natural auditory boundary exists in this particular region of the VOT continuum. The animals seemed to be very sensitive to differences near the phonetic boundary, producing small *jnd*s, and relatively insensitive to changes near the centers of phonetic categories, producing large *jnd*s.

Voice-onset time discrimination by monkeys

The 1981 discrimination test had not only provided evidence in support of enhanced discriminability at the boundary, but had also examined the CP hypothesis at a deeper level by showing how fundamentally different it was from what was predicted by Weber's law. In later studies (Kuhl & Padden, 1982) we accomplished the same thing using a simpler test. This new procedure was developed in order to conduct experiments that were more similar to those used with human listeners, particularly infants. The new procedure involved a standard discrimination technique in which pairs of stimuli that differed by a constant step size were tested.

We also moved to testing monkeys instead of chinchillas, and to a positive-reinforcement technique instead of avoidance conditioning. This technique involved training the monkey on a same–different task. The monkey initiated a trial by depressing a telegraph key. During training, we used stimuli that were easily discriminable, like a tone versus a noise or a click versus a buzz, and taught the animal to lift the telegraph key when the two stimuli were different. He was rewarded with a squirt of applesauce for doing so. If the stimuli were the same, the monkey was rewarded with applesauce for holding the key down until the end of the trial.

This procedure had several advantages. Once trained, animals could be tested on a variety of speech stimuli. Because it was a same-different procedure, the animals had no previous experience in categorizing the stimuli, making these tests more comparable to those performed using human infants.

The experiment was designed to test stimulus pairs from all three of the voiced–voiceless continua, bilabial, alveolar, and velar. Three pairs of stimuli were chosen from each: one "between-category" pair and two "within-category" pairs. The between-category pairs on each continuum were chosen to straddle the human phonetic boundary, whereas the within-category pairs were chosen to fall within a single category (one pair from the voiced and one pair from the voiceless categories). Although each of the stimulus pairs is physically separated by the same amount on the continuum, the CP model predicts that discrimination will be better for the between-category pairs than for the within-category pairs.

The data are shown in Figure 12.8. The percent correct discrimination scores for each between-category and within-category stimulus pair are shown. For each of the test series, animals performed better on the between-category pair than on either of the within-category pairs. That is, discrimination was enhanced for stimulus pairs that straddled the human phonetic boundary. This group trend was shown by each individual animal as well. In no case did an animal perform better on the within-category pairs for a series than on the between-category pair. Statistical analyses showed that the difference between discrimination scores on the between- and within-category pairs was highly significant. Thus, the existence of CP in animals was again strongly supported, this time with a new species and a new procedure.

Place-of-articulation discrimination by monkeys

Our new procedure had proven highly successful. Moreover, with the monkey we could confidently extend our investigations to a speech feature that required a frequency discrimination. The monkey's ability to resolve frequency more nearly approximates that of man. (See Kuhl, 1979b, for relevant psychoacoustic comparisons.)

The obvious choice of a speech feature involving frequency was the place-of-

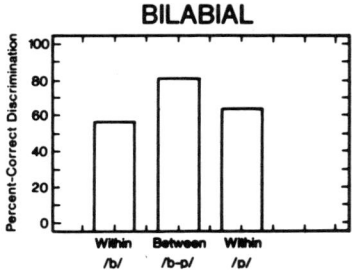

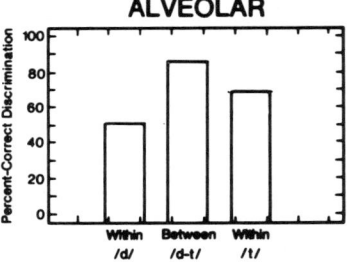

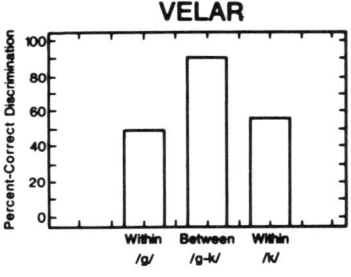

Figure 12.8. Average discrimination scores for monkeys tested with pairs of equidistant stimuli from three different voicing continua (bilabial, /ba-pa/; alveolar, /da-ta/; velar, /ga-ka/). Between-category pairs cross the human phonetic boundary in each case, whereas within-category pairs always fall within a single phonetic category. Best performance always ocurred on between-category pairs. (From Kuhl & Padden, 1982.)

articulation feature. In experiments on human listeners using computer-synthesized syllables, it has been shown that a change in the place of articulation from bilabial (/b/) to alveolar (/d/) to velar (/g/) can be governed by a change in the starting frequency of the second-formant transition. The rules for the /æ/ vowel context are as follows: When the starting frequency is low, /b/ is perceived; when it begins in the midfrequency range, /d/ is perceived; when the second-formant transition begins at a high frequency, /g/ is perceived. The place feature has always been of interest to speech theorists because, as shown in Figure 12.1, the rules given above change when the vowel is changed, showing that the acoustic events underlying our perception of the place feature are not constant in any absolute sense.

We wanted to test with animals whether there were any locations along a two-formant /bæ-dæ-gæ/ continuum where discriminability was enhanced, and if so, whether those particular locations coincided with the locations of human phonetic

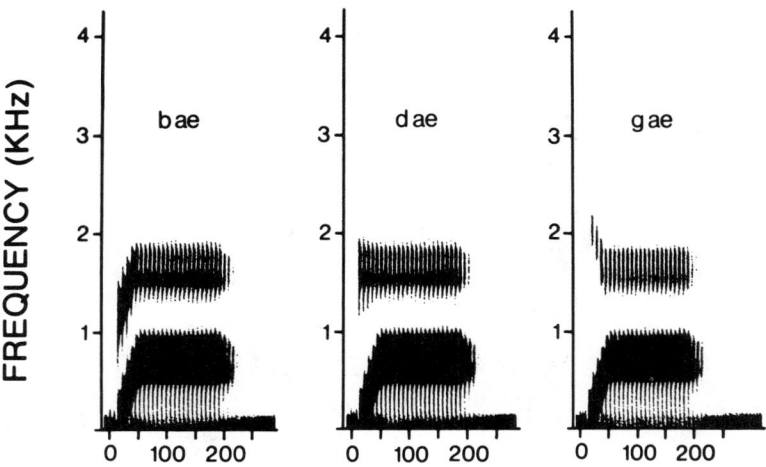

Figure 12.9. Stimuli from a place-of-articulation continuum in which the starting frequency of the second-formant transition is varied. Stimulus #1 is perceived as /bæ/; stimulus # 7 as /dæ/; stimulus #15 as /gæ/. (See Figure 12.1 for a comparison of the acoustic cues underlying the perception of the consonant /d/ in two other vowel contexts.) (From Kuhl & Padden, 1983.)

boundaries. Adults demonstrate increased discriminability in the regions of the /b-d/ and /d-g/ boundaries (Mattingly, Liberman, Syrdal, & Halwes, 1971). Infants tested with selected pairs of stimuli have been shown to discriminate only those pairs that straddled the adult-defined boundaries (Eimas, 1974). The same species and technique were used as in the 1982 study. Monkeys were tested in a same–different task using stimuli from a 15-step continuum ranging from /bæ/ to /dæ/ to /gæ/. The first, seventh, and fifteenth stimulus on the continuum are shown in Figure 12.9. Adults classify stimuli 1 to 4 as /bæ/, 5 to 11 as /dæ/, and 12 to 15 as /gæ/; it is important to note that the boundaries between categories are not simply based on a change from "rising" to "steady" to "falling" frequency transitions (Blumstein & Stevens, 1981), so it is not the detection of a simple acoustic feature that underlies the phenomenon.

Discrimination was tested for seven pairs of stimuli, each separated by two steps on the continuum (stimulus pairs 1 vs. 3, 3 vs. 5, 5 vs. 7, and so on). The results are shown in Figure 12.10. The average percent correct discrimination score is given for each pair. The data points are plotted at the stimulus number located midway between the two stimuli forming the pair (so the data point for the 1 vs. 3 stimulus pair are plotted at stimulus number 2). The locations of the human phonetic boundaries are marked by dashed vertical lines.

As shown, the best performance occurred on stimulus pairs 3 vs. 5, 9 vs. 11, and 11 vs. 13. These are exactly the pairs that involve stimuli from different phonetic categories for humans. Stimulus pairs were always separated by an equal physical

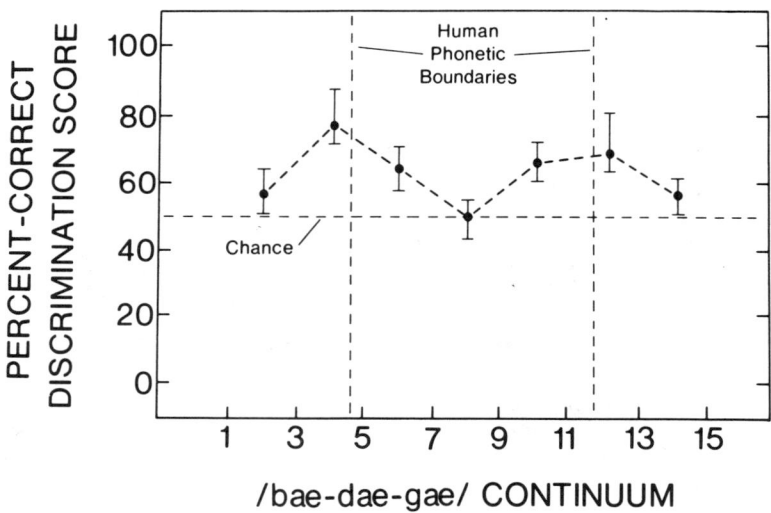

Figure 12.10. Average discrimination scores for monkeys tested with pairs of stimuli from a place continuum (/bæ-dæ-gæ/). The human phonetic boundaries between /b/ and /d/ and between /d/ and /g/ are marked with vertical dashed lines. Monkeys performed best when the stimulus pairs straddled human phonetic boundaries. (From Kuhl & Padden, 1983.)

distance on the continuum, but their perceived differences were not equivalent. Discriminability was poor when the stimulus pairs were from the same phonetic category but very good when they were from different phonetic categories.

Interpretation of the finding that animals' perception of speech is categorical

In five studies we have verified the existence of CP in animals. Both the categorization functions produced in the 1975 and 1978 experiments, and the discrimination functions produced in the 1981, 1982, and 1983 experiments mimic those seen in tests of CP in human listeners. Taken together, they serve as "existence proofs" that categorical perception of the voicing and place features (as realized using these stimuli) does not require specially evolved mechanisms. As speech theorists we must now decide what to make of this. What precise theoretical inferences should one make from demonstration experiments illustrating the existence of the categorical perception of speech in an animal?

Question #1: Are special mechanisms necessary for categorical perception?

Given the data discussed in this chapter, should we impute specially evolved mechanisms to account for CP?

The conservative posture is that one should impute special mechanisms only when there is no other reasonable explanation for the phenomenon in question. In 1967 we had no other reasonable explanation. Speech and nonspeech experiments completely diverged, and under those conditions it was reasonable to advance the argument that specially evolved mechanisms were responsible for the CP of speech. The claim, in fact, sharpened and focused the debate and was hence very helpful. But today speech and nonspeech findings are converging, providing no particular evidence favoring the special-mechanism argument, and allowing the other alternative to stand as an equally probable one. More to the point, we now have evidence that animals exhibit CP. The conservative approach would therefore be to await evidence strong enough to warrant again the claim that CP engages specially evolved mechanisms. This could come in the form of demonstrations in which humans succeed on speech tests where animals clearly fail.

The idea would be to continue to push the research program to its limits – to find out where the animal fails. Whatever animals can do can be handled by "auditory" mechanisms; what they cannot do may require higher-order "phonetic" ones. One must now undertake a series of more complex tests that involve more than the issue of the location of a boundary or enhanced discriminability for a given series of stimuli. These more complex tests should examine the rule-governed changes in the locations of the boundaries that occur in human adults when the rate of the utterance is changed (Miller & Liberman, 1979) or when the exact details of its synthesis are altered (Best, Morrongiello, & Robson, 1981).

These examples of "context effects" and "trading relations" represent a new line of evidence, which demonstrates the complexity of the underlying speech-processing mechanisms and adds support to the idea that special mechanisms are required for speech perception (Liberman, 1982). But here again it will be difficult to attribute these more complex effects to special mechanisms in the absence of tests (such as those with animals) that determine whether they can be accounted for by auditory processing.

Question #2: Do the animal data alter interpretations of findings on human infants?

The results of speech experiments on human infants are particularly intriguing. They strongly suggest that infants are born with the innate capacity to partition speech stimuli in ways that are conducive to the perception of phonetic categories. It is therefore very tempting to claim that these abilities are due to the workings of a mechanism that evolved especially for speech. Yet both the "special-mechanism" and the "general auditory" accounts predict that infants will demonstrate these effects at birth. The fact that they do so does not immediately rule out one or the other. Given the animal data, it does not follow that we are compelled to invoke special mechanisms to account for the basic CP effects in infants such as those involving the voicing feature (Eimas et al., 1971) or the place feature (Eimas,

1974). The animal demonstrations suggest that simple phoneme-boundary effects in human infants are not in themselves sufficient to warrant claims for the existence of specially evolved speech-processing mechanisms.

We then ask whether there are other data compelling us to impute special mechanisms in infants. One candidate is the recent evidence suggesting that context effects may exist in human infants (Eimas & Miller, 1980; Miller & Eimas, 1983; and Eimas, Miller, & Jusczyk in Chapter 5, this volume). Context effects in adults show, for example, that when the duration of a syllable is increased, the duration of the first-formant transition, which signals the difference between /b/ and /w/, must be made longer in order to maintain the /b/ percept. The infant studies consisted of discrimination tests in which pairs of stimuli that straddle the boundary on the "short" and "long" syllable continua are tested, as are within-syllable pairs on both continua. It is evidence that infants demonstrate context effects if they discriminate only those stimuli that straddle the two boundaries. Eimas and Miller (1980) have provided convincing evidence that two-month-old infants do show this effect.

At this time, tests of the context effect have not been completed in animals. The outcomes of such tests will be important, because the effects are difficult to explain by general auditory processing, and could be explained by a perceptual mechanism that takes articulation into account (Best, Morrongiello, & Robson, 1981). Obviously, the situation is more complex than it would be if the boundary were somehow "fixed" and impervious to the effects of changes in context, speaker, and rate. But the boundary values appear to be somewhat flexible, and any model attempting to account for speech perception will eventually have to explain that fact. If animals' boundaries were more fixed than humans' boundaries, it would be an outcome that would be interesting theoretically (Kuhl & Padden, 1983). We have shown in one test (Kuhl & Miller, 1978) that animals' voicing boundaries move with the place of articulation. However, until more tests of these effects are performed with both infants and animals, a "wait and see" posture seems to be the most appropriate.

Question #3: What can human infants do that animals can't?

No one predicted that monkeys and chinchillas would divide the speech continuum the way they do, so it does not seem wise to advance the claim that this or that *surely* won't be demonstrated. There are, however, logical places where an animal's performance could break down. Some of these – the trading relations and context effects – have already been mentioned. But there are other more complex things that young infants do, all of which are quite surprising. This chapter is not meant to encompass all of the recent work done on infants (see Kuhl, 1987, for review), but I will briefly mention three effects we have obtained in our own laboratory that seem to require a sophisticated perceptual organization of speech. They would make interesting tests for animals.

All three examples involve tests of infants' recognition of phonetic equivalence.

They go beyond tests of CP in one important way by examining infants' perception of equivalence for *discriminably different instances* representing a category. The first example is the detection of equivalence for two auditory signals that represent the same phonetic category but are easily discriminable from one another. An example of this is the detection of equivalence for two versions of the vowel /a/, one produced by a male, the other by a female. The two speakers' vowels are obviously acoustically discriminable, but they are perceived as equivalent in some sense to an adult because they represent the same vowel category. The question is, Do infants recognize their equivalence? If so, they would be detecting *auditory* equivalence classes for speech. Our studies show that infants, at least by six months of age, can indeed do this (Kuhl, 1979a, 1983, 1985a). Moreover, the data suggest that these equivalence classes may be represented by a "prototype" of the category (Grieser & Kuhl, 1983).

A second example of infants' more complex categorization abilities is their ability to detect cross-modal equivalents for speech. Studies in our laboratory show that infants detect equivalences between a vowel sound they hear and the sight of a person producing that sound, something like a primitive ability to "lip-read" (Kuhl and Meltzoff, 1982, 1984, in press). In this case, infants seem to be detecting *auditory-visual* equivalence classes for speech.

A third example involves infants' recognition of sensory-motor equivalences for speech. Here, infants show the ability to imitate speech sounds, and this indicates the recognition of equivalence between an auditory signal produced by someone else and the motor response necessary to reproduce it oneself. Our data show that these *auditory-motor* equivalence classes for speech are also displayed by infants (Kuhl & Meltzoff, 1982, in press). I will briefly discuss these three examples.

Infants' detection of auditory equivalence classes. Will infants perceptually group together sounds that belong to the same phonetic category, even though the variants are discriminably different? The test stimuli are chosen to represent difficult instances of categorization in speech research. One of these is the problem of the variation that occurs when different speakers produce the same sound. The problem occurs even when simple sounds like vowels are spoken, and computer speech-recognition programs have not solved it. In the current recognition systems, the computer has to familiarize itself with each new speaker's speech, and only a few speakers can be used. We conducted studies to see whether infants had a similar problem in categorizing the utterances produced by different speakers (Kuhl, 1979a, 1983).

The technique (shown in Figure 12.11) uses a simple conditioning procedure (Kuhl, 1985b). The infant sits on a parent's lap and is engaged by an assistant, who manipulates toys silently. A speech sound, such as the vowel sound /a/, plays repeatedly from the loudspeaker at the infant's left. The infant quickly learns that when the sound changes from the vowel /a/ to the vowel /i/ a bear playing a drum inside a black box on top of the loudspeaker is turned on for a short period of time.

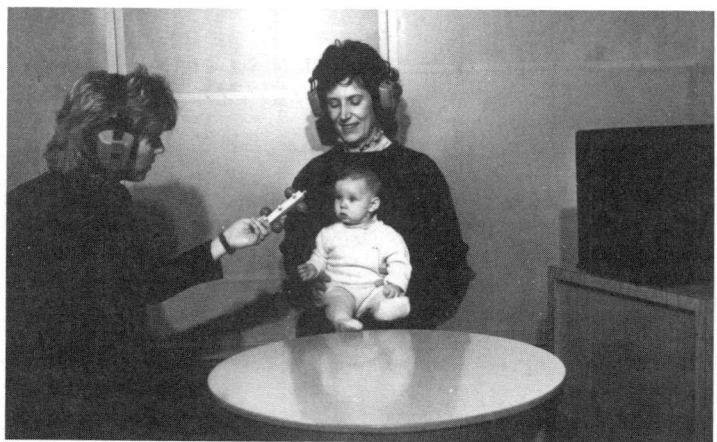

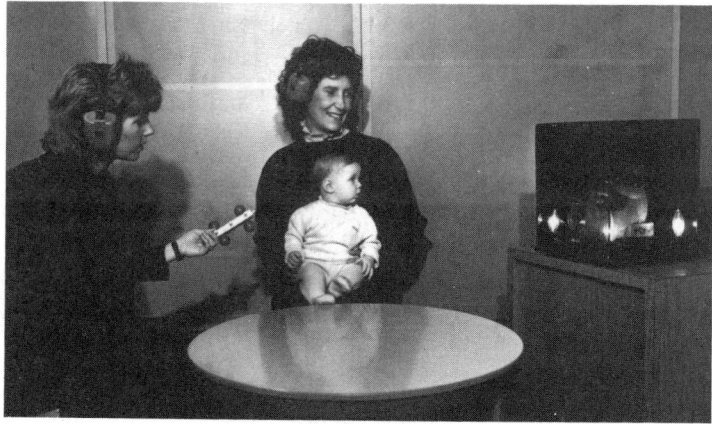

Figure 12.11. The head-turn technique used to study infants' auditory categorization abilities. Infants sit on a parent's lap and watch the toys held by an assistant while listening to sounds repeated over a loudspeaker located to their left. They quickly learn to produce a head-turn response toward the loudspeaker when the sound changes from one phoneme (/a/) to another (/i/) because it signals the opportunity to see an animated dancing bear. Once they are trained to distinguish the two sounds, generalization of the response to novel exemplars from both the /a/ and /i/ vowel categories is tested and infant's head-turn responses are monitored. Both the parent and the assistant wear headphones and listen to music that masks the stimulus change and prevents them from cuing the infant. (From Kuhl, 1986b.)

Eventually the infant anticipates the occurrence of the bear and produces a head-turn in the direction of the box when the sound /i/ occurs.

Once trained, the infant produces head-turning responses only when /i/ vowels occur, and does not turn during presentations of the vowel /a/. We want to know what infants will do when they are presented with new instances of /a/ and /i/ vowels, instances clearly different from the /a/ and /i/ stimuli heard during training. In our tests, infants were trained on the /a/ and /i/ vowels produced by a male speaker and then tested with brand-new instances of /a/ and /i/ produced by adult females or child speakers.

The data show that infants respond correctly to the new vowels on the very first trial (Kuhl, 1979a, 1983). Discrimination tests show that they have no trouble hearing the differences between the various /a/s, but they nevertheless can group them together perceptually. We have conducted these experiments with vowel categories that are very confusable – categories that computers cannot sort correctly – and the results are similar (Kuhl, 1983). Infants categorize the vowels correctly. They classify the sounds into their appropriate phonetic categories regardless of the speaker producing the sound.

A related finding from our laboratory (Grieser & Kuhl, 1983) suggests an even more sophisticated perceptual organization of vowel categories – one indicative of organization around a prototype. The question addressed in these studies was whether we could demonstrate an effect of stimulus "goodness" on infants' recognition of vowel categories (see Eimas, Miller, & Jusczyk in Chapter 5, this volume.) We tested whether infants' spontaneous tendencies to generalize to new instances of a vowel category were affected by the goodness of the stimulus that infants were initially trained to respond to.

To do this, we chose a variety of points in a two-formant coordinate vowel space corresponding to different locations in the /i/ vowel category. Adults rated the "goodness" of these vowels on a scale of 1 to 7. We chose one stimulus that was rated as a "good" /i/ and another rated as a "poor" /i/. Although they varied in "goodness," both were perceived as /i/ rather than some other vowel. We then created variant instances located in "rings" around the good and poor stimuli in the two-dimensional vowel space. The rings were located at four different distances, 30, 60, 90, and 120 mels, from these points.[1] On each of the four rings, eight stimuli were synthesized, for a total of 32 variants. Adults rated the goodness of the variants around the "good" and "poor" /i/s.

The tests on infants were designed to examine whether generalization around a "good" stimulus differed from generalization around a "poor" stimulus. The head-turn technique was used to examine infants' generalizations to variants around the two points. The results showed that generalization around the good stimulus was significantly broader than generalization around the poor stimulus. Moreover, the subtleties we saw in adults' goodness judgments were also replicated: Goodness around points was not defined solely in terms of psychophysical distance as measured in mels. It will now be interesting to examine the effect of stimulus goodness on categorization using a more "categorical" speech feature such as voicing or place in consonants. (See Miller, 1977, for relevant data on adults.)

These studies suggest that some points in vowel space are ideal candidates for category centers, because they are associated with perceptual stability over a broad array of category variants. Other points in vowel space are poor candidates, as perception is not stable and generalization to novel exemplars is weak. These data

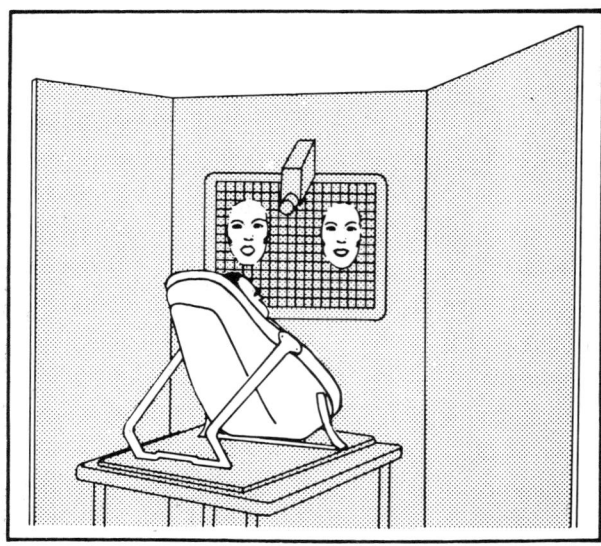

Figure 12.12. Infants' cross-modal speech-perception abilities are tested by presenting them with two facial images, one articulating the vowel /a/ and the other the vowel /i/. One or the other of the sounds is presented from a loudspeaker midway between the two facial images. The results show that infants look longer at the face that "matches" the speech sound they hear. (From Kuhl and Meltzoff, 1982.)

support the notion first expressed by Stevens (1972), who argued that vowel categories were organized so as to take advantage of the quantal nature of perception.

An effect of stimulus goodness in 6-month-olds that mimics the one exhibited by adults could indicate that infants organize vowel categories around a good central stimulus. This would be consistent with prototype theory (Rosch, 1973; see Medin & Barsalou, Chapter 16, this volume). It would be interesting to test whether the prototype effect requires experience in listening to or producing speech. We also intend to test these effects in animals. If the perceptual grouping of stimuli in vowel space is due to effects that are purely auditory, then it ought to be replicable in animals. But if it is due to speech-processing mechanisms that take articulatory dynamics into account, then animals should not display these effects.

Infants' detection of auditory-visual equivalence classes. Infants have demonstrated categorization abilities that go beyond those involving auditory perception. For example, a recent study from our lab tested the cross-modal perception of speech by infants (Kuhl & Meltzoff, 1982, 1984). We reported a study showing that 18- to 20-week-old infants relate the auditory and visual concomitants of speech. Figure 12.12 illustrates the technique (see also Massaro in Chapter 8, this volume). Infants were shown two filmed faces, side by side, of a woman articulating two different vowel sounds. One face displayed productions of the vowel /a/, the other of the vowel /i/. A single sound, either /a/ or /i/, was presented from a loudspeaker located midway between the two facial images (thus eliminating spatial cues). The two facial images articulating the sounds moved in perfect synchrony with one another.

Infants' visual fixations to the two faces were recorded. The hypothesis was that infants would prefer to look at the face that "matched" the sound. The results confirmed this prediction; infants looked longer at the face that matched the vowel they heard. The effect was strong – of the total looking time, 73% was spent on the matched face ($p < .001$) and 24 of the 32 infants demonstrated the effect ($p < .01$). There were no other significant effects – no preference for the face located on the infant's right as opposed to the infant's left side, or for the /a/ face as opposed to the /i/ face. There was no significant difference in the strength of the effect when the matching stimulus was located on the infant's right as opposed to the infant's left. (See Kuhl & Meltzoff, 1984, for full details.)

Thus, 4-month-olds perceive auditory-visual equivalents for speech. They recognize that /a/ sounds go with wide-open mouths and /i/ sounds with retracted lips. What accounts for infants' cross-modal speech-perception abilities? Have infants simply learned to associate an open mouth with the sound pattern /a/ and retracted lips with /i/? We do not favor a simple learning account for the phenomenon, whereby an arbitrary pairing is forged by associative learning (Kuhl & Meltzoff, 1984). But if not associative learning, then on what basis is the match between sound pattern and facial configuration made?

Two theoretical possibilities suggest themselves. One is that the effect derives from a phonetic representation of speech, the other that the effect occurs wholly independent of speech. Both accounts are fairly complicated and are taken up in detail elsewhere (Kuhl & Meltzoff, 1984). The main postulate of our "phonetic account" is that the perceived match between the acoustic and optic information is based on infants' knowledge of phonetics – in this case, their knowledge about the equivalence of phonetic information perceived by eye and by ear.

The second account runs very differently. It holds that the detection of a match is based on something else, something wholly independent of speech. By this account, the auditory and visual by-products of speech are related by some other property, one directed by simple physics. Our current experiments are aimed at separating the physical and phonetic explanations. We are testing whether nonspeech sounds that preserve a single feature of the vowels reproduce the cross-modal effect (Kuhl and Meltzoff, in press). Another way to test the physical account would be to present the stimuli to animals. Should the effect be replicable in monkeys, then one could claim that detecting the cross-modal match does not require a phonetic representation of speech.

Infants' detection of auditory-motor equivalence classes. Further evidence of infants' complex organization and representation of speech comes from experiments demonstrating that they are capable of vocal imitation. Imitation of speech shows that infants link specific articulatory maneuvers and their auditory consequences, and that they are capable of using this information to direct their articulators to match a given sound at will.

Our evidence of vocal imitation comes from the cross-modal experiments discussed above. In those experiments, infants vocalized; they "took turns," alternating their productions with the female speaker's vowels. Two important findings resulted from analyses of the vocalizations. First, infants matched the speech sounds they heard, both their prosodic characteristics (pitch contour and duration) and their formant characteristics (which determine vowel identity; Kuhl & Meltzoff, 1982, in press). Thus, infants are capable of imitating speech sounds.

Second, our studies showed that human speech is more effective in eliciting vocalization than is nonspeech stimulation. In some of our cross-modal experiments, infants saw faces articulating speech sounds, but heard nonspeech sounds (pure tones) rather than speech (Kuhl & Meltzoff, 1982, in press). We were interested in their responses to these nonspeech signals. Would they "talk back" to the faces when the faces produced pure tones rather than speech? The answer was "No." Infants who listened to nonspeech sounds did not produce speech. They produced some gurgles and grunts, but not speech. Apparently, infants talk only to faces that are talking to them.

In summary, human infants' perceptual organization and representation of speech is quite sophisticated – it encodes discriminably different auditory events as equivalent, it reflects the adult's rather complex definition of a "good" stimulus, and it relates speech information presented by eye to that presented by ear. The representation also includes auditory-motor linkages that allow infants to reproduce speech sounds they hear someone else produce. To be able to do this at six months of age is remarkable, and provides evidence of categorizational and representational abilities that go well beyond those required for CP.

Question #4: What is the status of the "auditory versus phonetic" distinction?

Early conceptualizations of the speech-perception process made a theoretical distinction between "auditory" and "phonetic" levels of processing. The distinction embodied an important conceptual point: the notion that at some point in the processing of sound, speech and nonspeech sounds were processed differently. At the time, the distinction was supported by a very clear dichotomy between the experimental results on speech and nonspeech – not only in the results of the CP studies reviewed here, but also in studies on hemispheric specialization (Kimura, 1967) and perceptual adaptation (Eimas & Miller, 1978).

The "auditory level" of analysis was operationally defined as the set of processes common to speech and nonspeech, whereas the "phonetic level" included processing that was unique to speech. Auditory processes were conceived to be those that produced a fairly simple, straightforward frequency-over-time transformation of the acoustic signal. This process was envisioned as one that resulted in the creation of a kind of "neural spectrogram." Phonetic processes somehow transformed widely diverse acoustic patterns into invariant percepts. As conceptualized, the "phonetic level" was the workhorse of perception.

The problem was that the "auditory level" was assumed to be a simple linear process. It was as though the sound spectrogram provided a direct analog of auditory processing. Investigators behaved as though the visual display represented what the ear did to sound, and this was misleading. What appeared to be physically equal changes in a dimension portrayed visually on a spectrogram were thought to be mirrored psychophysically at the level of the peripheral auditory system. What we now know about how the peripheral system transforms complex signals like speech suggests that this is wrong. Physiological and psychophysical studies indicate that even the processing of very simple sounds does not result in a linear transformation of acoustic information. Even for simple stimuli, combination tones, distortion products, and other nonlinear transforms abound. Studies of animals' neural responses to simple vowels show that even the preservation of simple formant-frequency information is not straightforward (Sachs & Young, 1979). We simply do not know how complex signals like speech are processed by the auditory system.

So although the "auditory versus phonetic" distinction is widely accepted it is very difficult to tease the two apart experimentally. At present, no machine behaves like an ear, so there is no accurate way to examine what auditory peripheral analysis does to the signal. This is why the development of an animal model of man's "auditory-level" processing was so important. An animal model provided an opportunity to examine auditory-level processing in the absence of higher-level influences. What resulted was a set of demonstration experiments showing that the "auditory level" was sufficient to exhibit CP; higher-order "phonetic-level" processing was not necessary. Eventually, we will understand the workings of the auditory system, which will enable us to program a machine to mimic the transformations it imposes. At that point, animal studies will not be necessary. Meanwhile, however, other tests of CP, including "trading relations" and "context effects," will continue to be examined by using a real (though not human) mammalian ear, rather than an ear simulated by computer. In addition, future tests on animals should focus on the detection of the higher-order equivalences that are recognized by human infants. Will animals recognize auditory equivalence classes? Will they detect a correspondence between the vowel sound /a/ and the sight of a person producing it? Will they imitate sounds presented to them? Surely these abilities must exceed even the chinchilla's or monkey's (surprising) abilities; but if history is a guide, we had better wait for the data.

Note

1. The "mel" scale adjusts the frequency of a stimulus to equate for perceived changes in its pitch; stimuli equally distant in mels are equally different in pitch, at least for simple pure tones.

References

Abel, S. M. (1972). Discrimination of temporal gaps. *Journal of the Acoustical Society of America, 52,* 519–524.
Abramson, A., & Lisker, L. (1970). Discriminability along the voicing continuum: Cross-language tests. *Proceedings of the Sixth International Congress of Phonetic Sciences* (1967, pp. 569–573). Prague: Academia.
Baird, J. C., & Noma, E. (1978). *Fundamentals of scaling and psychophysics.* New York: Wiley.
Best, C. T., Morrongiello, B., & Robson, R. (1981). Perceptual equivalence of acoustic cues in speech and nonspeech perception. *Perception and Psychophysics, 29,* 191–211.
Blumstein, S. A., & Stevens, K. N. (1981). Phonetic features and acoustic invariance in speech. *Cognition, 10,* 25–32.
Divenyi, P. D., & Danner, W. (1977). Discrimination of the time intervals marked by brief acoustic pulses of various intensities and spectra. *Perception and Psychophysics, 21,* 125–142.
Divenyi, P. D., & Sachs, R. M. (1978). Discrimination of time intervals bounded by tone bursts. *Perception and Psychophysics, 24,* 429–436.
Eimas, P. D. (1974). Auditory and linguistic processing of cues for place of articulation by infants. *Perception and Psychophysics, 16,* 513–521.
Eimas, P. D. (1975). Auditory and phonetic coding of the cues for speech: Discrimination of the /r-l/ distinction by young infants. *Perception and Psychophysics, 18,* 341–347.
Eimas, P. D., & Miller, J. L. (1978). Effect of selective adaptation on the perception of speech and visual patterns: Evidence for feature detectors. In R. D. Walk & H. L. Pick (Eds.), *Perception and experience.* New York: Plenum Press.
Eimas, P. D., & Miller, J. L. (1980). Contextual effects in infant speech perception. *Science, 209,* 1140–1141.
Eimas, P. D., Siqueland, E. R., Jusczyk, P., & Vigorito, J. (1971). Speech perception in infants. *Science, 171,* 303–306.
Grieser, D. L., & Kuhl, P. K. (1983). Internal structure of vowel categories in infants: Effects of stimulus "goodness." *Journal of the Acoustical Society of America, 74* (Suppl. 1), S102–103 (A).
Jesteadt, W., Wier, C. C., & Green, D. M. (1977). Intensity discrimination as a function of frequency and sensation level. *Journal of the Acoustical Society of America, 69,* 169–177.
Kimura, D. (1967). Functional asymmetry of the brain in dichotic listening. *Cortex, 8,* 163–178.
Klatt, D. H. (1975). Voice onset time, frication and aspiration in word-initial consonant clusters. *Journal of Speech and Hearing Research, 18,* 686–706.
Klatt, D. H. (1977). Speech perception: A model of acoustic-phonetic analysis and lexical access. In R. A. Cole (Ed.), *Perception and production of fluent speech* (pp. 243–288). Hillsdale, NJ: Erlbaum.
Kuhl, P. K. (1978). Predispositions for the perception of speech-sound categories: A species-specific phenomenon? In F. D. Minifie and L. L. Lloyd (Eds.), *Communicative and cognitive abilities – Early behavioral assessment* (pp. 229–255). Baltimore: University Park Press.
Kuhl, P. K. (1979a). Speech perception in early infancy: Perceptual constancy for spectrally dissimilar vowel categories. *Journal of the Acoustical Society of America, 66,* 1668–1679.
Kuhl, P. K. (1979b). Models and mechanisms in speech perception: Species comparisons provide further contributions. *Brain, Behavior and Evolution, 16,* 374–408.
Kuhl, P. K. (1980). Perceptual constancy for speech-sound categories in early infancy. In G. Yeni-Komshian, J. Kavanagh, & C. Ferguson (Eds.), *Child Phonology: Vol. II, Perception* (pp. 41–66). New York: Academic Press.
Kuhl, P. K. (1981). Discrimination of speech by nonhuman animals: Basic auditory sensitivities conducive to the perception of speech-sound categories. *Journal of the Acoustical Society of America, 70,* 340–349.
Kuhl, P. K. (1983). Perception of auditory equivalence classes for speech in early infancy. *Infant Behavior and Development, 6,* 263–285.
Kuhl, P. K. (1985a). Categorization of speech by infants. In J. Mehler and R. Fox (Eds.), *Neonate cognition: Beyond the blooming, buzzing confusion* (pp. 231–262). Hillsdale, NJ: Erlbaum.

Kuhl, P. K. (1985b). Methods in the study of infant speech perception. In G. Gottlieb and N. Krasnegor (Eds.), *Measurement of audition and vision during the first year of postnatal life: A methodological overview* (pp. 223–251). Norwood, NJ: Ablex.
Kuhl, P. K. (1986a). Reflections on infants' perception and representation of speech. In J. S. Perkell and D. H. Klatt (Eds.), *Invariance and variability of speech processes* (pp. 19–30). Hillsdale, NJ: Erlbaum.
Kuhl, P. K. (1986b). Theoretical contributions of tests on animals to the special-mechanisms debate in speech. *Experimental Biology, 45,* 233–265.
Kuhl, P. K. (1987). Perception of speech and sound in early infancy. In P. Salapatek & L. Cohen (Eds.), *Handbook of infant perception: Vol. II, from perception to cognition* (pp. 274–382). New York: Academic.
Kuhl, P., & Meltzoff, A. (1982). The bimodal perception of speech in infancy. *Science, 218,* 1138–1141.
Kuhl, P., & Meltzoff, A. (1984). The intermodal representation of speech in infants. *Infant Behavior and Development, 7,* 361–381.
Kuhl, P. K., & Meltzoff, A. N. (In press). Speech as an intermodal object of perception for infants. In A. Yonas (Ed.), *Perceptual development in infancy.* Hillsdale, NJ: Erlbaum.
Kuhl, P. K., & Miller, J. D. (1975). Speech perception by the chinchilla: Voiced-voiceless distinction in alveolar plosive consonants. *Science, 190,* 69–72.
Kuhl, P. K., & Miller, J. D. (1978). Speech perception by the chinchilla: Identification functions for synthetic VOT stimuli. *Journal of the Acoustical Society of America, 63,* 905–917.
Kuhl, P. K., & Padden, D. M. (1982). Enhanced discriminability at the phonetic boundaries for the voicing feature in macaques. *Perception and Psychophysics, 32,* 542–550.
Kuhl, P. K., & Padden, D. M. (1983). Enhanced discriminability at the phonetic boundaries for the place feature in macaques. *Journal of the Acoustical Society of America, 73,* 1003–1010.
Liberman, A. M. (1957). Some results of research on speech perception. *Journal of the Acoustical Society of America, 29,* 117–123.
Liberman, A. M. (1982). On finding that speech is special. *American Psychologist, 37,* 148–167.
Liberman, A. M., Cooper, F. S., Shankweiler, D. P., & Studdert-Kennedy, M. (1967). Perception of the speech code. *Psychological Review, 74,* 431–461.
Liberman, A., Harris, K. S., Eimas, P., Lisker, L., & Bastian, J. (1961). An effect of learning on speech perception: The discrimination of durations of silence with and without phonemic significance. *Language and Speech, 4,* 175–195.
Liberman, A. M., Harris, K. S., Hoffman, H. S., & Griffith, B. C. (1957). The discrimination of speech sounds within and across phoneme boundaries. *Journal of Experimental Psychology, 54,* 358–368.
Liberman, A. M., Harris, K. S., Kinney, J. A., & Lane, H. (1961). The discrimination of relative onset-time of the components of certain speech and nonspeech patterns. *Journal of Experimental Psychology, 61,* 379–388.
Lisker, L. (1975). Is it VOT or a first-formant transition detector? *Journal of the Acoustical Society of America, 57,* 1547–1551.
Lisker, L., & Abramson, A. S. (1964). A cross-language study of voicing in initial stops: Acoustical measurements. *Word, 20,* 384–422.
Mattingly, I. G. (1972). Speech cues and sign stimuli. *American Scientist, 60,* 327–337.
Mattingly, I. G., Liberman, A. M., Syrdal, A. K., & Halwes, T. (1971). Discrimination in speech and nonspeech modes. *Cognitive Psychology, 2,* 131–157.
Miller, G. A. (1956). The magical number seven plus or minus two: Some limits on our capacity for processing information. *Psychological Review, 63,* 81–97.
Miller, J. D., Wier, C. C., Pastore, R. E., Kelly, W. J., & Dooling, R. J. (1976). Discrimination and labeling of noise-buzz sequences with varying noise-lead times: An example of categorical perception. *Journal of the Acoustical Society of America, 60,* 410–417.
Miller, J. L. (1977). Properties of feature detectors for VOT: The voiceless channel of analysis. *Journal of the Acoustical Society of America, 62,* 641–648.

Miller, J. L., & Eimas, P. D. (1983). Studies on the categorization of speech by infants. *Cognition, 13*, 135–165.
Miller, J. L., & Liberman, A. M. (1979). Some effects of later-occurring information on the perception of stop consonant and semivowel. *Perception and Psychophysics, 25*, 457–465.
Miyawaki, K., Strange, W., Verbrugge, R., Liberman, A. M., Jenkins, J. J., & Fujimura, O. (1975). An effect of linguistic experience: The discrimination of /r/ and /l/ by native speakers of Japanese and English. *Perception and Psychophysics, 18*, 331–340.
Pisoni, D. B. (1977). Identification and discrimination of the relative onset time of two component tones: Implications for voicing perception in stops. *Journal of the Acoustical Society of America, 61*, 1352–1361.
Rosch, E. H. (1973). On the internal structure of perceptual and semantic categories. In T. E. Moore (Ed.), *Cognitive development and the acquisition of language* (pp. 111–144). New York: Academic Press.
Sachs, M. B., & Young, E. D. (1979). Encoding of steady-state vowels in the auditory nerve: Representation in terms of discharge rates. *Journal of the Acoustical Society of America, 66*, 470–479.
Stevens, K. N. (1972). The quantal nature of speech: Evidence from articulatory-acoustic data. In E. E. David, Jr., and P. B. Denes (Eds.), *Human communication: A unified view* (pp. 51–66). New York: McGraw-Hill.
Streeter, L. (1976). Language perception of 2-month-old infants shows effects of both innate mechanisms and experience. *Nature, 259*, 39–41.
Wier, C. C., Jesteadt, W., & Green, D. M. (1977). Frequency discrimination as a function of frequency and sensation level. *Journal of the Acoustical Society of America, 61*, 178–184.

13 Brain mechanisms in categorical perception

Martha Wilson

Adaptation-level theory provides a rationale for understanding and predicting many of the phenomena associated with categorical perception (CP). Moreover, the theory is consistent with current knowledge of brain organization, making it possible to investigate the neural substrates underlying CP in various sensory modalities. Hypothesized relationships between particular brain areas and modality-specific categorization processes were tested in neurologically intact and brain-damaged human and infrahuman subjects. In previous experiments with intact monkeys it was found that visual continua such as line length, orientation, and texture are perceived categorically; cortical lesions that spare the primary projection area and invade the inferotemporal visual area abolish the effect. Studies with human neurological patients also suggest that localized brain areas are critical for CP in different modalities. Subjects with damage to temporal-lobe structures failed to perceive stimuli on visual continua as members of perceptual categories, unlike other patients with lesions elsewhere in the brain. Perception of line length and hue appeared to be lateralized in different hemispheres because right-hemisphere temporal lesions affected the former whereas left-hemisphere temporal lesions unexpectedly affected the latter. Laterality effects were also found for tactile length and weight continua. The results for brain-damaged patients point to a right anterior focus for categorical perception of tactuospatial stimuli and a left-hemisphere and anterior focus for categorical judgments of heaviness. These results are interpreted in terms of current models of hemispheric specialization. More rigorous tests of the brain model for CP as an adaptation-level phenomenon will require the study of larger numbers of patients with circumscribed lesions. In addition to empirical findings relating CP to adaptation-level theory and to inferred brain functions, theoretical issues centering on prototypical stimuli, shifts in category boundaries, and the presumed uniqueness of speech signals are discussed.

Categorical perception (CP), a phenomenon first described by Liberman and his colleagues in studies of speech perception (Liberman, Cooper, Shankweiler, & Studdert-Kennedy, 1967; Liberman, Harris, Hoffman, & Griffith, 1957), continues to engage the interest of investigators, even though there has been little agreement about what processes might underlie this manner of perceiving. The fact that stimuli that are equally spaced on a physical continuum are perceived as if they belonged to one or another perceptual category, rather than appearing to vary continuously as a

---

Most of the research with human subjects that is described in this chapter was supported by a grant MH 36582 from the National Institute of Mental Health. I am grateful to Gustav W. Anderson, M.D. and Melville P. Roberts, M.D. for making it possible to study patients at the Hartford Hospital. I am also grateful to Barbara D. Streitfeld and Bette A. DeBauche for helpful discussion, and to W. A. Wilson for comments on an earlier draft.

function of their physical values, has represented a challenge to classical psychophysical theories. The aim of this chapter is to present some empirical data, as well as a theoretical rationale, which bear on some of the issues that have become intertwined with the discussion of CP.

One such issue centers on whether the speech mode represents a unique kind of perceptual activity, with one aspect of its uniqueness exemplified by the fact that speech continua, as opposed to nonspeech continua, are perceived in a categorical manner. There are now a number of reports that nonspeech continua are also perceived in categorical fashion (e.g., Healy & Repp, 1982; Miller, Wier, Pastore, Kelly, & Dooling, 1976; Pastore, Ahroon, Baffuto, Friedman, Puleo, & Fink, 1977; Zatorre & Halpern, 1979), but no single theoretical account that accommodates all of these results has been proposed. Another issue arises from the fact that speech functions are linked to the left hemisphere for most people. The association between speech stimuli and CP has led to the suggestion that a special speech decoder in the left hemisphere yields CP, whereas the right hemisphere participates in continuous perception (Liberman et al., 1967). Yet another issue involves differing explanations for shifts in category boundary as a function of experience (Diehl, Lang, & Parker, 1980; Remez, 1980; Sawusch & Nusbaum, 1979). Although these topics do not exhaust the questions that have aroused interest in the investigation of CP, they are questions for which some empirical answers can be given.

In an attempt to illuminate the neural mechanisms underlying CP, as well as perception in general, relationships between brain structures and perception were examined in nonspeech domains that have not been studied previously, including unidimensional continua in visual, tactile, and kinesthetic modalities. A single experimental paradigm was used throughout that yielded reliable evidence for CP in relatively few trials and was appropriate for use with brain-damaged subjects. For the purposes of these initial studies of the phenomenon at the level of brain mechanisms, perception was construed as categorical if the accuracy of discrimination across a category boundary was significantly better than within categories. Categorization of real-life items after circumscribed brain damage was also studied to compare the effects of short-term and long-term experience with stimulus items on category formation. The main purpose of all the studies described here was to examine the extent to which CP can be accounted for by more general principles of perceptual function and to relate behavioral CP findings to current knowledge of brain function.

Such an endeavor does not speak to the question of whether an understanding of the mechanisms involved in speech perception will require special explanatory principles, not derivable from accounts of other perceptual systems. A demonstration of CP in a nonspeech mode merely indicates that this way of perceiving stimuli on a continuum is not unique to the speech mode, whatever special status one might wish to assign to speech perception on other grounds (cf. Liberman et al., 1967; Repp & Liberman in Chapter 3, this volume). Nevertheless, finding similar kinds of processing mechanisms, such as CP, in speech and nonspeech modes alike, suggests that other similarities might be overlooked in the belief that speech is special. Just as a common plan can be discerned in the anatomical organization of perceptual systems, in spite of specializations within the constraints of the plan (Diamond, 1979), so it may be possible to define the communalities that exist in the formal aspects of all perceptual functioning while still recognizing the particularities that inhere in different systems. For this reason, the present interpretation of CP effects is based on a general theory of perception, namely, adaptation-level theory (Helson, 1948, 1964), without regard to the issues that divide theorists of speech perception, and in the hope that empirical findings can be understood as the outcome of general principles of perception.

The concept of adaptation level

In the last several decades, some form of central representation of experience that determines perception and action has been repeatedly postulated (Reed, 1969). The types of representation that have been proposed have ranged from the model-like feature representations of von Uexküll (1957), Sokolov (1963), and Mackay (1956), to Bullock and Horridge's (1965) more general "central state of expectation." As Reed points out, all these notions of an internal representation imply a centrally determined criterion for evaluating the effect of afferent stimulation.

Adaptation-level (AL) theory also emphasizes the need to appeal to a prevailing central state in order to define an effective stimulus, and to predict the perceptual outcome of stimulation (Helson, 1948, 1964). However, in contrast to the models referred to by Reed, AL theory ties the construct of an internal referent to physically defined variables at both the input and output stages of processing, and expresses the relationship between stimulus variables and perception quantitatively. The theory can therefore be tested on the basis of predictions that are generated in a rigorous way.

Briefly, the theory states that all stimulus inputs in a given domain are pooled, and their average value determines the level of stimulation to which the organism is adapted, or habituated. Because the adaptation level is defined as a neutral point of functioning, it can be represented by the stimulus value that elicits a null response. A wide range of experiments has shown that a weighted, logarithmic mean of the physical values of focal, background, and residual stimuli accurately predicts the level of adaptation, and thus the stimulus value that evokes a neutral response. The physical values that contribute to the adaptation level are weighted in terms of such quantifiable factors as frequency and recency. So, if the input can be specified in physical terms, the physical stimulus parameter's *value* that represents the level of adaptation is defined by the equation:

$$\log A = p \log \bar{X} + q \log B + r \log R,$$

where A is the adaptation level; $\bar{X}$ is the geometric mean of the stimulus values presented for judgment; B is a standard or anchor stimulus value; R is a remote anchor value, representing residual effects of previous experience; and *p, q,* and *r* are weighting constants that sum to unity (Helson, 1964, pp. 58–59).

The adaptation level is hypothesized to serve as an internal standard to which all stimulus input in a given sensory domain is referred. Stimuli with physical values greater than the value representing the adaptation level lead to one kind of perceptual response, whereas stimuli with values less than the value of the adaptation level lead to a complementary perceptual response. Thus, any perceptual continuum will be partitioned into two categories, with the boundary located at the neutral point. A finer partitioning could conceivably continue to occur as experience with restricted portions of the physical array proceeds (Pribram, 1960). The effective stimulus, in any case, is the discrepancy between the physical values of the adaptation level and stimulus input, rather than the physical value of the stimulus alone.

A number of phenomena in psychophysics and perception are encompassed by AL theory, among them selective adaptation, contrast, assimilation, and range-frequency effects. As the adaptation level varies with the stimulus history of the observer, or the addition of background or anchoring stimuli, the perceptual fate of physical stimuli is altered. For example, a stimulus that appears to be highly distinctive in one context, because its physical value makes it highly discrepant from the prevailing adaptation level, may lose its distinctiveness if the context is changed so that the adaptation level moves in the direction of the stimulus. Similarly, the "end" effects (Guilford & Dingman, 1955) or "edge" effects (Durlach & Braida, 1969) that are sometimes observed can be attributed to the fact that extreme values on a stimulus continuum are somewhat more easily discriminated and identified because they are maximally discrepant from the adaptation level (Capehart, Tempone, & Hébert, 1969; Wilson, 1971). If the stimuli on the continuum then assume new values, different ones will appear highly distinctive. Thus, AL theory emphasizes the *relativity* of perceptual judgment when only the physical values of stimuli are considered. At the same time, the theory allows for the *constancy* of perceptual judgment when the relationship between stimulus values and the adaptation level remains constant, or when stimuli always appear in a stable context.

AL theory also accounts for the finding that both identification and discrimination are history-dependent functions, in that both depend on the past and present experience of the observer. Rather than postulating that discrimination reflects the way that stimuli are assigned category labels, a more general account follows from the theory: Both identification and discrimination reflect the relationship of physical values to the current level of adaptation, and whereas different verbal labels may or may not arise as a consequence of the partitioning of a continuum, perceptual differences do arise in any case. Moreover, in terms of the theory, discrepancies from adaptation level may lead to two kinds of perceptual outcome. When stimuli take on values that lie on different sides of the adaptation level (between-category pairs), they will appear to differ *qualitatively* and *quantitatively* as a function of the psychophysical distance and direction of each stimulus from the neutral point. Stimuli with physical values that lie on one or the other side of the adaptation level (within-category pairs) will appear to differ only *quantitatively* because they will share the same perceptual quality. Therefore, within-category pairs should be more difficult to discriminate than between-category pairs, as observed in CP. Although step size (i.e., the physical difference between stimuli in a pair) affects both kinds of discrimination, it should be a more important factor in determining the accuracy of within-category discrimination because quantitative differences constitute the only attribute on which to base judgments. It follows, therefore, that perception is "categorical" when stimulus values lie on different sides of the adaptation level, and it is "continuous" when stimulus values lie on the same side of the adaptation level. If we are right in equating the concept of a category boundary for stimuli on a continuum with the adaptation level for the set, then CP can be discussed in the same theoretical framework as other perceptual phenomena.

Relationship of AL theory to other approaches

The attempt to bring the investigation of CP into the framework of more general theories of perception is not confined to AL theory, although it may be noteworthy that the first demonstration of CP in a nonspeech mode (Wilson, 1972) was motivated by AL theoretic considerations. In what follows, some of the more striking similarities and differences in approach between AL theory and other models will be summarized.

Signal-detection theory

The extension of signal-detection theory (SDT) as applied to CP phenomena by Macmillan (Chapter 2, this volume) has much in common with AL theory. First, they share the proposition that CP is not a mode of perceiving to be contrasted with continuous perception. Rather, both AL theory and SDT stress the relationship between the ability to identify stimuli on a continuum and to discriminate between selected pairs of such stimuli arises from a common process that is shared by both "continuous" and "categorical" modes of processing. Both theories deny that categorical judgment is mediated by labeling, a rather special claim in any case, as it rests on a particular experimental paradigm. Exponents of both SDT and AL theory agree that finding discontinuities in sensitivity to a continuous physical array is no more than a curiosity until the underlying mechanism can be spelled out.

As Swets (1971) has pointed out, AL theory and SDT share a common tenet that perceptual judgments are related to an internal criterion. Both the decision criterion in SDT and the adaptation level in AL theory reflect the direction and extent of bias in a perceptual system. Factors that contribute to bias (such as stimulus characteristics, long-term and short-term practice effects, immediate context, and relevance, to name a few) must be appropriately identified and weighted in order to describe the current processing space, or the level of adaptation; only then can behavior be described or predicted. Both theories partition the variables that determine psychophysical functions into those relating to immediate sensory input and those relating to stored information. Moreover, the role of sensory factors is conceptualized similarly in SDT and AL theory as both assume that at some level of the nervous system there is a physiological response encoding the physical properties of stimuli.

Differences between the two approaches arise, however, when the contributions of memory factors are considered. In SDT, when observers are said to be operating in the *trace* mode, the subject presumably maintains an image of the first stimulus in a pair in order to compare the second stimulus to its trace. When in the *context* mode, the comparison is said to be based on all of the stimuli presented. These two constructs are encompassed by a single one in AL theory, namely, the level of adaptation that establishes the basis of comparison, or internal referent, for all judgments. Perhaps it was because Durlach and Braida's (1969) theory addressed psychophysical issues in terms of auditory signals that the effects of variables associated with sequential presentation of two stimuli assumed a larger role than they play in AL theory, and therefore dictated a separate construct. In AL theory, the number of physical stimuli in a set is not a critical issue because the relationship of the physical values of stimuli to an internal referent, regardless of their number, determines their discriminability.

Translating Macmillan's (Chapter 2, this volume) concepts into AL theory terms, it follows that in what is called *fixed-level* discrimination, unless there are significant effects from residual factors, the adaptation level is determined solely by the two stimuli presented. Because the adaptation level is represented by the average of the two stimuli, sensitivity will be maximal, as one value will lie above the neutral point and the other will lie below it. *Roving-level* discrimination is said to occur when the physical values making up the pairs of stimuli to be discriminated are varied within blocks of trials. Unlike the rapid perceptual learning and high level of accuracy characteristic of fixed-level discrimination, in roving-level discrimination the terminal level of adaptation is established more slowly and discrimination will be more or less accurate depending on whether the stimuli in a given pair lie on the same or different sides of the physical value of the neutral point. Contrary to the assumption that fixed-level discrimination is independent of experience and represents sensitivity unbiased by memory noise, experience limited to two stimulus values still represents experience and still reflects the fact that the neutral point serves as a category boundary that anchors the stimulus continuum. Thus, one concept, the adaptation level, subsumes effects found in both experimental situations. Other factors, such as background stimuli and residual effects from previous experience, represent other potential influences on perceptual judgment in AL theory, but these are not explicitly identified as sources of variance in the SDT analysis.

Another concept that is treated differently in the two theories is that of perceptual anchors. In AL theory, anchors are defined as stimuli with physical values that are far from the adaptation level, or that are presented much more frequently than any single stimulus in the set to be judged. An anchor, therefore, in either case, exerts a greater influence on the adaptation level than do other stimuli in a set, pulling the neutral point in its own direction. The quantitative model for adaptation level predicts the location on a continuum of a region of increased sensitivity as the result of introducing anchors or standards. Depending on the physical values of the anchor and the stimuli being judged, introducing an anchor will shift the category boundary in one direction or the other, or, if its value lies at or near the adaptation level, will have no effect on judgments. In SDT, the existence of anchoring stimuli must be inferred from regions of heightened sensitivity if it cannot be shown that these are due to "natural boundaries," but no rationale for certain physical values acting as anchors has yet been provided. In terms of AL theory, "natural sensitivity" and the effects of anchors are not separable because regions of heightened sensitivity arising from the relationship of stimulus values on the continuum to the neutral point are equally natural whether they are due to the effects of explicitly introduced anchors on the adaptation level or to the partitioning of the continuum into those values that lie on either side of the adaptation level without benefit of anchors.

Finally, the most pronounced difference between SDT and AL theory lies in the differing assumptions about the processes that underlie perception. In AL theory, the establishment of neutral points as a function of all the stimuli experienced in a particular domain is conceived of as an automatic, physiological process leading to qualitative differences in identification and regions of heightened and reduced sensitivity. In SDT, in contrast, the factors that constrain performance are construed either as conscious or unconscious decision processes, or as interference that masks "true" sensitivity. Whereas it would be futile to deny that various forms of response bias can and do enter into perceptual judgments (Clark, 1966), the issue remains how best to characterize the underlying neural mechanisms that support perceptual processes. Clearly, all psychological explanation must ultimately be compatible with our knowledge of brain function; so the question is not whether physiological or mentalistic models are more appropriate. Rather, the issue concerns what processes are involved in perception. In support of a *sensory* as opposed to a *decisional* model of identification and discrimination, the phenomenological attributes of stimuli have been shown to change in a striking way when the relationship of the signal to the prevailing level of adaptation has been altered. A sensory model makes it unnecessary to hypothesize that some stimulus values have unknown qualities which make them inherently more memorable. This point is taken up in the next section, which relates AL theory to models based on prototypes.

Exemplars and prototypes

Also related to AL theory is the notion that categories are organized around prototypical stimuli that best exemplify the attributes characterizing a given category. A number of investigators have converged on this approach, although with somewhat different emphases (Keil, 1979; Posner & Keele, 1968; Rosch, 1973, 1975; see also Chapter 5 by Eimas, Miller, & Jusczyk; Chapter 8 by Massaro; Chapter 16 by Medin & Barsalou; and Chapter 18 by Bialystock & Olson, this volume). For

Rosch, the "family resemblance" that describes items belonging to a given category is something more than a list of shared features: the concept of "core meaning" is invoked to describe attributes shared to a greater extent by good examples than by poor examples (Rosch & Mervis, 1975). However, this description raises the problem of defining a category boundary. One category would presumably be demarcated from an adjacent one by the poorest examples of each category. Such a definition is not consistent with the crisp boundary effects seen in identification and discrimination. Nevertheless, the concept of prototypical stimuli fits well with other aspects of AL theory; highly representative items that act as prototypes are equivalent to stimuli that are very discrepant from the adaptation level. Capehart et al. (1969) were the first to suggest that the adaptation level serves as a category boundary, and that "the greater the incongruity . . . between the stimulus and the AL referent the easier the 'test' or comparison" (p. 416). They noted that stimuli with values distant from the neutral point produce unambiguous responses as measured by such indices as probability, latency, and amplitude. Their interpretation allows quantitative exploration of how prototypical stimuli function in perceptual judgment; it also removes some of the mystery surrounding the development of category structure (cf. Bornstein in Chapter 9, Eimas, Miller, & Jusczyk in Chapter 5, this volume).

Helson and Masters (1966) and Sarris (1967) investigated the inflection in the function describing the effectiveness of anchors or adaptors as their distance from the adaptation level was varied. Analogous experiments with speech sounds, discussed by Eimas et al. (Chapter 5), have yielded the same nonmonotonic functions as were found in the earlier work. AL theory, however, explains the effects of presenting better or worse exemplars of a category on judgments of other stimuli as well as the effects of varying stimuli in a set on judgments of prototypicality. Moreover, AL theory fares better in explaining how categories and representative stimuli arise in development. Rather than assuming that prototypical stimuli at a prephonetic level possess "some as yet unknown psychoacoustic properties" (Eimas et al., Chapter 5), AL theory postulates that experience with particular dimensions is pooled and averaged such that the distinctiveness of items that are discrepant from the average renders them immediately obvious and memorable. It is compatible with this account that highly representative items, once established and well anchored, may take on an independent life. Nevertheless, when changes in representativeness do occur as a function of contextual changes, it is difficult to reconcile these facts with the notion of privileged stimuli around which categories are formed.

Brain mechanisms and AL theory

Identifying brain structures and functions that subserve CP is only part of the larger problem of understanding brain mechanisms in perception. When it was believed that CP was limited to the speech mode, and when less was known about neural mechanisms in perception, it was more plausible to hypothesize that there were distinctive brain structures, organized in unique fashion, that processed speech signals in a categorical manner. Subsequently, facts about neural function in the visual system, in which perception was *not* believed to be categorical, were used to model neural processes in speech perception, which *was* believed to be categorical (cf. Remez in Chapter 6, this volume). Now, however, in order to understand the mechanisms underlying categorical perception of nonspeech stimuli (as in visual, auditory, tactile, and kinesthetic continua), a general theory of brain function and perception is called for.

AL theory not only provides a general account of both categorical and continuous perception for sensory systems, but it also leads to hypotheses about the nature of the neural mechanisms for perceiving physical stimuli as members of perceptual categories. On the assumption that all perceptual judgments are relative to the spatial and temporal context of the stimuli that give rise to them, the theory leads to the search for areas in the brain that sustain the effects of spatially and temporally integrated stimulus inputs. Moreover, the organization of such a system must allow for the modification of ongoing activity by current stimulus input as well as the evaluation of current input in terms of ongoing activity.

If we follow the path of stimulus input from the receptor surface to the cortical areas in which it is processed, there do not appear to be structures capable of evaluating stimulus input relative to ongoing activity until after the primary sensory areas (Wilson, 1978). In the visual system, striate cortex in the occipital lobe of the brain receives input from the retina via the primary visual relay nucleus of the thalamus, the lateral geniculate nucleus. In similar fashion, somatosensory input from skin, muscles, and joint receptors is projected through the posteroventral nuclei in the thalamus to cortex in the postcentral gyrus. These two cortical areas represent the primary sensory areas for vision and somatosensory function. In primates, these primary sensory systems are characterized by topographic organization and relatively rapid, faithful, and direct afferent input from receptor to cortex (Benevento & Rezak, 1976; Semmes, 1969). Cells in striate cortex appear to be involved in the analysis of restricted portions of the visual hemifield, in terms of such physical dimensions as length, width, orientation, and eye preference (Hubel & Wiesel, 1968). Similarly, recording from cells in postcentral cortex reveals modality-specific responses that are relatively faithful to the physical parameters of stimulation (Powell & Mountcastle, 1959; Werner & Whitsel, 1973). Thus, to a large extent, responses in these areas mirror some transformation of the physical values of stimulation.

Outside these primary sensory areas lie large expanses that were once assumed to be "association" cortex because they apparently lacked subcortical afferent input and presumedly did not respond electrophysiologically. However most, if not all, "association" cortex is now known to be sensory cortex (Diamond, 1979). There are multiple representations of the visual hemifields in prestriate cortex (Weller & Kaas, 1981), each such area apparently specialized for further analysis of visual stimulation (Zeki, 1978), and visually responsive cells are found in areas even farther from striate cortex in the inferior portions of the temporal lobe (Gross, Rocha-Miranda, & Bender, 1972). The somatosensory system is organized in an analogous way, with a number of somatic representations in the inferior and posterior parietal lobe (Burton & Robinson, 1981; Kaas, Sur, Nelson, & Merzenich, 1981). For both systems, it was once thought that such cortical areas outside the primary sensory area received all their afferent input from the primary area, but it is now clear that the erstwhile association cortex receives subcortical input from the thalamus as well. Diamond (1979) has argued that the organization of sensory systems can best be understood in terms of sensory fields, each such field subdivided into areas that are reciprocally connected but distinguished by different patterns of thalamocortical projections. Rather than postulating a serial processing model that starts with input to the primary sensory areas and continues across the cortex (Mishkin, 1979), this view emphasizes parallel projections from clusters of thalamic nuclei that subserve a given modality. For example, in the visual system, the lateral and inferior portions of the pulvinar nucleus of the thalamus project widely to subdivisions of visual cortex and in turn receive projections from cortical visual areas (Benevento & Rezak, 1976; Weller & Kaas, 1981). Similarly, in the somatosensory system, the medial pulvinar and lateral posterior nuclei have reciprocal connections with posterior parietal areas of cortex (Burton & Robinson, 1981; Lewis, Sakai, & Tanaka, 1981; Petras, 1971; Semmes, 1969).

Such anatomical arrangements may provide the neural substrate for reverberating circuits in which stimulus input can both affect, and be affected by, ongoing activity in the system. Cortical areas that lie outside the primary sensory areas, therefore, are more likely candidates than the core projection areas for subserving history-dependent processes such as those described at the behavioral level by AL theory. Wilson & DeBauche (1981) have proposed earlier that cortex in extrastriate areas such as prestriate or inferotemporal cortex is necessary for CP in the visual mode, as well as for other higher-order visual functions. By extension, parietal-lobe cortex outside the primary postcentral area is hypothesized to underlie CP in the tactile and kinesthetic modes.

This model assumes that stimulus input is projected directly to primary sensory areas and indirectly to other cortical subdivisions through thalamocortical and corticocortical projections, which are reciprocal. The interaction between the neural activity generated by a given stimulus and the ongoing level of activation in the relevant subdivision constitutes the output of the system, and thus the effective stimulus. Although it is necessary to postulate different ensembles of cells to subserve perception of each stimulus dimension in a modality, this assumption fits well with the finding of areas devoted to particular aspects of stimulation (Zeki, 1978). What is added here is the assumption that the activity of specific feature-detecting mechanisms does not in and of itself constitute perception even of elementary qualities. Rather, cells in sensory areas that respond preferentially to specific values

Brain mechanisms in categorical perception

of physical stimulation are hypothesized to send converging input to other cortical areas that sustain the effects of present and past stimulation. Such a model may even be useful in providing a clue to the functional significance of the multiple visual and somatic areas lying outside the primary sensory areas.

Methodology

Most of the results to be discussed were obtained by applying to human subjects the same paired-comparison procedures that led to the discovery that macaque monkeys tend to perceive visual stimuli in a categorical manner (Wilson, 1972). As Ehret (Chapter 10, this volume) points out, it is impossible to study CP phenomena in animals with the procedures used in standard experiments with humans, yet evidence for such phenomena can be gained indirectly. In the original study there were 10 stimulus items on each of three visual continua: length, orientation, and texture. First the animals were trained to choose one of the two endpoint stimuli in a set; then all the stimuli were presented in pairs for choice. In accordance with the methods of Guilford (1954), scale values were computed for the items in each set. I would argue that the scale values for the stimuli generate an identification function for the set because these values provide a measure of the degree to which each physical stimulus exemplifies the attribute designated for choice. The stimulus value that yields a scale value of 0 is defined as the adaptation level because it would elicit a neutral response by virtue of having been chosen 50% of the time.

To illustrate the procedure more concretely, suppose that subjects are asked to choose the longer of the two stimuli in each pair presented for judgment. One stimulus value on the continuum would be chosen half the time because it would appear equally often to be shorter and longer over all the comparisons. This physical value might coincide with one of the stimuli in the set, or it might lie between two of the stimulus values on the continuum. In either case, according to AL theory, the value eliciting a neutral response represents the internal standard for judgment of length, and the relationship of the physical values of the stimuli to the adaptation level determines how they will be identified and discriminated. Stimulus values that lie below the adaptation level should be chosen less often than chance because, on the average, such values will appear to be *short* whereas stimulus values that lie above the adaptation level should be chosen more often than chance because, on the average, they will appear to be *long*. Thus, the overall percentage of choices (correct and incorrect) of each stimulus value provides a measure of how that stimulus was identified. As Guilford (1954) points out, the resulting psychophysical function is formally equivalent to that generated by the constant method when a variable standard is used, as each stimulus, in effect, acts as a standard for every other stimulus. It is also difficult to see how this procedure differs in any fundamental way from the identification functions generated by asking subjects whether a given stimulus is a *ba,* a *da,* or a *ga.* By generating an identification function in this way, the location of a putative category boundary is established. The greater accuracy of between-category discrimination compared to within-category discrimination is then taken as evidence for CP.

It might be suspected that there is some circularity in this method for demonstrating categorical effects in perceptual judgments, but consideration of some possible outcomes of such an experiment demonstrates that this is not the case. Three hypothetical matrices are presented in Table 13.1 showing the proportions of choices of six stimuli paired in all possible combinations. These proportions could, of course, be converted to identification d' values, and compared with sensitivity d' values computed from discrimination data as described by Macmillan, Kaplan, & Creelman (1977) for two-interval, forced-choice procedures.

Matrix A shows a pattern of choices that would indicate an adaptation level between stimulus values 3 and 4, as would occur if only the set of stimuli being judged determined the level of adaptation. According to AL theory, stimulus values 1 to 3 would be perceived as belonging to one perceptual class, whereas stimulus values 4 to 6 would appear to belong to another perceptual class. If an anchor or standard greater than the physical value of stimulus 6 were presented before each pair was judged, AL theory predicts that the adaptation level would shift in the direction of the physical value of the standard, as shown in matrix B. Now stimulus values 1 to 4 fall into one category and values 5 to 6 fall into the other. These results follow from AL theory but in neither of these hypothetical sets of data is there any hint that perception is categorical.

If brain mechanisms indeed function so as to heighten sensitivity for pairs of stimuli that straddle the adaptation level, or, in other words, if the adaptation level serves as a category boundary, then results such as those depicted in matrix C would be expected. Here, the AL not only divides the continuum into categories in which stimuli are identified differently, as in A and B, but also discrimination of between-category stimulus pairs is seen to be perfect whereas discrimination of within-category stimulus pairs is seen to be at chance. In the experiments described later in the section on human brain damage, it is clear that the data approximate rather than reproduce these ideal results. Nevertheless, in all modalities studied, significant differences in accuracy have been found in different regions of the continuum, and these regions accord with deductions from AL theory.

Thus, given a particular identification function resulting from paired-comparison choices, there is no necessity for any particular pairs of stimuli on the continuum to be more or less difficult to discriminate. Yet, in the Wilson (1972) study, when discriminability of stimuli that lay on different sides of the adaptation level was compared to that of equally spaced stimuli that lay on the same side of the adaptation level, it was clearly shown that between-category discrimination was significantly better than within-category discrimination for all three dimensions studied. This empirical finding suggested that the adaptation level for a visual continuum serves as a category boundary if CP is defined by the relationship between identifi-

Table 13.1. *Matrices illustrating hypothetical distributions of choices in a paired-comparison task*

	A						B						C					
	1	2	3	4	5	6	1	2	3	4	5	6	1	2	3	4	5	6
1	*	.4	.3	.2	.2	.1	*	.4	.3	.3	.2	0	*	.3	0	0	0	0
2	.6	*	.4	.3	.3	.2	.6	*	.4	.4	.3	.1	.7	*	0	0	0	0
3	.7	.6	*	.5	.4	.2	.7	.6	*	.5	.4	.2	1.0	1.0	*	.5	.5	.4
4	.8	.7	.5	*	.5	.3	.7	.6	.5	*	.4	.2	1.0	1.0	.5	*	.5	.4
5	.8	.7	.6	.5	*	.4	.8	.7	.6	.6	*	.3	1.0	1.0	.5	.5	*	.4
6	.9	.8	.8	.7	.6	*	1.0	.9	.8	.8	.7	*	1.0	1.0	.6	.6	.6	*
p^a	.76	.64	.52	.44	.40	.24	.76	.64	.52	.52	.40	.16	.94	.86	.32	.32	.32	.24

[a]The proportion of choices (p) of each stimulus value over all comparisons is indicated at the bottom of the table.

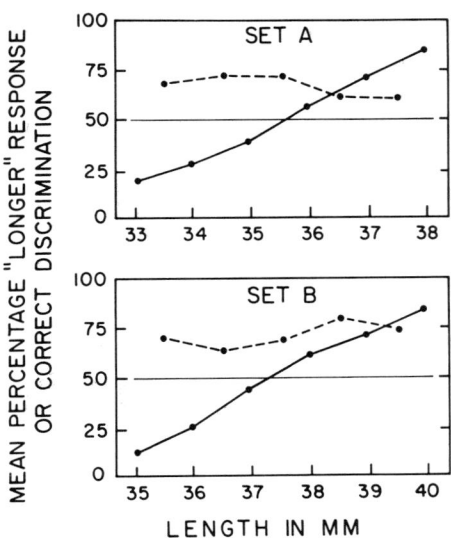

Figure 13.1. Identification (solid lines) and discrimination (dashed lines) between adjacent stimuli on the continuum for two sets of visual stimuli differing in length.

cation and discrimination functions, with a peak in discriminability at the category boundary.

Shifts in category boundary

If a category boundary can be equated with the adaptation level for a stimulus continuum, it follows that a boundary may vary both between and within individual perceivers. Shifts in category boundary, when experience is varied, are well documented, as shown in selective adaptation and contrast effects (cf. Diehl, 1981; see also Diehl & Kluender in Chapter 7, this volume). However, different category boundaries may be found among individual subjects owing to differences in background or residual factors even when experimental conditions are constant. AL theory explains both kinds of effects as a natural outcome of processes that underlie CP in all perceptual modes. Moreover, only when variability in the location of the category boundary is taken into account does the ubiquitous nature of the phenomenon manifest itself. In this section I will argue that the categorical nature of perception, in modes less firmly anchored than appears to be the case for speech perception, has often been obscured by the practice of averaging responses to physical values on the stimulus continuum across subjects who may have different boundaries for extra-experimental reasons. Lane (1965) also noted that category boundaries based on group identification functions do not always reflect individual performance.

The point is illustrated in Figures 13.1 and 13.2, which contrast the identification and discrimination functions obtained for visual judgments of line length when individual differences in category boundary *were* and *were not* taken into account.

Brain mechanisms in categorical perception

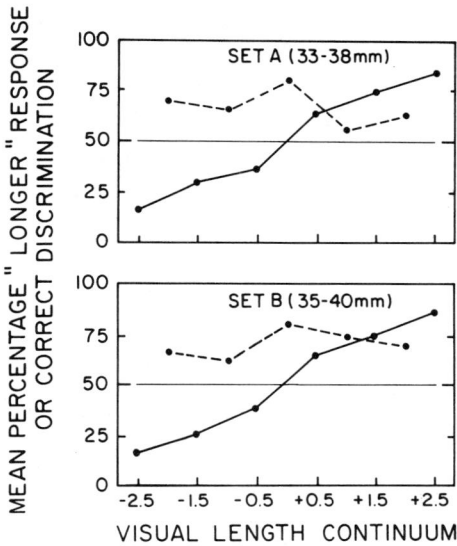

Figure 13.2. Identification (solid lines) and discrimination (dashed lines) between adjacent stimuli on the continuum for the two sets of stimuli shown in Figure 13.1. The stimulus values are represented in terms of step-differences from individual adaptation levels. A discrimination between −0.5 and +0.5 on the stimulus continuum thus represents a one-step, between-category discrimination for all subjects although the physical values of the stimuli differ depending upon the location of the category boundary.

In an experiment by Wilson, DeBauche, and Streitfeld (1983), 16 subjects judged two sets of equally spaced line lengths in a paired-comparison procedure, with each pair judged five times. Set A ranged from 33 to 38 mm in length, in 1-mm steps, and Set B ranged from 35 to 40 mm. Figure 13.1 shows that the identification functions based on the averaged responses of all subjects to the stimulus values on the continuum appear to be almost linear. The discrimination functions for one-step differences between stimuli, also shown in Figure 13.1, do not exhibit a peak in accuracy at the category boundary for either set of stimuli, a peak that should be observed if the stimuli were perceived as members of one or the other perceptual category. From these data it might be concluded that the perception of line length, unlike the perception of stimuli on a phonetic continuum, is not categorical.

A very different picture emerges when the discriminability of stimulus pairs along the continuum is assessed in terms of each subject's individual category boundary. For Set A, the boundary was found to lie between 34 and 35 mm for four subjects, between 35 and 36 mm for eleven subjects, and between 36 and 37 mm for one subject. For Set B, the boundary lay between 36 and 37 mm for four subjects, between 37 and 38 mm for nine subjects, and between 38 and 39 mm for three subjects. It is assumed from AL theory that all subjects adapted to the range of stimuli presented, but because no attempt was made to control for background or residual effects, these factors contributed to variability in the location of the boundary.

Representing stimulus values on the continuum in terms of their discrepancy from individual adaptation levels yields the identification and discrimination functions shown in Figure 13.2. That is, for Set A, the one-step difference between −0.5 and +0.5 represents the difference between 35 and 36 mm for eleven subjects, between

34 and 35 mm for four subjects, and so forth. When these individual differences are respected, identification functions for both sets of stimuli have steeper slopes across the boundary than elsewhere on the continuum, and the discriminability functions show a peak at the boundary characteristic of CP.

Figure 13.2 also illustrates the fact that the category boundary shifts to a higher value on the length continuum when the range of stimuli assumes higher values. Such effects due to changing the context in which stimuli are judged are analogous to the boundary shifts that occur when a standard is used or selective adaptation to a particular stimulus value has taken place (Helson, 1964). All these effects are predicted by AL theory as the value of the adaptation level is a weighted average of all the stimuli experienced in a given domain.

However, because the adaptation level or category boundary yielded by the paired-comparison procedure is defined as the stimulus value that elicits 50% choice, it might be assumed that the boundary would necessarily take on a different value when different values on the stimulus continuum are presented. This would be true only if discrimination were always perfect. Otherwise, the value of the boundary is free to vary and may occur at any location on the stimulus continuum. That is, there is no mathematical necessity for the category boundary to shift from its location on Set A to a higher value on Set B simply because the physical values of the stimuli increased. In fact, the value of the boundary did shift appropriately upward or downward for all subjects; as the discriminability data indicate, this was due to a new level of adaptation that led to changes in the way that stimulus values were identified *and* discriminated. As shown in Figure 13.2, the shift in peak discriminability follows the shift in boundary, and the difference in accuracy between one-step between-category discriminations and one-step within-category discriminations was significant for both Set A, $t(15) = 3.60, p < .005$, and for Set B, $t(15) = 2.86, p < .01$. So, whereas the difference between 35 and 36 mm was discriminated most accurately by the majority of the subjects on Set A, the difference between 27 and 38 mm was discriminated most accurately by the majority of subjects on Set B. We have also shown that predicted changes in discriminability occur when the same set of stimuli is judged in the presence of different anchor stimuli (Streitfeld & Wilson, 1983).

Identification functions were derived both from the paired-comparison choice data and from verbal labeling of each stimulus value as "long" or "short." These results are compared in Figure 13.3. In the panels on the left, functions are shown for two groups of subjects: those who were instructed in the paired-comparison procedure to choose the *longer* stimulus in each pair as opposed to those instructed to choose the *shorter* stimulus. The panels on the right show functions for the two groups, which differed in the order of testing. The only significant effect was due to varying the range of stimuli presented, $F(1, 12) = 226.87, p < .001$. It should be noted again that the boundary could have remained unchanged in the paired-comparison procedure as well as in the verbal labeling task when the stimulus range was varied.

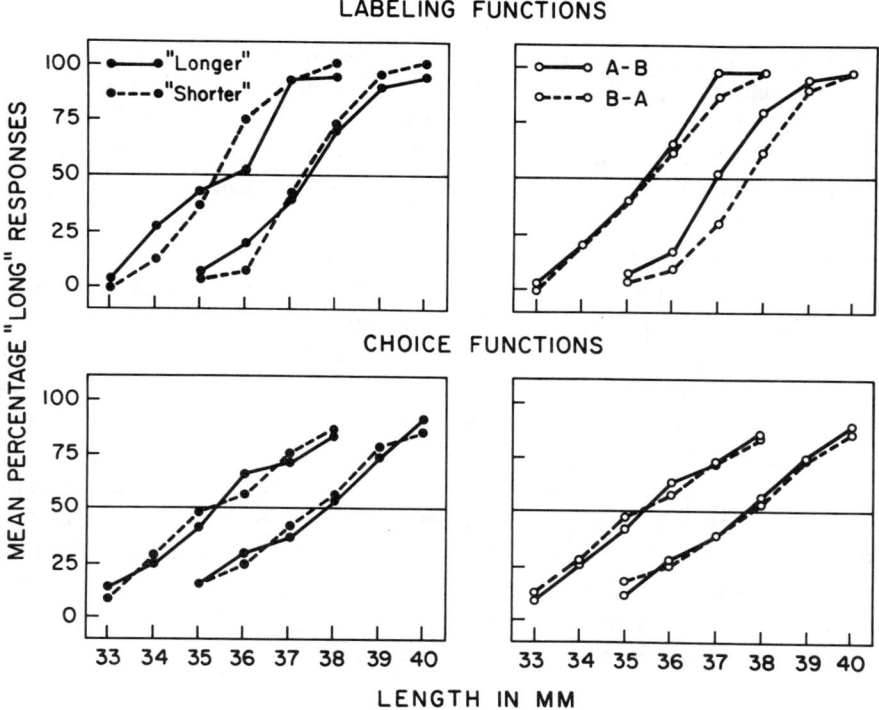

Figure 13.3. Identification functions as a function of instructions and order of testing for the two sets of visual length stimuli (set A and set B) shown in Figure 13.1, based on verbal labeling or on overall choices in paired-comparison testing. See text for details.

Although the group means did not differ significantly as a function of the procedure used, there are reasons to prefer the nonverbal method for obtaining identification data even for verbal subjects. Figure 13.3 shows that the curves based on paired-comparison choices vary less as a function of instructions or order of testing variables. In addition, the boundaries based on labeling data did not always predict the region of peak sensitivity in discrimination. This may be simply because the labeling data were less reliable, based as they were on fewer trials, or because the verbal labels were more subject to response bias. In either case, although the group results support the claim that the two procedures provide equivalent estimates of the adaptation level, the identification functions obtained from paired-comparison data gave a more accurate picture of how the stimuli in each set were perceived.

Speech perception and nonspeech perception obviously differ in the variability of the category boundary, both between subjects and within subjects. Studies of CP based on phonetic continua have often stressed the stability of values for the boundary, and indeed, Healy and Repp (1982) have put forth "context independence" as a necessary attribute of perception if it is to be considered categorical. Rather than disqualifying certain perceptual modes on this basis, the finding that perception can be both categorical *and* adaptable can be understood in terms of AL theory. Category boundaries may appear to be independent of context only because the context is relatively constant; but it does not follow that context is not important in determining how stimuli are perceived in speech and nonspeech modes alike (Wilson, 1972; Diehl et al., 1980; Sawusch & Nusbaum, 1979). When context is varied (e.g., by selective adaptation, by varying the range, frequency, intensity, or spacing of stimuli on the continuum, or by presenting a standard stimulus to which each stimulus is compared), the organism will adapt to a different level of stimulation unless the previous stimulus history has established a level of functioning that is so firmly anchored as not to be affected by the experimental manipulation that has occurred. It appears that there is a continuum of perceptual modes, some firmly tied to particular levels of adaptation because of the amount and constancy of previous stimulation, and others extremely labile because of the variability inherent in the stimulus environment. Perceptual systems that process wide variations in physical energy are labile mechanisms; there are wide swings in adaptation level as stimulating conditions assume very different values (DeValois, 1966; Michels & Helson, 1953). Natural speech stimuli, in contrast, are limited to those sounds produced by the human articulatory apparatus, and the congruence between the perception and production of speech sounds as well as the stability of category boundaries is, perhaps, not surprising for this reason (Wilson, 1972).

Categorization of semantic versus perceptual items

Up to this point I have stressed that categories emerge automatically from experience with a stimulus array because a category boundary is established automatically as the observer adapts to current stimulation. Whereas the quantitative form of AL theory requires that stimuli on a continuum be specified in physical terms, the concept of AL can be extended to any domain in which the stimuli can be ordered. Some data of Grossman and Wilson (1987) compared stimulus categorization in two knowledge domains: real-life, easily labeled items (fruits and vegetables) and two-dimensional perceptual items (green circles and blue squares). It was of interest to note the effects of changing the context in which items were presented on category boundaries and judgments of representativeness.

Subjects were asked to rate sets of stimulus items on a seven-point scale ranging from 1 (very, very fruit-like or very, very green-circle-like) to 7 (very, very vegetable-like or very, very blue-square-like), with a rating of 4 assigned to an item that appeared to be equally green-circle and blue-square-like, or equally fruit- and vegetable-like. Four overlapping sets of seven fruit and vegetable items, which were ordered according to Rosch's (1975) ratings, and three overlapping sets of seven perceptual items, constructed by combining Munsell hue samples with continuously varying shapes, were judged by observers in balanced orders. Four groups of subjects were tested, but only the results for neurologically intact controls and

Brain mechanisms in categorical perception

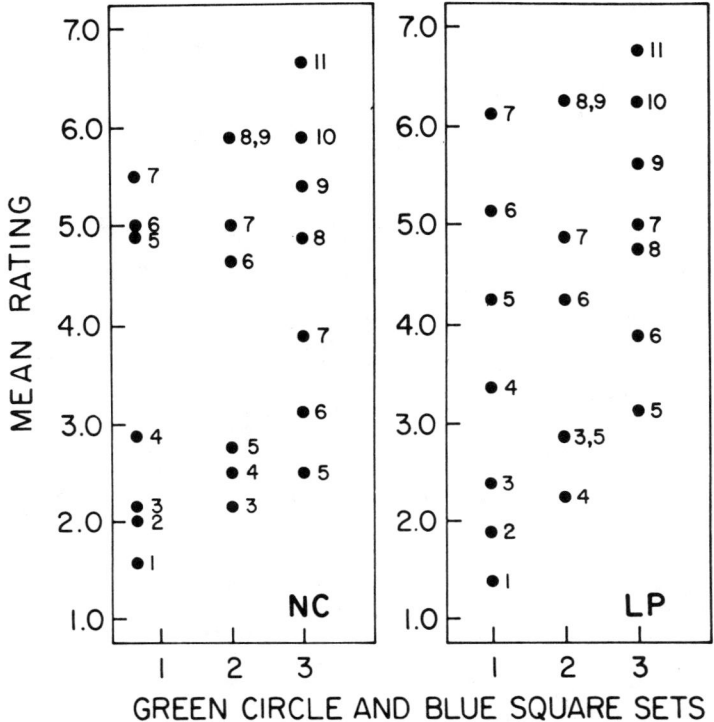

Figure 13.4. Ratings on perceptual items on a scale from 1 (very, very green circle-like) to 7 (very, very blue square-like) by normal control (NC) subjects and patients with left posterior (LP) brain damage. The Munsell hue notations for the items are 5G(1), 7.5G(2), 10G(3), 2.5BG(4), 5BG(5), 7.5BG(6), 10BG(7), 2.5B(8), 5B(9), 7.5B(10), 10B(11).

patients with left-posterior brain damage who were diagnosed as fluent aphasics will be summarized here.

As expected, the scale values of the hue–shape items shifted reliably as a function of the set in which the stimuli were presented for both groups of subjects, as did the location of the category boundary. As shown in Figure 13.4, not only items intermediate between green circles and blue squares, but also good exemplars of those qualities, were perceived as less representative as the context (the set in which an item was embedded) changed. In addition, it was not necessary to introduce highly representative tokens of a different category in order to shift the category boundary and alter the relative representatives of items.

Figure 13.5, shows the ratings of the meaningful, easily labeled items for the intact and brain-damaged groups. For the neurologically intact subjects, judgments of fruits and vegetables were not greatly affected by the range of stimuli in which a given item appeared. Ambiguous items were occasionally relabeled in terms of superordinate categories, but most items appeared to possess a fixed level of repre-

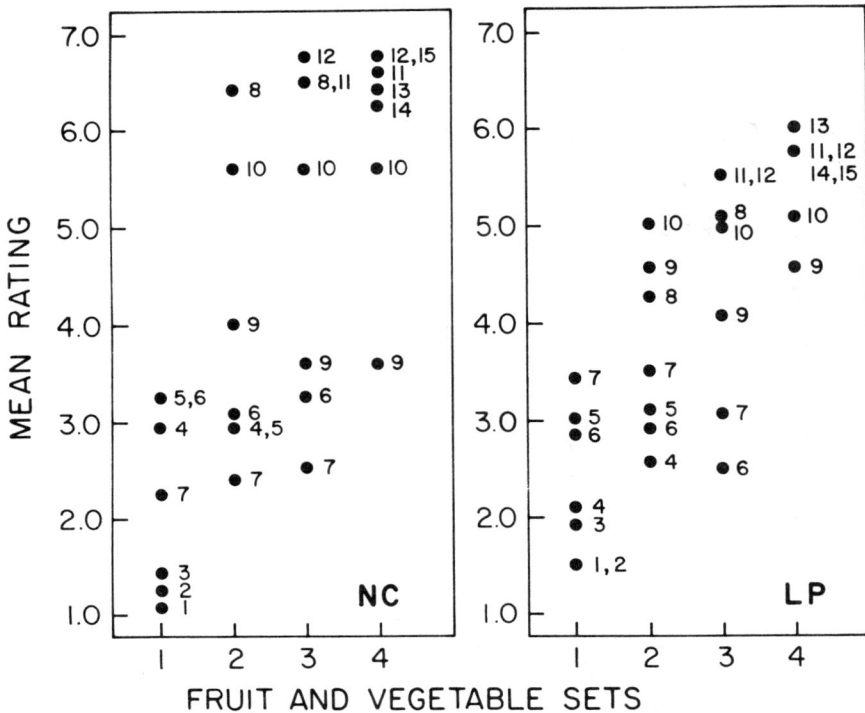

Figure 13.5. Ratings of semantic items on a scale from 1 (very, very fruitlike) to 7 (very, very vegetable-like) by normal control (NC) subjects and patients with left posterior (LP) brain damage. The items judged were apple(1), pear(2), cherry(3), cantaloupe(4), prune(5), raisin(6), pumpkin(7), avocado(8), olive(9), mushroom(10), wax bean(11), green onion(12), lettuce(13), green bean(14), and pea(15).

sentativeness; there appeared to be a firm category boundary between fruits and vegetables, regardless of the composition of the set. The patients with left-posterior brain damage, in contrast, frequently reassigned ambiguous items to different superordinate categories. There was also evidence that categories were more amorphous for the aphasic subjects as exemplified by ratings of adjacent items on the continuum. That is, the psychological distance between items was similar for between-category and within-category items. Moreover, highly prototypical items, particularly vegetables, were judged as less representative than they were by the normal control group.

These data could be interpreted as showing that in normal functioning there are two modes of stimulus categorization, one dependent on resemblance to prototypical stimuli and characteristic of the labeling of real-life, meaningful items such as fruits and vegetables, and one associated with relativistic judgments of physically continuous dimensions such as hue and shape. Repp and Liberman (Chapter 3, this volume) propose in a similar vein that selective adaptation and contrast effects in the auditory mode admit of explanation in terms of adaptation-level mechanisms, but they distinguish these phenomena from language-specific effects that demand other principles of explanation.

However, our data from brain-damaged subjects are compatible with another possibility, namely, that both higher-order semantic categories and abstract perceptual categories depend on similar, context-sensitive mechanisms, even though experiential factors produce different behavioral outcomes. Categories of meaningful, everyday items such as fruits and vegetables would be expected to be stable and relatively resistant to change, given the items' long history and vivid representation in observers' experiences. Hue–shape categories, in contrast, should reflect a more labile internal representation, resulting from stimulus values that typically vary over a large range in the environment. This would explain the similarities and differences across domains and groups: The perceptual ratings of both groups were influenced by the composition of the set, whereas the semantic ratings were uninfluenced by immediate context in the intact group and were significantly altered in the aphasic group. Because the ordering of stimulus items in terms of their relative representativeness did not differ for the two groups, it is likely that the aphasic subjects retained an appreciation of what is more or less typical of items in the superordinate categories. At the same time, the differentiating effect of a discrete boundary on judgments of near-boundary items was not seen in their ratings, and highly representative instances of a category were not given their due. Such findings are difficult to account for in terms of prototypes as the organizing principle underlying category formation. They suggest, rather, that all categories may arise from a common adaptation-level mechanism, a mechanism that leads to more or less permanent representations in the intact observer depending on the nature and history of the material that is experienced.

Effects of brain damage on categorical perception

The neural model for CP outlined in the section on brain mechanisms and AL theory hypothesized that extraprimary sensory areas are necessary for sustaining ongoing activity that acts as a reference level. This argument was based on the specificity of stimulus preferences and response properties of cells in primary sensory areas, which make it unlikely that they represent the physiological substrate for categories of experience. If this model is correct, a lesion in striate cortex should not interfere with CP in the visual domain unless damage is so extensive that perceptual functions are abolished, whereas damage to extrastriate areas may leave the organism without a standard for judgment, and hence a loss of CP. In a similar vein, Weiskrantz (1974) has characterized striate cortex and inferotemporal cortex in the monkey visual system in terms of feature-detecting and classifying functions, respectively. He further suggested that temporal-lobe areas are necessary for relating transformations of stimulus input to stored templates or models. The voluminous literature on the effects of brain lesions in humans also points to the importance of "association" cortex for higher-order perceptual processing, and implicates the right hemisphere in perceptual functions as opposed to those functions that are related to language (cf. Hécaen & Albert, 1978; Kolb & Whishaw, 1980; Luria, 1980).

Animal studies

Although there have been a number of investigations of categorical processes in animals (cf. Ehret, Chapter 10 and Snowdon, Chapter 11, this volume), lesion studies of brain–behavior relationships in CP are rare. Our first attempt to investigate cortical areas and CP used groups of macaque monkeys with bilateral damage to either lateral striate cortex or interotemporal cortex as well as unoperated controls. Three visual dimensions – length, orientation, and texture – were again studied. As reported by Wilson and DeBauche (1981), only the animals with inferotemporal lesions failed to perceive the stimulus continua in a categorical manner. However, their accuracy on within-category discrimination was no worse than that of animals in the normal control or lateral striate groups.

Some additional data that were not presented in Wilson and DeBauche (1981) are plotted in Figure 13.6. Here, identification and discrimination functions for the visual line-length continuum are shown for the three groups of monkeys. It is clear that the intact monkeys discriminated the stimuli more accurately when the two stimuli in a pair lay on different sides of the adaptation level. "End" effects can also be noted in that the extreme stimuli at either end of the continuum are differentiated from adjacent stimuli more accurately than are other pairs of within-category stimuli, and their special status is also reflected in the identification function.

In spite of their generally poor performance, the monkeys with lateral striate lesions exhibited a peak in discrimination accuracy at the category boundary. When performance on the larger step differences was analyzed, this group also performed as well as the control animals. These results imply an acuity loss with preserved stimulus categorization. Monkeys that had inferotemporal lesions, in contrast with those that had striate lesions, did not show any category boundary effects whatsoever. These results are consistent with the hypothesis that acuity functions depend on striate cortex and categorization functions depend on inferotemporal cortex.

Human studies

In order to extend these results to humans, and to other modalities and brain areas, an ongoing series of studies is being conducted with volunteer subjects who have suffered focal brain damage as the result of trauma, tumor, or cerebrovascular accident. Because the number of patients available for study to date is still small, the neural model proposed cannot be tested in detail and the results should only be considered suggestive. Nevertheless, findings have emerged that allow some tenta-

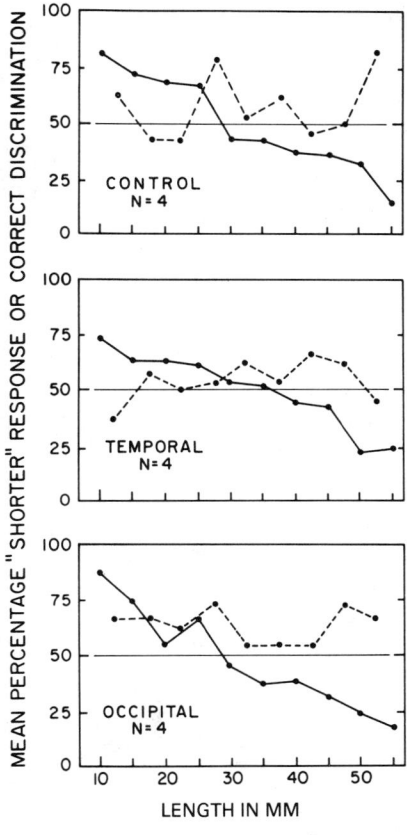

Figure 13.6. Identification (solid lines) and discrimination (dashed lines) between adjacent stimuli on a visual length continuum for intact and brain-damaged groups of macaques.

tive conclusions to be drawn about the relationship between various brain areas and categorical perception of stimuli in different modalities.

Four stimulus dimensions, two visual continua, and two tactual-kinesthetic continua were studied with the procedures outlined in the section on Methodology. Following paired-comparison testing, the category boundary was identified for each subject individually. Unbiased sensitivity measures, d', were calculated according to the methods given in Macmillan et al. (1977) for between-category and within-category discriminations, with one-step and two-step differences computed separately. For statistical purposes, the brain-damaged subjects were divided into groups with anterior versus posterior lesions (relative to the central sulcus as a boundary). The subjects were also compared in terms of whether the lesion was located in the right or left hemisphere. Mean d' values for between-category versus within-category discrimination, for combined one-step and two-step differences, were compared using two-tailed t tests for the groups described above. A summary of the results is plotted in Figure 13.7, and the results of the statistical tests are shown in Table 13.2.

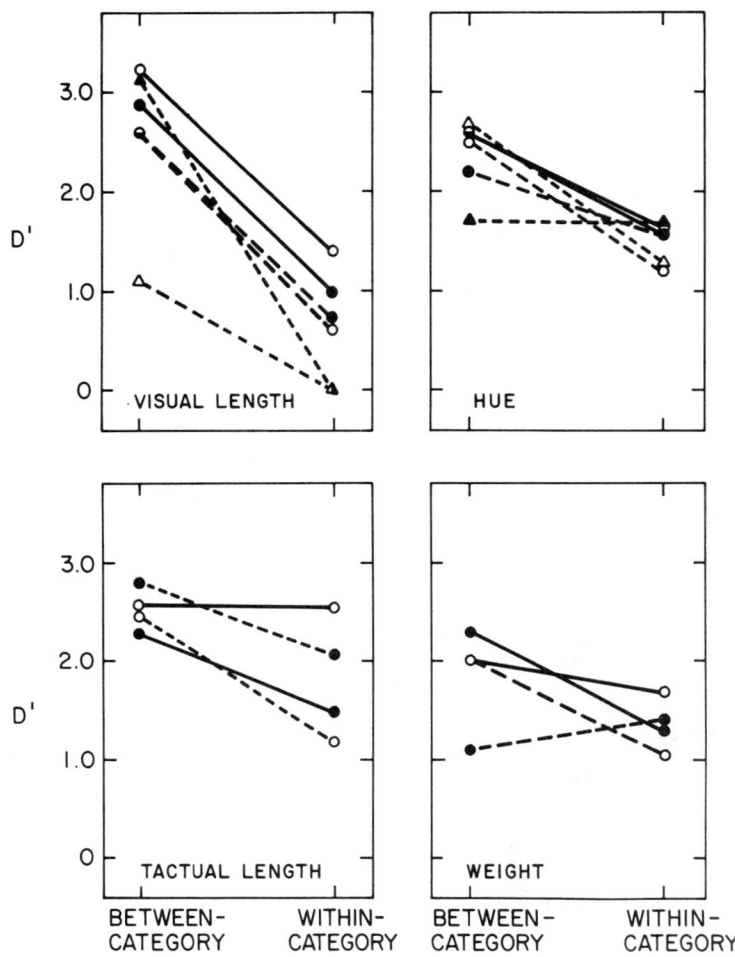

Figure 13.7. Mean sensitivity (d') on four stimulus continua for patients with brain damage. Anterior (solid lines, open circles); posterior (dashed lines, open circles); right-hemisphere (solid lines, closed circles); left-hemisphere (dashed lines, closed circles); right-temporal (triangles connected by dashed lines); left-temporal (solid triangles connected by dashed lines).

For the visual-length task, 19 subjects judged six line lengths ranging from 33 to 38 mm. Neither lateralization (right versus left hemisphere) nor localization (anterior versus posterior) effects on CP were evident; the differences between between-category and within-category sensitivity were significant for all groups. However, if we consider separately the two patients with lesions of the right temporal (RT) area who were tested, it appears that they did not demonstrate CP the way the other subjects with right-hemisphere or posterior lesions did, as illustrated in Figure 13.7 (upper left). The one patient with a left temporal (LT) lesion perceived visual line length in a highly categorical manner, as also shown in Figure 13.7.

Table 13.2. *Results of* t-*tests for categorical perception in four modalities*

	Visual dimensions					
	Length			Hue		
Group	t	df	p	t	df	p
A	7.52	7	.001	4.74	4	.025
P	5.35	10	.001	2.24	9	ns
R	8.12	13	.001	3.30	8	.025
L	3.05	4	.025	1.53	5	ns

	Tactual-kinesthetic dimensions											
	Length						Weight					
	C			I			C			I		
Group	t	df	p	t	df	p	t	df	p	t	df	p
A	—	3	ns	—	2	ns	—	4	ns	1.44	4	ns
P	3.60	6	.01	2.07	4	ns	1.92	11	ns	3.25	6	.025
R	1.88	6	ns	—	4	ns	2.12	12	ns	2.59	7	.025
L	1.26	3	ns	5.00	2	.05	—	3	ns	2.34	3	ns

Note: A = anterior, P = posterior, R = right hemisphere, L = left hemisphere, C = contralateral, I = ipsilateral. No entry indicates $t < 1.00$.

A different pattern of results was found for the hue-discrimination task (Figure 13.7, upper right). Six hues ranging from 7.5 G to 10.0 BG in equal Munsell steps were judged by 15 subjects. On this task, the between-category versus within-category difference in accuracy of discrimination is significant for the patients with anterior lesions but not for those with posterior lesions. Left-hemisphere damage but not right-hemisphere damage affected the degree to which perception was categorical. This suggests that the physiological substrate for hue categorization may be located in the left posterior region of the brain. Comparing performance of the three patients who had LT damage with that of two patients who had RT damage shows only the former to be markedly noncategorical. This apparently greater dependence of hue categorization on left-hemisphere function is difficult to reconcile with current ideas about lateralization, as color naming was not involved, and no obvious explanation is now forthcoming.

Turning to the tactual-kinesthetic tasks, further dissociations in structure-function relationships can be observed. For the tactile length discrimination, 11 subjects judged six lengths ranging from 13 to 23 mm, in 2-mm steps, by palpating the stimuli without visual guidance using the hand contralateral to their lesions. Figure 13.7 (lower left) illustrates that patients with anterior lesions failed to perceive the length stimuli categorically, whereas patients with posterior lesions did. The differences between between-category and within-category discrimination were not significant for either the right-hemisphere or the left-hemisphere groups, results that might be interpreted as suggesting that laterality is not critical. However, if the results are examined in the case of eight of the patients for whom data were also collected for the hand ipsilateral to the lesion, the patients with left-hemisphere lesions do show a significant difference in accuracy for between-category (d' = 3.03) versus within-category (d' = 2.27) discrimination, whereas the right-hemisphere patients do not. Because right-parietal lesions affected acuity but not CP, these results point to a right anterior focus for categorization of tactuospatial inputs. Contralateral acuity losses, in contrast, may arise from damage to either hemisphere (Corkin, Milner, & Rasmussen, 1970).

Discrimination of weights using the hand contralateral to the lesion was investigated in 17 subjects, who lifted opaque containers filled with appropriate amounts of lead shot and cotton. The stimuli on the continuum ranged from 110 to 160 gm in equal 10-gm steps. It appears from Figure 13.7 (lower right) that patients with anterior or left-hemisphere lesions failed to show CP whereas patients with posterior or right-hemisphere lesions did, but none of the differences in accuracy between the two types of discrimination attained significance. Again, however, data for the hand ipsilateral to the lesion allow a dissociation to be made between acuity losses, expected for the hand contralateral to the lesion, and deficits in CP, which may be lateralized to one or the other hemisphere. Table 13.2 shows that significant differences in sensitivity for between-category and within-category discriminations were obtained for patients with right-hemisphere or posterior lesions, and only anterior lesions or left-hemisphere lesions appeared to affect CP as opposed to sensory acuity. Thus, these results suggest that categorical judgments of weight may depend on an intact cortical area in the left-hemisphere or anterior region of the brain, or both.

This finding was again somewhat unexpected because right-hemisphere effects on higher-order perception are commonplace and left-hemisphere effects are usually thought to be restricted to speech functions. But it lends itself to recent theorizing more easily than do the results for hue perception. In studies of weight perception, McCloskey concluded that subjects make use of signals from centrally determined motor commands to judge heaviness: The discrepancy between an "expected" or "prepared for" weight and a weight that is being judged determines the perception of heaviness (McCloskey, 1974; McCloskey & Gandevia, 1978). Adaptation-level theory provides a rationale for what is "expected," namely, the level to which the perceiver is adapted, based on the pooling of previous kinesthetic inputs. The data from the weight-discrimination task point to the left hemisphere as the neural substrate for ongoing activity representing the level of adaptation for heaviness judgments. This proposed lateralization is consistent with Kimura's conception of left-hemisphere neural systems that control both manual activities and speech production (Kimura & Archibald, 1974; Lomas & Kimura, 1976).

Because subjects in the left-hemisphere group had suffered damage to parietotemporal as well as frontal areas, the results are quite consistent with Kimura's conclusion that overlapping left-hemisphere mechanisms are involved in programming motor response, manual as well as articulatory. She assumes that the left parietal region is involved in the general control of movements, and is important in providing input to more specific control systems in the left frontal cortex. Based on McCloskey's (1974) analysis of weight perception, one would expect that receptive as well as expressive functions would be represented in these control systems. That is, the left hemisphere appears to be critical for maintaining a record of kinesthetic experience that serves as the basis for programming motor acts. Such findings also agree with results in the monkey: Gentile (1972) reported that animals with lesions of the principal sulcus in the frontal lobes lose the ability to make "complex motor differentiations" when kinesthetic cues are the only available source of information. As she points out, Konorski (1967) had earlier proposed that prefrontal cortex is a gnostic area for kinesthesis.

However, performance of patients in the anterior group was also affected, and this raises the question of right-frontal as well as left-frontal involvement. The relevant results in the literature are also equivocal in that Kolb and Milner (1981) reported that right-frontal as well as left-frontal and left-parietal lesions impair the copying of motor acts whereas Kimura (1982) did not find deficits in motor programming after right-frontal damage.

Whatever the outcome of this issue, the left-hemisphere laterality effect observed for weight discrimination is hypothesized to depend upon left-hemisphere specialization for activities, both productive and receptive, in which kinesthetic cues contribute to motor programs. Similar ongoing neural activities representing past and present visuospatial and tactuospatial levels of stimulation are thought to be represented in the right hemisphere, which is consistent with Semmes's (1968) model of hemispheric specialization. Finally, the fact that input to either hand may lead to some degree of CP does not contradict the notion of hemispheric specialization for, as Bertelson (1982) points out, such results may occur with either strict or relative lateralization of function.

To summarize the results of these studies of brain-damaged subjects, impairments in perceiving stimuli categorically can be shown to be specific to a given mode of stimulation and to be dissociable from primary sensory deficits that lead to acuity losses. Although these results are tentative, they are provocative in pointing to different brain structures that may serve to maintain a record of experience in a particular sensory domain, a record that serves as an internal standard for judgment. As more cases with unilateral brain damage are studied, it should also be possible to evaluate the merits of models of lateralization implying strict localization versus those favoring relative specialization of one hemisphere over the other.

Concluding comments

These data show that visual, tactile, and kinesthetic stimuli are perceived as members of perceptual categories and that CP may accordingly be a very general, if not universal, characteristic of perceptual processing. Nor is this mode of processing limited to the left hemisphere; categorical perception of visuospatial and tactuospatial continua was more affected when brain damage was present in the right hemisphere, either because lateralization is relative and the neural mechanisms underlying CP in these domains are better represented in the right hemisphere or because lateralization is absolute, and input directed to the left hemisphere is transferred with some loss to the right hemisphere where it is perceived categorically (Bertelson, 1982). Kinesthetic stimulation, in contrast, was perceived less categorically when left-hemisphere brain areas were compromised. This result is compatible with other findings of left-hemisphere control of motor programs that depend on kinesthetic input. Results for hue discrimination are more difficult to explain in terms of current models of hemispheric specialization.

All the data presented were interpreted in terms of AL theory, which was also used to account for changes in identification and discrimination as a function of varying experience. It was suggested that the same principles of perceptual functioning could be applied both to short-term effects and long-term effects, rather than postulating separate kinds of mechanisms for different behavioral outcomes. For unidimensional perceptual stimuli, shifts in category boundary were shown to be a function of changes in adaptation level, which could be predicted from the range of physical values that were presented for judgment. In contrast to other accounts, which implicitly assume that a physical stimulus produces a constant effect, AL theory stresses the variable and adaptive nature of functioning in biological systems and suggests hypotheses about the neural basis of perception that are in accord with what is known about brain structure and function.

References

Benevento, L. A., & Rezak, M. (1976). The cortical projections of the inferior pulvinar and adjacent lateral pulvinar in the rhesus monkey (Macaca mulatta): An autoradiographic study. *Brain Research, 108,* 1–24.

Bertelson, P. (1982). Lateral differences in normal man and lateralization of brain function. *International Journal of Psychology, 17,* 173–210.

Bullock, T. H., & Horridge, G. A. (1965). *Structure and function in the nervous system of invertebrates.* San Francisco: W. H. Freeman. Cited in Reed (1969).

Burton, H., & Robinson, C. J. (1981). Organization of the SII parietal cortex: Multiple somatic sensory representations within and near the second somatic sensory area of cynomolgus monkeys. In C. N. Woolsey (Ed.), *Cortical sensory organization, Vol 1: Multiple somatic areas* (pp. 67–119). Clifton, NJ: Humana Press.

Capehart, J., Tempone, V. J., & Hébert, J. A. (1969). A theory of stimulus equivalence. *Psychological Review, 76,* 405–418.

Clark, W. C. (1966). The *psyche* in psychophysics: A sensory decision theory analysis of the effect of instructions on flicker sensitivity and response bias. *Psychological Bulletin, 65,* 358–366.

Corkin, S., Milner, B., & Rasmussen, T. (1970). Somatosensory thresholds. Contrasting effects of postcentral gyrus and posterior parietal-lobe excisions. *Archives of Neurology, 23,* 41–58.

DeValois, R. L. (1966). Neural processing of visual information. In R. W. Russell (Ed.), *Frontiers in physiological psychology* (pp. 51–91). New York: Academic Press.

Diamond, I. T. (1979). The subdivisions of neocortex: A proposal to revise the traditional view of sensory, motor, and association areas. In J. M. Sprague and A. N. Epstein (Eds.), *Progress in psychobiology and physiological psychology* (Vol. 8, pp. 1-43). New York: Academic Press.

Diehl, R. L. (1981). Feature detectors for speech: A critical reappraisal. *Psychological Bulletin, 89*, 1-18.

Diehl, R. L., Lang, M., & Parker, E. M. (1980). A further parallel between selective adaptation and contrast. *Journal of Experimental Psychology: Human Perception and Performance, 6*, 24-44.

Durlach, N. I., & Braida, L. D. (1969). Intensity perception. I. Preliminary theory of intensity resolution. *Journal of the Acoustical Society of America, 46*, 372-383.

Gentile, A. (1972). Movement organization and delayed alternation behavior of monkeys following selective ablation of frontal cortex. In J. Konorski, H.-L. Teuber, & B. Zernicki (Eds.), *The frontal granular cortex and behavior: Acta Neurobiologiae Experimentalis* (Vol. 32, pp. 277-304).

Gross, C. G., Rocha-Miranda, C. E., & Bender, D. B. (1972). Visual properties of neurons in inferotemporal cortex of the macaque. *Journal of Neurophysiology, 35*, 96-111.

Grossman, M., & Wilson, M. (1987). Stimulus categorization by brain-damaged patients. *Brain and Cognition*.

Guilford, J. P. (1954). *Psychometric methods* (2nd ed.). New York: McGraw-Hill.

Guilford, J. P., & Dingman, H. F. (1955). A modification of the method of equal-appearing intervals. *The American Journal of Psychology, 68*, 450-454.

Healy, A. F., & Repp, B. H. (1982). Context independence and phonetic mediation in categorical perception. *Journal of Experimental Psychology: Human Perception and Performance, 8*, 68-80.

Hécaen, H., & Albert, M. L. (1978). *Human neuropsychology*. New York: Wiley.

Helson, H. (1948). Adaptation level as a basis for a quantitative theory of frames of reference. *Psychological Review, 55*, 297-313.

Helson, H. (1964). *Adaptation-level theory: An experimental and systematic approach to behavior*. New York: Harper & Row.

Helson, H., & Masters, H. G. (1966). A study of inflection-points in the locus of adaptation levels as a function of anchor-stimuli. *The American Journal of Psychology, 79*, 400-408.

Hubel, D. H., & Wiesel, T. N. (1968). Receptive fields and functional architecture of monkey striate cortex. *Journal of Physiology, London, 195*, 215-243.

Kaas, J. H., Sur, M., Nelson, R. J., & Merzenich, M. M. (1981). The postcentral somatosensory cortex: Multiple representations of the body in primates. In C. N. Woolsey (Ed.), *Cortical sensory organization*, Vol. 1: *Multiple somatic areas* (pp. 29-45). Clifton, NJ: Humana Press.

Keil, F. C. (1979). *Semantic and conceptual development*, Cambridge, MA: Harvard University Press.

Kimura, D. (1982). Left-hemisphere control of oral and brachial movements and their relation to communication. *Philosophical Transactions of the Royal Society, London (B), 298*, 135-149.

Kimura, D., & Archibald, Y. (1974). Motor functions of the left hemisphere. *Brain, 97*, 337-350.

Kolb, B., & Milner, B. (1981). Performance of complex arm and facial movements after focal brain lesions. *Neuropsychologia, 19*, 491-503.

Kolb, B., & Whishaw, I. Q. (1980). *Fundamentals of human neuropsychology*. San Francisco: W. H. Freeman.

Konorski, J. (1967). *Integrative activity of the brain. An interdisciplinary approach*. Chicago: University of Chicago Press.

Lane, H. (1965). The motor theory of speech perception. *Psychological Review, 72*, 275-309.

Lewis, R. S., Sakai, S. T., & Tanaka, D., Jr. (1981). Thalamic projections of the posterior parietal area in the dog: Afferent organization and acetylthiocholinesterase histochemistry. *Society for Neuroscience Abstracts, 7*, 757.

Liberman, A. M., Cooper, F. S., Shankweiler, D. P., & Studdert-Kennedy, M. (1967). Perception of the speech code. *Psychological Review, 74*, 431-461.

Liberman, A. M., Harris, K. S., Hoffman, H. S., & Griffith, B. C. (1957). The discrimination of speech sounds within and across phoneme boundaries. *Journal of Experimental Psychology, 54*, 358-368.

Lomas, J., & Kimura, D. (1976). Intrahemispheric interaction between speaking and sequential manual activity. *Neuropsychologia, 14*, 23-33.

Luria, A. R. (1980). *Higher cortical functions in man* (2nd ed.). New York: Basic Books.
Mackay, D. M. (1956). Towards an information-flow model of human behavior. *British Journal of Psychology, 47,* 30–43. Cited in Reed (1969).
Macmillan, N. A., Kaplan, H. L., & Creelman, C. D. (1977). The psychophysics of categorical perception. *Psychological Review, 84,* 452–471.
McCloskey, D. I. (1974). Muscular and cutaneous mechanisms in the estimation of grasped weights. *Neuropsychologia, 12,* 513–520.
McCloskey, D. I., & Gandevia, S. C. (1978). Role of inputs from, skin, joints and muscles and of corollary discharges in human discriminatory tasks. In G. Gordon (Ed.), *Active touch: The mechanism of recognition of objects by manipulation: a multidisciplinary approach: Proceedings of a symposium held at Beaune, France, July, 1977, under the auspices of the International Union of Physiological Sciences* (pp. 177–187). New York: Pergamon Press.
Michels, W. C., & Helson, H. (1953). Man as a meter. *Physics Today, 6,* 4–7.
Miller, J. D., Wier, C. C., Pastore, R. E., Kelly, W. J., & Dooling, R. J. (1976). Discrimination and labeling of noise-buzz sequences with varying noise-lead times. *Journal of the Acoustical Society of America, 60,* 410–417.
Mishkin, M. (1979). Analogous neural models for tactual and visual learning. *Neuropsychologia, 17,* 139–151.
Petras, J. M. (1971). Connections of the parietal lobe. *Journal of Psychiatric Research, 8,* 189–201.
Pastore, R. E., Ahroon, W. A., Baffuto, K. J., Friedman, C., Puleo, J. S., & Fink, E. A. (1977). Common factor model of categorical perception. *Journal of Experimental Psychology: Human Perception and Performance, 3,* 686–696.
Posner, M. I., & Keele, S. W. (1968). On the genesis of abstract ideas. *Journal of Experimental Psychology, 77,* 353–363.
Powell, T. P. S., & Mountcastle, V. B. (1959). Some aspects of the functional organization of the cortex of the postcentral gyrus of the monkey. *Bulletin of the Johns Hopkins Hospital, 105,* 133–162.
Pribram, K. H. (1960). The intrinsic systems of the forebrain. In J. Field (Ed.), *Handbook of physiology: Neurophysiology* (Vol. 2, pp. 1323–1344). Washington, D. C.: American Physiological Society.
Reed, C. F. (1969). The solution of hidden figures: Brightness discrimination and eye movement. *Neuropsychologia, 7,* 121–133.
Remez, R. E. (1980). Susceptibility of a stop consonant to adaptation on a speech-nonspeech continuum: Further evidence against feature detectors in speech perception. *Perception and Psychophysics, 27,* 17–23.
Rosch, E. (1973). Natural categories. *Cognitive Psychology, 4,* 328–350.
Rosch, E. (1975). Cognitive representation of semantic categories. *Journal of Experimental Psychology: General, 104,* 192–233.
Rosch, E., & Mervis, C. B. (1975). Family resemblances: Studies in the internal structure of categories. *Cognitive Psychology, 7,* 573–605.
Sarris, V. (1967). Adaptation-level theory: Two critical experiments on Helson's weighted-average model. *The American Journal of Psychology, 80,* 331–344.
Sawusch, J. R., & Nusbaum, H. C. (1979). Contextual effects in vowel perception I: Anchor-induced contrast effects. *Perception and Psychophysics, 25,* 292–302.
Semmes, J. (1968). Hemispheric specialization: A possible clue to mechanism. *Neuropsychologia, 6,* 11–26.
Semmes, J. (1969). Protopathic and epicritic sensation: A reappraisal. In A. L. Benton (Ed.), *Contributions to clinical neuropsychology* (pp. 142–171). Chicago: Aldine.
Sokolov, Y. N. (1963). *Perception and the conditional reflex.* London: Pergamon Press. Cited in Reed (1969).
Streitfeld, B. & Wilson, M. (1986). The ABCs of categorical perception. *Cognitive Psychology, 18,* 432–451.
Swets, J. A. (1971). Comment: Adaptation-level theory and signal-detection theory and their relation to vigilance experiments. In M. H. Appley (Ed.), *Adaptation-level theory* (pp. 49–53). New York: Academic Press.

von Uexküll, A. (1957). A stroll through the worlds of animals and men. In C. H. Schiller (Ed.), *Instinctive behavior* (pp. 5–80). New York: International Universities Press.

Weiskrantz, L. (1974). The interaction between occipital and temporal cortex in vision: An overview. In F. O. Schmidt & E. G. Worden (Eds.), *The neurosciences, 3rd study program* (pp. 189–204). Cambridge, MA: M.I.T. Press.

Weller, R. E., & Kaas, J. H. (1981). Cortical and subcortical connections of visual cortex in primates. In C. N. Woolsey (Ed.), *Cortical sensory organization*, Vol. 2: *Multiple visual areas* (pp. 121–155). Clifton, NJ: Humana Press.

Werner, G., & Whitsel, B. L. (1973). Functional organization of the somatosensory cortex. In A. Iggo (Ed.), *Handbook of sensory physiology* (Vol. 2, pp. 621–700). New York: Springer.

Wilson, M. (1971). Shifts in categorization and identifiability of visual stimuli by rhesus monkeys. *Perception and Psychophysics, 10,* 271–272.

Wilson, M. (1972). Assimilation and contrast effects in visual discrimination by rhesus monkeys. *Journal of Experimental Psychology, 93,* 279–282.

Wilson, M. (1978). Visual system: Pulvinar-extrastriate cortex. In R. B. Masterton (Ed.), *Handbook of behavioral neurobiology*, Vol. 1: *Sensory integration* (pp. 209–247). New York: Plenum Press.

Wilson, M., & DeBauche, B. A. (1981). Inferotemporal cortex and categorical perception of visual stimuli by monkeys. *Neuropsychologia, 19,* 29–41.

Wilson, M., DeBauche, B. A., & Streitfeld, B. D. (1983, April). *Categorical perception of visual stimuli.* Paper presented at the meeting of the Eastern Psychological Association, Baltimore.

Zatorre, R. J., & Halpern, A. R. (1979). Identification, discrimination, and selective adaptation of simultaneous musical intervals. *Perception and Psychophysics, 26,* 384–395.

Zeki, S. M. (1978). Uniformity and diversity of structure and function in rhesus monkey prestriate visual cortex. *Journal of Physiology, 277,* 273–290.

Part V

Psychophysiological indices of categorical perception

14 Electrophysiological indices of categorical perception for speech

Dennis L. Molfese

This chapter provides a review of the auditory-evoked potential (AEP) and clinical neuropsychology literature related to categorical perception (CP). CP is initially described as a process in which equal-sized stimulus differences are more discernible across category boundaries than within. In the case of speech, these boundaries correspond to identification boundaries. A brief overview of electrophysiological recording techniques and the event-related potential literature provides background for the literature review on auditory-evoked potential. The research using this technique indicates that AEPs can be used to study this phenomenon. Furthermore, the technique may be useful for localizing the brain mechanisms responsible for CP and for tracing their development from early in infancy into adulthood. Apparently, both hemispheres can discriminate between stimuli from different phonetic categories. However, the right hemisphere appears to have an additional role in this process. This pattern of responding is not present at birth but appears by 2 months of age. Studies using nonspeech stimuli containing comparable temporal cues report similar patterns of results for children and adults. A review of studies investigating CP in both animal and human brain-damaged populations also indicates some involvement of the right hemisphere.

Voicing-contrast or voice-onset time (VOT) reflects the temporal relationship between laryngeal pulsing (e.g., vocal-cord vibration) and consonant release (e.g., the separation of lips to release a burst of air from the vocal tract during the production of bilabial stop consonants such as /b/, /p/). It has been reported that adult listeners can discriminate VOT differences between speech stimuli only to the extent that they can assign unique labels to them (Liberman, Cooper, Shankweiler, & Studdert-Kennedy, 1967). For example, listeners cannot discriminate between bilabial stop consonants with VOT values of 0 and +20 msec, perceiving both stimuli as /ba/. Stimuli with +40 and +60 msec VOT are both identified as /pa/, and subjects fail to discriminate between the +40- and +60-msec stimuli. Adults discriminate between and assign different labels to stimuli with VOT values of +20 and +40 msec. These stimuli are from different phonetic categories (/b/ vs. /p/). The 20-msec difference in VOT between speech syllables can only be detected when the VOT stimuli are from different phonetic categories. Consequently, changes in VOT appear to be categorical. Listeners can only discriminate between those sounds on

Support for this work was provided by the National Science Foundation (BNS-8004429 and BNS-8210846), March of Dimes (12-13), and the Office of Research Development and Administration (2-10481), Southern Illinois University at Carbondale.

the VOT continuum to which they can assign unique labels. Such findings, termed "categorical perception" (CP), have been consistently reported with adults in identification and discrimination studies (Liberman, Delattre, & Cooper, 1958; Lisker & Abramson, 1964, Abramson & Lisker, 1970) as well as with young infants in studies using the habituation of high-amplitude sucking as the discrimination measure (Eimas, Siqueland, Jusczyk, & Vigorito, 1971; Trehub & Rabinovitch, 1972; see also Eimas, Miller, & Jusczyk, in Chapter 5, this volume).

The studies with human infants have demonstrated that the CP for speech sounds differing in voicing does not require extensive experience in producing or listening to the sounds in question. Voicing contrasts are discriminated categorically in the first few months after birth (Eilers, Gavin, & Wilson, 1980; Eimas, 1974; Eimas et al., 1971; Lasky, Syrdal-Lasky, & Klein, 1975; Streeter, 1976). These results have suggested to some authors that the perception of speech sounds may involve an innate, special mechanism, unique to humans (e.g., Eimas 1974; Morse, 1974); others have questioned this interpretation (e.g., Butterfield & Cairns, 1974). There have been a number of studies with nonhuman primates to determine whether CP-like discrimination occurs in animals who cannot produce humanlike speech sounds. Waters and Wilson (1976), using a shock-avoidance paradigm, tested the ability of rhesus monkeys to establish a voiced–voiceless boundary and to discriminate contrasts along that continuum relative to their boundary. Their results indicated that nonhuman primates place the boundary for /ba/-/pa/ in the same region as adult humans do and that discrimination across this consonant boundary (between categories) was better than within categories. More recently, Kuhl and Padden (1983b) have confirmed this finding of categorical discrimination with rhesus macaque monkeys using a similar but more extensive set of synthetic-speech stimuli differing in voicing (/ba/-/pa/, /da/-/ta/, /ga/-/ka/). Evidence of CP for place-of-articulation contrasts has also been observed in rhesus macaques (Kuhl and Padden, 1983a; Morse & Snowdon, 1975; Sinnott, Beecher, Moody, & Stebbins, 1976). Finally, CP-like responding to voicing contrasts has even been reported in nonprimates such as chinchillas (Kuhl, 1981; Kuhl & Miller, 1975). It thus appears that one aspect of human-speech perception, categorical perception, is observable not only in young infants with minimal exposure to human speech, but also in nonhuman primates and in some cases even in nonprimates. Results from these animal studies have been interpreted as evidence that this aspect of speech perception is a property of the primate (if not the mammalian) auditory system, rather than being a special mechanism in humans (Kuhl, 1979; see also Chapter 11 by Snowdon and Chapter 12 by Kuhl, this volume).

From this brief outline it emerges that the temporal component of the voicing cue is processed by some mechanism active in the brain early in life, perhaps at birth (Eimas, Miller, & Jusczyk in Chapter 5, this volume) and possibly not unique to humans but a component of the mammalian auditory system. Moreover, this mechanism seems capable of categorically discriminating the VOT cue, whether or not it is embedded in the speech signal (Pisoni, 1977).

One question that has not been addressed directly with behavioral procedures concerns the localization of VOT mechanisms in the brain and how this organization may change during language acquisition. Given that VOT is an important cue for speech perception and that speech is generally thought to be controlled by the left (linguistic) hemisphere, it has been assumed that VOT perception is controlled by mechanisms specific to that hemisphere, but no systematic studies have been done.

My goal in this chapter is to review behavioral and electrophysiological studies of the nature, development, and organization of CP in the brain. It is interesting that there are many points of agreement between the earlier behavioral studies and the more recent electrophysiological studies. However, the newer techniques go beyond simply reinforcing our knowledge of what is already known in that they offer a way to address questions that have been raised but not pursued because of limitations of traditional behavioral methods.

Evoked potential procedures

The first series of studies involves recording brain activity detected by electrodes placed on the scalp. (For the purposes of this chapter, the review will focus on the auditory modality; material on visual-evoked responses and CP is ably reviewed in Chapter 15 by Regan.) Whereas a great deal of clinical research has focused on the use of the electroencephalogram (EEG) to study brain function, the majority of the work concerned with the perception of environmental events has used evoked-potential (EP) procedures. These involve recording the spontaneous electrical activity of the brain during the presentation of various stimuli. Unlike the standard EEG procedures, however, EP techniques attempt to establish strict temporal relationships between the onset of some stimulus event and the onset of changes in the various portions of the accompanying EEG pattern. Because of the small size of these electrical patterns (5 to 15 microvolts) relative to other electrical noise sources, researchers must usually repeat the stimuli a number of times in order to evoke multiple instances of the brain potentials. Next, these repeated evoked potentials are added together and averaged. The procedure averages out random noise that differs from presentation to presentation, thereby bringing out the waveform that is invariant across presentations. This average waveform is taken to reflect the brain activity elicited by the repeated stimulus event. Once the averaged EPs are obtained, a variety of different analyses can determine whether changes in certain stimulus features might produce corresponding changes in various portions of the brain response. In general, analyses focus on certain peaks in the waveforms that occur at various intervals following the onset of the stimulus event (Picton & Strauss, 1980; Vaughan, 1969). Such analyses may be as simple as directly measuring the amplitudes of peaks or the latencies between them or they may involve a complex factor analysis to reduce the complex waveform to a smaller set of simpler components not immediately apparent to direct inspection.

There is a great deal of evidence that the averaged EP can reflect changes in the neural activity of the brain during sensory (Regan, 1972, pp. 31–116) and cognitive processing (Donchin, Ritter, & McCallum, 1978, pp. 349–412). In the sensory case, so-called *exogenous* EP components appear to be relatively "impervious to variations of the psychological state of the observer" (Hillyard & Wood, 1979, p. 346). These components (which for the most part occur prior to 100 msec following stimulus onset) seem to be very stable from one individual to the next and are not usually altered by the subject's psychological state. Changes in these waveforms, whether in amplitude or latency, usually signal some problem with a receptor, pathway, or brain area represented by the component involved (Rockstroh, Elbert, Birbaumer, & Lutzenberger, 1982, p. 3). On the other hand, EP waveforms associated with cognitive or perceptual processes are usually referred to as "endogenous" components (Hillyard & Wood, 1979, p. 346). In general, the portion of the waveform that occurs after 100 msec will reflect this type of activity. Here, the various characteristics of the EP waveforms, although triggered by some stimulus, are affected by the cognitive–perceptual processes involved in processing the stimulus. Whereas the exogenous components are relatively stable across different subjects and mental states, the endogenous components may show great intersubject variability and may change across different tasks and states. For the research outlined below one would expect CP-like effects to elicit exogenous types of activity, given the consistent pattern noted across ages and tasks.

In general, there have been two different approaches to studying evoked potentials: (1) "defining the neuronal substrates of EPs *and* their relationship to behavioral events" and (2) "a purely empirical relation of EPs and behavior without recourse to neuronal mechanisms." There are a number of excellent papers that attempt to identify discrete brain sources responsible for generating the various components of the EP (Goff, Allison, & Vaughn, 1978; Klee & Rall, 1977), but the exact nature of these brain mechanisms remains in doubt and under discussion. At a grosser level, however, topographic studies do indicate that major portions of human EPs originate in the primary and secondary cortical areas specific to the modality involved in the detection of the stimuli presented (Simson, Vaughan, & Ritter, 1977a, 1977b; Vaughan, 1969). In particular, evoked potentials associated with auditory and visual presentations appear to be generated in the secondary cortex of the auditory and visual systems, respectively, as well as in the parietal association cortex (Simson, Vaughan, & Ritter, 1977a,b). At a grosser level, EP activity recorded over the left side of the head originates predominantly from the left hemisphere, whereas EP activity recorded over the right originates from the right hemisphere.

Auditory-evoked responses and voice-onset time

Studies by Dorman (1974) and Molfese and associates (Molfese, 1978, 1980; Molfese & Hess, 1978; Molfese & Molfese, 1979, in press) have used auditory EP procedures as well as behavioral techniques to study VOT processing in young infants, preschool-aged children, and adults. As in the habituation paradigms in infant research (see Eimas, Miller, & Jusczyk in Chapter 5, this volume), discrimination functions have been interpreted in the EP literature as evidence of a CP-like effect. A CP-like effect occurs if certain equal-sized differences are more discernible across category boundaries than within. EP responses that discriminate between two stimuli differing along some physical dimension are interpreted as reflecting between-category comparisons whereas the absence of discrimination with equal-sized stimulus differences is taken to reflect within-category comparisons. In the research outlined below, the test for a between-category difference involves a comparison of EP responses to the 20- and 40-msec stimuli whereas the within-category tests involve a comparison of responses to the 0- and 20-msec stimuli (category 1) and to 40- and 60-msec stimuli (category 2). When speech stimuli are used with these VOT values, the 0- and 20-msec stimuli are usually heard as voiced consonants (as in the case of the bilabial stop consonant /b/) whereas the 40- and 60-msec stimuli are heard as voiceless (as in the case of the bilabial stop consonant /p/).

In the first of the auditory-evoked-response (AEP) studies that attempted to assess whether AEPs could detect CP-like effects, Dorman (1974) recorded AEPs as part of a habituation paradigm. Typically, a habituation procedure involves the repetition of the same stimulus for some period of time during which a subject's responses to that stimulus begin to decrease in frequency or amplitude. At some point, when the response level has been sufficiently reduced, the experimenter stops presenting the "habituating" stimulus and begins presenting a new stimulus. If the subject can detect a difference between the habituating stimulus and the new one, the response level will increase. If, however, the subject is unable to distinguish between the habituating and the new stimulus, response levels do not show a "rebound" or dishabituation effect (a return to prehabituation levels). Dorman hypothesized that a portion of the AEP would decline with repeated presentations of the same stimulus. However, once a stimulus from a different phonetic category was presented, he expected the amplitude of the AEP component to increase. This increase was not expected to occur if the change was made from the habituating stimulus to a second stimulus from within the same phonetic category.

The AEPs of five experimental groups of adults (10 adults per group) were recorded from Cz (a location at the center of the scalp on the top of the head) referred to the right ear lobe. Four computer-synthesized consonant–vowel speech syllables were used. The initial bilabial stop consonant differed in VOT across the four stimuli. The first two consonants that belonged to one phonetic category were identified as /ba/ and had VOTs of 0 and 20 msec. The second phonetic category was represented by the two syllables with VOTs of 40 and 60 msec and were identified as /pa/. The syllables were 250 msec in duration and were repeated at a fixed interval of 1,750 msec. Group 1 listened to 20 presentations of the syllable with a VOT of 20 msec, followed by 20 presentations of the 0-msec stimulus. The next day this group heard first the 20-msec stimuli and then the 40-msec stimulus for a comparable number of times. Group 2 heard the same stimuli as Group 1 but in the reverse order. Group 3 listened initially to 20 trials of the 0- and 20-msec stimuli. They then heard one of these stimuli for 20 presentations, followed immediately by 20 presentations of the other stimulus. Group 4 listened to the same stimulus throughout. Group 5 listened to randomly ordered series of stimuli from both stimulus categories. AEPs were averaged separately for each stimulus and subject. The N1–P2 amplitudes (N1 range = 75 to 125 msec; P2 range = 175 to 225 msec) were then measured. The only significant effects noted were an increase in the peak-to-peak amplitudes of Groups 1 and 2 when the stimulus changed from one phonetic category to the other. Dorman interpreted these effects as demonstrating that AEPs could reflect the CP-like effects of voicing cues.

In a follow-up to this work, Molfese (1978) recorded AEPs from the left- and right-temporal regions of the scalp in 16 adults during a phoneme-identification task. Subjects listened to a randomly ordered series of synthesized bilabial stop consonants varying in VOT with values of 0, +20, +40, and +60 msec. They pressed one button after each stimulus presentation if they heard a /b/ and another button if they heard a /p/. Adults identified the stop consonants with VOT values of 0 and +20 msec as /ba/ approximately 95% and 93% of the time, respectively, whereas +40- and +60-msec VOTs were respectively identified 95% and 98% of the time as /pa/. AEPs to each stimulus were recorded during the identification task and were later analyzed using standard averaging techniques. Instead of using Dorman's procedure, Molfese applied principal components analysis to the entire AEPs rather than only a subset of points. This analysis indicated that two early AEP components recorded over the right-temporal region varied systematically as a function of the phoneme category of the evoking stimulus: Stimuli with VOT values of 0 and +20 msec elicited a waveform different from the one elicited by the +40- and +60-msec stimuli. No AEP differences were found between the 0- and +20-msec responses or between the +40- and +60-msec responses. These AEP patterns coincided with the /ba/ versus /pa/ identification boundaries. Components of the left-hemisphere responses differentiated the 0- and the +60-msec stimuli from the +20- and +40-msec stimuli. The left hemisphere appeared responsive to the boundaries or end values of the VOT stimulus set used but did not reflect the CP-like discriminations elicited over the right hemisphere (see also Chapter 13 by Wilson, this volume).

A parallel set of findings has been noted with nonhuman primates. Morse, Molfese, Laughlin, Linnville, and Wetzel (1987) tested a group of 15 1-year-old rhesus macaque monkeys with the same stimuli used by Molfese (1978). Auditory-evoked potentials were recorded from left- and right-temporal and parietal-scalp locations in response to a set of bilabial stop consonants that varied in VOT. Two regions of the AEPs (a negative peak at 150 msec and a positive peak at 390 msec) recorded from only the right-temporal scalp position were found to discriminate the two

CHILDREN VOT CENTROID

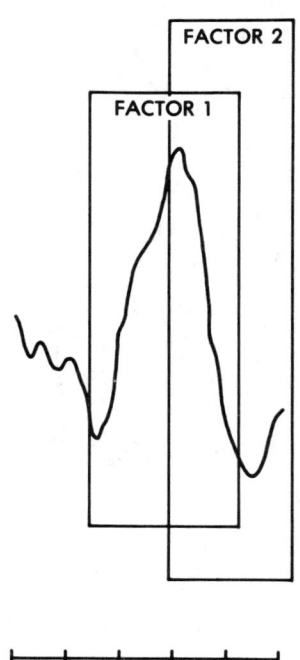

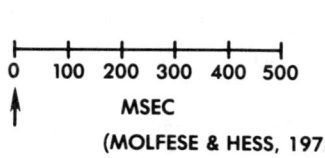

(MOLFESE & HESS, 1978)

Figure 14.1. The group averaged AEP (centroid) elicited in response to the different VOT stimuli from the various electrode sites. The areas labeled Factor 1 and Factor 2 were identified through factor analysis and analysis of variance steps as regions of the AEP, which systematically varied in response to changes in VOT. Calibration marker is 2 μV.

voiced from the two voiceless consonants. No within-category differences were noted.

Similar effects were also found with 3- and 4-year-old children in two studies, which used the velar stop consonants /k/, /g/ (Molfese & Hess, 1978; Molfese & Molfese, in press). In the Molfese and Hess study, AEPs were recorded from the left- and right-temporal regions of 12 nursery-school-aged children in response to a series of synthesized consonant–vowel syllables, which varied in VOT for the initial consonant (0, +20, +40, +60 msec). As with adults, one AEP component from the right-hemisphere electrode site only varied systematically as a function of phoneme category but did not change when elicited by VOT values from the same phoneme category. This component corresponds to the area inside the rectangle labeled Factor 2, as depicted in Figure 14.1. A second and distinct (orthogonal) AEP component (Factor 1 in Figure 14.1) also discriminated between VOT values along phoneme boundaries. However, in contrast to adults, this component was detected at recording sites over both hemispheres.

The changes in these AEP factors can be seen in individual AEPs, as illustrated in

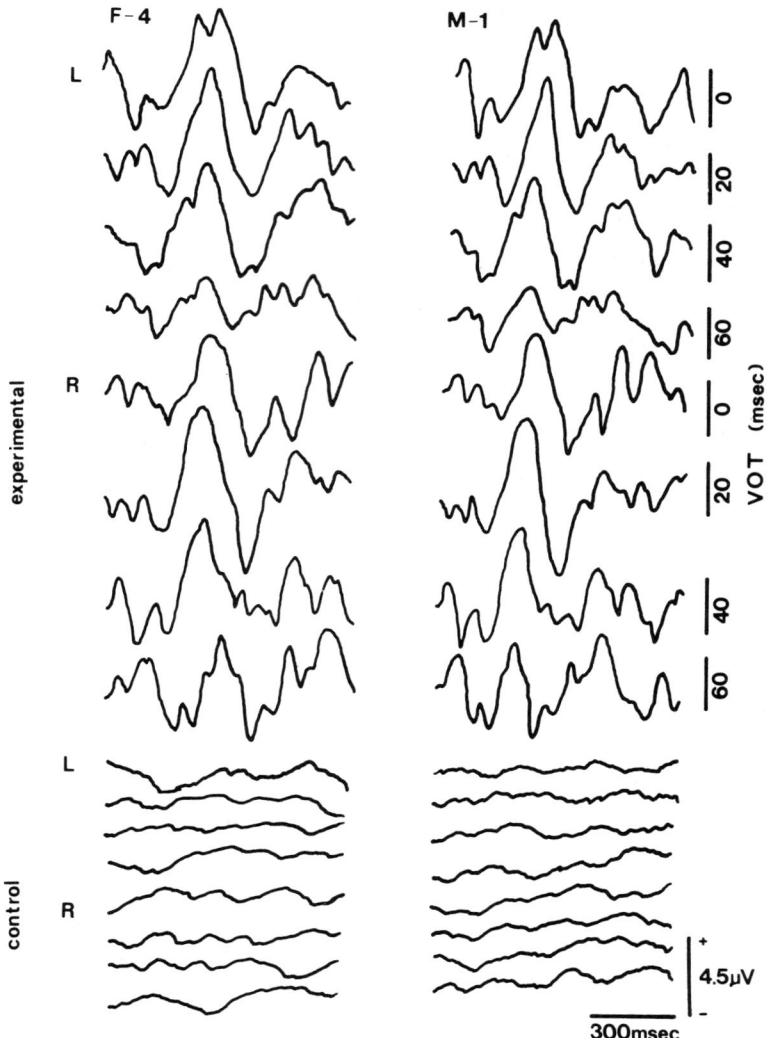

Figure 14.2. AEPs recorded from the left (L) and right (R) temporal regions in response to velar stop consonants, which varied in 20-msec steps along the voicing continuum. Time course is 900 msec with positive up. The top eight waveforms were AEPs recorded from a female while the top eight waves on the right were recorded from a male. The eight bottom traces on each side represent averages of the EEG recorded during nonstimulus periods.

Figure 14.2. Factor 2, as noted above, reflected changes in the second negative wave of the AEP. In both subjects presented in Figure 14.2, the second negative wave, which peaks at approximately 480 msec, appears more negative than the first large negative peak at approximately 170 msec for the 0- and 20-msec conditions in the right-hemisphere AEPs. However, right-hemisphere responses to the 40- and

60-msec stimuli do not produce a similar result. Rather, both the first and the second negative waves appear to peak at comparable levels. No such difference between the 0- to 20-msec responses when compared to the 40- to 60-msec responses can be noted in the left-hemisphere responses of either child. The bilateral-hemisphere effects that discriminated the 0- to 20-msec stimuli from the 40- to 60-msec stimuli (Factor 1) can also be seen in Figure 14.2. The distance from the first negative peak at 170 msec to the second positive peak at approximately 300 msec is larger for the AEPs elicited in response to the 0- and 20-msec stimuli than to the 40- and 60-msec stimuli. This is the case for both subjects and both hemispheres. In this case, then, one notes that in response to changes in VOT, the brain's responses from both hemispheres (as characterized by the AEPs) discriminated between sounds along phoneme-category lines. Later in time, only the right hemisphere responded in this manner. For these children, then, the AEP data can be interpreted as evidence for the presence of more than one perceptual mechanism in the brain that is sensitive to VOT changes and category boundaries. Moreover, as with adults, the right hemisphere appears to possess some ability to discriminate between VOT values at a time when the left hemisphere does not.

Evoked-potential procedures can be used to study CP in infants younger than those who can be effectively tested with the more standard conditioning procedures of Eimas, Miller, and Jusczyk (Chapter 5, this volume). Because the EP procedures do not require any overt behavioral response from the subject, they can even be used with newborn infants. Such tests at birth should allow researchers to determine whether at some level there is a brain response similar to that found with older children and adults that discriminate between, but not within, different phonetic categories.

Two further experiments found CP-like responses in infants over 2 months of age but failed to note such effects in newborns (Molfese & Molfese, 1979). In experiment 1, the four consonant–vowel speech syllables used by Molfese (1978) were presented to 16 infants 2 to 5 months old. AEPs to each stimulus were recorded from scalp electrodes placed over temporal areas (T_3, T_4) of the left and right hemispheres. With these infants, as with preschool children, one component of the cortical AEP from the right-hemisphere site discriminated between VOT values from different phoneme categories. A second AEP component over both hemispheres responded in a similar fashion. It is interesting that whereas this bilateral response did discriminate between stimuli from different categories, it also discriminated between stimuli from the same category. In experiment 2, 16 newborn infants were tested to determine whether these VOT discriminations were reflected in their AEPs. The same consonant–vowel speech stimuli and recording sites described for the older infants were used in the newborn study. Although both hemispheres were actively involved in the processing of the VOT stimuli, there was no evidence of any CP-like VOT effect similar to that found with older infants, children, and adults. From these data it would appear that the ability to discriminate VOT stimuli along phoneme boundaries is present in the early months of infancy but not at birth. Molfese and Molfese speculated that perhaps some period of maturation or experience is necessary before CP-like discriminations appear for VOT.

Are CP-like effects in EP studies restricted to speech stimuli?

Another question to be addressed in this chapter concerns the nature of the evoking stimulus needed to elicit these lateralized and bilateral AEPs. Are these responses elicited only by speech stimuli with temporal differences or do they reflect more fundamental auditory processing mechanisms sensitive to temporal information independent of other acoustic cues? Several studies were conducted to determine whether the AEP responses noted so far are specific to language stimuli. If similar electrophysiological effects could be found for both speech and nonspeech materials, some conclusions could be drawn regarding similarities in the underlying mechanisms. Specifically, if an acoustic temporal distinction does form the basis for phoneme distinctions, similar electrocortical responses should be elicited by both the VOT and the nonspeech materials with similar temporal lags. Because the processing of the 0- and +20-msec VOT stimuli in the right hemisphere has been found to be different from that of the +40- and +60-msec VOT stimuli, similar patterns of responding should be elicited by nonspeech temporal-lag stimuli. No differential left-hemisphere responses should be noted.

Four tone-onset-time (TOT) stimuli from Pisoni (1977) were used in this series of studies. Pisoni had presented eight subjects during an initial training period with a series of two-tone stimulus sequences. The stimuli for this tone onset time (TOT) training session consisted of two tones, a 500-Hz (Formant 1) and a 1500-Hz (Formant 2) tone. One training stimulus (-50 msec) was characterized by the first formant ($F1$) beginning 50 msec prior to the second formant ($F2$), whereas for the second training stimulus, $F1$ began $+50$ msec after $F2$. Both tones terminated together. Subjects were trained to press one button if they heard the -50-msec stimulus and a second button if they heard the $+50$-msec stimulus. Visual feedback was provided to all subjects after each response. After training, subjects were given identification tests (with no feedback) on the original training stimuli plus 9 other TOT stimuli that varied in 10-msec steps from -50- to $+50$ msec. In general, subjects identified the TOT stimuli from -50- to $+20$ msec as one stimulus whereas stimuli with temporal lags between $+30$ and $+50$ msec were identified as a different stimulus. Subsequent discrimination tests indicated that subjects could only discriminate between stimuli from different identification groups. Stimuli from the -50- to $+10$-msec category were discriminated from the $+30$- to $+50$-msec category. However, discrimination scores within a temporal category were at chance levels. In light of his finding that the discrimination boundaries for the TOT stimuli closely resembled those for the speech VOT stimuli, Pisoni concluded that VOT perception may depend on properties of the sensory systems sensitive to the temporal order between two events. VOT perception, then, would rely on acoustic-processing mechanisms sensitive to temporal lags between components of particular stimuli. Pisoni suggested that because of the salience of these differences, linguistic systems have incorporated this cue as a useful and important one for speech perception.

A subset of Pisoni's stimuli was used in the study to be outlined below. These stimuli contained temporal relationships comparable to the voicing contrasts of the synthesized-speech syllables previously used in our laboratory. Using these four TOT stimuli facilitated comparisons with the earlier electrophysiological research and permitted overall stimulus length to be controlled. Thus, AEP differences would not reflect overall differences in stimulus duration because all stimuli were 230 msec long. The four two-tone stimuli differed from each other in the onset time of the lower tone relative to the higher one. For the 0-msec stimulus, the lower tone began at the same time as the higher tone. The lower tone lagged 20 msec behind the higher tone for the +20-msec stimulus. For the +40-msec stimulus, the lower tone was delayed 40 msec after the onset of the higher tone, whereas the delay for the +60-msec stimulus was increased to 60 msec. Both tones ended simultaneously.

AEPs from four scalp sites over each hemisphere were recorded from 16 adults in response to each TOT stimulus. These responses were later analyzed using the principal components and analysis of variance procedures noted earlier. Nine factors accounting for approximately 81% of the total variance were isolated and identified. One portion of the AEP with a peak of 355 msec and common to all four electrode sites over the right hemisphere (Factor 8) discriminated the 0-msec and +20-msec TOT stimuli from the +40- and +60-msec TOT stimuli. No such changes were noted over the left-hemisphere electrode sites at the same latency. The left hemisphere did distinguish between TOT stimuli from within a category (e.g., it discriminated 0 msec from +20 msec and +40 msec from +60 msec). A second AEP component (Factor 3) with a peak latency of 210 msec occurred earlier in time and reflected the detection of CP-like boundaries over both the left and right parietal regions. An additional component (Factor 6) that indicated CP-like discrimination of these temporal cues occurred somewhat earlier (145 msec after the onset of the stimulus) over both hemispheres in the temporal and central cortical regions. These three AEP components are isolated in Figure 14.3. The right-hemisphere discrimination of the 0- to 20-msec stimuli from the 40- to 60-msec stimuli can be seen in Figure 14.4. Factor 8 influenced the size of the P330 and the N405 components.

The effect is perhaps more apparent if one inspects the relationship between the final two negative components of the right-hemisphere AEPs for the four TOT stimuli. These two late negative components reach equal levels of negativity (their lowest points) for the 0- and 20-msec stimuli whereas the final negative peak goes even lower for the 40- and 60-msec stimuli. No such effect can be observed for these components in the left-hemisphere AEPs. Processing of temporal information, then, appeared to involve both bilateral mechanisms localized in or near the temporal and parietal regions of both hemispheres and an additional but more generally

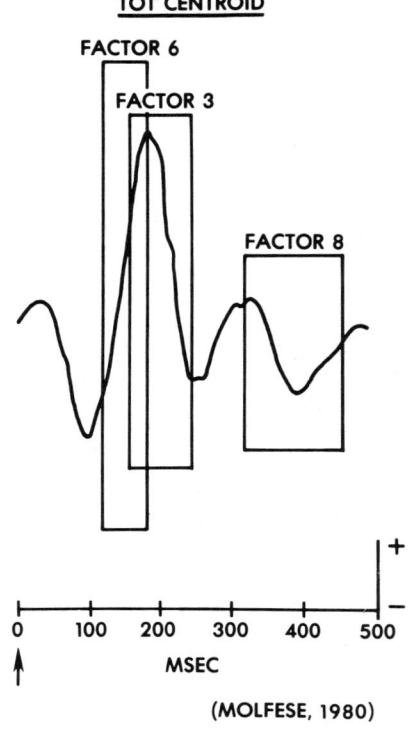

Figure 14.3. The group averaged AEP elicited in response to the Tone Onset Time stimuli. The areas of components of the waveform identified as varying as a function of temporal delays are indicated in the rectangles labeled Factors 6, 3, and 8.

located right-hemisphere lateralized process that occurred later in time. As with the subjects studied by Molfese and Hess, the bilateral effects occurred earlier in time than the right-hemisphere effect.

In a replication of this work and as an extension of Molfese and Hess's (1978) study with preschool children, Molfese and Molfese (in press) noted that comparable right-hemisphere responses were found late in the waveform that discriminated the 0- and 20-msec stimuli from the 40- and 60-msec stimuli. However, in this case the same portion of the right AEP changed for both the multiple-tone stimuli (which varied in the onset of the two tones in relation to each other) and the speech stimuli. Twelve children, 6 males and 6 females, were tested within 2 weeks of their third birthday. Each child listened to the same stimulus set used by Molfese and Hess (1978) as well as to the two-tone stimuli used by Molfese (1980). AEPs were elicited from scalp electrodes placed at temporal (T_3, T_4) and parietal (P_3, P_4) locations over both hemispheres. A late AEP component with a peak latency of 410 msec and occurring only over the right hemisphere electrode sites discriminated the 0-msec and 20-msec stimuli from the 40- and 60-msec stimuli. No such difference was noted over the left-hemisphere electrode sites. Given that the right-hemisphere lateralized component responded identically to both the speech VOT and the tone stimuli, it would appear that this portion of the waveform is indeed sensitive to the

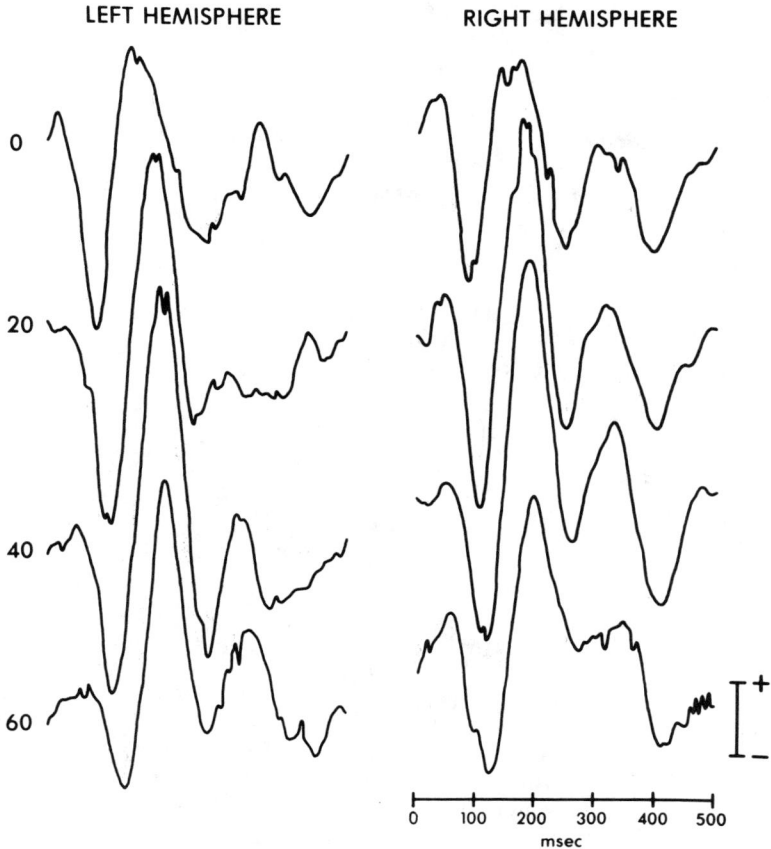

Figure 14.4. Group averaged AEPs recorded from the left and right hemispheres in response to the four TOT stimuli. Calibration marker is 2 μV.

temporal distinctions but ignores other acoustic differences (i.e., formant frequencies, number of formants, formant duration, etc.).

In an ongoing research project, Molfese has tested four children identified as language-delayed. These children, who range between 2.5 and 4.6 years, all share at least one trait – the absence of language production and little if any indication of language comprehension. Play-test audiometry indicated in all cases that air-conduction levels were in the normal range. These children were tested individually with data analyses focused on the single-trial responses of these children. Each child experienced the same stimuli and experimental treatments as the children described in Molfese and Hess (1978). An example of the AEPs for one of the children is presented in Figure 14.5. In this case, the averaged AEPs for a female (LDC #3, age 3 years, 4 months) are presented with left-hemisphere responses depicted on the left side of the figure and right-hemisphere responses on the right. Averaged AEPs

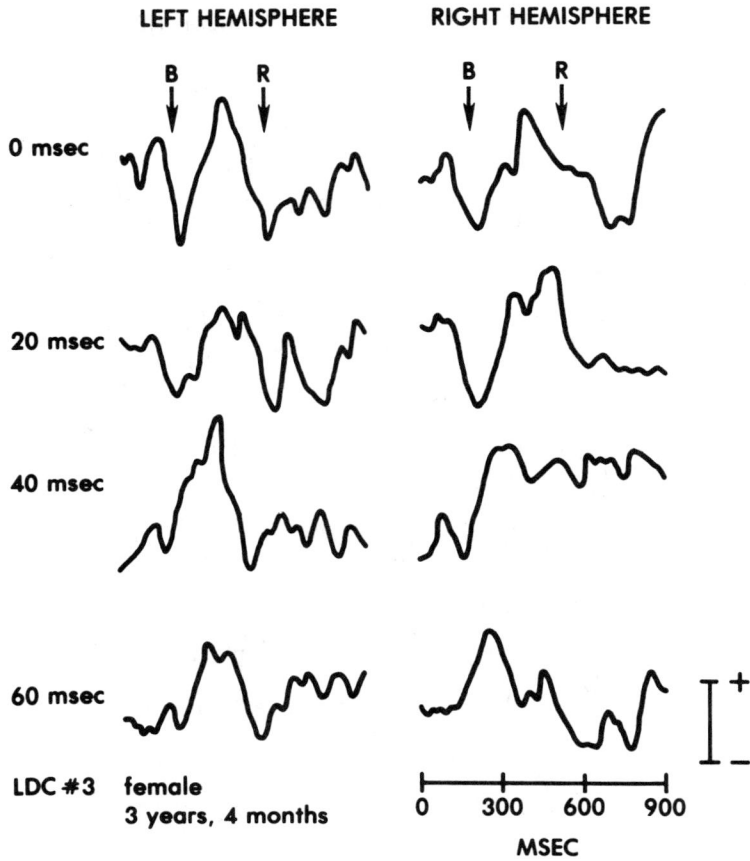

Figure 14.5. Left- and right-temporal-scalp-recorded AEPs to four VOT tokens. *B* indicates peak latency for bilateral component; *R* indicates peak latency for the right-hemisphere-lateralized component. Calibration marker is 4.5 μV with positive up.

are in response to the velar-stop consonants, which varied in VOT. The *B* at the top of the figure indicates where the peak for the bilateral response was noted by Molfese and Hess; the *R* indicates the region in which the right-hemisphere lateralized response occurred.

For LDC #3, the bilateral responses are similar to those reported with normal children for VOT changes. The P1–N2 amplitude is larger in both hemispheres for the 0- and 20-msec sounds than for the 40- and 60-msec sounds. However, the region in which the right-hemisphere lateralized response occurred for normal children does not show such a discrimination. In fact, the second negative wave and peak at approximately 500 msec is absent in this child in the right-hemisphere waveforms (but not in the left). When a stepwise discriminant analysis was applied to the single-trial data using the first 500 msec of AEPs from the normal children of

Molfese and Hess to classify this child, only the left hemisphere and the bilateral responses were correctly classified at least 70% of the time (where chance levels were 12.5 and 25%, respectively). It appeared, then, that the AEPs of this language-delayed child resembled those recorded from normal children except for the late, uniquely right-hemispheric CP-like discriminations. These were present in the normal children but absent in this child. Instead, the right-hemisphere responses of the language-delayed child over the 500-msec period appeared to be similar for the 0-, 20-, and 40-msec stimuli, which in turn differed from the 60-msec stimuli. That is, the right-hemisphere response discriminated the 0-, 20-, and 40-msec stimuli from the 60-msec stimuli. Similar effects have been noted for the other language-delayed children tested.

Effects of brain damage on categorical perception

Wilson (Chapter 13, this volume) has reviewed a number of papers dealing with CP in non-language-related tasks with brain-damaged subjects. A number of studies have also been conducted with human brain-damaged populations engaged in language tasks. Many of these brain-damage studies report right-hemisphere-related effects for VOT (Blumstein, Baker, & Goodglass, 1977; Miceli, Caltagirone, Gainotti, & Payer-Rigo, 1978; Oscar-Berman, Zurif, & Blumstein, 1975; Perecman & Kellar, 1981) whereas several others seem to indicate either a slight left-hemisphere advantage or the ability of both hemispheres to discriminate VOT categorically (Basso, Casati, & Vignolo, 1977; Blumstein, Cooper, Zurif, & Caramazza, 1977).

In the first of the studies noting a right-hemisphere role in VOT perception, Oscar-Berman et al. (1975) presented CV syllables varying in place-of-articulation, voicing, or both to 25 brain-damaged and 25 normal subjects. The brain-damaged subjects each had unilateral damage (16 left-brain, 9 right-brain). Nine left-brain and 3 right-brain subjects had anterior lesions and the remaining 7 left-brain and 6 right-brain subjects had posterior damage. The results of a dichotic task showed that the brain-damaged subjects made more errors than the normal controls, although the two brain-damaged groups were similar in error rate. The normal control subjects displayed a significant right-ear (left-hemisphere) advantage. The brain-damaged groups showed ear advantages that were ipsilateral to the lesion site. The findings of Oscar-Berman et al. are consistent with those reported by Johnson, Sommers, and Weidner (1977) and those reported by Schulhoff and Goodglass (1969), who found that the lesion site affects contralateral more than ipsilateral processing.

When Oscar-Berman et al. went on to examine the effects of the specific phonetic features, they found that when the dichotically presented stimuli shared common phonetic features, the performance of normal subjects and right-hemisphere-damaged individuals was better than when no features were shared. The left-hemisphere-damaged subjects, however, only benefited when the stimulus pair shared the feature "voice." In other words, the patients with an intact right hemisphere were able to make use of voice (but not place) information. Similar results were found in a study by Miceli et al. (1978), who also used stimuli differing in place and voice. Miceli and colleagues used a nondichotic technique to present pairs of synthetic CCVC (C = consonant, V = vowel) syllables to 42 normal control and 127 brain-damaged adults (43 right-brain, 48 left-brain without aphasia, 36 left-brain with aphasia). The consonants /p/, /t/, /k/, /b/, /d/, and /g/ were paired with /rin/ to form CCVC syllables (e.g., prin, trin). None of the syllables was a recognizable word in Italian, the native language of the subjects. The results of the test showed more voice than place errors for all subjects except the left-brain-damaged aphasic group. That group made fewest errors with voiced stimuli. Subjects with an intact right hemisphere performed better in discriminating voice information than patients with an intact left hemisphere.

Blumstein, Baker, and Goodglass (1977) also studied the processing of place and voicing features by brain-damaged and normal adults. There were 25 left-brain-damaged aphasic subjects, of whom 6 were classified as Broca's aphasics, 6 as mixed anterior, 6 as Wernicke aphasics, and 7 as residual posteriors. Pairs of real words and nonsense words that varied in place, voice, or both were used as stimuli in a nondichotic discrimination task. The fewest errors were made by Broca's aphasics. Mixed anterior patients made the most errors. The other two groups fell in between. Only the two posterior groups, the Wernicke's aphasics (who supposedly had a "normal" right hemisphere) and residual posteriors, showed a significant difference between the place and voicing features, with fewest errors on the voice contrasts.

In yet another study of voice and place features, Perecman and Kellar (1981) used a matching task with aphasic, nonaphasic, and normal subjects. The purpose of the study was to determine whether the differences between aphasic and nonaphasic subjects in the use of voice and place features were due to the time constraints involved in auditory presentation methods that interfere with linguistic-feature extraction by aphasics or whether the differences were due to linguistic representation of the features. There were 12 left-damaged aphasics (7 fluent and 5 nonfluent), 6 right-damaged nonaphasics, and 16 control subjects. Subjects were presented with two series of natural-speech stop-consonant triads representing voice or place features (/b/, /p/, /d/, /t/, /g/, and /k/). One series consisted of 18 triads in which two consonants in the triad shared the feature voice whereas the third consonant shared neither voice nor place with the other two consonants (e.g., /b/, /d/, and /k/). The second-triad series consisted of 36 triads in which one consonant pair shared voice (e.g., /b/, /d/), one pair shared place (e.g., /d/, /t/), and the third pair shared neither voice nor place (e.g., /b/, /t/). The consonant triads were repeated by an experimenter as often as necessary for the subject to make a judgment as to which two of the three sounds heard were most similar. Visual displays of the speech sounds heard on each trial were constantly available. The results showed that all three subject groups were able to use linguistic features to match sounds. However, when matches could be made on the basis of voice or place, aphasics (left-hemisphere-damaged subjects) matched more often using the voice feature. Normal subjects and right-damaged-nonaphasics used both features equally.

Perecman and Keller conclude from their investigation that voice and place require differential hemispheric processing. They suggested that voice can be processed by either the left or the right hemisphere. Damage to either hemisphere results in voice processing by the remaining undamaged hemisphere. This accounts for the similar performance on the voice feature by left- and right-damaged subjects. Place, however, seems to be processed by the left hemisphere. If the left hemisphere is damaged, place processing is affected. Such views are compatible with the electrophysiological research on voicing outlined earlier in this chapter indicating a right-hemisphere focus as well as a secondary focus across both hemispheres.

Not all of the clinical studies support the view that VOT is processed by right-hemisphere mechanisms (Basso et al., 1977; Blumstein, Cooper, Zurif, & Caramazza, 1977). However, they do tend to suggest that VOT is not processed exclusively by the left hemisphere. Basso et al. (1977) studied VOT perception in a group of brain-damaged Italian subjects, which included 50 left-brain-damaged patients with aphasia (dichotomized according to fluency and comprehension), 12 left-brain-damaged nonaphasics, 22 right-brain-damaged nonaphasics, and 53 controls. There were no significant differences between the groups in age, education, etiology of damage or time since damage. The stimuli were synthetic /da/ and /ta/ syllables with VOT values ranging in 10-msec steps between -150 and $+150$ msec. The normal subjects identified VOT values of -150 to 0 ms as /da/ and values of $+50$ to $+150$ ms as /ta/. For purposes of analysis, the upper boundary of /da/ was set at VOT values of -30 to $+30$ ms. The lower boundary of /ta/ was set between VOT values of $+10$ to $+60$ ms. These boundaries were based on the performance of the normal control subjects. All but one right-brain-damaged (nonaphasic) and all left-brain-damaged nonaphasics showed normal identification. Only 13 of the 50 left-brain-damaged aphasics showed normal identification. The identification performance of 33 of the remaining left-brain-damaged aphasics was so poor that *no* voice/voiceless boundary could be determined, although about half of these subjects showed a "trend" toward roughly correct identification. No significant relationship between fluency, comprehension abilities, and phoneme identification was found, although a significant positive correlation between Token Test scores and phoneme-identification deficits was found. The subjects with lower Token Test scores tended to have poorer phoneme-identification abilities.

In the second study, Blumstein, Cooper, Zurif, and Caramazza (1977) studied VOT perception in 16 left-brain-damaged aphasics (8 with posterior damage and 8 with anterior damage), 4 right-damaged nonaphasics, and 4 control subjects. The stimuli were /da/ and /ta/ syllables synthesized with VOT values ranging from -20 to $+80$ msec in 10-msec steps. The normal subjects identified stimuli with VOT values of -20 to $+20$ msec as /da/ and stimuli with TOT values of $+40$ to $+80$ msec as /ta/. The usual categorical perception of the VOT stimuli was found, in which subjects could discriminate between stimuli with VOT values of +25 and +40 msec and identified them as different phonemes (/da/ and /ta/, respectively). The subjects were unable to discriminate VOT values between −20 and +25 msec or between +40 and +80 msec. The four right-brain-damaged subjects showed VOT perception similar to that of the normal adults. Nine of 16 of the left-brain-damaged subjects also showed normal discrimination and identification of the stimuli. Of the remaining subjects, 4 could discriminate between the VOT stimuli but could not identify them and 3 could not discriminate or identify the stimuli. The only significant relationship between type of brain damage and performance was for the 4 Wernicke's aphasics, of which 3 could discriminate but not identify normally.

The right hemisphere and categorical perception

From the research reviewed here and in other chapters (see Wilson in Chapter 13, this volume) it appears that the right hemisphere plays some definite role in the process of CP. A common finding across the evoked-potential studies with both humans and animals that examine hemisphere differences is that CP-like effects are noted at electrode sites over the right hemisphere and that these effects are independent of any such left-hemisphere responses. Molfese and Molfese (1979) note such effects beginning at 2 months of age. Molfese and Hess (1978) and Molfese and Molfese (in press) note similar effects at 3 and 4 years of age and both Molfese (1978) and Molfese (1980) report these right-hemisphere effects with adults. Research with 1-year-old rhesus monkeys reveals comparable effects (Morse, Molfese, Laughlin, Linnville, & Wetzel, 1987). In all cases, the auditory-evoked potentials elicited by stimuli from one adult phonetic category differ from those elicited by a different category. Research conducted with brain-damaged humans has also noted a differential hemisphere effect in favor of the right hemisphere (Blumstein, Baker, & Goodglass, 1977; Miceli et al., 1978; Oscar-Berman et al., 1975; Perecman & Kellar, 1981). It appears, then, that the right hemisphere plays some marked role in CP.

It is also clear that this right-hemisphere ability is not limited to speech perception. The research reviewed by Wilson in Chapter 13 ably demonstrates this. Streitfeld (1982) has demonstrated that tests of visual length, visual texture, and tactile length all show more pronounced categorical effects when information is directed to the right hemisphere. This finding is reinforced by Wilson's study with brain-damaged patients in Chapter 13. Wilson asked subjects to make perceptual judgments concerning four stimulus continua: hue, visual length, tactile length, and weight. She concluded: "Subjects with [right temporal] damage did not perceive visual stimuli such as length or hue in a categorical manner." The auditory-evoked-potential studies with the TOT stimuli (Molfese, 1980; Molfese & Molfese, in press) also suggest that CP-like right-hemisphere effects can be found with nonspeech materials. In fact, the right-hemisphere categorical effects reported by Molfese and Molfese with 3-year-old children were identical for both the speech and the nonspeech stimuli. Thus, the right hemisphere appears to be involved in the categorical discrimination of material presented through either the auditory or the visual channel.

A final question concerns whether the right hemisphere works alone or in some interactive way with the left hemisphere in categorical judgement. In general, the literature reviewed thus far suggests that both hemispheres are involved, although perhaps at different levels. Wilson notes poorer CP for tasks involving weight perception with left-hemisphere-damaged subjects whereas right-hemisphere-damaged subjects perform more poorly on categorical judgements involving hue, visual length, and tactile length. As Wilson notes in the concluding section of her chapter, the CP mode of processing may not be limited to one hemisphere.

Categorical perception of visuospatial and tactuospatial continua was more affected when brain damage was present in the right hemisphere, either because lateralization is relative and the neural mechanisms underlying CP in these domains are better represented in the right hemisphere or because lateralization is absolute, and input directed to the left hemisphere is transferred with some loss to the right hemisphere where it is perceived categorically (Bertelson, 1982). Kinesthetic stimulation, in contrast, was perceived less categorically when left-hemisphere brain areas were compromised. This result is compatible with other findings of left-hemisphere control of motor programs that depend on kinesthetic input. Results for hue discrimination are more difficult to explain in terms of current models of hemispheric specialization.

The findings from the evoked-potential literature suggest that both the left and the right hemisphere are capable of responding to stimulation in a CP-like way. Molfese (1980), Molfese and Hess (1978), and Molfese and Molfese (1979) all note that the brain responses elicited contain at least two major regions of the brain wave that change systematically as a function of stimulus category. The first brain-wave component to occur in time for infants and children (generally around 100 msec in adults) is present over both hemispheres and seems to discriminate both between- and within-stimulus categories. The second component occurs later in time and is only detected by electrodes placed over the right hemisphere. These two components, then, do not appear to be exact duplicates of one another. Rather, they differ in both the time period in which they occur (with the bilateral brain response occurring first, to be followed by the right-hemisphere-lateralized response) and in the manner in which they respond. The left hemisphere appears capable at some level of making between-category discriminations. However, unlike the right hemisphere, the left is also capable of within-category judgements. This pattern of responding could indicate that information first comes into both hemispheres where it is initially encoded and processed at some level. This encoded information is then transferred from the left to the right hemisphere where additional processing of the right-hemisphere input is already in progress. At this point, cognitive factors may be engaged that attempt to categorize the material on the basis of the sensory information received, the subject's understanding of the present task, and the individual's cognitive state and experience. It is this final step that may be reflected in the additional right-hemisphere response.

Summary

Three general findings have emerged from this review: (1) Perception of the VOT cue across phoneme boundaries appears to be controlled by several cortical processes, some restricted to the right-hemisphere site and some apparently common to both hemispheres. (2) There is a developmental pattern to the emergence of mechanisms related to VOT perception. (3) The categorical effects do not appear to be restricted to language stimuli. Electrophysiological research has shown that VOT-related cues for speech perception are processed by a number of distinct mechanisms, some bilaterally represented and some lateralized to one cortical region. These mechanisms appear to change with development.

A number of attempts to identify CP effects in newborn infants have failed. At this point it appears that such effects may not appear until some time after birth. Certainly by 2 months of age the effects do appear to be present (Molfese & Molfese, 1979). At that point two temporally different electrophysiological responses can be elicited in response to changes in the VOT cue. One AEP component responsive to the VOT cue along phoneme boundaries was found in both hemispheres; a second component restricted to the right hemisphere responded in a similar fashion. These two different components (one bilateral and one right hemispheric), which perhaps reflect different mechanisms of processing, persist into early childhood and seem to reflect processes sensitive to category boundaries. It is only in the cortical responses of adults that substantially different responses are noted. With adults, two distinct right-hemisphere mechanisms are found, but no bilateral VOT mechanisms. Between 4 years and adulthood the bilateral VOT process either becomes lateralized to the right hemisphere or is replaced by a different mechanism, which is restricted to the right hemisphere.

It is important to note that the bilateral response common to both hemispheres in the young infants and preschool-aged children does not behave in the same way as the right-hemisphere response. Whereas the right-hemisphere response appears to discriminate between but not within categories, the bilateral response discriminates both between and within categories. It is not until adult subjects are tested that the bilateral effect is no longer seen. Rather, two right-hemisphere responses seem to emerge, both of which discriminate only between stimuli from different categories. Although the right-hemisphere response seems to have fairly rigid boundaries from even 2 months of age, perhaps the bilateral response allows some flexibility in tuning this mechanism by accommodating the perceptual demands of new environmental factors. The developmental process inferred from the evoked-potential studies reviewed above also appears to fit with the theoretical view offered by Eimas, Miller, and Jusczyk in Chapter 5. They note:

Thus, the initial categorical representations of infants must be malleable with respect to both category number and boundary location, so that with linguistic experience they can come to mirror the manner of categorization demanded by the parental language.

Finally, similar evoked-potential effects have been noted for both the speech and the nonspeech (tone) material. In both cases right-hemisphere effects were elicited from young children (Molfese & Molfese, in press) and adults (Molfese, 1980). In the one case where both the speech and nonspeech materials were presented to the same subjects (Molfese & Molfese, in press), an identical right-hemisphere effect was evoked. Given that identical responses appear to be elicited by both sets of stimuli, it would appear that the same mechanisms involved in the perception of the VOT speech cue could be involved in the perception of the nonspeech temporal cue.

References

Abramson, A., & Lisker, L. (1970). Discriminability along the voicing continuum: Cross-language tests. In *Proceedings of the Sixth International Congress of Phonetic Sciences, Prague, 1967* (pp. 569–573). Prague: Academic.
Basso, A., Casati, G., & Vignolo, L. (1977). Phonemic identification defect in aphasia. *Cortex, 13,* 85–95.
Blumstein, S., Baker, E., & Goodglass, H. (1977). Phonological factors in auditory comprehension in aphasia. *Neuropsychologia, 15,* 19–30.
Blumstein, S., Cooper, W., Zurif, E., & Caramazza, A. (1977). The perception and production of voice-onset-time in aphasia. *Neuropsychologia, 15,* 371–383.
Butterfield, E., & Cairns, G. (1974). Discussion summary: Infant reception research. In R. Schiefelbusch & L. Lloyd (Eds.), *Language perspectives: Acquisition, retardation, and intervention* (pp. 75–102). Baltimore: University Park Press.
Donchin, E., Ritter, W., & McCallum, W. C. (1978). Cognitive psychophysiology: The endogenous components of the ERP. In E. Callaway, P. Teuting, & S. H. Koslow (Eds.), *Event related potentials in man* (pp. 349–411). New York: Academic Press.
Dorman, M. (1974). Auditory evoked potential correlates of speech sound discrimination. *Perception and Psychophysics, 15,* 215–220.
Eilers, R., Gavin, W., & Wilson, W. (1980). Linguistic experience and phonemic perception in infancy: A cross-longitudinal study. *Child Development, 50,* 14–18.
Eimas, P. D. (1974). Linguistic processing of speech by young infants. In R. Schiefelbusch & L. Lloyd (Eds.), *Language perspectives: Acquisition, retardation, and intervention* (pp. 55–44). Baltimore: University Park Press.
Eimas, P., Siqueland, E., Jusczyk, P., & Vigorito, J. (1971). Speech perception in infants. *Science, 171,* 303–306.
Goff, E. R., Allison, T., & Vaughan, H. G., Jr. (1978). The functional neuroanatomy of event related potentials. In E. Callaway, E. P. Teuting, & S. H. Koslow (Eds.), *Event-related brain potentials in man* (pp. 1–79). New York: Academic Press.
Hillyard, S. A., & Wood, D. L. (1979). Electrophysiological analysis of human brain function. In M. S. Gazzaniga (Ed.), *Handbook of behavioral neurobiology* (Vol. 2, pp. 345–378). New York: Plenum Press.
Johnson, J., Sommers, R., & Weidner, W. (1977). Dichotic ear preferences in aphasia. *Journal of Speech and Hearing Research, 20,* 116–129.
Kimura, D. (1961). Some effects of temporal lobe damage on auditory perception. *Canadian Journal of Psychology, 15,* 156–165.
Klee, M., & Rall, W. (1977). Computed potentials of cortically arranged populations of neurons. *Journal of Neurophysiology, 40,* 647–666.
Kuhl, P. (1979). Models and mechanisms in speech perception: Species comparisons provide further contributions. *Brain, Behavior, and Evolution, 16,* 374–408.
Kuhl, P. (1981). Discrimination of speech by nonhuman animals: Basic auditory sensitivities conducive

to the perception of speech–sound categories. *Journal of the Acoustical Society of America, 70,* 340–349.

Kuhl, P., & Miller, J. (1975). Speech perception by the chinchilla: Voiced-voiceless distinction in alveolar plosive consonants. *Science, 190,* 69–72.

Kuhl, P., & Padden, D. (1983a). Enhanced discriminability at the phonetic boundaries for the place feature in macaques. *Journal of the Acoustical Society of America, 73,* 1003–1008.

Kuhl, P., & Padden, D. (1983b). Enhanced discriminability at the phonetic boundaries for the voicing feature in macaques. *Perception and Psychophysics, 32,* 542–550.

Lasky, R. E., Syrdal-Lasky, A., & Klein, R. E. (1975). VOT discrimination by four and six and a half month old infants from Spanish environments. *Journal of Experimental Child Psychology, 20,* 215–225.

Liberman, A. M., Cooper, F. S., Shankweiler, D., & Studdert-Kennedy, M. (1967). Perception of the speech code. *Psychological Review, 74,* 431–461.

Liberman, A. M., Delattre, P. C., & Cooper, F. S. (1958). Some cues for the distinction between voiced and voiceless stops in initial position. *Language and Speech, 1,* 153–167.

Lisker, L., & Abramson, A. S. (1964). Across language study of voicing in initial stops: Acoustical measurements. *Word, 20,* 384–422.

Miceli, G., Caltagirone, C., Gainotti, G., & Payer-Rigo, P. (1978). Discrimination of voice versus place contrasts in aphasia. *Brain and Language, 6,* 47–51.

Molfese, D. L. (1978). Neuroelectrical correlates of categorical speech perception in adults. *Brain and Language, 5,* 25–35.

Molfese, D. L. (1980). Hemispheric specialization for temporal information: Implications for the perception of voicing cues during speech perception. *Brain and Language,* 285–299.

Molfese, D. L. (1983). Event related potentials and language processes. In A. W. K. Guilliard and W. Ritter (Eds.), *Tutorials in ERPs.* Holland: Elsevier.

Molfese, D. L., & Hess, T. (1978). Hemispheric specialization for VOT perception in the preschool child. *Journal of Experimental Child Psychology, 26,* 71–84.

Molfese, D. L., & Molfese, V. J. (1979). VOT distinctions in infants: Learned or innate? In H. A. Whitaker & H. Whitaker (Eds.), *Studies in Neurolinguistics* (Vol. 4). New York: Academic Press.

Molfese, D. L., & Molfese, V. J. (In press). Right hemisphere responses from preschool children to temporal cues in speech and nonspeech materials: Electrophysiological correlates. *Brain and Language.*

Morse, P. A., Molfese, D. L., Laughlin, N. K., Linnville, S., & Wetzel, F. (1987). Categorical perception for voicing contrast in normal and lead-treated rhesus macaques: Electrophysiological indices. *Brain and Language, 30,* 63–80.

Morse, P. (1974). Infant speech perception: A preliminary model and review of the literature. In R. Schiefelbusch & L. Lloyd (Eds.), *Language perspectives: Acquisition, retardation, and intervention* (pp. 19–54). Baltimore: University Park Press.

Morse, P., & Snowdon, C. (1975). An investigation of categorical speech discrimination by rhesus monkeys. *Perception and Psychophysics, 17,* 9–16.

Oscar-Berman, M., Zurif, E., & Blumstein, S. (1975). Effects of unilateral brain damage on the processing speech sounds. *Brain and Language, 2,* 345–355.

Perecman, E., & Kellar, L. (1981). The effect of voice and place among aphasic, nonaphasic right-damaged and normal subjects on a metalinguistic task. *Brain and Language, 12,* 213–223.

Picton, T. W., & Stuss, D. T. (1980). The component structure of the human event related potential. In H. H. Kornhuber and L. Deecke (Eds.), *Motivation, Motor and Sensory Processes of the Brain-Electrical Potentials, Behavioral and Clinical Use* (pp. 17–49). Amsterdam: Elsevier.

Pisoni, D. B. (1977). Identification and discrimination of the relative onset time of two component tones: Implications for voicing perception in stops. *Journal of the Acoustical Society of America, 61,* 1352–1361.

Regan, D. (1972). *Evoked potentials in psychology, sensory physiological, and clinical medicine.* New York: Wiley.

Rockstroh, B., Elbert, T., Birbaumer, N., & Lutzenberger, W. (1982). *Slow brain potentials and behavior*. Baltimore: Urban & Schwarzenberg.

Schulhoff, C., & Goodglass, H. (1969). Dichotic Listening, side of brain injury, and cerebral dominance. *Neuropsychologia, 7,* 149–160.

Simson, R., Vaughan, H. G., Jr., & Ritter, W. (1977a). The scalp topography of potentials in auditory and visual discrimination tasks. *EEG, 42,* 528–535.

Simson, R., Vaughan, H. G., Jr., & Ritter, W. (1977b). The scalp topography of potentials in auditory and visual go/no go tasks. *EEG, 43,* 864–875.

Sinnott, J., Beecher, M., Moody, D., & Stebbins, W. (1976). Speech sound discrimination by monkeys and humans. *Journal of the Acoustical Society of America, 60,* 687–695.

Streeter, L. A. (1976). Language perception of 2-month-old infants show effects of both innate mechanisms and experience. *Nature, 259,* 39–41.

Streitfeld, B. D. (1982). *Categorical perception and the role of the right hemisphere in discrimination of visual and tactual-kinaesthetic stimuli.* Unpublished Ph.D. dissertation, University of Connecticut, Storrs.

Trehub, S., & Rabinovitch, M. (1972). Auditory-linguistic sensitivity in early infancy. *Developmental Psychology, 6,* 74–77.

Vaughan, H. G., Jr. (1969). The analysis of brain activity to scalp recordings of event-related potentials. In E. Donchin & D. B. Lindsley (Eds.), *Averaged evoked potentials: Methods, results, evaluations* (pp. 45–94). Washington, D.C.: NASA.

Waters, R. S., & Wilson, W. A., Jr. (1976). Speech perception by rhesus monkeys: The voicing distinction in synthesized labial and velar stop consonants. *Perception and Psychophysics, 19,* 285–289.

15 Evoked potentials and color-defined categories

D. Regan

This chapter reviews the color characteristics of EPs and draws attention to some simple (noncognitive) properties of EPs that might be confounded with EP effects associated with changes in perceived category. It is known that EPs are affected by cognitive variables (Hillyard, Picton, & Regan, 1978); whether correlates of perceived category can be observed in EP components remains to be established.

The interesting possibility that evoked potentials (EPs) might mark boundaries between perceived categories has so far been little explored. It seems reasonable to suppose that a clear boundary between perceived categories might be paralleled by a discontinuous change in some evoked-potential parameter. The studies described in this chapter do not directly address the question of perceived color boundaries, however. For the physical stimulus, color properties are uniquely described in terms of wavelength; however, at the level of sensation, very different color impressions can be produced by the same wavelength (Boynton, 1979). To date, evoked potential studies have compared EPs with light wavelength rather than comparing EPs with the sensation of color. (Molfese's chapter reviews EP studies of categorical perception in audition.)

Evoked-potential phenomenology is notoriously complex, however, and before interpreting EP observations in cognitive terms it is desirable to ensure that simpler explanations can be rejected. This chapter briefly reviews the effects of color on EPs; in particular, the effects of wavelength and chromatic contrast on EPs are examined in terms of early visual processing.

Evoked-potential data on color can usefully be grouped under two headings: EPs to spatially unpatterned stimulus fields and EPs to spatial chromatic contrast.

EPs to spatially unpatterned (diffuse) fields

This section describes the effects of wavelength on EPs produced by a diffuse field. An approximately diffuse field can be produced by means of an integrating sphere or by illuminating half a ping-pong ball placed over the eye. However, a uniform patch of light 10 to 60 degrees in diameter seems to give similar EPs, and high brightness can be obtained by using Maxwellian view, in which a lens forms an

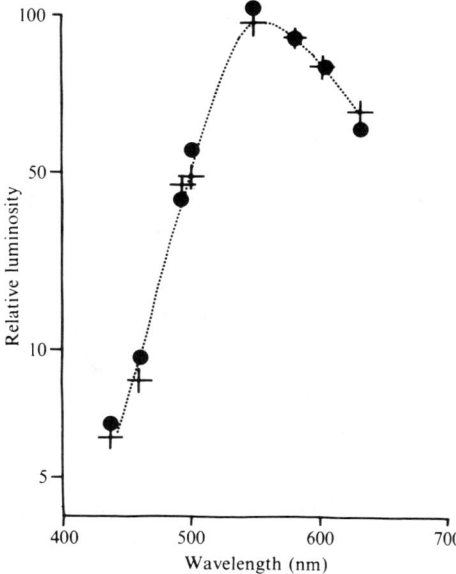

Figure 15.1. Relative sensitivity to lights of different colors measured by psychophysical heterochromatic flicker photometry (crosses) and by the evoked potential technique illustrated in Figure 15.2, that is, by measuring the luminance of colored lights that gave minimum amplitude of the 40-Hz EP. (From Regan, 1970a.)

image of the light source in the observer's pupil so the lens is seen as being uniformly illuminated (Westheimer, 1966).

Flickering a diffuse field produces EPs called "steady-state EPs" that can be analyzed into harmonic components of different frequencies. For example, a flicker of 20 cycles/sec will give an EP made up of frequency 20, 40, 60, and so on cycles/sec (Regan, 1966). In general, flicker produces an EP containing three different constituents, with quite different color properties (Regan, 1972a, 1975a). One constituent has a maximum amplitude at 10 cycles/sec (low-frequency component), the second (medium-frequency component) at about 16 cycles/sec and the third (high-frequency component) at about 40 to 50 cycles/sec. The three constitutents are emphasized at different electrode positions, and their relative amplitudes depend on both the individual subject and the flicker frequency. The three constituents originate in different regions of the brain (Regan, 1972a).

Figure 15.1 illustrates that the high-frequency constituent depends only on luminance and not at all on wavelength (Regan, 1970a). This EP component seems to be an electrophysiological correlate of luminance or brightness: The effects of subjective hue and subjective brightness are not confounded by this EP component. Figures 15.1 and 15.2 illustrate how it can be used to compare objectively the luminances of different wavelengths. (A similar technique can be used to compare sensitivity to different wavelengths in goldfish; Regan, Schellart, Spekreijese, & van den Berg, 1975.) The medium-frequency constituent, on the other hand, depends strongly on stimulus wavelength. It shows a large-phase lag that depends on stimulus wavelength, but not on flicker frequency, and this is difficult to explain

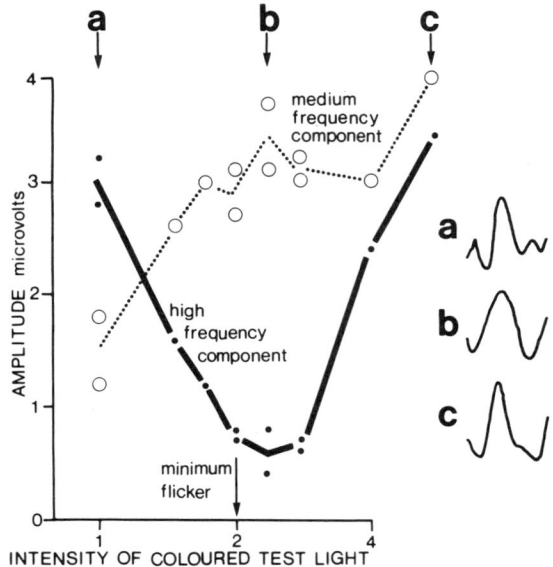

Figure 15.2. Two constituents in the same EP. A standard white light was alternated at 24 Hz in antiphase with a colored light whose luminance was adjusted until the subject saw minimum flicker (0 on abscissa). Then the colored light's luminance was altered in increments of 0.07 log units (18%). The three averaged traces were recorded at a, b, and c. At a and c there was strong subjective flicker, and no flicker at b. But the averaged EPs were similar at a, b, and c. The continuous line shows that the 40-Hz component of this EP falls to noise level at the minimum flicker point, but the larger 20-Hz component does not. (From Regan, 1970a.)

(Regan, 1970b, 1973a). Because the medium- and high-frequency constituents often coexist, and because their color characteristics are very different, the color properties of flicker EPs may seem complex unless the two constituents are separated. Contrary to some reports (Siegfried, Tepas, Sperling, & Hiss, 1965), the peak-to-peak amplitude of the averaged flicker EP does not provide a means of measuring luminance, because different constituents are confounded. This point is illustrated in Figure 15.2.

The distinction between transient EPs and steady-state EPs is that steady-state EPs are produced by "shaking the system gently," for example, by stimulating with flicker, and maintaining the stimulation until the visual system has settled down, whereas transient EPs are produced by "giving the system sharp taps," for example, with brief light flashes, the interval between successive flashes being long enough to allow the system to return to its prestimulus condition.

Several authors have described the color properties of transient EPs. Visual sensitivity to different wavelengths can be compared either by measuring EP amplitude (Armington, 1966; Siegfried, 1978) or by measuring latency (Klingamann, 1976; Wooten, 1972), although the precision seems somewhat less than that available with the method of Figures 15.1 and 15.2.

Transient EPs have been used as a means of investigating the processing of color information. A first step in this direction is to find whether light flashes of different wavelengths produce EPs that have different waveforms or distributions over the scalp. There is some evidence that responses to different wavelengths are generated in different regions of the brain (Clynes, Kohn, & Lifshitz, 1964; Regan, 1968). Wavelength-dependent differences between EPs can be enhanced by chromatic adaptation (Burkhardt & Riggs, 1967; Krauskopf, 1973; White, Katoaka, & Martin, 1977) and clarified by comparing monocular with binocular responses (White et al., 1977; Perry, Childers, & Dawson, 1969). In most of the studies discussed in this paragraph, large-stimulus fields of 11 to 25 degrees were used. Such large fields stimulate an inhomogeneous retinal area so that rod–cone differences and differences in color properties of different retinal regions might contribute to the observed EP effects. Siegfried (1970) found that EPs did not depend on wavelength when he recorded EPs to a small (2-degree) foveally viewed field. By using strong chromatic adaptation, however, Zrenner (1977) was able to show wavelength opponency (red–green opponency) even when using a foveal stimulus field of only 2-degree subtense.

Evoked potentials to chromatic contrast

The boundaries of real-world objects are commonly defined redundantly: Figure-ground segregation can be achieved by luminance, texture, or color difference, and perhaps also by motion contrast. An object can be seen even when its boundaries are defined only by a change in color, although visual acuity for this kind of object is considerably lower than for objects whose boundaries are defined by luminance difference. Whether or not a chromatic spatial boundary is visible seems to depend simply on whether the two colors are sufficiently different in hue.

Before discussing the results of EP studies (Estevez, Spekreijse, van den Berg, & Cavonius, 1975; Kinney & McKay, 1974; Regan & Sperling, 1971; Regan, 1972a,b, 1973b, 1975b; Regan & Spekreijse, 1974; Riggs & Sternheim, 1969), it is well to outline the pitfalls. When studying EPs to patterns defined by spatial color differences (i.e., chromatic contrast) the first prerequisite is to demonstrate that luminance effects are not masquerading as color effects. To ensure that there is negligible luminance contrast across the boundaries needs some technical care. A luminance match between two different colors is different for every individual, so the individual subject's eye should be used for this purpose. Heterochromatic flicker photometry is the standard method for matching luminances, but for our present purpose it is not entirely satisfactory: The precision may not be adequate; the match may depend on temporal frequency; a luminance match may not even be appropriate (see below).

One way of approaching this problem is to make many EP measurements around the best estimate of the match. Figure 15.3 illustrates this way of dissociating luminance and wavelength. The eye was stimulated by a checkerboard pattern

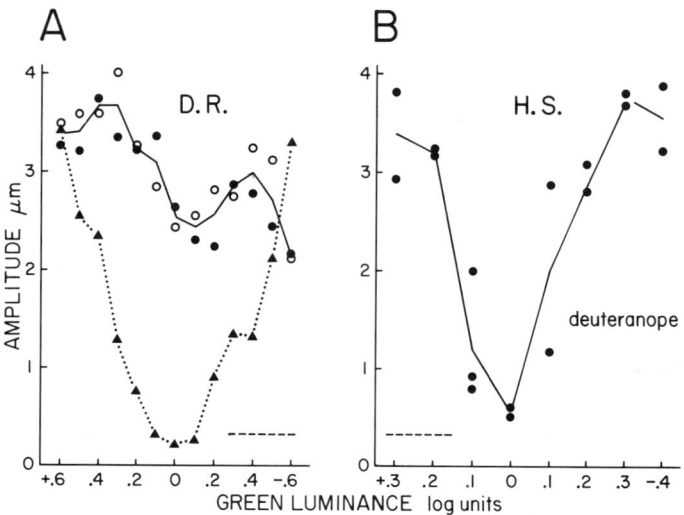

Figure 15.3. Evoked potentials for a pattern of red-and-green checks whose boundaries were defined by color difference alone. The luminance of the green checks was varied in steps of 0.1 log unit. Equiluminance was at 0 on the abscissa. Panel A (continuous line) is for a normally sighted subject. EP amplitude does not fall to 0 for any red/green balance. Panel B is for a color-blind subject. EP amplitude falls abruptly to noise level at the equiluminant point. (From Regan, 1973a.)

composed of alternate red-and-green squares. The intensity of the green squares was varied in steps of 0.1 log unit (abscissae), and EP amplitude was recorded for each green-red luminance balance (Regan, 1972a). A second control experiment is to vary the relative timing of red-and-green signals to ensure that the EP is not an artifact of differential delay between the two colors (Regan, 1973a; Regan & Sperling, 1971). In a normal eye, it was not possible to eliminate the EP for any balance of green-red luminance (Figure 15.3, open and filled circles). The situation was quite different in a red-green blind eye (deuteranope); for one unique balance of green-red intensity, EP amplitude fell to 0 with this subject (Regan & Spekreijse, 1974). The point made by Figure 15.3 is that a clear EP was recorded from the color-blind subject when the balance of green-red luminance was only slightly inaccurate. This EP must be due to luminance contrast; very little luminance contrast (about 5% to 10%) gives a clear EP, and this is well within the normal variability of luminance matches between different colors. Figure 15.3 shows that an EP produced by a pattern of two colors is not necessarily caused by the color difference: The luminances of the two colors must be very accurately matched in order to be sure that the EP does not originate from luminance differences. However, even this is not enough.

It is tempting to suppose that the presence of a clear EP for all ratios of green-red intensity is evidence for the existence of chromatic-contrast EPs. This is not neces-

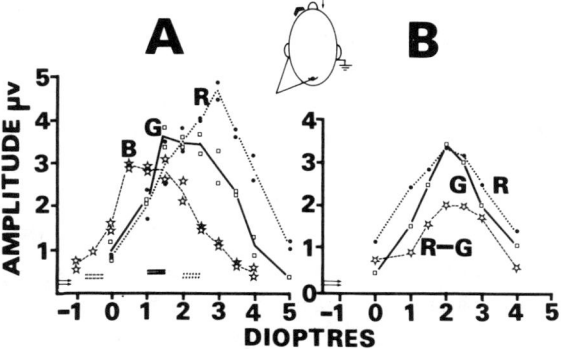

Figure 15.4. A. Pattern-evoked potentials to monochromatic red (R), green (G), and blue (B) checkerboard patterns. The eye's accommodation was paralyzed and lenses of different power were placed in front of the eye (abscissa). Due to the eye's chromatic aberration, red, green, and blue patterns were never in focus simultaneously. B. With the eye's chromatic aberration cancelled by optical means, the green (G) and red (R) patterns were both in sharp focus and gave the largest pattern EP with a 2.2-diopter lens in front of the eye. In this condition, an equiluminant pattern of red-and-green checks still gave an EP (R-G), showing that the chromatic-contrast EP is not an artifact of ocular chromatic aberration. (From Regan, 1973a.)

sarily so. For example, ocular chromatic aberration[1] can cause luminance-contrast EPs to masquerade as chromatic-contrast EPs. Consider the extreme case. Suppose that a pattern of small checks (sides of less than 0.3 degree) composed of blue-and-red squares falls on the retina. This is physically equivalent to a red/black checkerboard superimposed on a black/blue checkerboard, and indeed the stimulus can be generated in this way. Because of the eye's chromatic aberration, the two checkerboards cannot be in focus simultaneously. When the red/black checkerboard is in focus on the retina, the black/blue checkerboard is so blurred that it produces negligible pattern EPs. Consequently, the blue light can be ignored for pattern EPs even though it may be photometrically equal in luminance to the red light. One way of controlling for ocular chromatic aberration is illustrated in Figure 15.4 in the case of a pattern of red-and-green checks. This procedure cancels two kinds of chromatic aberration: longitudinal (i.e., focus difference) and transverse (i.e., magnification difference) (Regan, 1972a, 1973b). The red-and-green images are optically superimposed after being placed at different distances and being differentially magnified. When red-and-green retinal images are compensated in this way, genuine chromatic contrast EPs can be recorded (Regan, 1973b). Evoked potentials to red-black, green-black, and red-green checks have the same waveform and scalp distributions (Regan, 1973b), even when red-and-green cone types are separately stimulated (Spekreijse, Estevez, & Reits, 1977).

A possible explanation for these findings is that long-wavelength and medium-wavelength color signals generated by the checkerboard pattern remain segregated up to the point at which the EP is generated and there is active competition between these two signals (Regan, 1972a,b, 1973b, 1975a). There remains the question whether there are separate-contrast EP generators for each color channel or whether a single generator is addressed by all channels. Regan (1972b) found evidence for the first suggestion and Spekreijse et al. (1977) found evidence supporting the second idea.

An alternative explanation involves a chromatic-contrast channel in addition to luminance-contrast channels (Regan, 1973b). This idea can account for changes in the EP caused by altering the relative timing of red-and-green signals.

Special techniques have been developed to combat the variability of EPs so as to allow the color channels' red, green, and blue cone mechanism to be studied (Regan, 1974, 1975b). Different spectral sensitivity curves were obtained for red, green, and blue checks, consistent with the idea of three parallel color channels.[2] The sensitivity curves were consistent with the cone-cone interactions, for example, R+G and color-opponent (R−G) channels (Sperling & Harwerth, 1971).

Notes

1. For the same reason that a prism produces a spectrum, a simple lens has a shorter focal length in green light than in red light, and in blue light the focal length is shorter still. Consequently, the image of a white spot is a colored blur (chromatic aberration). Blue light is imaged closer to the lens than red light (longitudinal chromatic aberration), and the image of an extended object is bigger for red light than for blue light (lateral chromatic aberration) (Wyszecki & Stiles, 1967).
2. The relation between the short-, intermediate- and long-wavelength color mechanisms and perceived color categories is probably somewhat distant. The trivariance of color vision corresponds to the presence of three kinds of cone pigment in the retina, whereas perceived color depends on interactions between signals from the different classes of cone, on lateral interactions, and on the state of adaptation.

References

Armington, J. C. (1966). Spectral sensitivity of simultaneous electroretinograms and occipital responses. In H. M. Burian & J. H. Jacobson (Eds.), *Clinical Electroretinography, Vision Research* (Supplement 1), 225–235.

Boynton, R. M. (1979). *Human color vision*. New York: Holt, Rinehart, & Winston.

Burkhardt, D. A., & Riggs, L. A. (1967). Modification of the human visual evoked potential by monochromatic backgrounds. *Vision Research, 7*, 453–459.

Clynes, M., Kohn, M., & Lifshitz, K. (1964). Dynamics and spatial behavior of light evoked potentials, their modification under hypnosis, and on-line correlation in relation to rhythmic components. *Annals of the New York Academy Sciences, 112*, 468–509.

Estevez, O., Spekreijse, H., van den Berg, T. J. T. P., & Cavonius, C. R. (1975). The spectral sensitivities of isolated colour mechanisms determined from contrast EP measurements. *Vision Research, 15*, 1205–1212.

Gouras, P., & Eggers, H. (1982). Ganglion cells mediating the signals of blue sensitive cones in primate retina detect white-yellow borders independently of brightness. *Vision Research, 22*, 675–679.

Hillyard, S. A., Picton, T. W., & Regan, D. (1978). Sensation, perception and attention: Analysis using ERPs. In E. Callaway, P. Tueting, & S. H. Coslow (Eds.), *Event-related brain potentials in man* (pp. 223–321). New York: Academic Press.

Kinney, J. A. S., & McKay, C. L. (1974). Test of color defective vision using the visual evoked response. *J. Opt. Soc. Am., 64*, 1244–1250.

Klingamann, R. L. (1976). The human visual evoked cortical potential and dark adaptation. *Vision Research, 16,* 1471–1477.
Krauskopf, J. (1973). Contributions of the primary chromatic mechanisms to the generation of visual evoked potentials. *Vision Research, 13,* 2289–2298.
Perry, N. W., Jr., Childers, D. G., & Dawson, W. W. (1969). Human cortical correlates of colour with monocular, binocular and dichoptic vision. *Vision Research, 9,* 1357–1366.
Regan, D. (1966). Some characteristics of average steady-state and transient responses evoked by modulated light. *Electroencephalography and Clinical Neurophysiology, 20,* 238–248.
Regan, D. (1968). Chromatic adaptation and steady-state evoked potentials. *Vision Research, 8,* 149–158.
Regan, D. (1970a). Objective method of measuring the relative spectral luminosity curve in man. *Journal of the Optical Society of America, 60,* 856–859.
Regan, D. (1970b). Evoked potential and psychophysical correlates of changes in stimulus colour and intensity. *Vision Research, 10,* 163–178.
Regan, D. (1972a). *Evoked potentials in psychology, sensory physiology and clinical medicine.* London: Chapman & Hall. New York: Wiley.
Regan, D. (1972b). Evoked potentials to changes in the chromatic contrast and luminance contrast of checkerboard stimulus patterns. In G. B. Arden (Ed.), *The visual system* (pp. 171–187). New York: Plenum Press.
Regan, D. (1973a). An evoked potential correlate of colour: Evoked potential findings and single-cell speculations. *Vision Research, 13,* 1933–1941.
Regan, D. (1973b). Evoked potentials specific to spatial patterns of luminance and colour. *Vision Research, 13,* 2381–2402.
Regan, D. (1974). Electrophysiological evidence for colour channels in human pattern vision. *Nature, 250,* 437–449.
Regan, D. (1975a). Recent advances in electrical recording from the human brain. *Nature* (review article), *253,* 401–407.
Regan, D. (1975b). Colour coding of pattern responses in man investigated by evoked potential feedback and direct plot techniques. *Vision Research, 15,* 175–183.
Regan, D., Schellart, N. A. M., Spekreijse, H., & van den Berg, T. J. T. P. (1975). Photometry in goldfish by electrophysiological recording. Vision Research, *15,* 799–807.
Regan, D., & Spekreijse, H. (1974). Evoked potential indications of colour blindness. *Vision Research, 14,* 89–95.
Regan, D., & Sperling, H. G. (1971). A method of evoking contour-specific scalp potentials by chromatic checkerboard patterns. *Vision Research, 11,* 173–176.
Riggs, L. A., & Sternheim, C. E. (1969). Human retinal and occipital potentials evoked by changes in the wavelength of light. *Journal of the Optical Society of America, 59,* 635–640.
Siegfried, J. B. (1970). The relationship between stimulus wavelength and the waveform of averaged visual evoked cortical potentials. *American Journal of Optometry & Archives of the American Academy of Optometry, 47,* 282–287.
Siegfried, J. B. (1978). VECP: its spectral sensitivity. In J. C. Armington, J. Krauskopf, & B. R. Wooten (Eds.), *Visual psychophysics and physiology.* New York: Academic Press.
Siegfried, J. B., Tepas, D. I., Sperling, H. G., & Hiss, R. A. (1965). Evoked potential correlate of psychophysical responses: Heterochromatic brightness matching. *Science, 149,* 321–323.
Spekreijse, H., Estevez, O. & Reits, D. (1977). Visual evoked potentials and the physiological analysis of visual processes in man. In J. E. Desmedt (Ed.), *Visual evoked potentials in man* (pp. 16–89). Oxford: Clarendon Press.
Sperling, H. G. & Harwerth, R. S. (1971). Red-green cone interactions in the increment-threshold spectral sensitivity of primates. *Science, 172,* 180–184.
Westheimer, G. (1966). The Maxwellian view. *Vision Research, 6,* 669–682.
White, C. T., Katoaka, R. W., & Martin, J. I. (1977). Colour evoked potentials: development of a methodology for the analysis of the processes involved in colour vision. In J. E. Desmedt (Ed.), *Visual evoked potentials in man.* Oxford: Clarendon Press.

Wooten, B. R. (1972). Photopic and scotopic contributions to the human visually evoked cortical potential. *Vision Research, 12,* 1647–1660.
Wyszecki, G., & Stiles, W. S. (1967). *Color science.* New York: Wiley.
Zrenner, E. (1977). Influence of stimulus duration and area on the spectral luminosity function as determined by sensory and EP measurement. *Documents of the Ophthalmological Proceedings Series, 12,* 21–30.

Part VI

Higher-order categories

16 Categorization processes and categorical perception

Douglas L. Medin and Lawrence W. Barsalou

Although investigators who study categorical perception (CP) and those who study semantic categories both study categorization, they generally have not shared, compared, or integrated their findings. Our initial impression about these two areas of work was that their lack of communication reflected fundamental differences. After reviewing them, however, we were surprised to find numerous similarities. We first describe common issues that both areas face. These include: Specifying the attributes that represent categories and the relations that integrate attributes; identifying whether rules, central tendencies, ideals, exemplars, or boundaries underlie classification; characterizing the uses of categories, including classification, inference, generation, and productivity; explaining the relative roles of innate learning sensitivities and experience in category acquisition; identifying the mechanisms that underlie the dynamic flexibility of categories. We next review empirical similarities between the two lines of research. Categories in both areas exhibit sharp identification functions, within-category discriminability, typicality effects, and reference point effects. Both areas have also adopted similar theoretical approaches, including prototype theory, continuous versus discrete processing models, dual process models, and psychophysical models. Finally, we review points of future comparison that we believe are of particular interest and that might be useful in exploring the similarities and differences of categories in these two areas. These include: the locations, consequences, and uses of reference points in classification; the role of prototypes, exemplars, and other decision procedures in classification; the role of contextual priming in category flexibility; the roles of holistic and analytic processing in category processing; and the roles of cue validity and category validity in category processing.

Does the means by which a sound is classified as a /b/ or a /p/ have anything in common with how an animal is classified as a *fish* or a *bird?* The purpose of this chapter is to compare research associated with categorical perception in *sensory perception categories* with research on categorization in *generic knowledge categories*. Before going into these comparisons, it is important to distinguish between the two kinds of categories we will be examining. As will be seen, the distinction is elusive.

> This project was supported by Grant MH 32370 from the National Institute of Mental Health to Douglas L. Medin and by Grant IST 8308984 from the National Science Foundation to Lawrence W. Barsalou. We are particularly grateful to Arthur Samuel, Stevan Harnad, Dominic Massaro, and Gregory Murphy for their helpful comments on this paper. Any errors that remain are solely our responsibility. Reprint requests should be sent to either Douglas L. Medin, Department of Psychology, 603 East Daniel, University of Illinois, Champaign, IL 61820 or to Lawrence W. Barsalou, Department of Psychology, Emory University, Atlanta, GA 30322.

Sensory perception categories versus generic knowledge categories

Operational definitions. Perhaps the best way to define these two category types is operationally. Sensory perception categories (SP categories) are those categories studied by investigators interested in sensory processes and perception. Work on SP categories is often closely tied to psychophysical issues concerning how physical energy relates to perceptual experience. Examples of SP categories include categories of speech sounds (e.g., /b/), nonspeech sounds (e.g., plucks versus bows), colors (e.g., red), and so on; see Repp (1984) and the other chapters in this volume for reviews. People exhibit categorical perception when processing *some* SP categories.

In contrast, generic-knowledge categories (GK categories) are those categories studied by investigators interested in semantic analysis, memory organization, and abstract thought. Work on GK categories is often closely tied to cognitive science issues concerning knowledge representation and processing. Examples of GK categories include natural kinds (e.g., birds), artifacts (e.g., cars), and events (e.g., going to restaurants); see Medin and Smith (1984), Mervis and Rosch (1981), and Smith and Medin (1981) for reviews. So far, little if any thought has been given to whether people exhibit categorical perception when processing GK categories, although it is probably safe to say that most investigators who study GK categories implicitly believe that categorical perception occurs only for SP categories.

This initial distinction between SP and GK categories is hardly satisfying – defining these two category types by the investigators associated with them is like defining words by their page numbers in a dictionary. Clearly it would be advantageous to discover more theoretically relevant criteria. So far, however, we have not been able to define SP and GK categories rigorously, although we have discovered various aspects that are characteristic of these two category types. These characteristic aspects (which we discuss in the next section) should not be taken as definitional, because exceptions can be found to each of them. Our inability to define these two category types may reflect the fact that SP and GK categories are much less different than they initially appear.

Perceptual versus conceptual categories. One way SP and GK categories typically differ has to do with the abstractness of the attributes that define them.[1] The attributes used in classifying someone as a bachelor (e.g., adult, unmarried, male, human) seem much more abstract than the attributes that define SP categories (e.g., voice-onset time, formant transitions, brightness, color). This distinction is useful but does not provide an iron-clad principle because many GK categories are defined perceptually, at least to some extent. For example, Labov (1973) showed that people distinguish cups from bowls on the basis of their height-to-width ratio (although he showed that functional properties are important too). In general, classification with GK categories such as cars, people, houses, and so on often appears to depend heavily on perceptual properties (cf. Tversky & Hemenway, 1984).

Categorization processes and categorical perception 457

The nature of referents. SP and GK categories also typically differ with respect to the referents that instantiate them. The individual instances that instantiate GK categories are often permanent physical entities that persist over long periods of time and that may be important and distinct as individuals (e.g., particular dogs and cars). In contrast, instantiations of SP categories tend to be transient and not important as individuals (e.g., two different utterances of /b/). Although this distinction has some value, it too is not definitive. For example, individual members of some SP categories may be important and permanent (e.g., colors with respect to painting a house) and individual instances of some GK categories may be transient (e.g., thoughts).

Further distinctions. The fact that it is not easy to define SP and GK categories does not mitigate one's initial impression that they are very different. Beyond the characteristic aspects already mentioned, the representations of GK categories can often be more complex and contain more information than those of SP categories. GK categories may be integrated into more conceptual structures and into more elaborate ones than SP categories (e.g., hierarchies and cross-classifications). GK categories may enter into more complex combinations with each other than do SP categories (cf. Osherson & Smith, 1981). Additionally, GK categories may be less influenced by genetic predispositions and more influenced by experience than SP categories. In view of all these apparent differences, it is not surprising that there has been little cross-citation between the SP and GK categorization literatures.

Thesis

Given the obvious contrasts between SP and GK categories, it should not be surprising that we began this project as skeptics and did not expect to find more than superficial similarities between SP and GK categories. Had this review been done 10 years ago, we might well have maintained this initial impression. As other chapters in this volume bear out, however, work on SP categories has been developing rapidly, and it is interesting that much of this development turns out to be related to developments in work on GK categories. In fact, these parallels suggest that there are deep similarities between SP and GK categories.

An outsider's view of categorical perception

Before tracing some of the relations between SP and GK categories, we briefly present our view of current work on categorical perception (CP) in SP categories. Because much of the recent work on SP categories has focused on CP, and because CP is supposedly reserved for SP categories, we present our view of this work as a basis for our thesis. It is important to note that we do not intend to endorse any one particular approach or interpretation of CP, although we are probably guilty of selectively attending to observations and theoretical models that bring out similarities between SP and GK categories.

Definitions of categorical perception. In general, various investigators have defined CP in terms of identification performance, discrimination performance, or both. Some investigators interpret sharp identification functions at category boundaries as evidence of CP (e.g., Ehret in Chapter 10, this volume). Others define CP in terms of peaks in discrimination functions derived when the stimuli are equally spaced physically (e.g., Wilson in Chapter 13, this volume; or see Pastore in Chapter 1, this volume, for a closely related definition in terms of difference limens). Another discrimination-based measure requires that discrimination performance within a category be fairly flat (though it may be above chance) and worse than discrimination between categories (Eimas, Miller, & Jusczyk in Chapter 5, this volume). The third approach requires either that identification performance predict discrimination performance (Liberman, Harris, Hoffman, & Griffith, 1957), or at least that local identification and discrimination maxima coincide (Macmillan in Chapter 2, this volume). There simply is no uniform definition of CP.

Theories of categorical perception. CP is addressed by a variety of theories. The original theory of Liberman et al. (1957) assumes that discrimination performance is based solely on identification and predicts that discrimination within a category will be essentially at chance; in this strong form, the theory has received little support. There are a number of dual-process theories that can predict above-chance performance for discrimination within categories. Some of these theories rely on phonemic versus auditory processing (e.g., Fujisaki & Kawashima, 1970), whereas others replace the phonemic trace with a more neutral labeling notion (as in the trace versus context mode theory of Durlach & Braida, 1969) or propose that CP reflects memory limitations rather than perceptual processes (e.g., Hary and Massaro, 1982). A third class of theories claims that CP derives from relatively fixed differential sensitivity regions or thresholds (e.g., see Chapter 1 by Pastore). A fourth class of theories attributes CP either to reference points based on adaptation level and range effects or to prototypes that act as standards (see Chapter 3 by Repp & Liberman, Chapter 5 by Eimas et al., Chapter 8 by Massaro, and Chapter 13 by Wilson in this volume). A fifth possibility is that lateral inhibition is responsible for sharp discrimination at category boundaries (see Crowder, 1980), and a sixth is that decision processes are responsible for graded inputs being mapped onto less graded or even discontinuous outputs (see Chapter 8 by Massaro, this volume).

One other theory that has not directly addressed CP but that may be relevant is Lawrence's (1949, 1950) theory of acquired equivalence and acquired distinctiveness of cues. The basic idea is that categorization (treating two or more entities as equivalent) causes entities within categories to appear more similar and entities between categories to appear less similar than would be expected on the basis of perceptual similarity (see Medin, 1975, for a general review of this sizeable literature). This amplification of similarities and diminution of differences within categories could be partially responsible for the subjective experience that SP stimuli are categorically perceived (see Harnad in Chapter 19, this volume).

Initial conclusion. The other chapters in this volume give ample evidence that CP data can be accounted for by more than a single theory (e.g., dual processes, differential sensitivity regions, prototypes). Since all these accounts may be in some way capable of explaining CP, success at converging on good theories may be limited if observations are restricted to experimental operations that fall within the definition of CP. When more than one theory can handle a set of observations, it makes good sense to search for new observations. This represents no great insight on our part, and indeed over the last decade SP researchers have used an increasing variety of procedures and experimental manipulations. This broader scope of research has, among other things, laid the groundwork for our observation that similarities between SP and GK categories are more than superficial. In fact, much of the recent work in the two domains seems to be converging in interesting ways. Consequently, workers in both areas stand to benefit from comparing and exchanging methodological and theoretical tools.

Preview. The remainder of this chapter represents our attempt to justify the claim that much is to be gained from closer comparisons of SP and GK categories. In the next section we take up some basic issues in categorization that are central to both SP and GK categories, and in doing so, we will begin to note similarities between them. Besides providing initial comparisons of SP and GK categories, this section also lays the groundwork for the two subsequent sections, which represent the core of the chapter. The first of these describes what we believe are strong empirical and theoretical similarities between SP and GK categories. The second considers some of these points of comparison in greater detail and highlights possibilities for further cross-domain comparisons. The final section summarizes our conclusions.

Basic issues in categorization

The structure of information

Decomposition into attributes. Research on both SP and GK categories reflects a twofold consensus: (1) the concepts that represent categories can be analyzed into component parts or attributes, and (2) similarities between categories and among category members derive from their common and distinctive attributes (see Tversky, 1977). Thus robins are more similar to canaries than to squirrels because they share more attributes with the former than with the latter (for example, feathers, number of legs, beak). In addition, there are more attributes that distinguish robins from squirrels (e.g., feathers, hair) than distinguish robins from canaries (e.g., red, yellow). For the remainder of this chapter, we will assume that similarity is some function of the shared and distinctive attributes between concepts, although other factors must certainly be involved as well (Tversky, 1977).

Although the assumption that concepts can be decomposed into attributes is basic to work on GK categories, little progress has been made in identifying them (see Armstrong, Gleitman, & Gleitman, 1983). For example, attributes such as feathers, legs, and beaks are themselves abstract concepts, and the concept of a bird is certainly more than a list of attributes. In addition, attributes of GK concepts can range from fairly concrete ones (e.g., bright red feathers) to quite abstract ones (living, can get sick) and are often highly dependent on background theories and beliefs about the world. As argued by Murphy and Medin (1985), people's intuitive theories often make certain attributes salient while causing others to be ignored. In addition, theories often appear to play an important role in how perceptual attributes are interpreted. Palmer (1975), for example, shows how ambiguous line segments take on specific meanings as a function of the conceptual context in which they are perceived. Although little progress has been made in identifying the nature of the attributes that comprise GK concepts, the hypothesis that concepts can be decomposed into attributes has led to some theoretical progress (e.g., Rosch & Mervis, 1975; Rosch, Mervis, Gray, Johnson, & Boyes-Braem, 1976a; Tversky, 1977; Tversky & Hemenway, 1984). A more extensive discussion of attributes and dimensions in perceptual processing can be found in Treisman (in press).

In contrast, more progress seems to have been made in identifying the attributes that define SP categories. Some time ago linguists succeeded in describing the performative features that define phonemes. More recently, psychoacousticians have isolated the acoustic invariants of phonemes well enough to synthesize many SP categories artificially. These analyses have been corroborated by empirical findings (see Miller & Nicely, 1955).

The success in synthesizing speech from simple acoustic attributes may suggest that acoustic cues for phonemic categories are isolable and stable. Numerous SP theorists have emphasized, however, that the attributes associated with a particular phoneme may vary widely with speaker and phonetic context (Repp & Liberman in Chapter 3, and Diehl & Kluender in Chapter 7, this volume). Speech perception reflects real-world knowledge of speaker characteristics (e.g., rate, dialect, sex, age) as well as detailed knowledge of phonemic contexts. For example, voice-onset time (VOT) for naturally produced initial stops varies as a function of the following vowel, and listeners adjust their VOT boundaries in accordance with this interaction (Diehl, Lang, & Parker, 1980).[2]

There are at least two distinct views concerning attributes. One is that attributes are functional entities in the sense that they are identified by detectors in the nervous system. In the case of speech perception, this view has been criticized as oversimplified (Diehl & Kluender in Chapter 7, this volume); some even consider it to be experimentally disconfirmed (Remez in Chapter 6, this volume). An alternative view is that attributes are convenient fictions that allow one to bring out relationships among concepts. We prefer the latter view because it entails no assumptions about detectors.

Category structure. Numerous investigators have over the years noted that the attributes of exemplars can be related to category membership in a number of ways. To begin with, categories can be *defined*. More specifically, a category is defined if it is possible to specify a defining rule that identifies all of its members and only its members. In order to eliminate rules that do no more than enumerate the members of a class it is common practice to require that a rule involve information reduction. Even with this restriction there is an indefinitely large number of ways in which a category can be defined. For example, a category can have attributes that are jointly sufficient and singly necessary for category membership, that is, *only* members of the category possess all these attributes and *all* members possess each of them. We refer to this special case as a *well-defined category* (following Smith & Medin, 1981). For example, being adult, never married, eligible, living, male, and human are jointly sufficient and singly necessary for membership in the category bachelors. An example of a defining rule that is *not* a well-defined one is a disjunctive rule, according to which category members must satisfy any one of several sufficient conditions for category membership, but need not satisfy any one in particular. For example, a strike in baseball occurs either when a hitter swings and misses/fouls or when the ball is in the strike zone.[3] Many other forms of defining rules for category membership are also possible, such as exclusions, conditionals, and biconditionals (see Bourne, 1970; Bourne, Dominowski, & Loftus, 1979, p. 218). The key characteristics of defined categories are that membership is all or none and that membership can be unambiguously determined by reference to a rule.

More recently, work on GK categories has concentrated on *fuzzy categories*. In contrast to defined categories, a category is fuzzy if it is not possible to specify a rule that identifies all of its members and only its members. In addition, category membership is often not all or none. Consider Wittgenstein's (1953) example of games. No one has yet found a rule that discriminates all games from all nongames. Some attributes seem to be true of all games (e.g., occur in time, are an activity), but are so general as to be jointly insufficient. Other characteristic attributes set games apart to some extent from nongames, but none of these attributes are true of all games; they are therefore not singly necessary (e.g., involves competition, goal pursuit, and multiple participants is true of many games, but not all). Because no rule appears to distinguish games from nongames, and because category membership does not appear to be all or none, games are not a defined category. Instead, the characteristic attributes of games are structured such that each game has a strong similarity to a number of other games and not much similarity to nongames – what Wittgenstein referred to as a family-resemblance structure.

In further developing the family-resemblance principle and applying it to psychology, Rosch and her colleagues (reviewed in Rosch, 1978) proposed that attributes in the physical environment are not independent but occur in clusters of correlated attributes. Wings and beaks, for example, have a higher probability of physically co-occurring with flying and nesting than with gills and swimming. This correlational structure of the physical environment results in natural cuts between clusters of highly similar entities, and according to Rosch, people's most fundamental categories map onto these natural clusters. Given the difficulty of discovering rules for many natural categories, Rosch has argued that numerous categories owe their existence to the high within-category similarity and low between-category similarity that stem from the physical structure of the environment. That is, people do not form categories on the basis of rules, but instead form them on the basis of perceived similarity relations that stem from the structure of the physical environment. Alternative explanations of how categories are acquired can be found in Lakoff (in press), Murphy and Medin (1985), and Neisser (1987).

In general, GK categories appear to vary widely in their category structure. Some are definable by various kinds of rules that clearly specify category membership (e.g., bachelors, strikes in baseball, legal voters). Others are fuzzy, being only loosely related by similarity-based family resemblance (e.g., games, furniture, clothing). The current consensus is that most GK categories are fuzzy (Mervis & Rosch, 1981; Medin & Smith, 1984; Smith & Medin, 1981).

Although it is possible to specify ideal attribute values for exemplars of SP categories (e.g., /b/ is a bilabial, voiced, stop), it is not clear that these values provide a defining basis for membership. Evidence suggests that SP categories may often be fuzzy. Extensive literatures on trading relations (where one attribute need not be present if a compensatory attribute is) and context effects (where the attributes signaling a particular phoneme vary with the adjacent phonemes) demonstrate that speech perception can occur without ideal speech cues (for example, see Repp & Liberman in Chapter 3 and Diehl & Kluender in Chapter 7, this volume). In addition, naturally spoken exemplars of speech categories are often only intelligible in context, further suggesting that both less-than-defining cues and a wide variety of cues may play a role in classifying a speech sound into a particular category. Consequently, there may be no way to define membership in some SP categories. Finally, exemplars of many SP categories vary along critical continua (e.g., VOT) such that the category membership of exemplars near category boundaries may not be deemed as being as strong or as clear as that of exemplars close to the ideal values (see Chapter 5 by Eimas et al., this volume). Since it may not be possible to discover rules for SP categories, and since membership in SP categories may not always be all or none, SP categories, like GK categories, may often be fuzzy. A similar conclusion was reached by Heider (1971, 1972) with respect to color categories.

Bases of classification

Current work on GK categories has focused on how stimuli are classified into categories. Although the means of classification for a particular category is often closely related to its structure, with many categories classification can be accomplished in at least three distinct ways. We will use the defined category of bachelors to illustrate these. A more extensive development of these forms of classification can be found in Smith and Medin (1981).

Classification in GK categories

Classification by rules. When one knows a rule for a category, one can simply test exemplars against it for category membership. To determine whether an entity is a bachelor, for example, one could test for being adult, never married, eligible, living, male, and human; if the outcome of every test were positive, that entity would be classified as a bachelor. In general, this form of classification simply requires that each exemplar meet the defining criteria associated with its category.

Classification by prototypes. It has been argued that many GK categories are represented by *prototypes*. Generally speaking, the prototype of a category contains the characteristic attributes of its category's exemplars, namely, attributes that are highly probable across category members, but that are neither necessary or sufficient for category membership. For example, the prototype for bachelor might include attributes true of many bachelors but not all (e.g., goes to singles bars, drives a sports car, is heterosexual). The central assumption of this approach is that people often determine whether or not an instance belongs to a category on the basis of how similar it is to the category's prototype. Instances above some threshold of similarity to the prototype are classified as category members; all others are nonmembers. Another important assumption of this approach is that prototype classification can result in satisfactory (though not necessarily perfect) classification for categories lacking rules. With fuzzy categories, most stimuli sufficiently similar to the prototype are actually category members, and most insufficiently similar stimuli are actually nonmembers. Errors occur either when members fail to be similar enough to the prototype or when nonmembers are sufficiently similar. Whereas prototype classification may often result in correct classifications with bachelors, for example, it would clearly err in certain cases.

A further assumption of prototype classification is that ease of classification should vary with how similar an entity is to the prototype. The more similar a category member is to the prototype, the more easily it should be classified as a category member (e.g., Tom Sellick versus Pope John Paul with respect to bachelors). In contrast, the more similar a nonmember is to the prototype, the harder it should be to exclude it (e.g., Paul Newman, who is married, versus Meryl Streep). This differential ease of classification, which has been referred to as "typicality," "exemplar goodness," and "graded structure," has been observed extensively and is the most robust factor in classification performance we know of (see reviews by Medin & Smith, 1984; Mervis & Rosch, 1981). Note that the presence of graded structure tends to undermine the notion that categories are defined (but see Armstrong et al., 1983).

Prototypes do not contain only the characteristic attributes of their respective categories. As shown by Barsalou (1985), the prototypes of many GK categories contain ideal attributes that are often not characteristic of category members. With "things to eat on a diet," for example, exemplars become better examples of the category as their number of calories approaches the ideal value of zero. This reflects the fact that the prototype of this category contains the ideal attribute of zero calories, which clearly is not the characteristic value (i.e., central tendency) of the category. Barsalou (1985) also demonstrates that prototypes of GK categories may simultaneously contain some attributes that reflect the category's central tendency while containing others that represent their ideals.

Classification by exemplars. According to this view, people classify entities on the basis of their similarity to memories of previously experienced category members. Instead of testing a stimulus against a rule or a prototype that has been abstracted from experience with many members, they compare it with memories of specific category exemplars, each memory representing an encounter with an exemplar at a specific place and time.[4] Stimuli are assigned to the category having the most similar exemplar or exemplars. With respect to bachelor, an unidentified man might be compared to memories of previously encountered bachelors and would, if sufficiently similar to these exemplars, be assigned to the category. Similar to prototype classification, exemplar classification often leads to correct classifications but is not error-proof. In addition, it can also result in graded structure.

In summary, people could use any of the three classification strategies with defined GK categories. Obviously only the last two strategies can be used with fuzzy categories.

Classification in SP categories

Classification by ideals. Many SP theorists assume that people's knowledge of an SP category specifies attributes that its exemplars should ideally have. All exemplars of /b/, for example, should have the acoustic parameters of stops that are bilabial and voiced. The status of these ideals appears to vary from theory to theory. Some assume that these ideal parameters are the eliciting conditions of innate feature detectors. Others assume that they reflect the ideal way to generate SP exemplars during speech production. Still others implicitly assume that they enter into conventional linguistic rules as necessary and sufficient conditions for category membership. Many of the accounts along these lines seem to assume that ideal attributes are used in an all-or-none fashion; namely, either something possesses all of a category's ideal attributes and is therefore in the category or does not possess all the ideal attributes and is not in the category. Category membership is discrete or categorical as opposed to being graded. Classification by ideal attributes in SP categories is analogous to classification by rules in GK categories.

Classification by prototypes. More recent theoretical views of CP seem to have loosened the requirement that the exemplars of a SP category must possess all of its ideal attributes. Instead, a category's ideal values represent only the prototypical instance of the category, and exemplars can vary widely in the extent to which they approach the ideal. Work reflecting this view can be found in Samuel (1982) and in Repp and Liberman in Chapter 3, Eimas et al. in Chapter 5, Diehl and Kluender in Chapter 7, and Massaro in Chapter 8, this volume.

As with GK categories, the prototypes of SP categories could contain two kinds of attributes. SP prototypes could contain ideal attributes specified by innate feature detectors, production constraints, or linguistic convention. In such cases, prototypes would not necessarily contain the most characteristic attributes or the central tendency of their respective category. Alternatively the attributes in SP prototypes may not be ideal, but may simply reflect the central tendency (average) of the instances sampled. In either case, exemplars vary in their similarity to prototypes, and distance from prototypes determines ease of classification.

Classification by boundaries. A final classification strategy proposed by SP theorists is that people determine category membership on the basis of category boundaries rather than characteristic or ideal attributes (e.g., Pastore in Chapter 1, this volume). For example, any bilabial stop with a VOT less than 20 msec is a /b/, and any bilabial stop with a VOT greater than 20 msec is a /p/. As far as we know, this boundary strategy has not been addressed by GK theorists, although people probably use it with some GK categories. For example, voters and nonvoters are defined with respect to an age boundary, and some formal diagnostic categories used in psychiatry are defined with respect to boundaries (for example, "at least six of the following symptoms" – American Psychiatric Association, 1980). We return later to the roles of central tendency, ideals, and boundaries in classification.

Finally, we are not aware of any SP theorists who have addressed the use of exemplar strategies in SP classification (cf. Macmillan in Chapter 2 of this volume concerning context effects in "roving" discrimination).

Uses of categories

Understanding the uses of categories plays an important role in understanding their structure. We next consider four such processes and their implications for SP and GK categories.

Classification. The most obvious use of SP and GK categories is to classify various kinds of entities. Although SP and GK categories are both used for classification, the reasons for classification appear to be quite different. Classifying stimuli such as phonemes and colors often serves the purpose of making higher-order classifications – they are rarely ends in themselves. For example, classifying a sound as /b/ may serve the more basic purpose of determining that someone said the word bottle; and classifying a color as red may serve the more basic purpose of determining that something is a strawberry. In other words, classification with SP categories seems to serve to detect attributes that are relevant to higher-order classifications involving GK categories (see Harnad in Chapter 19, this volume).

In contrast, classification into GK categories appears to serve the purpose of inference and prediction.

Inference and prediction. Classifying an entity into a GK category provides access to what may often be a tremendous amount of information essential for knowing how to interact with that entity. Classifying something as a car, for example, permits inferences about what it is made of, how it operates, how to maintain it, how to sell it, and so on.

Classifying a stimulus into an SP category also provides access to knowledge that can be used for inference, however. For example, when speakers fail to generate all the attributes of a phoneme, the attributes actually produced may be sufficient to activate an SP category such that the missing attributes are inferred from its representation. It is also obvious that categorizing a sound as a particular phoneme results in predictions of what subsequent phonemes may follow.

Generation. Whereas classification involves going from exemplars to categories, generation involves going from categories to exemplars. With GK categories, generation typically takes the form of instantiation. When planning a camping trip, for example, one must instantiate the categories of clothing, tools, food, and so on. Although people may occasionally instantiate SP categories (e.g., picking a color), generation appears to be infrequent or to take a different form. For example, generation in speech categories typically takes the form of production. When producing an utterance, it is necessary to go from abstract phonemic representations to actions that produce the appropriate speech sounds. According to the motor theory of speech perception, the same representations are used for production and classification (see Repp & Liberman in Chapter 3 and Diehl & Kluender in Chapter 7, this volume, for two perspectives on this position). Although generation from both SP and GK categories involves deriving exemplars from category representations, that appears to be the extent of the similarity.

Productivity. Both SP and GK categories are used to construct higher-order categories. With SP, phoneme categories can be incorporated into representations of new words, and color categories can be incorporated into representations of new objects. GK categories such as disgusting, obnoxious, and flea can be combined to form more complex concepts such as digustingly obnoxious flea. Processing of both SP and GK categories appears to be highly productive in humans.

Category acquisition

Innate sensitivities for learning. There appear to be innate biases or natural partitions that influence the learning of both SP and GK categories. For SP categories, people seem to have differential regions of sensitivity along perceptual dimensions that probably have biological bases (Pastore in Chapter 1, this volume). Further evidence comes from studies showing that prelinguistic infants possess highly developed mechanisms for the perception of speech, or at least for particular kinds of acoustic signals (Eimas et al., in Chapter 5, this volume).

People also seem to have innate sensitivities for certain kinds of GK categories. Although a particular natural object (e.g., an apple) can be classified at a number of different taxonomic levels (e.g., food, fruit, apple, McIntosh apple), the *basic level* (apple in this case) has been shown to be the one most preferred by adults for classification (Murphy & Smith, 1982; Rosch, Mervis, Gray, Johnson, & Boyes-Braem, 1976a). Children show a natural affinity for concepts at the basic level, which they acquire before concepts at other levels (Anglin, 1977; Rosch, Mervis, Gray, Johnson, & Boyes-Braem, 1976a). In addition, cross-cultural work has shown that many cultures show maximal sensitivity for categories at the basic level and that cross-cultural differences in concepts are minimized at the basic level (e.g., Berlin, Breedlove, & Raven, 1973; Rosch, 1973, 1977). Whereas there may be a genetic disposition responsible for basic-level sensitivity, it is probably very different from any genetic dispositions responsible for sensitivities underlying SP categories.

The role of experience. The emphasis on innate biases must be tempered by the obvious fact that experience plays a significant role in the acquisition of both GK and SP categories. One of the most active areas of research in cognitive development for some time has addressed the issue of how children acquire GK categories. Investigators have addressed the question of whether children acquire functional attributes before perceptual attributes (Clark, 1973; Mervis, 1980; Nelson, 1974), the extent to which children classify by prototypes as opposed to rules (Keil & Kelly in Chapter 17, this volume), the order in which children acquire various kinds of ontological categories (Keil, 1979), the role of children's theories of the world in acquiring concepts (Carey, 1982), children's ability to acquire superordinate relations (Markman, 1979), the role of exemplar goodness in children's acquisition of categories (Mervis & Pani, 1980), whether children process exemplars analytically or holistically (Smith & Kemler, 1977), and numerous other issues.

Research on adult acquisition of GK categories has primarily examined the kinds of classification schemes people develop when learning categories (e.g., Bourne, 1970; Medin & Schaffer, 1978; Medin & Schwanenflugel, 1981; Medin & Smith, 1981; Rosch, Simpson, & Miller, 1976b); much of this work is reviewed by Smith and Medin (1981).

There is not a large body of research on the acquisition of SP categories beyond the work just cited on innate sensitivities. That perception may become categorical with experience has been well-documented in the case of musical categories (this work is reviewed by Repp, 1984; Repp & Liberman in Chapter 3 and Rosen & Howell in Chapter 4, this volume). Although work on adaptation (see Chapter 6 by Remez, Chapter 9 by Borstein, and Chapter 13 by Wilson, this volume) and on cross-cultural differences (e.g., Williams, 1977a,b) demonstrates the importance of experience in SP categories, little appears to be known about the role of experience in how children initially acquire SP categories. Eimas et al. (Chapter 5, this volume) present an interesting framework for exploring this issue.

Category stability and flexibility

Stability. For successful communication and social interaction, it is essential that people's conceptual systems be similar and relatively stable. Consequently it is important to determine the extent to which conceptual systems are stable between individuals and stable within the same individual across time. Very little work has addressed these issues, although Samuel (1982) has investigated individual differences in prototypes for /ga/ and /ka/ and for the boundary between them; McCloskey and Glucksberg (1978) have studied the stability of GK category boundaries; Bellezza (1984a,b,c) has studied the stability of exemplar generation in GK categories; and Barsalou (1987) has examined the stability of typicality gradients in GK categories. All of this work suggests that categories are *much less* stable than would be expected, both between and within individuals. Because innate sensitivities should contribute to stability, we expect SP categories to be more stable than GK categories.

Flexibility. One of the most impressive facts about human-classification performance with GK categories is its flexibility. As noted by Barsalou (1983), people readily construct new GK categories that are relevant to achieving novel goals. When confronted with having to survive a burning house, for example, people can construct categories relevant to successfully escaping (e.g., things to save from the house, ways to fight the fire, places to stay temporarily). Besides being able to easily construct goal-relevant categories, people readily cross-classify a given entity into a wide range of categories. A chair, for example, can be cross-classified as something to hold a door open, something to stand on to fix a light bulb, something to sell at a garage sale, and so on. Little work has addressed people's ability to form goal-relevant categories and to perform cross-classification.

Other work has demonstrated that typicality gradients within GK categories are extremely flexible. Roth and Shoben (1983) found that what is typical of a category varies widely as a function of its linguistic context (e.g., cows and goats are typical animals when the context is milking, but horses and mules are typical when the context is riding). They demonstrated such shifts in classification time as well as in typicality judgments. Barsalou and Sewell (1984) found that when people adopt the points of view of various cultures and subcultures, they perceive different prototypes for the same category. For example, a robin is a typical bird from the American point of view, but an ostrich is typical from the African point of view.

Although SP categories may have strong innate constraints that contribute to

Table 16.1. *Similarities and differences between sensory perception (SP) and generic knowledge (GK) categories with respect to basic issues in categorization*

Similarities	Differences
Category structure	
Decomposition into attributes	Attributes better specified for SP categories
Most categories are fuzzy	Larger variety of structures in GK categories
Classification	
Could use rules, prototypes, exemplars, or boundaries	Not much attention given to exemplar classification in SP categories or to boundary classification in GK categories
Uses of categories	
Classification	SP classifications typically subserve higher-order classifications; GK classifications typically subserve inference and prediction
Inference	More extensive for GK categories
Generation of exemplars	Retrieval of instantiations for SP categories; generation of actions for speeech categories
Productivity	
Acquisition	
Innate learning sensitivities	Perceptual sensitivity regions for SP categories; basic-level sensitivity for GK categories
Experience important	
Category stability and flexibility	
Categories appear sufficiently stable for communication	SP categories may exhibit more stability
Categories exhibit flexibility across contexts	GK categories may exhibit more flexibility

stability, adaptation and range effects certainly indicate that these categories are flexible to some extent (see Chapter 6 by Remez, Chapter 9 by Bornstein, and Chapter 13 by Wilson, this volume). In addition, Williams's (1977a) work with bilinguals shows that individuals can alter their category boundaries as a function of the language they are currently using (for a review of further work addressing this issue, see Repp & Liberman in Chapter 3, this volume). The impression that SP categories are less flexible than GK categories may reflect the fact that studies with SP categories often use synthetic stimuli divorced from their natural context. When richer settings are examined, context effects are abundant (Repp & Liberman in Chapter 3 and Diehl & Kluender in Chapter 7, this volume).

These issues are relevant to categories in virtually any stimulus domain. Although SP and GK categories differ to some extent on most issues, they generally appear to differ in degree rather than in kind. Table 16.1 summarizes what we perceive as the similarities and differences between SP and GK categories with respect to these issues. We now turn to what we view as the strong similarities between SP and GK categories.

Empirical and theoretical similarities between SP and GK categories

Empirical similarities

Sharp identification functions. One of the hallmarks of certain SP categories – those that exhibit CP – is sharp identification functions: People classify exemplars close to category boundaries just as accurately as they classify exemplars far from category boundaries (i.e., close to 100% accuracy in both cases). Such identification functions have been found for speech sounds (e.g., Liberman et al., 1957), nonspeech sounds (e.g., Miller, Wier, Pastore, Kelly, & Dooling, 1976), color categories (e.g., Bornstein in Chapter 9, this volume), and other visual stimuli (e.g., Pastore, 1978; Pastore et al., 1977). As discussed by Repp (1984) and other authors in this volume, SP categories vary substantially in the extent to which they exhibit CP, with some SP categories having very sharp identification functions and others showing much more continuous identification functions. In fact, Repp (1984) argues that CP can only be understood in terms of an interaction among particular perceivers, for particular stimuli, in particular tasks.

It has been a well-kept secret that many GK categories reveal the same sharp identification functions found in SP categories: People are close to 100% right in their classification of nearly all GK exemplars. People are generally no less accurate in classifying atypical exemplars close to boundaries (e.g., ostrich and penguin with respect to birds) than they are in classifying typical exemplars far from boundaries (e.g., robin and sparrow). The typical error rate in classification studies with GK categories is around 5%, with the error rates usually being slightly higher by a few percentage points for typical than for atypical exemplars (such studies are reviewed in Smith, 1978). GK categories do have unclear cases, that is, exemplars that are not classified the same way 100% of the time (e.g., Barsalou, 1983; McCloskey & Glucksberg, 1978). The number of such cases, however, is generally small relative to the number of other exemplars that are clearly classified; and proportionally it is probably about the same as the number of unclear cases in SP categories.

Although studies have found graded identification functions for certain GK categories (e.g., Labov, 1973), the fact that some GK categories exhibit sharp identification functions whereas others do not is analogous to the status of identification functions in SP categories. This suggests that sharp identification functions do not distinguish SP from GK categories, but instead depend on conditions that can occur for both category types.

Within-category discrimination. If perception were truly categorical, then people would not be able to discriminate members of the same category at all (i.e., they would be unable to tell two different exemplars of the same category apart). However, it has been unequivocally shown that people *can* discriminate exemplars from the same SP category. An analogous state of affairs exists for GK categories: Although GK categories often exhibit sharp identification functions, it is obvious that people can tell exemplars apart.

Even though people can discriminate exemplars within SP categories from one another, numerous studies have shown that discrimination across category boundaries is better than discrimination within categories, away from boundaries. More specifically, when discriminability is observed between stimuli of a constant difference along some critical continuum, it is typically found that sensitivity is highest around category boundaries. Although we know of no studies with GK categories that have directly explored this issue, we suspect that a similar effect would be found with some GK categories. As others have discussed (e.g., Pastore in Chapter 1, this volume) and as we will discuss in this chapter, the presence of reference points at category boundaries may be central to superior discrimination near boundaries. If this is true, then GK categories with reference points near boundaries may also exhibit superior discrimination near boundaries (e.g., for voters and nonvoters, which are separated by the reference point of age 18 at their boundary).

Typicality effects. Although most exemplars from SP and GK categories are identified with close to 100% accuracy, the members of a given category are not perceived as equivalent. A large literature on typicality judgments shows that people reliably perceive some exemplars of GK categories as being more representative of their categories than others (e.g., Rosch, 1973; Rosch, 1975b). With vehicles, for example, people perceive cars, boats, and skateboards as decreasing in typicality. Because no one has yet found a GK category without a typicality gradient, typicality gradients appear to be a universal property of GK categories (cf. Armstrong et al., 1983; Barsalou, 1983, 1985, 1987). There is a fair amount of evidence that typicality gradients also occur with SP categories. As shown by Samuel (1982) and Miller, Connine, Schermer, and Kluender (1983) for phonemes and by Heider (1971, 1972) for colors, subjects systematically judge some exemplars of SP categories as being more typical than others. (See also Eimas et al. in Chapter 5, this volume.)

Most important, typicality gradients predict ease of classification in both SP and GK categories. Typical members of both category types are classified faster than atypical members (see Massaro in Chapter 8, this volume, for SP categories; see Smith, 1978, and McCloskey & Glucksberg, 1979, for GK categories). Typicality effects have also been found in the acquisition of GK categories (e.g., Mervis & Pani, 1980; Rosch et al., 1976b) and in the generation of instances from GK categories (e.g., Barsalou, 1983, 1985; Mervis, Catlin, & Rosch, 1976). With SP categories, typicality has also been shown to predict adaptation effects (Bornstein in Chapter 9, this volume; Miller et al., 1983; Samuel, 1982).

Near-perfect identification, therefore, does not imply that SP and GK categories are true equivalence classes. Subjects reliably perceive exemplars in both SP and

GK categories as varying in how typical they are of their category, with this variance predicting important categorization phenomena such as classification, acquisition, generation, and adaptation.

Reference-point effects. Several authors in this volume have argued that reference points are critical for SP categories. For example, Pastore (Chapter 1) suggests that sharp discrimination peaks between categories occur because of salient reference points at category boundaries. As exemplars move away from a boundary and toward the center of their category, their magnitudes relative to the reference point become greater and, according to Weber's law, less discriminable (for pairs of exemplars that are a constant difference apart). For example, simultaneous air release and voicing provide a salient reference point on the VOT dimension such that increasing amounts of lag in voice onset become decreasingly discriminable (the same is true of increases in prevoicing on the other side of the reference point). Another example of a salient reference point is a flat formant transition, with increases in the rise (or fall) of formant transitions becoming decreasingly discriminable.

Analogous examples exist in GK categories. For example, a salient reference point that plays a role in discriminating voters from nonvoters is the age of 18. As voters become older (or younger) than 18, their values on the critical dimension probably become decreasingly discriminable. Along these lines, Holyoak (1978) has argued that people use reference points when deciding which of two GK concepts has a higher value on a test dimension (e.g., which is larger, a robin or an elephant?). More specifically, he found that the time taken to make such discriminations was well predicted by the ratio of magnitudes measured relative to salient reference points.

Another instance of reference points in GK categories has been explored by Rips and Turnbull (1980). They found that relative adjectives such as "large" and "small" have individual reference points associated with separate GK categories. For example, large and small map onto different reference points in the case of insects, mammals, and mountains (e.g., large means different things for each category). Rips and Turnbull also found that absolute adjectives such as blue have a single reference point that subserves all GK categories (but see Halff, Ortony, & Anderson, 1976) and that the average size of people serves as a global reference point for the adjectives of small and large.

Finally, Barsalou (1985) has shown that typicality gradients in GK categories are often determined by ideal reference points. "Foods to eat on a diet," for example, is structured with respect to the ideal reference point of zero calories, with exemplars increasing in typicality as their number of calories decreases. Such effects occur even in taxonomic categories. Typicality in fruit, for example, is determined to some extent by how close exemplars are to the reference point of ideal taste.

In all the above examples for both SP and GK categories, reference points are salient values on dimensions that structure categories. A qualitatively different way to view reference points is as the most representative instances of categories, that is, as their prototypes. Rosch (1975a) and Tversky (1977) have shown that prototypical exemplars act as reference points in similarity judgments, and Tversky and Kahneman (1983) have shown how the use of these reference points may lead to systematic biases in reasoning. There is no reason why the prototypical exemplars of SP categories cannot also be viewed as reference points. A problem that arises, however, is that discrimination is not at its best around the prototypes of SP categories (it is best at the boundaries). If prototypes act as reference points, then Weber's law predicts that discrimination should be excellent in their immediate vicinity. We will return to this issue later.

Theoretical similarities

Given the basic similarities in empirical findings for SP and GK categories, it is not surprising that there are corresponding theoretical similarities.

Prototype models. One of the most popular theories associated with work on GK categories proposes that concepts are represented by prototypes reflecting the central tendencies of categories (see Posner and Keele, 1968; Reed, 1972; Smith & Medin, 1981; Smith, Shoben, & Rips, 1974; Rosch, 1978). Recently this idea has been extended to SP categories (see Oden and Massaro, 1978; Samuel, 1982; Massaro in Chapter 8, this volume). In some cases this similarity even extends to adopting fuzzy set theory as the formalism to describe graded membership for both SP and GK categories (see Massaro, Chapter 8; Oden and Massaro, 1978; Mervis and Roth, 1981; Osherson and Smith, 1981; Roth and Mervis, 1983).

Continuous versus discrete processing models. Massaro and Cohen (1983) tested whether a categorical (i.e., discrete) processing model or a continuous processing model better predicted typicality judgments in SP categories. Their data favored a continuous processing model. An exactly parallel pair of processing models was evaluated in a series of studies on social categorization by Lingle, Altom, and Medin (1984), who found that some experimental procedures yielded data favoring the continuous model, whereas others favored the categorical model.

Dual-process models. A number of two-factor models have been proposed to account for performance with SP categories. (see Fujisaki and Kawashima, 1970; Massaro & Cohen, 1983; Macmillan in Chapter 2, this volume). Typically these models contain a discrete component that plays a central role in identification and a continuous component that underlies discrimination. Although we will not go into detailed comparisons, there are corresponding dual-process models associated with GK categories. For example, the model of semantic comparisons proposed by

Table 16.2. *Empirical and theoretical similarities between sensory perception (SP) and generic knowledge (GK) categories*

Empirical similarities	Theoretical similarities
Sharp identification functions	Prototype models
Within-category discrimination	Continuous versus discrete processing models
Typicality effects	Dual-process models
Reference-point effects	Psychophysical models

Smith et al. (1974) assumes that classification of exemplars into GK categories begins by considering overall similarity to prototypes, but for difficult decisions this is followed by a consideration of defining attributes.

Psychophysical models. Accounts of performance on both SP and GK categories have made ample use of signal detection models and other tools growing out of psychophysics. Macmillan (in Chapter 2, this volume) reviews the use of such models for SP categories. With respect to GK categories, Holyoak's (1978) reference-point model, Fried and Holyoak's (1984) distributional-classification model, and McCloskey and Glucksberg's (1979) random-walk classification model all borrow from signal detection theory. SP theorists have used adaptation-level theory (Wilson in Chapter 13, this volume), but we do not yet know of analogous applications by GK theorists.

A final point of interest concerning psychophysics comes from Noreen's (1981) mathematical analysis of possible decision rules for psychophysical tasks. For rules that apply to categorized stimuli falling along a continuous dimension (e.g., SP categories), Noreen showed that the optimal rule for deciding whether two such stimuli are the same or different involves first seeing whether they belong to different categories rather than first comparing their values on the continuous dimension.

In summary, both data and theory for SP and GK categories exhibit suggestive similarities, which we have summarized in Table 16.2. The next section reviews particular issues in categorization that are raised by our current knowledge and lack of knowledge about SP and GK categories. Future resolution of these problems may have important implications for our understanding of these two category types, as well as of categorization processes in general.

Points of future comparison

Reference points

Our review of the work on both SP and GK categories has led us to the conclusion that reference points are extremely important for both category types and probably for all category types. Reference points can be either salient values on dimensions that structure categories, or they can be prototypes that contain characteristic and ideal attributes of the category.

Locations of reference points. Reference points consistently crop up in several predictable locations. As has been well-documented for SP categories, reference points are often salient values from dimensions that occur at boundaries between categories and provide a salient basis for dividing their exemplars. For example, simultaneous acoustic parameters of air release and voicing provide a reference point on the VOT dimension that is used to partition phonemic categories. Reference points also occur in the centers of categories as prototypes that contain the characteristic attributes of their category (i.e. as the central tendency of their category). For example, the attributes comprising robins appear to approximate the central tendency of the bird category and may therefore serve as its prototype (Rosch & Mervis, 1975). Finally, reference points occur at other locations when they occur as ideals. With "things to eat on a diet," for example, typicality is determined with respect to the reference point of zero calories. Conversely, typicality for "things not to eat on a diet" is determined with respect to the reference point of indefinitely many calories. In neither category is the ideal the central tendency of the respective exemplars. Although ideals sometimes lie at the extreme ends of dimensions as they do in the examples just cited, they need not. In clothes to wear in the snow, for example, the ideal warmth a piece of clothing could provide would not lie at an extreme but in the vicinity of 98.6 degrees Fahrenheit.

Reference points can therefore occur in at least three places: at the boundaries of categories, at their centers, and at their ideals. We suspect that the locations of reference points differ substantially across category types. Perhaps one difference is that reference points are more likely to occur at the boundaries of SP categories than at the boundaries of GK categories. To some extent this may reflect greater innate constraints on SP categories than on GK categories. Although there is evidence for reference points occurring at both the centers and the ideals of GK categories (Barsalou, 1985), there has not been corresponding work with SP categories. More specifically, the issue of whether SP prototypes represent the central tendencies of their respective categories or ideals specified by innate constraints, production constraints, or linguistic convention has received little attention.

Consequences of reference points. In order to locate reference points, it is necessary to have a means of identifying them. We next discuss three consequences of reference points that can be used for this purpose: increased discrimination sensitivity, assimilation, and asymmetrical similarity relations.

Some accounts of discrimination sensitivity have stated that discrimination decreases with distance from reference points according to Weber's law. As pairs of exemplars a fixed distance apart move away from a reference point, their magnitudes relative to the reference point become greater and therefore less discriminable. This consequence of reference points can be used to identify them; reference points may be associated with regions of increased sensitivity (see Pastore in Chapter 1, this volume, for a more developed account).

However, there is at least one other explanation for improved discrimination around reference points at category boundaries (apart from Weber's law). Discrimination may be good for stimuli that straddle a reference point because they can be coded in qualitatively different ways (e.g., rising versus falling formant transitions; negative versus positive voice onsets). Stimuli that can be categorized in qualitatively different ways may be easier to discriminate than stimuli that differ to the same degree but are categorized identically.

Actually, reference points may produce three distinct categories of stimuli. In addition to stimuli that are clearly on one side of the reference point or the other, stimuli falling very near a reference point also form a salient category, namely, the category of stimuli that are not discriminable from the reference point (see Pastore et al., 1977, for a more complete discussion). For example, /b/ could be construed as the category of bilabial stops in which exemplars have VOTs that are not discriminable from simultaneity; /p/ would be those bilabial stops in which VOT is perceptibly positive; and prevoiced stops (which don't occur in English) would be those in which VOT is perceptibly negative. Similarly, with formant transitions, falling transitions may form one attribute, flat transitions may form a second, and rising transitions may form a third.

The point is that improved discrimination near reference points may in some cases simply be the beneficial outcome of these distinct coding schemes. Discrimination may be good near boundaries because stimuli are coded in qualitatively different ways, whereas discrimination may be poorer within categories because stimuli are all coded (qualitatively) in the same way. In general, it seems important to determine the relative extents to which discrete categorization versus Weber's law are responsible for improved discrimination near boundaries.

A second possible consequence of reference points – and one that seems diametrically opposed to the consequence of increased sensitivity just discussed – is assimilation to prototypes. Assimilation refers to the idea that exemplars near a prototype are somehow encoded more poorly than exemplars further away (Samuel, 1982). As a consequence, discrimination is poorer near prototypes than away from them. Samuel's notion of assimilation is quite speculative at this point and needs to be spelled out much more carefully. Are encodings of stimuli near a prototype distorted more toward the prototype? Do they have a higher probability of having the prototype literally substituted for them at encoding? Are they more susceptible to interference or forgotten more quickly for some other reason? Do stimuli far from the prototype receive more processing – given their atypicality – such that they develop sharper encodings or fade more slowly?

Along with Weber's law and qualitative coding, assimilation provides a third account of why discrimination peaks occur at the boundaries of some SP categories. According to the assimilation account, discrimination gets poorer for stimuli further from boundaries because assimilation to prototypes increases. In some sense, however, this is inconsistent with the Weber's law and qualitative-coding explanations just discussed. Whereas these two accounts propose that discrimination is best *near* reference points, the assimilation account proposes that discrimination is best *far* from reference points. One solution to this apparent inconsistency may be that when reference points are single values on a dimension, sensitivity in their vicinity is increased; but when reference points are multiple-attribute prototypes, sensitivity in their vicinity is decreased.[5]

Work clearly needs to be done to determine whether reference points increase or decrease sensitivity in their vicinity; different kinds of reference points may result in different patterns of sensitivity. In addition, it will be important to determine *why* particular kinds of reference points result in particular patterns of sensitivity. When sensitivity increases near reference points, for example, is it because of Weber's law or because of qualitivatively different coding? Finally, it will be important to determine what roles various kinds of reference points play in categorization. One possibility is that the kind of reference point people use when processing a category may depend on the particular task. One example that we will discuss later is that boundary reference points are used in discrimination tasks, whereas prototype reference points are used in classification tasks.

A final consequence of reference points is their effect on similarity judgments. Both Rosch (1975a) and Tversky (1977) have shown that GK prototypes and salient values from dimensions fit better into the *referent* position of similarity statements than into the *subject* position (i.e., statements of the form "A *subject* is similar to a *referent*"). For example, the statement "A pigeon is similar to a robin" is preferred to "A robin is similar to a pigeon" because robins are prototypical birds. Analogously, on the number line, "99 is similar to 100" is preferred over "100 is similar to 99" because 100 is a salient reference point. Not only do people prefer prototypes and salient values in the referent position; they also perceive the corresponding statements as describing a higher degree of similarity than their converses. In a further demonstration of this theme, Rips (1975) developed a scenario in which certain animals on an island were said to be ill. Subjects were asked to judge the likelihood that other animals might become ill. People were much more likely to infer that an atypical member of a category would become ill upon hearing that a typical member had become ill than to make the reverse judgment. Ortony (1979) has also done interesting work on asymmetries in similarity judgments. Although this approach to studying reference points has only been used to study reference points in GK categories, it might also be useful in identifying reference points in SP categories.

The use of reference points in classification. We just raised the possibility that subjects use boundary reference points in discrimination tasks and prototype reference points in classification tasks. In this section we consider issues involving the roles of reference points in classification.

People could either use boundary reference points or prototype reference points to classify SP exemplars. More specifically, people could classify an SP exemplar by determining its value relative to a boundary reference point (e.g., whether it has positive, simultaneous, or negative VOT) or by finding which prototype it is closest to (e.g., whether it is closer to the /b/ or /p/ prototype). These two classification procedures are very different in the assumptions they make about category representations. For the boundary strategy, category representations would have to contain attributes that specify *limits* on the attribute values that could be possessed by category members – such representations would not have to contain information about the characteristic or ideal attributes of the category. For the prototype strategy, the converse is true, namely, category representations need only contain information about characteristic and ideal attributes but not about the boundaries of the category.

The boundary and prototype accounts of classification are not easily discriminated by percent correct or reaction time. For percent correct, both accounts predict that subjects should be more accurate as exemplars move away from the boundary. According to the boundary model, which side of the boundary a stimulus lies on should become more discriminable as exemplars move away from the boundary. According to the prototype model, similarity to the correct prototype increases relative to similarity to incorrect prototypes as exemplars move away from the boundary. Both models also predict (for the reasons just given) that subjects should get *faster* as exemplars move further from the boundary. Consequently it is difficult to determine whether subjects are using boundary or prototype reference points in classification. However A. G. Samuel (personal communication) has pointed out to us that the boundary and prototype accounts of classification make different predictions for stimuli that lie on the *nonboundary* side of prototypes. The prototype view predicts that classification performance should worsen for these stimuli as they move further from the prototype. In contrast, the boundary view predicts that performance should keep improving as stimuli move further from the boundary.

For GK categories, little thought has been given to the possibility that people use boundary reference points during classification. Instead, every model we know of that uses reference points assumes that people use prototype reference points.

In general, we find it important to determine when and why people use boundary versus prototype reference points during classification. One factor that may influence the selection of reference points has to do with how categories contrast with one another. For example, if there are only two categories involved in a classification setting, then boundary classification is simpler than prototype classification. Boundary classification would require the use of only one reference point (one at the boundary between the categories), whereas prototype classification would involve two reference points (one for the prototype of each category). However, as the number of categories increases, prototype classification appears to become more parsimonious than boundary classification. This is because the number of prototype reference points increases linearly with the number of categories, whereas the number of boundary reference points increases at a positively accelerated rate (i.e., as each new category is added, it would seem to require a new boundary reference point at the boundary of *each* of the original categories). In addition, there may not be salient reference points at the boundaries of some categories. Consequently people may have no choice but to use prototype reference points.

Experience may also affect the use of reference points. Early during the learning of a category, people may have only a rough idea of the category and may therefore use a prototype acquired from their limited exposure to exemplars. With additional experience, however, they may discover a boundary reference point that more precisely discriminates categories. Consequently, people may shift from using prototype to boundary reference points with increasing sophistication. Another possibility is that people only develop and use boundary reference points to deal with atypical exemplars close to boundaries while continuing to use prototype reference points for typical exemplars.

Prototypes, exemplars, and decision rules

Prototypes versus exemplars. Although it may not be immediately obvious, excellent performance on prototypical stimuli and the presence of other typicality effects do not necessarily mean that subjects are using *prototypes*. Such observations are equally consistent with the assumption that subjects are instead using specific *exemplars* (i.e., memories of specific exemplars; but see note 4) to perform classification. Exemplar models have been constructed that can account for many findings originally explained by prototype models, including the fact that classification accuracy on specific old exemplars decreases over time more rapidly than classification accuracy on prototype patterns (Hintzman and Ludlam, 1980; Medin and Schaffer, 1978).

Investigators interested in SP categories might find it interesting to explore the possibility that SP classification involves comparing test items to exemplars as opposed to either boundary or prototype reference points. It is important to point out, however, that it is typically not easy to distinguish prototype and exemplar models. In addition, there are mixed models that rely on both prototype and exemplar information (e.g., Medin, Altom, and Murphy, 1984; Medin & Smith, 1981). Some of the more recent distributed memory models (e.g., Anderson, Silverstein, Ritz, and Jones, 1977; Eich, 1982; Hintzman, 1986; McClelland and Rumelhart, 1985) suggest some intriguing relationships between exemplars and prototypes.

Jacoby and his associates have recently reported some surprising findings concerning long-term effects of exemplars (see Jacoby and Brooks, 1984, for a review). They showed that presenting an instance of a concept lowers the perceptual threshold for later classification of *similar* instances of the same concept. For example, test items having the same irrelevant perceptual attributes as an initially encoded exemplar are classified more quickly than they would have been if that exemplar had not been presented or if an exemplar with different irrelevant attributes had been presented (Jacoby & Witherspoon, 1982). These exemplar effects persist over at least 24 hours (Jacoby and Dallas, 1981). These and related findings suggest that categorizing a stimulus involves more than simply activating a static representation during classification. We are not aware of any analogous findings with SP categories (although, as we will suggest, recently encoded exemplars might underlie adaptation and range effects).

Decision rules. Orthogonal to the prototype/exemplar issue is the question of how subjects integrate outcomes from the various attribute comparisons that occur during classification. More specifically, comparing a test stimulus to either prototypes or exemplars during classification involves comparing attributes of the test item to attributes of prototypes or exemplars in memory. Generally speaking, the test item is classified into the category whose prototype or exemplars best match it. The issue concerns how the outcomes of individual attribute comparisons are *combined* to reach a decision. Many classification models assume that the outcomes of attribute comparisons are combined according to an *additive rule*. Notably, this rule assumes that attribute comparisons are independent, that is, the outcome of one comparison does not affect any other comparison. An alternative possibility is that the outcomes of attribute comparisons are combined according to a *multiplicative rule*. According to this rule, outcomes are *not* independent; the outcome of one attribute comparison may affect the outcome of another, and the combination of outcomes is nonlinear (see the context model in Medin & Schaffer, 1978; the fuzzy set model in Oden and Massaro, 1978; the model proposed by Massaro in Chapter 8, this volume). In various contrasts of additive versus multiplicative integration rules, the data have primarily supported multiplicative rules, although additive rules are preferred under some conditions. In addition, Repp and Liberman (Chapter 3, this volume) and Diehl and Kluender (Chapter 7, this volume) provide numerous examples of dependencies among the outcomes of attribute comparisons during SP classification. It is important to point out that subjects could use multiplicative rules during either prototype or exemplar comparisons.

Flexibility

Adaptation and range effects. Although there have been numerous demonstrations of adaptation effects in SP categories, it is still not clear why they occur. Do adapters change prototypes, introduce new exemplars, change boundaries, alter ranges, fatigue detectors, or have some other effect? We find Remez's argument (Chapter 6, this volume) against adaptation of innate feature detectors for speech categories convincing (see also Diehl, 1981). It might be interesting to view adaptation in terms of the exemplar effects reviewed by Jacoby and Brooks (1984). More specifically, memories for specific exemplars may explain adaptation and range effects better than detector fatigue does. In this sense, the exemplar view is similar to adaptation level theory (see Wilson in Chapter 13, this volume), although the exemplar view would argue that exemplars themselves underlie adaptation, whereas adaptation level theory would argue that exemplars exert their effect by altering prototypes.

We are not aware of any demonstrations of range or adaptation effects with GK categories, but we believe these are important issues for research with these categories as well as with SP categories. Range often appears to be an uncontrolled variable, especially during typicality and similarity rating tasks. Regarding adaptation, it might be interesting to explore the role of abstractness. Does adaptation occur extensively with perceptual categories (e.g., SP categories), with concrete GK categories (e.g., birds, cars), and hardly at all with abstract GK categories (e.g., occupations, weekend activities)? Or do adaptation effects occur equally across all levels of abstraction? The exemplar effects reviewed by Jacoby and Brooks (1984) suggest that adaptationlike effects may occur widely across levels of abstraction.[6]

Priming by context. Priming effects have been reported for both SP and GK categories. As reviewed by Repp and Liberman (Chapter 3, this volume), semantic and syntactic contexts as well as local phonemic contexts can play a role in what people expect to hear. Priming effects are also ubiquitous in GK categories (e.g., Rosch, 1975b; Smith, 1978; Whitlow, 1986). Upon encoding a GK category name, for example, people expect its referent to be a typical rather than an atypical exemplar.

Most important, there seems to be flexibility in priming for both GK and SP categories. Earlier we discussed findings indicating that the particular prototypes primed for GK categories could be strongly influenced by linguistic context (Roth & Shoben, 1983) and by point of view (Barsalou & Sewell, 1984). Similar flexibility appears to exist for SP categories. As discussed by Repp and Liberman (in Chapter 3, this volume), the instance expected for a SP category can be affected by the preceding phonemic context, by the rate of speech, and by the characteristics of an individual speaker's voice.

Given the ubiquitousness and importance of flexibility in cognitive processing, it seems essential that future work be directed toward understanding this fundamental aspect of cognitive systems. Theorists frequently assume that category representations are static, with the same representation of a category being used on all occasions in which the category is processed. Yet it is becoming increasingly apparent that the representation used in processing a given category varies widely across situations and may rarely be the same in two different situations (Barsalou, 1987).

Processing variables

Holistic versus analytic processing. Although many GK categorization models assume that during classification people are assessing similarity between test items and prototypes (or between test items and exemplars), it is often unclear whether these judgments constitute holistic impressions of overall similarity or analytic integrations of attribute comparisons. In our discussion of additive and multiplicative integration rules earlier, we assumed that people process attributes separately prior to integration (i.e., analytic processing in the framework established by Garner [1974]). Under some circumstances, however, people seem unable to isolate the attributes of a stimulus so that they can be processed separately. As a result, such processing is more holistic (Garner, 1974).

The type of processing may depend on the stimulus domain. People are able to process the dimensions of *shape* and *size* analytically in the domain of geometric forms, whereas they are unable to process the dimensions of *hue, saturation,* and *brightness* analytically in the domain of colors (instead processing them holistically). The type of processing may also be related to development (e.g., Burns, Shepp, McDonough, and Wiener-Ehrlich, 1978; Kemler, 1983; Smith, 1981). As children grow older, they appear to shift from processing stimuli holistically to processing them analytically (see Keil & Kelly in Chapter 17, this volume). In addition, adults can be induced to process stimuli holistically under certain task conditions, such as under time pressure (e.g., Ward, 1983).

It is not clear whether the distinction between holistic and analytic processing also applies to SP categories. One possibility is that people prefer holistic processing during classification tasks and analytic processing during discrimination tasks. During classification, people may compare test items to prototypes or exemplars in a holistic manner. Rather than performing individual attribute comparisons and then integrating the outcomes, people may compare the gestalt of all attributes simultaneously to representations in memory. In contrast, having to discriminate between highly similar stimuli in same-different tasks may cause subjects to focus on specific dimensions relevant to making discriminations. This switch to analytic processing may cause stimuli that are subjectively perceived as identical during holistic identification to become perceived as different during analytic discrimination. Consequently, categories may be perceived as more "categorical" during classification processing than during discrimination processing.

Another possibility is that how people process speech stimuli depends on whether they are listening in a speech or nonspeech mode. When people listen to speech as part of natural language communication, they may tend to process stimuli more holistically. In contrast, when they listen to speech detached from communication contexts in laboratory circumstances with highly restricted ranges of stimuli, they may tend to process stimuli more analytically.

Cue validity versus category validity. Attributes that are highly diagnostic for category membership have high *cue validity,* which is the probability that something is a category member given that it has the attribute (i.e., cue). In contrast, attributes that are highly inferrable from category membership have high *category validity* – the probability that something has an attribute given that it is a category member. For example, "automatic transmission" has high cue validity for "vehicles" because anything possessing this property has a high probability of being a vehicle. In contrast, "four-legged" has high category validity for "dogs" because every dog has a high probability of having this attribute. Notably, automatic transmission has low category validity because many vehicles do not possess this property, and four-legged has low cue validity because many other categories exhibit this attribute.

Cue validity is central to classification, whereas category validity is central to drawing inferences from category membership. Depending on the relative extents to which categories are used for classification versus inference, their representations may be biased toward information high in cue or category validity. Although much work in cognitive psychology has associated inference with GK categories, people certainly also draw inferences on the basis of SP classifications. Such inferences may be necessary for repairing imperfections in natural speech signals. When speakers fail to provide all the attributes of a phoneme, the attributes actually provided may be sufficient to activate a SP category such that the missing attributes are supplied by its representation (as in the phonemic restoration effect). Such inferencing could cause people to "hear" phonemes that are not completely specified in the speech signal.

Evidence bearing on the way highly diagnostic and highly inferrable information is represented and processed in GK categories is sparse (although see Medin, Wattenmaker, & Michalski, in press; Tversky, 1977). Even sparser are theories that acknowledge and account for these two kinds of information. Although cue validity in GK categories has received some attention (see Jones 1983; Medin, 1982; Murphy, 1982; Rosch et al., 1976a), little attention has been given to how and when people make inferences from category representations to individual instances. Given that inference also occurs for SP categories, work is needed in this domain too. In addition, much remains to be learned about the role of cue validity in accessing SP categories (although see Repp and Liberman in Chapter 3 and Eimas et al. in Chapter 5, this volume, for relevant discussions).

In summary, there appear to be a number of areas of mutual concern for SP and GK categories. In fact, it appears that most issues of any concern in one area are relevant to the other area as well. These issues are summarized in Table 16.3.

Conclusion

Even minimal exposure to either the SP or the GK category literatures indicates that competing theoretical perspectives and diverse methodological techniques and issues abound. Regardless of the framework one adopts, however, we believe it important to bear ecological considerations in mind. Although manipulating variables in well-controlled and highly artificial laboratory settings is essential for the development and evaluation of theories, ultimately these theories must be about categorization in the real world. In both the SP and GK domains, there has been an increasing recognition that category representations are suffused with detailed

Table 16.3. *Points of future comparison between sensory perception (SP) and generic knowledge (GK) categories*

Reference points
Where reference points are located
  Boundaries
  Centers
  Ideals
Consequences of reference points
  Improved discriminability
  Assimilation
  Asymmetric similarity judgments
Uses of reference points in classification
  Boundary versus prototype classification

Prototypes, exemplars, and decision rules
The role of exemplars in classification
Additive versus multiplicative decision rules

Flexibility
Adaptation and range effects
  The role of exemplars
  The relationship between abstractness and adaptation
Contextual priming

Processing variables
Holistic versus analytic processing
  Differential use in discrimination and classification processing
  Differential use in speech and nonspeech processing
Cue validity versus category validity
  Representation and processing of highly diagnostic and highly inferrable information

---

knowledge that facilitates interaction with highly specific, natural contexts (e.g., Diehl & Kluender in Chapter 7, this volume; Murphy & Medin, 1985). Another ecological consideration has to do with the relation between speech perception and speech production. It would be surprising if speech perception turned out to have nothing to do with speech production, although the exact nature of this relation remains obscure.

We do not pretend that this review represents any kind of "objective" assessment of the similarity between SP and GK categories. These category types have both common and unique attributes; their similarity hinges on the extent to which one focuses on what is shared or what is unique. For some purposes it may be useful to focus on distinguishing attributes, but we have chosen to focus on the shared ones because doing so has strongly suggested common underlying categorization processes.

We noted many similarities between SP and GK categories with respect to basic issues in categorization. Both assume that concepts decompose into attributes and that these attributes form similar kinds of category structures. Classification in both domains could use rules, prototypes, exemplars, or boundary reference points. Categories in both domains are used for classification, inference, generation, and production. Category acquisition in both domains is affected by innate learning sensitivities as well as by experience. Finally, although categories in both domains exhibit stability, they also exhibit a high degree of adaptive flexibility.

Empirically, both domains show sharp identification functions, within-category discrimination, typicality effects, and reference-point effects. Such strong similarities suggest that similar categorization processes construct and operate on both SP and GK categories. Theoretical similarities parallel these empirical similarities. Both domains have used prototype models, continuous versus discrete processing models, dual-processing models, and psychophysical models. Because work with GK categories has been carried on in relative isolation from SP research and vice versa, these similarities in some cases have the character of independent discoveries. It would clearly be preferable, however, if contact were made between similar enterprises in the two areas.

Our conclusion that there are deep similarities between SP and GK categories came with at least as much a surprise to us as it might have for the reader. We hope that future reviews of these interrelationships can be written in terms not of surprise but of concrete progress.

Notes

1. For the remainder of the paper, we will use "attribute" when referring to any kind of feature, component, or property of a stimulus that can be represented by an information processing system. We make no assumptions about the format of these representations (e.g., whether it is propositional or analog) nor do we assume that the attributes correspond to innate detectors. By "concept" we mean a description of a class; normally the description is intensional, based on attributes possessed by some or all category members.
2. This discussion has assumed that the basic units of speech perception are phonemes. However, there is no consensus on this point because various investigators argue that other units (e.g., diphones, demisyllables) are basic. Although there is disagreement about the attributes of SP categories, much more progress in identifying attributes nevertheless appears to have been made for these categories than for GK categories.
3. Note that there is a problem with including disjunctive rules in the domain of defined categories. A disjunctive rule would allow a category to be defined by enumeration, which at best is a degenerate case of a defined category (e.g., the category of primary compass directions is either north, south, east, or west). On the other hand, requiring that a defined category must exhibit a many-to-one mapping also runs into problems (e.g., for categories with one member).
4. Actually this is only one sense of "exemplar" as it has been used recently in the GK category literature. Whereas some theorists call exemplars memories of specific encounters with category members (e.g., Hintzman, 1986; Jacoby & Brooks, 1984), others consider them generic representations of particular encounters that may develop after many encounters with them (see Medin & Schaffer, 1978). Whereas the former sense of "exemplar" refers to memories of specific episodes, the latter refers to generic representations that may result from processing episodes. This difference in definition bears little, if any, on our current discussion.
5. The following difference between single-valued reference points and multivalued reference points may result in different sensitivity patterns around them. Reference points that are single values on dimensions can result in stimuli being coded in qualitatively different ways with respect to them (i.e., above the

reference point or below the reference point). In contrast, multiattribute reference points do not create such clear divisions among stimuli. Instead, stimuli only vary in how *similar* they are on the constellation of attributes that comprise these reference points. The different ways in which these two kinds of reference points order stimuli may be responsible for different patterns of sensitivity.

6. Birnbaum's (1982) systextual design – embedding a factorial design in variable ranges of correlated attributes – may provide a good analytical tool for investigating these issues.

References

Altom, M. W., & Lingle, J. H. (1980). Episodic and categorical processes in impression change. In L. Ross (Chair). *Problems in reconceptualization: Integrating new facts with old concepts*. Symposium presented at the meeting of the American Psychological Association, Montreal.

American Psychiatric Association (1980). *The diagnostic and statistical manual of mental disorders* (3rd ed.). Washington, DC: American Psychiatric Association.

Anderson, J. A., Silverstein, J. W., Ritz, S. A., & Jones, R. S. (1977). Distinctive features, categorical perception, and probability learning: Some applications of a neural model. *Psychological Review, 84*, 413–451.

Anglin, J. M. (1977). *Word, object, and conceptual development*. New York: Norton.

Armstrong, S. L., Gleitman, L. R., & Gleitman, H. (1983). On what some concepts might not be. *Cognition, 13*, 263–308.

Barsalou, L. W. (1983). Ad hoc categories. *Memory & Cognition, 11*, 211–227.

Barsalou, L. W. (1985). Central tendency, ideals, and frequency as determinants of graded structure. *Journal of Experimental Psychology: Learning, Memory and Cognition, 11*, 629–654.

Barsalou, L. W. (1987). The instability of graded structure: Implications for the nature of concepts. In U. Neisser (Ed.), *Concepts and conceptual development: Ecological and intellectual factors in categorization*. Cambridge: Cambridge University Press.

Barsalou, L. W., & Sewell, D. R. (1984). Constructing representations of categories from different points of view. *Emory Cognition Project Technical Report* Number 2, Emory University.

Bellezza, F. S. (1984a). Reliability of retrieval from semantic memory: Common categories. *Bulletin of the Psychonomic Society, 22*, 324–326.

Bellezza, F. S. (1984b). Reliability of retrieval from semantic memory: Information about people. *Bulletin of the Psychonomic Society, 22*, 511–513.

Bellezza, F. S. (1984c). Reliability of retrieval from semantic memory: Noun meanings. *Bulletin of the Psychonomic Society, 22*, 377–380.

Berlin, B., Breedlove, D. E., & Raven, P. H. (1973). General principles of classification and nomenclature in folk biology. *American Anthropologist, 75*, 214–242.

Birnbaum, M. H. (1982). Controversies in psychological measurement. In B. Wegnener (Ed.), *Social attitudes and psychophysical measurement*. Hillsdale, N.J.: Erlbaum.

Bourne, L. E., Jr. (1970). Knowing and using concepts. *Psychology Review, 77*, 546–556.

Bourne, L. E., Jr., Dominowski, R. L., Loftus, E. F. (1979). *Cognitive processes*. Englewood Cliffs, NJ: Prentice-Hall.

Burns, B., Shepp, B. E., McDonough, P., & Wiener-Ehrlich, W. U. (1978). The relation between stimulus analyzability and perceived dimensional structure. In G. H. Bower (Ed.), *The psychology of learning and motivation* (Vol. 12). New York: Academic Press.

Carey, S. (1982). Semantic development: the state of the art. In E. Wanner & L. R. Gleitman (Eds.), *Language acquisition: The state of the art*. New York: Cambridge University Press.

Clark, E. V. (1973). What's in a word? On the child's acquisition of semantics in his first language. In T. E. Moore (Ed.), *Cognitive development and the acquisition of language*. New York: Academic Press.

Crowder, P. G. (1980). Disinhibition of masking in auditory sensory memory. *Memory & Cognition, 10*, 424–433.

Diehl, R. L. (1981). Feature detectors for speech: A critical reappraisal. *Psychological Bulletin, 89*, 1–18.

Diehl, R. L., Lang, M., & Parker, E. M. (1980). A futher parallel between selective adaptation and contrast. *Journal of Experimental Psychology: Human Perception and Performance, 6*, 24–44.

Durlach, N. T., & Braida, L. D. (1969). Intensity perception I: Preliminary theory of intensity resolution. *Journal of the Acoustical Society of America, 46*, 372–383.

Eich, M. A. (1982). A composite holographic associative recall model. *Psychology Review, 89*, 627–661.

Fried, L. S., & Holyoak, K. J. (1984). Induction of category distributions: A framework for classification learning. *Journal of Experimental Psychology: Learning, Memory and Cognition, 10*, 234–257.

Fujisaki, H., & Kawashima, T. (1970). Some experiments on speech perception and a model for the perceptual mechanism. *Annual Report of the Engineering Research Institute, 29*, 207–214.

Garner, W. R. (1974). *The processing of information and structure.* New York: Wiley.

Halff, H. M., Ortony, A., & Anderson, R. C. (1976). A context-sensitive representation of word meanings. *Memory & Cognition, 4*, 378–383.

Hary, J. M., & Massaro, D. W. (1982). Categorical results do not imply categorical perception. *Perception and Psychophysics, 32*, 409–418.

Heider, E. R. (1971). "Focal" color areas and the development of color names. *Developmental Psychology, 4*, 447–455.

Heider, E. R. (1972). Universals in color naming and memory. *Journal of Experimental Psychology, 93*, 10–20.

Hintzman, D. L. (1986). "Schema abstraction" in a multiple-trace memory model. *Psychological Review, 93*, 411–428.

Hintzman, D. L., & Ludlam, G. (1980). Differential forgetting of prototypes and old instances: Simulation by an exemplar-based classification model. *Memory & Cognition, 8*, 378–382.

Holyoak, K. J. (1978). Comparative judgments with numerical reference points. *Cognitive Psychology, 10*, 203–243.

Jacoby, L. L., & Brooks, L. R. (1984). Non-analytic cognition: Memory, perception, and concept learning. In G. Bower (Ed.), *The psychology of learning and motivation* (Vol. 18). New York: Academic Press.

Jacoby, L. L., & Dallas, M. (1981). On the relationship between autobiographical memory and perceptual learning. *Journal of Experimental Psychology: General, 3*, 306–340.

Jacoby, L. L., & Witherspoon, O. (1982). Remembering without awareness. *Canadian Journal of Psychology, 36*(2), 300–324.

Jones, G. V. (1983). Identifying basic categories. *Psychological Bulletin, 94*, 423–428.

Keil, F. C. (1979). *Semantic and conceptual development.* Cambridge, MA: Harvard University Press.

Kemler, D. G. (1983). Holistic and analytic modes in perceptual and cognitive development. In T. Tighe & B. E. Shepp (Eds.), *Perception, cognition, and development: Interactional analyses.* Hillsdale, NJ: Erlbaum.

Labov, W. (1973). The boundaries of words and their meanings. In C. J. Bailey & R. Shuy (Eds.), *New ways of analyzing variation in English.* Washington, DC: Georgetown University Press.

Lakoff, G. (in press). *Women, fire, and dangerous things: What categories tell us about the nature of thought.* Chicago: Chicago University Press.

Lawrence, D. H. (1949). Acquired distinctiveness of cues: I. Transfer between discriminations on the basis of familiarity with the stimulus. *Journal of Experimental Psychology, 39*, 770–784.

Lawrence, D. H. (1950). Acquired distinctiveness of cues: II. Selective association in a constant stimulus situation. *Journal of Experimental Psychology, 40*, 175–188.

Liberman, A. M., Harris, K. S., Hoffman, H. S., & Griffith, B. C. (1957). The discrimination of speech sounds within and across phoneme boundaries. *Journal of Experimental Psychology, 54*, 358–368.

Lingle, J. H., Altom, M. W., & Medin, D. L. (1984). Of Cabbages and kings: Assessing the extendability of natural object concept models to social things. In R. S. Wyer & T. K. Srull (Eds.), *Handbook of social cognition* (Vol. 1). Hillsdale, NJ: Erlbaum.

Markman, E. M. (1979). Classes and collections: Conceptual organization and numerical abilities. *Cognitive Psychology, 11*, 395–411.

Massaro, D. W., & Cohen, M. (1983). Categorical or continuous speech perception: A new test. *Speech Communication, 2*, 15–35.

McClelland, J. L., & Rumelhart, D. E. (1985). Distributed memory and the representation of general and specific information. *Journal of Experimental Psychology: General, 114*, 159–188.

McCloskey, M., & Glucksberg, S. (1978). Natural categories: Well-defined or fuzzy sets? *Memory & Cognition, 6*, 462–472.

McCloskey, M., & Glucksberg, S. (1979). Decision processes in verifying category membership statements: Implications for models of semantic memory. *Cognitive Psychology, 11*, 1–37.

Medin, D. L. (1975). A theory of context in discrimination learning. In G. Bower (Ed.), *The psychology of learning and motivation* (Vol. 9). New York: Academic Press.

Medin, D. L. (1982). Structural principles of categorization. In B. Shepp & T. Tighe (Eds.), *Interaction: Perception, development, and cognition*. Hillsdale, NJ: Erlbaum.

Medin, D. L., & Schaffer, M. M. (1978). A context theory of classification learning. *Psychological Review, 85*, 207–238.

Medin, D. L., & Schwanenflugel, P. J. (1981). Linear separability in classification learning. *Journal of Experimental Psychology: Human Learning and Memory, 7*, 355–368.

Medin, D. L., & Smith, E. E. (1981). Strategies and classification learning. *Journal of Experimental Psychology: Human Learning and Memory, 7*, 241–253.

Medin, D. L., & Smith, E. E. (1984). Concepts and concept formation. *Annual Review of Psychology, 35*, 113–138.

Medin D. L., Wattenmaker, W., & Michalski, R. (in press). Constraints and preferences in inductive learning: Comparing human and machine performance. *Cognitive Science*.

Mervis, C. B. (1980). Category structure and the development of categorization. In R. Spiro, B. C. Bruce, & W. F. Brewer (Eds.), *Theoretical issues in reading comprehension*. Hillsdale, NJ: Erlbaum.

Mervis, C. B., Catlin, J., & Rosch, E. (1976). Relationships among goodness-of-example, category norms, and word frequency. *Bulletin of the Psychonomic Society, 7*, 283–294.

Mervis, C. B., & Pani, J. R. (1980). Acquisition of basic object categories. *Cognitive Psychology, 12*, 496–522.

Mervis, C. B., & Rosch, E. (1981). Categorization of natural objects. *Annual Review of Psychology, 32*, 89–115.

Mervis, C. B., & Roth, E. M. (1981). The internal structure of basic and nonbasic color categories. *Language, 57*, 384–405.

Miller, G. A., & Nicely, P. E. (1955). An analysis of perceptual confusions among some English consonants. *Journal of the Acoustical Society of America, 27*, 338–352.

Miller, J. D., Wier, C. C., Pastore, R. E., Kelly, W. J., & Dooling, R. J. (1976). Discrimination and labelling of noise-buzz sequences of categorical perception. *Journal of the Acoustical Society of America, 60*, 410–417.

Miller, J. L., Conine, C. M., Schermer, T. M., & Kluender, K. R. (1983). A possible basis for internal structure of phonetic categories. *Journal of the Acoustical Society of America, 73*, 2124–2133.

Murphy, G. L. (1982). Cue validity and levels of categorization. *Psychological Bulletin, 91*, 174–177.

Murphy, G. L., & Medin, D. L. (1985). The role of theories in conceptual coherence. *Psychological Review, 92*, 289–316.

Murphy, G. L., & Smith, E. E. (1982). Basic-level superiority in picture categorization. *Journal of Verbal Learning and Verbal Behavior, 21*, 1–20.

Neisser, U. (1987). *Concepts and conceptual development: Ecological and intellectual factors in categorization*. Cambridge: Cambridge University Press.

Nelson, K. (1974). Variations in children's concepts by age and category. *Child Development, 45*, 577–584.

Noreen, D. L. (1981). Optimal decision rules for some common psychophysical paradigms. In S. Grossberg (Ed.), *Mathematical psychology and psychophysiology* (SIAM-AMS Proceedings, Vol. 13). Providence, RI: American Mathematical Society.

Oden, G. C., & Massaro, D. W. (1978). Integrating of featural information in speech perception. *Psychological Review, 85*, 172–191.

Ortony, A. (1979). Beyond literal similarity. *Psychological Review, 86,* 161–180.
Osherson, D. N., & Smith, E. E. (1981). On the adequacy of prototype theory as a theory of concepts. *Cognition, 9,* 35–58.
Palmer, S. E. (1975). Visual perception and world knowledge. In D. A. Norman & D. E. Rumelhart (Eds.), *Explorations in cognition.* San Francisco: W. H. Freeman.
Pastore, R. E. (1978). Phonemes and alphanumeric characters: Possible components of parallel human communication systems. *Visible Language, 12,* 27–42.
Pastore, R. E., Ahroon, W. A., Baffuto, K. J., Friedman, Puleo, J. S., & Fink, E. A. (1977). Common-factor model of categorical perception. *Journal of Experimental Psychology: Human Perception and Performance, 3,* 686–696.
Posner, M. I., & Keele, S. W. (1968). On the genesis of abstract ideas. *Journal of Experimental Psychology, 77,* 353–363.
Reed, S. K. (1972). Pattern recognition and categorization. *Cognitive Psychology, 3,* 382–407.
Repp, B. H. (1984). Categorical perception: Issues, methods, findings. *Speech and Language: Advances in Basic Research and Practice, 10,* 243–335.
Rips, L. J. (1975). Inductive judgments about natural categories. *Journal of Verbal Learning and Verbal Behavior, 14,* 665–681.
Rips, L. J., & Turnbull, W. (1980). How big is big? Relative and absolute properties in memory. *Cognition, 8,* 145–174.
Rosch, E. H. (1973). On the internal structure of perceptual and semantic categories. In T. E. Morre (Ed.), *Cognitive development and the acquisition of language.* New York: Academic Press, 111–144.
Rosch, E. H. (1975a). Cognitive reference points. *Cognitive Psychology, 7,* 532–547.
Rosch, E. H. (1975b). Cognitive representations of semantic categories. *Journal of Experimental Psychology: General, 104,* 192–233.
Rosch, E. H. (1977). Human categorization. In N. Warren (Ed.), *Studies in cross-cultural psychology.* London: Academic Press.
Rosch, E. H. (1978). Principles of categorization. In E. Rosch & B. B. Lloyd (Eds.), *Cognition and categorization.* Hillsdale, NJ: Erlbaum.
Rosch, E. H., & Mervis, C. B. (1975). Family resemblances: Studies in the internal structure of categories. *Cognitive Psychology, 7,* 573–605.
Rosch, E. H., Mervis, C. B., Gray, W. D., Johnson, D. M., & Boyes-Braem, P. (1976a). Basic objects in natural categories. *Cognitive Psychology, 8,* 382–439.
Rosch, E. H., Simpson, C., & Miller, R. S. (1976b). Structural bases of typicality effects. *Journal of Experimental Psychology: Human Perception and Performance, 2,* 491–502.
Roth, E. M., & Mervis, C. B. (1983). Fuzzy set theory and class inclusion relations in semantic categories. *Journal of Verbal Learning and Verbal Behavior, 22,* 509–525.
Roth, E. M., & Shoben, E. J. (1983). The effect of context on the structure of categories. *Cognitive Psychology, 15,* 346–378.
Samuel, A. G. (1982). Phonetic prototypes. *Perception and Psychophysics, 31,* 307–314.
Smith, E. E. (1978). Theories of semantic memory. In W. K. Estes (Ed.), *Handbook of learning and cognitive processes.* Hillsdale, NJ: Erlbaum.
Smith, E. E., & Medin, D. L. (1981). *Categories and concepts.* Cambridge, Mass.: Harvard University Press.
Smith, E. E., Shoben, E. J., & Rips, L. J. (1974). Structure and processes in semantic memory: A featural model for semantic decisions. *Psychological Review, 81,* 214–241.
Smith, L. B. (1981). Importance of the overall similarity of objects for adults' and children's classifications. *Journal of Experimental Psychology: Human Perception and Performance, 7,* 811–824.
Smith, L. B., & Kemler, D. G. (1977). Developmental trends in free classification: Evidence for a new conceptualization of perceptual development. *Journal of Experimental Child Psychology, 24,* 279–298.
Treisman, A. (in press). Properties, parts, and objects. In K. Boff, L. Kaufman, & J. Thomas (Eds.), *Handbook of perception and human performance.*
Tversky, A. (1977). Features of similarity. *Psychological Review, 84,* 327–352.

Tversky, A., & Kahneman, D. (1983). Extensional versus intuitive reasoning: The conjunction fallacy in probability judgment. *Psychological Review, 90,* 293–315.

Tversky, B., & Hemenway, K. (1984). Objects, parts, and categories. *Journal of Experimental Psychology: General, 113,* 169–193.

Ward, T. B. (1983). Response tempo and separable-integral responding: Evidence for an integral-to-separable processing sequence in visual perception. *Journal of Experimental Psychology: Human Perception and Performance, 9,* 103–112.

Whitlow, J. W. (1986). The nature of priming effects in semantic matching. *Journal of Experimental Psychology: Learning, Memory and Cognition, 12,* 353–360.

Williams, L. (1977a). The perception of stop consonant voicing by Spanish-English bilinguals. *Perception & Psychophysics, 21,* 289–297.

Williams, L. (1977b). Voicing contrasts in Spanish. *Journal of Phonetics, 5,* 169–184.

Wittgenstein, L. (1953). *Philosophical investigations.* New York: Macmillan.

17 Developmental changes in category structure

Frank C. Keil and Michael H. Kelly

There is increasing developmental evidence that there are qualitative shifts in the way word meanings are represented. This chapter explores possible parallels between shifts in semantic and conceptual development and corresponding shifts in perceptual development. The primary word meaning shift under discussion is called a "characteristic-to-defining" shift (c/d shift) and is related to the observations of Vygotsky and others that children seem to progress from highly instance-bound representations to more principled, definitional representations. The concept of the c/d shift is new, however, because the phenomenon does not seem to be a monolithic, stage-like metamorphosis of the child's entire conceptual structure. Instead, it occurs on a domain-by-domain basis, at very different points in development, depending on the domain involved. The c/d shift is from representations based on the characteristic features most typically associated with the instances of a concept to representations based on a relatively small number of defining features and/or dimensions that are used to structure the conceptual space. After briefly summarizing some data indicating the existence of the shift, we discuss possible reasons for its occurrence and the sort of general model that might best describe it.

As part of a more general framework for understanding the shift we consider perceptual categorization. The "integral-to-separable" shift seems to be an analogous process in perceptual development. A link between the two kinds of shift is made through a discussion of Rosch's work on prototype and basic level phenomena. In a common developmental pattern, children first treat all salient dimensions in a domain as equivalent in importance (classifying according to maximum similarity across all dimensions); then they came to perceive dimensions less holistically and organize a domain in a more theoretically coherent way, using a few meaningfully related dimensions. These parallels between the c/d shift and the integral-to-separable shift are then illustrated graphically to highlight equally important differences. The generality of this account is further examined in a discussion of developmental changes in phoneme similarity and the acquisition of syntactic categories. Finally, more detailed conjectures about possible common mechanisms underlying the shifts are considered.

The claim has often been made that children's category knowledge differs from that of adults and that dramatic changes occur with development. Proposals about the

Preparation of this chapter was supported by National Science Foundation grants BNS-81-02655 and BNS-8318076 to Frank C. Keil and a National Science Foundation predoctoral fellowship to Michael H. Kelly. The chapter was completed while Frank C. Keil was a fellow at the Center for Advanced Study in the Behavioral Sciences and was supported by the John D. and Catherine T. MacArthur Foundation, the Exxon Foundation, and the Alfred P. Sloan Foundation. We thank Jennifer Freyd for many helpful comments on previous versions of the paper.

nature of this change vary considerably, from the gradual hierarchical integration and differentiation theory of Werner (1948) to the more stagelike accounts offered by Piaget (e.g., 1970) and Bruner et al. (1966). Others, such as Vygotsky (1962), argue that categories change from instance-bound representations to more principled ones. All agree, however, that these underlying changes in category structure are reflected in concomitant changes in children's word meanings. In this chapter, we discuss a view that is close to Vygostky's because of its robustness and because it may describe one of the most general categorical shifts observed, one that applies not only to word meaning but also to perceptual processes and a wide range of other cognitive categories.

New techniques and recent studies have begun to provide a clearer idea of how this shift in category structure occurs for some word meanings and how it might be extended to other categories. In this chapter we first review the evidence that children's word meanings undergo qualitative developmental changes and that a similar shift occurs in perceptual development. We then attempt to specify the parallels between these two developmental changes. We believe that the changes both in the representation of word meanings and in perceptual categories can be subsumed under a general developmental progression from categories organized around typical exemplars to categories organized around defining or principled dimensions. In our conclusion, we make some conjectures about other cognitive and perceptual domains in which the shift might be observed as well as the mechanisms that might underlie this developmental shift.

The characteristic-to-defining shift in word meaning

Vygotsky felt that children's representations of the categories referred to by word meanings were fundamentally different from those of adults in that they were much more tied to concrete instances and less to underlying principles or definitions. Vygotsky's observations echoed the sentiments of observers of children for many centuries before him. Anyone who interacts with young children is struck by how their knowledge of some words often seems to be excessively swayed by particular examples. Anecdotes of this sort describe such things as the child who refuses to call a small hairless dog a dog or who insists that a party with funny hats and a cake must be a birthday party.

Such accounts fail, however, to provide precise descriptions of how the child's category structures change with age. It is assumed that the shift represents some global representational transformation such that, when it occurs, it applies to all the concepts available to the child, as if there were conceptual metamorphoses in which children's entire format for representing concepts changed in a fundamental way. Vygotsky made such a claim and did so for a strongly motivated reason: His view of changes in category structure was part of a broader theory of how language changes the nature of thought. He felt that only as one comes to internalize language does one gain the ability to represent concepts by any other means than concrete instances. Internalized language, according to Vygotsky, frees the child from relying on memories of specific instances and allows more principled representations to be formed. Vygotsky construed this internalization process as implying that the shift must occur at roughly the same time for all concepts, namely, at that point where language has become sufficiently internalized to enable children to distance themselves from particular instances and thereby to form more general, principled, rule-like representations.

Vygotsky was not alone in assuming that shifts of this sort were global. Analogous shifts discussed by Bruner, Olver, and Greenfield (1966), Werner (1948), and Piaget (Inhelder and Piaget, 1958) were also believed to reflect general changes in cognitive structure. If such accounts are correct, they have important implications for the generalizability of the shift to a wide variety of cognitive and perceptual categories. Cases of precise categorical knowledge in infants could not be explained by such a theory because the shift is normally supposed to occur when the child is between 5 and 7 years old. Similarly, cases of such a shift in much older children would be difficult to explain. The shift would have to be confined to a relatively narrow period in the course of development.

The all-or-none view may be wrong, however. There is increasing evidence suggesting that the shift does not occur in its entirety at a particular moment in development. The onset of the shift may depend on the particular area of knowledge being represented. Some domains may undergo conceptual reorganization in infancy, whereas others may be reorganized in adulthood. An important question, of course, is whether conceptual changes in children and adults have different causes and progress in different ways. It is conceivable that the mechanism underlying the shift from instance-bound to principled representation is similar for each category of knowledge, and each period of development. If so, the onset of the shift would depend more on what needs to be categorized and the knowledge needed to do so than on global aspects of cognitive development. The latter possibility has received increasing support from current investigations of the child's acquisition of word meaning.

Some of Vygotsky's initial observations about word meanings influenced a precursor to the view to be presented here, namely Carey's (1978) model of word meaning acquisition. Based on "haphazard-plus-missing features" Carey suggested that, early in development, many word meanings are represented in terms of haphazard examples, which can be highly idiosyncratic. With time, however, the child begins to add features to the meaning that are more systematic and principled. As an example of her model, she used the word "tall" and presented evidence that young children regarded "tall" as being closely tied to the meanings of specific words such that a child may know what it means for a man to be tall (head-to-toe extent) or for a house to be tall (roof-to-street extent), but may not have any generalized, abstracted understanding of "tall" independent of those contexts.

Werner (1948) also provided evidence that children cannot conceive of the meaning of a word apart from very specific situations of use. He argued, for example, that to the child, "size" does not mean an abstract dimension of measurement, but only a standard of comparison relative to specific objects. Thus, of a group of objects, the largest is the "mother," the second largest, the "aunt," and so on, down to the smallest "baby." According to Werner, objects "are ordered not according to size alone, but rather according to 'size' within a family" (p. 227).

Keil and Carroll (1980) tested these ideas more directly by presenting children with different sets of three objects and asking them whether one of the three was taller than the others. In some cases the objects varied in vertical extent (with width held constant) and in other cases they varied in width (with height held constant). Children were right for some objects, but wrong for others, indicating that they had not yet acquired a principled, context-independent meaning for "tall." More important was a finding in a second study showing that even for identical perceptual displays, whether or not "tall" was used correctly depended on the words used to identify the display. For example, children used "tall" appropriately when the display was identified as a house but not when it was labeled an arrow. Thus the difficulty they had in using "tall" was not a function of ease in perceiving tallness in the pictorial display, but rather depended on whether the labeled object (i.e., house vs. arrow) was typically categorized in terms of tallness (as verified by independent adult ratings). (Incidentally, adults who found the application of "tall" to some objects to be pragmatically odd – as in those objects, such as arrows, whose sizes are typically spoken of in terms of length, not height – were nonetheless easily able to pick out the right object as tallest by using the more systematic, content-independent meaning of "extent along the vertical dimension.")

These findings suggested that, at least for the spatial predicates used in the study, a shift from instance-bound to principled or rule-governed concepts occurred. Children seem initially to understand "tall" only with reference to things that are typically classified as tall or short. Later, they distance themselves from these instances and use the more systematic, context-dependent notion of vertical spatial extent, regardless of the objects involved. To make the account more general, however, a description of the shift in terms of changes in conceptual representation was needed. The semantic-memory literature, in particular the work of Smith, Shoben, and Rips (1974), suggested such a reformulation in terms of the characteristic and defining attributes of word meaning. Characteristic attributes are properties that are typically associated with objects referred to by a word but are not the ultimate criteria that determine referents. Defining features, on the other hand, are those that are the final arbiters of whether or not an example is a valid instance of the word. This account has been appropriately criticized on the grounds that few words have clear defining features that are necessary and sufficient to pick out referents (e.g., Smith & Medin, 1981). However, in order best to detect a conceptual shift from particular exemplars of a category to organizing principles, one needs to examine conceptual domains that are (in adults) clearly structured around particular defining dimensions. Given that a number of words from very different conceptual domains do have such features, the characteristic/defining distinction is

Table 17.1. *Examples of stories used in the characteristic-to-defining shift study*

Island	Uncle
+*Characteristic*/ −*Defining* There is this place that sticks out of the land like a finger. Coconut trees and palm trees grow there, and the girls sometimes wear flowers in their hair because it's so warm all the time. There is water on all sides except one. Could that be an island? −*Characteristic*/ +*Defining* On this piece of land, there are apartment buildings, snow, and no green things growing. This piece of land is surrounded by water on all sides. Could that be an island?	+*Characteristic*/ −*Defining* This man your daddy's age loves you and your parents and loves to visit and bring presents, but he's not related to your parents at all. He's not your mommy or your daddy's brother or sister or anything like that. Could that be an uncle? −*Characteristic*/ +*Defining* Suppose your mommy has all sorts of brothers, some very old and some very, very young. One of your mommy's brothers is so young he's only 2 years old. Could that be an uncle?

a good place to start examining semantic development, with the premise that the analysis might extend to other sorts of words as well.

If early knowledge about categories is based on common exemplars, then the attributes most often associated with these frequently occurring instances will predominate in the use and understanding of words that refer to those categories. This reliance on characteristic features should recede in importance as the child develops more analytic knowledge about the categories and starts to understand the dimensions or attributes necessary and sufficient for organizing those concepts. Thus, one can talk about a characteristic-to-defining feature shift as a more specific version of Vygotsky's instance-bound to principled shift.

Keil and Batterman (1984) documented this shift by presenting children with a variety of words that had both clear defining features and highly characteristic ones. Examples include "uncle," "island," "news," and the like. Two sets of stories were constructed for each term, one containing correct characteristic features but incorrect defining features (the $+c/-d$ case) and the other containing highly uncharacteristic features but correct defining ones (the $-c/+d$ case). Examples of these stories are presented in Table 17.1. Young children considered the $+c/-d$ stories as describing a valid instance of the word while the $-c/+d$ stories were consistently rejected. Thus a fellow who acts and looks like a typical uncle but is not related to you was judged as an uncle whereas someone who is two years old but your father's brother was rejected as a possible uncle. Older children gave the opposite pattern of responses, accepting the $-c/+d$ stories and rejecting the $+c/-d$ stories.

An equally important finding of this study was that the shift occurred at different times for different terms. Some terms were evaluated even by the youngest children by considering defining features whereas other terms were evaluated even by fourth graders by focusing on characteristic features. That the shift does not reflect a global change in representational structure is further supported by a follow-up study (Keil, 1986a) in which the shift was examined for terms from different conceptual domains or semantic fields (Lehrer, 1974), such as cooking and kinship. The shift occurred at nearly identical times for many terms drawn from the same field, but often at widely separated times for terms selected from different fields.

Why does the shift occur? Further work has shown that it cannot be accounted for either by changing patterns of adult input or by the idiosyncrasies of Western culture. For example, a study recently completed by Jeyifous and Keil (in preparation) suggests that parents give roughly the same ratio of defining and characteristic features to young and old children when defining concepts for them (even though their explanations vary with age of child in several other respects). The semantic-field data suggest that no general parental strategy change is involved, otherwise the shift ought to occur at roughly the same time for all concepts. Nor is the overall pattern of category development peculiar to Western culture; Jeyifous (1986) has uncovered similar patterns among the Yoruba in Nigeria.

There are many unresolved issues concerning the characteristic-to-defining shift and its implications for theories of semantic development in particular, and cognitive development in general. One important question concerns the scope of the shift: Is it restricted to the acquisition of word meanings or can analogs of the shift be found outside the realm of semantic development? Perceptual categorization is a promising field in which to look for parallels because developmental shifts recently proposed in this area are similar to the characteristic-to-defining shift in word meaning.

Perceptual categorization

Apart from its effects on the study of language development, Vygotsky's work has independently influenced research on the development of perceptual categories. In particular, Vygotsky's block studies suggested a model of how children learn to attend to various perceptual dimensions in categorization tasks. In those tasks children were required to sort groups of blocks into various categories on the basis of critical dimensions, such as size, shape, and color. Younger children tended to sort the objects on the basis of overall similarity between groups of blocks (i.e., on the basis of how similar they were along all the possible dimensions of comparison). With development, according to Vygotsky, "the grouping of objects on the basis of maximum similarity is superseded by grouping on the basis of a single attribute: e.g., only round objects or only flat ones" (1962, p. 77).

This phenomenon was replicated for many years, but only recently have advances in theories of category structure allowed us to understand in detail what is causing this shift in perceptual classification and how it relates to the characteristic-to-defining shift. The two most important advances are the work of Garner and of Rosch. Garner (1974) is now well known for his proposal of a dichotomy between

Developmental changes in category structure

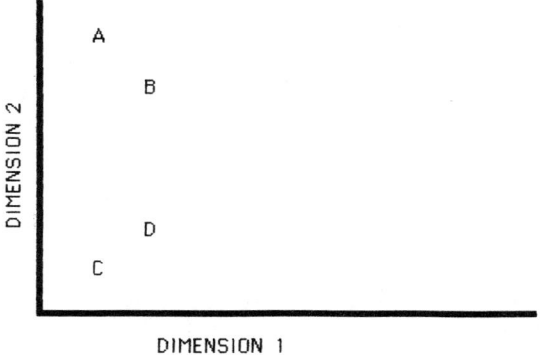

Figure 17.1. Abstract example of the integral/separable shift in perceptual development. Younger children tend to classify A with B and C with D because they are closest to each other in the multidimensional space, although sharing no common value on either relevant dimension. Older children classify A with C and B with D; objects that have a common value on at least one dimension although differing substantially on the other.

integral and separable dimensions in the psychological representation of categories. He proposed that some dimensions of category structure are easily isolable and can be dealt with psychologically as separate units. These might include shape, color, and size. Other dimensions, such as hue and saturation, might not be easily separable from the color they instantiate and thus can only be used independently to classify color after considerable practice and effort.

Garner's proposal led to the developmental speculation that performance on the Vygotsky block task might reflect an integral-to-separable shift. Younger children would treat dimensions such as color and shape as integral to the categories and would be unable to isolate them sufficiently for use in classification. Only later would the dimensions become separable. Kemler and Smith (1978), for example, have conducted a series of studies illustrating how young children often fail to isolate dimensions that older children can isolate. In their more recent papers they have generalized this account to a broader set of categories and drawn links to other work in developmental psychology. Kemler (1983), for example, argues that the integral-to-separable shift is similar to what has often been referred to in the developmental literature as a holistic-to-analytic shift (cf. Werner, 1948). One of the easiest ways to visualize the nature of the shift is to consider objects arrayed in a multidimensional space, as in Figure 17.1.

There are clearly two ways to organize the objects in this space. One way is to sort together those that are closest overall on the different dimensions. With such a technique, objects A and B would form one cluster, and C and D another. The other technique is to group together those objects that share the same values on various dimensions, as would be the case with objects A and C, and B and D. Of course, which strategy is chosen depends not only on the age of the subject, but the types of objects and dimensions involved. Even for adults many dimensions are such that overall proximity may be an easier strategy to use. For example, if there are no obvious boundaries or reference points in the continuum of a dimension, it is more difficult to determine whether two objects share the same value along the dimension. In the cases where the dimension itself consists of discrete attributes or some sort of categorical perception is involved, however, a separable strategy might be easier to use. Note that, as a matter of logic, any "wholistic" similarity could be used as a "principled" basis for categorization. The pertinent factors here are really (a) whether a property is *already* categorized or still *pre*categorical, (b) whether the property is continuous or discrete, and (c) how readily it can be discriminated or categorized. (These issues are discussed in Chapter 19 by Harnad, this volume.)

In the case of categorical perception (CP), perceivers divide up a physical continuum into discrete regions. To the extent that the dimensions specifying an entity are categorically perceived, they may be more likely to be seen separably. If discrete values are assignable, it may be easier to disentangle them from discrete values along other dimensions. Chapter 5 by Eimas, Miller, and Jusczyk and Chapter 9 by Bornstein (this volume) discuss the phenomenon of CP in infants with respect to color and speech sounds. It is interesting that, although young infants already perceive hue categorically, even adults do not normally see it as separable from saturation. Perhaps if saturation were also perceived categorically the two dimensions would be more naturally separable. (The case of speech is discussed in more detail later in this chapter.)

Children have more difficulty using some dimensions separably and are thus forced to rely on the strategy of minimal proximity in the dimensional space or overall similarity. This characterization of the developmental pattern illustrates in greater detail why the wholistic-to-analytic view of development could be valid.

Intuitively, the integral-to-separable shift also seems closely related to the characteristic-to-defining shift. Even the notion that the shift might occur at different times for different domains is compatible if one assumes that the degree of expertise needed to treat a dimension separately varies. Although Kemler and Smith have not discussed the expertise issue extensively in their writings, it is clear from their studies that adults who are given a great deal of experience with the integral dimensions of hue and saturation can learn to shift to sorting separably (see also Kemler, note 1). One way to see the connections between the two patterns of development more clearly is through Rosch's view of category structure.

Rosch's two biggest contributions to the study of categorical structure are the notions of the prototype and the basic level. Her well-known work on prototype structure (e.g., Rosch and Mervis, 1975) has been widely interpreted as showing that the classical views of category structure as consisting of lists of necessary and sufficient features are misguided. Membership in a category is often not an all-or-none affair but a graded phenomenon. The number of characteristics an object shares with other members of a category determines its own status within that category. No one feature is essential, but if an object has a high overall similarity to the most central members of a category, it is also a member.

The relations to the integral-separable distinction become especially clear when one scales prototype-based category structure in multidimensional space, as was originally done by Smith, Shoben, and Rips (1974). The prototype-theoretic basis for categorization in such spaces is essentially the same as integral categorization: Overall similarity on as many dimensions as possible determines membership in a category, rather than the possession of one or two criterial attributes (cf. Tversky & Gati, 1982).

Many have taken Rosch's work as suggesting that representations of categories and concepts can only be in terms of prototypes. This is not the view adopted here. A series of recent studies (e.g. Armstrong, Gleitman, & Gleitman, 1983; McNamara & Sternberg, 1983) reveals that adults do regard many concepts as having necessary, and often sufficient, features. Nonetheless, the prototype notion and the ways in which it can explain similarity judgments are useful constructs for interpreting the developmental patterns found in both the integral-to-separable shift and the characteristic-to-defining shift.

Rosch's studies do not allow us to make unambiguous inferences about what representational formats children are likely to be using when they show either integral or characteristic feature-based judgments. Smith and Medin (1981) present three different views that can approximately model the same phenomena: feature-based approaches, dimensional approaches, and exemplar-based approaches (see Medin & Barsalou, in Chapter 16, this volume). For our purposes it is not necessary to choose between these; it may well be that all three are involved to differing degrees with different types of concepts. In many of the developmental studies we have conducted on children the transcripts suggest that they are referring back to familiar exemplars. Moreover, Kemler (1983) argues strongly for exemplar-based representation in the early stages of learning about categories. In trying to characterize the commonalities between perceptual and conceptual categorization, however, we will find the dimensional view especially useful.

A second major contribution of Rosch is the idea of the basic level of categorization (Rosch, Mervis, Gray, Johnson, & Boyes-Braem, 1976), a level at which categories are most salient and easy to distinguish from each other. The basic level may help to predict the conditions under which the characteristic-to-defining shift will be most pronounced. Vygotsky's views are especially interesting here because he also argued that children form their first concepts at a middle level of generality. However, he believed that these concepts would not be understood in an adultlike manner until the superordinate and subordinate levels were also acquired. The construction of integrated conceptual systems, as opposed to the mere possession of isolated concepts, demands these two other levels, which then permit the child to think "vertically" by moving from one level of generality to the next. Thus, Vygotsky's views on the basic level differ critically from those of Rosch in his

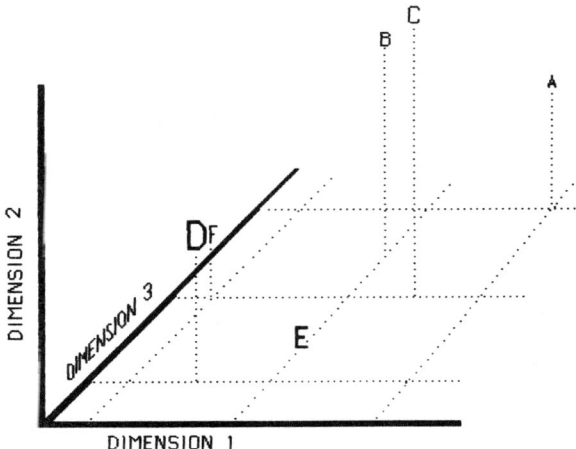

Figure 17.2. Abstract three-dimensional example of the integral/separable shift in perceptual development. Younger children tend to classify A, B, and C together and D, E, and F together because the members of each triplet are closer to each other in the multidimensional space than to any member of the contrasting triplet, although sharing no common value on any of the three relevant dimensions. Older children classify B with E, D with A, and C with F because they have common values on dimensions 1, 2, and 3, respectively, although each member of each pair differs substantially on the other two dimensions.

belief that the concepts of the basic level undergo a shift in representation as the superordinate and subordinate levels are formed.

At present, research on the characteristic-to-defining shift has not specifically addressed Vygotsky's hypothesis. However, the fact that the shift occurs on a domain-by-domain, rather than a term-by-term basis tentatively suggests that understanding the superordinate concept encompassing a set of terms might be a prerequisite for the shift. Whether acquisition of the superordinate level also affects the onset of the integral-to-separable shift remains to be seen. Vygotsky's hypothesis is important, however, because it portrays the various levels of conceptual generality during development in a dynamic, interactive manner. The child does not merely attach a superordinate concept to a preexisting slot in the conceptual hierarchy. Rather, the superordinate level is used to create such a hierarchy, which may require conceptual reorganization at the basic level.

Making more explicit the parallels

Stated in terms sufficiently general to apply to both the integral-to-separable shift and the characteristic-to-defining shift, the developmental pattern is as follows: Early in the acquisition of knowledge about categories children may know so little about the dimensions or organizing principles of a conceptual domain that they (1) cannot perceive in a separable manner the different dimensions that adults use to

Developmental changes in category structure

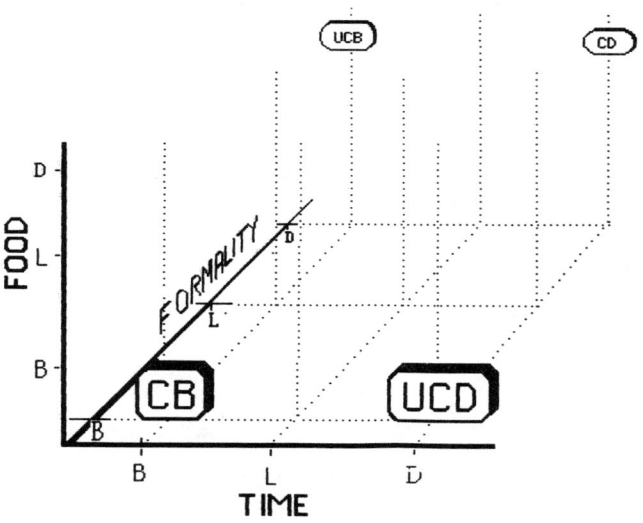

Figure 17.3. Idealized example of the characteristic/defining shift in word-meaning development. Younger children tend to classify UCD with CB and UCB with CD because they are more similar on more dimensions, although not on the defining one, time of day. Older children tend to classify UCD with CD and UCB with CB because they are similar on the defining dimension, time of day, even though they differ dramatically on the two characteristic dimensions of level of formality and types of food served. (Food type clearly does not vary as continuously as the other two dimensions.) [B = Breakfast; L = Lunch; D = Dinner; C = Characteristic; UC = Uncharacteristic.]

organize the domain or (2) although they can perceive these different dimensions, they do not know which are more important than others. Thus, they adopt the strategy of treating all dimensions as roughly equivalent and then they cluster items based on maximum similarity summed across all dimensions. With increasing knowledge and experience, they begin to perceive the dimensions less integrally or learn that a subset of those dimensions, perhaps only one, can be used as an efficient, or socially accepted, or theoretically useful means of organizing those items. There are many ways this shift can be influenced. For example, the weighting of dimensions, attributes, or exemplars may be closely correlated not just with their frequency but also with their salience. Thus, if a critical dimension is particularly salient it may help to organize the conceptual space in a separable or definitional way from the outset. Conversely, if it is very subtle in comparison to other dimensions, the shift may not occur until quite late or only for adults with a particularly relevant area of expertise.

The parallels can be visualized more concretely by assuming a dimensional form of representation and looking at different hypothetical cluster patterns in multidimensional spaces. Figures 17.2 and 17.3 show three-dimensional spaces for the integral/separable schema and for one of the characteristic/defining domains: meal terms (breakfast, lunch, and dinner). In Figure 17.2 the clusters B,C,A and D,F,E

are based on overall similarity on all three dimensions but precise values on any one dimension are not shared. Alternatively, clusters C,F and B,E and D,A are based on items having the same critical value on one dimension. The work of Kemler and Smith and others shows that young children tend to cluster the first way and older children, the second way. Figure 17.3 shows a closely analogous situation for meal terms. Young children are likely to call not only a characteristic breakfast (CB) "breakfast" but also an uncharacteristic dinner (UCD) because it shares the same value with breakfast on two of the three dimensions. They will also reject UCB because it only shares values on one dimension. Older children will call UCB "breakfast" and reject UCD because they pay more attention to the value on one dimension: time of the meal.

There are important differences between these two situations. In Figure 17.2 no one dimension is in principle any more important than any other and the main developmental pattern is the switch to viewing each dimension as an independent organizing principle as opposed to viewing all dimensions as a unified metric. In Figure 17.3 the developmental pattern is the recognition that one dimension in particular is the one along which the concepts should be organized and no other. If precisely the same developmental pattern occurred in 17.3 as in 17.2 then the children should shift toward classifying both UCB and UCD with CB, as they both share the same values with CB, but on different dimensions. In both the characteristic/defining and integral/separable shifts, however, the younger children do something very similar; they tend to cluster on the basis of overall similarity along all dimensions. What they shift to is different in the two cases, and is different yet again for natural kinds (Keil, 1986b); but the starting points are the same.

A related developmental pattern may be that young children often tend to overemphasize correlated properties of objects in their representations of them. In a recent study, Altman (unpublished) exploited the correlation between weight and size by allowing young children to play with two identically sized but differently weighted balls. When later asked to select from a set the pair of balls they had played with, the children consistently erred by choosing a pair in which the heavier one was also the larger one. They make similar distortions in their representations for age and size of silhouettes. These children seem to be so struck by the properties that commonly co-occur in objects that they cannot distentangle them and treat them in a separable manner. It is as if they are treating them integrally rather than separably. This is also a central notion in the construction of prototypes, where the correlations among features are what make the concepts rather than the features themselves.

Further examples and possible mechanisms

The question at hand is how general this developmental pattern is before it becomes too loose an analogy to be useful. There are two ways to consider its generality:

with respect to (1) other instances of shifts that seem to be similar and (2) the types of conditions that could motivate such shifts in conceptual representation.

Extending the examples. Two new cases of shifts in category structure help us explore the generality of the phenomenon: Shifts in phoneme similarity and the development of syntactic categories.

Shifts in phoneme similarity. Trieman and her colleagues (Trieman and Baron, 1981; Trieman and Breaux, 1982) have detected an integral-to-separable shift in the perception of similarity among syllables. Whereas older children and adults classify syllables together if they share an identical phoneme, younger children focus on overall similarity among syllable sounds. Thus, of the three syllables /bun/, /bis/, and /diz/, older children will co-classify the first two, which share the common phoneme /b/, whereas younger children will co-classify the last two, which are more similar overall. Trieman has also found that adults find it more difficult to remember paired associates whose syllables share a common phoneme than paired associates whose syllables sound somewhat similar globally, but share no phoneme. The reverse is true of children. It seems that the immediate perception of the common phoneme disrupts memorization processes or recall for adults. Trieman argues that the common phoneme does not cause problems for children because they do not perceive it. The syllable is perceived at an integrated, global level and cannot be parsed into its phonemic constituents.

These results, as well as others (e.g., Barton, 1980), have important ramifications for the categorical perception of speech. In particular, children may begin to learn the sounds of their language not by parsing words into their constituent phonemes, but by learning global similarities among common syllables. Only with further experience, perhaps even experience with reading, would the child be able to differentiate phonemic categories from an analysis of the internal structure of syllables.

The idea of the syllable as the initial basic level of speech representation rather than phonemes or distinctive features has seen increasing popularity (e.g., Menyuk and Menn, 1979). Eimas et al. (Chapter 5, this volume), for example, argue that dividing a word into phonemic segments might be an unlikely method of language learning. They also suggest that the eventual development of such segmentation might depend, in part, on learning to read. Evidence implicating the importance of reading has been provided by Morais, Cary, Alegria, and Bertelson (1979), who found that illiterate Portugese adults were much less sensitive to phonemic relations than their literate peers.

What are the implications of an integral-to-separable shift in speech perception for interpreting CP in infants? As many investigators of speech perception have argued, perhaps phonemic CP has nothing to do with our unique proclivity for language, but rather with general properties of the human auditory system, properties that might be shared with other species. Certainly the discovery that chinchillas perceive speech sounds categorically (see Kuhl & Miller, 1978 and Chapter 12 by Kuhl, this volume) much the way the human infant does would support such a view (see also Chapter 5 by Eimas et al. and Chapter 11 by Snowdon, this volume). Whatever the interpretation of these comparative investigations, the emphasis on CP in language development is complicated by the finding that young children beginning to learn language do not seem to perceive differences in speech sounds by way of phonemic contrasts. This paradox has led even those who believe in a speech-specific mode of perception to deny that CP supports the existence of this mode one way or the other (cf. Repp, 1982; and Repp & Liberman in Chapter 3, this volume).

Development of syntactic categories. Recent theories about the way children acquire formal lexical categories such as nouns, verbs, and adjectives have posited a type of characteristic-to-defining shift (see Maratsos, 1983; Maratsos & Chalkey, 1980). A formal lexical category, according to Maratsos (1983), is a group of semantically heterogeneous words that have common roles in a grammatical structure and are subject to similar morphological transformations. Thus nouns can vary in semantic content from the concrete and living, such as "boy" and "dog," to the abstract and mental, such as "truth" and "thought." They are united in a formal category despite diversity through their common roles as subjects and objects in sentences. In addition, they can all be combined with similar morphological markers to signify such things as plurality (e.g., "boys," "dogs," "truths," "thoughts") and can be concatenated with "the" to signify definite reference.

How do children acquire lexical categories? It seems they begin by focusing on semantic heterogeneity rather than structural homogeneity. For nouns, at least, they group together words that have highly characteristic features of nounhood, that is, concrete, physical objects. These nouns, of course, share the structural properties described above. After forming their prototype-based initial noun category, children abstract these structural rules and begin to use them in borderline cases. Thus, words that are not semantically very good "nouns" in that they do not refer to common physical objects are nonetheless grouped with the prototypical nouns because they share structural properties. With time, these more reliable structural tests supersede the characteristic, but unreliable, semantic properties and so become the defining features for nounhood (Maratsos, 1983).

Possible mechanisms for the shift. Given the many examples of the characteristic/defining shift in word meaning and the parallels to the integral/separable shift in perceptual development, one wonders not so much about their existence as about their causes. What motivates the shift? In this section, we will offer a few speculations concerning mechanisms, but much empirical and theoretical work remains to be done in this area.

The occurrence of the characteristic/defining shift on a domain-by-domain basis suggests that knowledge of a semantic domain is an important motivating factor. Relative knowledge, of course, calls to mind the expert/novice distinction that has become an increasingly important explanation of differences between children and adults on cognitive tasks. As in areas like memory (see Chi, 1978), the characteristic-to-defining shift may not result from global qualitative differences in cognitive functioning between children and adults, as Vygotsky would argue, but instead from local differences in knowledge. If correct, such an interpretation would predict analogs to the characteristic-to-defining shift in adults, depending on their status as a novice or expert in a particular area. Such an analog has been found by Chi, Feltovich, and Glaser (1981) in their investigation of classification differences between experts and novices in physics. Novices tend to classify physics problems in terms of their explicitly stated characteristic surface features (e.g., "blocks on an inclined plane"). Experts, on the other hand, classify the same problems in terms of the general, defining laws of physics they reflect (e.g., "Newton's second law").

Although the expert-novice distinction is valuable, it is still only a description of a particular factor that influences the characteristic-to-defining shift. Left to be explained is why quantitative increases in knowledge can result in an apparently qualitative change in representations of word meanings, physics problems (for example, see Chi et al., 1981), and so on. Some type of reorganization of this knowledge may drive the shift. Keil (1986b) has argued that this reorganization follows upon the crystallization of a set of theoretical principles that govern a particular domain. Thus, underlying the characteristic-to-defining shift is an atheoretic-to-theoretic shift in the organization of concepts in a domain. The principal motivation for this shift is the inherent atheoretical nature of conceptual domains organized around prototypes. These types of organizations cannot tell us, for example, *why* it is that the various featues typical of birds (e.g., beaks, feathers, wings) are so highly intercorrelated: They simply are. Given this fact, as well as an internal tendency toward principled organization of conceptual domains, one observes a shift away from prototype-based representations to theory-based representations.

Keil (1986b) has provided evidence for a prototype-to-theory shift through investigations of children's understanding of natural kind terms, such as animals and trees (cf. Putnam, 1975). For the young child, membership of an object in a natural-kind category depends on whether that object's features overlap extensively with those that characterize typical members of that category. If an object does not share enough of these features with typical members, or if the features are removed, it is not a member of the category. Thus, if a raccoon is altered to resemble a skunk perceptually and behaviorally, a young child will claim that the animal is no longer a raccoon, but a skunk. Older children, however, will claim that altering such features does not detract from the "essential" identity of the object. They often justify their answers with reference to the origins of the animal, its parents, offspring, and so on. Note that the older children do not have any detailed knowledge of why origins might be important. However, they have a rough "theory" that origins define an animal's identity, and this vague theory organizes their beliefs about the nature of the animal. The characteristic-to-defining shift in word meaning may be a special manifestation of this underlying prototype-to-theory shift. Thus, changes in the child's understanding of natural-kind words and words whose definitions consist of necessary and sufficient features may be the same phenomenon.

That a shift to theory-based organization of concepts can have an impact on the child's understanding of novel words is shown by Carey's (1978, 1985) investigations of the acquisition of the concept "animal." Young children organize their concept of "animal" around a prototype: people. When told, for instance, that people have "spleens," the child's tendency to generalize this attribute to other animals depends on their similarity to people. Thus, children generalize "spleen" to aardvarks more than to dodo birds, and to dodo birds more than to bugs. The centrality of human beings in the young child's concept of "animal" is further emphasized by the finding that children will generalize to bugs an internal organ attributed to people more than they will generalize to bugs an internal organ attributed to bees. This pattern reverses for adults, who, because of their taxonomic theories, treat "animal" as a separable category that divides into people, other mammals, birds, and so on. For young children, however, this concept is integral because it is organized around a single prototype.

Many other factors besides implicit theories could guide the characteristic-to-defining and integral-to-separable shifts. We mention a few here briefly:

Freyd (1983) has recently argued that a "shareability" constraint is imposed on the representation of concepts. By this, she means information that is often shared among members of a community will be transformed so that it is easily and efficiently communicated. This transformation will act to reduce a complex domain of knowledge to a few criterial dimensions and values along those dimensions. For example, the meanings of kinship terms could be defined along a number of dimensions as in maternal versus paternal relations, age, sex, sibling, and so on. Cultures, however, usually only select a subset of those dimensions as being relevant to kinship relations. To the extent that a body of information is to be widely shared among members of a community, there is a pressure on the community to organize that knowledge unambiguously along selected dimensions and on the individual to adhere consistently to those dimensions. Shareability does not predict which dimensions will be emphasized; rather, it suggests that once certain dimensions become emphasized on the societal level, they acquire a central organizing role in the conceptual representation of the individual. Tarr (1984) has provided evidence that communicative demands can influence the likelihood of a separable or integral organization of a multidimensional space; Jusczyk (1985) suggests that communicative pressure may even have similar effects at the phonemic level. There is a related line of research in social psychology on the effects of communicative settings on conceptual structure: Increased communicative demands can markedly influence conceptual structure toward a more conventionalized format (Krauss, Vivekanthan, & Weinheimer, 1968; Werner & Kaplon, 1963).

One final mechanism that could be related to the integral-separable shift is the word itself. Vygotsky (1979) argued that the word is not only a sign that "carries" or "conveys" meaning. It is also a tool that the child uses to sharpen understanding of the underlying concept and to home in on the adult category it designates. Vygotsky suggests the original function of the word is that of a tool rather than a sign. The word acts as an indicator that directs attention to the similarity between objects and aids in abstracting the dimensions of similarity. Attaching a lexical label to a concept seems to make the child focus more on specific contrasting features than on overall similarity. Clark's (1983) recent lexical contrast theory of meaning acquisition emphasizes a view similar to Vygotsky's.

Some recent evidence gathered by Markman and Hutchinson (1984) supports such a "directing" influence of words. It has been known for many years, and is discussed by Vygotsky and by Werner, that children often sort objects in terms of thematic rather than taxonomic relations. Thus, when presented with a dog, cat, and bone and asked which two belong together, younger children select the dog and bone whereas older children select the dog and cat. Markman and Hutchinson found, however, that when told that a dog is a "fep" and then asked to find another "fep," young children will select the cat rather than the bone. This work implies that children separate the category of "what goes together" from "what is called by the same name." The power of the word to direct attention to taxonomic relations with familiar as well as unfamiliar objects could extend into the integral-separable shift. Perhaps naming objects directs the child toward finding dimensional characteristics that form the meaning of this name. When in a standard integral/separable task children are asked to select the two things that go together, they tend to take the two objects with the greatest overall similarity. If they were asked to select the two things called by the same name, more separable responses might be observed. Perhaps if the experimenter gave the child different types of pretraining, say, by showing the child two objects that shared a dimension and telling the child either that these objects "go together" or "are both called 'fep'" one might observe more separable dimension-based responses in the test phase for the latter condition. Such experiments remain to be performed, but given the child's felicitously rapid learning of new words, such a "word-as-tool" view certainly seems possible. Viewed in the context of Harnad's chapter (Chapter 19, this volume), the sharing of names by two objects may force the child to use a more analytic strategy in searching for the defining features underlying the co-categorization, whereas merely being told that they "go together" in some open-ended way may favor a wholistic strategy.

Conclusions

In this chapter, we have described some widely observed developmental changes in category structure in order to explore their generality and their common mechanisms. We have suggested that the initial structure of category knowledge is similar across a wide range of cases of human categorization. Overall similarity among items is emphasized as organizing early category knowledge, with the consequence that no one dimension, feature, or principle is paramount in organizing the conceptual space. As representations of category structure develop, however, they diverge into a large number of different structural types that share the common theme of a shift toward an emphasis on just a few defining dimensions or principles as being primarily responsible for category structure. This general sort of shift is observed in categories as diverse as those for animals, syntax, and phonemes. We have speculated that the early representations are often exemplar-based models (see Kemler, 1983), although it may well turn out that different mechanisms (e.g., feature-based, exemplar-based, or dimensional ones) are at work in different category domains. We also argued that how and when the shift occurs is frequently a function of experience, knowledge, and expertise.

Although this chapter has focused primarily on changes in category structure with development, it does not assume that invariant patterns might not also be observed. On the contrary, we firmly believe that a variety of principles of category structure are determined by a priori domain-specific and domain-general constraints and predispositions. Even in the earliest stages, children do not select all the logically possible features or dimensions that could conceivably be used in a computation of overall similarity. Universally shared constraints could make some features more salient than others in organizing a domain and thus it is only within this subset of features that the shifts we have discussed are occurring. In addition, broad structural constraints on conceptual structure may be at work throughout the period during which knowledge differentiates and shifts away from early exemplar-bound representations. Thus, although children who organize their concept of hand tools around characteristic features may confuse one tool with another because of overall similarity, they tend to know simultaneously that all tools share certain structural properties that cannot be violated (e.g., not being alive). If early representations were completely based on overall similarity relations without any guiding constraints that laid down a skeletal conceptual framework, it is difficult to see how knowledge acquisition could proceed so successfully and quickly in the first place (see Keil, 1981). We therefore consider it essential that the developmental changes we have discussed here be viewed against a backdrop of constraints and predispositions that provide a kind of trellis within which the vines of categorical structure are able to differentiate.

References

Altman, R. (1984). Correlated features in development. Unpublished senior honors thesis, Cornell University.
Armstrong, S., Gleitman, L. R., & Gleitman, H. (1983). What some concepts might not be. *Cognition, 13,* 263–308.
Barton, D. (1980). Phonemic perception in children. In G. H. Yeni-Komshian, J. F. Kavanagh, & C. A. Ferguson (Eds.), *Child phonology. Vol. 2: Perception.* New York: Academic Press.

Bruner, J. S., Olver, R. R., & Greenfield, P. M. (1966). *Studies in cognitive growth.* New York: Wiley.
Carey, S. (1978). The child as a word learner. In M. Halle, J. Bresnan, & G. Miller (Eds.), *Linguistic theory and psychological reality.* Cambridge, MA: MIT Press.
Carey, S. (1985). *Conceptual change in childhood.* Cambridge, MA: MIT/Bradford Press.
Chi, M. T. H. (1978). Knowledge structures and memory development. In R. S. Siegler (Ed.), *Children's thinking: What develops?* Hillsdale, NJ: Erlbaum.
Chi, M. T. H., Feltovich, P., & Glaser, R. (1981). Categorization and representation of physics problems by experts and novices. *Cognitive Science, 5,* 121–152.
Clark, E. V. (1983). Meanings and concepts. In P. Mussen (Ed.), *Handbook of child psychology* (vol. 3). New York: Wiley.
Freyd, J. J. (1983). Shareability: The social psychology of epistemology. *Cognitive Science, 7,* 191–210.
Garner, W. R. (1974). *The processing of information and structure.* Potomac, MD.: Erlbaum.
Inhelder, B., & Piaget, J. (1958). *The growth of logical thinking from childhood to adolescence.* New York: Basic Books.
Jeyifous, S. (1986). Antimodemo: Semantic and conceptual development among the Yoruba. Unpublished doctoral dissertation, Cornell University.
Jusczyk, P. W. (1985). On characterizing the development of speech perception. In J. Mehler & R. Fox (Eds.), *Neonate cognition: Beyond the blooming, buzzing confusion.* Hillsdale, NJ: Erlbaum.
Keil, F. C. (1981). Constraints on knowledge and cognitive development. *Psychological Review, 88,* 197–227.
Keil, F. C. (1986a). On the structure dependent nature of stages of cognitive development. In I. Levin (Ed). *Stage and structure: Reopening the debate,* Norwood, NJ: Ablex.
Keil, F. C. (1986b). On the acquisition of natural kind and artifact terms. In W. Demopolous (Ed.), *Conceptual change.* Norwood, NJ: Ablex.
Keil, F. C., & Batterman, N. (1984). A characteristic-to-defining shift in the development of word meaning. *Journal of Verbal Learning and Verbal Behavior, 23,* 221–236.
Keil, F. C., & Carroll, J. J. (1980). The child's conception of "tall": Implications for an alternative view of semantic development. *Papers and Reports on Child Language Development, 19,* 21–28.
Kemler, D. G., & Smith, L. B. (1978). Is there a developmental trend from integrality to separability in perception? *Journal of Experimental Child Psychology, 26,* 498–507.
Kemler, D. G. (1983). Exploring and reexploring issues of integrality, perceptual sensitivity, and dimensional salience. *Journal of Experimental Child Psychology, 36,* 365–379.
Kemler, D. G. The effect of intention on what concepts are acquired. Manuscript submitted for publication.
Kuhl, P. K., & Miller, J. D. (1978). Speech perception by the chinchilla: Identification functions for synthetic VOT stimuli. *Journal of the Acoustical Society of America, 63,* 905–917.
Lehrer, A. (1974). *Semantic fields and lexical structure.* Amsterdam: North-Holland.
Maratsos, M. (1983). Some current issues in the study of the acquisition of grammar. In P. Mussen (Ed.), *Handbook of child psychology* (vol. 3.). New York: Wiley.
Maratsos, M., & Chalkey, M. A. (1980). The internal language of children's syntax: The ontogenesis of syntactic categories. In K. E. Nelson (Ed.), *Children's language* (vol. 2). New York: Gardner Press.
Markman, E. M., & Hutchinson, J. E. (1984). Children's sensitivity to constraints on word meaning: Taxonomic versus thematic relations. *Cognitive Psychology, 16,* 1–27.
McNamara, T. P., & Sternberg, R. J. (1983). Mental models of word meaning. *Journal of Verbal Learning and Verbal Behavior, 22,* 449–474.
Menyuk, P., & Menn, L. (1979). Early strategies for the perception and production of words. In P. Fletcher & H. Garman (Eds.), *Studies in language acquisition.* Cambridge: Cambridge University Press.
Morais, J., Cary, L., Alegria, L., & Bertelson, P. (1979). Does awareness of speech as a sequence of phones arise spontaneously? *Cognition, 7,* 323–331.
Piaget, J. (1970). Piaget's theory. In P. H. Mussen (Ed.), *Carmichael's manual of child psychology* (vol. 1). New York: Wiley.

Putnam, H. (1975). The meaning of meaning. In H. Putnam (Ed.), *Mind, language, and reality* (vol. 2). Cambridge: Cambridge University Press.

Repp, B. H. (1982). Phonetic trading relations and context effects: New experimental evidence for a speech mode of perception. *Psychological Bulletin, 92,* 81–110.

Rosch, E., & Mervis, C. (1975). Family resemblances: Studies in the internal structure of categories. *Cognitive Psychology, 7,* 573–605.

Rosch, E., Mervis, C. B., Gray, W. D., Johnson, D., & Boyes-Braem, P. (1976). Basic objects in natural categories. *Cognitive Psychology, 8,* 382–439.

Smith, E. E., & Medin D. L. (1981). *Categories and concepts.* Cambridge, MA: Harvard University Press.

Smith, E. E., Shoben, E. J., & Rips, L. J. (1974). Structure and process in semantic memory: A featural model for semantic dimensions. *Psychological Review, 81,* 214–241.

Tarr, M. J. (1984). *Shareability: Constraints on the sharing of knowledge.* Unpublished senior honors thesis, Cornell University.

Trieman, R., & Baron, J. (1981). Segmental analysis ability: Development and relation to reading ability. In T. G. Waller & G. E. MacKinnon (Eds.), *Reading research: Advances in theory and practice* (vol. 3). New York: Academic Press.

Trieman, R., & Breaux, A. M. (1982). Common phoneme and overall similarity relations among spoken syllables: Their use by children and adults. *Journal of Psycholinguistic Research, 11,* 569–597.

Tversky, A., & Gati, I. (1982). Similarity, separability and the triangle inequality. *Psychological Review, 89,* 123–154.

Vygotsky, L. S. (1962). *Thought and language.* Cambridge, MA.: MIT Press.

Vygotsky, L. S. (1979). The development of higher forms of attention in children. *Soviet Psychology, 18,* 67–115.

Werner, H. (1948). Comparative psychology of mental development (2nd. ed.). New York: International Universities Press.

Werner, H., and Kaplon, B. (1968). *Symbol Formation.* New York: International Universities Press.

18 Spatial categories: The perception and conceptualization of spatial relations

Ellen Bialystok and David R. Olson

The mental representation assigned to spatial displays in both perception and conception is described in terms of propositional representations that are both relational and categorical. Differences in the explicitness of these representations account for traditional distinctions between perception and conception. Differences in the richness of these representations account for distinctions between analogical and digital representational formats. The propositional representation consists of a predicate and two arguments. The first argument, the referent, specifies the features or objects being located; the second, the relatum, specifies the frame of reference in which that location is defined. The predicate is a categorical spatial concept that describes the relation between the object (referent) and the frame of reference (relatum).

A systematic means of operating on these propositional representations that yields the correct solution to a variety of spatial problems is proposed. These procedures, it is claimed, are sufficiently general to apply across a variety of spatial problems, yet sufficiently specific to yield the correct solution to each and to account for patterns of difficulty in observed responses. In addition, the development of these procedures can be traced through children of different ages who are able to solve increasingly difficult spatial problems. The procedures involve three steps, each of which corresponds to one of the three major components of the spatial proposition.

The perception and knowledge of spatial relations is an ideal domain for analysis of categorical processes. Phenomenally, space seems to be completely continuous and homogeneous, stretching without seam in three open-ended dimensions. In addition, more than other domains of knowledge, spatial relations have invited the invention of theories of noncategorical representations, such as mental images, to account for the apparently noncategorical nature of continuous space.

Work on the semantic representation of spatial relations by such writers as Bierwisch (1967), Miller and Johnson-Laird (1976), and Jackendoff (1983), however, has made it evident that at some point in the perception and interpretation of the physical world, spatial information must be translated, recoded, or transformed into relational structures that preserve properties like shape, size, orientation, direction, and dimensionality. Characterizing this translational operation is still an unsolved problem to which several chapters in this volume are directed. Yet there is little doubt that the end product of this operation is a set of categorical, semantic distinctions: *on/off, in/out, above/below,* and the like. These categories may be expressed either explicitly in spatial language or implicitly in the spatial representations of objects and events. The letters of the alphabet, for example, are treated as objects but involve a set of implicit spatial representations. Letters are either open or closed (e.g., *C* vs. *O*), constituent shapes either touch each other or are separated (*b* vs. *lo*), either angular or curved (*V* vs. *U*), are formed with distinctive up/down and left/right orientations, and so on. Any particular letter could be described as a collection of such binary contrasts.

Our central argument is that the mental representations of the spatial properties that give rise to distinctive objects, such as letters of the alphabet, and spatial concepts, such as *above* or *in front,* which are used in such relational constructions as "a car *in front* of a house," are structurally equivalent. Both are spatial, categorical, relational, and propositionally coded.

In advancing this view, we are collapsing some of the distinctions regarding representational format common in the literature. We argue that there is one kind of representational format, which may vary in explicitness and richness. Differences in explicitness account for the perceptual/conceptual distinction; differences in richness account for the analog/digital distinction. Only when representations are explicit and assigned to relations does space become an object of thought such that spatial relations become subject to intentional assignment and reassignment required to solve the spatial tasks that we shall describe. These representations, as we claimed, are necessarily categorical.

In some cognitive domains, the evidence for discrete perceptual categories consists of a "boundary effect" (see Harnad in Chapter 19, this volume) characterized by enhanced discriminability across a category boundary and decreased discriminability within a category. The exemplary case is that of phoneme discrimination (see Pastore in Chapter 1, this volume). For spatial categories, sometimes the boundaries are clear – the *touching/not-touching, pointed/curved, open/closed* features relevant to the recognition of letters of the alphabet would seem to be of this sort – whereas at other times the boundaries are vague but the central tendencies of the category are clear. The latter are "prototypical" categories (Rosch, 1977; Smith, Shoben, & Rips, 1974; see also Medin & Barsalou in Chapter 16, this volume). Although there are prototypical trees and shrubs, for example, the boundary is vague and the classes fade gradually into each other. The most conspicuous spatial categories of this sort are relative distinctions like *near/far, big/small,* and *tall/short.* So too, shape categories such as triangles, rectangles, and ellipses have prototypical members even if, upon examination, they also have sharply bounded features. Common object contrasts like *tree/shrub, chair/stool, bowl/plate* all involve prototypical members and vague boundaries.

It is not clear how the complex object categories relate to more fundamental, presumably universal, spatial categories and concepts. Some of the spatial distinctions that determine the assignment of objects to categories can be related rather directly to the biases of the perceptual system. Ogilvie and Taylor (1958, 1959) showed that for a fine wire to be visible in an oblique orientation, it had to be twice as thick as when it was in a horizontal or vertical orientation. Such acuities both reflect and are reflected in patterns of representation in memory. Thus, Lashley (1938) found that rats could learn to discriminate a horizontal pattern from a vertical one much more easily than a right-oblique from a left-oblique even if the two patterns were separated by 180 degrees in both cases. Similarly, Sutherland (1969) trained octopuses to respond to a rectangular bar placed in various orientations. Whereas they readily learned to discriminate horizontal from vertical orientations, there was no evidence of learning when they were required to discriminate opposite obliques. On the basis of a wide range of such evidence from nonlinguistic animals and linguistic humans, we have concluded that both the perceptual and the conceptual/linguistic systems reflect a profound bias toward seeing and interpreting objects in space in terms of primary categories of *front/back, up/down,* and *left/right;* spatial cognition is basically relational (Olson & Bialystok, 1983). This is a theme we pursue in this chapter.

There may well be special mechanisms for perceiving spatial relations just as there are special mechanisms for phoneme recognition. There is no good reason to believe that a spatial feature or predicate, such as *above,* is any more conceptual or "higher-order" or derived than the voice-onset time feature or predicate that distinguishes the phoneme /p/ from /b/. Nonetheless, our concern in this chapter is less with the ways in which the perceptual system delivers such properties than with an analysis of their structure and the ways in which they are used – first, to represent objects and events, and second, to represent the very spatial properties and relations that had earlier been implicit in those object and event representations. The former we refer to as the perception of objects; the latter, the perception of form.

Because spatial features are both categorical and relational, spatial stimuli fall into one category or another always relative to some frame of reference. This frame of reference constitutes one element of a spatial proposition. By using this theory, we avoid some of the problems associated with theories that postulate noncategorical forms of representation, such as mental images. These theories tend to overestimate the amount of information available in the representation and have difficulty in accounting for changes in the representations that occur with changes in the context of the display (Olson & Bialystok, 1983; Pylyshyn, 1981). Furthermore, mental representations in the form of images simply postpone the problem of specifying the interface between the structure of perception and the structure of language (Miller & Johnson-Laird, 1976). Similarly, verbal representations as a theory of spatial relations provide an inadequate account of spatial knowledge by restricting that knowledge to explicit spatial concepts and relations. Propositions provide an appropriate compromise between images and sentences: they have structure, they are not necessarily verbal or conscious, and yet they are translatable into verbal descriptions. Finally, they are syntactic objects upon which further computational operations may be performed.

The relational nature of spatial propositions is perhaps their most important advantage over other representational forms. Propositional representations of space are relational in that they relate objects, features, or other entities to implied or declared reference frames. Hence, the representation may change as the frames of reference change. Linguistic examples abound. The statement "Harry is tall" is constructed and interpreted only in terms of an implied standard of comparison. If Harry is an adult the mental representation of his height greatly differs from what it would be if Harry were a 4-year-old. We suggest that nonlinguistic spatial structural descriptions, constructed and used in the perception of objects in space, have the same contrastive, relational structure.

Structural descriptions of position are similarly relational. The position of an object, say a cup, is perceived in relation to some spatial reference frame, such as a table: *on* expresses a relation between a cup and a table. Similarly, representations of the internal structure of an object, its shape, specify the relations among component parts: The eyes have a location relative to the mouth and hair for example. Children have been shown to draw faces on the basis of precisely such information, establishing all internal relationships from the position of the eyes (Goodnow, 1972).

Again, we offer no account of how the visual system delivers such propositional representations aside from the conjecture that just as the perceptual system appears to impose category boundaries on acoustic signals to generate phonemes, so it may impose category boundaries on spatial information to generate spatial predicates. How that is achieved for either phonemes or spatial relations is not clear, but the problem is explored in Chapter 1 by Pastore, Chapter 9 by Bornstein, and Chapter 19 by Harnad. Our concern is with the structure and development of these categorical representations and their role in the perception and interpretation of the world.

The role of shape in object concepts

Whereas shape is a spatial property of a letter of the alphabet or a physical object, such as a ball, the shape is not the "object of perception"; rather, the ball is. For the child it is the ball that has permanence, function, name, and meaning (Nelson, 1974). But what is the mental representational form of the ball for the child? An abundance of evidence has shown that similarity judgments are based on spatial properties like location and shape (Anglin, 1977; E. Clark, 1973; Macnamara, 1982; Mervis, 1980; Nelson, 1973; Rosch, 1977). What then does the child "see"? The child sees the ball. Admittedly, in seeing the ball, the child sees something that is round. But whereas the child sees something round, the child does not see *that* it is round. The child knows it is a ball but does not know that it is round (Austin, 1962; Dretski, 1981).

What then is the relation between the roundness and the ball? The child perceives the ball by means of the spatial feature of roundness. But the shape, we may say, is implicit or instrumental or embedded in the perception and knowledge of the object. For an adult, either the object or its shape may be the object of perception and knowledge: The adult knows that it is a ball and that it is round. The former is part of the adult's knowledge of objects, the latter is part of the adult's knowledge of space. The problem to consider here is how the spatial information used by the child in recognizing the ball is transformed into the spatial knowledge possessed by the adult. In short, what is the relation between round as a perceptual feature of an object, and round as a concept?

To say that the shape feature of roundness is embedded in the concept of a ball is to say that although the feature is crucial to object identification, it cannot be used as a concept in its own right. A young child, that is, would resist classifying two different objects – for example, a ball and an orange – as equivalent. The categories governing classification in this case would be functional/interactive properties of the objects. When the shape feature of roundness is abstracted (however that occurs) from such objects, becoming an "object of perception" with its own distinctive meaning relative to the set of basic shapes – round, square, triangular, and so on – the child will have constructed a spatial concept and a new spatial category. This category (which we would also claim is categorical with respect to a set of alternatives) would then permit the classification of a ball and an orange as members of the same set (Olson, 1970).

In the example of the ball, *round* is initially part of a perceptual recognition routine, which, when combined with the significance or meaning of *rolls, bounces,* and *physical object,* yields the concept *ball.* When the feature *round* is isolated from that object to become an object of perception in its own right, with its own distinctive meaning, it has become a spatial concept. The new concept *round* is equivalent in status to the concept *ball* in that it can now be uniquely referred to and retrieved, manipulated, and imagined as an object of thought, and used as a basis for categorization. The extraction of spatial forms from object concepts – what we may refer to as the explication of spatial form – is the first, and major achievement in the development of spatial cognition (Olson & Bialystok, 1983).

Perception of objects and perception of form

We have introduced two uses for spatial information: one in which that spatial information remains implicit in the service of the perception of objects, the other in which it becomes explicit in the form of spatial concepts. Roundness is implicit in the recognition of a ball or a letter of the alphabet, but explicit in concepts like *round, sphere,* and *circle.* The notion that spatial information may be implicit in object recognition is well known. We may recognize a human face or other complex visual pattern and yet fail to identify the features that gave rise to the recognition. The temptation to be avoided is to assume that the implicit spatial information has a representational format different from that involved in the explicit conceptual representations of space. Both, we shall argue, are mentally represented by means of structural descriptions consisting of one or more ordered propositions that are built around a set of spatial predicates. The computational processes involved in assigning these propositions, although not precisely known, involve the sensory information from the display, the predicates or spatial concepts available for the interpretation of that display, and the experiences, goals, and expectancies that make some interpretations more probable than others.

There may be a relation between the use of spatial propositions for the perception of objects or form and the nature of the category boundary. Categories representing objects like balls or the letter C may be prototypical, characterized by clear exemplars but fuzzy boundaries. The features extracted from these objects to create categories representing forms, on the other hand, may be strongly bounded. Spatial predicates like *in/out, on/off, in front/behind,* and the like may be expected to have strict boundaries because they represent a single contrastive feature for which a binary test could be carried out somewhere in the perceptual system. Object concepts, being composed of sets of such predicates, cannot be judged on the basis of any one of them but rather from a sampling of characteristic features. Thus the abruptness of a category boundary is given, not by the difference between perception and conception, but by the difference between the representation of objects and the representation of forms.

This proposal is similar to that advanced by Smith et al. (1974) in their two-stage theory of semantic judgments. Subjects first make a fast, general judgment on the basis of prototypicality; only if that fails do subjects revert to a feature-by-feature comparison. The point to notice is that the object categories tend to be prototypical, whereas the feature categories tend to be categorical. Similarly, the features by which the prototypical object categories are judged are categorical. Furthermore, there is reason to expect that the feature categories are universal whereas the object categories reflect the more or less arbitrary conventions of the culture. Conceptual categories like balls and letters of the alphabet are clearly culturally defined, but predicates, like *above* and *below,* would appear to be universal. (The possession of terms for expressing these predicates is not, of course, universal.) What then is the structure of the spatial system used in perception and in thought?

Spatial propositions

If it is true, as we have suggested, that spatial information has the same propositional structure, whether it is implicit in the perception and memory of objects or explicit in spatial concepts, we must first discuss those propositional structures.

Spatial information, we hypothesize, is represented in the mind as a relation between a predicate and one or more arguments. Such representations would have the effect of forcing an apparently "seamless" physical space into discrete codes or categories of the mind. Perceptual events, as a consequence, would be restricted by the set of mental predicates available (as demonstrated by Sutherland's octopuses). Further, these mental representations, or structural descriptions, are activated in both the perception of objects and the perception of forms. In this section we shall outline this representational system and demonstrate the psychological reality of these representations by applying the theory to a series of problems in the field of spatial cognition; some we have studied ourselves, some have been made famous by others.

The specific propositional form adopted in this account for the representation of spatial information is the predicate calculus format discussed by Miller and Johnson-Laird (1976):

predicate (referent, relatum)

This formalism provides a means for generating and expressing an infinite number of spatial propositions that are not necessarily tied to a particular modality: They may represent either visual events or sentences or, further, either explicit or implicit spatial relations. The relational nature of spatial properties results from the fact that the propositions consist of a predicate and one or more arguments: The first argument is the "referent," the second the "relatum." A simple event, say, a cup on a table, would be represented mentally by a set of propositions including:

on (cup, table)

That representation characterizes a person's belief about a spatial relation, which could be expressed by a sentence, "The cup is on the table."

The predicate of the expression is roughly equivalent to a spatial concept. Basic spatial predicates would include such topological concepts as *open/closed, adjacent/nonadjacent,* and such Euclidean concepts, based on dimensionalized space, as *front/back, over/under, top/bottom, tall/short,* and *left/right.* Which of these are fundamental and which are derived by differentiation and combination of the fundamental ones is an important but unanswered question.

Predicates become concepts when they are associated with a linguistic form. This linguistic expression can take the form of verbs or prepositions to express relations – for example, *on, in, above* – or nouns to express constituents of objects – for example, *the top, the inside.* Hence, one hypothesis is that predicates are the outputs of the perceptual mechanisms, whereas concepts are the linguistic forms of those predicates. This would tie spatial concepts to language, leaving predicates basically nonverbal. It is the representation of essentially continuous physical space in terms of these spatial predicates that gives spatial cognition its categorical properties. (Note that we are not describing the mechanisms by which this is accomplished, but are simply characterizing the output of those mechanisms in a way that would explain certain properties of spatial cognition.)

The referent and the relatum are the features, objects, or events related by the predicate. The referent is typically the topic or subject and the relatum is the frame of reference.

Not every relation can be expressed by means of a single predicate. A right oblique, for example, is mentally represented by means of two predicates: *up* and *to the right* (Olson & Bialystok, 1983, Ch. 11). Other predicates may be generated by combining simpler, more primitive predicates. Thus *top* is derivable from *above* as follows:

top = *above* (properpart, H-axis)

That is, the part of the object that is above the midline horizontal axis provides one definition for the predicate *top*.

Whereas the perception of objects involves the relatively unintentional activation or assignment of spatial predicates to identifiable objects or constituents of objects, spatial cognition involves the intentional manipulation or reassignment of these spatial predicates to form new spatial propositions. We can use the classical conservation-of-liquids problem to illustrate this point. At one stage of development, the child's encounter with two beakers filled with water may generate the spatial representation:

taller (beaker 1, beaker 2)

That is, beaker 1 is taller than beaker 2. The conclusion from this display would be that beaker 1 contains more liquid than does beaker 2, given the salience of the vertical dimension in perception and the usual experience that taller vessels contain greater quantities. The activation of the predicate *taller* rather than other predicates would depend upon several factors: the salience of the property, the stock of available predicates, the purposes of the perceiver, and the like. The inference that beaker 1 contains more than beaker 2 is unconscious in that no special consideration of that usual conclusion or experience is required. The adult solution, however, requires the assignment of a predicate to the other spatial dimension, the relative width of the two beakers:

wider (beaker 2, beaker 1)

That is, beaker 2 is wider than beaker 1. When the child can voluntarily or intentionally reassign those predicates to the display and so recognize that there is a compensatory relation between the two predicates in the determination of volume, the conservation problem will be solved. This solution is more intentional than the former in that recognition of a problem in the conclusion that follows from the automatically assigned perceptual description is required in order to reassign those descriptions intentionally. (Again, there is no assumption that predicates *taller* or *wider* are primitives. Rather, they are probably derived from simpler predicates, such as extent combined with vertical or horizontal axis.)

If spatial cognition is to be characterized in this fashion, development can be seen as occurring in three ways: First there is the elaboration of spatial predicates whereby new predicates are added to the repertoire either by differentiating or combining existing ones. Evidence for the expanding stock of predicates and their combination may be seen in children's growing ability to differentiate *b* from *d* or left-obliques from right-obliques (Olson & Bialystok, 1983, Ch. 10). Second, there is the explication of these predicates to form spatial concepts. The child comes to know not only what balls are but also what round things are. Third, this explication permits children to voluntarily assign or reassign spatial predicates from new points of view, to imagine what an object looks like to another viewer, as in Piaget's famous three-mountain task described in the next section. What is invariant across development is the presence of some form of spatial propositions that constitute the mental representation of objects and events in the world. Following Frege (1952) we would argue that propositions, not concepts, are the basic units of mental life.

We turn now to the body of research on spatial thinking to examine the extent to which a representational theory of the sort described above can account for the available data.

A matrix for spatial problems

If space is perceived and operated upon in terms of categories, then the solutions children and adults offer to spatial problems should provide evidence for the existence of those categories. It must be demonstrable that the spatial structures and the operations on those structures we describe will provide a good model for the error scores and reaction times reported in the literature on spatial cognition.

To illustrate the application of this account of spatial mental representation, we will proceed by classifying a large number of spatial problems along two binary dimensions to create a four-celled matrix and then we will offer an account of how the problems in each cell are solved. The first dimension of the matrix differentiates those tasks in which a single object serves as a stimulus display from those in which a structured array of objects or features are used as the display. The second dimension reflects the type of spatial transformation. Either the position or the perspective of the viewer/subject is altered while the display remains invariant or the position or the structure of the display itself is transformed while the position of the viewer remains invariant. These options create the four types of problems shown in Table 18.1, with some examples of each.

The problem characterized as a viewer transformation of a single object display is best illustrated by Flavell, Botkin, Fry, Wright, and Jarvis's (1968) perspective problem, in which young children are asked what a doll looks like to a person viewing it from another side. Another example is asking the child to draw a patterned cup from a particular perspective in which the pattern is hidden (McLaughland, 1976, cited in Harris, 1977). Structurally equivalent to these are problems in which children are asked to locate spatial parts of objects, for example, *front,* and *back* (Harris & Strommen, 1974). Although the viewer does not actually move in these problems, the child's answer must account for the spatial structure of the display, which may conflict with the child's own ego-related spatial structure, that is, the child's own *front.* Thus two views must be reconciled to arrive at the appropriate spatial judgment.

Prototypical of the viewer transformation of an array display is the three-mountain task (Piaget & Inhelder, 1956), a small-scale geographic setting that children are asked to describe from various points of view. Huttenlocher and Presson (1973)

Table 18.1. *Matrix of spatial problems*

Transformation	Display	
	Object	Array
Viewer	Recognize object from another view (Flavell et al., 1968)	Three-mountain task (Piaget & Inhelder, 1956)
	Draw object (Harris, 1977)	Horse/cart perspective task (Huttenlocher & Presson, 1973)
	Locate spatial parts, e.g., find *front* (Harris & Strommen, 1974)	Describe spatial relation, e.g., What's *in front*? (Harris & Strommen, 1972)
		Construct block array (Harris & Basset, 1976)
		Map problems (Kosslyn et al., 1974)
Display	Rotation of abstract figures or objects (Shepard & Cooper, 1982)	Horse/cart rotation problem (Huttenlocher & Presson, 1973)
	Water-level problem (Piaget & Inhelder, 1956)	Rubik's cube
	Oblique recognition (Olson & Hildyard, 1977)	

constructed a similar problem in which a horse was attached to a cart by means of a removable harness on a circular supporting frame, permitting the horse to move around the cart or the cart to rotate while the horse remained fixed. The cart contained an array of three colored blocks, which the child had to describe from the horse's perspective after either the horse or the cart had moved. Harris and Basset (1976) contributed to problems of this type by asking children to reconstruct a color-coded linear sequence of blocks as it would appear from another perspective. Finally, as with object displays, array displays could involve not real movement but conflicting perspective by asking children to describe a relation between two objects, for example, "*a* is in front of *b*" (Harris & Strommen, 1972). The most complex of these problems involve cognitive maps or spatial layouts in which a complex set of propositions is required to express the internal structure of a display environment (Kosslyn, Pick, & Fariello, 1974; Yonas & Pick, 1975).

In display-transformation problems, a spatial manipulation is introduced to the stimulus materials and the subject must make a judgment about those materials after the manipulation. Adults (Shepard & Metzler, 1971) or children (Rovet, 1974) are asked to make identity judgments about pictured complex parts of three-dimensional figures that were either the same figure in a different orientation or different figures. The water-level problem introduced by Piaget and Inhelder (1956) is also of

Spatial categories

this type. Children are given a drawing of a tilted beaker and asked to draw a line indicating the water level in that container. Similarly, the oblique-recognition task given to both adults (Olson & Hildyard, 1977) and children (Bryant, 1974; Scher, 1980) requires that subjects examine a single stimulus – in this case, a line segment – and make a judgment about its orientation.

In the final cell, the manipulation is imposed upon an array of objects that may or may not maintain their internal structure. In Huttenlocher and Presson's (1973) horse-cart problem this is achieved when the cart moves rather than the horse. In this case, the perspective is constant, that is, the horse and child continue to view the display from the same viewpoint, but the array of blocks is rotated. A more complicated version of the same problem is Rubik's cube. Again, there are arrays of colored markers, but in this case the internal structure of those markers can also be altered. The solution requires finding the set of spatial transformations that will yield a particular configuration of the array components.

Although superficially different, the claim is that these problems are fundamentally equivalent because their solution depends upon the assignment and manipulation of spatial propositions constructed from a finite set of categorical relational predicates. Moreover, a single set of procedures governing the construction of these propositions underlies the solution to all the problems. If it can be demonstrated that the cognitive processes involved in perceiving and thinking about spatial relations manifest the categorical propositional structures we have described, then, even without precise mechanisms for translating continuous space into this system, it can nonetheless be taken as evidence that our perception, interpretation, and mental transformation of space is indeed categorical.

Solution to spatial problems

The solution to all these problems can be stated in three operations, each having an output that specifies one of the three constituents of the required spatial propositions of the general form:

predicate (referent, relatum)

1. Select referent: Identify critical features of display.
2. Find relatum: Assign axis or locate reference object in the display.
3. Assign predicate: Determine the spatial relationship between the referent and the relatum.

These operations become differentially implicated in the solution as a function of the position of the problem in the matrix. One or more of these operations, that is, may be especially difficult for a specific problem.

To illustrate the problem of object recognition from another perspective, "What does the doll look like to the observer?" requires that the child construct a proposition relating a critical feature of the doll (e.g., face) to the observer by means of a spatial predicate describing the axis (e.g., in front). Thus, the proposition *in front* (face, observer)

represents a relationship in which the observer sees the face of the doll. If the viewer were moved so that the axis defined by *in front* led to the critical feature *back* of the doll, the corresponding proposition would be

in front (back, observer)

In this case, the view of the doll available to the viewer is the one showing the doll's back. In both cases the solution requires the formation of a spatial proposition consisting of a predicate relating the referent to the relatum, the predicate being determined by the relatum. But the ease of that solution, or the facility with which the proposition can be constructed, depends upon the ability of the viewer to carry out intentionally each of the three operations. The difficulty in many cases arises from the explicitness (or rather, lack of explicitness) with which the relevant spatial concept is represented.

Select referent

The effect on problem difficulty of identifying the critical display features has been well documented (e.g., Flavell et al., 1968; Pufall & Shaw, 1973). To illustrate, we have shown (Olson & Bialystok, 1983) that a simple object presents different degrees of difficulty in the perspective problem as a function of the presence and detection of codable features. Children could solve standard perspective problems more easily for objects like dolls and cars, which possess intrinsic spatial tops and fronts, than for unfamiliar abstract figures, which did not. Presumably the propositions constructed in these cases made use of the known spatial parts of the referent. In addition, problems in which the child saw the *front* or *back* of the object were easier than those in which the child saw the *side*. Because the sides are symmetrical and confusable, it may be that their identification as a critical feature is more difficult, hence the proposition is not as simple to construct. More compelling, however, was the finding that children's ability to solve the perspective problem for the abstract figures (Shepard & Metzler, 1971) depended on ability to identify a critical, salient spatial part of that figure. There were significant and consistent differences in problem difficulty as a function of the presence or absence of a distinct codable "arm" pointing directly to the front of the observer. When such an arm existed, the problem was easier than when no such salient feature was available for constructing the representation.

Determine relatum

The most fundamental aspect of spatial cognition is determining the frame of reference and spatial axes or a reference object that may serve as the basis for assigning spatial properties to the referent. These relata are often implicit and presupposed rather than deliberately constructed. An important relatum is the viewer's own position, the ego-related frame of reference. Children's relative inability to deliberately construct alternative axes to serve as relata and their acceptance under some conditions of the implicitly generated ego-related relatum is often taken as evidence of egocentrism. Children, it is said, can *only* construct descriptions from their own viewpoint and, in more radical versions, are unaware that alternative viewpoints even exist (Laurendeau & Pinard, 1970; Piaget & Inhelder, 1956). The systematicity of egocentric errors, however, suggests that the difficulty arises not from children's absolute failure to adopt other perspectives, but from task conditions that make the determination of the appropriate relatum difficult.

In the study by Harris and Basset (1976), children were asked to reconstruct an array of three colored blocks as it would look from another perspective. All of the children began with the block that would be described as *in front* from the new perspective. Some of the children, however, were unable to use that block to project an axis and specify a new relatum from that point. Thus, they could identify the critical feature, namely, the block that would be "in front" of the observer (Step 1), but were unable to use that feature to establish a relatum (Step 2). Accordingly, the rest of the blocks were placed to replicate the current position, and the child was described as having committed an egocentric error. But because locating the block that would be "in front" for the new perspective was easily accomplished, a pervasive judgment of egocentrism seems unwarranted. The child's problem, rather, was being unable to override the current ego-related relatum with one intentionally constructed from the position of the critical block.

An important influence on the ease of assigning axes to displays is the degree of congruity between the axes automatically assigned to that display in ordinary perception and the axes that must be intentionally assigned to solve the current problem. Although both descriptions are achieved by constructing propositions from the same set of spatial categories, the axes automatically assigned during perception are somewhat more primary. The difficulty in deliberately assigning alternative axes during spatial cognition will depend in part on the correspondence between the two descriptions. The simplest case is a problem involving a 0-degree transformation – the two descriptions in this case are identical.

Overcoming a perceived and automatically assigned relatum is also a primary source of difficulty in the oblique-discrimination task. Similarity judgments for horizontal- and vertical-line segments are consistently easier for both adults and children to make than are judgments for diagonal-line segments. The frame in which the line segments are presented automatically evokes the perception of horizontal and vertical structural axes (Arnheim, 1974; Palmer, 1977). Line segments that correspond to those axes, namely, verticals and horizontals, are easily represented and recognized. Line segments that cannot be coded in terms of those axes, however, are problematic. The representations of oblique-line segments in variable positions require that new horizontal and vertical axes be assigned to each particular line segment to yield dual predicate descriptions, such as "up and right." These

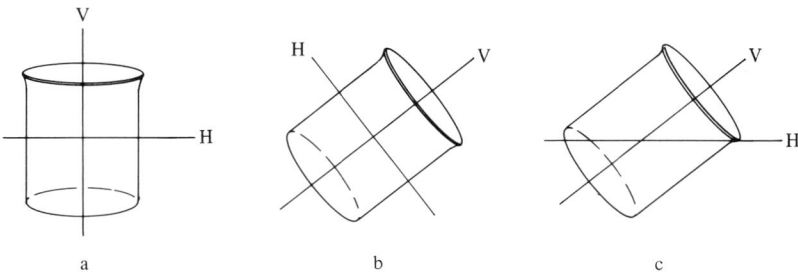

Figure 18.1. Role of conflicting axes in the solution to the water level problem. (a) The axes of the flask and the axes of the environment coincide. (b) In a tilted flask, the axes of the flask differ from those of the environment and children often assign the water level on the basis of the axes of the flask. (c) The correct solution comes from the differentiation of the axes of the flask from the axes of the environment and assigning the water level on the basis of the latter.

local axes potentially conflict with the automatic horizontal and vertical axes assigned to the whole display in perception. Children in fact succeed in the task by coding the line segments in terms of salient features of the display, such as corners, rather than in terms of the underlying spatial dimensions, thus avoiding the problem of resolving conflicting axes or relata (Bryant, 1974; Scher, 1980).

A variation of the same phenomenon underlies the water-level problem (Piaget & Inhelder, 1956). Having identified the critical feature of the display (in this case, the beaker), the child must decide whether the horizontal line indicating the water level should be placed with respect to the beaker, as is usually the case (see Figure 18.1a,b), or with respect to the spatial environment, as is the case here (see Figure 18.1c). The latter choice calls for a deliberate judgment to override a compelling perceptual tendency. Adults, too, have been shown to vary in this decision as a function of their knowledge of the principle of water-level invariance (Howard, 1978).

The two steps discussed so far – selecting the referent and the relatum – also interact to make spatial problems more or less difficult to solve. A variation in the problem used by Huttenlocher and Presson (1979) illustrates this point. The material was a diamond-shaped array of four colored objects. In addition to altering whether the transformation was applied to the viewer position (viewer rotation) or the display (array rotation), they asked two kinds of questions to elicit the responses. The first, called "appearance questions," presented the child with full pictures of all the possible outcomes and asked the child to select the arrangement of objects that showed the correct answer. The second, called "item questions," systematically asked the child to tell what object would be in each of the four positions: front, back, left, and right.

The percentage of errors committed on each of their problems for each of these question types is as follows:

Spatial categories

	Appearance	Item
Array rotation	15	32
Viewer rotation	56	20

Huttenlocher and Presson explain these findings with a series of descriptions concerning the difficulty of mentally imagining and transforming the displays under the various conditions. Our account of this interaction between problem type and question type is in terms of the contribution of each question type to the first two steps in the process of constructing the relevant spatial propositions under each type of transformation.

Consider first the results for the appearance questions for the two problem types. When the array moves, children easily select the picture showing the whole array after the transformation; when the viewer position changes, children are unable to predict the arrangement of the objects from the new position. This difference may be attributable to the ease of identifying the critical feature of the referent, namely, what will be *in front* of the viewer after the transformation. If the array is moving, that identification is easy because the child is in effect told to imagine what the display would look like if it were rotated so that the "ball," for example, became "in front." Consequently, the picture showing the ball in front must be correct. For the viewer rotation, the child must imagine how the display would look from another side. That requires the assignment of the *in front* relationship from the new location and orientation of the viewer to determine which object will be in front. Failure to determine that feature leaves the child with no strategy with which to assess the alternative response pictures.

The perspective task is simplified in the item questions. Children are told to imagine themselves moving, but this time the structure of the question reveals its solution. Rather than confronting uninterpreted displays, the child is guided through a reconstruction of the correct display by telling one at a time what is in front, in back, and so on. That is, the question provides the child with the predicate and requires only that the child generate the necessary referent from the given relatum. When steps are structured in this way, item questions are relatively easy.

The ease or difficulty of constructing the proposition can also account for the question type differences for the array rotation. In these problems, simply identifying what will be in front is adequate to the solution because the internal structure of the display is never violated. Thus appearance questions are easy because only one feature of the display need be coded. Item questions are more difficult because the critical object, the referent, must be used to construct a front–back axis, the relatum, in order to determine the location of the other three objects. Appearance questions can be made just as difficult by including distractors for which the internal structure has been violated, thus forcing the child to encode all the internal relationships from the new relatum, as is necessary for the item questions (Bialystok, 1986).

It remains a matter of some controversy as to just what is the relevant relatum used by younger children in constructing the proposition representing the position of an object in the rotated display. We argue that the relatum used for representing the location of the ball is the observer:

in front (ball, observer)

in which the predicate *in front* marks that the ball is in front of (and adjacent to) the observer's front. Given such a representation, the child simply looks for a picture featuring the ball. Huttenlocher and Presson (1979) and Huttenlocher and Newcombe (1984), on the other hand, argue that the relatum (using our theoretical language rather than theirs) used in representing the location of the ball is the other object in the display:

in front (ball, other object)

in which the predicate marks the relation between the ball and the display (when viewed from some specified viewpoint). We suggest that children first note relations between observer and object; later, when they learn to reassign axes to the display, rather than to the single object, they will have the machinery to construct relations like those described by Huttenlocher and her colleagues.

Assign predicate

It is in the assignment of a predicate specifying the relationship between the referent and the relatum that the continuous or categorical nature of spatial concepts is most critically tested. The propositional description requires that these relationships be expressed in terms of bounded digital categories that may be altered through computation. Support for the argument that these relationships are continuous and altered analogically is given by the linear relationship between the time required to solve a rotation and the angular distance through which the figure has moved (Shepard & Cooper, 1982). We claim, along with others (Hinton, 1979; Just & Carpenter, 1976, 1985), that the continuous motion is an illusion, and that the apparently linear function can be explained through other means.

To solve the rotation problem used by Shepard and Metzler (1971), for example, a proposition must be constructed relating a critical feature of the first display to the relatum, which would generally be the display object itself:

at the top (long arm, object 1)

That is, the long arm is at the top of object 1. The viewer then searches object 2 for the analogous constituent and codes that relation:

front (long arm, object 2)

That is, the long arm is at the front of object 2. Next, the viewer computes the value for the relationship between this arm across the two displays, a value we call r:

Spatial categories 527

r(long arm [object 1], long arm [object 2])

This predicate would specify in ordinary language terms both a distance and direction of rotation, for example, a quarter turn to the right (around a front/back axis) (cf. Hinton, 1979). This procedure may be sequentially applied to as many critical features as necessary to arrive at a judgment of similarity for the two objects. As long as the value *r* continues to describe the spatial relation between the comparable components, the two objects are considered to be the same.

To the extent that a categorical value for *r* can be assigned, the process of comparing the two objects is computational. The boundaries that specify the categories for *r* seem to be based on the perceptual structure of a circle (cf. Arnheim, 1974). Just and Carpenter (1976), using eye-movement data, for example, report that the size of the computational step is about 50 degrees, a distance that corresponds roughly to 45 degrees, or one-eighth of a circle. A partition of space into quadrants, which are then divided in half, then, could provide the boundaries for the distance moves. In addition, in a study of children's rotation of abstract shapes, an examination of errors in both selecting and reconstructing the correct shape after a given rotation showed no effect of linear distance, but did show strong effects of quadrants: 90-degree transformations were consistently easier than any other displacement (Bialystok, 1986). The interpretation is that the value for the predicate *r* is based on a category of distance that has as its primary boundaries a quarter turn through circular space.

The three steps involved in the construction of the spatial proposition provide a computational solution to spatial problems based on the existence of spatial predicates that are more or less bounded and are consistent with the performance of adults and children in actually solving these problems. In what remains, then, we discuss the nature of these spatial predicates and their categorical properties.

Spatial predicates as spatial categories

Spatial categories, whether exhibited in simple shapes or in elementary spatial relations, are the manifestation of certain mental structures having the form of spatial propositions. The structure of these propositions is a set of predicates that relate objects, features of objects, or constituents of objects to certain frames of reference. Such propositions, we have argued, are the elementary units of perception and thought. In addition, although we have not addressed the question of just how the perceptual systems deliver these propositional structures, we take them to be the output of the perceptual process and the input to conceptual thought. As Fodor (1983) says: "The perceptual processes must represent the world so as to make it accessible to thought" (p. 68).

We have further tried to show that both the perception of spatial relations and intentional thought about spatial relations involve using the same types of spatial propositions. They differ in that in perception they are automatically assigned whereas in thought they are intentionally assigned. One cannot avoid seeing a diagonal line relative to its position in a display. The position serves as an automatically assigned relatum to the referent line. In spatial thought the frame of reference is intentionally assigned for some purpose. Yet both involve the representation of the line relative to some frame of reference. The relational, propositional code is not what differentiates perception from thought; it is rather that the latter is subject to revision and reassignment. Perhaps this is an example of what Pylyshyn calls "cognitively penetrable" (Pylyshyn, 1984).

Where do these spatial categories and spatial predicates come from? Rock (1983) has argued that constructive theories of perception must ultimately be linked either to neurological receptors, as the Gestalt school attempted to do, or else derived from a conceptual basis. There have been attempts to identify sensory receptors specifically attuned to the spatial properties we have described in some psychophysical experiments. Best known are the detectors that have a selectivity for orientation of line (Hubel and Weisel, 1959; Olson, 1970; Sutherland, 1969). There is every reason to believe that additional sensitivities will be identified with further research.

Two points about the search for specialized sensors are worth noting. First, the selectivities that have been discovered are essentially congruent with the predicates we have discussed. That is, the categories of thought, in some cases, may be reflected in the peripheral organs. Harnad, in Chapter 19, suggests that innate (or learned) feature detectors may yield bounded categories that subsequently serve as atoms for spatial propositions. Whereas we basically agree, we would add that *spatial* features are primarily, if not exclusively, relational rather than substantive. Spatial predicates relate features rather than being features themselves.

The second point about the psychophysical findings is that the spatial detectors thus far discovered do not approximate the richness of our conceptual structures for the representation of spatial relations. Can conceptual alternatives provide an equivalent basis for category formation? Clearly natural kinds, like dogs and trees, are categories, but can these categories affect the detection of spatial relations? Probably not. Rather, such categories make use of the available spatial predicates. But what about the complex predicates, like *top* and *taller,* that are assembled out of simpler ones?

Our suggestion, mentioned earlier, is that the basic set of predicates for which the perceptual system seems to be specialized is largely specified innately. Learning and development increase that stock of predicates by differentiation, by combination, and then explication, largely through language. Siegel and Siegel (1977), for example, have demonstrated that the categorical perception of musical intervals is a function of musical training. Proffitt and Halwes (1982) argue that there are modifications in category boundaries as a function of the language and culture of the perceiver. We are left with the view that some spatial categories reflect perceptual biases of the knower, whereas others evolve through experience, culture, and growth. It must not be assumed, however, that perceptual sensitivities can be exhausted by such simple mechanisms as feature detectors. Is it inconceivable, for example, that there are detectors for such predicates as *in front* or *above?* At best, one may hope to find mechanisms that code and preserve such relations (however they may do that), but they cannot be thought of as simple feature detectors.

Are these categories invariant or do they vary across contexts? It may be that categories directly reflecting innate perceptual sensitivities differ from derived categories in this matter. The innate categories may be reflected directly in the arrangement of our perceptual apparatus and the kind of information to which it responds. H. Clark (1973) has argued that it is our asymmetrical body structures – with eyes at the front and gravity pulling in one direction – that are responsible for our representation of the primary spatial dimensions in the environment. Accordingly, categories such as *up/down, front/back* may have precise boundaries and display relative invariance across contexts. Indeed, if an object is turned upside down, even adults have difficulty deciding what to call the top; they are in a conflict between the top specified by their own orientation in space, and the top dictated by the canonical object itself. Furthermore, as we have seen, the biggest problem for children in solving spatial cognitive tasks occurs when the spatial properties of the ego are out of congruity with those of another viewer or the display.

In spite of the important role of context in the perception of spatial relations and in the reassignment of these representations on the basis of alternative frames of reference, spatial cognition remains categorical and relational. Having imposed a propositional structure in the course of perceiving objects and events in the world, people have the basic machinery required to solve a full range of spatial–cognitive problems. Such problems, we have argued, depend upon representing an often continuous physical space in terms of appropriate propositional structures and then operating upon those structures to produce a solution. That these propositional structures are often language-like is not an argument against them. The odd fact is that the relations between spatial and linguistic cognition should have taken so long to discover.

References

Anglin, J. M. (1977). *Word, object, and conceptual development*. New York: Norton.
Arnheim, R. (1974). *Art and visual perception: A psychology of the creative eye*. Berkeley: University of California Press.
Austin, J. L. (1962). In G. L. Warnock (Ed.), *Sense and sensibilia*. Oxford: Oxford University Press.
Bialystok, E. (1986). Implicit display structure as a frame of reference. In *Different frames of reference in children's spatial representation*. Symposium conducted at the American Psychological Association Convention, Washingtion, D. C.
Bierwisch, M. (1967). Some semantic universals of German adjectivals. *Foundations of Language, 3,* 1–36.
Bryant, P. E. (1974). *Perception and understanding in young children: An experimental approach*. London: Methuen & Co.
Clark, E. V. (1973). What's in a word? On the child's acquisition of semantics in his first language. In T. E. Moore (Ed.), *Cognitive development and the acquisition of language* (pp. 65–110). New York: Academic Press.
Clark, H. H. (1973). Space, time, semantics, and the child. In T. E. Moore (Ed.), *Cognitive development and the acquisition of language* (pp. 27–63). New York: Academic Press.

Dretski, F. (1981). *Knowledge and the flow of information.* Cambridge, MA: MIT-Bradford.
Flavell, J. H., Botkin, P. T., Fry, C. L., Wright, J. W., & Jarvis, P. (1968). *The development of role-taking and communication skills in children.* New York: Wiley.
Fodor, J. (1983). *Modularity of mind.* Cambridge, MA: MIT Press.
Frege, G. (1952). *Translations from the philosophical writings of Gottlob Frege.* (P. T. Geach & M. Black, Eds.), Oxford: Blackwell.
Goodnow, J. J. (1972). Rules and repertoires, rituals and tricks of the trade: Social and informational aspects to cognitive and representational development. In S. Farnham-Diggory (Ed.), *Information processing in children* (pp. 83–102). New York: Academic Press.
Harris, L. J., & Strommen, E. A. (1972). The role of front-back features in children's "front", "back", and "beside" placement of objects. *Merrill-Palmer Quarterly, 18,* 259–271.
Harris, L. J., & Strommen, E. A. (1974). What is the "front" of a simple geometric form? *Perception & Psychophysics, 15,* 571–580.
Harris, P. (1977). The child's representation of space. In G. Butterworth (Ed.), *The child's representation of the world* (pp. 83–93). New York: Plenum Press.
Harris, P., & Basset, E. (1976). Reconstruction from the mental image. *Journal of Experimental Child Psychology, 21,* 514–523.
Hinton, G. (1979). Some demonstrations of the effects of structural description in mental imagery. *Cognitive Science, 3,* 231–250.
Howard, I. P. (1978). Perception and knowledge of the water-level principle. *Perception, 7,* 151–160.
Hubel, D. H., & Weisel, T. N. (1959). Receptive fields of single neurons in the cat's striate cortex. *Journal of Physiology, 148,* 574–591.
Huttenlocher, J., & Newcombe, N. (1984). Children's representation of information about location. In C. Sophian (Ed.), *The origins of cognitive skills.* Hillsdale, NJ: Erlbaum.
Huttenlocher, J., & Presson, C. C. (1973). Mental rotation and the perspective problem. *Cognitive Psychology, 4,* 277–299.
Huttenlocher, J., & Presson, C. C. (1979). The coding and transformation of spatial information. *Cognitive Psychology, 11,* 375–394.
Jackendoff, R. (1983). *Semantics and cognition.* Cambridge, MA: MIT Press.
Just, M., & Carpenter, P. (1976). Eye fixation and cognitive processes. *Cognitive Psychology, 8,* 441–480.
Just, M. & Carpenter, P. (1985). Cognitive coordinate systems: Accounts of mental rotation and individual differences in spatial ability. *Psychological Review, 92,* 137–176.
Kosslyn, S. M., Pick, H. L., & Fariello, G. R. (1974). Cognitive maps in children and men. *Child Development, 45,* 707–716.
Lashley, K. S. (1938). The mechanism of vision: XV. Preliminary studies of the rats' capacity for detailed vision. *Journal of General Psychology, 18,* 123–193.
Laurendeau, M., & Pinard, A. (1970). *The development of the concept of space in the child.* New York: International Universities Press.
McLaughland, D. (1976). A second cup? A re-examination of young children's drawings of a familiar object. *Final Honours Thesis,* University of Lancaster.
Macnamara, J. (1982). *Names for things.* Cambridge, MA: MIT Press.
Mervis, C. B. (1980). Category structure and the development of categorization. In R. J. Spiro, B. C. Bruce, & W. F. Brewer (Eds.), *Theoretical issues in reading comprehension* (pp. 279–307). Hillsdale, NJ: Erlbaum.
Miller, G., & Johnson-Laird, P. N. (1976). *Language and perception.* Cambridge: Cambridge University Press.
Nelson, K. (1973). Some evidence for the cognitive primacy of categorization and its functional basis. *Merrill-Palmer Quarterly, 19,* 21–39.
Nelson, K. (1974). Concept, word and sentence: Interrelations in acquisition and development. *Psychological Review, 81,* 267–285.
Ogilvie, J. C., & Taylor, M. M. (1958). Effect of orientation of the visibility of a fine line. *Journal of the Optical Society of America, 48,* 628–629.

Ogilvie, J. C., & Taylor, M. M. (1959). Effect of length on the visibility of a fine line. *Journal of the Optical Society of America, 49,* 898–900.
Olson, D. R. (1970). Language and thought: Aspects of a cognitive theory of semantics. *Psychological Review, 77,* 257–273.
Olson, D. R., & Bialystok, E. (1983). *Spatial cognition: The structure and development of the mental representation of spatial relations.* Hillsdale, NJ: Erlbaum.
Olson, D. R., & Hildyard, A. (1977). The mental representation of oblique orientation. *Canadian Journal of Psychology, 31,* 3–13.
Palmer, S. E. (1977). Hierarchical structure in perceptual representation. *Cognitive Psychology, 9,* 441–474.
Piaget, J., & Inhelder, B. (1956). *The child's conception of space.* New York: Norton.
Proffitt, D. R., & Halwes, T. (1982). Categorical perception: A contractual approach. In W. B. Weimer & D. S. Palermo (Eds.), *Cognition and the symbolic process* (Vol. 2). Hillsdale, NJ: Erlbaum.
Pufall, P. B., & Shaw, R. E. (1973). Analysis of the development of children's spatial reference systems. *Cognitive Psychology, 5,* 151–175.
Pylyshyn, Z. W. (1981). The imagery debate: Analogical media verus tacit knowledge. *Psychological Review, 88,* 16–45.
Pylyshyn, Z. W. (1984). *Computation and cognition: Toward a foundation for cognitive science.* Cambridge, MA: MIT Press.
Rock, I. (1983). *The logic of perception.* Cambridge, MA: MIT Press.
Rosch, E. (1977). Human categorization. In N. Warren (Ed.), *Studies in cross-cultural psychology* (Vol. 1, pp. 1–49). New York: Academic Press.
Rovet, J. (1974). *Can spatial skills be acquired via film? An analysis of the cognitive consequences of visual media.* Unpublished doctoral dissertation, University of Toronto.
Scher, A. (1980). *On spatial cognition: Process and development.* Unpublished doctoral dissertation, University of Calgary.
Shepard, R. N., & Cooper, L. A. (1982). *Mental images and their transformations.* Cambridge, MA: MIT Press.
Shepard, R. N., & Metzler, J. (1971). Mental rotation of three-dimensional objects. *Science, 171,* 701–703.
Siegel, J. A., & Siegel, W. (1977). Absolute identification of notes and intervals by musicians. *Perception & Psychophysics, 21,* 143–152.
Smith, E. E., Shoben, E. J., & Rips, L. J. (1974). Structure and process in semantic memory: A featural model for semantic decisions. *Psychological Review, 81,* 214–241.
Sutherland, N. S. (1969). Shape discrimination in the rat, octopus, and goldfish. *Journal of Comparative and Physiological Psychology, 67,* 160–176.
Yonas, A., & Pick, H. L. (1975). An approach to the study of infant space perception. In L. B. Cohen & P. Salapatek (Eds.), *Infant perception: From sensation to cognition. Volume 2: Perception of space, speech, sound* (pp. 3–31). New York: Academic Press.

Part VII

Cognitive foundations

19 Category induction and representation

Stevan Harnad

Categorization is a very basic cognitive activity. It is involved in any task that calls for differential responding, from operant discrimination to pattern recognition to naming and describing objects and states-of-affairs. Explanations of categorization range from nativist theories denying that any nontrivial categories are acquired by learning to inductivist theories claiming that most categories are learned.

"Categorical perception" (CP) is the name given to a suggestive perceptual phenomenon that may serve as a useful model for categorization in general: For certain perceptual categories, within-category differences look much smaller than between-category differences even when they are of the same size physically. For example, in color perception, differences between reds and between yellows look much smaller than equal-sized differences that cross the red/yellow boundary; the same is true of the phoneme categories /ba/ and /da/. Indeed, the effect of the category boundary is not merely quantitative, but qualitative.

There have been two theories to explain CP effects. The "Whorf Hypothesis" explains color-boundary effects by proposing that language somehow determines our view of reality. The "motor theory of speech perception" explains phoneme-boundary effects by attributing them to the patterns of articulation required for pronunciation. Both theories seem to raise more questions than they answer, for example: (i) How general and pervasive are CP effects? Do they occur in other modalities besides speech-sounds and color? (ii) Are CP effects inborn or can they be generated by learning (and if so, how)? (iii) How are categories internally represented? How does this representation generate successful categorization and the CP boundary effect?

Some of the answers to these questions will have to come from ongoing research, but the existing data do suggest a provisional model for category formation and category representation. According to this model, CP provides our basic or elementary categories. In acquiring a category we learn to label or identify positive and negative instances from a sample of confusable alternatives. Two kinds of internal representation are built up in this learning by *acquaintance:* (1) an *iconic* representation that subserves our similarity judgments and (2) an analog/digital feature-filter that picks out the invariant information allowing us to categorize the instances correctly. This second, *categorical* representation is associated with the category name. Category names then serve as the atomic symbols for a third representational system, the (3) *symbolic* representations that underlie language and that make it possible for us to learn by *description*.

This model provides no particular or general solution to the problem of inductive learning, only a conceptual framework; but it does have some substantive implications, for example, (a) the "cognitive identity of (current) indiscriminables": Categories and their representations can only be provisional and approximate, relative to the alternatives encountered to date, rather than "exact." There is also (b) no such thing as an absolute "feature," only those features that are invariant within a particular context of confusable alternatives. Contrary to prevailing "prototype" views, however, (c) such provisionally invariant features *must* underlie successful categorization, and must be "sufficient" (at least in the "satisficing" sense) to subserve reliable performance with all-or-none, bounded categories, as in CP. Finally, the model brings out some basic limitations of the "symbol-manipulative" approach to modeling cognition, showing how (d) symbol meanings must be functionally anchored in nonsymbolic, "shape-preserving" representations – iconic and categorical ones. Otherwise, all symbol interpretations are ungrounded and indeterminate. This amounts to a principled call for a psychophysical (rather than a neural) "bottom-up" approach to cognition.

An empirical approach to problems of philosophy?

In contemporary cognitive science certain long-standing problems of philosophy appear to be taking on an optimistically empirical form. One of these – not one I propose to take up here – is the "other minds" problem. Comparative psychologists, behavioral biologists, neurobiologists, and computer scientists are actively investigating criteria for attributing consciousness to organisms and mechanisms other than ourselves (Griffin 1978; Searle 1980; Harnad 1982a). What is interesting about these new approaches to problems like the other-minds problem is that they appear to be working their way free from the purely a priori considerations that had restricted philosophers to a number of alternative "isms," with no objective way to decide among them.

A priori problems no doubt remain, but the new empirical inquiries seem to be wresting some portions of the old subject matter from the grasp of undecidability. Cognitive science promises a better functional understanding of the organisms and mechanisms, including ourselves, whose performance we judge (intuitively) to be either conscious or unconscious. This new functional information about what sorts of mechanisms can and cannot successfully generate conscious-like performance may then go on to educate our intuitions about what is and is not conscious. Even the celebrated "Turing Test" (Turing, 1964) seems to be undergoing a metamorphosis from a thought-experiment into an operational criterion (Harnad, in preparation, a).

The other-minds problem, however, is mentioned here only to set the stage for describing a series of six problems (also largely philosophical ones until recently) that are more directly related to the theme of this volume:

1. *The problem of induction* is the first and most important of these problems: How does one arrive at "successful" generalizations from finite samples of instances?
2. *The problem of mapping words onto the world:* What is the relation between words and the world they describe? How is it established?
3. *The problem of meaning holism:* Is a word's meaning isolable from the meaning of the rest of the lexicon, or can the revision of one meaning necessitate the revision of all meanings?
4. *The problem of knowledge-by-acquaintance versus knowledge-by-description:* What is the difference between what is (or can be) known through direct sensory experience and what is (or can be) known through verbal description?
5. *The problem of elementary percepts and the problem of atomic terms:* What are the units of perception and how do the words we use in our description themselves get their meanings if they are to break out of the circle of dependence on prior descriptions (and prior words, etc.)?

6. *The problem of universals:* What is the essential difference between an object and a feature?

The unifying theme of this chapter is that contemporary research on categorization suggests a way of drawing some epistemological aspects of these problems into the realm of decidability. However, let me also quickly acknowledge that other aspects (particularly ontological ones) will remain untouched:

In the case of induction, neither the fallibilist's problem of "inductive risk" (the ever-present logical possibility that today's provisional generalizations will fail to hold tomorrow) nor the even more profound sceptic's problem of grounding induction noninductively (the apparent impossibility of validating the inductive process itself by any means that do not themselves already rely on induction) are not illuminated appreciably by what will be discussed here (just as the problem of equating qualitative experience with physical states is not resolved by work on the functional and behavioral correlates of consciousness in the case of the other-minds problem).

As to the words/world problem: There are a host of difficulties with the idea of "reference" that we owe to Frege (e.g., 1952 translation), Goodman (1954), Quine (1960), and Putnam (1975). One is the observation that the meaning of a word cannot be simply the object it refers to because, as Frege's morning-star/evening-star example shows, different words, with different meanings, can have the same referent (e.g., Venus), even unbeknownst to the speaker. There are also problems about what the connection between a word and its referent is, and how it is established. The model to be presented here will, it is hoped, cast some modest light on such difficulties, but it certainly cannot settle most of them to anyone's satisfaction. The treatment of meaning holism and concept revision will also no doubt be too epistemic[1] for the concerns of most philosophers.

The acquaintance/description dichotomy will also be limned in part, but the irreducibility of experience itself (Nagel, 1974) will remain as untouched as the nature of consciousness in the case of the other-minds problem (of which the acquaintance/description problem is, of course, merely a variant).

The model's application to the elementary-percepts and atomic-terms problem will likewise bypass the questions about irreducibility that are held by some philosophers to be the fundamental ones. And of course no real ontological issues will be broached by this treatment of our concepts of universals.

For each aspect of these longstanding problems that will be seen to be left untouched, however, I hope some aspects will have to be viewed in a new way as a result of this discussion, with some of the attendant questions even turning out to be posable in an empirically decidable form. For example, in the case of induction, there will be a description of the general features of the kind of mechanism needed to extract the regularities underlying instances by inductive generalization (if and when successful induction is possible). In the words/world case, a three-level representational system will be proposed to mediate between the world and the words one uses to describe and understand it. Holistic meaning revision will arise as a consequence of the convergent nature of this representational system and its relation to input data and the objects generating it. The acquaintance/description split will find its counterpart in the hybrid system of representation itself, with the two-level "acquaintance" system serving as the locus of elementary percepts and the grounding for the atomic terms of the third, "descriptive" system. The object/feature dichotomy will also find a natural counterpart in the proposed dual acquaintance system and its relation to the descriptive system. (All this should become clearer as the chapter progresses.)

This synthesis will be undertaken within the general framework of a theory of categorization. To close this introductory section I will now simply reformulate the six problems I have mentioned in categorization-theoretic terms:

The problem of induction (1) is the problem of extracting reliable categories from experience, that is, the problem of detecting and encoding – on the basis of a finite sample of instances of members and nonmembers of a set of underlying categories – the regularities or *invariants* that are sufficient to allow further instances to be categorized "correctly." The words/world problem (2) is the problem of matching the category representation to the instances encountered so as to yield "correct" categorization. Direct experience will be a prerequisite for forming the perceptual categories in the dual acquaintance system, whereas verbal descriptions will be the chief source of the symbolic categories of the descriptive system (4). Word/world coordination will involve a specific interaction of all three representational systems, with the names of the perceptual categories serving as the atomic terms for the verbal categories (5). The universals (6) for which we have concepts will be the invariant features underlying categorization that have themselves become categories. Last and most important, the "correctness" of categorization will turn out to be fundamentally an *approximate* rather than an exact matter, depending on the range and the confusability of the instances the categorizer has sampled to date. However, this approximateness of categories, especially verbal ones, will be seen to be an advantage rather than a handicap, giving the verbal system the potential for the universal expressive power of natural language and guaranteeing (insofar as a guarantee is possible, given inductive risk) that meaning revision, though holistic and approximate (3), will always converge.

Approximationism

Approximation and context-driven convergence. "Approximation" is a key concept in the present approach. In fact, if one wished to classify the approach in terms of an "ism" of the sort that the philosophical versions of these problems have generated, the best descriptor would be "approximationism" or "convergentism." The idea is that all of our categories turn out to be approximate rather than "exact" ones (in some realist's sense of "exact"); we converge on these approximations by accumulating data from experience and continually updating the categories in accordance with the constraints and contingencies of experience so as to yield an approximate match that is adequate for the sample of categorization problems we have faced to date (with the past always subsumed as a special case). Whether this inductive process is best viewed as "optimization" or as "satisficing" (i.e., provisionally making do – Simon, 1957) turns out to be a metaphysical question to which there appears to be no *general* answer (if we are indeed the kinds of categorizing devices I will describe), although there can be local answers in particular cases. What seems undeniable is that, whether it converges on an optimum or it merely satisfices, the induction of categories is an *approximate* process.[2]

It is easy to give concrete examples of the sense in which categories are approximate. Consider a simple problem in machine vision: Suppose all that a visual-scene analyzer had to do was to tell apart trees from animals, that is, to categorize all instances of trees as trees and all instances of animals as animals. Suppose, by way of further simplification, that trees and animals were the only patterns the analyzer ever encountered, and suppose (to simplify still more) that the patterns were already suitably smoothed and parsed so that they only appeared in standard positions, with figure and ground, parts and whole, already appropriately sorted.[3]

Now it is evident that with nothing to worry about but sorting trees and animals under these canonical conditions, a very simple rule would work quite well, for example, counting the number of legs, L, and calling an instance a tree if L was less than or equal to 1 and an animal otherwise. Obviously such a rule could only work with well-smoothed and parsed instances and with no anomalous ones (such as storks standing on one leg, trees with split trunks, or tables). But, as an approximation, the rule would successfully sort the standard cases described. As anomalies were introduced, the rule could be elaborated so as to tighten the approximation in accordance with the new contingencies. It is also apparent that if this view of categorization is a representative one, better and better approximations are all one can ever expect. No "essence" of a tree or of an animal could ever be captured by a process such as this. All that one could hope for would be the extraction and encoding of those invariant properties that will reliably subserve the categorizations one must make.

A picture versus a thousand words. A few other cases will have to be described to set our intuitions about approximation securely. Approximation is what is at issue in the observation that "a picture is worth a thousand words." In fact, in a formal sense (one that is in most cases trivial or inconsequential, yet true), a picture is always worth more than an infinite number of words, the reason being that a verbal description will always fall short. Words obviously fall short when they leave out some critical feature that would be necessary to sort some future or potential anomalous instance; but even if one supposes that every critical feature anyone would ever care to mention has been mentioned, a description will always remain essentially incomplete in the following ways:

(a) A description cannot convey the qualitative nature of the object being described (i.e., it cannot yield knowledge by acquaintance), although it can converge on it as

closely as the describer's descriptive resources and resourcefulness allow. (Critical here will be the prior repertoire of direct experiences and atomic labels on which the description can draw.)
(b) There will always remain inherent features of the object that will require further discourse to point out; an example would be a scene that one had neglected to mention was composed of a prime number of distinct colors.
(c) In the same vein, there would be all the known and yet-to-be-discovered properties of prime numbers that one could speak of – all of them entailed by the properties of the picture, all of them candidates (albeit far-fetched ones) for further discourse "about" the picture.[4]
(d) Finally, and most revealingly, there are the inexhaustible shortcomings of words exemplified by all the iterative afterthoughts made possible by, say, negation: for example, "the number of limbs is *not* two (three, four, . . . etc.)." The truth of all these potential descriptions is inherent in the picture, yet it is obvious that no exhaustive description would be possible. Hence all descriptions will only approximate a true, complete "description."

The context of alternatives and the context-dependence of categorization. There will be an idiosyncratic – but, I believe, well-motivated – use of the word "context" in this chapter; its meaning is perhaps best illustrated here. It applies equally to the tree-versus-animal discrimination problem mentioned earlier and to the (ostensibly trivial) negative/iterative case (d) just described. Every category has (at least) one *context* associated with it, namely, the relevant set of confusable alternatives amongst which the categorization is to be made.[5] For example, the context of the tree/animal categorization consisted of highly smoothed and parsed instances of trees and animals (in two-dimensional projection). In this context, a limb-count and comparison with the number 1 is sufficient to give rise to successful categorization. With the introduction of sleeping storks, bifurcated tree trunks, or tables, the context is widened and the approximation must be tightened to take into account more kinds of cases.[6]

The point is that successful categorization depends on finding the critical features on the basis of which reliable, correct performance can occur. These will depend, not on the inherent "features" of any particular instance (there are an infinity of them), but on the context: the range of confusable alternatives involved, the specific contrasts to be made, the invariant features that will reliably subserve successful categorization. And because ranges can change (and instantiation and categorization are never-ending processes), all categories and the features on which they are based will always remain provisional and approximate.

Convergence, category revision, and holism. The following generalizations can at this point be made about approximation and convergence: For convergence of a category-induction problem to be possible, the instances must contain an invariant basis for "correct" sorting. (i) If they do not have an invariance then the problem is insoluble, indeterminate, or ill-defined. Given that there is invariance inherent in the instances, there is still the question of whether or not the induction can find it. (ii) If the only means of finding the invariance is random trial-and-error, and time or capacity constraints make a combinatorial search unrealistic, convergence will again fail to occur. (iii) If, however, the invariance can be converged upon after a finite, reasonably small set of instances has been sampled – either because of prior simplifying constraints on the search or because of prior approximations and successful analogies – then the categorization can converge.

Note, however, that even here convergence will be context-relative, provisional, and approximate because (a) future instances could again diverge (a widening of the context), requiring a new or revised solution (a tightening of the approximation), and because of (b) factors of "underdetermination" and parsimony (to be discussed below). It can be shown information-theoretically (Dretske, 1983; Garner, 1974; Harnad, in preparation, b; Olson, 1970; Sayre, 1986) that *the context of confusable alternatives* determines the minimum quantity of information that will be required to discriminate reliably among them (and complexity theory [Chaitin, 1975] suggests methodological constraints for preferring a minimum).[7]

Underdetermination of category invariance. Two further illustrations should suffice. The first comes from a problem in the philosophy of science: the underdetermination of theories by data. It is always true in a trivial sense and often true in a substantive and practical sense that data are compatible with more than one theory that explains them (in fact, with an infinite number of theories). In practice, there may be two or more rival theories attempting to account for the same data. These theories will differ in their generality and their parsimony (some will account for more data, some will do so with fewer parameters) as well as in their predictions. Where predictions differ, "testability" presumably prevails, "normal science" occurs, and theories can be chosen and revised on the basis of subsequent evidence. It is obvious that this too is an approximate process; existing and future data provide the "context," as governed by the constraints and contingencies of the real world (as well as the limitations of our existing categories, our imaginations, and our ability or luck in extracting the features that "work").[8]

The theories can be viewed literally as descriptions of the invariants underlying the data – as making explicit the sorting rules for "correctly" classifying the events, objects, and properties of the real world, present and future – in other words, as attempted solutions to a categorization problem. Again, "correct" is problematic because the categorization is clearly provisional, not obviously optimal rather than "satisficing," and, as ever, approximate. Underdetermination implies approximationism, and it is hence likely that what can be discovered about the cognitive processes underlying the formation of perceptual and verbal categories will apply to scientific theory-construction too.

Overdetermination, Occam, and optimization. Underdetermination requires a word to be said about overdetermination (imparsimony) as well: It is certainly true that neither with respect to the truth of scientific theories nor with respect to the validity and veridicality of perceptual and verbal categories is there any a priori reason for Occam's razor to prevail. God never promised a parsimonious universe, and there is no logical reason that an N-parameter account should be truer than an $N+1$-parameter account of the same data. Similarly, there is no logical reason why, in our tree/animal categorization problem, the algorithm should have been the simplest one, namely, the comparison of the limb count with unity. First of all, the most parsimonious rule could be inefficient: It could take too long to implement; or it could simply be the case that the mechanism one is attempting to model happens to use a more redundant rule, perhaps for reliability, robustness, or speed (say, limb-count plus a calculation of the ratio of the length of the perimeter to the area or the principal axis, yielding a second parameter).

Redundancy and efficiency are mainly optimization matters. In principle, minimal rules must be preferred if an approximate process is to converge rather than go on forever (for example, by testing far-fetched, higher-order number-theoretic properties). But this is a methodological principle, not a logical one, and may be violated in practice. It is a logical matter, however, to note that the *decidability* of a question of parsimony can only rest on the availability of discriminating data. If there is no way ever to know whether a mechanism (or a universe) is better described by an N-parameter account or an $N+1$-parameter account, then the matter is probably better consigned to the domain of a priori questions that this discussion must bypass.

For our purposes, as long as there is a potential widening of the empirical context that can decide between a more and a less parsimonious algorithm (say, by showing that one of them sorts more instances or does it better in some sense), then an empirical choice can be made. Otherwise, the theory that overdetermines the data is to be provisionally rejected. Underdetermination of theories by data is a complicated enough fact of life without compounding it by overdetermining the data through an arbitrary, redundant proliferation of parameters.

Analog representations, analog/digital conversion, and "digital/digital" transformations. Finally, some mention should be made of the celebrated "analog/digital" distinction (Goodman, 1968; Lewis, 1971; Pylyshyn, 1984; Harnad, 1982b, and in preparation, a). Because this entire chapter could easily be devoted to this highly relevant issue, at the expense of describing the actual model being proposed, I will make a few quick points pertinent to the question of approximationism without providing all the supporting arguments: In important respects the formation of perceptual categories is a process of analog-to-digital (A/D) conversion.[9] In such a process some information is always lost (A/D transformations are approximations).

For example, the readout of any "digital" watch, no matter how precise, will always quantize time approximately, be it to the closest second, millisecond, microsecond, or what have you. The quantization is the digitization: A minimal atomic unit is selected that sets the "grain" or level of resolution of the system. Note that grain cuts both ways, however. After all, even an "analog" watch has limits on its resolving capacity, and its crystal pacemaker's oscillations (inasmuch as they are countable) are "digital." None of this requires a foray into quantum physics or concerns about whether physical processes are ultimately continuous or discrete. Biology and cognition occur at levels where the granularity is (roughly speaking) known and not really at issue. There is no real continuity in the nervous system, only continuity simulated by the deliberate blurring of grain or by insufficient resolving power to make discrete discriminations in certain regions. Hence it must be immediately pointed out that even the "continuous" representations that we will be assigning to the analog or iconic component of our dual acquaintance system will only have *simulated* continuity or pseudocontinuity rather than "real" continuity. In this sense, a real object will always be worth a thousand times (or even an infinite amount) more than a retinal image or a "mental" one. That is, even what we are calling an analog representation will be an approximation relative to the object it represents. This kind of approximation, however, is rather different from the kind of approximation involved in verbal description, and it is in some ways much less interesting, for it is still *shape-preserving* rather than symbolic; nevertheless, it will be shown to *mediate* verbal representations in an important way.

For now, let us note only that we are dealing with at least two orders of approximation: The first is the approximation involved in whatever structural information is lost in an analog transformation (because of grain, resolving capacity, and any other dimension or range of variation not faithfully preserved in the image). This itself involves some approximation (information loss): the object-to-icon (O/I) transformation. Next there is the further approximation involved in selectively extracting invariant features (and discarding other variation that is not invariant across instances) in the service of category formation: This is the icon-to-atomic-category (I/C) conversion.[10]

Finally, there is the atomic-category-to-verbal-category and the verbal-to-verbal category conversion involved in symbolic description: These will be called the categorical-to-symbolic (C/S) and symbolic-to-symbolic (S/S) transformations. It is decidedly an understatement to call the last of these – the remarkable natural-language phenomenon of translatability (Steklis & Harnad, 1976) – a "D/D" conversion. But what the three prior stages of A/D conversion (O/I, I/C, C/S) and the fourth stage of D/D (S/S) do illustrate is the extensive degree to which category formation is indeed a process of approximation.

Categorical perception

Discrimination, identification, and categorical perception. Having set the stage with this extended discussion of approximationism, I will now describe the kinds of data and findings that have motivated the model to be proposed here. First, there is the psychophysical evidence concerning our *relative discrimination* performance: the kinds of stimuli we can tell apart (when they are presented simultaneously or in immediate succession) by making a same/different judgment, by stimulus-stimulus matching (picking which of several stimuli is most similar to the target stimulus), or by stimulus-response matching (copying, mimicking, or some other analog response). Same/different judgments can provide evidence about the size of the *jnds* (just-noticeable differences) between stimuli and matching can be used to derive multidimensional measures of similarity or proximity between stimuli. What must be emphasized in the case of the relative discrimination data is that they depend either on the simultaneous presence of the stimuli being compared or on their successive presentation within a short enough time interval to allow brief iconic images to mediate the comparison. The discrimination is *relative* because it involves pairwise comparison, rather than being an absolute judgment about a stimulus in isolation.

Absolute discrimination, on the other hand, requires an autonomous judgment about the stimulus being presented, not a comparison with an accompanying stimulus. Absolute judgment calls for a unique discriminating response, which can either be a specially trained operant response or, more generally, a verbal label. In this chapter, absolute discrimination will henceforth be referred to as "identification" and relative discrimination simply as "discrimination." As I have pointed out elsewhere (Harnad, 1982b), "absolute" and "relative" are in any case partially misleading descriptors, because absolute discriminations are always made relative to an implied context of alternatives (i.e., they are context-dependent in the sense described earlier), whereas relative discriminations (and their underlying representations) are somewhat context-independent, and in that sense more "absolute."

For the purposes of categorization theory, the last three decades of research on discrimination and identification can be grounded in George Miller's synthesis in his celebrated 7 ± 2 paper (Miller, 1956; Broadbent, 1975). Miller noted that whereas discriminability seems to vary with the sensory modality and dimension involved, identifiability seems to have modality-independent constraints that are governed by learning, encoding (i.e., representation), and memory. How many stimuli you can discriminate will depend on the sensory dimension in question, but how many you can identify depends on what the confusable alternatives are (i.e., the informational context) and how you encode them: Discrimination is modality dependent and identification is representation dependent.

Even before Miller's observations, however, there had been indications that there might be interactions between identification and discrimination, or at any rate that discrimination too could be affected by experience and learning (Lawrence, 1950; see also E. J. Gibson, 1969). In particular, it was noted that mere exposure could sharpen discriminability and that certain kinds of differential experience could enhance some perceived differences and diminish others. But if discriminability was modifiable then perhaps psychophysical assumptions about stable, isotropic *jnd* continua were too rigid. Stability and isotropy were challenged separately. Helson (1964) showed how discrimination could vary with adaptation level (see Wilson, Chapter 13, this volume) and research on color perception (see Bornstein, Chapter 9) and phoneme perception (Macmillan, Chapter 2) showed that uniform physical continua were not necessarily uniform or continuous perceptually.

Phoneme perception and the motor theory. Apart from questions about plasticity and anisotropy in sensory continua, the role of experience and learning – and especially that of the motor system and language – in our discriminative performance became an object of attention and speculation. The finding in phoneme perception had been that discriminability was greater across the "boundaries" between two different phoneme categories (e.g., /ba/ and /da/) than it was within the categories, even when physically equal stimulus differences were involved. Now because phonemes were assumed to be acquired, man-made categories, it was hypothesized that language somehow mediated these dramatic boundary effects (which are subjectively perceived as not merely quantitative but also qualitative). In particular, according to the "motor theory of speech perception" (Liberman, Harris, Hoffman, & Griffith, 1957), the reason that /ba/ and /da/ were "categorically" (i.e., discontinuously) discriminated was that their perception was mediated by a motor template derived from the way the sounds had to be articulated in order to be spoken: The perceptual discontinuity was mediated by the motor discontinuity.

The hypothesis of an analog motor template depended on a number of assumptions that did not remain unchallenged for long. One was the "speech is special" assumption, according to which perceptual discontinuities of this sort (henceforth referred to as Categorical Perception or CP) should be unique to speech. An early critique of the motor theory by Lane (1965), however, showed that CP-like effects could occur in other modalities. Another assumption of the motor theory had been that phoneme-category boundaries are acquired in learning how to speak, but it was later found that prelinguistic infants exhibit CP effects in phoneme discrimination (see Eimas, Miller, & Jusczyk in Chapter 5, this volume). It had also been assumed that phoneme CP was unique to human beings, but it was subsequently observed in nonhuman species (with no apparent humanlike vocalizations to "mediate" them – see Chapter 10 by Ehret, Chapter 11 by Snowdon, and Chapter 12 by Kuhl, this volume).

Some attempts were made to patch up the motor theory and to hold onto the speech-is-special hypothesis by recasting it in evolutionary form, suggesting that there had been natural selection for enhanced discrimination of certain categories of audition because of its congruity with vocal categories. In addition it was conceded that these categories may have been even more favored because they had been "prepared" by chance congruence with phylogenetically older auditory discontinuities (of unknown functional significance).

This uneasy synthesis is more or less the current status of the motor theory. The model to be proposed in this chapter will attempt to pick out the salient features of the motor theory and the "speech is special" theory that might be worth preserving; but first let us look briefly at the parallel developments in color CP.

Color perception and the "Whorf Hypothesis." Influenced by the "Whorf Hypothesis" that language somehow determines our view of reality, Berlin & Kay (1969) conducted extensive cross-cultural investigations to show that color-boundary effects are governed by vocabulary and that the categories of colors we can discriminate depend on the colors we name. The findings indicated that the phenomenon is ambiguous. There is some effect of color-names, but there also appear to be universal perceptual constraints at work, underlying not only the boundary effects but even the degrees of freedom that different languages have in their color naming. The current view is that color categories are largely governed by innate, species-specific color-detecting mechanisms, but that there is also some color-boundary plasticity that can be modulated by experience and naming (see Chapter 9 by Bornstein, this volume), especially in the young.

Unanswered questions about categorical perception

On the basis of the color and phoneme CP data as well as the various critiques and elaborations of the motor theory and the Whorf hypothesis that have appeared to date, a number of prominent unanswered questions about the generality and particulars of the CP phenomenon suggest themselves. Many of these questions have already been posed in the introductory chapter to this volume and by several of the other contributors. By way of motivating the representational model to be proposed in this chapter, I will now state the most prominent of these unanswered questions here, together with a number of provisional replies and hypotheses that point toward a coherent framework for unified CP research in the more general context of category formation:

1. Is CP uniquely related to or dependent on language, or are there instances of nonlinguistic CP? If CP is defined as enhanced discriminability between categories and enhanced similarity within categories (relative to some objective, category-independent metric) then it is not unique to language or uniquely dependent on language. However, language is unique in its potential to mediate CP because it provides the labels and the descriptions that subtend most of our categories.

2. What is the relation of the Whorf Hypothesis to CP? The Whorf Hypothesis originally concerned a putative influence of syntactic categories on perception – it was claimed that the Hopi, lacking a future tense in their language, had no concept of the future (Whorf, 1964) – but the idea has always been vague and difficult to test (cf. Bloom, 1981; Liu, 1985). A CP version of the Whorf Hypothesis could be formulated as follows: The perceptual and conceptual discriminations we make are governed by the categories we name and by our representations of the invariant features underlying the categorization. To the extent that discriminability could be demonstrated to be influenced by learned names and descriptions, this version of the Whorf Hypothesis would be supported.

3. Is speech special, and if so, is its special status connected with CP? Speech is special in the following respects: It is the chief human medium of commu-

Category induction and representation

nication: linguistic communication. Speech-sound categories (phonemes) are special in that they have motor analogs – the auditory stimuli can be not only perceived but also *produced* by the perceiver. This perception/production congruence is also not unique to speech (gesture, for example, shares the same motor-analog property [Steklis & Harnad, 1976], as do facial expression, singing, dancing, etc.). Speech-sound categories exhibit CP (phoneme boundaries), but because of the special perception/production congruence in speech, it is not yet clear whether this is a representative or an anomalous form of CP.

4. Is CP uniquely related to or dependent on communication, or are there noncommunicational instances of CP? Phoneme CP is communication related. So are most of the existing examples of CP-like effects in animals, which tend to involve species-specific signaling systems (see Ehret in Chapter 10, this volume). Color CP, however, is not obviously communicational, although it may be influenced by language. It is not yet clear whether any arbitrary operant response can "label" categories and generate boundaries or whether language and other communicational systems and contexts are especially involved.

5. Is CP uniquely related to or dependent on motor activity, or are there purely sensory instances of CP? There are three ways motor activity could be crucial to CP: (a) in analog form (as dictated by the "motor theory of speech perception"), (b) in furnishing the arbitrary names and symbolic descriptions provided by language, or merely (c) as an operant source of arbitrary or functional discriminating responses. Whether the motor system is crucially involved in CP in any of these ways is not yet known. It is logically possible that CP could be mediated purely by sensory matching (with one stimulus serving as the instance and the other as the "label") but it would be difficult to demonstrate that covert language had not played a role in human experiments; possibly animal experiments on stimulus/stimulus CP could clarify this, although there too an overt operant response is likely to be necessary (cf. Premack, 1976). CP effects arising purely as a result of sensory preconditioning seem unlikely, but they remain a logical possibility.

6. What is the current status of the "motor theory"? The motor theory is currently moot. Its ontogenetic version seems to be contradicted by developmental data and its phylogenetic version seems weakened by comparative data. However, it is still not eliminated as a possible special factor in the case of speech-sound CP.

7. What is the role, if any, of analog representations, sensory or motor, in CP? Moot. The role of the motor system has not been sorted out, nor has the role of analogs. A further complication comes from the fact that analog matching is one of the measures of relative discrimination itself. CP can probably occur without motor analogs, but motor analogs probably strengthen it, and hence may indeed have been capitalized upon in some instances by evolution, as the later motor theories have claimed (see Chapter 12 by Kuhl, this volume).

8. Is CP unique to audition, or does it occur in other modalities as well? CP clearly occurs in vision too (color CP); audition may be a special case (apart from the chameleon) because of its production-analog character and its (consequent) preferred evolutionary status as a signaling system (Steklis & Harnad, 1976).

9. Is auditory CP unique to speech? No, there are now numerous instances of nonspeech auditory CP (see Rosen & Howell in Chapter 4, this volume).

10. Is CP unique to human beings, or do other species exhibit it as well? Nonhuman species exhibit CP-like effects too (see Chaptes 10, 11, and 12, this volume). The role of CP in comparative cognition and comparative communication is an important topic for future research.

11. Is CP a learned or an innate phenomenon or both? This is one of the most critical unanswered questions about CP. Experience can demonstrably modulate CP boundaries (see Chapter 3 by Repp & Liberman, Chapter 4 by Rosen & Howell, and Chapter 9 by Bornstein, this volume) but it is not yet known whether it can create them de novo or alter them radically or permanently.

12. Are there short-term and long-term CP effects? There are short-term, habituation-like effects and task-dependent stimulus-range effects for sure (see Chapter 2 by Macmillan & Chapter 13 by Wilson, this volume). Long-term effects have not yet been carefully tested. Learned CP boundaries would be the most convincing demonstration of a long-term effect, but long-term or permanent movement of a preexisting boundary would also be an important finding.

13. Does CP imply total within-category indiscriminability or merely enhanced within-category similarity and enhanced between-category distinctiveness? The overstatement of within-category reductions in discriminability (with claims that within-category differences are indiscriminable) has resulted in much misunderstanding of CP. There never has been total within-category indiscriminability, nor would that make psychophysical sense: It would require a category one *jnd* wide! There has also not yet been a clear demonstration of the time-course of acquired CP in which discriminability within and between categories is compared before and after CP training. For innate CP it would be hard to establish a baseline to assess what was enhanced and what was diminished.

14. Are CP boundaries fixed or plastic? Short-term plasticities have been demonstrated. Long-term plasticity remains to be investigated, both early in development and at maturity.

Category induction and representation 549

15. Is CP purely a continuity/discontinuity phenomenon? Psychophysical studies of CP are of course based on perceptual discontinuities. So are models that posit thresholds or all-or-none feature detectors. However, as long as a similarity metric can be inferred from the data (e.g., by psychophysical scaling techniques [Tversky, 1977], or even with event-related potentials – see Chapter 14 by Molfese and Chapter 15 by Regan, this volume), the requisite boundary effects on discrimination can in principle be demonstrated without any real physical continuum or continuity being involved.

16. Does CP have a temporal counterpart? First of all, auditory CP usually involves a temporal (horizontal) component as well as a synchronous (vertical) one (see, for example, Chapter 1 by Pastore and Chapter 10 by Ehret, this volume). In addition, the kind of "rechunking" experiment Miller (1956) described (e.g., the recoding of 0/1 binary digit sequences into bigger chunks for better recall by using their overlearned decimal names) involves the temporal domain. Moreover, direct experiments on temporal discrimination remain to be tried. Anything that can be coded into a Millerian "chunk" can be a category and can hence give rise to CP effects.

17. Is CP just a concrete perceptual effect or does it occur with abstract categories as well? Abstract CP remains to be investigated, but it is certainly possible in principle. Moreover, in the present model it will be hypothesized that the feature extraction required to form categories in the first place necessarily involves abstraction.

18. What is the relation of CP research to natural category research? CP research is unified by a discriminability paradigm that permits within- and between-category similarities to be tested; CP research has also until now been concerned largely with concrete perceptual categories (see Chapter 1 by Pastore, this volume). Natural category research (although it began with color categories; see Chapter 9, this volume) has chiefly been preoccupied with (a) how long it takes subjects to judge an instance to be a member of a category, (b) how typical a member they judge it to be, and (c) what features or rules they *report* using in order to perform the categorization (see Chapter 16 by Medin & Barsalou and Chapter 17 by Keil & Kelly, this volume). Typically the categories are already well learned and the membership judgments are reliable; the relation of typicality judgments and categorization latency to within- and between-category discriminability is not known, although it should certainly be investigated. Models arising from the two different approaches differ. It is time to unify these two areas of categorization research, along with the older concept formation research (Bruner, Goodnow, & Austin, 1956).

19. What is the relation of CP research to work on feature detectors in neuroscience? As yet, minimal. Some CP modelers are thinking in terms of feature detectors (see the critical review in Chapter 6 by Remez, this volume), especially in the case of categories that look innate (see Chapters 5, by Bornstein, 9, by Ehret, and 10, by Eimas et al.). However, the difficult cognitive problem of category acquisition does not yet have a neural basis to draw on, although some of this may eventually emerge from human ERP (event-related potential) studies (see Chapters 14, by Molfese, and 15, by Regan) and from more basic work on sensory psychophysics and higher sensory and cognitive functions.

20. What is the relation of CP research to Gibsonian work on "direct perception"? The Gibsons were among the first to be interested in perceptual learning (E. Gibson, 1969). Of course, the ecological-optics approach (Gibson, 1979) does emphasize the detection of invariants (see also Neisser, 1987). However, the notion of direct, unmediated "pick-up" has so far not proven useful in modeling invariance extraction in category formation, particularly in the important cases in which learning is involved. CP seems more amenable to a constructive (Rock, 1983) and perhaps even a computational approach (Ullman, 1980).

21. What is the relation of CP research to research on pattern recognition and artificial intelligence? To date, statistical pattern recognition research has not been successful in developing models with realistically general categorization capabilities (Minsky & Papert, 1969).[11] Artificial intelligence (AI) has tended to focus on specialized problems requiring considerable built-in symbolic knowledge (Schank, Collins, & Hunter, 1986) and, as in the primate "language" studies (Premack, 1976), the symbol manipulation has been considerably overinterpreted (Searle, 1980, Harnad, in preparation, a). The higher cognitive problems in categorization research call for an inductive approach that AI will only be able to provide if it attempts to construct more general, all-purpose category learning models. (The model to be proposed in this chapter, for example, is potentially computer testable, and its further development could be guided by both perceptual-learning and simulation data.)

22. What is the relation of CP research to contemporary philosophy of cognitive science? The CP view is fundamentally at odds with the "panpropositional" (or "symbol-crunching") view, according to which most of the cognitive work is done by mental "sentences" (much as in current AI; Pylyshyn, 1980, 1984; Fodor, 1975, 1980). This sentential view seems to be ungrounded; in particular, the meanings of the atomic terms of its sentences cannot simply be derived from still more sentences without infinite regress. According to the model proposed here, *the meanings of elementary symbols must be grounded in perceptual categories*. That is, symbols, which are manipulated only on the basis of their form (i.e., syntactically) rather than their "meaning," must be reducible to nonsymbolic, *shape-*preserving representations. Semantics can only arise when the interpretations of elementary symbols are "fixed" by these nonsymbolic, iconic representations and their causal connections to input and output from the world. The view is "bottom-up," but psychophysical rather than neural; and it emphasizes the crucial grounding function of nonsymbolic (iconic and categorical) representations.[12] It is best described as "robotic functionalism," as opposed to the currently regnant "symbolic functionalism."

A three-level representational system: An iconic and categorical acquaintance system and a symbolic description system

Iconic and categorical representations. The model is quite simple. It was originally proposed in order to account for the kinds of differences that appear to underlie hemispheric lateralization (Harnad, Doty, Goldstein, Jaynes, & Krauthamer, 1977; Harnad 1982b), but it is by no means committed to left/right differences (which may turn out to have been exaggerated in the flurry of research stimulated by the dramatic split-brain findings). The hypothesis is that whenever the categorizer encounters a sensory input, not one, but *two* kinds of representation of the stimulus object begin to be established (if they do not exist already) or become activated (if they already exist).

The first kind of representation is *iconic,* being an analog of the sensory input (more specifically, of the proximal projection of the distal stimulus object on the device's transducer surfaces). This iconic representation (IR) is "unbounded," in that it is not governed by a category boundary. (The sense of this will become clearer soon.)

It is perhaps misleading to describe the IR as "a" representation, because, by its nature, it will in fact be many (mostly very similar) analog representations; the differences among these will arise from the instance-to-instance variation of the input class in question. To oversimplify: Suppose the input was a species of mushroom. The instances would vary in all the ways such a mushroom could vary; not only in size, form, and color, but also in position, surroundings, and time of day. It is even misleading to speak of the instances that activate an IR as being any single class of inputs at all (except at the metalevel), for to the iconic system they would blend continuously into one another, with nothing setting them apart except perhaps whatever *natural* boundaries there may be amongst the variations from instance to instance: In nature the mushroom may never grow upside-down or appear suspended in mid-air; or there may exist no intermediate forms blending continuously from it into a toadstool.

So analog representations are unbounded in the sense that nothing reliably links them to a shared category except whatever natural similarities and differences they may have.[13] The latter would unite somewhat the IRs activated by inputs that had some overall configural similarity (in vision this would perhaps be overall topographic form) that they did not happen to share with any other input.[14]

But apart from such "ecological" boundaries, iconic representations would blend continuously into one another, sharing the same analog representational substrate to the degree that they shared overall physical similarities of configuration or shape. Note that, apart from possibly subserving some none-too-reliable "natural categorization," these IRs would not be very useful for categorization and identification (i.e., for absolute discrimination).[15] On the other hand, IRs would be ideal for relative discrimination, in that they faithfully preserve the iconic character of the input for such purposes as same-different judgments, stimulus-matching, and copying. These are all fundamentally noncategorical tasks, in which categorization would probably introduce biases that would distort the analog, holistic character of the raw, unfiltered inputs.

At the same time that IRs were being strengthened by repeated exposure to a class of inputs, however, another kind of representation would be forming: The "bounded" *categorical* representation (CR) would have (a) a category boundary and would be (b) highly context-sensitive (with "context" here being used in the specialized sense introduced earlier: the sampled set of instances of relevant and confusable alternative categories) and (c) feedback- or consequence-dependent. In the case of the mushroom-discrimination problem, the context would be all the kinds of mushrooms with which the one in question could be confused. Now if toadstools were the only existing alternative, and they were all separated fortuitously by a reliable natural shape-gap of some kind, then perhaps the CR would be redundant (except in collecting this naturally disjoint class of instances under a collective label). But if there were any possibility of confusion – as there would be in many natural, nontrivial (i.e., underdetermined) categorization problems – then the CR would have to assume a form that was radically different from the IR. Note that IRs would be the result of an analog transformation, preserving – except perhaps for some acquired and innate smoothing and some of the unavoidable information loss mentioned earlier in connection with analog transformations – the spatiotemporal structure (i.e., the physical "shape") of the input or proximal stimulus. The CR could not afford to do this, at least not indiscriminately; in fact, the CR would have to eliminate most of the raw configural structure, retaining only what was *invariant* in all of the uninformative and irrelevant instance-to-instance variation of the mushroom in question and invariantly *absent* from instances of other categories of mushroom within the same context of alternatives (e.g., toadstools). In other words, the CR would have to include a kind of A/D (analog/digital) filter that could reliably sort the mushroom instances into their appropriate, bounded categories using distinctive, confusion-resolving features.[16] In our terms, however, the filter would be more perspicuously described as I/C (iconic-to-categorical) rather than A/D, for even invariant features would be (minimally, selectively, and partially) shape-preserving, and hence not yet arbitrary formal symbols: not yet fully "digitized."

Active versus passive filtering. It is not clear whether the categorical representation should be equated with the I/C filter itself, or with a filtered instance or even a filtered IR. The model is currently not specific enough to be committed to any of these three interpretations. It is clear that some interaction among input instances, stored IRs, and stored filters will be involved in categorization, but the question of whether or not to posit more content to the CRs than the filter itself seems somewhat premature at this point and in any case would not substantively alter this account.

More important is the question of the *nature* of the I/C filtering function of the CRs. It seems unlikely that these will be passive filters, simply selectively detecting some stimulus feature (such as straightness) and then sorting according to its presence or absence (e.g., in the context of "rectilinear" versus "curvilinear" planar forms). Passive feature-detection no doubt occurs, but active, constructive filtering may be even more important. Some computation would be called for in arriving at conjunctive and disjunctive invariants (e.g., small *and* rectilinear, small *or* rectilinear) by induction, although once found to be reliable, they could of course be detected holistically. A task that was more like prime-number detection (which I of course do not suggest we do perceptually or "on-line") would require active computational processes, however. Perhaps the identification of the closed planar rectilinear forms (particularly those with more than seven sides) represents a categorization problem of the latter kind. The "analysis-by-synthesis" variant of the motor theory (Stevens & Halle, 1967) also suggests that there is active filtering in phoneme perception; temporal processes seem by their nature to require active, "real-time" filtering and integration. But even classical instances of "unconscious inference" underlying perceptual constancies seem to involve constructive rather than passive filtering (Rock, 1983). Finally, abstract categorization problems (e.g., deciding whether a given mathematical function is differentiable or whether a given letter string is a word) seem especially to call for active processing in order to be solved correctly. Note also that the active process could itself be either analog or A/D (as in mental rotation [Shepard & Cooper, 1982], or in categorical perception) or it could even be symbolic (as in mental counting or inference [Fodor, 1975]) or hybrid.[17]

The issue of whether CRs involve passive or active filtering (or even whether the filtering is conscious or unconscious [Holender, 1986]) does not affect the general hypothesis that bounded representations are formed by the detection and encoding of the features that are sufficient to sort negative and positive instances correctly. Not even questions of optimality (necessity, sufficiency, exhaustiveness, parsimony, efficiency, speed, robustness, reliability, etc.) are critical to the basic constraint that CRs must be very different from IRs. Whereas IRs preserve analog structure relatively indiscriminately, CRs selectively reduce input structure to those invariant features that are sufficient to subserve successful categorization (in a given context). It remains to add that the categorization must be *expressed* or acted upon in some form, and that although any differential response would do, the vast repertoire of arbitrary[18] labels that (later) constitutes the lexicon of a language is the natural source for the differential responses associated with every categorization. Hence CRs are not only filtered (or filters) but they are labeled: Associated with the CR of the positive instances of each category (in a given context) is the category name.

At this point we can again turn to the CP phenomenon to note that, just as IRs can account for discrimination performance, CRs can account for identification. And, most important, the CP "boundary effect," that is, the enhancement of between-category differences and within-category similarities, can be seen as a natural interaction between the two kinds of representation, with the filtered invariants of the CRs biasing the analog structure of the IRs (see Figure 19.1). Another important point is that, up to now, both kinds of representation and their effects arise from *direct acquaintance* with the instances; hence both are perceptual representations (one more concrete than the other). The labels of the CRs, however, have been hypothesized to correspond to the linguistic lexicon, and our vocabulary certainly does not arise purely by perceptual acquaintance. Moreover, there is so far something uncomfortably extensional and referential about this system of labels; that is, they seem to stand for or refer to a set of instances, and we know that there are problems with referential theories of linguistic meaning (Frege, 1952; Putnam, 1975).

Symbolic representations. This is the juncture at which the *description* system must be introduced; but first a simplifying assumption will be made (one that will no doubt give rise to some strong objections, particularly from "speech act" theorists [e.g., Searle, 1969]): For the purposes of this theory of categorization, no generality is lost if the only kind of linguistic act taken into consideration is the declarative sentence. Even more specifically, it will be assumed that all declarative sentences can be reformulated and meaningfully treated as propositions about category membership. That is, what is predicated about the subject of a proposition is that it is a member of some category or other. For example, the foregoing sentence can be (tediously) reformulated as making the proposition that "all (sentences that make) predications are (members of the category of) sentences that assign category membership."

With this simplifying assumption one can state the hypothesis that the description system assigns category membership "by dictum" (so to speak). Instead of constructing an invariance filter on the basis of direct experience with instances, it operates on *existing* labels, and constructs categories by manipulating these labels, in particular, assigning membership on the basis of stipulated rules rather than perceptual invariants derived from direct experience.

Consider the same categorization problem "solved" two different ways.[19] Let the problem be the very first one we considered, that of telling apart trees and animals (in a smoothed context without anomalies and with "limbs" already categorized). The solution by the acquaintance system ("de re") requires sampling instances of trees and nontrees and (presumably) converging on the $L \leq 1$ invariant by induction. The result is a CR, which consists of an $L \leq 1$-filtered, labeled representation plus an appropriately biased population of IRs. The solution by description ("de dicto") is to *recombine* the existing label repertoire (which includes "limbs," numbers, and whatever the tree/animal instances are collectively called in their superordinate context) and stating the rule: "It's a tree if it has one limb or less, an animal otherwise."[20]

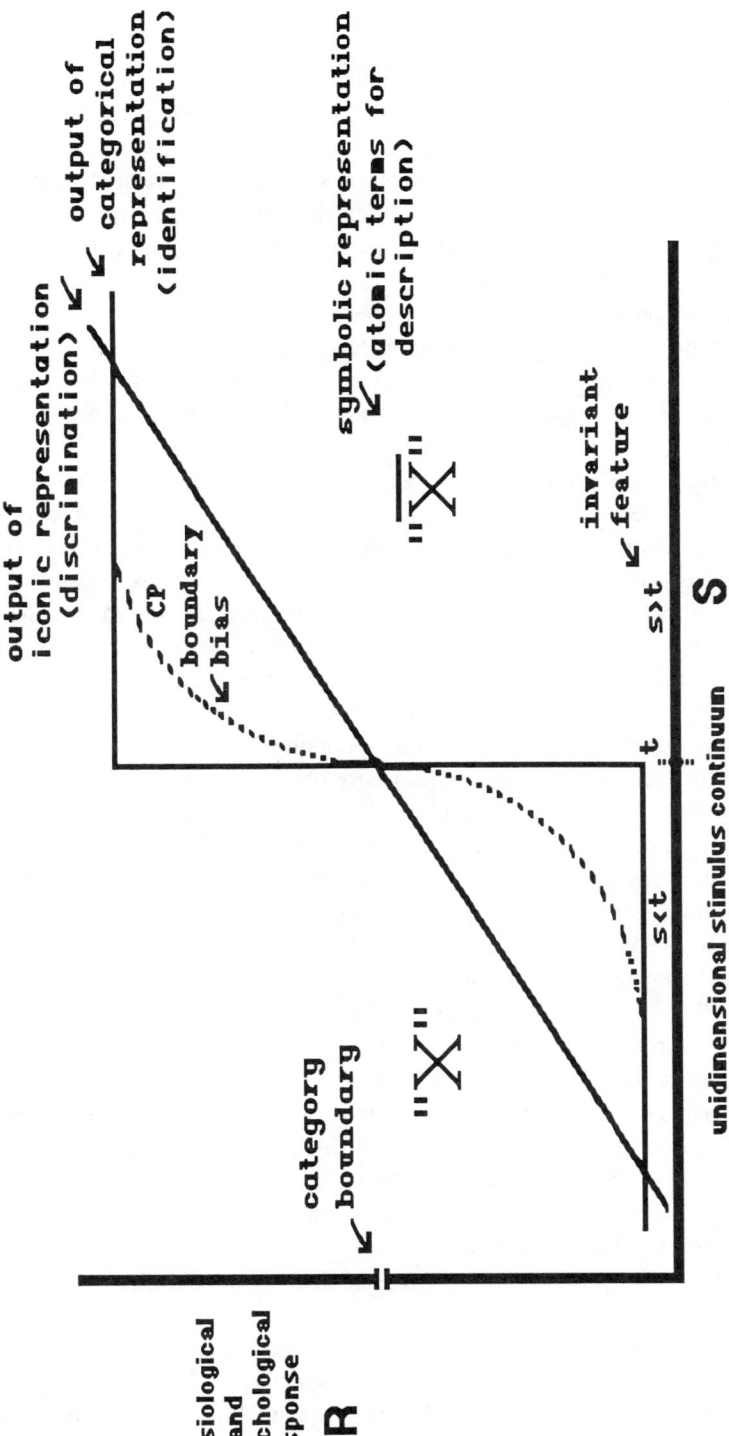

Figure 19.1. Idealized depiction of the input/output relations among the three kinds of representation (iconic, categorical, and symbolic) for a simple one-dimensional stimulus continuum, S. The iconic representation (in accordance with Weber's Law) is proportional to S (actually, log S/S'). The categorical representation is an all-or-none function of the invariant features (e.g., $s > t$, t = threshold, in this simple quantized continuum) and determines the category boundary. (In reality there is always some variability at the boundary.) "X" and "$\overline{X}$" (i.e., "not-X") are the symbolic representations (i.e., the labels for the stimulus category and its complement in this dichotomous context). Combining these into propositions yields further symbolic representations. The dotted line shows the CP boundary effect: the biasing influence of the category boundary on perceived similarity, as reflected in anisotropies in the Weber function. This is the effect of naming on perceiving, as represented in this model by the interaction between the iconic and the categorical representation.

The principle is simple: Descriptions spare us the need for laborious learning by direct acquaintance; however, they depend on the prior existence of a repertoire of labeled categories on which the combinatory descriptions can draw. Hence *symbolic* representations (SRs), which are encoded as mental sentences, define new categories, but they must be grounded in old ones; the descriptive system as a whole must accordingly be *grounded* in the acquaintance system.[21] Moreover, apart from the obvious parasitism of description on acquaintance, there is nothing to prevent redundant representations from being formed. There could, for example, be both a CR and an SR for the tree/animal categorization above. And whereas, apart from its grounding function, the acquaintance system has a certain primacy with respect to concrete categories, the descriptive system will obviously loom increasingly large with abstract ones.

The idea of abstraction needs some further elaboration in the context of this model. Note that an element of abstraction was already involved in the I/C process. The CR really *is* an abstraction from the raw instances: It consists of the invariant features sufficient to subserve the categorization, with everything else discarded. Hence it is not true that the CR is merely an *extensional* representation (as the IRs are, perhaps). It does not encode the totality of the instances; only their invariant properties. Hence it is an *intensional* rather than an extensional representation, preserving and expressing invariants, properties, relations, rules.[22]

Now recall the recurrent caveat I have been mentioning, about invariants "in a given context." The fact is that the same instance (or object, if you will) can appear in many different contexts (indeed, an infinity of them), depending on the relevant alternatives, confusabilities, and contrasts involved. Consequently, an instance can have (and activate) many different CRs, each associated with a different context. Each context will in general involve superordinate categorizations, with their own attendant invariants. (For example, the context of the tree/animal discrimination could have been living things, concrete objects, things I have in my backyard, drawings, etc.) Whether or not this locally hierarchical representational system is strictly hierarchical throughout is an open question (Keil, 1979), but I suspect not. In any case, the fact that different features of an instance will be encoded in different CRs associated with different contexts suggests that objects and properties are represented in similar ways in this system. "Apples" (which are objects, presumably) will have CRs that select for redness, roundness, and so on. "Red things" and even "redness" (they have somewhat different contexts) will likewise have their own CRs (with all three kinds counting apples as instances). The process of forming bounded representations *is* the process of abstraction, and CRs consist of abstracted features (or their detectors; cf. Chapter 6 by Remez, this volume).

CRs are representations of the members of the category that they discriminate. They accomplish the absolute discrimination by selectively filtering features. Hence, cognitively speaking, objects are the instances that CRs sort and properties are the means by which CRs sort them. But nothing prevents an instance from being an instance of a property, in which case its CR will again sort it by (higher-order)

Category induction and representation 557

properties. The only difference between whether something is an object or a property in this representational system is whether it is encoded as a category (in which case it is treated as an object) or it is merely used as an invariant in the encoding of a category (in which case it is just a property). Again, in practice, as with CRs and SRs for the same "thing," properties that are encoded in the CRs from some subordinate category will also tend to be members of superordinate categories themselves, although again some bottom-level object versus first-level feature distinction must ground the system. Once features get named, however, it is natural that the work of making further categorical distinctions should be taken over by the symbolic system, not only because words and other formal symbols are preferable to concrete representations in dealing with abstractions, but also because of the remarkable capacity of natural language to describe anything (to as close an approximation as one can express the need for [Steklis & Harnad, 1976]).[23]

Limits of the model. It remains to state candidly what this model has *not* done before summarizing what it has attempted to do and returning briefly to describe its bearing on the philosophical questions that were alluded to at the outset. This model has *not* provided an algorithmic solution to the problem of induction (cf. McClelland et al., 1986); it has not given a general (or even a particular) formula that will find the invariants underlying any given (underdetermined) categorization problem. The model is only a sketch of some of the general features it might be useful for such an inductive device to have, if such a device is possible at all. Cognitive nativism – the idea that categories are not learned but inborn – is a vast null hypothesis. For some theorists it seems plausible to accept this null hypothesis a priori (Chomsky, 1980; Fodor, 1981, 1985), or at least on persuasive current evidence. If the nativistic null hypothesis is right, then the evidence to date is entirely consistent with CP's being nothing but a (special, or possibly general) innate mechanism. This of course passes the inductive burden for "learning" CP categories to evolution (Harnad, 1976) or perhaps, with the "new preformationism," the inductive burden can be discarded altogether (Eldredge & Cracraft, 1980). The present model is frankly inductivist and still envisions that the burden can be shouldered without consigning the origins of our categories to the Big Bang.

Apart from being inductivist but failing to provide any inductive algorithms, the present model also goes considerably beyond the data, not only generalizing CP a good deal past what has as yet been investigated, but not even accounting for the existing data in the most parsimonious way: Simple, task-specific feature detectors would have been enough; the existence of three representational systems is hardly forced on us by the evidence.

On the other hand, the model does synthesize CP findings with identification performance data in general, and it does pursue a rather suggestive developmental and representational link between identification in psychophysics and identification in pycholinguistics. It also suggests that the "categorical perception" literature may have more in common with other lines of research on category cognition (e.g.,

Neisser 1987) than merely the name: Categorical perception may provide the groundwork for category cognition. The model itself also attempts to resolve some of the disputes about whether representations are "imagistic" or "propositional" (Kosslyn, Pinker, Smith, & Shwartz, 1979; Pylyshyn, 1981). Answer: Some of each, and more besides. Finally, some productive contact is made with certain long-standing philosophical problems. I will close by describing the model's implications for the problems raised at the beginning of the chapter.

Philosophical implications

The problem of induction. If any nontrivial induction actually does occur in cognition, then a category-representing architecture of the kind I have described could accomplish it in principle. All-purpose learning algorithms have not been proposed, but the narrowing of the scope of the problem provided by the idea of context, invariants, and the context-relativity of categorization, as well as the general limits and advantages suggested by approximationism and convergence, perhaps recast the empirical side of the induction problem in a more tractable form.

The word/world problem, meaning holism, and concept revision: According to this model, a potential dissociation between words and the world (i.e., an indeterminacy about how words pick out their referents, which ones they pick out, and what the link between them is) is mediated by the dual-acquaintance system. The (always provisional and approximate) match between words and world is grounded in our perceptual categories, which are based on the invariants that are sufficient to subserve reliable categorization, that is, object-sorting. Word meanings are context-relative and local, on the one hand, and, because contexts are interrelated (both vertically and horizontally) and always susceptible to widening by experiential contingencies, meanings are also perpetually subject to holistic revision and updating, with new categories and their representations always subsuming old ones as special cases (i.e., as having been rougher approximations to *the same thing*).[24] When the word/world relation is recognized to be approximate rather than exact – mediated by our provisionally successful categories rather than some absolute or ontic standard of veridicality, with convergence and a steady tightening of the approximation guaranteed by the cumulativity of the category formation process itself – the word/world link looks somewhat more secure.[25]

The acquaintance/description problem. The differences between sensory and verbal information and what one can expect from them are reflected in the model in a rather natural way. Again, the several levels of approximation involved in forming each of the representations and the nature of the dependence of the description system on the acquaintance system seem to mirror some of the phenomenology. The problem of "qualia" (the irreducible qualitative nature of subjective experience) is of course hardly solved here, but it is put in the context of other irreducibles and approximations.

Elementary percepts and atomic terms. Here the proposal is rather bold and specific. CP (rather than *jnd*s) furnishes our elementary percepts, whose names serve as the atomic terms of our propositions. Experiential data and invariance-filters ground these symbols with their initial meanings, and symbol recombinations in propositions generate the rest. Once symbols are grounded, a good deal of redundancy and cross-talk become possible between perceptual and verbal representations. Rival approaches that rely exclusively on a single symbolic description system are seen, despite the acknowledged power and scope of symbol manipulation, to be fundamentally ungrounded, with symbol meanings indeterminate apart from the theorist's interpretation. Given the power of symbolic representation to approximate any other kind of representation, however, it remains an open question (and probably in part a contingent one having to do with time and capacity constraints, efficiency and robustness considerations, and other questions of optimization) just *how much* iconic and categorical representation is needed in order to ground the symbolic system. The burden of the argument of this chapter was to show that this amount is of necessity not zero.

The problem of universals. What is primary in cognition is categorization. Categorization always involves the sorting of instances (in a context) according to invariant features. The level of encoding is different for an instance and for its (intracontextual) features. This would be the representational basis of the object/feature distinction in cognition. Then, of course, features can themselves be treated as "objects," with their own higher-order features, and so on. For a cognizer, an "object" is merely a member of a set of instances that is categorized in a certain way on the basis of certain features. Needless to say, this model of how objects and features are represented says nothing whatever about what really "exists" behind instances, that is to say, behind appearances. It only addresses the *concept* of universals, suggesting one mechanism that appears as if it would be able to handle appearances adaptively – if, that is, things are indeed as they appear.

The other-minds problem revisited. Appearance is of course that persisting philosophical problem that no amount of cognitive science will resolve. Everything that has been conjectured here about the nature of the representations that generate both CP effects and general categorization performance would be equally true of (a) a device that *behaved exactly as if* it saw, felt, believed, and meant things (but did no such thing, being an insentient automaton, devoid of all qualitative experience) and of (b) a device (like ourselves) that *really did* see, feel, believe, and mean things – in other words, one that really had a mind, rather than merely appearing to have one. This categorical distinction, like the problem of whether the members of any other category we have are *in reality* the way they appear, seems to exceed the resolving capacity of the approximationist variety of representational device that we ourselves are (according to the present model), no matter how tight we make the approximation, and irrespective of whether we are wearing our cognitive scientists' hats, our philosophical apparel, or our ordinary folk costumes.

Notes

1. That is, it will only be concerned with our *concepts* of what there is in the world, how we get those concepts, and how we revise them as our data-base grows, rather than with the question of what there really is in the world, and how we "know" it (Harnad, in preparation, b).

2. At the very least, the surviving aspects of the old problems of induction – temporal risk and the ungroundedness of induction – guarantee that our categories will always remain approximate in *those* respects.

3. All of the preconditions would of course have to be based recursively on the successful solution of prior categorization problems of the same kind.

4. The inexhaustibility of their list of potential "entailments" is of course not unique to pictures; it is shared by propositions (e.g., axioms) and is in fact mediated by propositions *about* pictures. But pictures (and objects) differ from propositions in that they inherently contain (in analog form) the information to answer (in the particular) an infinity of potential questions that propositions can raise. (I ignore here the sentence/proposition distinction.) In my view, so-called propositional models of cognition (Fodor, 1975, 1980; Pylyshyn, 1980, 1984) mistakenly put an unsupportable burden on propositional representations in failing to distinguish between, on the one hand, what *is* and *is not* encoded propositionally (presumably neither of these classes is empty in practice) and, on the other hand, what *can be* encoded propositionally (answer: *anything* – to an approximation – in principle, but not necessarily or optimally so in practice). And to the extent that propositions are doomed to be approximate, they of course cannot encode "everything."

5. The context consists of the sampled members of the category itself plus the sampled members of its *complement* of relevant alternative categories. The context is usually itself an actual or potential higher-order category.

6. Because the constraints and contingencies of categorization problems are in principle open, it is not out of the question that successful performance should happen to depend on (say) the limb-count's *not* being equal to a prime number, or to 227, or what have you.

7. I also conjecture that (1) approximationism, (2) context-dependence, and the fact that contexts themselves are *neither* (3) "modular" (i.e., independent and isolable from one another [*pace* Fodor, 1985]) *nor* (4) incommensurable (*pace* Kuhn, 1970) imply meaning "holism" (Quine, 1953): A change in the meaning of one term – i.e., a change in the invariants that determine that category as a consequence of a widening of the context of confusable alternatives – can in principle change the meaning of all other terms.

8. Minsky's (1961) "credit assignment problem" – the problem of determining to which candidate features (from among an infinity of candidates) to assign credit in revising a pattern recognition model so as to handle new, anomalous patterns that cannot be successfully sorted using the current feature-set – is just a special case of underdetermination, and hence cannot be expected to have a general, principled solution any more than the problem of finding the "right" scientific theory to account for empirical data (or the general problem of induction) can. The constraint that the context of a category must be bounded and complemented (i.e., that the complement of a category cannot be either empty or "everything there is") may play a role in ensuring that category induction can converge despite underdetermination (see Harnad, 1982b). Approximateness itself plays a similar converging role.

9. For now I will conform to the provisional definition that a (physical) transformation from an object X to another object Y is *analog* to the degree that the process P that generates the (physical) properties of Y from the properties of X (i.e., causally connects them) is *invertible*. In practice, this will mean that P is formally describable as a continuous, invertible function mapping isomorphic properties between X and Y (although the properties themselves need not be continuous). By contrast, a transformation from X to Y is *digital* to the degree that it is *not* a physically invertible one between properties, but a *formal* one, depending on conventional rules for manipulating arbitrary symbol tokens in Y that can be *interpreted* as "standing for" properties of X. A/D conversion would be a two-stage process according to this definition, involving (1) discretization and dimensional reduction (which still preserve some physically invertible structure) and (2) symbolization (in which the vestiges of physical shape are transformed into formal code).

Note that this definition is nonstandard and controversial. Not only does it define "analog" and "digital" (a) as matters of degree and (b) as dependent on an invertible physical transformation or causal connection, but it even implies that (c) a "dedicated" *digital* computer – one that is hard-wired to its transducer inputs and its effector outputs – is for that reason *analog* to a degree (namely, the degree to which the hard-wired physical processes are invertible). The hypothesis that we are such hybrid "dedicated" systems, and that the hard-wiring of any internal symbolic "modules" we may have to our afferent and efferent systems serves to "fix" their symbolic interpretations – setting their encryption/decryption relations physically – is closely related to the "grounding" arguments that will be made later in this chapter.

10. Note that this is all still analog, for it still preserves some of the *shape* of the input, albeit in a highly reduced and abstracted form. I/C conversion is really a transformation from macro-icons to micro-icons, the former preserving context-independent, holistic, configural properties of the proximal stimulus, the latter selectively reduced to only those properties that are invariant in a specific context of confusable alternatives.

11. The subject is far from closed, however, with the new work on formal learnability (Osherson, Stob, & Weinstein, 1986) and on connectionism (Ballard, 1986; McClelland and Rumelhart, 1986) reopening the topic of general induction.

12. Without "homuncularity," that is, without the need for something/someone else to "look at" or "interpret" the icons. Homuncularity has been used as one of the arguments against "copy" theories of perception.

13. The fortuitous gaps, niches, and correlations in the variation – otherwise potentially continuous and omnidirectional – among the instances on which they are based provide an important constraint on iconic representations (as well as on the categorical representations to be introduced later). However, although the fact that the world is thus conveniently partitioned into many disjoint "natural kinds" is a significant simplifying factor for some categorization problems, it by no means represents a general solution to the problem of category acquisition. For example, the problem of perceiving "object constancy" under spatial transformations still requires the selective detection of invariants. Any domain in which instances vary continuously is a potential problem. So is any domain in which the variation, though discrete, is so complex, subtle, or confusable – i.e., *underdetermined* – as to necessitate selective search and filtering. Finally, there is the domain of abstract "objects," whose instances vary along conceptual rather than physical dimensions. (For example, along what dimensions of variation are prime numbers or well-formed sentences or existentialist writing similar or different?)

14. This kind of holistic resemblance, helped out by some convenient natural gaps in variation, is the only sort of thing I can imagine being "picked up" in a direct, passive, Gibsonian fashion by a perceptual system that was neither pretuned innately toward specific trigger features nor actively processing information (cf. Neisser 1987). External *invariants* must certainly underlie all successful categorizations, but how much internal processing is required in order to detect, select, and use them is an empirical matter depending on the degree of underdetermination of the particular category and context in question. Invariants may come at a higher processing price than a Gibsonian mechanism can "afford."

15. For similar reasons, nondirected or "ad lib" similarity of the sort studied and modeled by Tversky (1977) seems unlikely to explain how we categorize. Categorization is an *imposed* rather than an ad lib task. Hence the relevant dimensions of similarity must be found and selected by active processing guided by feedback from the consequences of *mis*categorization. (This is related to the distinction in AI between "supervised" and "unsupervised" learning models.) In nontrivial (i.e., confusable, underdetermined) categorization problems the solution is not obvious in the precategorical (ad lib, unsupervised) similarity structure.

16. It seems to be a point of logic rather than one of theoretical preference that if a categorizer is able to perform error-free categorization then that performance must be based on detecting and using some set of features that is *sufficient* to serve as a basis for the successful categorization (though not necessarily "necessary" or exhaustive, because, especially with underdetermination, there might be other features that would suffice too). The putative alternatives to the "classical" necessary/sufficient-features approach to category cognition – originating with Rosch (Rosch & Lloyd, 1978) and attributed to Wittgenstein, 1953 – seem to be based on confusions among the following additional (and independent) factors:

(1) Some categorization is not all-or-none; there may be no "X's," just things that are X to greater or lesser degrees (e.g., the category "big"). (2) Some categorization performance may not be reliable; subjects may sometimes miscategorize, or there may be some instances whose membership is uncertain or graded or probabilistic (e.g., the category "guilty"). (3) The subject may not be aware of the features he is using; the ones he verbalizes may indeed be neither necessary nor sufficient, but then they're not the ones he's using. (4) There is an element of arbitrariness in what one does and does not choose to call a "feature" (as opposed to a "metafeature"); there is no logical or practical reason why features cannot be disjunctive, negative, conditional, relational, polyadic, or probabilistic – or even derivable only by complex computational, constructive, algorithmic, propositional, or "model-driven" processes – as long as they are grounded in reliable, detectable, invariant properties of the instances being categorized and they are sufficient to subserve successful categorization. (5) All categories are provisional and approximate.

Hence, at least insofar as our reliable, overlearned, all-or-none, *bounded* categories are concerned – and these are the categories (e.g., "bird" and "pet") that tend to be used in the experiments stimulated by Rosch's work – both the existence and the use of (singly) sufficient (and disjunctively necessary) sets of features seems inescapable. The origin of the putative alternatives to this – nonnecessary/sufficient "prototypes" and "family resemblances" – seems to be attributable to a focus on typicality judgments and reaction times rather than categorization per se, together with a reliance on the subject's (and perhaps the experimenter's) introspections as to the basis for the categorization. The real basis for categorization can only be found by inference, as tested by models that attempt to generate reliable categorization performance when confronted with the same instances that subjects can categorize successfully.

17. Symbolic and hybrid processes – and "theory-driven" categorization in general (if the theory is explicitly represented) – require a third kind of representation, which will be introduced shortly. Note that the tripartite representational architecture being proposed here stands in distinct contrast to both dual encoding (imagistic/verbal) models (e.g., Paivio, 1986) and monolithic computational approaches to cognition (Pylyshyn, 1984).

18. The question of analog versus arbitrary responses, though pertinent to question 3 raised earlier (in the section on unanswered questions about CP), will not be discussed here (see Harnad, 1982b, and, for a rival approach, Pylyshyn, 1984).

19. In both cases, "tabula rasa" assumptions cannot and will not be made; in other words, some prior categories will already be assumed to exist, either innately or by prior recursion based on the same learning principles being described here.

20. A more natural example would be first learning by acquaintance to label "horse" and "stripe" and then learning by description rather than acquaintance that "zebra" = "horse" & "stripes."

21. The advantage of learning categories by description is that it allows instances to be sorted correctly without any prior acquaintance merely by *combining* the symbols for prior categories in a proposition; but, to avoid infinite regress, categories learned by description must be grounded either in (1) already grounded categories or in (2) categories learned by acquaintance or "known" innately (i.e., "learned" by evolution).

Although there is no space to elaborate the point here, I conjecture that the problem of ungroundedness is responsible for (1) McCarthy and Hayes's (1969) "frame" problem (i.e., the enormous difficulty that pure symbol-manipulating programs have in determining what has been altered and what has remained constant after any given change has taken place) as well as for (2) the common criticism that AI's symbolic meanings are not "intrinsic" but "derived" (e.g., Searle, 1980). There is also an interesting connection with (3) Minsky's (1961) "credit assignment" problem and with (4) underdetermination and approximationism in general.

A rival approach that also singles out the special problem of the relation between symbolic and nonsymbolic (transducer/effector) processes is that of Pylyshyn (1984), but the two approaches diverge radically concerning the autonomy of the symbolic level (i.e., groundedness and "modulability"). A transduction-based critique of Searle (1980) as well as of the autonomy of symbol-manipulation in cognition (what Searle calls "Strong Artificial Intelligence") is to be found in Harnad (in preparation, a).

22. CRs only encode rules implicitly, whereas SRs encode them explicitly (cf. Chapter 17 by Keil & Kelly and Chapters 18 by Bialystok & Olson, this volume).

23. I do not have a theory for the expressive power of language, but I suspect that there is an analogy

between the possibility of generating all further categories from a grounded set of prior categories by recombining their symbols and the possibility of deriving all (provable) theorems from a set of axioms and derivation rules. What and how much constitutes a grounded set is an open question.

24. This amounts to a denial of radical incommensurability in concept revision, even after cataclysmic "paradigm shifts" (Kuhn, 1970). The argument is also related to the "translatability thesis" (Steklis & Harnad, 1976).

25. Among other things, it follows from this model that all of our cognitive categories have to be approximate as between the "earth/twin-earth" examples of Putnam (1975; or between Goodman's [1954] "green" and "grue," or among the alternate interpretations of Quine's [1960] "gavagai" and other such examples of representational indeterminacy), for distal differences not reflected in the proximal stimulation would have the same IRs, CRs, and SRs in this system. Potential problems arising from this would appear to be blocked by the following two principles: (1) "The cognitive identity of indiscriminables" (i.e., narrow approximationism: what you can't tell apart is the same to you) and (2) "Methodological epiphenomenalism considered as a research strategy in cognitive psychology" (i.e., only aspire to model categorization performance capacity, rather than qualitative content).

References

Ballard, D. H. (1986). Cortical connections and parallel processing: Structure and function. *The Behavioral and Brain Sciences, 9,* 67–119.
Berlin, B., & Kay, P. (1969). *Basic color terms: Their universality and evolution.* Berkeley: University of California Press.
Bloom, A. H. (1981). *The linguistic shaping of thought: A study on the impact of language on thinking in China and the West.* Hillsdale, NJ: Erlbaum.
Broadbent, D. E. (1975). The magic number seven after fifteen years. In A. Kennedy & A. Wilkes (Eds.), *Studies in long term memory.* London: Wiley.
Bruner, J. S., Goodnow, J. J., & Austin, G. A. (1956). *A study of thinking.* New York: Wiley.
Chaitin, G. (1975). Randomness and mathematical proof. *Scientific American, 232,* 47–52.
Chomsky, N. (1980). Rules and representations. *Behavioral and Brain Sciences, 3,* 1–61.
Dretske, F. I. (1983). Precis of "Knowledge and the flow of information." *Behavioral and Brain Sciences, 6,* 55–90.
Eldredge, N., & Cracraft, J. (1980). *Phylogenetic patterns and the evolutionary process.* New York: Columbia University Press.
Fodor, J. A. (1975). *The language of thought.* New York: Crowell.
Fodor, J. A. (1980). Methodological solipsism considered as a research strategy in cognitive psychology. *Behavioral and Brain Sciences, 3,* 63–109.
Fodor, J. A. (1981). The present status of the innateness controversy. In *RePresentations.* Cambridge, MA: MIT/Bradford Press.
Fodor, J. A. (1985). Precis of "The modularity of mind." *Behavioral and Brain Sciences, 8,* 1–42.
Frege, G. (1952). *Translations from the philosophical writings of Gottlob Frege.* (P. Geach & M. Black, Eds.). Oxford: Oxford University Press.
Garner, W. R. (1974). *The processing of information and structure.* Hillsdale, NJ: Erlbaum.
Gibson, E. J. (1969). *Principles of perceptual learning and development.* Englewood Cliffs, NJ: Prentice-Hall.
Gibson, J. J. (1979). *An ecological approach to visual perception.* Boston: Houghton Mifflin.
Goodman, N. (1954). *Fact, fiction and forecast.* University of London: Athlone Press.
Goodman, N. (1968). *Languages of art.* New York: Bobbs-Merrill.
Griffin, D. R. (1978). Prospects for cognitive ethology. *Behavioral and Brain Sciences, 1,* 527–538.
Harnad, S. (1976). Induction, evolution and accountability. *Annals of the New York Academy of Sciences, 280,* 58–60.
Harnad, S., Doty, R. W., Goldstein, L., Jaynes, J., & Krauthamer, G. (Eds.). (1977). *Lateralization in the nervous system.* New York: Academic Press.
Harnad, S. (1982a). Consciousness: An afterthought. *Cognition and Brain Theory, 5,* 29–47.

Harnad, S. (1982b). Metaphor and mental duality. In T. W. Simon & R. J. Scholes (Eds.), *Language, mind and brain.* Hillsdale, NJ: Erlbaum.
Harnad, S. (in preparation, a). Minds, machines and Searle.
Harnad, S. (in preparation, b). Uncertainty and the growth of knowledge (review of Dretske: *Knowledge and the flow of information*).
Helson, H. (1964). *Adaptation-level theory: An experimental and systematic approach to behavior.* New York: Harper and Row.
Holender, D. (1986). Semantic activation without conscious identification. *Behavioral and Brain Sciences, 9,* 1–66.
Keil, F. C. (1979). *Semantic and conceptual development: An ontological perspective.* Cambridge, MA: Harvard University Press.
Kosslyn, S. M., Pinker, S., Smith, G., & Shwartz, S. P. (1979). On the demystification of mental imagery. *Behavioral and Brain Sciences, 2,* 535–548.
Kuhn, T. (1970). *The structure of scientific revolutions.* Chicago: University of Chicago Press.
Lane, H. (1965). The motor theory of speech perception: A critical review. *Psychological Review, 72,* 275–309.
Lawrence, D. H. (1950). Acquired distinctiveness of cues: II. Selective association in a constant stimulus situation. *Journal of Experimental Psychology, 40,* 175–188.
Lewis, D. (1971). Analog and digital. *Nous, 5,* 321–327.
Liberman, A. M., Harris, K. S., Hoffman, H. S., & Griffith, B. C. (1957). The discrimination of speech sounds within and across phoneme boundaries. *Journal of Experimental Psychology, 54,* 358–368.
Liu, L. G. (1985). Reasoning counterfactually in Chinese: Are there any obstacles? *Cognition, 21,* 239–270.
McCarthy, J., & Hayes, P. (1969). Some philosophical problems from the study of artificial intelligence. In B. Meltzer & D. Richie (Eds.), *Machine intelligence* (Vol. 4). Edinburgh: Edinburgh University Press.
McClelland, J. L., Rumelhart, D. E., and the PDP Research Group. (1986). *Parallel distributed processing: Explorations in the microstructures of cognition.* Cambridge, MA: MIT Press (2 volumes).
Miller, G. A. (1956). The magical number seven, plus or minus two: Some limits on our capacity for processing information. *Psychological Review, 63,* 81–97.
Minsky, M. (1961). Steps towards artificial intelligence. *Proceedings of the Institute of Radio Engineers, 49,* 8–30.
Minsky, M., & Papert, S. (1969). *Perceptrons: An introduction to computational geometry.* Cambridge, MA: MIT Press.
Nagel, T. (1974). What is it like to be a bat? *Philosophical Review, 83,* 435–451.
Neisser, U. (1987). *Concepts and conceptual development: Ecological and intellectual factors in categorization.* New York: Cambridge University Press.
Olson, D. R. (1970). Language and thought: Aspects of a cognitive theory of semantics. *Psychological Review, 77,* 257–273.
Osherson, D. N., Stob, M., & Weinstein, S. (1986). *Systems that learn.* Cambridge MA: MIT/Bradford Press.
Paivio, A. (1986b). *Mental representations: A dual coding approach.* Oxford: Oxford University Press.
Premack, D. (1976). Mechanisms of intelligence: Preconditions for language. *Annals of the New York Academy of Science, 280,* 544–561.
Putnam, H. (1975). *Mind, language and reality.* New York: Cambridge University Press.
Pylyshyn, Z. W. (1980). Computation and cognition: Issues in the foundations of cognitive science. *Behavioral and Brain Sciences, 3,* 111–132.
Pylyshyn, Z. W. (1981). The imagery debate: Analogue media versus tacit knowledge. *Psychological Review, 88,* 16–45.
Pylyshyn, Z. W. (1984). *Computation and cognition.* Cambridge, MA: MIT/Bradford Press.
Quine, W. V. O. (1953). *From a logical point of view.* Cambridge, MA: Harvard University Press.
Quine, W. V. O. (1960). *Word and object.* Cambridge, MA: MIT Press.
Rock, I. (1983). *The logic of perception.* Cambridge, MA: MIT Press.

Rosch, E., & Lloyd, B. B. (1978). *Cognition and categorization.* Hillsdale, NJ: Erlbaum.
Sayre, K. M. (1986). Intentionality and information processing. *Behavioral and Brain Sciences, 9,* 121–166.
Schank, R. C., Collins, G. C., & Hunter, L. E. (1986). Transcending inductive category formation in learning. *Behavioral and Brain Sciences, 9,* 699–686.
Searle, J. R. (1969). *Speech acts.* Cambridge: Cambridge University Press.
Searle, J. R. (1980). Minds, brains and programs. *Behavioral and Brain Sciences, 3,* 417–457.
Shepard, R. N., & Cooper, L. A. (1982). *Mental images and their transformations.* Cambridge, MA: MIT/Bradford Press.
Simon, H. A. (1957). *Models of man: Social and rational.* New York: Wiley.
Steklis, H. D., & Harnad, S. R. (1976). From hand to mouth: Some critical stages in the evolution of language. *Annals of the New York Academy of Sciences, 280,* 445–455.
Stevens, K. N., & Halle, M. (1967). Remarks on analysis by synthesis and distinctive features. In W. Wathen-Dunn (Ed.), *Models for the perception of form.* Cambridge, MA: MIT Press.
Turing, A. M. (1964). Computing machinery and intelligence. In A. R. Anderson (Ed.), *Minds and machines.* Engelwood Cliffs, NJ: Prentice-Hall.
Tversky, A. (1977). Features of similarity. *Psychological Review, 84,* 327–352.
Ullman, S. (1980). Against direct perception. *Behavioral and Brain Sciences, 3,* 373–415.
Whorf, B. L. (1964). *Language, thought and reality.* Cambridge, MA: MIT Press.
Wittgenstein, L. (1953). *Philosophical investigations.* New York: Macmillan.

Author index

Abbs, J. H., 233, 234
Abel, S. M., 155n8, 368
Abramov, I., 291
Abramson, A. S., 41–4, 92, 100, 105, 118, 142–3, 145, 147, 155–6n10, 162, 171, 185, 204–5, 229–31, 244–5, 349, 350, 362–3, 365, 422
Ades, A. E., 61, 73, 74, 79, 123, 124, 152, 211, 234
Ahroon, W. A., 36–7, 40, 120, 245, 258, 265, 297n1, 388, 470, 476
Aibel, I. S., 103
Ainsworth, W. A., 96, 162, 232
Albert, M. L., 408
Alegria, J., 182, 186
Alegria, L., 503
Alfonso, P., 102
Allison, T., 424
Altman, 502
Altom, M. W., 473, 479
Anderson, J. A., 219, 479
Anderson, N. H., 274
Anderson, R. C., 472
Anderson, R. M., Jr., 202
Anglin, J. M., 467, 514
Aplin, R. N., 106
Arai, S., 102
Archibald, Y., 412
Armington, J. C., 446
Armstrong, S. L., 460, 463, 471, 499
Arnheim, R., 523, 527
Aslin, R. N., 42, 44–5, 106, 143, 167, 169, 171–2, 188n8, 221, 237, 262, 292
Atal, B. S., 243
Atkinson, J. E., 228
Austin, G. A., 549
Austin, J. L., 514

Baer, T., 96, 103
Baffuto, K. J., 36–7, 120, 245, 258, 265, 297nl, 388, 470, 476
Bagley, W. L., 104
Bailey, P.J., 98, 189n15, 204, 211, 218

Baird, J. L., 368
Baker, E., 435, 436, 438
Ballard, D. H., 561n11
Barclay, J. R., 167, 262–3
Barlow, H. B., 206, 219
Barney, H. L., 204
Baron, J., 503
Barsalou, L. W., 10, 13, 19, 82, 174, 380, 393, 461, 464, 470, 471, 472, 475, 481, 499, 512, 549
Barton, D., 503
Basset, E., 520, 523
Basso, A., 435, 437
Bastian, J., 144, 155n8, n9, 360, 361
Batterman, N., 495
Bauers, K., 334
Beare, A. C., 288, 290
Beecher, M. D., 207, 304, 306, 307, 323, 334, 341, 351, 422
Beer, C. G., 321
Bekesy, G. von, 58
Beletsky, L. D., 312
Bellezza, F. S., 468
Bellugi, U., 337
Bender, D. B., 207, 396
Benevento, L. A., 395, 396
Berger, L. R., 321
Berger, R. S., 40
Berlin, B., 290, 292, 296, 337, 467, 545
Berliner, J. E., 61, 71, 74, 80
Bertelson, P., 182, 186, 413, 414, 503
Bertoncini, J., 164, 181
Best, C. T., 47, 106, 169, 189n15, 375, 376
Bever, T. G., 179, 180, 206
Bialystock, Ellen, 20–2, 82, 175, 393, 513, 515, 517, 518, 522, 525, 527, 562n22
Bierwisch, M., 511
Birbaumer, N., 424
Birnbaum, M. H., 486n6
Bisti, S., 206
Blair, W. F., 310
Blank, M. A., 179
Bloom, A. H., 546
Blumstein, S. E., 95, 107n1, n5, 166, 179,

187n4, 188n6, 205–6, 212–16, 227, 233, 236–7, 243, 248n2, 265, 435, 436, 437, 438
Boas, F., 289
Bogert, C. M., 246
Bomba, P. C., 174, 175
Bond, Z. S., 104
Bondarko, L. V., 206
Bornstein, M. H., 6, 9, 13–14, 34, 81, 115, 172, 174–5, 210, 289, 290, 291, 292, 296, 297n1, 323, 342, 394, 468, 469, 470, 471, 498, 514, 544, 546, 548, 550
Borst, J. M., 204
Botkin, P. T., 519, 522
Bourbon, W. T., 266
Bourne, L. E., Jr., 461, 467
Boyes-Braem, P., 460, 467, 483, 499
Boynton, R. M., 287–8, 289, 290, 444
Brady, S. A., 94, 150, 151
Braida, L. D., 5, 48, 54, 59, 60–77, 78, 80, 81, 82, 83n3, n7, 93–4, 123, 152, 155n7, 245, 390, 392, 458
Breaux, A. M., 503
Breedlove, D. E., 467
Bregman, A. S., 136, 247n1
Brill, S. L., 163
Broad, D. J., 239
Broadbent, D. E., 104, 232, 240, 544
Broen, P. A., 119, 171
Brooks, L. R., 479, 480, 481, 485n4
Brooks, R. J., 321
Bruner, J. S., 492, 493, 549
Bryant, J. S., 215, 216
Bryant, P. E., 521, 524
Buchwald, S. E., 143, 156n10, 185, 232, 245
Bullock, T. H., 389
Bunnell, H. T., 102
Burdick, C. K., 307
Burkhardt, D. A., 447
Burns, B., 482
Burns, E. M., 35, 122, 153
Burton, H., 396
Butterfield, E., 422

Cairns, G., 422
Caltagirone, C., 435, 436, 438
Campbell, J., 247n1
Capehart, J., 390, 394
Capranica, R. R., 246, 311–12
Caramazza, A., 105, 435, 437
Carbone, E., 105
Carden, G., 100, 101, 169, 170
Carey, S., 467, 493, 506
Garney, A. E., 39, 59, 148, 167, 306
Carpenter, P., 526, 527
Carrell, T. D., 103, 166, 169, 172, 221
Carroll, J. J., 494
Carter, B., 186
Cary, L., 182, 186, 503
Casati, G., 435, 437

Cassirer, E., 200
Catlin, J., 296, 471
Cavonius, C. R., 447, 450
Chaitin, G., 541
Chalkey, M. A., 504
Chao, S., 312
Chapin, C., 187n4
Chen, M., 239
Cheney, D. L., 321, 334, 335
Chi, M. T. H., 505
Childer, D. G., 447
Chomsky, N., 183, 206, 207, 227, 241–2, 557
Clark, E. V., 467, 507, 514
Clark, H. H., 529
Clark, L. F., 128
Clark, W. C., 393
Clarkson, M. G., 165
Clarkson, R. L., 172
Cleveland, J., 334, 346, 347
Clifton, R. E., 165
Clynes, M., 447
Coe, C. L., 338
Cohen, L. B., 174
Cohen, M., 473
Cohen, M. M., 266, 269, 271, 274, 280
Cole, R. A., 96, 104
Collins, G. C., 550
Conant, J. B., 273
Connine, C. M., 96, 177–8, 188n12, 471
Convis, C. L., 232
Cooper, F. S., 24n2, 32, 54, 60, 78, 89, 92, 107, 114–18, 141–2, 152, 163, 173, 187n4, 204–5, 210, 212, 221, 229, 231–2, 236, 240, 243, 247, 255, 264–5, 301–2, 356, 358, 365, 387, 388, 421, 422
Cooper, L. A., 21, 526, 533
Cooper, W. E., 96, 187n3, 200, 212, 213, 214, 231, 234, 435, 437
Corbit, J. D., 33, 34, 95, 187n4, 188n11, 211, 227, 233, 350
Corkin, S., 412
Cracraft, J., 557
Craik, F. I. M., 40
Creelman, C. D., 30, 33, 48, 58, 59, 62, 64, 66, 70, 73, 78, 123, 154–5n7, 167, 302, 306, 398, 409
Crimmins, D. B., 40
Crowder, P. G., 458
Crowder, R. G., 57, 80, 92, 93
Cumming, W. W., 291, 296
Cutler, A., 180
Cutting, J. E., 33, 35, 40, 69, 119, 120, 121, 125, 126–8, 129, 130–2, 133–8, 173, 214, 258, 260, 304, 306, 318, 340

Dallas, M., 480
Danner, W., 365
Darwin, C. J., 94, 150, 151, 212
Dawson, W. W., 447

DeBauche, B. A., 396, 401, 408
Dechovitz, D., 104, 105, 170, 229, 244
Delattre, P. C., 107, 117, 163, 204, 212, 229, 231–2, 422
Delgutte, B., 128, 133
Denes, P., 240
DeValois, K. K., 207, 291
DeValois, R. L., 207, 291, 404
Dewson, J. H., 307
Diamond, I. T., 389, 395, 396
Diehl, R. L., 12, 34, 93, 95, 143, 156n10, 163, 175, 185, 200, 212, 213, 214, 218, 219, 231, 232, 234, 245, 246, 247n1, 388, 400, 404, 460, 462, 465, 466, 469, 480, 484
Dimmick, F. L., 296
Dingman, H. F., 390
Divenyi, P. D., 365
Dollard, J., 187n4
Dominowski, R. L., 461
Dommerques, J. V., 180
Donald, L., 95, 96
Donchin, E., 424
Dooling, R. J., 35, 41, 46, 54, 59–60, 74, 121, 145, 146, 243–4, 245, 304, 306, 318, 340, 361, 388, 470
Dorman, M. F., 102, 128, 189n15, 205, 424, 425, 426
Dosanjh, D. S., 47
Doty, R. W., 551
Dretske, F. I., 514, 541
Droczek, L. A., 341
Durlach, N. I., 5, 48, 54, 59, 60–77, 78, 80, 81, 82, 83n3, n7, 93–4, 123, 152, 155n7, 245, 390, 392, 458

Eccardt, T., 98, 102, 128, 168, 179, 232
Edman, T. R., 205
Ehret, G., 14–15, 81, 115, 121, 187n2, 246, 304, 307, 313, 314, 316, 317, 322, 323, 325–7, 336, 340, 342, 350–1, 397, 408, 458, 545, 547, 549, 550
Eich, M. A., 479
Eilers, R., 422
Eilers, R. E., 150, 151, 152
Eimas, P., 234, 237, 350, 360, 361
Eimas, P. D., 7, 10–11, 16, 19, 33, 34, 42, 43, 44, 92, 93, 95, 103, 115, 118, 121, 127, 144, 150, 155n8, n9, 161, 167, 168, 170, 171, 172, 173, 179, 181, 187n4, n5, 188n7, n11, 200, 207, 211, 213, 214, 227, 233, 234, 244, 274, 304, 333, 349, 358–9, 368, 375, 376, 379, 382, 393, 394, 422, 425, 440, 458, 462, 465, 467, 468, 471, 498, 503, 504, 545, 550
Ekman, G., 290
Elbert, T., 424
Eldredge, N., 557
Elman, J. L., 93, 95, 143, 156n10, 185, 218, 219, 232, 234, 245, 266
Elsner, N., 307

Emlen, S. T., 321
Endman, M., 165
Erickson, D. M., 47, 99, 168, 170, 229, 244
Erman, L. D., 242
Espmark, Y., 321
Estevez, O., 447, 449, 450
Evans, E. F., 212
Ewan, W. G., 227

Fagan, J. F., III, 174
Fairbanks, G., 230–1
Falls, J. B., 321
Fant, C. G. M., 204, 205
Fant, G., 179, 200, 206, 227, 228
Fariello, G. R., 520
Feldtkeller, R., 325
Feltovich, P., 505
Fennel, R. D., 242
Ferguson, C. A., 184, 186
Fernald, A., 169, 172, 181
Ferrero, F. E., 154n6
Fertig, R. H., 239
Fink, E. A., 36–7, 120, 245, 258, 265, 297n1, 388, 470, 476
Fiorentini, A., 206
Fisher, F. W., 186
Fitch, H. L., 47, 99, 103, 168
Flanagan, J. L., 228
Flavell, J. H., 519, 522
Flege, J. E., 106
Foard, C. F., 121, 173, 213, 340
Fodor, J., 21, 527, 557, 560n4, n7
Fodor, J. A., 163, 550, 553
Foreit, K. G., 95, 96, 105
Foss, D. J., 179
Fourcin, A. J., 43, 151, 152
Frauenfelder, U., 178–9, 180
Frege, G., 519, 537, 554
French, J. A., 334
Freyd, J. J., 506
Fried, L. S., 474
Friedman, C., 36–7, 120, 245, 258, 265, 297n1, 388, 470, 476
Frishkopf, L. S., 246
Fromkin, V., 206
Frost, N., 184
Fry, C. L., 519, 522
Fry, D. B., 92, 118
Fujimura, O., 106, 171, 173, 229, 245, 304, 306, 358
Fujisaki, H., 33, 55, 56, 57, 58, 92, 93, 94, 101, 102, 122, 123, 153, 257, 458, 473
Funkenstein, H. H., 207

Gainotti, G., 435, 436, 438
Ganong, W. F., III, 90, 94, 95, 104, 105, 212, 213
Gans, S. J., 103, 169, 172
Garner, W. R., 482, 496–7, 541

Garnes, S., 104
Garrett, M. F., 163
Gati, I., 499
Gavin, W. M., 150, 151, 152, 422
Gelman, R., 174
Gentile, A., 413
Gerhardt, H. C., 307, 310, 311, 320, 321, 325
Gerstman, L. J., 117, 124, 125, 133, 136, 204, 229, 245
Gewirth, L., 107n1, n5
Gibson, E. J., 544, 550
Gibson, J. J., 119, 188n13, 550
Glackin, R., 307
Glaser, R., 505
Gleitman, H., 460, 463, 471, 499
Gleitman, L. R., 460, 463, 471, 499
Glucksberg, S., 468, 470, 471, 474
Goff, E. R., 424
Goguen, J. A., 271, 272
Goldberg, R. F., 76
Goldsmith, J., 165, 181
Goldstein, L., 551
Goldstein, M. H., 246
Golowner, L., 40
Goodglass, H., 435, 436, 438
Goodman, N., 537, 542, 563n25
Goodnow, J. J., 514, 549
Gordon, J., 287, 289, 290
Gottlieb, G., 312–13
Gray, W. D., 460, 467, 483, 499
Green, D. M., 59, 262, 368
Green, K., 103, 104
Green, S., 323, 334, 341, 351
Greenfield, P. M., 493
Grieser, D. L., 178, 376, 379
Griffith, B. C., 6, 7, 31, 33, 55, 118, 255, 274, 301, 302, 304, 306, 357, 387, 458, 470, 545
Griffin, D. R., 536
Grosjean, F., 232
Gross, C. G., 207, 291, 396
Grossman, M., 404
Guilford, J. P., 296, 390, 397

Haack, B., 304, 307, 313, 314, 316, 317, 322, 323, 325–7, 342
Haggard, M. P., 168, 170, 229, 230–1, 244
Halff, H. M., 472
Hall, J. L., 243
Hall, L. L., 212, 215, 216
Halle, M., 200, 202, 204, 206, 207, 227, 231, 236, 553
Halpern, A. R., 154n2, 388
Halwes, T., 31, 47, 99, 118–19, 168, 173, 304, 306, 318, 373, 528
Hamernik, R. P., 47
Harnad, S., 22–4, 61, 174, 178, 201, 219, 262, 336, 459, 498, 507, 512, 514, 528, 536, 541, 542, 543, 544, 547, 548, 550, 551, 557, 560n1, n8, 562n18, n21, 563n24
Harris, K. S., 6, 7, 24n2, 31, 32, 33, 54, 55, 60, 78, 89, 92, 116, 118, 138–9, 141, 142, 144, 146, 154n7, 155n8, n9, 210, 236, 255, 264, 274, 301, 302, 304, 306, 357, 360, 361, 387, 458, 470, 545
Harris, L. B., 42, 219
Harris, L. J., 519, 520
Harris, P., 519, 520, 523
Harvey, N., 118
Harwerth, R. S., 450
Hary, J. M., 41, 77, 78, 132, 258, 259, 304, 306, 458
Hayes, P., 562n21
Healy, A. F., 57, 67–9, 71, 73, 80, 83n4, 92, 93, 388, 403
Hébert, J. A., 390, 394
Hécaen, H., 408
Heider, E. R., 296, 462, 471
Heinz, J. M., 204
Heinz, R. D., 307
Helmholtz, H., 7
Helson, H., 122, 211, 234, 389, 390, 394, 402, 404, 544
Hemenway, K., 456, 460
Henderson, D., 47
Hennessy, B. L., 42, 44, 45, 106, 143, 172, 262
Herbert, J. A., 297n1
Herriman, E., 229
Herrnstein, R. J., 187n2
Hess, T., 424, 427, 432, 433–5, 438, 439
Hildyard, A., 521
Hillenbrand, J., 165, 245
Hillenbrand, J. M., 163, 164
Hillyard, S. A., 424, 444
Hinde, R. A., 341
Hinton, G., 6, 526, 527
Hintzman, D. L., 479, 485n4
Hirsch, I. J., 41, 42, 46, 138–9, 140, 141, 145–6, 155n7, 244, 325
Hiss, R. A., 446
Hodun, A., 338, 344
Hoffman, H. S., 6, 7, 31, 33, 55, 118, 225, 274, 301, 302, 304, 306, 357, 387, 458, 470, 545
Holender, D., 553
Holmberg, T. L., 163, 164
Holyoak, K. J., 472, 474
Horridge, G. A., 389
House, A. S., 187n4, 210, 230–1, 239
Howard, I. P., 524
Howell, P., 7, 8–10, 40–1, 43, 69, 76, 79, 80, 83n5, 118, 128, 129–30, 131, 133, 135, 136, 139, 145, 149, 154n4, 155n9, 170, 173, 214, 259, 260, 306, 467, 548
Hoy, R. R., 307, 309
Hubbard, M. R., 296
Hubel, D. H., 34, 206, 219, 395, 528
Huber, F., 307, 308, 309
Hughes, G. W., 204
Humboldt, W., 289

Hunter, L. E., 550
Hurvitch, L. M., 207
Husaim, J. A., 174
Hutchinson, J. E., 507
Hutchinson, R. E., 321
Huttenlocher, J., 519–20, 521, 524–5, 526
Hyde, S. R., 202
Hyman, L. M., 239–40
Hyman, R., 184

Ingemann, F., 229, 245
Ingram, D., 186
Inhelder, B., 493, 519–21, 523, 524
Isenberg, D., 128
Ishizaka, K., 228

Jackendoff, R., 511
Jacobs, G. H., 291
Jacobson, J. Z., 166, 187n4
Jacoby, L. L., 479–80, 481, 485n4
Jakobson, R., 200, 206, 227
Jameson, D., 207
Jarvis, P., 519, 522
Jaynes, J., 551
Jenkins, J. J., 106, 171, 172, 173, 205, 245, 304, 306, 358
Jesteadt, W., 368
Jeyifous, S., 496
Johnson, D. M., 460, 467, 483, 499
Johnson, J., 435
Johnson-Laird, P. N., 511, 513, 517
Jones, G. V., 483
Jones, R. S., 219, 479
Jusczyk, P. W., 7, 10–11, 16, 19, 34, 44, 93, 95, 100, 101, 107n3, 115, 121, 127, 150, 161, 164, 165, 167, 169, 170, 171, 172, 173, 177, 183, 186, 188n8, 207, 212, 221, 234, 237, 244, 247n1, 304, 349, 358–9, 368, 375, 376, 393, 394, 422, 425, 440, 458, 462, 465, 467, 468, 471, 498, 506, 545, 550
Just, M., 526, 527

Kaas, J. H., 395, 396
Kahneman, D., 473
Kanamori, Y., 102
Kaplan, H. L., 30, 33, 48, 58, 59, 60, 62, 64, 66, 70, 73, 78, 123, 154–5n7, 167, 302, 306, 398, 409
Kaplan, J. K., 42
Kaplan, J. N., 338
Kaplon, B., 506
Kasuya, H., 102
Katoaka, R. W., 447
Katz, J., 164, 165
Kawashima, T., 33, 55, 56, 57, 58, 122, 123, 153, 257, 458, 473
Kay, P., 290, 292, 296, 545
Keating, P. A., 94, 105
Keele, S. W., 162, 184, 393, 473

Keil, F. C., 20, 82, 393, 467, 482, 494, 495, 496, 502, 505, 508, 549, 556, 562n22
Kellar, L., 34–5, 153n2, 304, 306, 318, 435, 436, 437, 438
Kelly, Michael H., 20, 82, 467, 482, 549, 562n22
Kelly, W. J., 35, 41, 46, 54, 59–60, 74, 121, 145, 146, 243–4, 245, 304, 306, 318, 340, 361, 388, 470
Kemler, D. G., 467, 482, 497, 498, 499, 502, 508
Kessen, W., 174–5, 290
Kewley-Port, D., 107n1, n5, 132, 187n4
Kiang, N. Y.-S., 128
Kido, K., 102
Kimura, D., 382, 412–13
Kinney, J. A., 31, 32, 33, 137–9, 141, 146, 154n7, 360, 361, 447
Kiparsky, P., 186
Klatt, D. H., 178, 179, 183, 186, 188n14, 202, 204, 205, 229, 230–1, 240, 243, 244, 356, 362
Klee, M., 424
Klein, R. E., 167, 171, 422
Klingamann, R. L., 446
Kluender, K. R., 12, 34, 95, 96, 163, 175, 177–8, 188n12, 200, 218, 247n1, 400, 460, 462, 465, 466, 469, 471, 480, 484
Kohn, M., 447
Kolb, B., 408, 413
Konishi, M., 246
Konorski, J., 413
Kosslyn, S. M., 520, 558
Krauss, R., 506
Krause, S. E., 240
Krauskopf, J., 447
Krauthamer, G., 551
Kuhl, P. K., 7, 16, 43–4, 106, 115, 122, 146–7, 148, 163, 164, 165, 167, 173, 178, 187n2, n4, 232, 244, 274, 301, 304, 307, 319, 340–1, 356, 359, 360, 361, 362, 364, 365, 367, 368, 370, 371, 376, 377, 379, 380–1, 382, 422, 504, 545, 548
Kuhn, T., 560n7, 562n24
Kunasaki, O., 101, 102

Labov, W., 456, 470
Ladefoged, P., 104, 105, 185, 202, 232, 240
Lahiri, A., 207n1, n5
Lakoff, G., 462
Lane, C. E., 38
Lane, H., 31, 32, 33, 92, 115, 122, 137–9, 141, 146, 154n7, 360, 361, 400, 545
Lane, M., 24n5
Lang, M., 218, 231, 234, 388, 460
Lapointe, S. G., 187n3
LaRiviere, C., 229
Lashley, K. S., 513

Lasky, R. E., 167, 171, 422
Latta, J., 246
Laughlin, N. K., 426, 438
Laurendeau, M., 523
Lawrence, D. H., 458–9, 544
Lazarus, J. H., 33, 257, 304, 306, 319, 337, 352
Leben, W., 165
Lehiste, I., 230–1
Lehrer, A., 496
Lenneberg, E. H., 206
Lesser, V. R., 242
Lettvin, J. Y., 207, 246
Levitt, A. G., 100, 101, 104, 105, 169, 170
Lewis, D., 542
Lewis, R. S., 396
Liberman, A. M., 5, 6, 7, 8, 10, 22n2, 31, 32, 33, 47, 54, 55, 60, 78, 79, 89, 92, 98, 99, 102, 103, 106, 107, 114, 115, 116, 117–19, 128, 137–9, 141, 142, 144, 146, 152, 153, 154n7, 155n8, n9, 163, 164, 168, 169, 170, 171, 173, 179, 186, 187n4, 189n15, 204, 205, 210, 212, 221, 229, 231–2, 236, 240, 243, 244, 245, 246, 255, 264, 265, 274, 279, 301, 302, 304, 306, 318, 323, 356, 357, 358, 360, 361, 365, 373, 375, 387, 388, 406–7, 421, 422, 458, 460, 462, 465, 466, 467, 469, 470, 480, 481, 483, 504, 545, 548
Lieberman, P., 187n4, 233, 234
Lifshitz, K., 447
Ligon, D., 321
Lillehie, R. A., 341, 346
Lim, J. S., 61, 74, 83n7
Lindblom, B., 228, 231, 239, 243
Lingle, J. H., 473
Linnville, S., 426, 438
Lisker, L., 41, 42, 43, 44, 47, 100, 105, 142, 143, 144, 145, 147, 155n8, 155–6n9, 162, 170, 171, 185, 204, 205, 229, 230, 231, 239, 244, 349, 350, 360, 361, 362–3, 365, 422
Littlejohn, M. J., 310
Liu, L. G., 546
Lloyd, B. B., 561n16
Locke, S., 34–5, 153n2, 304, 306, 318
Lockhart, R. S., 40
Loftus, E. F., 461
Logan, R., 32, 41
Lomas, J., 412
Lopes, L., 272
Lorenz, K. Z., 14, 302, 320
Lotz, J., 245
Loveland, D. H., 287n2
Lowerre, B. T., 240
Lubker, J., 228
Luce, R. D., 55, 59, 273
Ludlam, G., 479
Luria, A. R., 408
Lutzenberger, W., 424

MacAdams, S., 136
McAllister, R., 228
McCallum, W. C., 424
McCarthy, J., 562n21
McClasky, C. L., 172
McClelland, J. L., 479
McCloskey, D. I., 412, 413
McCloskey, M., 468, 470, 471, 474
McCulloch, C., 208
McCulloch, W. S., 207, 246
McCusker, S. B., 93, 218, 234
MacDonald, J., 274
McDonough, P., 482
Mace, W., 188n13
McGuirk, F. D., 297n1
McGurk, H., 173, 174, 274
MacKain, K. S., 106
McKay, C. L., 447
Mackay, D. M., 389
Macken, M. A., 185
McLaughland, D., 519
Macmillan, N. A., 5–6, 9, 30, 31, 33, 41, 48, 58, 59, 60, 62, 64, 66, 69–70, 73, 76, 77, 78, 79, 94, 97, 116, 119, 121, 122, 123, 154–5n7, 167, 245, 255–6, 257, 302, 306, 337, 340, 352, 391, 392, 398, 409, 458, 465, 473, 474, 544, 548
McNabb, S. D., 266
Macnamara, J., 514
McNamara, T. P., 499
MacNeilage, P. F., 141, 142, 210, 243
Maddieson, I., 154n3
Maffei, L., 206
Maier, V., 319
Maital, S., 292, 296
Mandler, R., 170, 229, 244
Mann, V. A., 99, 101, 102, 104, 231
Manning, A., 302
Maratsos, M., 504
Markl, H., 314
Markman, E. M., 467, 507
Marler, P., 303, 321, 323, 333, 334, 337, 351
Martin, J. G., 102
Martin, J. I., 447
Masataka, N., 319, 343
Massaro, D. W., 13, 19, 41, 77, 78, 90, 100, 132, 162, 176, 188n11, 210, 257, 258, 259, 262, 266, 269, 271, 272, 274, 280, 304, 306, 393, 458, 465, 471, 473, 480
Masters, H. G., 394
Mateer, C., 216
Mattingly, I. G., 31, 32, 118–19, 164, 173, 357, 360, 373
Mattingly, J. G., 304, 306, 318
Maturana, H. R., 207, 246
May, J., 104
Medin, D. L., 10, 13, 19, 82, 174, 188n9, 380, 393, 456, 458, 460, 461, 462, 463, 467, 473,

Medin, D. L. (*cont.*)
 479, 480, 483, 484, 485n4, 494, 499, 512, 549
Mehler, J., 178–9, 146, 180, 181
Meltzoff, Z., 377, 380–1, 382
Menn, L., 184, 186, 503
Menyuk, P., 184, 503
Mervis, C. B., 184, 188n9, 296, 394, 456, 460, 462, 463, 467, 471, 473, 475, 483, 498, 499, 514
Merzenich, M. M., 327, 396
Metzler, J., 520, 522, 526
Miceli, G., 435, 436, 438
Michalski, R., 483
Michels, W. C., 404
Mikos, M. J., 94, 105
Milewski, A. E., 174
Miller, C. L., 307
Miller, G. A., 23, 54, 81, 114, 123, 206, 293, 336, 358, 460, 511, 513, 517, 544, 549
Miller, J. D., 35, 41, 42, 43, 46, 54, 59–60, 74, 121, 145, 146, 147, 148, 167, 173, 187n2, 243–4, 245, 304, 306, 307, 318, 319, 340–1, 359, 361, 362, 364, 365, 367, 388, 470, 504
Miller, J. L., 7, 10–11, 16, 19, 34, 44, 96, 99, 100, 102, 103, 104, 115, 121, 127, 167, 168, 169, 170, 171, 177–8, 179, 181, 187n3, n5, 188n7, n12, 200, 211, 213, 214, 218, 229, 232, 234, 237, 349, 358–9, 375, 376, 379, 382, 393, 394, 422, 440, 458, 462, 465, 467, 468, 471, 498, 545, 550
Miller, N. E., 187n4
Miller, R. S., 467, 471
Mills, C. B., 180
Mills, J. H., 47
Milner, B., 412, 413
Minifie, F., 232
Minsky, M., 550, 560n8, 562n21
Mishkin, M., 396
Miyawaki, K., 106, 171, 173, 245, 304, 306, 358
Moffat, A. J. M., 325, 327
Moffitt, A. R., 161
Moiseff, A., 309
Molfese, D. L., 18, 44, 115, 121, 263, 424, 426, 427, 428, 430, 435–6, 437, 438, 444, 549, 550
Molfese, V. J., 424, 427, 428, 430, 438–9, 440, 441
Moncrieff, R. W., 210
Monroe, M. D., 296
Moody, D. B., 207, 304, 306, 307, 323, 334, 341, 351, 422
Morais, J., 182, 186, 503
Morgan, K. A., 163, 164
Morrongiello, B., 47, 169, 189n15, 375, 376
Morse, P. A., 43, 151, 152, 169, 304, 307, 340, 341–2, 422, 426, 438

Morton, J., 210
Moskowitz, A. I., 184
Mountcastle, V. B., 395
Mudry, K. M., 246
Murphy, C., 169, 173
Murphy, G. L., 460, 462, 467, 479, 483, 484
Murray, J., 121, 150, 169, 173
Myers, J. L., 278–9
Myers, M., 169, 172

Nagel, T., 537
Neely, R. B., 242
Neisser, U., 24n4, n7, 202, 462, 550, 558, 561n14
Nelson, K., 467, 514
Nelson, R. J., 396
Nemser, W. J., 245
Newcombe, N., 526
Newman, J. D., 207, 246, 346
Newport, E. L., 214, 337
Newton, Isaac, 287
Nicely, P. E., 206, 460
Nigro, G. N., 95, 213
Noma, E., 368
Noreen, D. L., 474
Norman, D. A., 272, 276, 279
Norris, D., 180
Nowikas, K., 32, 41
Nusbaum, H. C., 80, 94, 234, 388, 404

Oden, G. C., 90, 100, 162, 188n11, 266, 272, 274, 473, 480
Ogilvie, J. C., 512
Ohala, J., 228
Öhman, S. E. G., 102
Ojemann, G., 216
Olivier, D. C., 296
Oller, D. K., 151, 152
Olson, D. R., 20–2, 82, 175, 393, 513, 515, 517, 518, 521, 522, 528, 541, 562n22
Olver, R. R., 492, 493
Ortony, A., 472, 477
Oscar-Berman, M., 432, 435
Osherson, D. N., 272, 457, 473, 561n11

Paap, K. R., 257
Paccia, J. M., 187n3
Padden, D. M., 44, 244, 370, 376, 422
Paivio, A., 562n17
Palmer, S. E., 460, 523
Pani, J. R., 467, 471
Papert, S., 550
Parducci, A., 34, 116, 119, 122
Parker, E. M., 218, 231, 234, 247n1, 388, 460
Pastore, R. E., 4–5, 9, 13, 32, 35, 36–7, 38, 40, 41, 42, 46, 54, 59–60, 69, 74, 120, 121, 127, 128, 145, 146, 153n2, 154n2, 173, 222, 243–4, 245, 258, 265, 297n1, 304, 306, 318,

Author index 573

337, 340, 349, 352, 361, 388, 458, 465, 467, 470, 471, 476, 512, 514, 549
Payer-Rigo, P., 435, 436, 438
Pelamatti, G. M., 154n6
Penfield, W., 216
Perecman, E., 435, 436, 437, 438
Perey, A. M., 42, 44, 45, 56, 60, 66–7, 106, 143, 167, 172, 262
Perry, N. W., Jr., 447
Pesetsky, D., 98, 102, 128, 168, 179, 232
Petersen, M. R., 207, 323, 334, 351
Peterson, G. E., 204, 230–1
Petras, J. M., 396
Petzold, P., 93, 94
Piaget, J., 492, 493, 519, 520–1, 523, 524
Pick, H. L., 520
Picton, T. W., 444
Pinard, A., 523
Pinker, S., 558
Pisoni, D. B., 33, 42, 44, 45, 55, 56, 57, 60, 63, 64, 65, 66–7, 73, 95, 99, 103, 106, 121, 132, 143, 145–6, 150, 153, 163, 166, 167, 169, 171, 172, 173, 188n8, 205, 206, 210, 211, 214, 221, 234, 235, 237, 243–4, 257, 262, 276, 279, 301, 302, 304, 306, 319, 337, 352, 361, 365, 422, 430–1
Pitts, W. H., 207, 246
Plomp, R., 243
Ploog, D., 246
Pola, Y. V., 317, 343, 344, 350, 352n1
Pollack, G. S., 307, 309
Popov, A. V., 307
Port, R. F., 47, 106, 232
Posner, M. I., 162, 184, 393, 473
Powell, T. P. S., 395
Prather, P., 180
Premack, D., 547, 550
Presson, C. C., 519–20, 521, 524–5, 526
Pribram, K. H., 202, 390
Price, P. J., 104, 105
Proffitt, D. R., 528
Pufall, P. B., 522
Puleo, J. S., 36–7, 40, 120, 245, 258, 265, 297n1, 388, 470, 476
Purks, S. R., 61, 74
Putnam, H., 505, 537, 554, 563n25
Pylyshyn, Z. W., 20, 513, 528, 542, 550, 558, 560n4, 562n17, 562n18, n21
Pynn, C. T., 78, 123, 155n7

Quine, W. V. O., 537, 560n7, 563n25

Rabinovitch, M., 422
Rabinowitz, W. M., 61, 74, 83n7
Radley, J.-P. A., 204
Rakerd, B., 105
Rall, W., 424
Raphael, L. J., 102, 128, 162, 205, 240
Raskin, L. A., 292, 296

Rasmussen, T., 412
Raven, P. H., 467
Ray, V. F., 289, 291
Rayment, S. G., 166, 187n4
Reddy, D. R., 240, 242
Reed, C. F., 389
Reed, E. S., 188n13
Reed, M. A., 169, 172, 173
Reed, S. K., 473
Regan, D., 6, 18, 423, 424, 444, 445, 446, 447, 448, 449, 450, 549, 550
Reits, D., 449, 450
Remez, R. E., 11–12, 34, 80, 95, 119, 127, 132, 169, 188n11, 214, 216, 221, 234, 262, 388, 395, 460, 468, 469, 480, 550, 556
Repp, B. H., 5, 8, 10, 24n2, 33, 47, 57, 67–9, 71, 73, 79, 80, 83n4, 89, 92, 93, 94, 98, 101, 102, 104, 106, 116, 118, 123, 128, 115n10, 163, 166, 168, 175, 179, 188n9, n10, n11, 210, 229, 231, 232, 247, 255, 265–6, 276, 279, 304, 306, 323, 388, 403, 456, 458, 460, 462, 465, 466, 467, 469, 470, 481, 483, 504, 548
Rezak, M., 395, 396
Riggs, L. A., 34, 447
Rilling, M. E., 266
Rips, L. J., 472, 473, 474, 477, 494, 499, 512, 516
Ritter, W., 424
Ritz, S. A., 219, 279
Roberts, L., 216
Roberts, M., 95, 177, 211, 229, 230–1
Robinson, C. J., 396
Robson, R., 47, 169, 189n15, 375, 376
Rocha-Miranda, C. E., 207, 396
Rock, I., 202, 528, 550, 553
Rockstroh, B., 424
Roeder, K. D., 246
Rosch, E. H., 184, 188n9, 296, 336, 380, 393, 394, 404, 456, 460, 461–2, 463, 467, 471, 473, 475, 477, 481, 483, 496, 498–9, 512, 514, 561n16
Rosen, S. M., 7, 8–10, 40–1, 43, 69, 76, 79, 80, 83n5, 94, 128, 129–30, 131, 133, 135, 136, 138–9, 145, 149, 154n4, 155n9, 170, 173, 214, 234, 259, 260, 306, 467, 548
Rosenblum, L., 35, 154n2
Rosner, B. S., 33, 40, 60, 67, 69, 73, 75–6, 77, 79, 83n3, n6, 120, 121, 125, 126–7, 129, 130–2, 133–8, 173, 214, 258, 304, 306, 318, 340
Ross, G. S., 174
Roth, E. M., 468, 473, 481
Rothenberg, M., 228
Rovet, J., 520
Rowell, T. E., 341
Ruben, R. J., 307
Rubin, P. E., 169, 221
Rudnicky, A. I., 104

Rumelhart, D. E., 272, 479
Runeson, S., 179

Sachs, M. B., 307, 383
Sachs, R. M., 123, 365
Sakai, S. T., 396
Sales, G. D., 314
Samuel, A. G., 39, 59, 90, 96, 176, 188n12, 214, 306, 323, 465, 468, 471, 473, 476, 478
Sandell, J. H., 291
Sarris, V., 394
Savage, A., 341
Savin, H. B., 179, 180, 206
Sawusch, J. R., 80, 93, 94, 95, 99, 107n3, 177, 212, 213, 214, 218, 234, 235, 247n1, 266, 388, 404
Sayre, K. M., 541
Schaffer, M. M., 467, 479, 480, 485n4
Schank, R. C., 550
Scharf, B., 325, 327
Schermer, T., 104
Scheirer, C. J., 40
Schellart, N. A. M., 445
Scher, A., 521, 524
Schermer, T. M., 96, 177–8, 188n12, 471
Schleidt, W. M., 314
Schmuckler, M. A., 35, 154n2
Schneider, W., 238
Schroeder, M. R., 243
Schulhoff, C., 435
Schwab, E. C., 80, 94
Schwanenflugel, P. J., 467
Searle, C. L., 166, 187n4
Searle, J. R., 536, 550, 554, 562n21
Segui, J., 178–9, 180
Selfridge, O. G., 200, 201
Seligman, M. E. B., 335
Semmes, J., 395, 396, 413
Sewell, D. R., 468, 481
Seyfarth, R. M., 321, 334, 335
Shankweiler, D. P., 114, 115, 116, 117–18, 119, 141, 152, 186, 205, 206, 229, 232, 236, 240, 243, 247, 265, 356, 358, 365, 387, 388, 421
Shankweiler, D. S., 163, 173, 187n4
Shaw, R. E., 188n13, 522
Shepard, R. N., 21, 520, 526, 553
Shepp, B. E., 482
Sherrick, C. E., 244
Shiffrin, R. M., 238
Shigeno, S., 92, 93, 94
Shoben, E. J., 468, 473, 474, 481, 494, 499, 512, 516
Shuvalov, V. F., 307
Shwartz, S. P., 558
Siegel, J. A., 122, 153, 264, 528
Siegel, W., 122, 153, 264, 528
Siegfried, J. B., 446, 447
Silverstein, J. W., 219, 479
Sim, L., 338

Simon, C., 43, 151, 152
Simon, H. J., 93, 218, 234, 539
Simpson, C., 467, 471
Simson, R., 424
Singer, L. T., 174
Sinnott, J. M., 304, 306, 307, 341, 422
Siqueland, E. R., 44, 121, 150, 161, 167, 171, 174, 207, 244, 304, 358–9, 368, 375, 422
Smith, D. G., 312
Smith, D. P., 290
Smith, E. E., 188n9, 272, 456, 457, 461, 462, 463, 467, 471, 473, 474, 479, 481, 494, 499, 512, 516
Smith, G., 558
Smith, H. J., 346
Smith, J. C., 314
Smith, L. B., 121, 166, 169, 173, 186, 467, 482, 497, 498, 502
Smith, N., 165, 181
Smith, N. V., 186
Smith, P. T., 279
Snowdon, C. T., 15–16, 43, 106, 115, 122, 187n2, 303, 304, 307, 317, 334, 338, 340, 341–2, 343, 344, 346, 347, 350, 351–2, 408, 422, 504, 545
Sokolov, Y. N., 389
Soli, S. D., 81, 103, 150, 151
Sommers, R., 435
Souther, A. E., 232
Speigel, M. F., 322
Spekreijese, H., 445, 447, 448, 449, 450
Spelke, E. S., 174
Sperling, H. G., 446, 447, 448, 450
Stark, R. E., 172
Starkey, P., 174
Stebbins, W. C., 207, 304, 306, 307, 323, 334, 341, 351, 422
Stecher, B., 232
Steklis, H. D., 543, 547, 548, 557, 563n24
Sternberg, R. J., 499
Sternberg, S., 277
Sternheim, C. E., 447
Stevens, K. N., 38, 54, 74, 95, 107n1, n5, 115, 120, 121, 127, 166, 179, 187n4, 188n6, 204, 205, 206, 210, 213, 227, 229, 231, 233, 234, 236–7, 239, 244, 248n2, 265, 279, 350, 380, 533
Stevens, S. S., 79
Stevenson, J. G., 321
Stiles, W. S., 450n1
Stob, M., 561n11
Strange, W., 106, 119, 171, 172, 173, 205, 245, 304, 306, 358
Strauss, M. S., 174
Streeter, L. A., 44, 167, 171, 359, 422
Streitfeld, B. D., 401, 402, 438
Strommen, E. A., 519, 520
Studdert-Kennedy, M., 24n2, 32, 54, 60, 78, 89, 92, 93, 95, 98, 114, 115, 116, 117–18, 119, 123, 127, 141, 152, 163, 173, 179,

187n4, 205, 206, 210, 214, 218, 229, 231, 234, 236, 239, 240, 243, 247, 255, 264, 265, 279, 301, 302, 356, 358, 365, 387, 388, 421
Summerfield, A. Q., 45–6, 95, 98, 103, 150, 151, 168, 170, 173, 177, 189n15, 205, 211, 216, 229, 230–1, 232, 244, 245
Sur, M., 396
Sussman, H. M., 233, 234
Sutherland, N. S., 513, 516, 528
Swets, J. A., 40, 59, 262, 391
Swinney, D. A., 104, 180
Syrdal, A. K., 31, 118–19, 173, 304, 306, 318, 373
Syrdal-Lasky, A., 167, 171, 422
Szczesiul, R., 32, 35, 41, 154n2

Tallal, P., 172
Talmage-Riggs, G., 346
Tanaka, D., Jr., 396
Tarr, M. J., 506
Tartter, V. C., 211
Tash, J., 211, 214, 276, 279
Tautz, J., 325
Taylor, M. M., 512
Tees, R. C., 171
Tempone, V. J., 390, 394
Tepas, D. I., 446
Theiois, J., 277
Thomas, E. A. C., 278–9
Thomas, E. C., 128
Thorpe, W. H., 321
Thorson, J., 308, 309
Thurstone, L. L., 268
Torgerson, W. S., 154n7
Trehub, S., 422
Treisman, A., 460
Trieman, R., 503
Tseng, C., 187n4
Turing, A. M., 536
Turnbull, W., 472
Turvey, M. T., 164, 188n13
Tversky, A., 459, 460, 473, 477, 483, 499, 549, 561n15
Tversky, B., 456, 460

Ullman, S., 550

Vagges, K., 154n6
van den Berg, T. J. T. P., 445, 447, 450
van den Broecke, M. P. R., 69, 128–9, 130, 132
van der Hulst, H., 165, 181
van Heuven, V. J. J. P., 69, 128–9, 130, 132, 136
Vaughan, H. G., Jr., 424
Verbrugge, R. R., 105, 106, 119, 171, 173, 232, 245, 304, 306, 358
Vertovec, Ann, 346–7
Viemeister, N. F., 39, 59, 148, 167, 306
Vignolo, L., 435, 437

Vigorito, J., 44, 121, 150, 161, 167, 171, 207, 244, 304, 358–9, 368, 375, 422
von Frisch, K., 291
von Uexküll, A., 389
Vygotsky, L. S., 492–3, 495, 496, 497, 499–500, 505, 507

Walley, A. C., 100, 101, 121, 150, 169, 170, 173, 186
Walter, D. G., 277
Ward, T. B., 482
Ward, W. D., 35, 122, 153
Warfield, D., 307
Watanabe, T., 128
Waters, R. S., 106, 147–8, 304, 307, 319, 340, 422
Waterson, N., 184
Watson, C. S., 80, 266, 322
Wattenmaker, W., 483
Weber, T., 308, 309
Wegel, R. L., 38
Weidner, W., 435
Weinstein, S., 561n11
Weisel, T. N., 528
Weiskopf, S., 174–5, 290
Weiskrantz, L., 407
Weisstein, N., 34, 202, 208
Weller, R. E., 395, 396
Werker, J. F., 106, 171
Werner, G., 395
Werner, H., 492, 493–4, 497, 506, 507
Westheimer, G., 445
Wetzel, F., 426, 438
Whalen, D. H., 101
Whishaw, I. Q., 408
White, C. T., 447
Whitfield, I. C., 212
Whitlow, J. W., 481
Whitsel, B. L., 395
Whorf, B. L., 6, 289
Wickelgren, W. A., 179, 206, 276, 279
Widen, B., 39
Widin, G. P., 59, 148, 167, 306
Wielgus, V., 32, 41
Wiener-Ehrlich, W. N., 482
Wier, C. C., 35, 41, 46, 54, 59–60, 74, 121, 145, 146, 243–4, 245, 304, 306, 318, 340, 361, 368, 388, 470
Wiesel, T. N., 34, 206, 219, 395
Williams, L., 105, 143, 149, 155–6n10, 171, 185, 245, 468, 469
Wilson, A., 304, 307, 319
Wilson, M., 17, 24n6, 34, 80, 97, 116, 119, 121, 122, 202, 210, 234, 297n1, 323, 349, 390, 391, 395, 396, 397, 401, 402, 404, 408, 423, 432, 435, 436, 458, 468, 469, 474, 481, 544, 548
Wilson, W. A., Jr., 106, 147–8, 340, 422
Wilson, W. R., 150
Winitz, H., 229

Winship-Ball, A., 338
Winter, P., 207, 246
Witherspoon, O., 480
Wittgenstein, L., 461, 561n16
Wolf, C. G., 212
Wollberg, Z., 207, 246
Wood, C. C., 33, 48, 54, 74, 166, 302
Wood, D. L., 424
Wooten, B. R., 446
Wright, A. A., 291, 296
Wright, J. W., 519, 522
Wyszecki, G., 450n1

Yeni-Komshian, G. H., 105
Yonas, A., 520
Young, E. D., 383

Zadeh, L. A., 271
Zatorre, R. J., 90, 154n2, 388
Zeki, S., 291, 396
Zippelius, H. M., 314
Zoloth, S. R., 207, 323, 334, 351
Zrenner, E., 447
Zurif, E. B., 105, 435, 437, 438
Zwicker, E., 243, 325

Subject index

a priori constraints, 2, 508, 557, 561n13
absolute categorization, 29–30, 33, 35–6, 39, 45, 48–9
absolute discrimination, 544, 552, 556
absolute identification, 92
absolute threshold, 35, 322
absolutely discrete perception, 32
absoluteness criterion, 92
abstract categories, 556
abstract categorization problems, 553
abstraction 11, 456; in adaptation, 481; in animals, 303, 310; of categorical representatives, 174; CP and, 549; in representational system, 556–7
ABX task, 55, 56, 58, 59, 66–7, 82, 114, 118, 125, 129, 130, 135–6, 138, 306, 346, 368; bias in, 60
acoustic context, 232, 235
acoustic continua, 3, 29; discrete categories in, 337; location of boundaries on, 89–112; perception of, in infants, 167–8
acoustic contrasts, 121
acoustic correlates, 236–7, 239, 246
acoustic cues, 5, 128, 204–6, 212, 221, 356; extrasyllabic, 232, 236–7; isolable, stable, 460; and location of boundaries, 91, 98–9, 107; redundant, 238; within-syllable, 232
acoustic discontinuity, natural, 151, 561n13
acoustic events, 372; processing of, 187n1
acoustic information, 47, 173, 383; in speech signal, 165–6
acoustic invariance hypotheses, 107n1, 166, 233, 265
acoustic outputs, 227, 230, 232, 240
acoustic patterns, 119, 204, 205
acoustic signal: orthogonal substructures of, 227, 228; parallel transmission of segment information to, 205
acoustic theory of speech production, 162, 227
acoustic variability, 117, 162–3, 210; and invariant cues, 204–6
acquaintance, direct, 544, 556

acquaintance system: two-level, 538, 543, 551–8
acquired similarity (principle), 9, 187n4
acuity, test of, 368–70
acuity functions, 408, 412, 413
adaptation, 15, 91, 293, 324, 333, 469; in animal communication, 303; in category acquisition, 467–8; see also selective adaptation
adaptation effects, 6, 34, 234, 480–1; predicted by typicality, 471, 472; prediction of, 221
adaptation level, 323, 391, 392, 407, 458, 544; as category boundary, 394, 398–400, 408, 414; concept of, 389–91; and stimulus values, 398
adaptation-level (AL) theory, 17, 349, 389–91, 412, 474, 481; brain mechanisms and, 394–7, 414; qualitative/quantitative form, 390–1, 393, 394, 401–4; and relation to other approaches, 391–7
"adapting stimuli," 80
adaptiveness of categorization, 337, 352
adjectives, 472, 504
aerodynamic processes, 239, 244
affiliative speech, 340
affordances, 24n4, 550, 561n14
affricate–fricative contrast, 121, 125–6, 130, 132, 136, 153
affricates, 124–5
Aguaruna Indians, 337–8
AL theory, see adaptation-level (AL) theory
alertness level, 323
all-or-none categories, 19, 461, 464, 561–2n16
ambiguity vs. conflict, 278–80
amplitude, 394, 421, 445
analog/digital (A/D) conversion, 4, 21, 542–3
analog/digital distinction (spatial representation), 512, 526–7
analog/digital filter, 262, 552, 553, 554
analog information, 21
analog representations, 542–3, 547–8, 551–2
analog stimulus traces, 22
analog transformation, 552

577

analysis, pandemonium model of, 200–2
analysis-by-synthesis, 7, 8, 236, 553
analytic processing, 467, 481–2
anatomy, 291
anchor(s), 6, 79, 80, 94, 245, 389–90, 394; location of, 77 stimuli of (changes in discriminability with different), 402
anchoring paradigm, 94–5
animal studies, 1; brain mechanisms in CP, 408; and category boundary differences, 43–4; and comparisons with humans, 246–7, 360, 364, 365, 366, 367, 372–4, 375, 376–7; and comparison with infants, 375–7; CP, 301–33, 397, 422
animal vocalizations, 8, 14, 246–7; animal perception of, 334–6; categories/subcategories in, 338, 339t; distress, 338–40; see also species-specific sounds
animals, 17, 187n2; auditory sensitivities in, 146–7, 150, 151; and boundary locations, 7, 9, 106; categorization of human speech by, 318–19; categorization tests on, 335–86; and color categories, 14, 289, 290–1; and communication signals, 14–15, 81, 337; CP in, 15, 16, 43–4, 115–16, 340–52, 547; CP in, interpretation of finding, 374–83; and processing of speech stimuli, 383; psychophysical model of, speech recognition in, 244–5; range effects in, 147–8; specialized speech perception mechanisms in, 207; speech perception, in, 359–83; testing methods on, 306–7; see also call types (animal communication)
anisotropy, 13
anurans, 309–12
appearance, 524–5, 559
approximation: and context-driven convergence, 538–9; two orders of, 543
approximationism, 538–43, 558, 559, 562n21
arousal level, 307, 323
articulation, 106, 116, 122, 128, 376; differences in, 168; discontinuous, 141–5; in motor theory, 117; and perception, 115, 117–18; see also place of articulation
articulatory apparatus, 210
articulatory explanations, CP in speech, 113–60, 547
articulatory gestures, 99, 120, 125, 137; phonemically distinct, 143–4
articulatory/phonatory configuration, 230, 232
articulatory-referential theory, 119–20
articulatory system, 186–7n6
artifacts, 40–1, 456
artificial intelligence (AI), 1, 550
aspiration, 185
aspiration noise, 47, 137, 150–1
assimilation, 390; as consequence of reference points, 475, 476–7
assimilation effects, 221
"association" cortex, 395–6, 408

asymmetrical similarity relations, 475, 477
atheoretic-to-theoretic shift, 505, 554ff
atomic terms, 536, 537, 538, 540, 559
attention, 18, 172, 238, 307; dishabituation of, 174
attributes, 460, 501; acquisition of, 467; and category structure, 461–2; characteristic/ideal, 18, 478; comparisons of, 480, 482; cue/category validity of, 482–3; in SP/GK categories, 19ff, 456, 459–61, 465
audition, 7–8, 90, 548; perceptual categories in, 287–300; and perceptual parallels with vision, 293–6
auditory abilities, general, 221
auditory analysis of speech sounds, 182, 184–5, 186, 381–2
auditory continua, 38; neural substrates underlying CP in, 395
auditory cortical neurons, 212
auditory discontinuities, 123, 146–7, 150, 265
auditory equivalence classes, 383; infants' detection of, 377–80, 382
auditory-evoked potentials (AEPs), 18, 263, 423, 438; stimulus evoking, 430–35; and voice-onset time, 424–30
auditory explanations, CP in speech, 113–60
auditory-feature detectors, 211–14, 216, 221
auditory hypothesis, 91, 96–7
auditory-information processing, categorization processes in, 255–83
auditory-intensity perception, 54–5, 60–77
auditory mechanisms, general, 211–12
auditory-memory limitations (CP), 257, 261
auditory mode, 247, 266
auditory-motor equivalences for speech, infants' recognition of 10, 16, 377, 381–2
auditory-nerve-firing patterns, 128, 133
auditory onset time continua, 41–3
auditory patterns, 23, 214; nonspeech, 172–3
auditory-perception literature, 32, 46, 47
auditory processes: role of, in adaptation, 211–14; vs. specialized phonetic mechanisms, 355, 360, 361, 362, 375–6, 380, 382–3; and speech sounds, 132–6, 137
auditory processing, 187n1, 243–7, 383; mechanism of, sensitive to temporal information, 430–1
auditory psychophysics, 29ff, 53ff, 368
auditory sensitivities: accounting for, 150–2; in animals, 146–7; estimation of, 82; inborn, 16, 115, 116; region of, 120–1
auditory sensitivity P (C/A), 55–7
auditory-sensitivity theory, 120–1, 124, 125, 133, 148, 149–52; assessment of, 126; conjunction with other theories, 129–32, 137, 152–3
auditory stimuli, 34–6; "demonstrations" of CP in, 33

Subject index

auditory system, 16, 90, 503; inborn sensitivities, 115, 120–1; in infants, 116; and perceptual transfer function, 38; peripheral, 383
auditory threshold, 47
auditory-visual equivalences for speech, infants' recognition of, 377, 380–1
autosegmental phonology, 181
avoidance-conditioning procedure, 362
axis(es) (spatial), 521, 522, 523–4, 525, 526

basic level (theory), 467, 498, 499–500
behavior(s): adaptive, 333; and continuous/categorical perception, 263; EPs relation to, 424; and species-specific calls, 307
behavioral methodologies, 17, 423, 425
between-boundary discrimination, 545
between-category discrimination, 261, 263, 337–40, 358, 367–8, 398, 422, 425, 458, 512, 549; in AL theory, 390–1, 398–400, 402, 406, 409–12; in animals, 315–16, 340–1, 342, 370, 371; brain function and, 388; enhanced, 548; hemispheric specialization and, 439, 440; in infants, 358–9; in representational system, 554; and SP/GK categories, 471; test for, in EP, 425, 429
between-category similarity, 462
bias, 60, 80, 81, 90; in auditory detection, 213; in CP testing, 307, 554–5; innate, 323; in perceptual system, 391, 512–13, 528; semantic, 104, systematic, 473; in testing procedures, 346
bias-edge effect, 80
bilinguals, 142–3, 185, 232, 245, 349, 469; color category identification, 290
binary-feature matrix, 100
biological determination, 164; of categorization, 172, 175
biological predisposition, 14, 15, 457; in learning, 467; sensitivity for categorization processes, 467; speech perception, 7, 44, 97; *see also* innateness
biomechanical processes, 239, 244
birds, 303, 312–13, 322, 333
blackbirds, 307
block studies (Vygotsky), 496–7
Block's law, 47
body structures, asymmetrical, 529
boundary effects, 4–5, 13, 14, 512; anchor effects, natural/learned, 31; multiple, 5; in representational system, 554
boundary location, 322; and AL theory, 390; fixed, 99; language and, 349, 350; rule governed changes in, 375
boundary reference points, 477–9, 485
brain: and AL theory, 394–7; function of, in perception, 393; nature, development and organization of CP in, 422, 423–41
brain areas: AEP in, 430–5; and CP of stimuli in different modalities, 409–13; EP in, 424–30, 444, 446
brain damage, 388, 408–13, 435–8; and categorization of semantic vs. perceptual items, 405–7; effects of, on CP, 407–13, 435–8; and hemispheric effect on CP, 439
brain mechanisms in CP, 387–417
brain structures: and perception, 388–9; unique to speech processing (theory), 394–5
brightness, 288, 482; subjective, 444
Broca's aphasics, 436
bullfrogs (*Rana catesbeiana*), 246, 311–12, 318

call-type recognition, 318, 319–20, 322; selective attention in, 323
call types (animal communication), 302, 303, 312, 317–18, 319–22, 340, 343, 351; discrimination of, 334; labeling, 344, 346; learning and, 322; research on, 320–1
carrier frequency (animal CP), 304, 309
categorical model (speech perception): and identification-reaction times, 276–80; and rating responses, 266–8, 269–71; rejection of, 280
categorical partitioning, 13, 262; fuzzy-logical model, 254–83
categorical perception (CP), 89; in AL theory, 395; analog representations in, 547–8; in animals, 15, 16, 43–4, 115-16, 340–52, 547; in animals, interpretation of finding, 374–83; and audition, 359, 548; brain mechanisms in, 387–417; categorization processes and, 455–90; characteristics of, 114–15; conditions for, 301–2; as continuity/discontinuity phenomenon, 549; vs. continuous perception, 6, 13, 53–85, 255, 258, 261–6, 273–6, 277, 391; criteria for, 32, 36, 38; defined, 30, 32–3, 89, 336, 456; and direct perception, 550; discovery of, 357–8; distinct from categorical perception results, 257–61; effects of brain damage on, 407–13, 435–8; in EP studies, 430–5; evidence against, 280; evidence for, 258–61; evidence for, of species-specific sounds, 307–19; expectation of occurrence of, 303, 308, 321; explanations of, 265–6; functional significance of, 336–40; furnishes elementary percepts, 559; as general universal characteristic of perceptual processing, 413–14; generalized to categorization, 22–4; historical review of, 31–3; as hypothesis about origins of spatial categories, 22; interpreter influence in discrimination of, 306; and key-stimuli, 319–27; as learned, 358–9; measurement of, 304–7; mechanisms of, 323–7, 328; as model for category cognition, 3–4; models of, 273–6, 543–58; and motor activity, 547; naturalistic view of, 332–54; necessity of specialized mechanisms for, 374–5, *see also* specialized mechanisms; new test for, 266–71, 273–6; observed by practice of averaging val-

categorical perception (CP) (*cont.*)
ues, 400–4; operational definition of, 29; in other modalities than speech, 13–17; and parallels between vision and audition, 293–6; processes underlying, 387–8, 400; provisional criteria for, 15; relation of Whorf Hypothesis to, 546; and relation to communication, 547; and relation to philosophy of cognitive science, 550–1; right hemisphere and, 437, 438–9; separable dimensions in, 498; of sound signals, animal studies in, 301–31; of space, 521; as special, 13, 14, 53, 340–1, 422; in strict sense, 352; study of, 5, 254, 255–61; unanswered questions about, 546–51; unique to human speech/general perceptual mode (debate), 301, 340–2, 545; usefulness of, 306, 328, 352; *see also* infants, CP in

categorical perception (CP) theory, 457–9; refutation of, 280; strong form, 458

categorical representations (CRs), 61, 201, 551–8, 559; in infants, 10, 161, 162, 163, 171, 174, 176–7; in nonhuman organisms, 187n2

categorical-to-symbolic (C/S) transformation, 543

categoricity, 214

categories, 302; absolute discrete, 33; acquired, 2; bounded, 8, 528; concrete, 556; decomposition of, into attributes, 459–61; defined, 461; discrete, 337; functional significance of, 336–40; relation of infant and adult, 170–2; stability/flexibility, 468–70; uses of, 465–6; *see also* perceptual categories

categorization: active vs. passive filtering in, 552–4; adaptive, 337, 352; basic issues in, 459–70; basis for, 11, 526n16; changes in, causes by repetitive stimulation, 215–16; cognition primary in, 559; context-relativity of, 558; "correctness" of, 538–43; CP generalized to, 22–4; difficulty in, 356–7; distance from discrimination, 288–9; functional significance of, 15, 346; GK/SP category comparison in, 474–83; of human speech by animals, 318–19; hypothesis about processes underlying, 90–1; iconic representations in, 552; in infants, 183; learned, 323–4; natural, 552; as problem, 1–4; "pure," 352; of semantic vs. perceptual items, 404–7; sensory and decision processes in, 261–6, 271, 280; sharp, 114; of speech, 113, 161–72, 226–53; successful, 540, 560n6

categorization function: affricate/fricative distinction, 126f, 129–32; animals, 374

categorization processes: and CP, 455–90; inherent to human perceptual systems, 162

categorization research, 19, 537

categorization tests in animals and infants, 355–86

categorization theory, 538

category acquisition, 466–8, 472, 550; experience in, 479; GK/SP categories, 485; typicality effect in, 471

category boundary effect (*see also* boundary effects), 32, 41, 48, 54, 78, 79; anchor concept of, 74; intensity theory of, 61; and plucks and bows, 69

category boundary(ies) 4, 23, 124, 440, 514; acquisition of, 545; adaptation level as, 394, 398–400, 408, 414; in AL theory, 392; arbitrary, 121–2; auditory constraints on, 243; with categorical representations, 552; classification by, and SP categories, 465; and context independence, 404; defining, 394; differences in, 43–6; as discontinuity, 36; discrete, 20; effect of experience on, 548; evoked potentials (EPs) as, 443; $F1$-cutback continuum, 145; fixed, 116; flexible, 266, 350; fuzzy, 512, 514, 516; and individual recognition, 348–50; learned-label theory, 122; location of, 5, 38–9, 89–91, 147–8, 169–70, 171, 244–6, 302; location of, and color, 292; location of, and prototypes, 178; methods of obtaining, 90; modification of, 34; modification of, as function of language, 528; in motor theory, 7–8; place of articulation and, 42; plasticity in, 17, 548; precision in, 336, 529; reference points at, 471, 473, 475, 476; rise time and, 120; sharp identification functions at, 458; shifts in, 91, 129, 350, 468, 469; shifts in, as function of experience, 388, 400–4, 407, 414; shifts in, with anchors, 393; in spatial categories, 512, 514, 516; for stimuli on continuum with adaptation level for set, 391, 398–400, 404, 407; and trading relationships, 47; vague, 512; voiced–voiceless contrasts, 185; VOT, 42; *see also* phonetic boundaries

category cognition, 557–8; CP as model for, 3–4

category distinctions, prelinguistic, 106

category formation: approximation in, 543; in infants, 164; invariance extraction in, 550

category generation, 472

category learning, 23–4, 550

category membership, 483, 562n16; attributes in, 461–2, 463; graded, 498–9; natural kind, 505–6; propositions about, 554; rules in, 461–2, 464, 554

category representations, knowledge in, 483–4

category revision and approximation, 540–1

category structure, 175–8, 461–2; developmental change in, 394, 491–510; reference points in, 473; and word meaning, 492–6

category-tuning, 292

category validity, cue validity vs., 482–3

cats, 307

ceiling effects, 68, 81, 129, 165

Subject index

central nervous system, 322
"central state of expectation," 389
central tendency (characteristic values): category membership, 464, 465, 473; reference point of, 475
chance performance, 32, 114; auditory stimuli, 35, 36; and phoneme categories, 118; visual stimuli, 37, 38
characteristic attributes (word meaning), 494-6
characteristic features, 20; of spatial categories, 516
characteristic-to-defining shift, 20, 499, 500-7, 508; in development of syntactic categories, 504; experience and, 498; mechanism underlying, 492, 493, 504-7; in word meaning, 492-6, 506, 507
children: and auditory-evoked potential (AEP) studies, 427-30, 432-35; category acquisition by, 467; developmental change in categorization by, 20, 491-2, see also development; EPs in, 440; VOT processing in, 425, 427-9; see also infants
chimpanzees, 333
chinchillas, 16, 43-4, 106, 146-7, 148, 167, 173, 244-5, 307, 319, 324, 340-1, 359, 376, 419, 504; discrimination of *jnd* voice-onset time, 368-70; voice-onset-time generalizations, 362-4
chirps, 119, 211, 212, 334; of insects, 307
choice rule, 273
chromatic adaptation, 446
chromatic contrast, 443, 446-9
chromatic spectrum, perceptual representation of, 28/-9, 290-1, 292
chromaticity, 287
chunks, 10, 22
class-membership functions, 272
classification, 11, 455; bases of, 462-6; basic level, 467; in category acquisition, 467; category use in, 465-6; by children, 467; "correct," 541; cue validity central to, 483; decision rules in, 480; differential ease of, 463; flexibility in, 468-70; GK/SP categories, 463-4, 484-5; holistic vs. analytic processing in, 481-2; in SP categories, 464-5, 479-80; typicality and, 471, 472; use of reference points in, 477-9
classification tasks: holistic processing of, 482; prototype reference points and, 477
coarticulation, 101-2, 162, 231-2, 239
coding, qualitative, 476, 477
cognition: automatic/controlled processes in, 238; comparative, 548; computational approaches to, 562n17; in CP, 1-25; foundations of CP in, 22-4; induction in, 558; labels in, 10; primary, in categorization, 559; propositional models of, 560n4
cognitive categories, 82

cognitive demons, 201, 202, 206, 213, 218
cognitive development, 1, 493, 496; category acquisition in, 467
cognitive economy, 15, 336, 340
cognitive literature, 40
cognitive maps, 520
cognitive modeling, 1, 2
cognitive nativism, 557; *see also* innateness
cognitive processes, 172; as propositional, 20-1
cognitive processing: EP and, 424; flexibility in, 481; and hemispheric specialization, 439
cognitive psychology, 178, 358, 483
cognitive science, 242, 456; feature-detector theory in, 206; problems of philosophy in, 536-8, 550-1
cognitive structure, 493
"cognitively penetrable," 528
color, 6, 14, 20, 446, 456, 465, 497; and CP in infants, 498; multidimensionality in, 81; processing of, 482; sensation of, 443; and speech, 293-6; typicality gradients of, 471; wavelength properties of, 443, 445-6
color boundaries, 6, 443
color categories, 14, 462, 466, 549; and animal studies, 289, 290-1; cross-cultural, 289-90, 291; evoked potentials and, 443-51; identification of, 470; in infants, 175, 290, 296; modifiability of, 292; physiology of, 281; visual EPs in study of, 18
color cohyponyms, 288
color CP, 14, 547, 548
color naming, 288-9, 290, 292; determines color discrimination, 546; focal colors in, 296
color perception, 2, 287-300, 544; in animals, 341-2; and Whorf Hypothesis, 545-6
color-scaling experiments, 287-8
color space, 288
color spectrum, 3
color vision, 333; categories/subcategories of, 338, 339t; physiological bases for, 6; trivariance of, 449n2
common-factor theory, 121
communication, 15; comparative, 548; and conceptual structure, 506; relation to CP, 547
communication repertoire, 336-7
comparative judgment (law of), 268
comparative psychology, 1
compensation, 102, 242, 244-6
complexity theory, 541
computational demons, 201, 202, 206
computational power, 239-43, 246
computational theory, 12, 550
computers, 1, 23, 356-7, 377
concept formation research, 549
concept revision, 536, 537, 558
conception as source of perception, 528
conceptual categories, 516; vs. perceptual categories, 456

conceptual/linguistic system, 513
conceptual reorganization, onset of, 493, 495–6
conceptual structure, 508
conceptual systems, 499; stability/flexibility, 468–70
conceptualization of spatial relations, 511–31
conditional-avoidance paradigm, 43
conflict (speech event) vs. ambiguity, 278–80
confusable alternatives, 540, 544, 552; context of, 541
congruence, and perception/production of speech sounds, 404, 547
conjunction, 272
connectionism, 561n11
consciousness, 536, 537
consequence-dependency, 552
conservation-of-liquids problem, 518
consonant release, 421
consonant stop, 153n1; *see also* stop consonants
consonant-vowel syllables, 64–5
consonants, 31, 73, 123, 153, 336; discrimination of, 340; identification/discrimination (intensity theory) of, 66–9; identification of, 92, 205
constant fundamental frequency wave forms, 125–6
constraints: in development of category structure, 508; in discrimination, 166–7; in induction problem, 541
constructive approach, 550
context, 23, 168–9, 234, 236, 246, 394; of categorical representations, 484, 552, 556, 558, 559, 560n5; in categorization, 540; of confusable alternatives, 23, 541; and convergence, 541; in discrimination, 340, 544; effects of, on category boundaries and judgments of representativeness, 404, 405, 407; and indiscriminability, 15; in perception of spatial relations, 529; and phoneme boundary placement, 116, priming by, 481; and speech perception, 460; widening of, 541, 542
context coding, 71–3, 77, 78, 124; effect of training on, 67; model of, 74
context coding mode, 123, 152, 153
context dependence/independence, 403, 540, 544
context effects, 78, 80–1, 83n4, 375, 383, 462; and CP in infants, 376; and invariance of acoustic cues, 236, 237; in roving discrimination, 465; in speech perception, 12
context influences (CP), 258–61
context/location calls, 317
context mode, 392; efficiency of, 70–3; identification and fixed/roving discrimination of, in estimation of memory variance, 65–70; intensity resolution, 61, 62, 63, 64, 77, 80
context sensitivity, 92, 407
continuity/discontinuity phenomenon, CP as, 4, 549

continuity of phenomena and mechanisms (across species), evolutionary assumption of, 332, 333
continuous discrimination in humans, 345–6
continuous identification, SP categories in, 470
continuous model (speech perception): identification-reaction times of, 276–80; rating responses of, 268–71
continuous perception, 5, 29, 153n2, 544; in AL theory, 395; in animal categorization, 311, 319–20, 321, 322; auditory stimuli, 35, 38; CP distinct from, 6, 13, 53–85, 255, 258, 261–6, 273–6, 277, 280, 304–6, 391; identification/discrimination relation in, 78–9; models of, 273–6; in right hemisphere, 388; in test for CP, 266–71
continuous processing, 188n14; in infants, 179
continuous representations, simulated/pseudo, 542–3
continuous sensory information, 262–3
continuous vs. discrete processing models: GK/SP categories in, 473, 485
contrast, 91, 234, 390, 540
contrast effect(s), 92–3, 94, 97, 234, 400, 407; adaptation, 218; prediction of, 221
convergence, 23, 459; approximation and, 538–9, 540–1, 542, 558; context-driven, 538–9; in meaning revision, 538; in speech/nonspeech findings, 361, 375
coo-calls, 323, 334, 341, 346
copying, 552
"core meaning" (concept), 394
cortex, 407–8, 413; and visual system, 395–6
cotton-top tamarins (*Saguinus oedipus*), 334, 341–2
CP literature, 31–3, 34–9, 40, 557–8; intensity theory in, 63–73
credit assignment problem, 560n8, 562n21
crickets, 246, 307–9, 325
critical band, 325–7
cross-classification, 468
cross-cultural differences in category acquisition, 468
cross-cultural studies: and color categories, 289–90, 291, 296; and speech, 295
cross-language comparisons, 105–6, 142–3, 182, 245, 358
cross-model perception of speech in infants, 377, 380–1
cue (concept), 98
cue-integration effects, 98–9, 100, 101
cue validity vs. category validity, 482–3
cues, 102, 356, 463; acquired equivalence/distinctiveness of, 458–9; relevant, for phonetic categories, 227, 229–30
cultural relativism, 289, 291
culture(s): and category acquisition, 467; and characteristic-to-defining shift, 496; and color discrimination, 14; and color naming, 292;

Subject index

effect of, on category boundaries, 528; and object categories, 516; and prototype perception, 468; and shareability constraint on representation of concepts, 506; and subordinate categories, 337–8

data reduction, 235
decidability, 542
decision criterion, 391
decision-making levels, feature-detector hypothesis and, 235–6
decision processes, 13, 393, 458; in categorization, 261–6, 271, 280; in speech recognition, 12
decision rules, 236; in classification, 480, 482; discrete, 263–4; for psychophysical tasks, 474
decision stage, 265–6, 306
decisional model, 393
declarative sentence, 554
defined categories, 19
defining features, 20; in word meaning, 494–6
defining (principled) dimensions, 492
demons, 212, 214, 273; *see also* cognitive demons; computational demons
DeMorgan's Law, 272
description: experience and, 23; as representational system, 20, 22
description system, symbolic, 538, 551–8
detecting, detection, 206, 441
detection theory, 59, 302
development: in auditory sensitivities, 151–2; in category structure, 491–510; and color categorization, 292; in emergence of VOT perception mechanisms, 440; in event-related potentials, 18; and holistic vs. analytic processing, 482, 507; in representations of children's categories, 20; and spatial categories, 528–9; in spatial cognition, 518–19; in speech processing, 172
developmental psychology, 497
dialect, 238, 239–40, 338, 346, 351
difference limen (DL), 30, 31, 35–6, 37, 39–40, 43–5, 48, 140, 458
difference limen (DL) function, 30–1
diffuse field(s), 443–6
digital/digital (D/D) transformation, 542–3
dimensional approaches, 499, 508
dimensionality, 81–2, 511
dimensions, 501
direct perception theory, 119, 127, 132, 188n13, 550, 561n14
direction, 511
discontinuities, 3, 14, 391, 545; acquired, 9, 23; natural, 15, 16, 151; psychoacoustic, 79; psychophysical, 38–9; sources of, 13; in speech perception/production, 6–7, 8–9; *see also* auditory discontinuities
discrepancies from adaptation level, 390–1, 394, 401–4, 412

discrete perceptual processing into absolute categories, 29–30, 33, 48–9
discrete processing model, 473
discrete-state models, 54
discreteness, 30, 33, 58
discriminability, 30, 120; enhanced, at boundaries, 358, 367–8, 370–1, 372–4; in infants, 44–5, 167, 174–5; learned names and descriptions in, 546; measurement of, 36; reference-point effects in, 472–3, 475–6; of rise times, 128–9; subordinate-category, 15–16; tone intensity, 83n7; variability in, 115, 544; visual stimuli, 37–8; and VOT, 114, 244–5, 370–1; within-and-cross-category, 43–4
discrimination, 2–3, 419; in adaptation-level theory, 17; in animals, 16, 303, 307; better-than-predicted, 55, 68; between/within category, 175–7; boundary in, 5, 394; constraints on, 166–7; distinct from categorization, 288–9; as history-dependent function, 390, 414; and identification, 255–61, 273–6, 280, 543–4; in infants, 10, 183; initial plosives, 138–40, 141, 144; of *jnd* in voice-onset time in chinchillas, 368–70; and label learning, 9; levels of, 166, 167; monotonic/nonmonotonic, 358; place of articulation in monkeys, 371–4; poor, within phoneme category, 114–15; prediction of, 55, 58–9; reliance on category labels in, 92; reliance on memory in, 306; as representational system, 20; is sense modality dependent, 544; sensory/decisional models of, 393; time-dependent memory variance in, 63–5; in visual/auditory perception parallel, 293–5; *see also* fixed discrimination; roving discrimination
discrimination function, 22; affricate/fricative distinction, 125, 126f, 129–32, 136; in animals, 307, 374; better-than-predicted, 33; brain mechanisms in CP, 408; correlated with identification function, 13, 30, 54, 60–77; as evidence of CP (animals), 306, 310–11, 312, 322, 425; individual differences and, 400–2; isomorphic, 337–40; in motor theory, 118, 119; musical pitch studies, 122; nonmonotonic, 166; peaks in, 458; shape of, 73–7
discrimination peak(s), 32, 36, 118, 119, 120, 244, 472; affricate/fricative distinction in, 125, 126, 136; at boundaries, 114, 166, 476–7; explanations of, 55; in infant CP, 167; initial plosives, 140, 141, 142–3, 144, 149; in plucks and bows, 69; reasons for, 123–4; and shift in phonetic boundaries across languages, 105–6; in trained subjects, 59–60; VOT, 75–6
discrimination performance, 13, 19; average, 31, 33; in definitions of CP, 458; effect of practice on, 39–40; iconic representations account for, 553–4; in infants, 220–1; phonetic

discrimination performance (cont.)
  boundary location and, 105–6; time course of changes in, 23
discrimination sensitivity as consequence of reference points, 475–6, 477
discrimination tasks: analytic processing in, 482; auditory memory in, 257, 261; boundary reference points and, 477; in intensity theory, 61–3
discrimination tests: animal CP, 308–9, 312, 313, 314–17, 318; and boundary location, 302; infant CP, 376, 379
dishabituation, 307, 422
disjunction, 272
disjunctive rules, 485n3
display transformation problem, 519, 520–1, 524–7
distinctive feature (concept), 10, 200–3, 206
distinctive feature theory, 214, 227
distinctive features: as basic level of speech representation, 503; binary nature of, 207; search for invariant acoustic correlates of, 236–7
distributional-classification model, 474
divergence, 541; in animal studies, 375; in speech/nonspeech findings, 361
divergent evolution, 333
domain(s), 173, 482; characteristic-to-defining shift in, 494–5, 500; 505, 508; conceptual reorganization in, 493
dual-coding model, 257, 562n17
dual-process memory model, 122–3
dual-process model, 33, 54, 55–8, 59, 63, 65, 68, 69, 122–3, 152, 153, 173, 458; GK/SP categories in, 473–4, 485
duration, 92, 324–5, 343, 344–5, 347–50, 355, 382; critical, 15; and monotonic discrimination relationship, 358; sound, 304
duration continuum, 319; and CP in animals, 316, 317

ear advantages, 432–3
echoic memory, 22, 33, 122, 123, 551ff
ecological-optics approach, 550
ecology, 14–15, 207, 320, 352, 551; in GK/SP comparison, 483–5
economy: articulatory, 239; principle of, 336
"edge" effects, 390
efficiency, 542, 553
egocentrism, 523, 529
ego-related frame of reference (relatum), 523
eight-response identification trials: VOT, 75–6
electroencephalogram (EEG), 423
electrophysiology, 34, 204; indices of CP for speech, 421–41; of sensory processes, 206–7
elementary percepts, 536, 537, 538, 559
empirical similarities between SP/GK categories, 470–3, 485

encoding, 538, 544; implicit/explicit, 562n22; of instances, 557, 599
"end" effects, 390, 408
energy peaks in spectrum, 325, 327
English language, 171, 180, 239–40, 241, 292; articulatory discontinuity in, 142–3; boundary locations in, 105–6; color categories in, 290, 292; phone distinction in, 204; voiced/voiceless sounds in, 137; voicing changes in, 185; VOT continuum in, 149–50
environment, 15; and animal CP, 304; categorization of information in, 175; correlational structure of, 461–2; language and, 358, 359
equivalence classes, 10, 173, 174; in infants, 16, 163–6; SP/GK categories as, 471–2
error sources (spatial cognition), 519, 523, 524–5
ethology, 14–15, 320
Euclidean concepts, 519
European honeybee, 291
event-related potentials (EP), 17–18, 549, 550; averaged, 423–4; to chromatic contrast, 446–9; and color-defined categories, 443–51; neuronal substrates of, 424; procedures in, 423–4, 438; to spatially unpatterned (diffuse) fields, 443–6
events, 456
evolutionary theory, 557; continuity of phenomena and mechanisms across species in, 332, 333; divergent/convergent, 333; motor theory of speech perception in, 545, 548
exemplar-based models, 479–80, 499, 508
exemplars, 296, 501; and adaptation and range effects, 480–1; AL theory and, 393–4; analytical/holistic processing of, 467; categories organized around, 492, 495; category membership, 462, 463; classification of, 470, 471, 474, 478–9; classification of, by GK categories, 464; classification of, by SP categories, 465; clear, 512, 514, 516; generation and, 466, 468; in GK/SP categories, 485; goodness of, 463, 467; long-term effects of, 479–80; similarity to prototypes, 465, 473, 475, 476–7, 478, 479–80; theories of, 485n4
expectations, 18, 516; and within-category discrimination, 349, 350
experience, 10, 15, 22, 59, 124, 153, 323, 457; in AL theory, 388, 392; anchors acquired through, 77; with caller, 349, 350; in categorization, 237, 238, 538–9; and characteristic-to-defining shift, 498, 508; in classification, 464; and color categorization, 14, 292; and description, 23; in development of category structure, 501; direct, with instances, 554, 556; effect of, on category boundaries, 548; effect of, on identification and discrimination, 390, 544, 545; in GK/SP categories, 485; and infant speech perception, 164; irreducibility of, 537; and learning CP, 358–9; necessary to

CP, 430, 440; pooled, averaged, 394; in producing/hearing speech sounds, 422; and prototype effect, 380; in representational system, 559; residual effects of, previous, 390; role in category acquisition, 467–8; role of, in category boundary shifts, 388, 400–4, 407, 414; role of, in use of reference points, 479; selective attention and, 322; short/long-term effect of, on category formation, 388; in spatial categories, 516, 528; in speech perception, 97, 503; in verbal description, 540; *see also* linguistic experience
experimental design, 54, 59–60, 61, 274, 328; in animal studies, 363–4, 371
experimental manipulation, 97, 98, 101, 102, 459; in phoneme boundaries, 116
experimental method (CP), 2–3, 5–6; speech CP, 11–12
expert/novice distinction, 505
expertise and characteristic-to-defining shift, 498, 508
explanation of CP: approaches to, 116–24; assessment of, 124–52
explicitness, representational format, 512, 522

faces, 8, 10
factor analysis, 420
factorial design, 274
"family resemblance," 394, 461–2, 562n16
feature-based approaches, 499, 508
feature categories, universality of, 516
feature detection, 12, 23; active/passive, 553–4
feature-detection models, 11–17, 188n11, 205–6; compared to other theories, 210; physiological mechanisms in, 206–7; rejection of, 214–19; tests of, 207–10
feature-detector hypothesis, 233–4, 246; arguments against, 234–6
feature detectors, 12, 21–2, 202, 361, 396, 460; all-or-none, 549; appeal of, 206–10; arguments against, 234–6, 239; fatigue in, 212, 213, 215, 218, 219, 234, 481; hard-wired, 350; hierarchies of, 214, 216, 220; as innate biological mechanisms, 237; learned, 22; neuroscience of, 549–50; outputs of, 234–6; phonetic, 95; selective adaptation and, 233–4; in spatial categories, 528–9; in speech, 33–4; task-specific, 557; *see also* phonetic feature detectors
feature evaluation in fuzzy-logic model, 272–3, 277–8, 279
feature integration, 99–100; in fuzzy-logic model, 273, 274
feature representations, 389
features, 188n9, 549; identifying critical, 522, 525, 540; informational underdetermination of, 23; necessary and sufficient, 498, 506, 561n16; object(s) difference from, 537, 538, 559; search for, 23; sufficient to serve as basis for categorization, 561-2n16; *see also* distinctive features
Fechner's Law, 29
feedback, 23–4, 145; with categorical representations, 552
field cricket (*Grylius campestris*), 308–9, 318
figure-ground segration, 446
filtering: active vs. passive, 552–4; selective, 556
filtering mechanisms, 227, 228
filters, nested, 200
fishes, 333
fixed discrimination, 5, 65–70, 74–6, 79, 245; and AL theory, 392; intensity theory, 61–3; learning in, 80; in VOT experiment, 75–6
flexibility: category, 468–70; in GK/SP categories, 480–1
flicker frequency, 444–5
flicker-fusion, threshold for, 4–5
flickering visual stimuli, 36–7, 39
floor effects, 81, 129
flying crickets (*Teleogryllus oceanicus*), 309
focal colors, 296
$F1$-cutback continuum, 137–41, 145–6
$F1$ onset frequency, 150–2
form perception, 10–11; and perception of objects, 515–16
form processing, 482
formant transition, 136, 167–8, 472, 476; feature integration, 100; selective adaptation, 211–12, 213; speech sounds differing in, 304; stop consonants, 102
formants, 115, 227; second, 118–19;
frame of reference: determination of, 522–6; spatial features in, 513, 514, 527, 528, 529
"frame" problem, 562n21
French language, 105, 180
frequency, 91, 116, 119, 121, 124, 355; in AL theory, 389; in animal studies, 304, 371–4; *jnd* and, 368; in monotonic discrimination relationship, 358; pattern–nonspeech categorization, 304
frequency bandwiths, 15, 325, 342
frequency range, 304, 343
frication, 169–70
fricative/affricate boundary, 105
fricative-affricate continua, 33
fricatives, 81, 101, 124–5, 136; categorized by infants, 164; intensity theory, 67–9, 73; production of, 99, 101
frogs, 207, 246, 303, 309–12, 322, 325
functional attributes, 467
functional significance of CP, 336–40, 346
fuzzy categories, 461, 462, 463, 464
fuzzy logic (concept), 271–2
fuzzy-logical model of categorization behavior, 13, 254–83

fuzzy-logical model of perception (FLMP), 271–3, 275; ambiguity vs. conflict in, 278–80
fuzzy set model, 480
fuzzy set theory, 473

games, 461
generalization, 14, 15; of characteristic-to-defining shift, 493, 503–4; inductive, 536, 537; of phonological rules, 186–7; "successful," 536
generation: category, 472; GK/SP categories in, 466, 485; of instances, 471
generic knowledge (GK) categories, 19, 456; acquisition of, 466–8; and category structure, 461, 462; classification in, 463–4; decomposition of, into attributes, 460; instantiations of, 457; vs. sensory perception categories, 455, 456–7, 459, 469t, 470–85; stability/flexibility of, 468–70, 485; uses of, 465–6
genetic predisposition; *see* biological predisposition
Gestalt school, 528
gesture, 547; discrete productive, 118, 119; *see also* articulatory gestures
glides, 168
global sequential (range-frequency) effects, 94–5
goal-relevant categories, 468, 516
Goeldi's monkeys (*Callimico goeldi*), 313, 317–18, 343
goldfish, 444
goodness: category of, 96, 175–6; exemplar of, 394; phonetic categories of, 175–6; stimuli of, 379–80, 382
goodness judgments, 13
goodness of fit, 256, 270
gorillas, 333
graded categories, 19
graded identification functions, 470
graded structure, 463, 464
grain, granularity, 16, 542–3
great apes, 333
green treefrog (*Hyla cinerea*), 307, 310–11
groundedness, 550, 552, 557, 559, 562n21
grounding problem, 3, 23, 556ff
guessing, 115, 270–1

habituation (animal CP), 307
habituation of high-amplitude sucking, 422
habituation paradigms, 425
"haphazard-plus-missing features," (model), 493
hard-wired functions, 350, 352; color categories, 292; *see also* innateness
harmonic structure, 165
HARPY (model), 240, 242
Haskins Laboratories, 229, 243, 247
Haskins model, 54, 55–8, 59, 69, 144
head-turning response, 44, 163-4, 378–9
hearing, 7–8
HEARSAY (model), 12, 242

heart-rate orienting response, 307
Helmholtz resonators, 227
hemispheric specialization, 382, 413, 414, 439, 440, 551; CP/continuous perception in, 388; *see also* brain; lateralization
heterochromatic flicker photometry, 446
hierarchical analyzer, 200–2
hierarchical integration and differentiation theory, 492
hierarchy, 16, 500; of feature detectors, 214, 216, 220; in representational system, 556; sensory-perception and generic knowledge categories in, 19
high-amplitude sucking procedure, 166, 422
higher-level knowledge model, 12
higher-order categories, 5, 18–22
higher-order classifications, 465–6
higher-order interactions, 5, 9
history-dependent processes, 396; *see also* experience
holistic processing, 467, 481–2
holistic representation, 20
holistic-to-analytic shift, 497–8, 507
homuncularity, 561n12
homunculus, 11–12, 21, 214
Hopi (tribe), 546
horse-cart problem, 520, 521
house mice (*Mus musculus*), 307, 313–17, 318, 325, 342
hue, 18, 20, 438, 446, 482, 497, 498; discrimination in animals, 341–2; hemispheric specialization in discrimination of, 414; judgments of, 406–7; subjective, 444; visual categorization of, 287–92; voicing and, 293–6
hue categories, 287–9, 290–1, 296; perceptual development and, 292
hue-discrimination task, 411
human/animal parallels (speech perception), 364, 365, 366, 367, 372–4; where they break down, 360, 375, 376–7
human-performance modeling, 1, 2
human studies, brain mechanisms in CP, 408–13
human-vision literature, 34

icon-to-atomic-category (I/C) conversion, 543, 552, 553
iconic and categorical acquaintance system, 551–8
iconic representations (IRs), 61, 201, 544, 551–8, 559
ideal attributes in category membership, 462, 464, 465
ideal form (CP), 122–3, 264
idealization (strategy), 227
ideals: boundary, 341; classification by, in SP categories, 464, 465; reference points in, 475
identifiability: modality-independent constraints on, 544

Subject index

identification, 2–3, 5, 19, 22, 60, 393, 422; in adaptation-level theory, 17; boundary in, 394; discrimination and, 58–60, 78–9, 81, 123, 255–61, 273–6, 280, 543–4; in estimation of memory variance, 65–70; in feature detector model, 188n11; as history-dependent function, 390, 414; iconic representations in, 552; and label learning, 9; multiresponse, 58; as representational system, 20, 544; roving, 6; sensory/decisional models of, 393
identification boundaries in animals, 16
identification/discrimination task as measure of CP, 258–61, 273–6, 280
identification function, 22, 167, 557; brain mechanisms in CP, 408; and correlation with discrimination function, 13, 30, 54, 60–77; history-dependent, 349; individual differences in, 400–2, 403; method for eliciting, 397–400; in motor theory, 118, 119; sharp, 114, 118, 119, 264; sharp, in SP/GK categories, 470, 471, 485
identification labeling, 13
identification performance, 19, 245; in categorical/continuous models, 273–6; CRs account for, 553–4; in definition of CP, 458; time course of changes in, 23
identification-reaction time, 13, 276–80
identification tasks: affricate/fricative distinction in, 135–6; and intensity theory, 61–3; six-response, 76; two-response, 80–1
image demons, 200–1, 206, 213
imparsimony, 541–2
imprinting, 10, 313, 322, 323
indeterminacy, 563n25
indiscriminability, 15–16, 548
individual differences, 351–2; and category boundaries, 400–4; in infant speech perception, 164; in speech production, 377; in stability of conceptual systems, 468; and within-category discrimination, 338, 346, 349–50, 351
individual recognition (animal communication), 302, 303, 314, 318, 320, 321, 322, 323, 347–50
individual-specific differences, 333
Indo-European languages, 290, 292
induction, 2, 22, 539, 554; problem of, 536, 537, 538, 540–1, 557, 558; ungroundedness of, 560n2
inductive risk, 537, 538
infant studies, 127, 237, 422; animal data compared with, 375–7; category boundaries in, 44–5
infants, 17; and acquisition of language, 161–95; auditory sensitivities of, 151; categorical knowledge in, 493; categorization of speech sounds in, 207, 244, 356; categorization tests in, 355–86; color categories in, 14, 289, 290, 292, 296; CP boundaries in, 7, 9, 10; CP in, 16, 115–16, 121, 163, 166–70, 293, 295, 307, 437, 493, 498, 503–4, 545; discrimination capabilities of, 150; event-related potentials (EPs) in, 18; evoked potentials in, 429–30; imitation of speech in, 381–2; phoneme boundary effect in, 367–8; precocious abilities of, 220–1; recognition of phonetic equivalence in, 376–82; sensitivity to potential phonetic boundaries in, 106; speaking-rate effects in, 103; special mechanisms as cause of CP in, 375–6; speech perception in, 161–95, 295, 358–9, 440, 467; speech processing in, 180–2; speech-specific motor-theoretic effects in, 16; VOT processing in, 425, 429–30
inference(s), 7, 466, 483, 485, 553, 562n16
inferotemporal cortex, 407, 408
information, 10–11, 188n6; ambiguous/conflicting, 278–80; continuous, 264, 271–3; required for discrimination, 541; about speaker, 340; structure of, 459–62; syllabic, 235; for unambiguous phonetic categories, 227, 232, 238–43; value of, 262
information-integration theory, 274
information loss in categorization, 542–3
information processing, 340; need for specialized, 235; redundancy in, 238
information reduction, 461
informational capacity, limits on, 23
innate feature detectors, 237, 464, 480–1, 528; in color CP, 14; in SP prototypes, 465
innate mechanisms (CP), 15, 207, 237, 303, 322; in color perception, 546; for speech perception, 422
innate sensitivities, 8–9; in category acquisition, 466–7, 468
innateness: of anchors, 6; of auditory CP in animals, 16; of capacity to partition speech stimuli, 375–6; category, 550; of constraints, 475, 557; of CP, 2, 121, 548; in perceptual system, 179; of phonetic knowledge, 381; of spatial detectors, 528–9
insects, 14, 303, 307–9, 322, 333
instance-bound features (categories), 20, 541, 559
instantiation, 466, 540; encoding, 557, 559; experience, 554, 556; in GK categories, 457
integral-to-separable dimensions shift, 20, 497–8, 500–7; and category membership, 499
integration, 98–9
intensity, 58, 304, 355, 358
intensity resolution, 123
intensity resolution theory, 60–73; revised, 61, 73–7
internal representation, see mental representation
internal standard of judgment, 391, 392, 413
internalization of language, 493
interval-identification functions, 122
intonation, 165
intuitive beliefs, 460

invariance: finding, 540–1, 550; underdetermination of, 541; *see also* acoustic invariance hypotheses
invariance filter, 553, 554, 559
invariants, 24n4, 187–8n6, 539, 540; acoustic variation and, 204–6; conjunctive/disjunctive, 553; external, 561n14; extracting, 538, 543; in given context, 556, 557, 558, 559; picked out by categorical representations, 552, 553, 554, 556
irreducibility, 537, 558
isolation peeps, 338–40
isomorphism, 291, 337–40
isotropy, 544

Japanese language, 106, 358
Japanese macaques (*Macaca fuscata; M. nemestrina; M. radiata*), 44, 323, 334, 341, 351
judgmental effect, 93–4, 116, 119, 124
just noticeable differences *(jnds)*, 147, 544, 559; monotonic/nonmonotonic, 368, 369–70; stable, 544

key (sign) stimuli, 14–15, 302–3, 310, 327–8, 350–1; hypotheses concerning relation between CP and, 319–27; releasing mechanisms and, 320
kinesthetic modality, neural substrates underlying CP in, 388–9, 395, 396, 412–14
knowledge: in category representations, 483–4; and characteristic-to-defining shift, 505, 508; in development of category structure, 500–1; early, 495; limited, 39–40; required for representation of speech, 181; selective attention and, 322; and speaking-rate effect, 103; in speech recognition, 12, 242; *see also* tacit knowledge
knowledge acquisition, 508
knowledge-by-acquaintance, 539–40; vs. knowledge-by-description, 536, 537, 538, 558
knowledge-by-description, 536, 537, 538, 558

label learning, 9–10, 23; *see also* learned-label theory
labeling, 114–15, 349, 458; overlearned, 57; psychophysical, 22, 24
labeling function, 140; effect of practice on, 39; as evidence of CP, 304–6, 307, 309, 310–11, 312, 317, 318, 343; isomorphic, 337–40; sharp, 122, 125
labeling task, 125, 130
labeling tests, 304–6; animal CP, 308, 313, 314–17, 318, 322; and boundary location, 302
labels, 10, 20, 22; in categorical representations, 391, 553, 554; learned, 115, 116; prior existence of repertoire of, 554, 556; unique, 421–2
LAFS (Lexical Access From Spectra), 12, 240–2

language, 1, 7, 20, 89, 172, 232, 553; and category boundary shifts, 105–6, 349–50, 469, 545, 546: and color categories, 292; and constraints on speech production, 239–40; constraints on variation of sounds of, 202–3; and CP, 5, 13–14, 358–9, 546; determines view of reality, 13–14, 545–6; experience in, 171–2; labels in, 10; and location of color boundaries, 6; perceptual structure and, 513; relativism in, 289; role of, in discrimination, 545–6; selective adaptation effects of, 95–6; sound structure of, 184; and spatial concepts, 517, 528–9; speech categorization in, 113; and stored representations of speech, 181–2; symbolic descriptions of natural, 22, 23; universalism in, 289–90
language acquisition, 10, 177, 423, 433–5, 503–4; in infants, 161–95; speech-perception capacities in, 182–7
"language of thought," 21, 22
language processing: higher-order, 240; specialized mechanisms for, 355–60; vertical nature of, 153
language stimuli in AEPs, 430, 440
languages, 171; and differences in articulatory-acoustic patterns, 105–6; phone distinctions in, 204; voicing contrasts in, 185; and VOT continuum, 149–50
laryngeal vibration, 113–14, 421
latency, 394, 424, 445
lateral inhibition, 458
laterality, 412, 413
lateralization, 410, 411, 412, 413, 414, 551
learnability, formal, 561n11
learned-label theory, 9, 22, 79, 115, 116, 121–4, 125, 148, 554; in conjunction with other theories, 126–8, 129–32, 136–7, 152–3
learned phenomenon, CP as, 548
learning, 8, 10, 23–4, 60, 187n4, 544; in animal CP, 303, 321–3; in categorization, 323–4; and CP, 2, 5, 15, 23, 304, 323, 358–9; effect on identification and discrimination in, 544, 545; in infant's recognition of phonetic equivalence, 381; innate sentivities for, 466–7; in pandemonium model, 202; passive, 154n2; perceptual, 78, 79, 80, 550; of phoneme categories, 152; and predicates, 528–9; psychophysical label, 22; to read, 186; in representational system, 22–3, 556, 558; of species-specific vocalizations, 350–1; and speech perception, 9, 115, 165
learning explanations of CP in speech, 113–60
left hemisphere (brain), 414; in CP, 388, 439, 440–1; damage to, 409–13; EP activity in,

424, 426, 427, 429, 430–38, 440, 441;
  speech functions linked to, 388, 412, 423
length, 397, 408, *see also* line length
levels-of-processing, 40, 382–3; category structure in, 176–8; units in, 178–9
lexical categories, 504, 551ff
lexical contrast theory, 507
lexical rules in infants, 161, 162, 182–7
lexicon, 554; acquisition of, 182–7, 551ff
line length, 400–1, 410, 411
linguistic function: abilities, 205; analysis, 206, 209–10; categories, 337, 338, 340; cognition, 529; communication, 547; context, 468–481; contrasts, 204, 206; convention, 465, 475; experience, 43, 91, 122, 125, 171–2, 177, 180, 181, 182, 207, 440; form, 517; knowledge, 210; meaning (referential theories of), 554; naming, 22; organization, 289; processing, 152, 177; representation, 436–7; rules, 464; "set(s)", 245; systems, 431
linguistic-feature extraction, 436
linguistics, 242; descriptive, 204; in feature-detector model, 199, 206, 216, 219, 221
lip reading, 8, 377
listener factors, 92, 105–6
local-context effects on boundary locations, 103, 104, 105
local determinacy (assumption), 235, 236
local sequential effects, 92–4
localization, 410, 413
long-term effects (CP), 17, 548
loudness, 79, 258
low-threshold theory, 36, 55, 58
luminance, 18, 444, 445, 446
luminance effects, 446–9

macaque monkeys, 207, 244, 397, 408
machine vision (problem), 539
magnitude estimation, 92
mallard ducks, 323–13, 318
mammals, 121, 207, 313–18, 322, 325, 333; range effects, 147–8
manner of articulation, place of articulation vs., 229
mapping, 48; of acoustic information, 168, 240; between sound and percept, 355–6; words onto world, 536, 537, 538, 558
match/mismatch detection, 18
maturation, 292, 427; *see also* development
Maxwellian view, 443–4
meaning, 23; core, 394; of words, 536, 537, 559
meaning holism: approximation and, 540–1; problem of, 536, 537–8, 558
meaning revision, 538
measurement error, 33
"mel" scale, 383n1
memorization processes, 503

memory, 55, 79, 93, 336, 505, 544; in AL/STD comparison, 392; in animal CP, 303; in CP, 123, 304, 306; long-term, 6; organization of, 456; patterns of representation in, 513; psychophysics of, 206; retrieval processes in, 336; short-term, 6, 210
memory constraints, 352
memory limitations (CP), 257, 261, 458
memory models, 479
memory modes, efficiency of, 70–3
memory variance, 62; in discrimination, 63–5; identification and fixed/roving discrimination in estimation of, in context mode, 65–70, 78
mental image, 511, 513
mental representations: in dual acquaintance system, 543; of spatial information, 516–19; stable/labile, 407
mental rotation, 553
mental sentences, 550
"method of limits" procedure, 369
methodology, 280, 352; adapted to natural conditions, 332, 334–6; of brain mechanisms studies, 397–400
mice, 246, 322, 325–7
"minimal acoustic cues," 212
miscategorization, 561n15, 562n16
models, 1, 80; classification of, 480; cognitive functions, 1, 2; context coding, 74; continuous perception, 273–6; CP, 273–6, 543–58; exemplar-based, 479–80, 499, 508; generalization of CP to categorization, 22–4; limitations of, 78, 81–2; neural, 199–225; nonspeech CP, 34–9; psychophysical, 5–6, 29–52, 54–60; speech CP, 11–17; speech perception, 207–8, 233; speech processing, 178–9; speech production, 227–8; speech recognition, 12, 240–3; STD, 58–60; threshold, 55–8; two-process, 9
monkeys, 16, 106, 324, 341, 352, 376; brain-damaged, 407, 413; and color categories, 291; forest-living, 333; and place-of-articulation discrimination, 371–4; and voice-onset-time discrimination, 370–1
Moog synthesizer, 125
morphological structures, adaptive, 333
motivation, 327, 328; animal CP, 317, 319, 321–3
motor activity, 547; brain area in control of, 412–13, 414
motor economy, 336, 340
motor mediation in speech discontinuities, 9
motor performance, 1
motor theory of speech perception, 6–8, 9, 12, 16, 107, 115, 116, 121, 124, 125, 148, 152, 240, 358, 365, 466; analysis-by-synthesis variant in, 553; in conjunction with other theories, 126–32, 136–7, 152–3; current status of, 545, 547; as explanation of CP, 117–

motor theory of speech perception (*cont.*) 20; meaning of, 141–5; phoneme perception and, 545
multidimensional space, 188n9; cluster patterns in, 501–2; organization of, 506; prototype-based category structure in, 499
multidimensionality, 6, 81–2
multiplicative integration rule, 480, 482
mushroom-discrimination problem, 551, 552
music, 8, 34–5, 80, 122, 467
musical intervals, 35, 528
musicians, 153n2

name, category, 553
naming, 20, 22, 557
natural behavior(s), 315, 316–17
natural boundary (concept), 74–5, 393, 551, 561n13
natural category research, 549
natural context, 334–5; learning in, 331–2; testing in, 307
natural kinds, 456, 505–6, 561n13
natural language, 538, 557
natural listening situation, 167, 172
natural perceptual boundaries, 360, 361, 365, 367; in animal studies, 364, 370
natural selection, 16, 333, 545
"natural sensitivity," 5, 16, 393
natural speech, 229, 404, 482, 483
naturalistic approach, 332–54; characteristics of, 332–6
necessary and sufficient features, 498, 506, 561n16
negation, 272
negative/iterative problem (description), 540
negative VOT boundary, 44–5
nervous system, 14, 17, 392
neural detectors, 11–12
neural elements, 205–6
neural information processing, 300
neural mechanisms, 2, 200, 324
neural models (speech perception), 199–225
neural quantum theory, 58
neural spectrogram, 12, 235, 243, 383
neurological substrates (perception), 291, 292, 293, 528
neurons, 202
neurophysiology: and color vision, 296; in feature-detector model, 199, 206–7, 216, 218, 221
neuroscience, feature detection in, 549–50
neutral point (AL theory), 392, 393, 394
neutral trials, 279–80
"new preformationism," 557
noise, 9, 18, 36, 37, 79, 328, 423; in animal CP, 303, 304; aspiration of, 47, 137, 150–1; in continuous vs. categorical perception, 264; damage-risk criteria for, 47; duration of, 102
noise-buzz, 35, 41–2, 45–6

noise hypothesis, 39–40
noise-lead time, 304
noise-onset-time (NOT) continuum, 41–2, 46
noncategorical aspects (CP), 39–43
noncategorical representations, 511, 551
nonhuman species: CP in, 13–17, 340–52; *see also* animals
nonlinguistic CP, 170–2, 546
nonspeech, 103, 118–19, 136, 139, 144, 148, 243–4, 318–19, 395, 456; in AEPs, 430–35; auditory detectors of, 212, 213–14; categorization of, 304; categorization of, by infants, 172–5; discrimination of, by infants, 221; EP, 438–9, 441; identification of, 470; infants' reaction to, 382; models and demonstrations of, 34–9; processed differently from speech, 115, 382–3; sequential effects of, 92–3, 107
nonspeech analogs, of affricate/fricative contrast, 125–6; to $F1$ cutback, 138–41; to voicing continuum, 145, to VOT stimuli, 150, 244–5
nonspeech auditory patterns, 172–3, 548
nonspeech continua, 40–1, 120–1, 124, 125, 137, 145, 388; perception of, by infants, 161–2
nonspeech domains: brain structure/perception relation in, 388–9; continuous vs. categorical perception in, 129–30, 263
nonspeech perception, 212, 265; variability of category boundary in, 403–4
nonspeech processing, 188–9n15
nonspeech tests (CP), 360–2
nonsymbolic representations, grounding function of, 550–1
normalization, 98, 248n2
nouns, 504, 517

object(s), 1, 6, 21, 466; classification of, 18–22; difference of, from feature(s), 537, 538, 559; grouping of, 496–7; in multidimensional space, 497–8; perception of, and perception of form, 515–16; in representational system, 556–7; sorting of, 507, 558; in verbal description, 540
object categories: culture and, 516; and relation to spatial categories, 512–13
object concepts, role of shape in, 514–15
object constancy, 561n13
object perception in pandemonium model, 202
object perception theory, 119
object recognition: identification in, 22; spatial propositions in, 521–2, 526, 527
object-to-icon (O/I) transformation, 543
oblique-discrimination task, 523–4
oblique-recognition task, 521
Occam's razor, 541–2
octopuses, 516
ocular chromatic aberration, 448
oddity design task, 306, 368

Subject index

old-world monkeys, 307, 341
olfactory perception, 210
ongoing activity as reference level, 395-7, 407, 412
ontological categories, acquisition of, 467
operant conditioning, 307, 377-8
operant testing procedure, 16, 334, 335-6
optimality, 553
optimization, 539, 541-2, 559
orangutans, 333
orientation, 174, 397, 408, 511; within-between category differences (infants), 174-5; of line, 528
orthogonality principle, 227, 228, 229
"other minds" problem, 536, 537, 559
overdetermination, 541-2
overlearning, 6, 23-4, 57, 238, 322

paired-comparison procedure, 397, 401, 402, 403, 409, 544
pandemonium, 206, 218, 273
pandemonium model, 11-12, 200-3, 219, 262
panpropositional view, 550
paralinguistic discrimination system, 338, 340, 351-2
parallel discrimination tests, 23
parameter setting, 183
parietal association cortex, 421
parsimony, 173, 218, 234, 236, 541, 542, 553, 557; in classification, 479
pattern analysis; pandemonium model of, 11-12, 200-3
pattern classification, 273, 278-9
pattern playback schematic spectrograms, 138
pattern-recognition, 238, 550
perceived similarity structure, 23
percent correct, 5, 59, 458, 478
percent within-category discriminability, 4
perception, 221; biologically based linguistic mode of, 44; as both categorical and adaptable, 404; brain structures and, 338-9; categorization in, 1, *see also* categorical perception (CP); follows production, 117, 142-3, *see also* motor theory of speech perception; fuzzy-logical model of, 271-3; history-dependent, 349; integral-to-separable shift in, 20; mechanisms of, 322; of objects/forms, 515-16; physiological mechanisms of, 206; process underlying, 393; and production, 266; relativism in, 289; of spatial relations, 511-31; specialized mechanisms for, 355-6; theories of, 389, 391-7, 528; and thought, 527-8; units of, 178-82, 536, 537, 538, 559; *see also* continuous perception; direct perception theory
perceptual adaptation, 382
perceptual analysis: basic unit of, 206; mechanism of, 212, 213
perceptual anchors, 55, 74-7; in AI/SDT comparison, 392-3; interior, 74-6

perceptual attributes, acquisition of, 467
perceptual boundary, 302, 390; cross-language differences in, 182; shift in, in animal studies, 365-8; *see also* boundary effects
perceptual categories, 456; overdetermination of, 541-2; underdetermination of, 541; in vision and audition, 287-300
perceptual categorization: development in, 496-500; neural substrates in, 291
perceptual coding, two-factor theory of, 93-4
perceptual compensation, 248n2
perceptual/conceptual distinction, 512, 526-7
perceptual confusability, 81; *see also* confusable alternatives
perceptual constancy, 7, 10, 162, 163; in infants, 16
perceptual-cue integration, 98-9
perceptual dimensions, 73; qualitative/quantitative, 258, 261; shifts in, 20
perceptual discontinuities, 120; category boundaries indicative of, 44; TOJ threshold as, 43
perceptual economy, 336, 340
perceptual function, CP accounted for by, 388
perceptual items vs. semantic items, 404-7
perceptual judgment: categorical effects in, 398-400; relativity/constancy of, 390; subliminal time course in, 18
perceptual learning, 78, 79, 80, 550ff
perceptual mechanisms, 320, 336; in animal/human comparisons, 319; possible, in CP, 323-7
perceptual processes; developmental changes in, 492, 496-500
perceptual processing, 336; CP as general/universal characteristic of, 413-14; higher-order, 408; in human/animal comparisons, 341
perceptual representation, 554
perceptual responses, 29-30
perceptual sensitivity, 209-10
perceptual space, 320
perceptual structure and language structure, 513
perceptual system, 170, 172; biases in, 512-13; biological determination in, 172, 179; labile/stable, 404, 407; modification of ongoing activity in, 395-7, 407, 412; units of information in, 178-82
perceptual theory, 293-6
perceptual threshold(s), 36
perfect proportions (problem of), 60
perspective problem, 519, 522
perspective task, 525
phoneme(s), 7, 8, 184, 293, 323-4, 481; analysis of words into, 185-6; attributes of, 460; as basic level of speech representation, 485n2, 503-4; classification of, 465; invariant features of, 54; and relation to its acoustic realization, 117; and selective attention in CP, 322-3; as special, 547; as typicality gradients, 471; voice-onset-time continuum between, 319

phoneme boundary(ies), 6, 9, 114, 115, 116, 118, 121, 125, 136, 142-3, 547; AEPs and, 427, 429, 440; affricate/fricative distinction, 135; innate vs. learned, 141; location of, 147, 150, 151
phoneme boundary effect, 166, 320, 367-8; in infants, 167, 376
phoneme categories, 118-19, 120, 255; learning of, 152; and SP, 466
phoneme CP, 14
phoneme discrimination, 323, 427, 512, 514
phoneme-identification task, 423
phoneme perception, 553, 554; and motor theory, 545
phoneme recognition, 356, special mechanisms for, 513, 514
phoneme similarity: shifts in, 503-4
phonemic processing, 95-7, 189n15, 355; categories, 460; codes, 180; contrasts, 125, 144, 150; labels, 114, 115, 122; restoration effect, 483; sensitivity, 82; sensitivity P(C/L), 55-6; variation, distinctive feature concept of, 200-3; vs. auditory processing, 458
phonetic processing: boundaries, 89-112, 362-4, 365-8, 376; categories, 90, 170-2, 188n11, 226-32, 243, 337, 338, 340, 346, 352; categorization, 12, 171, 232, 351-2; classification, 239; communication, 91; context and location of boundaries, 91; contrasts, psychoacoustic principles for, 243-4; detector view, 207; development, 205; discrimination, 338; environment, 168; equivalence, infants' recognition of, 376-82; feature detectors, 92, 199-225; features, accurate and rapid perception of, 234-5, 340; general auditory processes and, 355, 360, 361, 362, 375, 382-3; hypothesis, 91, 96-7, 100; learning, 106; level (language), 355-60; level of analysis, 212-13, 382-3; mode (speech perception), 247, 266; perception, 7, 200-3, 205-6; repertoire, 7; representation of speech, 381; segments 89, 204, 205
phonological features, detector output as, 234-5
phonological processes, language- or dialect-specific, 239-40, 241
phonological rules, 241, 242
phonological system: acquisition of, 182-7; in infants, 161, 162, 182-7
phonology, 165, 181, 184
phrase-structure grammar, 241-2
phylogeny, 333, 337
physics: of color, 288, 296; in infants' recognition of equivalence clauses, 381
physiology: adaptive, 333; of color categories, 289, 291, 296; control processes (speech production), 239
picture(s) more valuable than words, 539-40
pigeons, 291, 296, 307

pitch, 92, 122, 153, 165, 382; cue value of onset of, 231; perfect, 154n2
place continua, 33, 124, 142
place cues, invariant, 236
place features, 374, 375
place-of-articulation, 16, 42, 43, 44, 96, 102, 146-7, 148, 212, 336; acoustic invariance, 236-7; in brain-damaged subjects, 435-8; and category boundaries, 99, 100, 102, 376; contrasts in, 422; correlates of, 179; discrimination of, 340; discrimination of, by monkeys, 371-4; in infant/adult categories, 170-1; vs. manner of articulation, 229; perception of, 118; and phoneme boundary, 151; selective adaptation of, 212-13; template defining, 188n6; voice-onset time and, in animal studies, 365-8
place value: initial stops in, 236-7; VOT variation as function of, 239, 244
playback experiments, 334-6, 338, 345, 346
plosive consonants 153; classifications of, 113-14; perception of, 118, 123, voiced/voiceless, 114, 116-17; voicing distinction in, 124, 137-52
plucks and bows, 126, 127, 128-30, 132, 135, 136, 214, 258-60; continuum of, with edge anchors, 76-7, 79, 80; intensity theory of, 69-70, 73
point of view: influence of, on prototype, 481; in solution of spatial problems, 523
Polish language, 94, 105
positive-reinforcement technique, 371
practice, 5, 46
practice effects, 39-40, 42-3
precompilation (strategy), 241
predicate calculus format, 517-19
predicates, 513, 514, 515-16; assignment of, in solution of spatial problems, 521-7; explication of, 518-19; finite set of, 516, 521, 528-9; source of, 528-9; and two arguments, 516-19
prediction(s), 389; of adaptation, 215; of discrimination, 58-9, 255-61; GK categories in, 466
predispositions and development of category structure, 508, see also biological predisposition
prefrontal cortex, 413
prephonetic levels of processing, 176-8
prepositions, 517
presentation of standards, 80
prestriate cortex, 395-6
primates, 207, 422; auditory-evoked-response (AEP), 426-7; language studies in, 550; sensory systems in, 395; trichromatic, 291; visual system in, 296
prime numbers, 540; detection of, 553
priming (effects) by context, 481

Subject index

proactive effects, 93
probability, 272, 394
problems of philosophy (cognitive science), empirical approach to, 536–8, 558–9
processing: 162, 167, 170, 171, 175; mechanisms of, 388–9; on-line, 186–7; organization of, 182; units of, 178–82
processing modes, psychophysical approach to, 53–85
processing space, 70–3, 80
processing variables in GK/SP categories, 481–3
production constraints, 465, 475
production mechanisms, 336
productivity, 466
pronunciation, 186
properties in representational system, 556–7
propositional representations of space, 513–14
propositions, 20–2, 513, 560n4; as basic units of mental life, 519, 527; about category membership, 554; around set of spatial predicates, 515–16; symbol recombinations in, 559
prototype matching (fuzzy-logic model), 273, 275–6, 279
prototype model, 11, 478, 479; in SP categories, 473, 485
prototype reference points, 477–9
prototype structure, 498–9, 502
prototype theory, 380
prototype-to-theory shift, 505–6; 551ff
prototype(s), 13, 19, 79, 90, 91, 100, 162, 175, 188n11, 266, 562n16; AL theory and, 393–4, 406, 407; assimilation to, 476–7; in category structure, 178; classification by, 467; conceptual domains organized around, 505; in developmental changes in category structure, 20, 506; exemplars as, 465, 473, 475, 479–80; in explanation of infant categorization, 174; in feature integration, 273, 275–6; flexibility in, 91; in GK/SP categories, 463–5, 485; identification of, 6; individual differences in, 468; in infants' recognition of equivalence classes, 377, 379, 380; influenced by linguistic context, 481; nature of, 188n9; phonemic segments of, 185–6; reference points and, 473, 475; refining of, 184–5; representations of speech, 10, 184–5; and selective adaptation, 96, 97; shift in, to theory, 505–6, 551ff; as standards, 458
prototypical categories, spatial, 512, 516
prototypicality, 516
psychoacoustics, 54, 69, 79, 100–1, 105, 242; and constraints in speech categorization, 243–7
psycholinguistics, identification in, 557
psychology: of color naming, 288, 291; in feature-detector model, 199, 206, 219, 221
psychometric function(s), 146
psychophysical aspects: of CP, 1–25, 244; of discontinuities, 38–9, 90; labeling, 22; of partitioning of variables, 392; of processing modes, 53–85
psychophysical model (speech perception), 5–6, 29–52, 244–5, 247; GK/SP categories in, 474, 485
psychophysical scaling techniques, 549
psychophysical specializations, universal, 341
psychophysical studies on color categories, 289–90
psychophysics, 2, 206, 261–2, 271, 358, 388, 456; auditory, 368; of categorical perception, 2–3, 17–18; of color discrimination, 288; of color vision, 296; contrast phenomena in, 211; of critical bands, 327; distinct from psychoacoustics, 54; identification in, 557; nonspeech, 93–4; one-dimensional, 82
pygmy marmoset (*Cebuella pygmaea*), 15, 313, 317, 318, 343–5, 346–8, 349, 350

"qualia," problem of, 558
qualitative perceptual dimensions (CP), 3, 258, 261, 476

random-walk classification model, 474
range, 91, 116, 119, 121, 122, 123, 124
range effects, 34, 94–5, 136, 458, 469; in animals, 147–8; exemplars and, 480–1
range-frequency effects, 94–5, 97; in AL theory, 390
range manipulations, affricate/fricative distinction in, 129–30
rate normalization effect, 232
rate of speech, 116, 162, 187n3, 481; and acquisition of language, 182, 184; and effects on labeling VOT stimuli, 151; infants' perception of, 161, 168–9; and location of boundary, 91, 102–3, 375
rating judgments, 266–71, 280
reaction times, 478, 519; identification responses, 276–80; and visual/auditory perception parallels, 293
reading, 186, 503
real-life items, categorization of, after brain damage, 388, 404–7
recency in AL theory, 389
"rechunking" experiment, 549
red-winged blackbirds (*Agelaius phoeniceus*), 312, 318
redundancy, 238, 542, 555, 559
reference, 245, 537
reference-point effects, SP/GK categories of, 472–3, 485; *see also* anchor(s)
reference-point model, 474
reference points: at category boundaries, 471, 477–9, 485; external, 5, of GK/SP categories, 474–9
referential theories, 554

referents, 457; in word meaning, 494
relative discrimination, 543-4, 547, 552
relative-onset time, 140
relative-timing continua, 9
relativism, 289, 291
relativist hypothesis, 13-14
releasers, *see* key (sign) stimuli
repetition rate, frequency of, 215, 304, 324-5
representation of speech, 219; organized into network, 183-4, 185-6; prelexical, 179-82; segmental/syllabic, 179-82, 184
representational format, singular, 512
representational systems, 20; experience in, 559; three-level, 22-4, 537-8, 546, 551-8
representation(s), 2, 5, 6, 18-19, 90, 102, 499, 544; bounded, 61, 552, 553; change from instance-bound to principled, 492, 495; in children's categories, 20; continuous, 542-3; correlations between stored and generated, 178, 179, 181-7, 188n11; of experience (theory), 389-91; flexibility in, 481; of GK/SP categories, 457; imagistic/propositional 558; integral and separable dimensions of, 497-8; intensional, 556; nature of, 599; shareability constraint on, 506; unbounded, 61, 551, 556; units of, 178-9; *see also* categorical representations (CRs); symbolic representations (SRs)
representations of spatial properties and objects/concepts structural equivalence, 512, 513, 515, 529
representativeness: in AL theory, 394; reference points and, 473
resolution-edge effect, 80
response bias, 104, 393; SDT model of, 58, 59, 81
response latency, 341
response(s): changes in, 80-1; contrast in, 84
retinal ganglion cells, 207
retinal stimulation, 219
rhesus macaques *(Macaca mulatta)*, 340, 341, 419
rhesus monkeys, 43, 147-8, 307, 319, 419, 435
right hemisphere (brain), 408; continuous perception in, 388; and CP, 434, 435-6, 437-8; damage to, and CP, 409-13, 414; and EP (activity), 424, 426, 427, 428-9, 430-8, 440, 441
rise time(s), 35, 121, 258-60; affricate/fricative analog, 126, 128-9, 130-2, 133-7; defined, 120; and fricative noise, 125; and nonspeech CP, 304; perception of, 120, 127-8, 173; and plucks and bows, 69; and sawtooth stimuli, 40-1
root-mean-squared deviation (RMSD), 256-7, 276
roving discrimination, 5, 6, 78, 79, 245, 465; and AL theory, 392; in estimation of memory variance, 65-70, 74-5; intensity theory of, 61-3; learning in, 80

Rubik's cube, 521
rule(s), 539; additive integration of, 480, 482; and category membership, 461-2, 464, 554; classification by, 463, 467, 541; disjunctive, 461; encoding, 562n22; of GK/SP categories, 485; governing changes to boundary location, 375; linguistic, 464; minimal, 542; and multiplicative integration, 480, 482; phonological, 186-7, 241, 242; relating acoustic properties of speech to its perception, 355-6

salience, 165, 166
same-different discrimination, 21, 57-8
same-different judgments, 543-4, 552
same-different procedures, 64, 306
same-different task, 59, 60, 368
satisficing, 539, 541
saturation, 20, 288, 482, 497, 498
sawtooth continua, 125-6, 127, 128; affricate/fricative distinction, 130, 132, 136
sawtooth stimuli, 40-1, 136
scalp electrical activity, 17-18
second-formant transition, 3, 341, 372
secondary cortex, 44
segment identification, 204, 205
segmental-context effects, 101-2, 103, 124
segmentation, 162-3, 166, 181, 204-6, 237; phonemic, 185-6; prelexical representations of speech, 179-80; temporal basis for, 179
selective adaptation, 11-12, 33-4, 95, 323, 404, 406-7; in AL theory, 390; effects of, 42, 400; in feature-detection model, 209-10, 233-4; phonetic feature detectors and, 211-19; procedures in, 177-8; stimulus-sequence effects, 95-7
selective attention, 9, 10, 18, 20, 47; in animal CP, 321-3; and location of boundary effect, 5; as mechanism of CP, 323-4, 328
selective attention model, 15
selective pressure, 247, 303
semantic analysis, 456
semantic and syntactic effects, boundary location of, 104-5
semantic bias, 104
semantic comparisons (model), 473-4
semantic context, 104, 481
semantic development, 495-6
semantic integration, 240
semantic items vs. perceptual items, 404-7
semantic judgments, two-stage theory of, 516
semantic-memory literature, 494
semantic-network theory, 242
semantic representation of spatial relations, 511-12
sensation, 54-5
sensitivity(ies), 6, 81, 98; in AL/SDT comparison, 392, 393; area of natural, 74-6, 77, 79, 81; context, 92, 407; differential, 90, 91, 458; discrimination peaks and, 55; and experi-

mental design, 54; in identification/discrimination, 74–5, 78–9; inborn, in auditory system, 115, 120–1; innate, for learning, 466–7; innate, to potential phonetic boundaries, 106; natural, 5, 16, 393; perceptual learning in, 80; in SDT model, 58–60; to speech source, 104; visual, 292
sensorimotor performance, 15
sensory adaptation, 17
sensory areas, extraprimary, 407
sensory continua, 29, 544, 545
sensory cortex, 395–6
sensory domains: adaptation level in, 390; categorization in, 175
sensory effect, 93–4
sensory factors, 392
sensory fields, 396
sensory information, continuous, 262–3
sensory matching, CP, 547
sensory modalities, 12, 544; CP of stimuli in, 409–13; neural substrates underlying CP in, 388–9, 395–7, 413; *see also under specific type, e.g.,* tactile modality
sensory model (perception), 393
sensory motor equivalences for speech, infants' recognition of, 377, 381–2
sensory perception (SP) categories, 19; acquisition of, 466–8; category structure of, 462; classification in, 464–5; and CP, 456, 459; decomposition of, into attributes, 460; vs. generic knowledge categories, 455, 456–7, 459, 469t, 470–85; instantiations of, 457; stability/flexibility of, 468–70; uses of, 465–6
sensory processes: in categorization, 261–6, 271, 280; electrophysiology of, 206–7
sensory processing, 115; EP and, 421
sensory psychophysiology, 2
sensory representation, 2, 12
sensory systems, 430; organization of, 396
sensory-trace mode (memory), 123, 153, 551ff
sensory variance, 61, 62, 64, 70, 74, 78
sentences, 20; mental, 550
sequential effects, 80
shape, 406–7, 482, 497, 511; in iconic/categorical representations, 552; representations of, are relational, 514; role of, in object concepts, 514–15
shape categories, 512
"shareability" constraint, 506
shock-avoidance paradigm, 419
signal detection models, 474
Signal Detection Theory (SDT), 5–6, 40, 49n4, 54, 61, 262, 265; AL theory compared with, 391–3; CP models 58–60; psychophysical theory of, 54, 58–77; tests of, 70
signaling systems, 547
silence duration, 47, 102, 105, 144
similarity, 23, 141, 166; acquired (principle), 9, 187n4; in category membership, 499; empirical, in GK/SP categories, 470–3, 485; and function of attributes, 460; perceived, 23; phoneme, 503–4; theoretical, 485; within-category, 462
similarity judgments, 473, 523–4; based on spatial properties, 514, 527; effect of reference points on, 477
similarity (strategy), 496, 498, 501, 502, 503, 507, 508
simplification (strategy), 227
simultaneity, 140, 145
simultaneity-successive thresholds, 46
sine-wave analogs, 169, 221
sine-wave stimuli, 169
sinusoidal stimuli, 40, 126–7, 128, 138
situation: and discrimination, 338; and word meanings, 493–4
size, 20, 482, 497, 511; as concept, 494
"slit"–"split" contrast, 47
social categorization, 351, 473
soma to sensory function, 395, 396
sorting, 1, 22, 507, 558
sound continuum, control of (experiments), 302–3
sound-energy concentration, 304, 325
sound parameters (CP), 304
sound/percept relation: mapping, 355–6; mediating mechanism of, 358
sound-producing mechanisms, 227–8
sound signals: categorical perception of – animal studies, 301–31; discrete – animals, 303
sound structure of language, 184
sound synthesizing, 342, 343, 344–5, 346–8, 349–50, 352; *see also* synthesized (synthetic) speech
source/filter interaction (speech production), 228
space: continuous and homogeneous, 511, 516; CP of, 519–21; *see also* multidimensional space
Spanish language, 142–3, 152, 153, 171; boundary locations in, 105; voicing changes in, 185; VOT continuum, in, 149–50
spatial categories, 511–31; invariance of, 529; spatial predicates as, 527–9
spatial cognition, 515, 517; categorical and relational, 513, 517, 529; development of, 518–19; error scores and reaction times in, 519
spatial concepts, test of continuous or categorical, 526–7
spatial features, both categorical and relational, 512–14, 517, 529
spatial form, explication of, 515
spatial information, 515, 516–17; translated into relational structure, 511–12
spatial perception, 21
spatial predicates: as spatial categories, 527–9; *see also* predicates

spatial problems: matrix for, 519–21; solution to, 521–7, 529
spatial propositions, 513–14, 516–19; in development, 519; and solution to spatial problems, 521–7
spatial relations, perception and conceptualization of, 511–31
spatial representation, propositional theory of, 21–2
spatiality (CP), 549
spatially unpatterned (diffuse) fields, 443–6
spatiotemporal structure of categories in iconic/categorical representations, 552, 553
speaker characteristics, 460, 481
speaker-normalization effects, 103–4
specializations, general, 205
specialized mechanisms, 173, 207, 341, 355–86, 422; evidence for, 355–60; for higher-order processing, 355–60; infant studies in, 375–6; necessity of, 360, 361–2, 374–5; for perceiving spatial relations, 513
specialized processes vs. auditory processes, 355, 360, 361, 362, 375–6, 380, 382–3
species recognition, 318
species-specific features, 333; recognition of, (in animals), 14, 303, 307, 310, 312, 313–18, 320, 321, 322
species-specific sounds, 14, 341, 342–5, 350–2; evidence for CP of, 307–19; learned, 350; perception of, 352; two-stage model for processing, 351–2
spectral composition and animal call signals, 310
spectral mechanisms, 165, 325–7, 449
spectral-onset characteristics, 183–4
spectral patterns, 304
spectral similarity, 93
spectral templates, 237, 240–1
spectral-trading relations, 104
speculative physiology, 206
speech, 16; auditory (continuous/categorical perception of), 274–6, 278, 279; categories/subcategories in, 338, 339t; categorization of, by animals, 318–19; and color, 293–6; compared with animal vocalizations, 246–7; electrophysiological indices of CP for, 421–41; as special, 16, 32, 115, 243, 244, 247, 266, 361, 389, 545, 546–7; special-mechanisms debate in, 355–86; as unique perceptual activity, 388
speech categorization, psychoacoustic constraints on, 243–7
speech CP, 503–4; auditory, articulatory, and learning explanations of, 113–60; electrophysiological indices for, 421–41; generalization of, to general CP, 9–10, 16; in infants, 295; models for, 11–17; as special domain, 6–8, 9; and speech production, 15, 547; theories of, 8–10

speech-identification task, 92, 264
speech perception, 5, 54, 97, 348–50; in animals, 359–83; articulatory knowledge in, 117–18; categorical, 6–11, 265, 358, 388, see also speech CP; constrained by tactic knowledge, 107; discreteness issue in, 58; and human/animal parallels, 360, 364, 365, 366, 367, 372–4, 375, 376–7; in infants, 161–95; integral-to-separable shift in, 503–4; interpretation of finding of categorical, in animals, 374–83; in language acquisition, 182–7; mechanism of, 422–23, 429, 440; mediated by phonemic labels, 115; models of, 207–8, 233; modes of, 247, 266; neural models of, 199–225; speaker characteristics and, 460; as special, 14, 118; and speech production, 6–8, 107, 484; theories of, 178–9, 188n11, 210; variability of category boundary in 403–4; see also motor theory of speech perception; specialized mechanisms
speech perception literature, 30, 31–3
speech-perception tests, 302
speech-phoneme boundaries, 302
speech processing: brain structures unique to, 394–5; in infants, 180–2
speech production, 5, 119, 227, 466; compensation for interactions in, 231–2; constraints on, 240; mechanisms of, 162–3; phonetic segments in, 227–8, 229–30; psychophysics of, 206; and speech perception, 107, 358, 484; tacit knowledge in, 239–40
speech recognition: accuracy in, 238; acoustic cues in, 238–43; and animal communication signals, 246–7; failure of machine, 356; feature-detector hypothesis in, 233–4; invariant acoustic correlates in, 236–7; models of, 12, 240–3; tacit knowledge in, 239–40; theory of, 226, 227, 237–47
speech signal(s), 167; acoustic information in, 165–6; and correspondence with phonetic categories, 226–32; idiolectal of vocal-tract-specific, 240; infants' perception of, 161, 183; segmental distinctions in, 162–3, 179; variable, 172, 175
speech-sound discrimination, 306
speech-sound identification (tests), 92
speech sounds, 456; acquired distinctiveness of, 138; animal perception of, 307, 341; animal similarities to, 341–2; auditory processes and, 132–6, 137; categorical representations of, 187n2; categorization of, 226–53; constraints on variation in, 202–3; and CP in infants, 498; CP of, 146, 148, 149–50, 337–8; cues in categorization of, 462; discrimination of, 338; discrimination of, by infants, 221; identification of, 188n11, 470; perception of, 2, 208–9, 352, see also speech perception; processed differently from nonspeech, 382–3
speech-specific patterns, 93

speech-specific phonetic processing, 265-6
speech stimuli, 482; in AEPs, 430-35; and CP, 388; in EPs, 438-9, 440, 441
speech-structure effects, 106
speech-synthesis-by-rule systems, 136; *see also* synthesized (synthetic) speech
squirrel monkeys, 246, 338-40, 346
stage theory, 492
staircase procedure, 44, 368-9
statistical decision theory, 36
STEPIT (computer program), 269-71
Steven's Power Law, 29
stimulation: brain areas and, 396-7; and level to which organism is adapted, 389
stimuli, 6, 37, 43; subliminal/supraliminal, 35, 36, 37
stimulus difference, 30, 89
stimulus duration, 42, 43
stimulus input: evaluation of, in terms of ongoing activity, 395, 396-7; pooling, averaging of, 389, 390, 400, 412
stimulus-interaction results, 38, 39f
stimulus presentation (experiments), 306, 335
stimulus repetition, 420, 422
stimulus/response matching, 544
stimulus-sequence effects, 91-7, 107
stimulus sets, 54; dimensionality of, 81-2
stimulus/stimulus matching, 543-4, 547, 552
stimulus-structure effects, 92, 97-106
stimulus values, 389-90, 395; and adaptation level, 398, 401-4; location of, 390-1; and relation to internal reference, 392
stop consonant-semivowel distinction, 168, 171, 179
stop consonants, 3, 100, 101, 141, 164, 212; contrast effects of, 94; and place of articulation, 170-1; place value of, 236-7; production of, 421; stimulus-sequence effects on, 92; voicing judgments for, 229, 230-1; word-initial, 233
stops, voiced/voiceless, 362-3
stream segregation, 136
stress level, 162, 246
striate cortex, 407, 408
structure(s): of GK/SP categories, 457; of information, 459-62; of language, 186
stumptail macaque (*Macaca arctoides*), 341, 346
subliminal stimuli: auditory, 35, 36; visual, 37
subordinate categories, 337-8, 340, 352, 557
subordinate levels (representation), 499-500
summation model, 12
superordinate categories, 254, 336, 337-8, 405, 406, 407, 556, 557
superordinate levels (representation), 499-500
superordinate relations, 467
supraliminal stimuli: auditory, 35, 36; visual, 37
Swedish language, 290
syllabic codes, 180
syllable duration, 168-9

syllable-repetition rate, 308, 309
syllables, 184; as basic level of speech representation, 503; as basic unit of perceptual analysis, 206; as tone-bearing units, 181
symbolic description, 543
symbolic description system, 538, 551-8
symbolic knowledge, 550
symbolic representations (SRs), 2, 201, 554-7, 559
symbolic-to-symbolic (S/S) transformation, 543
symbols: discrete, 21; grounded, 550, 552, 557, 559
sympatric treefrogs (*Hyla cinerea, H. gratiosa, H. squirella; H. versicolor, H. chrysocelis*), 320-1
syntactic categories, 504
syntax, 105, 240, 355, 481
synthesized (synthetic) speech, 89, 104, 114, 169, 175-6, 229-30, 356, 422, 425, 431, 460; rating responses, 269-71
systextual design, 486n6

tabula rasa mechanisms, 23-4
tacit knowledge, 231, 232, 236, 239-40, 243, 244, 245, 247; organization of, 240; in speech perception, 12, 107
tactile length, 438
tactile modality: neural substrates underlying CP in, 388-9, 395, 396, 413-14
tactual-kinesthetic tasks, 411-12
Tamil (langauge), 142
task type and reference points, 477
task variables, 123
taxonomic relations, 507
taxonomy, 55
templates, 237, 407, 561n16; optimal, 107n1; *see also* exemplars
temporal cues and AEPs, 427-32
temporal lobe, 396
temporal mechanisms (CP), 324-5
temporal-order identification, 41-3, 46
temporal-order information, 365
temporal-order judgment (TOJ) threshold, 42-3
temporal patterns in animal CP, 304
temporal processes, 553
temporal proximity, 93
temporal risk, 560n2
temporal structure in animal call signals, 310
temporal-trading relations, 105
temporality (CP), 549
testability, 541
tests, testing: in animal CP, 302-7; and animals' perception of speech, 359-83; bias in, 346; and CP, 266-71, 319-20, 324, 328, 383; and discrimination, 368; with feature-detector model, 207-10; and within-category discriminability, 336
texture, 397, 408, 446; visual 435
Thai language, 44, 105-6, 171

thalamus, 207, 219, 396
theoretical similarities in SP/GK categories, 473–4
theories, underdetermination of, 541, 542
three-mountain task, 519–20
threshold (traditional) models (CP), 4–5, 55–8, 59, 60, 265
thresholds, 549; absolute, 35, 322; perceptual, 36
Thurstonian models, 54, 59; scaling, 61; tools, 81
timbre, 55, 56, 67–8, 69, 73
time, units of processing in, 178–9, 180, 482
time-series elaborations, 23
toads, 309–12
tonal patterns, 322
tone, 181
tone intensity, 71, 83n7, 173–4; and identification/discrimination relation, 78; perception of, 82
tone-onset time (TOT), 432, 438; perception of, 172–3
tone-onset-time (TOT) continua, 42, 45–6, 146, 150
tone-onset-time (TOT) stimuli, 430–1
topographic form, 551
topographic organization, 395
topographic studies, 421
topological concepts, 517
trace coding, 73
trace decay, 63
trace mode, 392; efficiency of, 70–3; and intensity resolution, 61, 62, 67; time-dependent memory variance in, 63–5
trace parameter, 5–6
trace variance, 62
trace vs. context mode theory, 458
trademarks (distinctive features), 233
trading relations, 5, 47–8, 375, 376, 383, 462; phonetic 98–9, 100; among sources of information, 161, 168–9, 170; speaking-rate effects of, 102, 103
trained operant response, 544
training, 23, 77, 116, 122, 172, 306, 548; and animal tests, 307, 315, 322, 323, 335, 362, 363, 369; in discrimination tasks, 306; effects of, 59–60, 67, 145–6; studies in, 164, 262–3, 378–9
transient EPs, 445–6
transition duration, 168–9, 172–3
translatability, 543, 563n24
tree-vs.-animal discrimination problem, 539, 540, 542, 554–6
trial-and-error method, 540
truth values (fuzzy logic), 271, 272, 273
"tuning," 361, 362
"Turing Test," 536
21FC discrimination task, 70, 77
two-interval, forced-choice procedures, 59, 398

typicality, 18–19, 463, 561n16
typicality effects, 479; in SP/GK categories, 471–2, 485
typicality gradients, 468, 471, 472
typicality judgments, 473, 549

UCLA Phonological Segment Inventory Database, 154n3
ultrasound, 313–17, 327, 342
uncertainty, 37, 39–40
unconditioned response (animal CP), 307
unconscious inference, 7, 553
underdetermination, 541, 542, 561n13, n14, n16, 562n21
ungroundedness (problem), 562n21
unidimensionality, 73, 81
units of processing, 171–82, 185–6, 188n6
universalism, 13–14, 289; in cross-cultural studies, 289–90; in infant studies, 290; in physiological studies, 291
universals, problem of, 537, 538, 559
utility of phenomenon to organism, 332, 333
utterance rate, 232, 235, 246; tacit knowledge and, 239; *see also* rate of speech

verbal categories, over-/underdetermination of, 541–2
verbal descriptions, 536, 539–40
verbal information, 558
verbal label, 544
verbal labeling task, 402, 403
verbal memory, 257
verbs, 504, 517
vervet monkeys (*Cercopithecus aethiops*), 321, 334
viewer transformation of array display (problem), 519–20, 524–7
viewer transformation of single object display (problem), 519, 523–7
vision, 11, 21, 548; perceptual categories in, 287–300; perceptual parallels with audition, 293–5
visual acuity, 446
visual categorization of hues, 287–92
visual-evoked responses, 420
visual form categories, 18
visual information, 274
visual length, 438
visual modality, neural substrates underlying CP in, 388–9, 395–6, 413–14
visual patterns, 23; categorization of, by infants, 172, 173–5; perception of, by infants, 161–2
visual process: speech process analogy with, 207; structural hypotheses re, 219; visual processing in EPs – color, 443–9
visual speech, continuous/categorical perception of, 274–6, 278, 279
visual stimuli, 36–8; identification of, 470
visual system, 514; and color naming, 292;

Subject index

feature detectors in, 11, 34; neural connections in, 206, 207, 395–6; stimulus input, 395
visual texture, 438
vocal apparatus, 227–8, 230, 421
vocal communication, naturalist approach to, 333
vocal imitation by infants, 381–2
vocal sound production, 205
vocal tract, 107, 142, 227; characteristics of, 235, 238, 240; components of, 238; size of, 103–4, 232, 435–8
vocal-tract resonators, 227–8
voice-onset time (VOT), 67, 79, 81, 137, 324–5, 336, 472; in animal CP, 319; auditory-evoked responses and, 424–35; categorization of, 167, 173; and category boundary, 244–6, 349; changes in, are categorical, 421–2; discrimination of, 417–23, 437; discrimination of, by monkeys, 370–1; discrimination of *jnd*s, by chinchillas, 368–70; generalization of, by chinchillas, 362–4; and high sensitivity and interior anchor, 75–6, 77; hue and, 293; measurement of, 142–3; and place of articulation in animal studies, 365–8; reference point in, 473, 375; selective attention and, 322; speech sounds differing in, 304; temporal aspects of, 170; variations in, 239, 460; and voiced/voiceless stops, 230–1, 233
voice-onset-time (VOT) continua, 33; classification of plosives in, 107; and discriminations, 340, 341; division of, 171; identification boundaries of, 43–4; infant studies in, 44–5; partitioning of, across language, 149–50; perception of, in animals, 146–8; time-varying, 41–2; within- and cross-category discriminability, 43–4
voice-onset-time (VOT) mechanisms, localization of, 423, 429
voice-onset-time (VOT) perception, 430–1; basis of, 150–2; in brain-damaged subjects, 435–8
voice-onset-time (VOT) stimuli, nonspeech analogs to, 244–5
voiced affricate/fricative pair, 124
voiced/voiceless boundary, 422, 425, 437
voiced/voiceless stops, 230–1, 233
voiceless affricate/fricative distinction, 124–37, 141–2; and first demonstration of CP, 125
voicing, 16, 99, 105, 422; hue and, 293–6
voicing boundary(ies), 100, 170
voicing contrast(s), 41, 42–3, 341, 350, 421–22; cross-language, 105; discrimination of, by infants, 422; and language acquisition, 185; and word-initial stop consonants, 233
voicing cues, 229–30, 232; temporal components of, 422
voicing distinctions, 211–12; acoustic elements in, 204–5; in plosive consonants, 124, 137–52; in stop consonants, 171

voicing feature, 374, 375; and boundary shifts, 365–8
voicing judgments: and initial stops, 229, 230–1; and stops in word-medial position, 229–30
vowel-duration differences, 239–40
vowel identification, 382; stimulus-sequence effects in, 92
vowel length, 162, 187n3
vowels, 42, 94, 117, 123, 153; categorization of, by infants, 165; contrast effects of, 92–3; duration of, 103; and identification/discrimination, 64–5, 66–9, 73; perception of, 118; production of, 239

water-level problem, 520–1, 527
waveform, 18, 424; continuous acoustic, 205; invariant, 423
wavelength: effects of, on EPs, 443–6; hue and, 288, 289, 290, 292; and luminance, 446–9; and VOT, 293; within/between category differences (infants) in, 174–5
Weber's law, 9, 35, 36, 37, 41, 54, 69, 83n7, 128, 131, 132, 140, 155n9, 244, 260, 368, 472, 473, 475, 476, 477; denied in CP, 358, 361, 370–1
weight perception, 412, 413, 438, 439
Wernicke's aphasics, 436, 438
white noise, 128, 132, 155n9
white-throated sparrows (*Zonotricha albicollis*), 321
Whorf Hypothesis, 6, 13–14, 545–6
within-category discrimination, 166–7, 254–5, 261, 263, 337–40, 367–8, 398, 422, 425, 458, 512, 545, 549; in AL theory, 390–1, 398–400, 402, 406, 409–12; in animal studies, 340–1, 342, 346, 370, 371; brain function and, 388; of GK/SP categories, 470–1, 485; hemispheric specialization and, 439, 440; in infants, 167, 358–9; in naturalistic approach, 336, 352; test for, in EP, 425, 427, 429
within-category similarity, 462; enhanced, 548; in representational system, 554
within-class discrimination in animal categorization, 309, 315–16
word (the) as tool, 507
word meaning, 536, 537, 559; characteristic-to-defining (principled) shift in, 492–6, 506, 507; developmental changes in, 492–6
word meaning acquisition (model), 493, 551ff
word recognition network, 184, 185–7
words: new, 466, 506; and relation to world, 536, 537, 538, 558; shortcomings of, for description, 540

yelling model, 12
"yells," 202
yes-no tasks, 59
Yorubas, 496